YOU CAN MAKE IT...
IN
ARCHAEOLOGY!

First published in 2002 by Miles Kelly Publishing,
Bardfield Centre, Great Bardfield, Essex CM7 4SL

Printed in Italy

ISBN 1-84236-098-1

24681097531

Series Editor: Paula Borton
Assistant Editor: Nicola Sail
Cover Illustration: The Maltings
Layout Design: Mackerel

YOU CAN MAKE IT...
IN
ARCHAEOLOGY!

by Freya Sadarangani

Illustrations   Martin Remphry

Titles in the Series:

Contents

About the Author:

Freya Sadarangani studied classical studies (classical civilisations, Latin and stuff) at Manchester University, and then did a postgraduate degree in archaeology at University College, London. Her interest in archaeology turned into an obsession at the age of six when she realised she could fund her craving for gobstoppers by digging up artefacts from her Mum's back garden, displaying them in the garden shed, and charging the neighbours an entrance fee of a penny!

She has spent time excavating in Peru and is currently working for an archaeological company in London, spending her days rummaging around in muddy, wet holes in search of ancient goodies.

Chapter 1

Back to reality

You're trekking through the South American
jungle in search of the golden idol of the Incas.
The humidity is stifling. Your whip hangs loosely by
your side. You check your ancient map and see
that you must be close now. And then there it is,
immersed in jungle vines, the entrance to the lost
temple of the Incas. You cautiously brush the vines
away and take a first step into the dark stone
passageway. You claw through the spider webs that
bar the way. You walk further into the vaults of
the temple, careful to avoid the crossbow booby-
traps that may be triggered at any second. You
pick your way over the decaying human bodies
that litter the path. And now you're sweating. Your

pulse is racing. There's a light at the end of the passageway. You know you're close now. And then, there it is, glinting in a ray of the sun, the golden idol of the Incas. It's everything that you imagined – truly magnificent. After years of searching, here it is finally in your grasp. It must be booby-trapped, so you take a sack of sand of similar weight and in one swift movement exchange the idol for the sand. You stand motionless for a second. A sigh of relief. It seems to have worked. But then…an almighty roar. Huge cracks start appearing in the walls. The ceiling comes crashing down. You start to run. Arrows are flying in every direction. You race through the passageways. A massive boulder tears through the passageway hot on your heels. You…

Hold on! Time out! Reality check!

What?

Well, this book's about how to become an archaeologist, not how to direct a Hollywood film.

Oh. But I thought you were taking me through a day in the life of an archaeologist.

I don't know how to break this to you, but that was not archaeology. Running through booby-trapped temples, risking your life in search of golden idols is not an archaeologist's average day at work.

So what is? Fighting Nazis and the forces of evil?

Well, no. First off, you've got to clear from your mind those images of Indiana Jones and Lara Croft. Archaeology is more *Time Team* than *Tomb Raider,* I'm afraid.

Okay, but I still get to use a whip and a gun, don't I?

Er, perhaps if you were a lion tamer.

As an archaeologist though you'd probably be armed with a shovel, a mattock (these can be just as effective when dealing with any stray Nazis on the loose), a brush (not quite as effective), and most important of all – the essential tool of the archaeologist's trade – a trowel. With these tools archaeologists can dig and poke around in the ground.

So that's what archaeologists do, dig big holes in the ground?

Well, kind of. But it's a little more complicated than that…

Over the next few chapters we're going to lift the lid on what an archaeologist actually does. You're going to find out what the highs and lows of being an archaeologist are, and how exactly you can 'make it' in archaeology.

So what are you waiting for?

Chapter 2
The right stuff

So what does an archaeologist do?

Before we go any further fill out this short questionnaire to see if you've got what it takes to become an archaeologist:

Have you got the right stuff?

1 It's Tuesday night and you're deciding what to watch on TV. You've got a choice between *Time Team* and *Meet the Ancestors*. Do you...

a) watch *Time Team* and record *Meet the Ancestors*?

b) turn the TV off. You'd prefer to play tiddleywinks?

2 It's first period on Monday morning and Mrs Pastit (hypothetical history teacher) is talking about the pyramids of Egypt. Do you...

a) listen intently and take lots of notes?

b) invest in some matchsticks to prop your eyes open?

3 You're an archaeologist

Am I?

No, but try and imagine you're one. Your supervisor (the boss) tells you to excavate a deep cesspit (pit of poo). Do you...

a) jump in and only wince slightly when it splatters all over your face?

b) make a run for it?

4 You're still an archaeologist. You're working outside and it starts to snow. Do you...

a) mutter under your breath, put on your winter woollies and carry on working?

b) throw down your tools, resign, and become a chartered accountant?

If you've answered mostly 'a' then you've got what it takes! Not only are you interested in archaeology but you're also prepared to do nasty dirty jobs and work in hard conditions. If you've answered 'b' for questions 3 and 4, well then you're just a wimp!

Okay, you're still reading, you must have answered mostly 'a'. So now to the matter in hand. We've established that archaeologists are not superheroes. They don't raid tombs and they don't have to be black belts in karate, so what does an archaeologist actually do?

Well, archaeologists are like detectives...

Oooh, do you mean solving murders and chasing crooks?

Er no, not exactly. I mean in the way that they have to do a lot of detective work. Archaeologists try to figure out what life was like in ancient times. They have to look for clues that will help them understand how ancient cultures developed, lived and died.

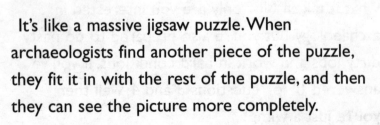

It's like a massive jigsaw puzzle. When archaeologists find another piece of the puzzle, they fit it in with the rest of the puzzle, and then they can see the picture more completely.

But how do they find the pieces of the puzzle?

By finding artefacts.

What are they?

They're physical things that have been left by ancient people – like a clay pot, or a stone tool, or even their bones – they can be anything.

Oooh I know, like Indiana Jones finding the Lost Ark of the Covenant or Lara Croft finding the Magical Triangle?

Well, in theory, yes (although you do know that the Magical Triangle is complete fiction, don't you?). More often than not, though, archaeologists don't find the Holy Grail or the Ark of the Covenant. More frequently they uncover an ancient rubbish dump – and get just as excited!

Doesn't sound very exciting.

Well it can be. People's rubbish can tell us loads about them. Try looking in your rubbish bin and see what it says about you. That mouldy banana skin, those smelly chicken bones, that broken plate; they all say something about you and the society that you live in.

So here comes the science part! Archaeologists mainly find these artefacts by digging in the ground. Either because they were buried by ancient peoples in the first place, or because over the centuries they've been covered over by layers of soil, demolished buildings, decayed vegetation etc... Underneath the modern layers are older layers, and in these layers are older artefacts and features...

Uh? What are features?

Sorry, I was getting ahead of myself. Well, features are things like rubbish pits. Imagine, if you will, that you're living in Britain in 100 BC and you want to get rid of your rubbish (no dustmen in those days you know). So, you dig a hole in the ground and throw in your broken bits of pottery (you had a bit of a tantrum last night) and your fish bones from last night's supper which are beginning to pong. 2100 years later an archaeologist comes along, removes all the modern and older layers that have accumulated above your rubbish pit. The archaeologist can see where your pit is – not because he/she's got super powers – but because it's a different colour and texture from all the soil around it (plus there's a telling fish bone sticking out of it). So the archaeologist digs out the contents of your pit – the bits of pottery, the fish bones, and the soil that's in it – and is left with the hole that you dug in the first place, before you filled it in. The pit is the feature and the pottery and fish bones are the artefacts.

Still with me?

Good. So to recap, archaeologists take off the modern layers and then record and remove the older layers, features and artefacts that they find underneath. And this, my friends, is what's called an **excavation**.

Which reminds me, before we go any further, here are a few terms and phrases that are used by archaeologists.

Archaeological lingo

In the field = on an excavation or doing a survey. So, 'Hi, my name's Norman and I'm working in the field' does not mean that Norman is spending his days surrounded by butterflies and daisies in a nice green field. It translates as 'Hi, my name's Norman and I'm working on an excavation at the moment'.

On site = on an excavation. This is because archaeologists are very silly and need two terms that mean the same thing.

A dig = an excavation. Just in case two terms aren't enough.

Trench = hole. This is what archaeologists work in when they're excavating. They're a bit like the World War One trenches – wet, muddy, and infested with rats and lice.

Finds = artefacts. So archaeologists will cry from their muddy trenches, 'Eureka,

I've found a find!' – this is because archaeologists like tongue twisters.

Skellie = skeleton. This is because archaeologists are very unimaginative people.

Culture = group/society (rough definition). Archaeologists while away many an evening discussing the correct definition of 'culture' – this is probably because archaeologists need more hobbies.

Archaeology is a long and complicated process, and it requires many people with different skills to help in that process. Archaeology isn't just about digging up artefacts.

No?

No. Just as there are archaeologists that work 'in the field' excavating bits of history, there are those archaeologists that spend their time in laboratories analysing those bits of history; whether it's a gold Celtic necklace, a cremated

Roman body – or even a bit of decayed Egyptian poo!

Fact File

Archaeologists go potty for pottery.

Even the smallest fragment (sherd) of pottery can drive archaeologists wild with excitement. This is not because archaeologists are sad individuals who need to get out more, it's because you can date pottery – and I don't mean that archaeologists take pieces of pottery on dates to the cinema. No, I mean that archaeologists can tell when the piece of pottery was made.

You see, archaeologists don't just dig random holes all over the world, pick out all the ancient artefacts they can get their hands on, and then throw them into museum cases. Archaeology is a little more complicated than that. In most archaeological investigations there are in fact seven separate stages (with digging just being one of them) to the whole process. Because there are so many different stages, there are many different types of archaeologists who are skilled in doing all the different jobs.

So, here are the seven stages of the archaeological process:

Generally, the first stage is **Research**. Archaeologists don't just start digging in the ground without researching the area first. So they go to libraries and look at tattered old maps and old records to find out who lived there and what buildings used to stand there. This way they can decide where the best place to excavate is, since if there have been loads of buildings on the site the archaeology might have been destroyed. Plus, archaeologists want to know if they're going to come across a smelly old 20th century outdoor toilet before they start digging.

Next, archaeologists have to do a **Survey** of the area. By doing a survey of an area archaeologists can decide where the best possible place to dig is (i.e. where you're going to find the most remains). To do this, archaeologists go 'field walking' – and no, this doesn't mean that archaeologists go skipping arm in arm through lush, green meadows (well, actually they do, but only in their free time). 'Field-walking' means that archaeologists systematically walk through an area and any artefacts that they find on the surface of the ground are recorded and collected.

Other survey techniques include sticking various probes in the ground to find out if there's anything underneath by taking sonar, radio wave, electrical, or magnetic readings (ask your physics teacher). Another method is aerial photography. Not all crop circles and crop marks are made by aliens, you know. Some of them at least are visible because there's an archaeological feature underneath. So, archaeologists get to go up in aeroplanes and take pictures of the ground.

The next stage is the one everybody thinks archaeology is about – **Excavation.** More on this later in Doris's Diary.

The fourth stage is **Artefact processing.** Archaeologists have to clean all the mud off and catalogue all the artefacts that were found during the excavation. This is a very boring job, but hey, somebody's got to do it.

After they've been cleaned, the artefacts don't just get thrown into a museum, they have to be analysed first. So this is the fifth stage – **Analysis.** Archaeologists have to study the artefacts to find out how they were used and when they were made. More on this in Chapter 5.

Once the excavation's finished and everything's been analysed, archaeologists have to write a report on everything they've found and what it all means. This is the next stage, **Reporting**. Archaeologists need to be very clever to do this because they have to look at all the pieces of the jigsaw they've found and fit them together to build the whole picture.

The last and final stage of the process is **Preservation.** All the artefacts that were found have to be stored somewhere – in a museum or in a university.

So you see, there are loads of different stages in archaeology. Because of this, there are loads of different jobs in archaeology. So you need somebody to do the research, you need daredevil photographers who are willing to hang out of low-flying planes, you need people who are experts in human bones, pottery, glass etc… and you need people who are field archaeologists (excavators).

To bring you a bit closer to the sort of day a field archaeologist has, I'm going to introduce you to Doris. Doris is an archaeologist that works 'in the field' and she looks as normal as you or I. She doesn't have a beard, she doesn't wear Jesus sandals, nor does she wear a silly brimmed hat or PVC catsuit with an ammunition belt tied round her waist. No, she looks completely normal.

Anyway, Doris works for an archaeological company in Grimsby. She's part of a team that excavates bits of land that are about to be built on by new buildings. So she spends most of her time working on building sites.

This is **Doris's Diary:**

1st March

6.00am
Alarm goes off.

7.30am
Arrive at work. Slip into my fetching cagoule and stylish Wellington boots. Trowel in hand, I walk onto site.

7.35am

John (the supervisor) tells me where he wants me to start digging. So here goes...

8.00am

Spent the last half hour clearing modern rubble. But I'm all set now.

9.00am

Thought I'd found a 17th century pit underneath the rubble, spent an hour exposing it and then carefully excavating it. Found a bit of early 17th century pottery in it. But then, right at the bottom, two massive lumps of concrete and a biro pen. If this is a 17th century pit, I'll eat my hat.

10.00am

This is more like it. Found part of a wall underneath the modern concrete dump. Looks 17th century. Better clean it up and start recording it.

10.05am

Started exposing and cleaning the wall, and found a tile floor - must be in some sort of room - cool!

11.00am

It's nice and clean now, better get a quick photo of it and start recording it.

1.00pm

Phew, that took ages. I've just finished measuring and drawing every single brick of the wall - from the top and from the sides. Feeling a bit cross-eyed now. Never-mind, time for lunch.

2.00pm

Okay, now for the paper work...

2.30pm

Paper work finished. Have recorded every possible thing about the wall and floor. From what they're made of, to when I think it was made. Okay, so now for one of the bits I love most about archaeology, I get to demolish it with a big hammer...

3.00pm

Phew, that's better. It's amazing how demolishing an ancient wall can be so therapeutic! Better clear up the rubble and see what's underneath.

4.00pm

Looks promising, there seems to be some sort of pit underneath, and it's got a bit of Saxon pottery poking out of it. Could be a Saxon rubbish dump. Anyway, home-time now. The Saxon rubbish pit will have to wait till tomorrow.

So there you have it. As you can see, Doris's day didn't involve raiding golden idols from temples, or crazy shoot-outs with Nazis, or even fighting ancient stone statues that have come to life. It involved excavating and recording the remains of a 17th

century wall in Grimsby.

Not much adventure in that.

Mmmm. I can tell that you weren't all that impressed by Doris's day. But you see, her day *was* an adventure – she found a wall and floor that had not been seen for centuries. It was another piece of the jigsaw puzzle.

Yeah, but…

Okay, so you want adventure. I'll give you adventure!

Read on for the more adventurous sides of archaeology…

Chapter 3

Adventure

Okay, let's face it – working as an archaeologist in Grimsby is not the most adventurous of jobs or locations (no offence, Doris!). But the good news is, that you don't have to excavate 17th century walls in Grimsby.

I don't?

No. As an archaeologist you've got options. You could be excavating tombs in the Egyptian desert, you could be mapping temples in the jungles of Mexico, or you could even be excavating Roman boats from the bottom of the ocean.

Adventurous enough for you?

In fact, the history of archaeology is littered with stories of adventure.

Fact File

Archaeologists go gooey for graves

Not only do we archaeologists get to work with some dead interesting people, we also get to work with interesting dead people. You see, most ancient cultures would put artefacts (or 'grave goods', as archaeologists call them) into the graves of dead people so that the dead person could use them in the afterlife. Archaeologists love finding grave goods because these can tell them loads of things about ancient cultures.

How about Howard Carter?

Who?

Howard Carter. He was responsible for making one of the most significant archaeological discoveries of all time – the tomb of the Egyptian Pharaoh Tutankhamun. Since almost all Egyptian tombs were robbed by *tomb raiders* (yes, Lara, that includes you) at one point or another, very little was known about the contents of Egyptian pharaonic tombs. That was until 1923, when after years of searching, Carter finally found the tomb of the child king Tutankhamun in the Valley of the Kings. Miraculously it had lain almost undisturbed for around 3000 years, and was found packed with the

most amazing objects – oodles of jewellery, statues, golden thrones, crowns, beds, chariots, intricate model boats, board games, remnants of food, a boomerang (?!), shrines of gilded wood, and the mummified body of Tutankhamun himself. All in all, it was an incredible discovery, and archaeologists have learnt more about the burials of Egyptian pharaohs from this one discovery than they have from any other. What's more, Carter himself became an instant celebrity.

Fact File

The Curse of Tutankhamun

By 1927, everybody that had excavated or worked on Tutankhamun's tomb was dead, apart from Howard Carter. Was this a coincidence, or was it…duh duh duh… the Curse of Tutankhamun? In fact at the time, newspapers went wild with stories of the curse and predictions of who would be next. The story sparked hundreds of extremely bad films of mummies coming back to life and exacting their revenge on archaeologists that had violated their tombs. Anyway, it all turned out to be a load of codswallop – firstly, there's no mention of curses in the ancient texts of Egyptian religion, secondly, everyone that had died, died of natural causes, and thirdly, Howard Carter lived to a ripe old age. Surely if there was such a thing as the Curse of Tutankhmun, Carter would have been the first to pop his clogs.

Underwater archaeology

If you love archaeology, love being underwater, and you don't mind killer sharks and jellyfish, then this is the job for you! Underwater archaeology is not just about finding ancient shipwrecks either, but about finding whole cities, villages, harbours etc. that after centuries of rising sea levels are now underwater.

In principle, underwater archaeology is really no different to excavations on land, just more complicated, a lot more dangerous – oh, and you have to communicate with sign language (it's a little difficult to talk underwater, unless 'glug, glug' means anything to you).

To become an underwater archaeologist you need specialist training – not only do you have to be a qualified archaeologist (more on how you do that in Chapter 4), but you also have to be a qualified diver – with hundreds of dives under your belt. You also need to be trained in all the methods and techniques that archaeologists use underwater. All of this requires a lot of training. At the very least you will need to do an MA (more on what that means later) in underwater archaeology at university. And even when you are fully qualified, getting a job as a professional underwater archaeologist isn't a cinch. As with a lot of professions there aren't always enough jobs to go round.

But before you even think about entering down that path, the best thing to do is a dive. You never know how you're going to react underwater until you've experienced being 4.5 metres under the water breathing through an oxygen tank – even the biggest, hardest blokes can start screaming for their mummies.

And remember, even underwater archaeology isn't always glamorous. Recent excavations around the harbour at Alexandria (Egypt) had to be stopped in the afternoons because all the city's sewage was being pumped into the water – lovely!

The great thing about archaeology is that you don't have to be 15 metres underwater to experience a bit of adventure. Working on land can be just as adventurous. For a start you can work anywhere in the world.

Yeah, but even if I was an executive for some big international business I'd still get to work abroad.

Sure. But not in the same way. Business executives only get to see the insides of airports and conference rooms. As an archaeologist you *really* get to travel. You get to meet real people (not people in suits), you get to eat real local foods (not three-course meals in your hotel room), and you get to live in remote places. You could be working in the deepest, darkest jungle, or on a remote mountaintop, or in the middle of the desert, or even in the North Pole – wherever tickles your fancy.

Unfortunate Fact

Before you get too carried away with the idea of adventurous deep-sea dives or excavating burials packed full of treasure in the jungles of Central America, a word of warning – a lot of the work can be tedious and mind-numbingly boring. You can spend days upon days just cleaning the dirt off a skeleton before you can even take it out of the ground, or months upon months meticulously mapping a shipwreck. So even if you're excavating a site in the Egyptian desert, most of your days tend to be like Doris's.

Fortunate Fact

Fortunately, the heart-stopping, mouth-watering, rendered speechless moments in archaeology make it all worthwhile.

What's more, archaeologists normally dig up artefacts that are a lot older than a 17th century wall. Often, archaeologists excavate artefacts that are thousands and thousands of years old.

Thirdly, archaeologists often dig up things that are a lot more exciting than a boring old wall in Grimsby. They excavate ancient cities – like Pompeii, the Roman city that was entombed by the ash and larva from a volcanic eruption (see fact file), they excavate incredible ancient graves, they excavate the ancient palaces of Egyptian pharaohs, they excavate the houses of early farming communities that existed around 8000 years ago, they uncover amazing paintings of animals on cave walls that were painted by cave-dwelling humans around 20,000 years ago. In short, archaeologists dig up a lot of mind-bogglingly extraordinary stuff.

Fact File

Pompeii

In August AD79 in southern Italy, near the Roman city of Pompeii, Mount Vesuvius erupted, covering Pompeii in several metres of volcanic ash. Although the eruption was a terrible tragedy, it was (and still is) an archaeologist's dream come true – it meant that an exact moment in time was captured forever. The people of Pompeii had no time to pack up their belongings and make a run for it – so not only did archaeologists find the people of Pompeii lying under the ash, but also their houses, their shops, their temples, their furniture, their belongings, their food etc… It's like seeing a day in the life of a Roman city. Excavations at Pompeii have been going on for ages and will still be going on in years to come.

If all this interests you (if it doesn't you've probably got a screw loose somewhere) then you'll be wondering what you have to do to become an archaeologist. So before you rush out and buy a trowel, read on to find out how to make it in the world of archaeology.

Chapter 4

Making it in archaeology

For the majority of archaeologists this is a contradiction in terms. 'Making it' and 'archaeology' are words that don't often appear in the same sentence!

Why?

Well, very few people 'make it' in archaeology. It's a long and difficult path to the top. To become a successful archaeologist you're going to have to be patient (it could take a lifetime), often do jobs that you'd rather not do, be **very** dedicated, do lots of studying, and not mind being permanently skint.

Still interested??

Er, I think so – it depends what happens when I do make it.

Well, 'making it' in archaeology isn't exactly the same as making it as a movie star, for example. It's not like you'll be making a fortune, or you'll be invited to the latest premier. And you certainly won't be supping on oysters and lobster while sipping expensive champagne.

I won't?

No. I'm afraid it'll be more a case of baked beans on toast with a bottle of cheap bubbly from Asda.

Oh right, so what's the point?

Well, if you are one of the lucky ones, and do 'make it', these are the sorts of things that may happen to you –

You may be involved in some amazing discoveries. Who knows, you may be the next Howard Carter. Or you may find evidence of new cultures that were never before known about.

You'll get to direct your own excavations.

Your theories may become facts. Who knows, you could be the one to prove and convince everyone that yes, Stonehenge was in fact built by life forms from outer space (joke!).

Your name and theories will be in print. Bookshops will have whole shelves stacked full with all the books that you've written.

You may even get to be on TV because some discovery channel programme wants you to talk about your theories (note – you may need a beard to do this).

If any or all of the above appeals to you (not necessarily the beard part), then you'll want to know how to get there.

WARNING. It's not easy and you may have grey hair and wrinkles before you get to the top. Only the people that *really really really* love archaeology need read on...

You can't just get to the top by doing an A-level

in archaeology, you know. No. You might need lots of silly letters before and after your name (all shall be revealed later), and you need experience of working 'in the field'.

How to become a field archaeologist

A field archaeologist is somebody who is mainly involved in the survey and excavation aspects of archaeology (i.e. they work in the field, like Doris). Every budding archaeologist needs experience in working as a field archaeologist.

Why?

Because it's the basis of all archaeology.

Oh.

In fact, you'll find that pretty much everybody involved in any part of the archaeological process (whether they're an Egyptian poo specialist, or a specialist in bricks) was a field archaeologist to start with.

Unfortunately you can't just wake up one day and decide, 'Oooh, I know, I think I'll get a job as a field archaeologist today.' You need experience, and you need qualifications before anyone's going to pay you to dig.

Bummer!

And normally the only way to become a field archaeologist is to work initially as a volunteer.

Volunteer? Does that mean I don't get paid?

Afraid so. And if you've never dug before you may even have to pay for your board and lodging. If you are thinking about volunteering you have to shop around a bit – some organizations will charge you a lot of money just for the privilege of working for free.

The amount of time you have to volunteer before you become a professional archaeologist, and therefore get paid, generally depends on whether you've got a degree (more on this later). If you haven't got a degree then you'll probably need wealthy parents because you may be working for months, even years before anyone's going to pay you a penny.

Okay, so let's assume you've just got your degree, you've notched up a couple of months of experience as a volunteer field archaeologist, what next?

Well, if you're really lucky you'll be able to get a job as a professional field archaeologist.

Why do I have to be lucky? Surely once I've got a degree and loads of experience everyone's going to want to employ me?

Afraid not – it's a case of too many archaeologists and too few jobs. But there are jobs out there.

Anyway, if you're good, after a few years of working as a professional field archaeologist you may get promoted to supervisor. This doesn't mean that you get to put your feet up, drink cocktails in the sun, and just boss people about. Okay, you do get to boss everybody about, but there's a little more to it than that. Supervisors are in charge of the day-to-day running of the excavation and they're often in charge of writing the reports after the excavation has finished.

But the really big cheese of an excavation is the director or manager. They get to run the whole show.

Before we go any further, I think it's only right that I should be completely honest with you and warn you of the lows of being a field archaeologist. Like all jobs, there are highs and there are lows. Here are just a few of them –

Being a field archaeologist
Low 👎

You have to work outside in the winter – in icy rains, in the snow, in cold winter winds. This can be really unpleasant and soul destroying, particularly when you have to break through the layers of ground frost before you can even start digging! Or when you have to spend hours trying to get rid of the icy rainwater from the hole that you're working in.

High 👍

You get a great tan in the summer. And all your friends are jealous of you because they have to work in stuffy offices.

Low 👎

You spend all day covered in mud.

High 👍

No one wants to sit next to you on the bus home, so you get two seats all to your self.

Low 👎

You never get to wear nice clothes to work (because they'd get ruined).

High 👍

Tramps don't ask you for money because they think you're one of them.

Low 👎

Sometimes the work can be really physically demanding – wielding mattocks, shovelling dirt, wheeling heavy wheelbarrows can all be exhausting, and you can ache in places that you never knew existed!

High 👍

You develop muscles on your muscles. You never have to 'work-out'. And you get so fit that you don't pant, dribble or collapse when running for a bus.

Low

You get blisters and calluses on your hands from the tools that you use.

High

They make you look more interesting.

Low

You have to work and sometimes live in some really scummy situations – with no running water, no bathing facilities, you may even have to sleep in a tent!

High

You're at one with nature!?! (yeah, right.)

Low 👎

The toilets where you're working/living can be worse than the portaloos at Glastonbury Festival. And sometimes there are no toilets at all, just bushes...

High 👍

Er, there isn't one.

Low 👎

You get paid peanuts. You'll never own a Versace frock (unless you buy one secondhand from Oxfam), and you won't be driving a Porsche convertible with inbuilt 'surround-sound' stereo (unless you've got a part-time job as a chauffeur).

High

Peanuts are tasty.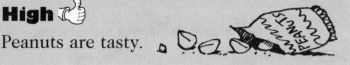

Low 👎

You may have to
spend months away
from your friends
and family because
you're working on
an excavation in
Cambodia.

High 👍

Who cares – you're in Cambodia!
Anyway, you can make new friends.

Okay, so there are a few lows – aren't there in every job?! But if you were to ask any archaeologist, he/she would say that without a doubt, the pros outweigh the cons.

The coolest things about being a field archaeologist are – you never know what you're going to find, you get to be the first person to see things that haven't seen the light of day for hundreds or thousands of years, and you learn something new pretty much everyday. I bet you don't get that sort of job satisfaction as a chartered accountant.

Anyway, back to making it as an archaeologist. Although you don't have to be Einstein to become an archaeologist, to become a *successful* archaeologist, you're going to need qualifications and you're going to need lots of them!

Qualifications

First off, you're going to have to get a BSc or BA in archaeology.

What on earth does that mean?

Well, BSc stands for Bachelor of Science, and BA stands for Bachelor of Arts…

I didn't realize that I'd have to be unmarried all my life just because I want to be an archaeologist.

No, no. Not that sort of bachelor. 'Bachelor of Arts' is just a term for a degree (although archaeologists do find it hard to get anyone to marry them, due to the fact that they're permanently dirty and smelly). Anyway, if you do a BA or BSc in archaeology, you'll learn all about archaeology. You'll also get some experience of working 'in the field'. Your degree will take you three to four years to do, and once you've finished you get to have letters after your name. So you'll no longer be just boring old Joe Bloggs, you'll be **Joe Bloggs BA** or **Joe Bloggs BSc**

But I'm not called Joe Bloggs!

Er…I was using it as an example.

Anyway, lots of archaeologists stop here – they get a degree and then work as field archaeologist and eventually become a supervisor and so on. However, some archaeologists decide to follow more of an academic path and study at university for a few more years.

What! Are they mad?

Probably. But you see, the more qualifications that you have as an archaeologist, the more chance you have at doing your own thing. So, the next stop for studious archaeologists is an MA or an MSc

A what?

MA stands for Master of Arts and MSc stands for Master of Science – they're the qualifications that come after your first degree. It's at this point that you can start to specialize in the area that interests you, such as a particular culture – like the Incas, the Celts, or the Vikings – or a particular country, like the archaeology of Africa. You see, the more you specialize in a particular area, the more you'll become hot property. I mean, let's face it, you can't know everything about everything, can you? But if you know everything about one thing then you're a specialist. And when you're a specialist you're a valuable person to know and employ.

Anyway, this will take you one to two years to do and when you've finished you'll no longer be Joe Bloggs BA

I won't?

No, you'll be Joe Bloggs MA or Joe Bloggs MSc

Okay so you've got your BA or BSc in archaeology and you've passed your MA or MSc, next, is the crème de la crème of university qualifications – a PhD.

Uh?

PhD. It stands for Doctor of Philosophy...

But I don't want to be a philosopher. Come to think of it, I don't want to be a doctor either – I get squeamish when my nose bleeds.

No, no, not that sort of doctor. A 'doctor' can mean somebody that has achieved the highest level of university degree – in the same way that A-levels are the highest qualifications you can get at school. And 'philosophy' doesn't only mean 'what's the meaning of life?', it can also mean 'advanced study'. So, to put it simply, a PhD is the highest degree you can do, and it means that you're extremely clever. And what's more, you'll no longer be called Joe Bloggs MA. You'll be Dr Bloggs.

Anyway, when you do a PhD you really specialize in the particular area that you're interested in – like Inca human sacrifices. By the end of it (it takes a minimum of three years) you'll know all there is to know about Inca human sacrifices and you'll have come up with fantastic, ground-breaking theories about it.

Okay, so you've now got an impressive list of qualifications, you're Dr So-and-so, you've got oodles of experience working 'in the field'. The only problem it has all taken so long you're now 75 years of age with false teeth and a zimmer frame, and are therefore in no fit state to direct any excavation or appear on TV (only kidding!).

Chapter 5
It's not all digging

Digging may not be your cup of tea. And if it's not, then don't fear! There are many other jobs in archaeology that are just as important, but don't require you to spend your day in a muddy, wet hole.

If you love peering down microscopes and dressing up in a long white coat then this could be for you. So for all you budding scientists out there, listen up, here are a few of the other jobs in archaeology…

Dating Specialists

Archaeology needs specialists in dating…

People that have got loads of girlfriends or

boyfriends? I don't see why that...

No, no. Not that sort of dating. Archaeological dating is about being able to say how old something is. Ancient artefacts aren't found with labels on saying 'made in England in 1321 BC', you know! But there are a number of scientific techniques that enable you to work out the age of an artefact (give or take a hundred years). So take Jim, for example. He spends his day dating wood by looking at tree rings (this is called dendrochronology). Or take Lucy – she spends her time in a lab using carbon-14 to date artefacts.

4,736
4,737
4,738
4,739
4,740
4,741
4,743
4,744

Wow, it's all so much clearer now.

Okay, brief explanation: every year a tree grows a new layer of wood (this is called a tree ring). If it's been a good summer the tree ring will be wider, and if it's been a bad summer the ring will be thinner.

Still paying attention? Good, I'll continue...

So, Jim can then match the pattern of the rings with the records that he has, to find out when the tree was growing, and when it was cut down.

Zzzzzzzzzz

Carbon-14 dating only works for organic artefacts – like animals and plants. Carbon-14 is a radioactive carbon atom that is found in all plants and animals – even when they're dead. In any sample it takes 5568 years for half the carbon-14 to decay. So Lucy can measure how much carbon-14 there is left in a sample and can then tell how old it is.

Zzzzzzzz

Okay, I get the message. For more information, ask your science teacher – at the very least, it might make a nice change from dissecting frogs first thing on a Monday morning.

If you fancy yourself in a white lab coat as a dating specialist then you'll need to be good at science and more than likely, you'll need a BSc in archaeology.

If dating doesn't grab you, however, then what about becoming a human osteologist?

Human osteologists

Human whaty whatists?

Human osteologists are people who study human remains – their skeletons and stuff.

Well, why didn't you say that in the first place?

Because we archaeologists like to use long, complicated words – it make us feel big and clever.

Anyway, take Olga – she's an osteologist – and she spends her days analysing bones. Because she's so clever and knows all there is to know about human bones she's able to look at a skeleton and tell how the person died, what their diet was like, how old they were when they died, what sex they were, what horrible diseases they had etc...

Now, this job is not for the more faint-hearted of you. It can be pretty gruesome. If you don't mind spending your days with bits of dead people, then this could be the job for you. But remember, it's not just bones that you might be studying. If you're working in somewhere like Egypt, where they often mummified their dead, or in a really icy-cold climate (where bodies get frozen), the bodies may still have skin and hair, fingernails, and even the contents of their stomachs may have survived.

Fact File

Yuk

Horrible things happen when people are buried in lead coffins. Lead coffins are completely air-tight which means that when the body inside starts rotting, the gases it gives off can't escape. So when some poor unsuspecting archaeologist opens the coffin hundreds of years later, the gases mix with the sudden rush of oxygen and gooey slime explodes all over their face. And that's not all, if the person had some awful disease, the virus could still be living in the coffin just waiting to attack some poor inquisitive archaeologist. So, beware of lead coffins.

If you're really interested in becoming a specialist in human or even animal remains then you'll need to be good at science, particularly biology, and there again, you'll probably need to do a BSc in archaeology.

If looking at mouldy old bones or decomposing skin under a microscope doesn't grab you (I can't imagine why it wouldn't), then what about being an environmental archaeologist?

Environmental Archaeologists

Archaeologists don't just look at ancient people,

and their artefacts. To understand them more, archaeologists also look at the different and changing environments those people lived in.

Why?

Well, it helps us see more of the whole picture. We are a product of our environment, after all.

Sounds a bit deep for me.

Well, think about it, if you were born a few thousand years ago...

What, like my headteacher? (Tee hee!)

You would have been much more affected by the environment. The type of climate you lived in, the

sorts of vegetation and animal life around – all would determine how you lived. You don't even have to go back a thousand years. You'd live a very different life if you were living in the North Pole to the kind of life you'd have in the jungles of Africa, wouldn't you? For a start, you'd have to make very different houses – not much wood in the North Pole.

And because environments are constantly changing (did you know that elephants and hippos used to roam around London 130,000 years ago?), archaeologists think this is one of the reasons that causes human societies to change, because they have to adapt to a different environment. Archaeologists also think that changes in the climate caused some societies to disappear because they couldn't adapt to those changes.

So what exactly does an environmental archaeologist do?

Well, take Roddy, for example, he's an environmental archaeologist and he just *lurves* soil, he spends hours upon hours sieving it or putting it in flotation tanks. The only thing he likes more than soil is what he finds in it, like bits of pollen, small animal bones, snail shells etc...

This is not because Roddy is a weird nutter, it's

because with the things that he finds, he can reconstruct what the environment and climate used to be like a long time ago. Clever, huh?

So if soil and snail shells do it for you and you want to become an environmental archaeologist, then you'll also need to be good at science, and I know I've said this before, but you'll probably need to do a BSc in archaeology.

If none of the above grabs you, then what about becoming a finds specialist?

Finds Specialists

Finds specialists are people who analyse ancient artefacts. You see, not only do you need people with special knowledge on different cultures, different time periods, dating techniques, and so on, archaeology also needs people that are specialists in the artefacts that are found through excavation – like bricks for example.

Uh? But a brick's a brick.

Actually it's not. Throughout history, the brick has been made differently at different times. Remember Doris's wall? Well, before she demolished it, she would have saved a couple of bricks and sent them back to the laboratory for Bryan, the brick specialist. He would have looked at them, measured them, analysed what they were made of, and would then probably have said 'Ah ha, yes ... a perfect specimen of *redus brickus*. Typical of the make and design of bricks that were made and used for houses in Grimsby during the late 17th century'.

For every type of artefact that field archaeologists excavate – like pottery, stone tools, bronze swords – there are specialists that will be able to examine them and tell who made it (not whether Bill or Bob made it, but what culture made it), what it is, how it was made, what it was used for, and when it was made – clever, huh?

So there are pottery specialists, wood specialists, jewellery specialists, textiles specialists and so on. If you have a bit of a thing for Viking helmets and swords, prehistoric pottery, or just about anything, you can make a career out of it. Oh, and the white laboratory coat is optional.

Fact File

How did they do that?

Archaeologists are inquisitive creatures, they love to dabble in experimental archaeology – they make reconstructions of things that they find to work out how ancient people would have made and used them. They like to pretend that they're prehistoric cave dwellers and have a go at making stone tools by bashing two bits of flint together. They like to build big Viking longships and then try and sail them from A to B. Sometimes they succeed and sometimes they fail. Recently, archaeologists tried to build a miniature Egyptian pyramid, using the same tools, techniques and methods as the ancient Egyptians – they failed miserably.

Conservators

Conservators are people that treat ancient artefacts to stop them from decaying. You see, certain materials like wood and human flesh (organic materials) can be preserved for thousands of years if they're buried in certain conditions – like bogs, arid deserts, or in ice. But when archaeologists dig them up, the artefacts start to decay. So archaeology needs people like Hugh, the conservator. Hugh's able to take artefacts and treat them with special chemicals to prevent them from rotting into nothing. Conservators also re-build ancient buildings that have been partially destroyed or are falling down, or re-paint ancient paintings that have started to decay. In fact many of the ancient monuments you may have visited — like the Acropolis in Athens, and the Tower of London — have all been partially rebuilt.

Fact File

Body in the Bog

Conservators also conserve human bodies. When the upper half of a 2000-year-old man was found in Cheshire, he still had most of his skin and flesh because they'd been preserved in a bog. Even the contents of his stomach had survived – apparently his last meal had been a griddle cake (a rough bread). The poor man had been hit on the head, knifed, strangled, and then chucked into a bog. When he was found, conservators had to treat him with special chemicals and water so that he wouldn't rot away. They did such a good job that you can still see him today in the British Museum. He is now so famous he even has his own name – 'Lindow Man'.

If a white lab coat does nothing for your complexion, and the smell of laboratories makes you feel sick, then there are a few other jobs in archaeology that might interest you.

Photographers

Archaeology always needs photographers because everything that is found during an excavation needs to be recorded. So take Richard the photographer, for example, he spends his day photographing excavations, as well as the artefacts that are found, and sometimes he even gets to hang out of a low-flying plane to take photographs from the air. So if you fancy yourself as a bit of a David Bailey and you've got a bit of thing for archaeology then this could be the job for you. All you need is to be a dab hand with cameras (some sort of photography qualification is required) and some knowledge and experience of archaeology.

Computer Analysts and Stuff

Archaeologists aren't behind the times. Oh no, we're modern people who have taken archaeology (kicking and screaming) into the 21st century. Nowadays computers are an essential part of archaeology. Without them we'd just fall apart. This is not just because we'd no longer be able to play solitaire on them, it's also because computers are used for so many things – like drawing reconstructions and analysing many different types of data. Remember Doris's wall and pit? Well, the plans that she drew would have been given to Carole, the computer whizz who would have then re-drawn them on to her computer along with everything else that had been found on the excavation.

So if you're a bit of a whizz on computers, this could be the type of job for you. You'll need a lot of specialist training on all the different types of packages that archaeologists use, and again, experience as a field archaeologist would be very useful.

Illustrators

Not everything is done on computers though. Archaeologists still use good old-fashioned pencil and paper sometimes. So there are professional archaeological illustrators like Sam, who spends his day meticulously drawing artefacts or entire

scenes of what life used to be like in ancient times on the basis of what was found during an excavation.

For this you need an eye for detail, qualifications in art/graphic design, knowledge of archaeology, and sometimes, you need a good imagination.

Not being a field archaeologist

There are advantages to working in a laboratory, or at a computer etc, but it's not all a bed of roses, you know. So here are some of the pros and cons...

Con

Field archaeologists get better tans than you in the summer.

Pro

Field archaeologists look sixty years old when they're only thirty – all that sun and windburn takes its toll. Whereas you'll look sweet sixteen all your life.

Con

Not much exercise in looking at stone tools under microscopes. So if you want to keep fit you'll have to go jogging at the weekends.

Pro 👍

At least you don't have to start wielding heavy mattocks and shovels around first thing on a Monday morning.

Con 👎

Whilst field archaeologists spend their days digging in the glorious outdoors on some Tibetan mountaintop, or underwater archaeologists spend their afternoons on the Mediterranean seabed, you'll be cooped up in some boring old office or laboratory.

Pro 👍

You won't get eaten by a killer shark or charged by some wild Tibetan mountain goat.

Chapter 6

Alternatively...

If none of the jobs mentioned so far grab you, then don't worry. You can still be involved in archaeology without being stuck in a wet hole all day as a field archaeologist, or looking at a mouldy old thigh bone under a microscope as an osteologist, or sieving soil as an environmental archaeologist and so on.

I can?

Sure you can. Here are a few other jobs that just may tickle your fancy.

Museum Curator

If you love ancient artefacts, then what about becoming a museum curator?

What do they do?

Well, curators look after a museum's collections – they're in charge of acquiring the artefacts, researching them, cataloguing them, storing them, displaying and explaining them to the public. In short, they're managers of museum collections.

So, how do I become a museum curator?

Well, if you want to be in charge of an archaeological collection you'll need to have a good knowledge of archaeology, you'll need a qualification in museum and heritage studies, and you'll need good managerial skills. Voluntary work experience in a museum would also be a bonus.

Archaeological Documentaries

If you're torn between a career in television and a career as an archaeologist, then why not work in archaeological documentaries?

What, like Time Team *and* Meet the Ancestors?

And all the rest. Archaeological documentaries are all the rage at the moment.

You could get a job as a development researcher – somebody that comes up with the original idea for a documentary, like *Roman Cesspits In London*, or as a researcher – somebody who has to research all the Roman cesspits in London. Or you could even be the presenter of the documentary – you'll probably need to be a middle-aged man with a lot of facial hair to do this, though (that seem to be the general requirement).

So how do I get into archaeological documentaries?

Well, nothing is set in stone, but it would help if

you had some knowledge of archaeology and some experience and qualifications in media.

Amateur Archaeology

If the idea of professional archaeology doesn't, appeal to you, then all is not lost. You can still survey, excavate, and analyse artefacts, but as an amateur archaeologist.

An amateur archaeologist is not someone who's pants at archaeology, it's somebody who loves archaeology but doesn't want to make a career out of it, so they do archaeology as a hobby at the weekends.

The great thing about amateur archaeology is that you can choose how involved you want to be – you can excavate sites every single weekend, or if that's too much you can excavate four days a month. Okay, not getting paid is a bit of a downer, but if you're working as a chartered accountant Monday to Friday, you'll probably be earning oodles of cash anyway. Another cool thing about amateur archaeology is that you can choose what you want to do – you can choose to excavate and record, you can choose to survey, you can choose to sort out the artefacts – or you can have a go at doing everything.

There are loads of amateur archaeological societies all over the country that you can join. And you can get involved at any age. If you want to excavate, though, you'll probably need to be sixteen years or over.

Oh, and you don't need any prior experience or any particular qualifications to join. You just need a few quid to pay for your membership, a real enthusiasm for archaeology, and a few free weekends.

Chapter 7

You've got the bug

If you've read this book and you still want to be an archaeologist, well then you're beyond help. It's a sad state of affairs, but once you've got the archaeology bug, there's no cure for it.

Okay, so you're not old enough to become an archaeologist right now. But this doesn't mean you have to sit in your classroom just dreaming of a time when you can spend your days in a muddy wet hole, or looking at mouldy old Egyptian poo down the lens of a microscope.

I don't?

No. There are a number of things that you can do right now to get involved in archaeology. After all, before you sign your life over to an existence of poverty and mud, it's best to be sure that you really are interested in archaeology, and a good way to do that is to learn as much as you can about ancient cultures.

So here are some top tips on what you can be doing now:

1 Join your local historical and archaeological societies. These societies will know all about the history and archaeology in your area, and you can get involved in all the work that they do. Get on to the Internet or ask your teacher where your local historical/archaeological society is.

2 Badger your mum or your school to take you to museums. Visiting archaeological museums is the best way to learn about

ancient cultures. Seeing artefacts and learning about them really helps to bring the past to life. Remember, museums aren't the stuffy, boring places that they used to be. Some museums now have interactive displays and organize workshops where you can handle the artefacts, and you're shown how they were made and used.

3 Log on to the Council for British Archaeology's web site (www.britarch.co.uk), and click on 'Young Archaeologists Club' – you can get loads of information here on various events put on throughout the country.

4 Visit historical and archaeological sites. If you've never visited Stonehenge or Hadrian's Wall then GO. England is littered with historical and archaeological sites that you can visit – whether they're stone circles, castles, churches, walls or barrows. There's

bound to be at least one near where you live.

5 And what about when you go on holiday? Don't just lounge around on the beach, or play in the swimming pool, go and visit all the historical and archaeological sites in the area. Remember, the more you know the better.

6 Watch archaeological documentaries. Take advantage of the number of archaeological documentaries that are on TV at the moment. You can learn so much. Amongst other things, you can learn about the new discoveries all over the world and you can see how an excavation is actually done.

7 And most important of all: READ. And I don't mean reading Tomb Raider comics either. There are thousands of books on ancient civilizations and cultures to read, there are magazines, and there's the Internet.

Chapter 8

A load of old fossils

Okay, you're probably wondering why we haven't discussed digging up dinosaur bones yet…the reason is that palaeontology (the study of dinosaurs) has got nothing to with archaeology.

Uh? But I've seen Jurassic Park, *I thought archaeology and palaeontology were one and the same.*

Well, there are a few similarities – they both involve a lot of detective work, they both dig in the ground, and they're both interested in finding the remains of what were once living things that died many, many years ago. However, whereas archaeologists are primarily interested in humans that existed a long time ago and all the things they left behind, palaeontologists tend to look at creatures, now fossilized, that lived at a time before we humans even existed – like dinosaurs.

So if you're a one-track, single-minded archaeology fiend then you needn't read any further. But if, however, you're completely dotty about dinosaurs then read on...

So, palaeontology (pronounced palley-on-tology, in case you didn't know) is the study of extinct, fossilized animals, and palaeontologists are people who study them.

How do they study them?

They look at all the fossilized remains of the animals – their bones, their teeth, their eggs, and sometimes they even look at their fossilized poo (which palaeontologists call coprolites because 'poo' is not a long enough word for them). Remarkably, palaeontologists even occasionally find fossilized footprints.

Fact File

In the beginning

When fossilized extinct animals were first discovered, the church claimed that they were animals that had been washed away and killed in the great flood (the great flood in the Bible). Well, there certainly wouldn't have been any room for two *Tyrannosaurus rexes* on Noah's Ark, would there? After decades of debate and discovery it was proved that dinosaurs and other animals existed on earth many, many millions of years before humans did (in fact the first dinosaurs evolved on earth around a staggering 245 million years ago). Amazingly some people still don't believe it.

Anyway, so when a palaeontologist finds the fossilized skeleton of a dinosaur, he/she can match it to a type of dinosaur that they already know about. So, for example, Peter the palaeontologist

would uncover a dinosaur skeleton that has four legs, a long neck, a long tail, no sharp teeth etc. and would say, 'Aha, I've found a *Diplodocus*'.

What if it's a type of dinosaur that no one has found before?

Good question. Palaeontologists are constantly finding new species of dinosaur. If you unearth the skeleton of a dinosaur that's never been found before, it's up to you to name it, but remember you have to give it the longest, most complicated name you can possibly think of! You'd then have to analyse all its features to discover what it ate (was it a herbivore, omnivore, or carnivore), what did it look like, how did it walk etc.

Fact File

Oops!

Sometimes when palaeontologists put together skeletons or try to understand them, they get it a bit wrong. When the first reconstruction of *Tyrannosaurus rex* was made, his eyes were put in his nasal socket. A big boob was made recently when the fossils of a creature was found that had the head of a primitive bird, and the teeth and the tail of a land-bound little dinosaur – they called it *Archaeoraptor*. Many a debate was to be had about this creature, it was seen as the 'missing link' between dinosaurs and birds. A while later it was discovered to be a fake – the dinosaur tail had just been glued to the bottom of the bird!

So, where do palaeontologists find dinosaur skeletons?

They find their fossilized remains in rocks.

In rocks? How did they get there?

Okay, well there are three categories of rock – igneous rocks, sedimentary rocks and metamorphic rocks.

How interesting.

Actually it is. You see, igneous rocks (like granite) are cooked by volcanoes and then blasted out as lava during an eruption. The lava and volcanic ash can then trap any poor unsuspecting animal that might be around at the time. So the animal gets trapped and then eventually becomes fossilized. Sedimentary rocks (like limestone, sandstone, and chalk) are created by the build up of layers of mud or sand that eventually become squashed into stone. So when some poor dinosaur (or any living thing – plant or animal) dies on one of

these layers it gets covered over by more layers and becomes fossilized in the rock. Metamorphic rocks (like slate) are made by the cooking of sedimentary or igneous rocks by volcanic activity. Any fossil remains in the rocks get burnt.

The great thing about rocks is that each layer contains a different level of radioactivity.

Why's that so great?

Well, palaeontologists can measure the level of radioactivity, and then date the layer and the fossils within it.

What, to the exact year?

Give or take a few million years.

Because palaeontologists find dinosaurs in rocks they need to use very different tools to archaeologists. They use things like pneumatic drills, and dentist's drills, chemical baths, even Plaster of Paris to wrap bones in.

Qualities you need to become a palaeontologist.

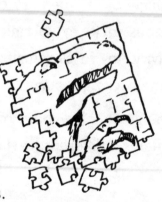

1 You need to be a dab hand at doing jigsaw puzzles. You'll be spending many a day fitting together old fossilized bones.

2 You need to be very, very patient. It takes a long time to find fossils, a long time to clean them, a long time to remove them, a long time fitting their bones together, a long time to study them etc... By the time you've finished the whole process and your dinosaur skeleton is finally hanging in a museum, you'll probably be a fossil.

3 You need to be pretty fit. A lot of palaeontology is done in inhospitable areas – up cliffs, in caves, in gorges etc. so you'll be exhausted just from the walk to work. And once you get to work you'll be hammering and chipping away at rock all day. So if you're a person who is rather challenged in the fitness department, then get fit!

4 You need to be good at science.

5 And finally, you need to be a fossil fanatic.

So how do I become a palaeontologist?

With a lot of hard work! Like archaeologists, you'll probably need to volunteer on a field excavation for a while (I'm afraid you can't do that until you're a bit older). And like archaeologists, you'll need to do a lot of studying.

Most palaeontologists are experts in geology (the study of rocks) and zoology (the study of animals that are around today), so you'll have to study these subjects. For now, though, you need to be good at science, and get the best possible grades you can.

That's a wrap

So you've made it to the end of the book. This has got to be a good sign – not only does it mean that you can read (which will certainly help you on your way to becoming an archaeologist/palaeontologist) but it also means that all this talk of mud, hard work, or forever empty pockets hasn't completely put you off! And it shouldn't. Because although being an archaeologist or palaeontologist is not always a bed of roses and 'making it' is no cinch, they are (without a doubt) two of the most interesting, exciting, different and fun jobs around.

So go on, get yourself down to your local hardware shop and invest in a trowel.

Penguin Reference Books
A Handbook of Management

Thomas Kempner is Principal of the Administrative Staff
College, Henley, and Professor and Director of Business
Studies at Brunel University. He graduated in Economics from
University College, London, and subsequently worked at the
Administrative Staff College, Henley, and at the University
of Sheffield. In 1963 he started the Management Centre at the
University of Bradford and became Professor of
Management Studies as well as the Centre's first director.
Professor Kempner is the author of numerous articles and
several books on management topics. He is the editor of the
Pelican Library of Business and Management, a business
consultant, and also the director of several companies.
Among his publications are *A Guide to the Study of
Management* (1969), *Management Thinkers* (co-edited,
1970), and *Business and Society* (with K. Macmillan and
K. Hawkins, 1974).

A Handbook of
Management

Edited by Thomas Kempner

Penguin Books

Penguin Books Ltd,
Harmondsworth, Middlesex, England
Penguin Books, 625 Madison Avenue,
New York, New York 10022, U.S.A.
Penguin Books Australia Ltd,
Ringwood, Victoria, Australia
Penguin Books Canada Ltd, 2801 John Street,
Markham, Ontario, Canada L3R 1B4
Penguin Books (N.Z.) Ltd,
182–190 Wairau Road, Auckland 10, New Zealand

First published by Weidenfeld & Nicolson 1971
Revised edition published by Penguin Books 1976
Reprinted 1977
Copyright © Thomas Kempner, 1971, 1976

Made and printed in Great Britain by
Richard Clay (The Chaucer Press) Ltd,
Bungay, Suffolk
Set in Monotype Times

Introduction

A Handbook of Management has been written to provide a handy reference book on the main concepts and ideas which underpin the work of management. The authors hope that it will provide useful information in a complex subject for both managers and students – indeed the two are often the same.

Our main purpose was to help managers survive in an increasingly complex and jargon-obsessed society.

The subjects of management studies are many and varied; there are few topics which can be regarded as completely useless to managers. Nevertheless certain boundaries have become established – at least for the time being. This handbook contains the topics and subjects generally regarded as essential. These include:

1. The relevant parts of the social sciences applicable to management: Economics, Sociology and Psychology. They describe the underlying or background situations which all managers face – that is, the behaviour of individuals and groups at work and in society as a whole, their reactions to monetary and other stimuli and the process of social, political, economic and technological change.

2. The quantitative aspects of management – the process of measurement analysis and comparison of the available data.

3. The functional areas such as Marketing, Production, Personnel, Finance.

4. The integration of management activities through the subject of 'Business Policy' which includes strategy formulation and planning. It is under this heading that specific attention is given to the future prospects of all parts of the organization.

Each author has tried to take a concise and synoptic view of the topics which comprise his subject area, giving as much coverage as possible and yet without producing a book of impossible length.

How to Use This Book

This handbook divides the subject matter of management into eleven main headings, each of which is covered by an entry giving a brief overview of that subject. The eleven headings are:

1 Business Policy and Corporate Planning.
2 Industrial Relations, Trade Unions and Collective Bargaining.
3 Industrial and Occupational Psychology and Ergonomics.
4 Industrial and Commercial Law.
5 Management Accounting and Financial Management.
6 Industrial Sociology (including Organization and Structure).
7 Quantitative aspects of Management (including Statistics, Operational Research and Computer Applications).
8 Economics, Econometrics and Managerial Economics.
9 Personnel Management.

10 Marketing (including Purchasing and Public Relations).
11 Production Management.

To obtain an overview of the whole field of management the reader can simply look up the entries under the eleven main headings.

To obtain a more detailed view of the subjects covered by a main heading, the reader should refer to the synoptic index (pages 9–25). Here, under each of the eleven main headings, are listed the whole range of topics which fall within them, as well as cross-references (⇨ see; ⇨ see also) to the major links between topics.

Throughout the handbook cross-references are included in most entries. These should be read to obtain a fuller grasp of the topic concerned.

Most entries also contain reading references to the leading books on the topic, which will help the reader to build up his own library on the fields which concern him.

N.B. The Industrial Relations Act, 1971, to which a number of references are made in the text has been substantially repealed. Further legislation is proposed.

List of Contributors

with their Initials and Subjects

A.J.A.A.	A. J. A. Argenti Management Consultant	Business Policy
N.H.C.	Dr N. H. Cuthbert Senior Lecturer in Industrial Relations, The Management Centre, University of Bradford	Industrial Relations and Trade Unions
E.E.	Dr Elwyn Edwards Reader in Ergonomics, University of Loughborough	Industrial and Occupational Psychology and Ergonomics
W.F.F.	Dr W. F. Frank Head of the Department of Legal Studies, Lanchester Polytechnic	Industrial and Commercial Law
C.M.H.H.	C. M. H. Hutchinson British American Tobacco Ltd	The Managerial Grid
E.A.L.	E. A. Lowe	Management Accounting and Finance
M.J.C.M.	Dr M. J. C. Martin	Quantitative Aspects of Management
I.C.McG.	I. C. McGivering Reader in Organizational Behaviour, The Management Centre, University of Bradford	Industrial Sociology and Behavioural Studies
L.T.S.	Dr L. T. Simister	Economics
L.S.	L. Stephens Former Director, Institute of Personnel Management	Personnel Management
R.W.	R. Wild Professor of Management Studies, Administrative Staff College, Henley-on-Thames	Production Management
G.S.C.W.	G. S. C. Wills Professor of Marketing and Logistic Studies, School of Management, Cranfield Institute of Technology	Marketing

Synoptic Index

Business Unionism ⟫ Trade Union Membership; Trade Union Officers
Check-off ⟫ Collective Bargaining
Closed Shop ⟫ Agency Shop; Approved Closed Shop
Collective Bargaining
Commission on Industrial Relations
Committee of Investigation ⟩ Court of Inquiry
Communism and Trade Unions ⟩ Trade Union – Communism
Company Bargaining ⟩ Collective Bargaining; Workplace Bargaining
Company Union ⟫ Trade Union Types
Conciliation ⟩ Industrial Conciliation
Confederation of British Industry
Contribution Deduction Schemes ⟩ Check-off
Court of Inquiry ⟫ Industrial Conciliation (Law); Industrial Dispute; Industrial
　　Arbitration Board; National Industrial Relations Court
Craft Union ⟩ Trade Union Types – Craft Union
Demarcation ⟩ Trade Union – Demarcation
Department of Employment
Dilution
Disclosure of Information
Dispute ⟩ Industrial Dispute
Effort Bargaining ⟩ Collective Bargaining
Employers' Association ⟫ Collective Bargaining
Employers' Federation ⟩ Federation
Federation ⟫ Employers' Association
General Union ⟩ Trade Union Types – General Union
House Union ⟩ Company Union
Incomes Policy ⟩ Prices and Incomes Policy
Industrial Democracy ⟫ Participation
Industrial Dispute
Industrial Relations
Industrial Relations Act
Industrial Relations Code of Practice
Industrial Relations Commission ⟩ Commission on Industrial Relations;
　　Industrial Relations – Reform in Great Britain.
Industrial Relations – Reform in Great Britain
Industrial Union ⟩ Trade Union Types – Industrial Union
Joint Industrial Council ⟫ Joint Consultation
Labour Relations ⟩ Industrial Relations
Lock-out ⟫ Strike; Industrial Dispute
Pay Board ⟩ Prices and Incomes Policy
Payroll Deductions ⟩ Check-off
Plant Bargaining ⟩ Workplace Bargaining
Political Levy ⟩ Trade Union – Politics
Price Commission ⟩ Prices and Incomes Policy
Prices and Incomes Policy
Procedure Agreement

10

Productivity Bargaining ⟱ Collective Bargaining; Prices and Incomes Policy
Restrictive Labour Practices
Royal Commission on Trade Unions and Employers' Associations ⟩ Industrial
   Relations – Reform in Great Britain
Shop Steward
Sole Bargaining Agent
Staff Association ⟩ Company Union
Strike – and other Industrial Action
        Causes
        Forms
        Remedies
        Statistics
Trade Association ⟩ Employers' Association
Trade Union – Communism
          Demarcation
          Government and Administration
          Jurisdiction
          Membership
          Officers
          Politics
          Structure
Trade Union and Labour Relations Act
Trade Union Types – Craft Union
          General Union
          Industrial Union
          White Collar Union
Trades Council
Trades Union Congress
Union Shop ⟩ Closed Shop
Unofficial Strike ⟩ Strike – Causes, Forms, Remedies, Statistics
Wage
Wage Drift
Wage Systems
White Collar Union ⟩ Trade Union Types – White Collar Union
Whitley Committee ⟩ Joint Industrial Council
Whitley Council ⟩ Joint Industrial Council

3. *Industrial and Occupational Psychology and Ergonomics*

Acuity ⟩ Hearing, Vision
Adaptation ⟱ Ergonomics
Adaptive Control ⟱ Cybernetics
Ageing
Anthropometry
Aptitude Tests ⟱ Intelligence; Psychology
Attitude Scales ⟱ Personality

Reaction Time
Redundancy (of information)
Rest Pauses ◊ Fatigue
Safety ◊◊ Accident Prevention
Seating ◊ Posture
Sex Differences
Skill
Somatotype
Sound ◊ Hearing; Noise
Speech
Stability ◊ Feedback
Stereotypes
Taylor, F. W. ◊◊ Scientific Management
Temperature ◊ Heat
Threshold ◊◊ Ergonomics
Tracking ◊◊ Ergonomics
Vibration
Vision
Work ◊ Muscular Work
Zipf's Law

4. *Industrial and Commercial Law*

Agency
Apprenticeship, Contract of
Arbitration, Commercial
Arbitration, Industrial ◊◊ Collective Bargaining; Lock-out; Strike; Industrial
    Arbitration Board
Bankers' Commercial Credits
Bankruptcy
Bills of Exchange ◊ Negotiable Instruments
Bills of Lading
Charter Party ◊◊ Bills of Lading
C I F Contracts
Collective Agreements (in Law)
Commercial Law
Company Law
Contracts of Employment
Cooling-off Order
Copyright
Disabled Persons' Employment
Dismissal of Employees (Law)
Employer's Liability ◊◊ Factory Law
Factory Law ◊◊ Employer's Liability
Fair Wages Clause ◊◊ Collective Bargaining
F O B Contracts

Goodwill (in Law)
Guarantees
Hire Purchase Law
Industrial Arbitration Board ⟫ Arbitration, Industrial
Industrial Conciliation (in Law) ⟫ Collective Bargaining
Industrial Court ⟩ National Industrial Relations Court
Industrial Injuries
Industrial Law
Industrial Training Act ⟫ Industrial Training
Industrial Tribunals
Insurance ⟩ National Insurance; Insurance Law
Insurance Law ⟫ National Insurance
International Labour Organization
Joint Stock Company ⟩ Company Law
National Industrial Relations Court
National Insurance ⟫ Insurance Law
Negotiable Instruments
Office Employment
Partnership
Patents
Picketing
Redundancy Payments Act
Registered Trade Unions ⟩ Trade Union – at Law
Resale Price Maintenance (Law) ⟫ Monopoly Policy; Restrictive Practices
Restraint of Trade
Right to Work
Sale of Goods
Strike – and the Law ⟫ Strike – forms; Industrial Disputes
Trade Marks
Trade Union – at Law ⟫ Collective Bargaining; Shop Steward; Strike
Truck Acts
Unfair Dismissal ⟩ Dismissal of Employees
Unfair Industrial Practices
Wages Councils ⟫ Collective Bargaining

5. *Management Accounting and Financial Management*

Absorption Costing
Accountancy
Accountancy Conventions
Accounting
Accounting System
Assets
Auditing
Balance Sheet ⟫ Assets; Claims; Capital; Valuation of Assets
Break-even Analysis ⟫ Marginal Costing

Synoptic Index

Replacement Cost Accounting ⟡ Changing Price Levels
Reserves ⟡ Claims
Responsibility Accounting
Risk and Uncertainty (in Financial Management)
Shares ⟡ Claims
Sinking Fund
Stabilized Accounting ⟡ Changing Price Levels
Standard Costing
Stewardship Accounting ⟡ Accountancy Conventions
Taxation, Accounting Treatment of
Transfer Pricing
Valuation of Assets ⟨⟩ Depreciation
Working Capital

6. *Industrial Sociology*

Accountability ⟡ Responsibility
Alienation ⟨⟩ Authority; Job Enlargement; Morale; Specialization
Anomie
Attitude Survey ⟨⟩ Attitude Scales
Authority ⟨⟩ Leadership; Power; Status
Brown, Wilfred ⟡ Functional (1); Line and Staff (2)
Bureaucracy
Capitalism
Centralization ⟡ Delegation
Chain of Command ⟨⟩ Authority; Delegation; Line and Staff
Charisma ⟨⟩ Authority
Classical Organization Theory ⟨⟩ Organizational Theory
Communication ⟨⟩ Authority; Information Theory
Communication Networks ⟨⟩ Authority; Delegation
Conflict ⟨⟩ Authority; Power
Coordination ⟨⟩ Communication; Organization
Culture ⟨⟩ Social System
Decentralization ⟡ Delegation
Delegation ⟨⟩ Authority
Department
Discipline ⟨⟩ Authority; Norm; Social Control
Division of Labour ⟡ Specialization
Dysfunctional ⟡ Functional (2)
Fayol, H. ⟨⟩ Classical Organization Theory
Follett, Mary Parker ⟡ Authority
Formal Organization ⟨⟩ Bureaucracy; Organizational Theory; Social System
Functional (1) ⟨⟩ Authority; Line and Staff
Functional (2)
Group ⟨⟩ Conflict; Socio-Technical System
Group Methods of Training

16

Synoptic Index

Taylorism ◊ Scientific Management
Technology and Organization ◊◊ Socio-Technical System
Time Span of Discretion ◊◊ Job Analysis
Unity of Command ◊◊ Authority; Functional; Responsibility
Values ◊◊ Norm; Role
Weber, Max ◊ Bureaucracy
Woodward, Joan ◊ Technology and Organization

7. *Quantitative Aspects of Management (including Statistics, Operational Research and Computer Applications)*

Acceptance Sampling ◊ Quality Control
Allocation Problems ◊◊ Mathematical Programming
Arithmetic Unit ◊ Computer
Assignment Method ◊ Mathematical Programming
Average ◊ Measures of Location
Binary Scale ◊◊ Computer
Binomial Distribution ◊◊ Frequency Distributions
Central Processor ◊ Computers
Competitive Problems ◊◊ Decision Theory; Simulation
Computer Program
Computers
Confidence Level ◊ Hypothesis Testing
Correlation and Regression ◊◊ Statistics
Critical Path Method ◊ Network Analysis
Data Processing (Automatic/Electronic/Integrated)
Decision Theory ◊◊ Decision Trees; Business Policy
Degrees of Freedom ◊ Statistical Tests
Errors (Types I and II) ◊ Hypothesis Testing
Expected Value ◊ Measures of Location
Forecasting Techniques (Short Term)
Frequency Distributions ◊◊ Statistics
Games, Operational and Business ◊ Competitive Problems; Simulation; Decision
   Theory
Hardware/Liveware/Software ◊◊ Computers
Heuristic Programming ◊◊ Simulation; Computers
Histogram ◊ Statistics
Hypothesis Testing ◊◊ Statistical Tests; Statistics
Information Retrieval
Input/Output Devices and Media (of Computers)
Inventory or Stock Control Problems
Library (computers) ◊ Hardware/Liveware/Software
Linear Programming ◊ Mathematical Programming
Liveware ◊ Hardware/Liveware/Software
Management Science(s) ◊◊ Operational Research
Mathematical Programming

18

Mean ⟡ Measures of Location
Measures of Dispersion ⟡⟩ Statistics
Measures of Location ⟡⟩ Statistics
Median ⟡ Measures of Location
Mode ⟡ Measures of Location
Model ⟡ Operational Research
Network Analysis
Normal Distribution ⟡ Frequency Distributions
Off-Line/On-Line ⟡⟩ Computers
Operational Analysis ⟡ Operational Research
Operational Research (OR)
Percentiles ⟡⟩ Measures of Dispersion and Location
Peripheral Equipment (Computers) ⟡ Computers
PERT ⟡ Network Analysis
Poisson Distribution ⟡ Frequency Distributions
Population ⟡ Statistics
Probability
Programmers ⟡ Computer Program
Quality Control
Quantitative Methods
Queueing Problems
Range ⟡ Measures of Dispersion
Real Time ⟡ Off-Line/On-Line
Regression ⟡ Correlation and Regression
Replacement Problems
Risk Analysis ⟡⟩ Capital Budgeting; Discounted Present Value
Routing Problems ⟡⟩ Linear Programming
Sampling ⟡⟩ Statistics
Scheduling Problems ⟡ Sequencing Problems
Search Problems ⟡⟩ Operational Research
Simplex Method ⟡ Mathematical Programming
Simulation (computer)
Software ⟡ Hardware/Liveware/ Software
Standard Deviation
Statistical Tests
Statistics
Stock Control ⟡ Inventory or Stock Control Problems
Storage Media (Computer) ⟡⟩ Input/Output Devices and Media
Systems Analysis and Design ⟡⟩ Operational Research
Time Sharing
Transportation Method ⟡ Mathematical Programming
Variance ⟡ Measures of Dispersion

8. *Economics, Econometrics and Managerial Economics*
Balance of Payments
Business Motivation ⟡⟩ Motivation

Competition ⟫ Market Models and Competition
Consumption Function ⟫ National Income Accounts; The Multiplier
Cost-Benefit Analysis
Cost Functions ⟫ Costs; Costing Systems
Cost of Living ⟡ Index Number of Retail Prices
Costs ⟫ Cost (in accounting systems); Cost Functions
Demand (Theory of) ⟫ Demand Functions; Prices (Theory of); Pricing (Market Pricing); Elasticity
Demand Functions ⟫ Demand; Prices (Theory of); Elasticity
Econometrics ⟫ Forecasting
Economics
Elasticity ⟫ Demand; Demand Function; Prices (Theory of)
Employment
Exports ⟡ Balance of Payments
Fiscal Policy ⟡ Forecasting for the Economy; Monetary Policy
Forecasting for the Economy: Short-term
Forecasting: Medium-term
Gross Domestic Product (GDP) ⟡ National Income Accounts
Gross National Product (GNP) ⟡ National Income Accounts
Growth in the Economy; Determinants
Growth: Measurement
Growth of the Firm ⟫ Patterns of Growth
Horizontal Integration ⟡ Patterns of Growth
Imports ⟡ Balance of Payments
Index Number of Industrial Production
Index Number of Retail Prices
Index Numbers
Inflation
Input/Output Analysis
Investment in the Economy: Determinants ⟫ Growth
Lateral Integration ⟡ Patterns of Growth
Location of Industry and Regional Problems
Macro-Economic Models ⟫ Economics
Managerial Economics ⟫ Economics
Market Models and Competition ⟫ Competition
Model (in Economic Analysis) ⟫ Economics; Econometrics
Monetary Policy
Monopolistic Competition ⟡ Market Models and Competition
Monopoly ⟡ Market Models and Competition; Monopoly Policy
Monopoly Policy ⟫ Restrictive Practices
The Multiplier ⟫ Employment; Growth in the Economy
National Income Accounts ⟫ Forecasting for the Economy
Oligopoly ⟡ Market Models and Competition
Patterns of Growth ⟫ Growth of the Firm; Corporate Planning; Business Policy
Perfect Competition ⟡ Market Models and Competition
Planning (in the Economy)

Prices (Theory of) ⟡ Transfer Pricing; Demand; Demand Functions; Pricing (Market Pricing)
Production Theory
Profits
Regional Problems ⟡ Location of Industry
Restrictive Practices ⟡ Monopoly Policy; Resale Price Maintenance Law
Vertical Integration ⟡ Patterns of Growth

9. *Personnel Management*

Absenteeism
Accident; Industrial
Appraisal ⟡ Performance Appraisal
Apprentice Training ⟡ Industrial Training
Dismissal Procedure ⟡ Grievance Procedure; Dismissal of Employees (Law)
Employee Services ⟡ Welfare
Equitable Payment ⟡ Time Span of Discretion; Job Analysis
Executive Development ⟡ Management Development
Factory Inspector
Fringe Benefits ⟡ Entries on Wages
Further Education
Grievance Procedure
Group Incentives ⟡ Wage; Wage Systems
Group Methods of Training
Group Selection Methods ⟡ Selection
Incentives ⟡ Motivation; entries on Wage
Induction
Industrial Disease ⟡ Industrial Injuries
Industrial Relations Officer (Ministry of Labour) ⟡ Manpower Adviser (Department of Employment and Productivity)
Industrial Training
Industrial Training Boards
Job Analysis ⟡ Personnel Management; Merit Rating
Job Description ⟡ Job Analysis; Job Evaluation
Job Enlargement
Job Evaluation ⟡ Job Analysis
Job Specification ⟡ Job Analysis, Job Evaluation
Joint Consultation ⟡ Joint Industrial Council; Collective Bargaining
Joint Consultative Committee ⟡ Joint Consultation
Labour Stability ⟡ Labour Turnover
Labour Turnover
Management Development
Manpower Adviser (Department of Employment and Productivity)
Manpower Planning
Medical Services ⟡ Factory Law; Industrial Disease
Merit Rating ⟡ Job Analysis

21

Occupational Training ⟡ Industrial Training
Operator Training ⟡ Industrial Training
Overtime
Payment by Results ⟡ Entries on Wage
Performance Appraisal
Personnel Management
Personnel Management Adviser ⟡ Manpower Adviser
Personnel Manager ⟡ Personnel Management
Personnel Officer ⟡ Personnel Management
Personnel Policy ⟡ Personnel Management
Piece Rates ⟡ Wage Drift; Wage; Wage Systems
Plant Bargaining ⟡ Workplace Bargaining
Profit Sharing ⟡ Entries on Wage
Recruitment
Redundancy
Retirement Policy ⟡ Ageing
Salary Structure
Scanlon Plan
Selection ⟡ Aptitude Tests
Selection Tests ⟡ Selection; Aptitude Tests
Sensitivity Training ⟡ Group Methods of Training
Severance Pay ⟡ Redundancy
Severity Rate ⟡ Accident Prevention
Shift Work
Skills Analysis ⟡ Job Analysis
Staff Appraisal ⟡ Performance Appraisal
Staff Assessment ⟡ Performance Appraisal
Staff Management ⟡ Personnel Management
Staff Status
Suggestion Schemes
Supervisory Training ⟡ Industrial Training
Training ⟡ Industrial Training
Training Officer
Training within Industry (TWI)
Turnover ⟡ Labour Turnover
Wage Incentive Schemes ⟡ Entries on Wage
Welfare
Workplace Bargaining
Works Committee ⟡ Joint Consultation
Works Council ⟡ Joint Consultation

10. *Marketing (including Purchasing and Public Relations)*

Advertising
Audience Measurement
Automatic Vending ⟡ Retailing

24

Method Study ⇌ Work Study

Motion Study ⇌ Method Study; Gilbreth

Multiple Activity Chart ⇌ Gantt Chart; Method Study; Process Charts

Pacing (in Assembly or Flow Line Work)

Performance Rating (in Time Study) ⇌ Time Study

Planned Maintenance ⇌ Preventive Maintenance

Plant Layout

Plant Layout Techniques

Predetermined Motion Time Study (PMTS) ⇌ Work Measurement; Time Study; Synthetic Timing

Preventive Maintenance ⇌ Maintenance

Priority Rules ⇌ Sequencing and Dispatching Problems

Process Charts ⇌ Method Study

Production Lines ⇌ Assembly Lines

Production Management

Production Planning and Control ⇌ Jobbing Production; Assembly Lines

Ratefixing ⇌ Work Measurement

Ratio Delay Study ⇌ Work Sampling

Sequencing and Dispatching Problems ⇌ Production Planning and Control

Simo Charts ⇌ Method Study; Therbligs; Process Charts

Synthetic Timing ⇌ Time Study; Work Study

System Loss ⇌ Work Measurement

Therbligs ⇌ The Gilbreths; Method Study; Simo Charts

Time Study ⇌ Work Measurement; Synthetic Timing

Value Analysis ⇌ Method Study

Work Design ⇌ Ergonomics

Work Measurement ⇌ Work Study; Time Study

Work Planning Chart ⇌ Multiple Activity Chart

Work Sampling ⇌ Sampling

Work Study ⇌ Method Study; Work Measurement

A

Absenteeism Time away from work from sickness or other cause. A distinction is made between voluntary and involuntary absenteeism. Absence is described as voluntary when there is no acceptable reason for it and it could have been avoided; it is described as involuntary when it is the result of sickness, accident, a breakdown of transport or other cause which is largely outside the control of an employee. Rates of absenteeism are calculated as a percentage of hours lost in relation to normal working hours, so that comparisons can be made between individuals, departments, factories and classes of worker (e.g. married and single women, works and office staffs, etc.). A survey of absence rates made in 1955–6 in some 70 firms in a cross section of British industry, but excluding coal-mining and docks, showed an average for men in manufacturing industry of just under 4% with variations from 3% to 4·5%, compared with 6·3% in the distributive trades. For women the average absence rate in manufacturing industry was 6·5%, with variations from 6·4% to 7%. The rate for women in the distributive trades was not available, but it is known to be substantially higher than for men. When the facts about absenteeism are known an investigation on the causes may reveal variations in the effectiveness of supervision, particular pressures of work, the effect of different levels of earning or methods of payment, conflicts between responsibilities at home and at work, the state of the labour market for particular kinds of worker, and so on. In many cases a thorough diagnosis of the facts and causes of absenteeism will lead to remedial action by changes in personnel policy. If absences through sickness or accident are analysed separately, they may bring to light defects in medical services, in sickness pay schemes or in methods of ⟡ Accident Prevention. L.S.

British Institute of Management, *Absence from Work: Recording and Analysis* (1955), *Absence from Work: Incidence, Cost and Control* (1961); *Fringe Benefits, Labour Costs and Social Security*, Eds., G. L. Reid and D. I. Robertson (Allen & Unwin, 1965).

Absorption Costing ⟡ Overheads.

Acceptance Sampling ⟡ Quality Control.

Accident, Industrial An accident occurring in a place subject to the *Factories Act* is notifiable to the Factory Inspectorate if it causes either loss of life or disables an employed person for more than three days.

In 1967 there were 304,016 accidents at work, 564 of which were fatal. These included 247,058 (342 fatal) involving factory workers; 46,475 (197 fatal) in building and construction; and 9,117 (23 fatal) in works at docks, wharves and quays, other than those employed for shipbuilding.

The fatalities for 1967 represent a 20% drop on the 1966 figure but the upward trend in all accidents continued with an increase of 2·5% in 1967 over 1966. H.M.

Factory Inspectorate's estimate of the time lost through accidents at premises subject to the *Factories Act* in 1967 was slightly under 7·5 million working days. N.H.C.

D.E.P. Gazette (1968).

Accident Prevention The steps which are taken to increase the safety of employees with a view to reducing both the total number of accidents and the number of serious accidents. The process starts with a detailed record of accidents which is analysed to show what kinds of accident occur, where they occur and to which categories of employee they occur. Widely used measures of standards of safety are the frequency rate, which shows the number of accidents which have happened in a given period in relation to the man-hours worked, and the severity rate, which indicates the number of hours lost through accidents in relation to the man-hours worked. A policy of accident prevention aims: (1) to make the conditions of work as safe as possible by good 'housekeeping', proper maintenance and the enclosure of dangerous machinery and processes (incorporated when possible in the original design of the machine or plant); (2) to provide protection to the employee when some dangers are unavoidable, e.g. by safety devices, protective clothing and eye shields, etc.; (3) by organization, supervision and training to encourage employers to adopt safe working methods, e.g. by the appointment of a Safety Officer, establishment of a Safety Committee and by the safety training of young employees. Minimum standards are laid down in the ◊ Factory Law and regulations. As a large majority of industrial accidents do not occur on machinery, but result from handling goods, falls and the use of handtools, etc., training and supervision are as important to the prevention of accidents as the enclosure or guarding of dangerous parts of machinery. It is common knowledge that some people have more accidents than others, but research shows that factors such as the nature of the job, the amount of exposure to risk, the climate of work (e.g. the strength or weakness of supervision), and individual fatigue play a bigger part in causing accidents than 'accident proneness'. Nevertheless research has been undertaken and tests have been devised to discover the human traits which are the basis for 'accident proneness', and to use this information in selecting people for jobs of varying risk. ◊◊ Ergonomics; Critical Incidents Technique in Accidents. L.S.

R. D. Reamert, *Modern Safety Practices* (J. Wiley, 1958).

Accountability ◊ Responsibility.

Accountancy ◊◊ Accounting. The practical art of the accountant. The term also refers to the generally accepted rules and conventions of practising accountants (◊◊ Accountancy Conventions). Sometimes these rules of accountancy practice are referred to variously as 'postulates', 'principles' or 'standards'; but, in view of the arbitrariness and lack of scientific criteria in much of accountancy, which may well be unavoidable, such terms seem presumptuous. As one eminent writer observed 'the work of the accountant and the writings on accounting, until very recently proceeded by a sort of patchwork and tinkering' (J. B. Canning, 1929).[1] 'Much has changed since . . . Yet, the fundamentals of our discipline have not yet

1. *The Economics of Accountancy* (Ronald Press, 1929).

found a formulation that is general and rigorous enough' (R. Mattessich, 1964, when referring to Canning's dictum).[1] E.A.L.

Accountancy Conventions The generally accepted practices of accountants. ⟨⟩ Accountancy. Some of the principal conventions and assumptions are as follows:
1. The Accounting Entity
By convention, an entity is defined as the unit or organization which is treated as the separate whole for the purposes of accounting control. The entity is not necessarily coextensive with a legal entity. For example, the various branches or departments of a firm may be treated as separate entities. A 'group of companies' will generally be treated as an entity for purposes of publication of financial accounts (⟨⟩ Consolidated Accounts).
2. The Going Concern Assumption
In preparing financial accounts an assumption is made, where nothing is specifically known to the contrary, that a firm has an indefinitely long existence and will continue in its present kind of business indefinitely. Accordingly valuations are made on the basis that assets will continue to be used for their present purposes and therefore may not reflect market values (⟨⟩ Valuation of Assets).
3. Money Values
In preparing accounts, accountants have traditionally used historical monetary values despite their recognition of the fact that 'real' economic values may well be changing and will differ. Accountants often state that to do otherwise would lessen the objectivity of statements and cause confusion. However, it is clear that the basis of this convention is now changing (⟨⟩ Changing Price Levels, Accounting for).
4. Conservatism
As a general rule accountants tend to select that basis for measurement which gives the most unfavourable interpretation of events. This convention gives rise to particular precepts, such as: 'Do not anticipate gains but provide for all foreseeable losses.' 'Write off any assets value if it is doubtful.' 'Asset values should generally not be written up.' 'Value stock-in-trade at the lower of cost or net realizable value.' 'Under-statement of asset values is commendable.' It can be argued that such rules may tend to bring accounting into disrepute as a science of measurement.
5. Objectivity
In order to serve as a basis for accounting measurement evidence must be easily and clearly verifiable. Hence the emphasis by accountants on original costs or certifications by 'experts'. Clearly such objectivity may result in the sacrifice of relevance in accounting statements.

Other conventions of note relate to stewardship, the matching of costs and revenues in profit calculations, consistency, materiality, time intervals for accounting periods, etc. E.A.L.

K. MacNeal, *Truth in Accounting* (University of Pennsylvania Press, 1939).
K. MacNeal, 'What's wrong with Accounting' reprinted in *Studies in Accounting*, ed. W. T. Baxter and S. Davidson (Sweet & Maxwell, 1962).

1. *Accounting and Analytical Methods* (Irwin, 1964).

Accounting An analytical method may perhaps best be defined as a technique (and in this sense a statistical technique) for collecting, analysing, summarizing and presenting financial data relating to a particular entity or organization, so as to describe its financial position and the changes therein. As such it should be distinguished from accountancy, which is the practical art of professional accountants (⟡ Accountancy).

The entity in question is most likely to be a business firm but similar accounting principles may be applied also to the affairs of a nation (the National Income 'Blue Book' is an example) and its agencies (e.g. statutory bodies like the BBC and the various Nationalized Industries); non-profit making bodies, as they are conventionally called (e.g. churches, clubs, hospitals, etc.); a household; an individual in his private capacity.

The use of this analytical method will enable an entity to run its affairs in a more systematic administrative manner and also give useful information about the efficiency with which it is carrying out its task. For the concept of financial efficiency, or effectiveness of expenditure, is just as applicable to a church as to an ordinary business.

Accounting method is based upon the essentially simple notion that any asset or resource has two important aspects: (1) its money value and (2) the corresponding money claim on that asset accruing to the party who has a legal claim arising from it (whether as owner or as a creditor). The accounting system of any business is a collection of accounts in which an up to date record is constantly maintained of the assets belonging to the entity, as they change their form and value through business transactions and market forces, and of the corresponding claims arising from these events (⟡ Valuation of Assets).

In the language of the book-keeper, this duality of accounting method is termed 'debit' and 'credit'. Other descriptions of this fundamental duality may be given in terms of inputs and outputs, costs and revenues, assets and claims. Since the Asset and Claim aspects of any transaction, expressed in monetary values, must be identical it is of course clear that any properly kept set of books of account must 'balance'.

The primary impetus to the development of accounting lies in the usefulness of an accounting system to an organization. At the everyday level of importance, it is the means by which vast numbers of contractual obligations are recognized in terms of their monetary implications. Within organizations it is the accounting system which keeps track of all the flows of resources (goods, capital equipment, persons employed, etc.) between the various managers and factories which are responsible and accountable for their proper use. Further the system also controls their use by means of the application of efficiency criteria concerning the outputs to be expected from given amounts of such resources.

At a higher level of economic control, the use of basic accounting statements enables interested parties in any arm to watch effectively over their particular interests and, perhaps even more crucially, it enables the management to assess its present financial and economic status and to examine the consequences of past important decisions and therefore to plan better for the future. E.A.L.

H. C. Edey, *Introduction to Accounting* (Hutchinson, 1963); M. J. Gordon

and G. Shillinglaw, *Accounting: A Management Approach*, (Irwin, 1964);
R. J. Bull, *Accounting in Business* (Butterworth, 1969); G. J. Staubus, *A. Theory of Accounting to Investors* (University of California Press, 1961).

Accounting System The accounting system of an organization consists of all those policies, procedures, records and reports of a financial nature which assist in managerial administration, planning and control.

The diagram below gives a description of an accounting system:

It is important to note that the system not only consists of the double-entry book-keeping system but also of the source documents, reflecting the basic observation of business transactions and events, as well as the policies, procedures and

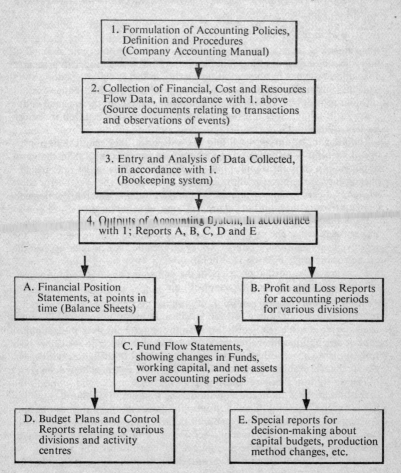

definitions formulated at top-management level concerning accounting information.

The design of efficient accounting systems is a difficult task since on the one hand it is essential that the system should, from a planning view point, be flexible, that is capable of giving multipurpose information quickly; on the other hand, from a control viewpoint, it should give uniform and consistent standards of performance so that valid comparisons can be made (◊ Management Accounting; ◊ Costing Systems). E.A.L.

W. R. Dobson, *Management Information* (Gee, 1966); for wider implications of accounting systems see also R. A. Johnson, F. E. Kast, and J. E. Rosenzweig, *The Theory and Management of Systems* (McGraw-Hill, 2nd ed., 1967).

Activity Sampling ◊ Work Sampling.

Acuity ◊ Hearing; Vision.

Adaptation If a sensory input is maintained at a constant level over a period of time, the subjective impression of its magnitude tends to decrease. This process of adaptation probably has biological significance in that it directs attention away from the constant features of the environment and highlights the dynamic ones.

Odour provides the most dramatic example of adaptation; the apparent disappearance of odours after a period of exposure is well-known. In other sensory modalities, the effect is less marked.

The mechanisms involved fall into two categories; they may be either peripheral or central. In the case of audition, for example, neural discharge in response to a constant stimulus falls off to about half its initial rate, but this phenomenon takes place in much less than one second. The longer-term effect whereby we learn to ignore continued sounds is central in origin: the neural signals continue to reach the brain but fail to affect conscious awareness.

Dark adaptation is something of a misnomer, since it involves an increase in sensory sensitivity. The range of adaptation of the eye is quite enormous, the sensitivity varying with the ratio of 5000:1 between the dark adapted eye and the eye perceiving bright light (◊ Threshold).

More generally, adaptation refers to the human capability of adjustment to environmental variability (◊ Homeostasis). E.E.

Adaptive Control Classical control theory is largely concerned with the problems of minimizing the difference between an actual output value of a system and a fixed reference value (◊ Feedback). Adaptive control involves the additional sophistication of having the reference value itself also subject to regulatory control in order to improve the performance of the system in a changing environment. A hypothetical example may best illustrate the significance of adaptive control.

The governor of a steam engine is perhaps the best known, and historically the earliest, example of automatic regulation using feedback. The control characteristics of such a device are, however, fixed at the time of its design and manufacture. An adaptive governor would be one with variable characteristics which would, in turn, be controlled by the output of other systems. Thus, for example, if the object of an adaptive governor were to minimize the cost of operating a vehicle, the adjustment of the governor would vary in relation to such economic factors as the cost of fuel, the hourly pay of the crew, and the rates of depreciation of the machinery at various operating speeds. Thus an adaptive control system of this type would be utilizing a versatile form of self-regulation appropriate to a changing environment (⟡ Cybernetics). E.E.

Advertising The process of persuasively communicating information concerning a product or service to its market. It employs the printed and spoken work as well as visual material. It is undoubtedly on a par with personal salesmanship (⟡ Selling) as a vitally important element in marketing communications (⟡ Marketing Communications Mix). The effective creation of advertising involves the use of marketing research (⟡ Marketing Research), the formulation of a creative brief, the visualization of the context of illustrative material, the writing of the copy or words involved, the preparation of art work, the purchase of space in the relevant medium and the supervision of production. In particular the task of purchasing media space involves the use of sophisticated methods of measuring their penetration and effectiveness (⟡ Audience Measurement), and minimizing the cost of reaching defined audiences. The pattern of expenditure in Britain during the decade since the introduction of commercial television has been transformed and the main media employed are indicated together with their amounts (see table, page 34).

This level of total expenditure in 1965 constituted 2·1% of the national income; at this level it is exceeded only by the USA where the comparable figure was 2·7%. £420 m. of UK advertising in 1967 was placed in the various media via agencies, three-quarters of whose income comes from the 15% commission received on billings from the media proprietors. The major professional organization is the Institute of Practitioners in Advertising, founded in 1917. It operates its own system of examinations and in 1965 its membership was 270 agencies and 5,000 individuals; and in 1972 its membership was 270 agencies and 2,000 individuals. G.S.C.W.

B. B. Elliott, *A History of English Advertising* (Business Publications, 1962).

Advisory, Conciliation and Arbitration Service (ACAS) This body was established to provide advisory services to employers on industrial relations and manpower utilization; to provide conciliation and mediation as a means of avoiding and resolving disputes; to make facilities available for arbitration; and to undertake enquiries as a means of promoting the improvement and extension of collective bargaining.

The Service was set up on an administrative basis on 2 September 1974, and is being established on a statutory basis when the Employment Protection Bill becomes an Act. (This had not yet occurred at the time of going to press, September 1975.) It is governed by a Council of ten, comprising a full-time Chairman and nine part-time members of whom three are nominated by the TUC, three by the CBI and three are independent. The Council directs the work of nine regions staffed by some 180 Industrial Relations Officers employed on advisory work and conciliation on collective issues, and by approximately 70 Conciliation Officer Tribunals (COTS) who handle conciliation on individual unfair dismissals cases.

Also under the Council's management are the five functional headquarters

Total Advertising and Sales Promotion Expenditure by Media

Media	£ million				Percentage of Total			
	1969	1970	1971	1972	1969	1970	1971	1972
PRESS								
National newspapers	76	75	76	130	14·0	13·5	12·9	18·4
Regional newspapers	56	59	67	188	10·3	10·7	11·3	26·5
Magazines and periodicals	49	47	50	60	9·0	8·5	8·4	8·5
Trade and technical journals	50	53	52	61	9·2	9·6	8·8	8·6
Other publications	4	4	4	15	0·7	0·7	0·7	2·1
Press production costs	29	34	39	44	5·3	6·1	6·6	6·2
TOTAL PRESS	264	272	288	498	48·5	49·1	48·7	70·3
Television	129	125	143	176	23·7	22·6	24·2	24·9
Poster and transport	21	22	23	26	3·9	4·0	3·9	3·7
Cinema	6	6	6	7	1·1	1·1	1·0	1·0
Radio	1	1	1	1	0·2	0·2	0·2	0·1
TOTAL	421	426	461	708	77·4	77·0	78·0	100·0

Source: Advertising Association

branches: one each for advice, for conciliation, and for arbitration, all taken over from the Department of Employment; and two for longer-term investigations, functions taken over from the late Commission on Industrial Relations.

Although the functions of the Service have previously been provided elsewhere, it is thought to possess three major advantages over previous arrangements. First, since these functions are now removed from government control the Service can operate, and be seen to operate, impartially. Second, as the Service is operating (to date) in an environment free from both statutory pay restraints and the legal framework of the *Industrial Relations Act*, now removed from the Statute Book, it can win public acceptability. Third, since the functions are merged in one body, cases can easily and quickly pass where appropriate from one function to another, for example from conciliation to arbitration or investigation. N.H.C.

Ageing At no time in life is the human organism in a completely stable state. The processes of growth and development continue through infancy, childhood and adolescence, culminating in a peak period of adulthood between about 20 and 25 years of age. Thereafter, in the case of most physical and mental functions, the ageing process begins. This is characterized by a slow but steady decline which continues its course until death.

Some decrements in sensory sensitivity, short-term memory and speed of movement are likely to be measurable by the time an individual reaches his early 30s. It is unusual for such decrements to amount to an occupational or everyday handicap, particularly as their effect is masked by the acquisition of experience. After the passage of a further decade, however, persons engaged upon work involving speed, stress, unfavourable environmental conditions, high energy outputs or severe irregularities in working conditions are likely to find their work load intolerable.

A good deal can be done, by the application of human engineering principles, to relieve the stresses placed upon the ageing worker. In particular, older workers should not be required to cope with tasks involving a high degree of novelty, tight tolerances, machine pacing of work, high levels of energy expenditure or severe environments. That is to say, all the factors which make work onerous to the younger man are likely to have more marked effects upon older work people. E.E.

A. T. Welford, *Ageing and Human Skill* (OUP, 1958).

Agency An agent, in law, is a person who has authority to enter into a contract on behalf of another party, known as his principal. The agent's authority may either have been conferred on him expressly by his principal or its existence may be implied by law. Thus, where someone by words or conduct leads others to believe that a certain person is his agent, he will be responsible for any contractual commitments entered into by this apparent agent, even if he had acted without any express authority.

Where the agent has his principal's express authority, he may, but need not, be acting under a contract with the principal. Where such a contract exists, the agent is under an obligation to the principal to perform the agency transaction and he is entitled to claim from the principal the agreed remuneration for his services. In the absence of such a contract the agent may refrain from acting on the principal's behalf and if he has acted for him he is not entitled to remuneration.

Apart from general agents there exist also certain classes of special agent whose authority is generally determined by commercial custom or by statute. These include mercantile agents (factors), estate agents and brokers. w.f.f.

G. H. L. Fridman, *The Law of Agency* (Butterworth, 3rd ed., 1971).

Agency Shop A workshop or other workplace in respect of which, under the ◊ *Industrial Relations Act*, 1971, repealed 1974, all the employees therein must belong to a particular trade union, or, if they did not wish to be union members, must pay a contribution to the union concerned equal to the union subscription (excluding optional additions), or the equivalent amount to an agreed charity. An agency shop was governed by an agency shop agreement between the union, or joint panel of unions, and the employer(s), or ◊ employer's association concerned.

An agency shop agreement could be secured voluntarily but a registered union which already had negotiation rights could secure an agency shop agreement, if necessary after a successful ballot conducted by the ◊ Commission on Industrial Relations, by action in the ◊ National Industrial Relations Court. A successful ballot occurred where a majority of those eligible to vote, or not less than two-thirds of those voting, voted in favour. Procedures were also laid down for employees wishing to challenge the continuation of an agency shop.

It was an ◊ Unfair Industrial Practice for an employer not to implement an agency shop agreement after the Court had ruled in its favour. It was not an unfair industrial practice for an employer to take action against an employee for refusing to comply with the courses of action to which that employee was committed where an agency shop agreement existed.

The agency shop is sometimes regarded as a species of post-entry ◊ closed shop. This and the ◊ approved closed shop were the only two forms allowed under the *Industrial Relations Act* ◊ *Trade Union and Labour Relations Act*. n.h.c.

Alienation A negative emotional state. Alienation may be manifest in apathetic withdrawal, blind unthinking obedience or aggressive destructive acts. The term was first introduced into sociology by Karl Marx (1818–83) (K. Marx, *Economic and Philosophical Manuscripts*, 1844). In the Marxist view, the worker was deprived of any opportunity for personal involvement in his work by the system of property ownership typical of the capitalist system. The modern sociologist accepts the fact of alienation but not the Marxist explanation of it, preferring to attribute alienation to the size of the industrial organization, the impersonality of the system, the elaborate techniques of control and the minute sub-tasks in which the individual is required to specialize. In a recent study of alienation in four different industries, Robert Blauner identified four types which were commonly experienced by the industrial worker. These were *powerlessness*, experienced when the individual is subjected to controls which he is unable to influence; *meaninglessness*, which occurs when the individual is unable to perceive the basic purpose of his own work either to his own personal needs or to the purposes of the organization as a whole; *isolation*, which arises from the absence of meaningful social identifications; and *self-estrangement* which he experiences when work becomes simply a means to an end, a temporary activity undertaken solely because of the need to earn a living.

These various forms of alienation are not uniformly experienced by all industrial workers but the incidence of alienation is sufficiently widespread to cause concern. The more enlightened industrial managements, therefore, are inclined to welcome the existence of a trade union organization as a partial antidote to powerlessness and to seek ways of making work more meaningful. ⟡ Anomie; Authority; Job Enlargement; Morale; Participation; Specialization. I.C.MCG.

Robert Blauner, *Alienation and Freedom* (University of Chicago, 1964).

Allocation Problems A company may manufacture a number of different products and there may be a 'best' way of making each. However, the company may have insufficient resources available to make each product in its 'best' way. The problem is to decide which allocation of resources provides the 'best' way of making all the products taken together. A number of operational research techniques have been developed to solve this problem (⟡ Mathematical Programming) and the answer thus obtained is better than that given by common sense.

As well as in production planning, allocation problems also occur when deciding: (a) where to build a new plant; (b) how to allocate workers to jobs; (c) how to plan the distribution of finished products from factories to customers, so as to minimize transport costs. M.J.C.M.

Patrick Rivett and Russell L. Ackoff, *A Manager's Guide to Operational Research*, pp 38–41 (J. Wiley, 1963).

Allowances (in Work Measurement) The Standard Time for a job must include an allowance to compensate for necessary rest and relaxation, delays and interruptions in the normal job cycle.

An allowance is added to the Basic Time for the job (i.e. the time required assuming continuous working at the standard rate) to produce the Standard Time (i.e. the time required assuming continuous working at the standard rate, and permitting necessary relaxation, interruptions, delays, etc.) ⟡ Work Measurement.

Allowances, normally given as a percentage of Basic Time, usually include:

(1) Relaxation Allowance. (a) Fatigue allowance to give the worker opportunity to recover from the physiological and psychological effort required by the job. This allowance depends on the job, the worker and the environment, e.g. energy required; types of movement; visual movements; comfort; atmospheric and thermal conditions, etc. (b) Personal Needs.

(2) Contingency Allowances, to compensate for the time required to perform necessary additional activities which because of their intermittent and irregular nature were not included in the Basic Time, e.g. consulting drawings, etc.

(3) Tool Allowance to compensate for adjustment and sharpening of tools.

(4) Reject Allowance, necessary where a worker must necessarily produce a proportion of defective items.

(5) Excess Work Allowance, to compensate for extra work necessary because of a temporary change in the standard conditions.

(6) Interference Allowance, to compensate for time necessarily lost because of the synchronization of stoppages on two or more machines attended by one worker. ⟳ Machine Assignment and Interference. R.W.

R. M. Currie, *The Measurement of Work* (BIM, 1965).

Anomie A social condition characterized by the absence of a clear and consistent normative structure.

A highly integrated community develops norms which regulate personal behaviour and interpersonal relationships and define the limits of individual aspiration. Within such a community the individual knows what is expected of him and his conformity is rewarded with the approval and support of his fellows. The system provides security and emotional support for its members and is conducive to the maintenance of their mental health. Conversely, the absence of clear norms leads to individual doubts and anxieties and the loss of supportive social relationships.

The term anomie was first introduced into sociology by Emile Durkheim at the end of the nineteenth century. In a classic study (*Suicide*, 1897), he showed, *inter alia*, a positive relationship between suicide rates and anomie. More recently, the concept has been shown to be related to the incidence of various forms of social deviation and individual stress.

In the industrial organization some degree of anomie may be manifest in the absence, or break-up, of closely knit social groups by technological requirements. Consequently, the persons so affected may be deprived of meaningful social relationships and, if lacking compensatory job commitment, become alienated. Blauner's category of alienation 'isolation' is closely related to anomie. ⟳ Alienation; Institution; Morale; Norm; Role conflict; Socio-Technical System; I.C.MCG.

R. K. Merton, *Social Theory and Social Structure* (Free Press, 1957).

Anthropometry The study of the size and shape of the body. In its applications in industry it is concerned with the sizing of clothing, equipment and buildings to ensure compatibility with human measurements. Three particular observations are worthy of note:

(1) Anthropometry is concerned with the variability in human measurements and not merely with the 'average man'. Thus hardware must be constructed to suit as large a proportion of individuals as possible, with an appropriate range of adjustments provided where practicable ⟳ Percentiles.

(2) It is important in any particular application to obtain data from the relevant population. There are differences between the sexes, between races, between different age groups and between different occupational groups.

(3) It is important to study human movements and not merely static sizes. More headroom is required, for example, for a person descending a staircase than for the same person ascending.

Numerous compilations of anthropometric measurements for a variety of population groups are available. E.E.

C. T. Morgan *et al.*, *Human Engineering Guide to Equipment Design* (McGraw-Hill, 1963).

Appraisal ◇ Performance Appraisal.

Apprentice Training ◇ Industrial Training.

Apprenticeship, Contract of A contract of apprenticeship does not today differ significantly from other ◇ Contracts of Employment. An apprentice is merely a special type of servant, differing from other servants in that the consideration for his services is represented by the master's duty to teach him the basic skills of the trade or profession concerned. Although many apprentices are infants (under 18 years of age) this is not essential and an adult could be apprenticed as well. The apprenticeship agreement, unlike other contracts of employment, must be made in writing and is often made in the formal manner as a deed. Although it may be desirable to make an infant apprentice's parent or guardian a party to the contract, it is not essential that they should be associated with it. Since, however, in earlier days the master occupied a quasi-parental position *vis-à-vis* the apprentice, it is even today not possible for a master to sue the apprentice for breach of contract, but he could sue the apprentice's parent or guardian if he was a party to the contract. Where the apprentice has failed to keep his part of the bargain, the master may take him before the local magistrates with a view to having the apprenticeship agreement cancelled. w.f.f.

   G. J. Webber, *Batt's Law of Master and Servant*, Ch. 15 (Pitman, 1967).

Approved Closed Shop A form of ◇ closed shop allowed by the ◇ *Industrial Relations Act*, 1971, repealed 1974. The conditions governing such a closed shop were extremely restrictive.

   Where an approved closed shop agreement existed, it was a condition of employment that an employee be a member of the registered trade union(s) concerned (◇ Trade Union – at Law) or pay the appropriate union contribution to a charity. Under such an agreement it was not an ◇ Unfair Industrial Practice for an employer to refuse to engage a worker who was not a member of the appropriate union(s) for any reason and refused to become a member; or to dismiss, penalize or otherwise discriminate against a worker on the ground that he was not a member for any reason, was not specially excepted, or had refused or failed to pay appropriate contributions to a charity.

   An approved closed shop could only come about if there was a joint registered union(s)–employer(s) application to the ◇ National Industrial Relations Court which must be satisfied, after an investigation by the ◇ Commission on Industrial Relations, that an ◇ Agency Shop would be inadequate to ensure 'the principle of free association in independent trade unions'; that an approved closed shop was necessary to maintain reasonable terms, conditions and continuity of employment; and that it was necessary for promoting and maintaining stable collective bargaining arrangements and for preventing collective agreements from being frustrated.

   Where the National Industrial Relations Court was satisfied and the employees concerned agreed, if necessary after a ballot producing a majority of those eligible to vote, in favour, or a two-thirds majority of those voting, in favour, then the

Court would assent to an approved closed shop agreement between the union(s) and employer(s) concerned.

When the Industrial Relations Act appeared on the statute book it was envisaged that the approved closed shop provisions would apply to few cases, and that in particular it would accommodate unions operating in areas where employment is casual and intermittent or where recruitment and organization are especially difficult, though where union membership makes for greater stability of the industry in question, e.g. Equity and the Musicians' Union in the entertainment industry, and the National Union of Seamen in shipping. N.H.C.

Industrial Relations Act, 1971, Ch. 72, H M S O, ss. 17, 18; Schedule I.

Aptitude Tests For purposes of selecting personnel for courses of training, it is desirable to have available a predictive index of potential ability. Thus aptitude tests (as opposed to tests of existing achievement or proficiency) have been developed.

The method of construction of these tests begins with a careful analysis of the demands of a particular job, and the formulation of a large number of trial test items, each of which relates to some aspect of that job. Scores obtained by persons already known to possess job proficiency are obtained, and in this way the validity of the proposed test items may be empirically examined. ⧔ Intelligence.

Large numbers of aptitude tests have been designed and developed for such purposes as aircrew selection, and for measuring artistic, clerical, mechanical and musical aptitudes.

Batteries of aptitude tests along with intelligence and personality ratings are also in frequent use for purposes of vocational guidance ⧔ Intelligence, Psychology. E.E.

Arbitration, Commercial A method of settling commercial disputes by referring them for adjudication to a nominated person or group of persons who will decide the issue by means of an arbitration award after having given both sides an opportunity of presenting their respective cases. Reference of a dispute to arbitration has generally to be made in writing and is governed in the U K by the provisions of the Arbitration Act 1950. Valid arbitration awards are enforceable in much the same way as judgments of a court of law.

Commercial arbitration is often preferred to judicial proceedings in a court of law for the following reasons:

(1) The arbitrator or arbitrators may be selected by the parties to the dispute from among persons who combine a knowledge of the law with knowledge of the particular commercial or technical problems that are involved in the dispute. The arbitrator, unlike a judge, may use his practical experience of commerce in reaching his award.

(2) Arbitration proceedings may be conducted privately and not necessarily in open court. This is particularly useful where some confidential information is likely to be disclosed in the course of the proceedings.

(3) Arbitration proceedings may be held where and when the parties wish and some of the delays of the law may thus be avoided, though the arbitration award

may be subsequently challenged in the courts in which case much of the time saved will be lost.

(4) It is doubtful whether arbitration is much less costly than court proceedings, but some economies may be made in the number of expert witnesses who will have to be called. w.f.f.

F. Russell, *Law of Arbitration and Awards* (Stevens & Sons, 1970).

Arbitration, Industrial The settlement of a trade dispute, i.e. one concerning wages and other conditions of employment, by the award of an independent third party who may be either an individual or an arbitration board or tribunal. Industrial arbitration must not be confused with ◊ Commercial Arbitration. While the latter is governed by the Arbitration Act 1950, this Act does not apply to industrial arbitration proceedings.

The awards of an industrial arbitrator are not as such legally binding in English law and will only be enforceable if adopted by the parties and embodied in individual contracts of employment. This applies even to the awards of the ◊ Industrial Arbitration Board set up in 1919 as a permanent arbitration tribunal for industrial disputes. It is only under wartime conditions that industrial disputes are made legally binding by emergency legislation. This has been the case in Britain in both the last wars. Under normal peacetime conditions, not only will these awards not be legally binding, but the parties to a dispute are not even compelled to agree to go to arbitration. Arbitration is thus entirely voluntary, while in wartime it is likely to become compulsory, at least to the extent of strikes and lockouts being outlawed until the dispute has been heard by an appropriate arbitration body. When the Employment Protection Bill becomes law, the functions of the Industrial Arbitration Board will be transferred to the newly set up Central Arbitration Committee, constituted in a similar way to the Industrial Arbitration Board, but forming part of the new Conciliation and Arbitration service. ◊ Collective Bargaining; Lockout; Strike; Advisory, Conciliation and Arbitration Service. w.f.f.

I. G. Sharp, *Industrial Conciliation and Arbitration in Great Britain* (Allen & Unwin, 1950).

Arithmetic Unit ◊ Computers.

Assembly Line Balancing One requirement for the efficient operation of assembly or flow-line type production is that each station on the line requires an equal amount of time to perform their respective operations. The work content for the complete assembly line must therefore be allocated in, as near as possible, equal amounts to each station, otherwise inefficiencies will be introduced, as operators at stations with less work either wait for the arrival of work from the previous station on the line, or work more slowly to compensate. ◊ Assembly Lines.

The assembly line balancing procedure takes no account of 'human' characteristics since the object of the exercise is normally to balance the standard times (determined by work measurement) for each station. This assumes that a given constant time will be required by the operator at each station, whereas in fact an operator's cycle time will vary because of variations in work method mistakes, faulty materials, etc. ◊ System Loss.

Assembly Lines

Assembly line balancing considers the situation as deterministic and constant, as for example a transfer line consisting entirely of machines.

Given the required line output (P) the cycle time (C) can be calculated:

e.g. $P = 60$ per hour. $C = \dfrac{1}{P} = 1$ min.

The work to be performed on the line can be broken down into a set of minimum rational work units, i.e. the smallest logical units of work. The problem is then to allocate these units of work to work stations to satisfy the following constraints and requirements:

(1) Precedence constraints, i.e. certain units must appear in a certain order, e.g. holes must be drilled before being tapped.

(2) Zoning constraints, i.e. it may be necessary for (a) certain units to occur at the same work station, e.g. because they both require the same piece of expensive equipment; (b) certain units *not* to occur at the same work station, e.g. because they involve work on opposite sides of the job.

(3) Equal Work Content (ti) at each station.

(4) Station Work Contents, or maximum station work content (ti max) equal to the required cycle time (C).

Requirements (3) and (4) together ensure that total balancing loss is minimized and spread evenly over all stations.

N.B. Balancing Loss = Total Allowed Time − Total Work Content
$$= n(C) - \Sigma_1^n t_i$$
$$\text{or} \quad = n(t_i \max) - \Sigma_1^n t_i$$

Numerous methods have been developed for solving the Assembly Line Balancing problem; however, because of the complexity of the situation no rigorous method is available to obtain an optimal solution for the general practical case.

One of several heuristic procedures is normally used, to obtain a near optimal solution, perhaps the best known being the ranked positional weight technique. ⟫ Heuristic Programming. R.W.

R. Wild, *Mass Production Management* (Wiley, 1972).

Assembly Lines (Flow or Production Lines) Assembly and flow lines are the chief method of production used for high quantity standardized items.

The operations necessary for completion of the job are located at successive stations on the lines, an approximately equal amount of work being undertaken at each station.

This method of production has the following characteristics:

(1) Minimum distance moved by product. Hence minimum handling and minimum space required. (2) Job Specialization, hence little training necessary, and a high level of performance possible. (3) Minimum work in progress, hence minimum production time. (4) Inflexibility, hence dependence upon continued, stable, quantity demand for standardized product. (5) Maximum resource utilization.

Even with complete line balancing, i.e. equal standard times at each station, under-utilization of resources may occur because of the variability of operation times resulting from human error, faulty material, etc. (System Loss.) Too rigorous pacing of work may also result in the production of defective or incomplete work. ⟡ Assembly Line Balancing; System Loss; Pacing.

Production planning for this type of production is comparatively complex because of its inflexibility. Continuous supply of raw material and sub-assemblies is essential, and output rate is effectively fixed.

$$\left(\text{Output rate/hr} = \frac{1}{\text{Cycle Time (hrs)}}\right)$$

However, production control is comparatively simple.

Job simplification has been a continuing trend since the beginning of industrial engineering and assembly line work incorporates many of the traditional concepts of work design. Recently, however, there has been a counter trend, i.e. job enlargement, based on the theory that oversimplification of work will affect the needs of the individual and lead to diminishing economic returns. ⟡ Job Enlargement.

Perhaps the two principles of assembly or flow line work which are most questionable are the principles of work simplification and pacing. Assembly lines differ a great deal in the extent to which these principles are adopted. Cycle times vary from a few seconds to several hours and similarly situations where work is rigorously paced often exist alongside assembly lines incorporating large buffer stocks.

Assembly-line manufacture is normally in anticipation of demand, i.e. for stock, unlike jobbing manufacture which is in response to demand, i.e. direct to customer order. ⟡ Pacing.

Two basic types of assembly or flow line exist – 'Non-Mechanical Lines' and 'Moving Belt Lines'. In the latter, items, either removable from or fixed to the line, are carried past stations by a mechanical transfer device. On such lines the mechanical pacing effects (⟡ Pacing) may be high, and incomplete items may be produced. Mechanical pacing is absent on non-mechanical lines, since items are passed from station to station on completion; however, for effective operation, such lines must normally operate with buffer stocks of work in progress between stations (⟡ Buffer Stocks). R.W.

R. Wild, _Mass Production Management_ (Wiley, 1972).

Assets An asset may be broadly defined as a valuable possession or, alternatively, as any economic resource which is expected to yield future benefits to its owner. ⟡ Valuation of Assets.

Legally, an asset is an enforceable right or relation between persons. For example, in the case of business assets, such as a machine, the law recognizes and will enforce a right of the owner to 'quiet possession' as against other parties. In the case of a debt, which is an intangible right, the law recognizes the debtor–creditor relation by enforcing payment, once the debt has been proven.

In balance sheets, assets are classified into two main categories, namely 'Current Assets' and 'Fixed Assets'. Current assets consist of (1) cash, (2) items which are held with a view to conversion into cash in the ordinary course of business (e.g. trade debtors, stocks of finished output, investments held as near cash, and (3) assets which will be used up shortly in the ordinary course of business or production, e.g. payments in advance for rent, rates, insurances, etc., work-in-progress, raw materials stocks.

Assets which are intended to be held for the longer term (more than one year) for use in ordinary business and manufacturing operations, are classed as fixed assets, e.g. plant, fixtures, transport vehicles, factory premises.

Thus it is clear that it is the *intention* of the owner which is paramount in this classification of assets. A motor vehicle is a fixed asset when used as transport but to a motor vehicle manufacturer it is stock-in-trade, a current asset.

It is often the practice to divide up the category of fixed assets into the three categories of 'intangible', 'fixed' and 'investments' where appropriate. Intangible assets are those fixed assets which are not represented by material possessions (other than investments) e.g. patents, trade-marks, ⟡ Goodwill. Investments, the remaining, non-material, asset category, consists of those investments held not for quick conversion into cash but for purposes of economic integration or of control of other companies, as in the case of groups of companies ⟡ Claims; Consolidated Accounts. This conventional subdivision of assets can have grave drawbacks in terms of realistic decision-making about asset disposition. E.A.L.

Assignment Method ⟡ Mathematical Programming.

Attitude Scales Individual responses, evoked by particular stimuli, tend to fall into relatively stable and consistent patterns, which may conveniently be described as attitudes. Thus, for example, a person's reaction to one particular policeman on one occasion will be, to some extent, predictable from a knowledge of his semi-permanent attitude towards the police. Sets of such attitudes, integrated into a total complex behavioural system, comprise the individuality characteristic of each human being. ⟡ Personality.

Attitude Scales, derived usually from questionnaire data, set out to evaluate the direction of a person's attitude, the magnitude of its deviation from a central value, the tenacity with which it is maintained, and its relative importance within the total personality organization.

For purposes of industrial management, attitudes are relevant in such areas as job placement, studies of job satisfaction and the identification of occupational difficulties, in addition, of course, to applications within the field of consumer research. E.E.

Attitude Survey The systematic collection of attitudinal data, usually for the purpose of predicting behaviour, testing reactions to specific phenomena, or ascertaining the relationship between attitudes and other variables.

The data may be collected in a variety of ways but the most common are probably by interview, by questionnaire, by ⟡ Attitude Scales, and, for the more sophisticated, by the use of projective techniques. As techniques of attitude scaling and measurement have developed, so has the use of attitude surveys increased and opinion polling is now an established profession. Attitude surveys are a valuable research tool in the hands of the trained psychologist or sociologist but despite an apparent simplicity the design and conduct of such a survey contain many pitfalls.

It is necessary to be absolutely clear what data are needed and how they can best be collected; what population is to be studied and what kind and size of sample is to be drawn; how the questions should be phrased and by whom and where the questioning should be carried out; what statistical analysis is appropriate and what inferences may properly be drawn. Additionally, it must be borne in mind that attitudes are often ephemeral and subject to considerable influence from perhaps temporary circumstances. ⟡ Attitude Scales. I.C.MCG.

A. N. Oppenheim, *Questionnaire Design and Attitude Measurement* (Heinemann, 1966); C. Sellitz *et al.*, *Research Methods in Social Relations* (Methuen, 1959); S. L. Payne, *The Art of Asking Questions* (Princeton U.P., 1951).

Audience Measurement Definition and quantification of the readers/viewers/ listeners reached by a medium to determine the impact achieved by advertisements placed within the particular medium. Measurement for press media is made by sample survey, of which the most comprehensive is the syndicated *National Readership Survey*, conducted by the Institute of Practitioners in Advertising (IPA) annually since 1957. Individual press media also publish details of their own readership predominantly in the form of the *Media Data Form* which is registered with and authenticated by the IPA. Major controversy centres around the value of such data as a guide to the effectiveness of any advertisement set amongst it (⟡ Advertising) and also on the relevant way in which the measurement of readership should be made. An affirmative reply to the question that a given medium, e.g. a newspaper, has been seen is frequently supplemented by questions to ascertain the level of reading and noting of particular elements. An additional measure of page traffic, the propensity to read particular positions within papers as well as particular pages, is also frequently implied. Readership should be clearly differentiated from circulation which is a measure of the number of copies distributed. The methodological problems of readership research are particularly well treated in W. Belsen, *Studies in Readership* (Business Publications, 1963). For TV the equivalent audience measurement is again syndicated under the control of the advertising profession. Similar methodological problems of the extent to which viewing can be adequately defined present themselves, and ratings are obtained by metered measurement of the time a TV set is switched on in a sample of homes. Cinema audience measurement is normally made in terms of box office unit receipts, poster and outdoor sites by a measure of passers-by, and radio listening by sample survey methods. G.S.C.W.

Auditing The principal function of an auditor (when appointed for the purpose of the audit of a limited company) is to certify that a company's annual accounts show a 'true and fair view' of the company's affairs. The auditor is also required to certify that proper books of account have been kept and that the annual accounts are in accord with the books. The meaning of the terms 'true and fair' and 'proper books' is not obvious but accountants acting as auditors have generally interpreted these terms to mean that the books and accounts are in accordance with currently accepted principles of accountancy. ⟡ Accountancy Conventions. Auditing practice does not however consist only of the application of accounting principles. At least as important is the verification of the books and accounts with independent evidence, as to the transactions entered into by the company and as to its present financial status in terms of the values of assets and liabilities. The verification process consists mainly of the examination of documents such as invoices, receipts, contracts, documents of title, etc., as well as an investigation of the company's administrative system in order to determine whether it is such as to encourage fraud, embezzlement or defalcations. Owing to the size of the task, it is generally accepted practice that auditors should carry out intelligent test checks of the company's system of accounting and administration and original documents rather than carry out an exhaustive check.

The use of statistical methods for sampling for this purpose is growing. Accountants are also beginning to see auditing in terms of an audit of management efficiency and to use appropriate methods of investigation for this purpose also. E.A.L.

> R. K. Mautz, and H. A. Sharaf, *The Philosophy of Auditing* (American Accounting Association, Madison, Monograph No. 6, 1961).

Authority The right to use power. In the formal organization this right is usually defined and the definition promulgated so that all members of the organization understand the extent of the authority vested in their own positions and in the positions held by others. It is axiomatic that such authority should be just sufficient to enable the proper discharge of the duties assigned to the position and that the incumbent should be held accountable for its proper use.

Authority is not power itself and it is quite possible to have one without the other. For example, the ineffective supervisor may have authority but little power and there are many situations in which individuals have power without authority. ⟡ Power. Incidentally, in so far as there exists a *right* to strike, those participating in an official strike are exercising not only power but authority. Authority is more likely to be acceptable to subordinates when the superior is respected personally and technically, and when his manner of exercising authority is in accordance with their expectations and values.

Organizations differ in the extent to which they rely on authority as a means of achieving control or motivation. An authoritarian organization is one which relies on authority and in such organizations there is usually a heightened status consciousness and an emphasis on ⟡ Social Distance. Authoritarianism tends to reduce upward communication, to discourage subordinates from using initiative and to minimize their personal involvement in the tasks which are allocated to them. Current thinking favours a superior–subordinate relationship in which the exercise of authority is replaced by personal influence through ⟡ Leadership: a concept of teamwork in which the superior perceives his role as one involving his working with, rather than his being placed over, his subordinates. This concept was first introduced into the management literature by Mary Parker Follett (1868–1933) with her distinction between 'power with' and 'power over'. ⟡ Discipline; Leadership; Power; Responsibility; Social Distance; Status. I.C.MCG.

> J. M. Pfiffner and F. P. Sherwood, *Administrative Organisation* (Prentice-Hall, 1960); H. G. Metcalf and L. F. Urwick, *Dynamic Administration: the collected papers of Mary Parker Follett* (Pitman, 1941).

Automatic Vending A method of ⟨⟩ Retailing where a vending machine automatically provides merchandise and thereby completes a sales transaction on the insertion of coins or notes. At the Census of Distribution in 1961 the value of such sales was estimated at £4·2 m. This does not include machines owned by user companies, but only returns by auto-vending machine companies. More recent figures suggest a substantial growth, with sales of hot beverages alone estimated at around £4 m. during 1968. About 80,000 new vending machines were sold during 1968 of which 30,000 were for hot beverages. This method of retailing has significant potential, for although it is currently not a low-cost method of selling, it has inherent cost advantages over more labour-intensive methods. It is in terms of labour that one of the greatest cost pressures exists in retailing. There are four major types of vending machines: (a) package vendors for wrapped items, e.g. nylons, biscuits, bars of chocolate, (b) bulk vendors, e.g. hair cream, petrol, (c) bottle vendors, e.g. cold drinks, (d) cup vendors, e.g. hot drinks. Vendors in category (c) are rapidly being replaced by (d) style machines because of problems of acceptance and disposal of waste. This method of distribution has grown substantially in the 1960s, but has an extensive history in 'slot machines' (category (a)) which were traditionally used on railway stations. An extensive evaluation of this method of retailing has been carried out in North America, see M. Marshall, *Automatic Merchandising* (Harvard University Press, 1954); and the Economist Intelligence Unit in the July 1969 issue of *Retail Business* carried out a special report on this industry in Britain. G.S.C.W.

Automation In mechanized systems, the primary source of power and some simple repetitive control operations are typically provided by machinery. In such systems, the main load of detecting, measuring, calculating, communicating, inspecting, controlling and decision-making is undertaken by the human operator. When a substantial amount of these information-handling functions are carried out by machine, the system may be said to be automated. Obviously, automation is a matter of degree, and its level is defined by the extent to which 'intelligent' (i.e. information handling) behaviour may proceed without human intervention.

The word 'automation', which was coined in Detroit in the mid-fifties, has caused a good deal of misunderstanding and misapprehension in industry. It remains, none the less, a useful word to describe the present trend towards the carrying out by machine of a variety of functions which have traditionally been regarded as a uniquely human capability. These functions stand in contrast to the energy-generating tasks which were taken over by machine during the first industrial revolution.

Sir Leon Bagrit, in the 1964 Reith Lectures, described the elements of automation as 'the three Cs', i.e. Communication, Computation and Control. Each of these Cs has been the subject of very considerable development during the course of this century.

Just after the turn of the century, Marconi's successful experiments in long-distance communication heralded the beginning of the revolution in information transmission technology. Since this time developments have been made in several directions leading to such practical systems as colour television, aircraft communications and satellite links. ⟡ Information Theory.

The history of computers can be traced back to the mechanical inventions of Pascal and Leibniz in the seventeenth century, through the nineteenth-century contributions of Babbage and Hollerith to the emergence of the electronic analog and digital machines of today. The electronic computer has revolutionized scientific, technical and business computations and has made possible the rational solution of problems which in a previous era were left unsolved.

Automatic control, (⟡ Feedback) as typified in a simple form by the governor, has made possible the elimination of the need for human intervention for purposes of providing the regulation of systems. The advantages of automatic control elements may include speed, reliability, accuracy and cost.

Inevitably there have been economic, political, educational, managerial and social consequences of automation, not all of which are favourable either to the individuals concerned or to society at large. A good deal of research and of implementation of research in the social sciences needs to be done if the full benefits of the technological innovations are to be reaped. E.E.

L. Bagrit, *The Age of Automation* (The 1964 Reith Lectures) (Penguin Books, 1966).

Average ⟡ Measures of Location

B

Balance of Payments The purpose of a balance of payments statement is to show what a country pays and receives in the course of its international transactions. As an example the UK Balance of Payments for 1972 is given below.

United Kingdom Balance of Payments 1972[1]

		£m.
A.	***Current Account***	
	Visible Trade	−692
	Invisibles	+729
	Current Balance	+37
B.	***Currency Flow and Official Financing***	
	Current Balance	+37
	Investment and other capital flows	−690
	Balancing item	−612
	Total Currency Flow	−1265
	Allocation of Special Drawing Rights (+)	+124
	Total	−1141
	Financed as follows:	
	Net transactions with overseas monetary authorities	+449
	Official reserves (drawings on +/additions to, −)	+692

1. *Economic Trends*, HMSO, June 1973.

The visible balance measures the difference between a country's exports and imports of manufactured and semi-manufactured goods, raw materials, fuel and foodstuffs. As is evident from the above account and others for previous years there is normally a debit balance on visible trade for the UK.

The invisible account is concerned with the payments and receipts derived from the provision of services. It includes payments and receipts derived from shipping, air freight, tourism and insurance; income earned and paid on overseas investment and foreign-owned home investment; current government expenditure abroad on the maintenance of forces and the provision of grant aid to underdeveloped countries.

Taken together these two give our current balance which could be broadly said to represent our profit or loss in day-to-day dealings. During the last few years the UK has had a considerable credit balance from the invisibles account to buttress visible trade deficits.

Balance Sheet

If the country's current account transactions were our only dealings with the world then the balance of payments accounts would be quite simple. For example, a surplus on current account would allow us to build up our reserves or repay short-term debt. However, there are other transactions which are reflected in the item 'Investment and other capital flows'. These transactions include long-term loans between the British Government and Governments overseas, borrowings abroad by the British Government and nationalized industries, investment by firms in overseas industries and by overseas firms in British industries, and British borrowing from the 'Euro-dollar' market. When the total effect of all these recorded capital transactions is added to the current balance the total never adds up exactly to the amount of foreign currency the country has in fact gained or lost which is known precisely by the Bank of England. Hence a 'balancing item' is added to the accounts.

These three sub-totals yield the second important total from the accounts which is the total currency flow and this is adjusted by our receipt of Special Drawing Rights. When there is a loss, as in 1972, then it has to be covered by the Government drawing on the reserves and borrowing from the International Monetary Fund or other sources overseas. When there is a gain, as in 1971, the Government can build up the reserves or pay off such borrowing.

It is important to realize that we are dealing here with 'flow' and not 'stock' concepts. The account tells us nothing basically about the structure or size of a country's overseas assets and liabilities. From a less abbreviated account, however, we could learn more about the payments and returns associated with these assets and liabilities. L.T.S.

Balance Sheet May be defined as a statement in money terms of the assets, liabilities and capital relating to a business or other organization. However, one might be tempted to infer from such a definition that its construction represents an attempt to value that entity. Conventional balance sheets are not drawn up with this purpose in mind however. A reading of the Recommendations of The Institute of Chartered Accountants in England and Wales, for instance, will make this clear. Fixed assets are generally stated at cost less 'reasonable' depreciation, and current assets at the lower of the costs or market value, in some cases, and realizable value in others, and therefore a conventional balance sheet is usually not a statement of the net worth of an entity. ⪧ Assets; Claims; Capital; Valuation of Assets.

A balance sheet is according to present-day conventional practice rather a historical document reporting on the stewardship and accountability of the management of the entity and providing, when comparisons are made between successive balance sheets and with those of other concerns, information as to the absolute and relative growth and profitability of the organization. It is however necessary to emphasize that present controversy gives rise to somewhat different practices. Some balance sheets give information which enables an intelligent reader to come closer to a reasonable view of the present worth of the business. For the general form of a balance sheet ⪧ Claims. E.A.L.

H. C. Edey, *Introduction to Accounting* (Hutchinson, 1963).

50

Bankers' Commercial Credits Of considerable importance in international trade. An exporter who has agreed to supply goods to a foreign customer will wish to have some guarantee of being paid when the goods are delivered. He may insist, therefore, as part of the deal that a reputable British bank should undertake to pay for the goods. The buyer will then have to approach his own bank to arrange for him the opening of such credit. The importer's bank, if satisfied as to the customer's credit rating, will then contact its agents or correspondent bank in Britain, asking that they should open an irrevocable documentary credit in the exporter's favour, accepting responsibility for reimbursing the British bank in due course. The exporter will then be informed by the British bank of their willingness to honour drafts, ◊ Negotiable Instruments, up to a stated maximum amount, provided that these drafts are accompanied by the appropriate shipping documents. Unless these documents are produced in the exact form stipulated in the bank's letter of confirmation to the exporter, the bank will not be obliged to accept the draft. The documents will then be forwarded by the bank to the instructing bank in the importer's country who will reimburse them and hold the documents until the importer has paid the amount involved and the charges incurred. The documents in question are those that are needed to claim the goods from the carrier who has been conveying them to the importer's country. w.f.f.

C. M. Schmitthoff, *Export Trade: Law and Practice of International Trade* (Stevens & Sons, 1975).

Bankruptcy The name given to legal proceedings the purpose of which is to secure the assets of a person who is unable to pay his debts, with a view to realizing these assets and using the proceeds to satisfy, in part or in full, the claims of his creditors. In this way the interests of all parties can be safe-guarded: the creditors are treated equitably and the debtor, once discharged from bankruptcy, will be able to start again in business without the burden of the old debts. Only individuals can be made bankrupt; a joint stock company that is unable to pay its debts will be wound up (liquidated) compulsorily.

Any creditor or group of creditors, or indeed the debtor himself, may present to the court a bankruptcy petition (provided the debts owing to them exceed £50), which must indicate that the debtor has committed an 'act of bankruptcy'. If the court is satisfied that an act of bankruptcy has been committed, i.e. the debtor has done something indicating his inability to pay his debts, a receiving order will be made against him allowing the official receiver to take charge of the debtor's assets. The creditors will then meet and will decide whether to ask the court to declare the debtor bankrupt. If this is done, a trustee in bankruptcy will be appointed who has to take over the bankrupt's assets, realize them and distribute the proceeds among the creditors, acting throughout under the supervision of the court. The bankrupt will be publicly examined as to the whereabouts of his assets and the reasons for his inability to pay his debts. If his conduct has been blameless, he may in due course apply to be discharged from bankruptcy which means that he will no longer be liable on the unpaid balance of his debts. w.f.f.

R. V. Williams, *Law and Practice in Bankruptcy*, Eds. M. Hunter and D. Graham (Stevens & Sons, 1968).

Bargaining Agent ◊ Sole Bargaining Agent.

Bargaining Unit Under the ◊ *Industrial Relations Act*, 1971, repealed 1974, a bargaining unit was a body of employees grouped together for ◊ Collective Bargaining purposes in respect of matters not dealt with 'under more extensive bargaining arrangements'.

The expression quoted from the Act allowed of situations where negotiations were conducted at different levels.

The ◊ Industrial Relations Code of Practice gives criteria for determining the limits of a bargaining unit. These include terms and conditions of employment, job content, and the training, experience and qualifications required. There should be a substantial degree of common interest among the employees concerned. For the sake of consistency and to reduce fragmented bargaining, the bargaining unit should encompass as wide a group as is practicable.

When proposals were made for establishing or varying a bargaining unit, the first aim of management and union(s) should have been to reach voluntary agreement. Where this proved impossible, either or both parties might seek advice and conciliation from the ◊ Department of Employment. The ◊ Commission on Industrial Relations might have been brought in voluntarily. Failing a solution by any of these means, the employer, a registered trade union, an individual employee in certain circumstances, or the Secretary of State for Employment might have applied to the ◊ National Industrial Relations Court for a settlement.

A bargaining unit could consist of a company (or its employer equivalent, e.g. a public corporation, a local authority); a factory or department; a particular grade, or similar grades, of employee; or a particular occupation.

A trade union with negotiation rights in the bargaining unit might be a 'sole bargaining agent'. ◊ Sole Bargaining Agent; Collective Bargaining; Industrial Conciliation; Trade Union – at Law.

Despite the repeal of this legislation the concept of the bargaining unit remains useful for practical purposes. N.H.C.

 Industrial Relations Act, 1971, Ch. 72, HMSO, ss. 44 *et seq.*; Industrial Relations Code of Practice, HMSO 28 February 1972, ss. 74–81.

Batch Production Falls between Jobbing production and Mass (Assembly Line) production, in that products are produced neither as single unique units nor continuously as standardized items.

Either (1) a standard range of products is available and sufficient orders exist to facilitate batch manufacture even though individual orders exist only for small quantities; and/or (2) individual orders are received for fairly large quantities of special products.

The nature of the product and demand will determine whether the production layout approaches that of mass production, i.e. layout by product or that of the jobbing shop, i.e layout by process. Furthermore, the nature of the product and demand will determine whether products are made in anticipation of demand for stock, or are made to customer order.

Normally, a compromise situation exists. Either sufficient standard products exist, or products contain sufficient common or similar parts to justify large batch manufacture on a group of facilities reserved or designed for this purpose. Additionally, general purpose equipment is normally available for production in small quantities, to customer order.

Production planning and control in Batch Production therefore consists of elements of the processes adopted in Assembly line, and Jobbing Shop procedure, plus procedures to deal with the problems unique to this type of production, e.g. Economic Batch Sizes, etc. ⟡ Batch Sizes. R.W.

Batch Sizes (Lot Size; Economic Lot Size) Careful determination of the size and frequency of the production or purchase of batches or lots of items, is an important method by which total costs can be reduced. ⟡ Batch Production; Inventory Problems.

For example, in production the total annual cost of setting up and preparing machinery for the manufacture of a certain part will clearly depend upon the number of occasions such set-ups are necessary, and hence for a given demand will reduce with increasing batch size. A similar situation exists in purchasing since total ordering costs will reduce as order quantity increases.

Conversely, the total costs of carrying stock will increase as stock and hence either manufactured or purchased batch size increases.

When production or purchasing in batches is necessary, the economic batch size may be determined, often accurately and analytically.

Example. In the simple situation where (1) Demand is known and constant. (2) Production or purchased parts move into stock together. (3) No shortages occur.

$$\text{Economic batch size} = \sqrt{\frac{2RS}{I}}$$

where R = Annual demand
S = Set-up or Order Cost
I = Stock-keeping cost/part/year

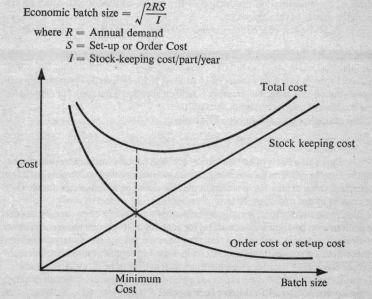

53

Bills of Exchange

Analytical solutions are also available in more complex and realistic situations, e.g. where shortages, quantity discounts, variable stock-keeping costs, probabilistic demand, etc. are allowed. R.W.

J. Magee and D. M. Boodman, *Production Planning and Inventory Control* (McGraw-Hill, 1967).

Bills of Exchange ⟡ Negotiable Instruments.

Bills of Lading A person who wishes to send a consignment of goods by sea will enter into a contract of affreightment with a carrier by sea. This contract is evidenced by a document known as a bill of lading. A bill of lading differs from a ⟡ Charter Party which represents a contract for the hire of an entire ship. A bill of lading not only contains the terms of the contract of affreightment but it also acts as a receipt for the goods shipped and by mercantile custom it has come to represent a document of title to the goods to the extent that a transfer of the bill of lading is taken to mean that the property in the goods represented by the bill is being transferred. In this way the property in goods which are still afloat may be transferred to a buyer who will pay for them on receipt of the bill of lading. Bills of lading are generally issued by the shipowner or charterer of a ship in sets of three, one being retained by the master of the ship on which the goods are carried, while the other two are handed to the consignor of the goods. He will then dispatch one copy by airmail to the consignee with the other copy being sent separately by surface mail. The recipient of the bill of lading may endorse it to a third party who would then on production of the bill be entitled to claim the goods from the master of the ship. W.F.F.

E. R. H. Ivamy, ed. *Payne's Carriage of Goods by Sea* (Butterworth, 1972).

Binary Scale This is used to represent numbers in a computer rather than the familiar decimal scale. The latter, 'a ten state' scale, uses the arabic digits 0–9 inclusive, and is based on powers of 10 (that is, 1, 10, 100, etc.). The conventional method of writing a decimal number is really a shorthand notation for expressing the coefficients and successive powers of 10.

For example, decimal number 329 is really:

$$3 \times 10^2 + 2 \times 10^1 + 9 \times 10^0.$$

The choice of a basis of 10 is arbitrary and was probably originally determined by the number of digits on two hands, which would provide a convenient basis for counting. Other scales are in common use, for example, a duo-decimal scale (12) to convert inches to feet, and a tertiary scale (3) to convert feet to yards.

Electronic circuits represent digits and hence numbers in a computer, by adopting alternative configurations or states for each digit. It is much more convenient to design 'two state' rather than 'ten state' circuits so, in a computer, the binary rather than the conventional decimal scale is used to represent numbers. Further, a computer makes decisions which require alternatives to be formulated logically. These formulations must be expressed electronically and a 2-valued, or binary, logic is preferable to a 10-valued or decimal one.

It is interesting to note that in GB the binary scale is used every day to convert pints into quarts and 10 shillings into pounds sterling.

In computer applications, the binary scale uses the two digits, 0 and 1, and is based on powers of 2. By analogy with decimal numbers, binary numbers are expressed as the coefficients of successive powers of 2.

For example, the binary number 1101 is really: $1 \times 2^3 + 1 \times 2^2 + 0 \times 2^1 + 1 \times 2^0$, and its decimal representation is: $8 + 4 + 0 + 1 = 13$.

The decimal number 329 can be written in binary as: 101001001.

That is, $1 \times 2^8 + 0 \times 2^7 + 1 \times 2^6 + 0 \times 2^5 + 0 \times 2^4 + 1 \times 2^3 + 0 \times 2^2 + 0 \times 2^1 + 1 \times 2^0$.

That is, $1 \times 256 + 0 \times 128 + 1 \times 64 + 0 \times 32 + 0 \times 16 + 1 \times 8 + 0 \times 2 + 1 \times 1 = 329$

Binary arithmetic is analogous to decimal arithmetic and is illustrated by two simple sums expressed in binary and decimal arithmetic:

110101	53		11010	26
10001	17 +		10001	17 −
1000110	70		1001	9

Similar analogies hold for multiplication and division and are described in the specialist textbooks on computers. Binary code, i.e. the number system to the radix 2, is of especial significance as it is the natural language of many two-state physical components used within a digital system. (Switches, for example, are either open or closed; relays are either energized or de-energized.) Hence the allocation of 0 and 1 to the alternative states of such components provides a convenient way of performing arithmetic operations. Furthermore, since 1 and 0 may conveniently represent respectively 'true' and 'false' there are useful analogies between binary arithmetic and two-state symbolic logic. M.J.C.M.

John C. Cluley, *Electronic Computer*, pp. 65–72 (Oliver and Boyd, 1967).

Binomial Distribution ⬦ Frequency Distributions.

Blackleg A blackleg or 'scab' is a member of a work-group, usually also a trade unionist, who breaks the cohesion of the work group in an ⬦ Industrial Dispute with an employer by taking independent action. Thus any worker who refuses to take part in a strike, regardless of whether or not he is a trade unionist, is a blackleg. Blacklegging is a more serious offence in the trade union calendar than mere non-unionism.

Some union rule books carry the ultimate sanction of expulsion for blacklegging but the moral stigma alone is so great that the incidence of this offence is relatively rare. The fear of being 'sent to Coventry' and other forms of ostracism by workmates both at work and elsewhere is usually sufficient to ensure conformity.

Blacklegs especially recruited for the purpose have sometimes been used by employers as strike-breakers. Historically troops have been used as blacklegs and on other occasions have been called in to protect blacklegs. N.H.C.

V. L. Allen, *Trade Union Leadership* (Longmans Green, 1957).

Branch and Bound Technique Many decision problems can be usefully represented in the form of a tree, e.g. the determination of the optimum order in which to execute three tasks can be represented as follows:

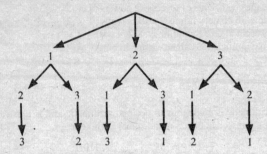

Two decision levels are evident. Firstly, deciding whether to place 1, 2, or 3 first, and, secondly, which of the remaining two to place second. This is a simple example, but in a complex case the number of branches to the tree may be considerable and consequently some method of arriving at an optimal solution without evaluating all possible alternatives is desirable.

The Branch and Bound algorithm was developed as a method of solving precisely this type of problem and relies on an intelligent search of the decision tree. Two concepts are involved and these are described with reference to the above three-task example.

Branch

When a task is committed to the sequence a Node is produced, and further branching from that Node commits the remaining jobs to the sequence, i.e. if Task 1 appears at the first Node further branching produces the Nodes at which 2 or 3 are committed to the sequence.

Bound

The 'Lower Bound' is calculated for each Node and represents the merit of the solution from that point, e.g. in the above example our objective is to minimize time required to complete all three tasks. The Lower Bound will give the minimum processing time for the solutions emanating from that Node.

The use of the Lower Bounds enables us to concentrate on the most promising sequences, and provisionally to neglect the unpromising ones, i.e. we branch from the Nodes with the lowest lower bounds. By this procedure we are able to make an intelligent branch rather than a random one.

The Branch and Bound method was developed in 1963 for the solution of the 'Travelling Salesman' problem, which involves the routing of a salesman from a base, once through several locations and back to base, in minimum distance or time. More recent applications have included (1) the special case of the Sequencing problem where jobs have to be processed in the same order on each machine; (2) Plant Location problems; (3) Electrical circuit design ⟨⟩ Decision Theory; Decision Tree. R.W.

F. S. Hillier and G. J. Lieberman, *Introduction to Operations Research* (Holden-Day Inc., 1967).

Branding The ascription to a product or service of a name other than the producing company's full name, in order the more effectively to identify it and to differentiate it from other similar goods or services. At its most successful it may become the generic term for describing the category to which it belongs, e.g. as Hoover did for vacuum cleaners. Such a high level of awareness can create an insistence by customers which can force distribution in consumer markets. The phenomenon of branding is less common in industrial markets and in the sale of technical products. The efficacy of branding lies in its ability to coalesce the constellation of ideas and concepts surrounding a product or service and thereby facilitate the communication process; this is generally termed the brand image and reflects at any point in time the overall status of users' perceptions of a company's offering. Where a company makes a range of products it may do so under a house brand name, e.g. the Dulux range of painting and decorating products. Common branding across a product range offers economies in promotion, but calls for a sustained and consistent planning and presentation of constituent products. Major new developments, out of tune with an overall image for a brand name, are frequently launched under a different brand name. It is also becoming familiar for large distributors to adopt house branding of which the pioneer in Britain has been Marks and Spencer, with its St Michael brand. An organization's own corporate identity is susceptible to similar analysis, but where brand names adopted differ from the company name any corporate image is normally less apparent. G.S.C.W.

Breakaway Union A new trade union formed by a group of dissident members having withdrawn from an existing trade union.

Secession from a trade union and the formation of a breakaway occurs when a section loses confidence in the union and develops different goals, and when that section is large enough and active enough to form an independent body.

While the rights of workers to join unions of their own choice need to be respected, the right to break away and form a new union has always been condemned as likely to undermine the strength of the parent union; to encourage discontented members to seek a solution outside the union rather than internally through the democratic process; and to weaken the unity of the trade union movement. The formation of a breakaway union is the most serious crime in the trade union calendar.

The larger, more complex, more centralized unions with a heterogeneous membership can better withstand external stresses because of their numerical strength, but are more vulnerable to internal stress than the smaller, more homogeneous and less centralized unions. Thus the Transport and General Workers' Union has suffered breakaways in the National Amalgamated Stevedores' and Dockers' Union and in the National Passenger Workers' Union; and the Aeronautical Engineers' Association is a breakaway from the former Amalgamated Engineering Union. Breakaway unionism may come about through the enhanced status of a membership group, now acquiring a feeling of exclusiveness, for example the National Association of Signalmen aims to provide for their now high-status workers an organization similar to that provided by the footplatemen's and salaried staffs' unions, and separate from the National Union of Railwaymen which is formally responsible for the organization of signalmen.

The official policy of the ⟨⟩ TUC is to refuse to affiliate a new union if there is already one in existence organizing the type of worker concerned. Employers are reluctant to incur the ire of powerful, established unions by dealing with breakaways; indeed an employer may not bargain with a breakaway even if it represents a majority of those employed by the firm.

Public policy has tended to discriminate against breakaway unions and their formation in the civil service has compelled the government as an employer to define its policy towards them. Following the report of the Terrington Committee (Cmd. 8470) the government will not recognize for bargaining purposes any new union unless it can prove that existing associations have failed and were unable to look after the interests concerned. In practice this is extremely difficult.

It can be argued that more inter-union competition would stimulate the trade-union movement, but liberal and sensible union policies can only be developed in conditions of reasonable security. Nevertheless the right of trade union members to vote with their feet is the ultimate right in the face of poor or unrepresentative leadership. Successful breakaway unions are few in Britain, and win recognition only by their own unrelenting efforts. N.H.C.

S. W. Lerner, *Breakaway Unions and the Small Trade Union* (Allen & Unwin, 1961).

Break-even Analysis The study of how costs and profits vary with the volume of production, using accounting methods of analysis. The technique can be illustrated by reference to the following diagram:

Break-even Chart for Next Planning Period

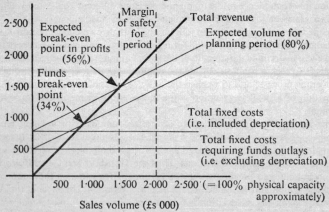

In this traditional form, total cost in relation to volume is shown as a straight-line relationship, extending from zero production to a point indicating 100% of production capacity. Since sales generally represent a mixture of many products, production capacity is usually measured in terms of sales volume rather than physical units. The chart is an oversimplification because it is generally thought by accountants that the straight-line relation is only valid around 'the relevant range of volume'; that is to say in the capacity range in which the firm expects to operate, say from about 60% to 100%. The projection back to the cost axis is only made in order to give a general explanation concerning the nature of fixed costs. The sales revenue line will generally be at a 45 degree angle to both axes, since output is in terms of sales volume. Consequently sales price changes will affect the slope of the cost line, *not* the total revenue line, in this particular representation.

The name generally given to this kind of analysis is somewhat misleading since its uses are meant to be wider than the ascertainment of the break-even point. This point cannot be looked upon as a guide to managerial decisions generally.

Probably the most important aspect of this simple budgeting model is that it turns a profit target into a general operation plan. That is to say a given profit target on the break-even chart gives a production manager an output target and the sales manager a sales target. However, unless this chart is used very carefully it can, in view of its limitations (particularly its validity within only limited ranges) and the assumptions made, be badly misinterpreted (e.g. about constant prices, product mix, cost relationships).

The wider uses of a break-even analysis approach are often referred to by various names, such as marginal or direct costing, contribution accounting, incremental profit analysis. ⟡ Marginal Costing; Costs. E.A.L.

    R. I. Tricker, *The Accountant in Management* (Batsford, 1967), Ch. 9, 'Strategic Decision', esp. Appendix.

Bridlington Rules ⟡ Trade Union – Jurisdiction.

Brightness The intensity level of both a physical stimulus and the corresponding subjective sensation are sometimes referred to as 'brightness'. The relation between these objective and subjective levels is not a simple one. The ambiguity in meaning is removed by the use of the term *Luminance* to describe the stimulus level and *Luminosity* for the subjective level.

The amount of light radiated by a source is termed *Luminous Flux*, the unit of which is the *Lumen*. (Approximately 1200 lumens are radiated by a 100-watt tungsten bulb.) The *Illumination* of a surface is defined by the luminous flux per unit area falling upon it. Thus the units are either lumens/sq. ft (also called ft-candles) or lumens/sq. metre (also called lux). The Luminance emitted by a surface is a function of both the incident light and the reflecting characteristics. The unit of Luminance, the Foot-lambert, is defined as the emission from a perfect reflector having the illumination of 1 lumen/sq. ft.

    Brightness contrast provides a measure of the difference between the luminance of a viewed object (e.g. a letter on a road sign) and the luminance of the background (e.g. the field area of a sign). The contrast is expressed as,

$$\frac{B_1 - B_2}{B_1} \times 100$$

where B_1 is the higher luminance and B_2 the lower. Visual performance is facilitated by high values of contrast.

Luminosity, or apparent brightness, depends not only upon luminance but also upon such factors as colour, contrast and state of adaptation of the eye. ⟡ Colour; Illumination; Vision. E.E.

E. J. McCormick, *Human Factors Engineering* (McGraw-Hill, 1964).

Brown, Wilfred ⟡ Functional (1); Line and Staff (2).

Budgeting (Short-term) An accounting budget is a short-term (annual) plan of action made in terms of physical resources and their monetary equivalents. A budget must necessarily begin with a financial objective, if it is to be a business plan, e.g. a specified rate of return on capital or the maximization of sales revenue given a minimum specified rate of return on capital invested. The complete plan of action in terms of subsidiary operation budgets for sales, production selling and distribution, administration and finance, is then prepared so as to arrive at a budgeted manufacturing, trading and profit and loss account, showing how the historical accounts should turn out if all matters go according to plan. The implications for cash flows, changes in stocks, debtors and creditors are then calculated and given a separately determined figure for additions to fixed assets (⟡ Capital Budgeting), and a budgeted ⟡ Balance Sheet can be prepared, showing the expected financial position at the end of the budgeting period.

Theoretically the budgeting process should consist of the formulation of various alternative plans of action from which the 'best' in terms of achievement of objectives is selected. However, in practice, such is the present state of the methods of budgeting, the only budget which is fully written down is usually the one which is to be accepted. Mathematical programming methods may however help in the future to improve this aspect of budgeting.

It is important to stress the control functions of the short-term budget, as well as those of planning. Provided that the budget plan is fully worked out in substantive and physical terms as well as financial terms, a budget provides a specification of activities and targets for all levels of management and therefore also acts as a management control device. ⟡ Control. E.A.L.

H. C. Edey, *Business Budgets and Accounts* (Hutchinson, 1960); Y. Ijiri, *Management Goals and Accounting for Control* (North Holland Publishing Co., 1965).

Buffer Stocks (in flow lines) All stocks in manufacturing systems act as a form of buffer between, or means of disconnecting, supply and demand (⟡ Inventories or Stocks). Such a function is vital in certain types of flow line production system (⟡ Assembly Lines) where without interstation buffer stocks considerable underutilization of resources would occur. Non-mechanical type flow lines generally operate with capacity for buffer stocks between stations. The larger such stocks, the lower the amount of idle time or delay at stations, and the lower the operator pacing effect (⟡ Pacing). R.W.

R. Wild, *Mass Production Management* (Wiley, 1972).

Bureaucracy An organizational form possessing to a high degree the characteristics enumerated below. The use of the term in sociology can be attributed to the German scholar Max Weber (1864–1924) (M. Weber, *The Theory of Social and Economic Organisation*). It is important to recognize (1) that the term is used by the sociologist in a non-pejorative sense and (2) that bureaucratization is a matter of degree – *all* organizations exhibit some characteristics of bureaucracy even if only slightly. These characteristics were described by Weber as follows: (1) the duties and responsibilities of all members of the organization are clearly defined; (2) the various positions in the organization are arranged hierarchically with each office responsible to a superior and responsible for subordinates (with the exception, of course, of the extreme top and bottom of the pyramid); (3) an elaborate system of rules governs the manner in which each official carries out his duties. Decisions are recorded and preserved so as to constitute precedents to guide future decisions; (4) each official holds office on the basis of merit formally attested and is subject to systematic selection and training (seniority and merit were considered to be synonymous); (5) each official carries out his duties without regard to any personal or family commitment, impartially and without emotion. His authority is confined to the discharge of his official duties and he is motivated both by a sense of duty and by the promise of a career.

Weber recognized that no bureaucracy existed in absolute form but he believed that the more closely an organization approximated to the 'ideal type', the greater would be its efficiency. To some extent his belief has been justified by the development of bureaucratic traits in industrial organizations over the last generation or so. There has been an increasing emphasis on specialization within the ranks of management and an increasing importance of formal qualifications; the greater size and complexity of organizations have necessitated the development of more elaborate administrative procedures; and the need for coordination and control has brought a corresponding need for accurate specifications of duties and relationships. On the other hand, experience supplemented by formal research suggests that certain dysfunctions seem to be inherent in the bureaucratic form; there is a tendency for rules and procedures to become ends in themselves and for the hierarchical principles to result in too great a reliance on the use of authority with its concomitant discouragement of personal initiative. Weber's seminal work, however, has helped to stimulate the research interest of the sociologist in problems of organizational behaviour. ⟢ Classical Organization Theory, Formal Organization. I.C.MCG.

Peter M. Blau, *Bureaucracy in Modern Society* (Random House, 1956).

Business Motivation Any analysis of the firm needs as an integral part a definition of the goal(s) of the firm. Whilst information on demand and cost functions and market structures may be available, goal(s) need to be defined so that the information may be effectively used. It is also true that adequate definition of the goal(s) may conceivably alter the information required to achieve the goal(s).

Traditionally economists have approached the firm from an optimizing standpoint and at its simplest the goal of the firm has been taken as the maximizing of profits. It should be stressed, however, that for a long time the firm was not really

61

the centre of interest for economists, but was merely a convenient building block in an elaborate theoretical structure that determined prices and hence allocated resources.

With the growth of the modern corporation and the division between ownership and management, the traditional theory has come under increasing fire from specialists in administrative theory as well as some economists. This is quite apart from earlier critics who argued that the traditional entrepreneur might also be interested in other things beside maximizing profits. The newer critics argue that the nature of the modern corporation is such that maximizing of sales receipts is a much more plausible goal. This is partly because the professional managers are concerned with the competitive position of the company and partly because they are naturally concerned with their own rewards. Both of these, it is argued, are more closely geared to absolute sales receipts than profits. Of course, the shareholders are not forgotten entirely and this goal incorporates a minimum profit constraint.

Both these goals are developed from an optimizing standpoint. Over against these are goals which have been developed from a 'satisficing' standpoint. Their roots are in psychology rather than classical economic theory; in particular in the view that the motive to act stems from drives, and action terminates when the drives are satisfied. By 'satisficing' is meant being satisfied with some standard of achievement below the maximum possible and thus the goals which would follow from this approach are achieving a certain level of profit, or a certain share of the market, or a certain level of sales.

The latest work in this field concentrates more closely upon the managers and postulates that they are utility maximizers. By this we mean that the managers wish to maximize their utility (or satisfaction) from being managers. Their utility is said to be dependent upon such things as the size of their salaries, profits, security, congenial working conditions, power, etc., and the operations of the firm are viewed from this standpoint.

The recent work in this field has coincided with an upsurge in the use of computers for analysis of problems and this has led to the development of computer models of firms to simulate decision processes. Whilst this work is still in its infancy some successes have been obtained in using these models to predict company decisions. ⟨⟩ Motivation. L.T.S.

R. Cyert and J. March, *Behavioural Theory of the Firm* (Prentice-Hall, 1963); O. E. Williamson, *The Economics of Discretionary Behaviour* (Prentice-Hall, 1964).

Business Policy A general rule or set of rules laid down to guide executives in making their decisions. They are therefore statements of the type 'When faced with a situation of the type X, always choose course of action A, rather than B or C...'

Policy statements are usually broad and far-reaching in their effect on the company and it may require only a comparatively few such statements to define the character of a company completely. To achieve this complete delineation, policy statements must be made covering three aspects of a company: its objectives, the means by which it is intended to achieve these, and the constraints (see below). Policy decisions are more often made as a result of moral, political, aesthetic or personal considerations than as the result of logical or scientific analysis, and are usually made by the owners or the directors of a company rather than by executives at the lower or middle levels.

The subject of Business Policy had received little systematic thought until recent years when Management Techniques for use in this area began to be devised ⟨⟩ Corporate Planning, Decision Theory, Company Models: of these the first is probably the only technique that attempts to systematize all areas of policy while the latter two tend to be more useful in the area known as strategy (⟨⟩ Strategy, Tactics). There is in fact considerable confusion as to the distinction between policy and strategy but it may be said that policy decisions refer more often to the character or nature that the company wishes to adopt, while strategy refers to the means to be employed in bringing about these desired characteristics.

The three areas of the company in which policy decisions are required are considered individually in their sections (⟨⟩ Objectives, Means, Constraints), but the following is relevant here. The nature or character of a company – and indeed of every organization of every type – is made up of two elements: the purpose of the organization and how it chooses to go about the task of fulfilling it; and this in turn can logically be split into two elements: those actions that it will take to achieve its objectives (i.e. means) and those that it will not take even though they may have helped it to achieve its objectives (i.e. constraints). The decision as to its objectives must be the first to be taken for unless these are known, no appropriate strategy can be selected to achieve them. Normally the founders of the company state explicitly or implicitly what the purpose of the company is (and the pursuit of profit must be the main or perhaps the sole purpose of any company) and this decision is unlikely ever to be changed radically, for any major change made to the fundamental objectives of a company may so alter its character that it ceases to be a company as such and becomes instead a charity or a nationalized organization or some other type of organization not having the pursuit of profit as one of its fundamental objectives. It may be possible for changes to be made in some of the less fundamental objectives set for a company as such, but there must be some doubt as to whether an objective that can be altered frequently is an objective at all. In general, the more precisely the objectives are defined, the more accurately can strategy be devised to achieve them, and the more precisely can the progress of a company towards its objectives be judged.

Once the objectives are known, it is then necessary to decide what strategy is to be adopted to achieve them. However, strategic decisions are usually circumscribed by the policy decisions of the owners or directors who may state in broad terms both what may and may not be done. Whether, for example, the company is to remain in private hands or seek a public quotation, whether to remain independent or to merge, to remain only in the present area of business or to diversify (⟨⟩ Diversification, Patterns of Growth), and if so into what areas of business.

Thus many of these strategic decisions can be, and are, taken at the instigation of the owners or directors on the basis of their own personal inclinations but such decisions can also be taken as a result of cold analytical calculation in view of all the relevant facts; the extent to which personal as opposed to analytical considerations enter into these decisions depends upon how far the owners or directors feel that the decision is liable to affect the nature or character of the company and how far the decision can be said to be of purely practical importance. Many decisions, especially those concerned with constraints, can only be regarded as Policy, the attitude of the company towards its employees or government officials for example.

In general, policy decisions are the broad, far-reaching guide-lines laid down by owners or directors to shape the company so as to reflect their personal beliefs as to what sort of a company they wish to run and how it should behave. Strategic decisions, on the other hand, are mainly concerned with the long-term actions necessary to put the policy decisions into effect and these are usually taken by senior executives after considerable study and rational analysis of the alternatives. A.J.A.A.

> H. I. Ansoff, *Corporate Strategy* (Pelican Books, 1968); A.J.A. Argenti, *Corporate Planning* (Allen & Unwin, 1968).

Business Unionism Trade unionism viewed as a business, with the leader's job to sell his members' labour at the highest obtainable price.

Business unionism is a concept originating in the USA where trade unionism is concerned almost exclusively with larger wage packets, shorter working hours, better fringe benefits, etc., i.e. with the protection and improvement of the economic position of members rather than with political and social reform. In Britain there has been a mixture of both; throughout the 20th century many trade unions have supported the Labour Party, financially and otherwise. At the same time, British unions have moved nearer to the business union form.

In so far as it may be said to operate in Britain, business unionism is associated with the changing structure of the trade union movement. New techniques, services and skills have changed the workforce, with increasing emphasis on white collar and female employment. ⟪⟫ White-collar unions are a twentieth-century phenomenon, and, reflecting the changing political attitudes of their members, are on the whole more interested in business unionism than political commitment to the Labour Party. ⟪⟫ Trade Union – Politics.

The growth in size of British unions since 1918 is also significant. The larger the membership, the more a union may veer towards business unionism. Increasing size means more professional officials and the danger of lower membership participation, with still greater reliance on full-time officials. In some large unions senior officials may virtually appoint their own successors, a situation quite alien to the theory of British trade-union democracy. If officials get results in terms of larger pay packets, however, the members may well be satisfied. Even the bargaining activities of part-time officers at the level of the work place, ⟪⟫ the Shop Stewards, clearly evidence an interest in economic rather than political goals, although in the USA much of this would be conducted by full-time union 'business managers'. ⟪⟫ Trade Union – Membership; Trade Union – Officers. N.H.C.

> H. A. Turner, *Trade Union Growth, Structure and Policy* (Allen & Unwin, 1962); R. Taft, 'On the Origins of Business Unionism', *Industrial and Labour Relations Review*, October 1963.

C

Capital, in accounting and economics In contrast to income, capital may generally be defined as a stock of wealth, income being a flow of goods and services through a period of time. Capital comprises all material objects and other 'real' assets which form the means of production of goods and services. The conceptual basis of valuation of economic capital is in terms of the present value of the future services and satisfactions or incomes to be derived from it. ⇨ Valuation of Assets.

Accountants use the term capital in somewhat different ways, for instance when referring to:

(1) *Owners' Capital* as the money amount attributed to the total claim of the owners of the business. This total claim will be equal to the difference between the stated values of assets and liabilities in a balance sheet. ⇨ Claims.

(2) *Classification of Expenditures* as capital income. A capital expenditure is one which results in the acquisition of an asset for purposes of increasing the earning power of the business when the earnings benefit is likely to extend over a number of years. Such an expenditure is usually termed a fixed asset and will be subject to depreciation charges.

(3) *Asset Definition.* For example, fixed capital is used to denote fixed assets and working capital to denote the difference between current assets and current liabilities. This usage is somewhat misleading and reference should be made to assets not capital.

(4) *Capital Gains*, as profits not arising in the 'ordinary course of business'.
E.A.L.

> E. O. Edwards and P. H. Bell, *Theory and Measurement of Business Income* (University of California Press, 1961); I. Fisher, *The Nature of Capital and Income* (Macmillan, 1906).

Capital Budgeting Refers to the investment decision-making procedures of firms. These procedures consist of five principal components:

(1) The search for feasible projects.

(2) The evaluation of feasible projects and the specific projects to be implemented.

(3) The agreement of the amount to be invested in each accounting period.

(4) Decision upon the sources of finance for projects.

(5) The economic and financial 'auditing' of past investment decisions made so as to improve future decisions.

A satisfactory criterion for evaluating the desirability of investment projects should deal with all of the first three aspects mentioned above. The fourth component may be termed a method of 'feedback' for improving the workings of the criterion.

A number of criteria of varying degrees of sophistication are used in practice, the principal ones are the following:

Qualitative Methods (i.e. those which do not use a framework of mathematical measurement).

(1) Degree of necessity, i.e. invest by renewing those capital items which have ceased to function.

(2) 'Squeaky Wheel' Principle, i.e. invest by renewing those items which appear (or sound) most dilapidated.

(3) Executive judgement, i.e. intuitive judgement and experience; executives meet (or otherwise decide) to agree upon a list of projects to be implemented.

Quantitative Methods

(4) Size of Division or Department, i.e. allocated funds to the various parts of organization according to some measure of relative size.

(5) Payback Period Measure ⟨⟩ Payback Period.

(6) Discounted Cash Flow Methods: (a) Internal Rate of Return, (b) Present Value Criterion.

The above methods are given in order of increasing sophistication. Methods 1, 2, 3 and 4 as such do not allow in any scientific way for the important factors affecting the profitability of an investment. The ⟨⟩ Payback Period measure of return has serious defects and of the two discounted cash flow methods ⟨⟩ Present Value is generally to be preferred to the ⟨⟩ Internal Rate of Return approach. R A T

H. Bierman and S. Smidt, *The Capital Budgeting Decision* (Macmillan, 1900),
J. F. Weston and D. H. Woods, *Theory of Business Finance: Advanced Readings* (Wadsworth, Belmont, 1967).

Capital, Cost of The cost of capital is the minimum rate of return which an investment project must be expected to earn if it is to be worth while ⟨⟩ Capital Budgeting. This criterion of worthwhileness can only be arrived at in the light of some objective for the investing organization, e.g. maximizing the present value of shareholders' interests in the company; achieving a certain rate of expected dividend to shareholders, etc.

'What is the cost of capital?' This problem causes much controversy amongst business and managerial economists. Basically there are two schools of thought: the traditional school looks upon the cost of capital as the weighted average of the various kinds of equity and debt capital of the firm. It follows from this line of thought that there is an optimal capital structure for a firm. The other school of thought, led by Modigliani and Miller, contends that apart from taxation aspects of the problem there is no optimal capital structure for a firm and that the cost of capital is equal to the expected rate of return on investment for firms subject to the same degree of risk.

The approaches outlined above are clearly very different from traditional accounting thinking on the cost of capital. Conventionally the accountant has seen this cost as the out-of-pocket interest expense recorded in the profit and loss account. According to this view the funds derived from shareholders are viewed as costless, or if dividends are recognized as a cost then retained earnings are costless. A more realistic approach suggests that funds can only be costless if they have no alternative investment opportunities. The cost of capital is then that rate of return on the alternative investment opportunity yielding the highest return. However, the presence of financial risk and uncertainty makes measurement of alternatives so that they are comparable immensely difficult ⟡ Risk and Uncertainty. E.A.L.

A. A. Robichek and S. C. Myers, *Optimal Financing Decisions* (Prentice-Hall, 1965).

Capital Market The capital market, through which limited companies raise the long-term finance necessary for additional investment in plant, factories, working capital, etc., consists of all those institutions concerned with the issue of shares and securities to investors. The principal institutions directly involved are issuing houses and underwriters. The general functions of an issuing house are to act firstly as an intermediary between, and sponsors of, its client, the company raising capital. The issuing house advises the company on all aspects of the issue, in particular the type of share or debenture loan to issue, the method of issue and the price and other terms of offer. It also generally acts as the main underwriter initially, but the large insurance companies often underwrite the issue at a later stage. Sub-underwriting through a large number of institutional investors is also generally arranged for the whole or most of the issue.

The most usual methods of issue are:

(1) A public issue, by which the company offers the shares or loan directly to the public.

(2) An offer to existing shareholders, i.e. a 'rights' issue.

(3) An offer for sale, by which the company sells the shares to an issuing house which then sells on its own behalf to the public.

The Stock Exchanges are legally quite separate from the institutions of the issuing market but economically they are completely interlinked as parts of the capital market. Although a company is not directly involved in Stock Exchange dealings, except in having to register transfers of share and loan ownership, it is only if the company has obtained a quotation for its share and loan issues that investors will find its securities attractive. E.A.L.

A. J. Merrett, M. Howe and G. D. Newbould, *Equity Issues and London Capital Market* (Longmans, 1967); H. E. Dougall, *Capital Markets and Institutions* (Prentice-Hall, 1965).

Capital Structure The capital structure of a business can be measured by the ratios of the various kinds of permanent loan and equity capital to total capital. The term 'gearing' is used to refer to the proportion of loan to equity (or alternatively total) capital. 'Financial leverage' is another term used to express the same kind of idea but is sometimes used to measure capital structure in a slightly different way: that is by the ratio of debt (both short- and long-term) to total assets or alternatively by the ratio of long-term debt to total assets. ⟡ Assets. Whilst both measures of leverage are useful it can be argued that the first is preferable in that it more clearly measures the risk connected with trading on debt, since current liabilities, as a class of claims, may be regarded also as a permanent part of capital. Clearly the use of leverage carries with it the possibility of higher gains for ordinary shareholders. When the rate of return on total assets exceeds the cost of debt, ordinary shareholders obtain increased returns through leverage but when it is less their returns are reduced by leverage. What is the 'right' amount of leverage must depend heavily on the riskiness and other characteristics of the industry.

The concepts of leverage and gearing·and the idea of financial risk connected with them can be used to formulate alternative theories of the cost of capital and valuation of equities. E.A.L.

E. Schwartz, 'Theory of the Capital Structure of the Firm', *Journal of Finance*, 14 March 1959, Chicago.

Capitalism An individual system characterized by the private ownership of resources by individuals or public companies, competition in pursuit of financial profit and minimal regulation of activities by the government.

The term has connotations more emotional than scientific and it is probably reasonable to suggest that it be more properly classified as a political than as an economic concept. Its supporters claim that a capitalist system maximizes production, stimulates enterprise and invention, distributes resources in the most socially advantageous way and results in a high degree of individual freedom. Its critics deny that production for financial profit necessarily results in the most socially desirable utilization of resources, argue that freedom in a capitalist system is heavily dependent on the possession of personal wealth and that the system results in a steadily increasing social inequality which is not only unjust but also politically explosive.

This is not the place to attempt an evaluation of the capitalist system but it is relevant to note the tendency for the governments of 'capitalist' countries increasingly to undertake a general direction of the economy, to regulate the activities of private businesses and to make direct provision of social services particularly in the fields of education, health, housing and welfare. Conversely, 'socialist' countries appear to be tending to permit, even to encourage, a measure of competition amongst production units and to permit a measure of influence on productive resources of a market demand. I.C.MCG.

J. K. Galbraith, *American Capitalism* (Houghton Mifflin, 1954); J. K. Galbraith, *The Affluent Society* (Houghton Mifflin, 1958); A. Berle, *The American Economic Republic* (Sidgwick & Jackson, 1963).

Capitalization Rate ◊ Price–Earnings Ratio.

Cash Flow ◊ Funds Flow Analysis.

Cell Production The 'cell' system of work organization may be employed in batch production when group technology is adopted (◊ Group Technology). A cell consists of a group of workers and machine tools whose task is the manufacture of one or more groups or families of components. Such cells are often arranged in a manner which facilitates item flow (◊ Mass Production) and because of the difficulty in balancing resources in these cells, workers are generally required to exhibit some flexibility, i.e. to operate more than one machine. This flexibility may, if coupled with the delegation of some responsibility for work scheduling, etc. to the workers in the cell, give rise to a form of semi-autonomous work group of the type often advocated in mass production (◊ Group working). R.W.

Central Processor ⟡ Computers.

Centralization ⟡ Delegation.

Chain of Command The vertical arrangement of direct authority relationships. Also called 'the scaler-chain' or 'the line'. The length of the chain is the number of persons who constitute the superior/subordinate continuum. It is widely considered to be desirable to keep the chain of command as short as possible otherwise problems of remoteness and rigidity are likely to be experienced. ⟡ Authority, Delegation, Line and Staff. I.C.MCG.

Changing Price Levels, Accounting for It has long been recognized that the conventional basis of accounting in terms of historical cost (i.e. in terms of the purchasing power of the £ at the date when an asset was acquired or revalued, a liability was incurred or capital was raised) produced results which may differ significantly from those when the effects of inflation are taken into account. In recent years the increasing rate of inflation has caused considerable attention to be paid to this problem, the main objective being to put users of financial statements, particularly managements and shareholders, in a better position to appreciate the effects of inflation on costs, profits, depreciation, return on capital, distribution policies (including dividend covers), borrowing powers and future cash requirements.

There are two main methods of taking inflation into account. One method, known as replacement cost accounting, charges in the profit and loss account the replacement cost of items wholly or partly used up: for example, if raw materials have risen in value since bought, the amount charged in the profit and loss account would be the current cost of buying an equivalent quantity of the same raw materials (whether these were in fact bought or not); as fixed assets would cost more to replace than their original cost, the annual depreciation charge would be increased to cover the replacement cost.

An argument used against replacement cost accounting is that it does not distinguish increased costs due to changes in technology, or in supply and demand, from increased costs due simply to inflation. This difficulty is avoided by the approach proposed by the Institute of Chartered Accountants in England and Wales. This approach modifies the historical cost convention by proposing that 'historical costs should be converted from an aggregate of historical £s of many different purchasing powers into approximate figures of current general purchasing power'. Both the 'historical cost' and the 'converted' figures would be published for all quoted companies.

The proposed basis of conversion, in broad terms, is to segregate items into 'monetary' and 'non-monetary' items and to increase the latter in proportion to the inflation which has occurred since their acquisition or last revaluation. The proposed index for the conversion process is the Consumer Price Index produced by the Central Statistical Office. E.A.L.

R. S. Gynther, *Accounting for Price Level Changes: Theory and Procedure* (Pergamon Press, 1966).

Charisma An endowment of outstanding leadership qualities or powers of personality. The term has been taken by sociology from ecclesiastical history where it meant 'the gift of divine grace'. Some writers, following the sociologist Max Weber, regard charisma as a source of authority. It is suggested, however, that confusion is less likely if charisma be regarded not as a source of authority but as a source of power, as we have defined these terms. In this sense a person with authority will have that authority enhanced if he also possesses charisma whilst a person lacking authority may yet wield considerable influence over others through the possession of charismatic qualities. The precise qualities which would constitute charisma are likely to vary from one situation to another and, indeed, from one individual to another, and for that reason cannot usefully be enumerated ⟡ Authority, Leadership. I.C.MCG.

Charter Party A contract between a shipowner and a person wishing to hire the ship, whereby the latter, the charterer, hires or charters the ship for a particular period of time or a specified voyage. The term is derived from the Latin *carta partita* (a split-up document) which refers to the medieval practice of writing the terms of the contract on a piece of parchment which was then split down the middle, with each party retaining one half of the document.

In an ordinary charter the shipowner retains control over the ship and its crew but has to place the ship at the disposal of the charterer for the purpose and the time stated in the charter party. If the charterer is unable to fill the available capacity of the ship with his own cargo, he may decide to carry the cargoes of other people and for this purpose issue to them ⟡ Bills of Lading. W.F.F.

Carver on Carriage by Sea (Sweet & Maxwell, 1971).

Check-off An arrangement whereby employers deduct trade union contributions from the wages or salaries of members in their employment and pay them over to the union(s) concerned.

Check-off is an American term and others are often employed in Britain, for example, 'payroll deductions', 'contribution deduction schemes'.

The practice has grown rapidly in recent years and now affects approximately two million trade unionists, or one union member in five. Most of those workers are employed in the public sector but it is estimated that about 1200 private firms have agreed to the arrangement.

Union attitudes towards the practice have changed in recent years. The collection of contributions either at the branch or by workshop representatives, often ⟡ Shop Stewards, was formerly regarded as a guarantee of union independence and an essential point of contact between members and their union. It has now been realized that this traditional method produces arrears of contributions, accounting and human problems, and a significant loss of revenue. Failure to collect contributions encourages lapsing of membership and problems of qualifications for benefits. The check-off helps to solve such problems and in practice does not on the whole seem to harm union independence or to damage contacts between the union and its members. There is doubt in some cases about its impact on attendances at branch meetings.

Employers are coming to see the check-off as a concession which can be used in ⟨⟩ Collective Bargaining; as an inexpensive gesture of goodwill to trade unions or as a means of encouraging union financial stability and thus responsible trade unionism.

The check-off appears to have had little effect on the growth or containment of the ⟨⟩ Closed Shop, and it is possible to operate it in a way which safeguards the position of those union members who wish to contract out of the political levy. ⟨⟩ Trade Union – Politics. N.H.C.

Royal Commission on Trade Unions and Employers' Associations, Research Papers 8, *Three Studies in Collective Bargaining* (HMSO, 1968).

CIF Contracts Cost, insurance, freight contracts are contracts for the sale of goods which are performed by the seller handing to the buyer the documents which represent the goods. These are the documents which entitle the buyer to claim the goods from the carrier and they include ⟨⟩ Negotiable Instruments, the insurance policy in respect of the goods, the invoice and the necessary consular certificates which prove the origin of the goods. On delivery of the documents by the seller, the buyer has to pay for the goods and he may not delay payment until he has actually taken physical possession of the goods. All expenses at the receiving end, including the cost of unloading and landing the goods and customs duties, will have to be borne by the buyer. While the goods are in transit they are at the buyer's risk and he will have to accept the documents and pay for them even though the goods have been lost, being of course protected by the insurance policy taken out on his behalf by the consignor of the goods. The price of the goods includes all insurance and freight charges, but does not include the above-mentioned expenses to be borne by the buyer. W.F.F.

D. Sassoon, *C.I.F. and F.O.B. Contracts* (Sweet & Maxwell, 1975).

Claims (or Equities) Valuable possessions owned by a business are generally called assets. Each asset owned gives rise to a corresponding claim (or equity) which accrues to the person contributing the asset. Claims are classified in a balance sheet either as liabilities or capital. Liabilities arise where the claimant has a non-ownership interest in the organization, that is to say is legally entitled to satisfaction of the debt arising from the asset contributed. Liabilities are usually subdivided as between current liabilities, those which are payable within one year, e.g. trade and expense creditors, and longer-term liabilities, e.g. debentures and other long-term loans. In financial discussion, debentures are often referred to quite realistically as long-term capital.

Capital, the other principal claim, is a residual, being generally the excess of the stated value of assets over all liabilities. Clearly capital could also be negative. As defined for balance sheet purposes, it is also referred to as 'the equity' or 'net worth' of the business, and in the case of a limited company is usually classified into the following main categories:

(1) Issued Shares representing the claims arising from the capital contributed in the form of cash or other assets by shareholders.

(2) Capital Reserves, representing claims arising from shareholder contributions, e.g. a share premium account; from profits or surplus not arising in the

'ordinary course of business', e.g. profits on fixed assets, fixed assets revaluations; or from profits set aside specifically as being available for dividends.

(3) Revenue Reserves representing transfers from Profit and Loss account, not available for dividends.

(4) Retained Profits, representing the balance of profits, after all appropriations in respect of dividends, taxes and transfers to reserves have been made.

The principal claim categories are illustrated in the sample sheet below:

Assets			£	*Claims*		£
Intangible Assets				*Capital*		
Goodwill, at cost	100,000			Issued – Ordinary Shares		200,000
Patents and Trade Marks, at cost	20,000		120,000	Capital Reserves		55,000
				Revenue Reserves[1]		25,000
				Retained Profits		40,000
						320,000
Fixed Assets						
	at cost	*less deprcn.*	*balance at date*	Future Tax Reserve		30,000
						350,000
Property	150,000	15,000	135,000			
Plant	240,000	130,000	110,000	*Liabilities – Long-term*		
Fixtures	65,000	20,000	45,000	7% Debentures		100,000
				290,000		
	£455,000	165,000				
Current Assets						
Stocks and Work-in-Progress at lower of cost or market value		85,000		*Current*		
Marketable Investments, at cost held for the short term (market value £21,500)		20,000		Trade and Expense Creditors	106,000	
				Current Taxes	5,000	
Trade Debtors		45,000		Dividends	10,000	121,000
Cash at Bank and in Hand		11,000	161,000			
			£571,000			£571,000

1. The legal distinction between capital and revenue reserves was removed by the Companies Act 1967.

E.A.L.

Classical Organization Theory That approach to the development of organizational theory which is exemplified by the writings of, most notably, Henri Fayol, Luther Gulick, L. F. Urwick, J. D. Mooney and A. C. Reiley. The approach is characterized by an attempt to identify the important elements in the process of administration and the features common to administrative structures so that there can be developed a set of principles which would serve as a guide to good practice. Recognizing the considerable advantages accruing from the division of labour, the classical theorists sought to ascertain the basis or bases on which such division should take place and the most effective means of ensuring the coordination and unified direction of the organizational sections thus created. Considerable emphasis is placed on the precise definition of tasks and of the relationships between tasks. Control is achieved through a reliance on a system of checks and the use of authority.

The writings of the classical theorists have fallen into some disfavour. The principles which they advanced proved to be of less value than was hoped; they were not always consistent one with another and some were little more than exhortations. There was too much concern with what ought to be and this tended to inhibit the more rigorous investigation of actual behaviour and its causes and consequences. Without such investigation, the attempt to formulate principles of universal application was premature. It may be suggested that the main contribution of the classical writers was threefold: (1) they pioneered the idea that management was a suitable subject for intellectual analysis; (2) they developed a set of concepts and a terminology which have provided a foundation on which subsequent theorists have built; (3) criticism of their work has stimulated the recent rapid growth in the number of empirical studies of organizational behaviour ⟨⟩ Henri Fayol, Organizational Theory; Scientific Management. I.C.MCG.

E. Dale, *Management: Theory and Practice*, Pt. 3 (McGraw-Hill, 1965).

Closed Shop A work place in which a job is only to be obtained and retained if employees become and remain members of a particular trade union, or of one of a specified number of trade unions.

The closed shop affects about 3·75 million workers, approximately 16% of all employees, or one worker in 6. Of Britain's trade unionists, about 39% are in closed shops, or 2 out of 5. The closed shop is most prevalent in manufacturing industry, where about 26% of the labour force is affected, closely followed by transport, with 22%.

The closed shop is prevalent among craftsmen, traditionally groups wishing to protect their skill monopoly; casual workers, where there is little or no job security, for example, seamen, dockers, wholesale market workers and film and television technicians; trades with a high labour turnover and/or problems of contact, for example, building workers, engineering workers, road haulage workers and miners; process workers in iron and steel manufacture where historically there were union recognition problems; musicians and other artists in the entertainment industry where there are wide fluctuations in demand for labour, little job security and frequent unemployment; and employees of cooperative societies and some local authorities which have employer-initiated closed shops.

The most significant variations of the closed shop are functions of the form it takes; the manner of its enforcement; and the scope of its application.

The two main forms are the 'pre-entry closed shop' (USA – 'closed shop') where the worker has to join the union or be accepted by it, before he can be engaged by the employer; and the 'post-entry closed shop' (USA – 'union shop') where the employer is free to engage a non-unionist so long as he agrees to join the union immediately or shortly after engagement. The pre-entry closed shop is associated with job entry control by a trade union and can affect all grades of worker from the skilled to the relatively unskilled. In the case of skilled work where accredited apprenticeship is a necessary qualification for the job, the union may limit entry to its membership to qualified apprentices and then seek to limit the number of apprentices trained, bargaining with employers to get a fixed proportion of apprentices to trained craftsmen. This form is known as the 'craft qualification shop'. The case of relatively unskilled work is known as the 'labour supply closed shop'. Sometimes the ⟨⟩ Check-Off is a substitute for the closed shop, but in practice they often complement each other.

Variations in the manner of enforcement of the closed shop range from the formally recognized closed shop, the subject of a written agreement between union and employer; through the informally recognized variety with no agreement but a possible screening by management for union membership of applicants for jobs; to the union-enforced closed shop, where the employer is not prepared to agree to the practice and union members refuse to work with non-members. In some cases managements have forced the closed shop on their employees.

Application of the closed shop varies widely in scope. Sometimes the most that is involved in refusing to belong to a union is the loss of a particular job in a particular location; by agreeing to be moved to a similar job within the same works the employee can evade the effects of the closed shop. Where an entire plant is affected there may be variations in the prevalence of the closed shop from one plant to another within the same town or region. There are relatively few occupations comprehensively closed to the non-unionist throughout the UK; printing is one of them.

Sometimes social and economic pressures are made very strong in order to induce a man to join a union, for example his tools are 'mislaid'; he may be 'sent to Coventry'; management, fearing trouble, may tell him they 'prefer' workers to belong to a union and give him the least remunerative work.

The man is not excluded from the job, nor do union members strike. This is a 'semi-closed shop'. All other workplaces are 'open shops'.

When participating in job regulation, unions have three objectives: maximizing membership, disciplining membership in relation to union workplace rules, and controlling entry to the job. Thus the closed shop cannot be explained simply by reference to its relative disadvantages to employers, or in terms of union solidarity. It should be seen as a device which unions want to assist in dealing with particular problems concerned with organizing, controlling, or excluding specific categories of worker. This explains why some groups with a high density of union organization do not insist on the closed shop; it also provides a reason for its complexity of type. It is designed to solve pressing and immediate problems and it cannot guarantee that no future organizational problems arise. Unions with a closed-shop tradition may be helped, hindered, or even destroyed by changes in technology, markets or leadership.

While from the trade-union point of view it may be functionally necessary, operation of the closed shop sometimes results in the restriction of individual liberty and it may have disadvantageous economic effects. In its pre-entry form it is sometimes used to deny whole classes of worker the right to compete for particular jobs. American experience indicates that the practice cannot be eliminated by legal enactment.

Like any other union demand, the closed shop can be the subject of ⟨⟩ Collective Bargaining. Management may demand, for example, a limitation of the right to strike in exchange for recognition, and in several industries formal recognition has been accompanied by an arbitration agreement containing a no-strike clause. Strikes to impose or maintain the closed shop are a fraction of all strikes but are a rough indication of demands for the practice and employer resistance to it. ⟨⟩ Strike – Statistics. The practice is not a historical relic, but an increasingly common contemporary phenomenon.

Some members of the professions, such as teachers, are also trade union members and their position in relation to the closed shop is similar to that of other trade unionists. Far more professional workers are members of a ◊》 Profession, some of which operate practices analogous to the closed shop. In the case of barristers and veterinary surgeons, for example, membership of their respective associations is a condition of employment. In the case of registered professions, monopoly resides in those on the state-held register. Even without legal monopoly, institutional monopolistic advantages accrue to associations which can make membership a hallmark of qualification. All unregistered professions are prone to closed shop.

The *Industrial Relations Act*, 1971, repealed 1974, made void all pre-entry closed-shop arrangements and agreements. Under the Act an employee had the right to belong to a registered union of his choice or not to belong to any kind of union.

Unless an agreement for an ◊》 agency shop or an ◊》 approved closed shop existed, it was an ◊》 unfair industrial practice for an employer to refuse to engage a worker or otherwise to penalize him for exercising his rights on union membership, and for another person to put pressure on an employer so to do. Thus it was an unfair industrial practice for a trade union (◊》 Trade Union – at Law) or organization of workers or an official of either to call, organize, procure, finance, or threaten a strike (◊》 Strike – and the law) or sanctions short of a strike (◊》 Strikes – and other industrial action) to induce an employer to comply with a pre-entry closed-shop arrangement or agreement.

The ◊》 agency shop, sometimes regarded as a species of post-entry closed shop, and the ◊》 approved closed shop, were the only two forms of closed shop allowed under the *Industrial Relations Act*.

Despite the Act's provisions voiding the traditional closed shop in Britain, it continues to flourish in practice. The ◊》 *Trade Union and Labour Relations Act*, 1974 reinforces the closed shop situation by its concept of the 'union membership agreement or arrangement'. N.H.C.

W. E. J. McCarthy, *The Closed Shop* (Blackwell, 1964).

Coding and Classification ◊ Group Technology.

Collective Agreements in Law In recent years fundamental changes have taken place in the legal status of collective agreements. Before the *Industrial Relations Act*, 1971 collective agreements were held not to be legally binding contracts because it was assumed that the parties to such an agreement did not intend it to have legal consequences. Section 34 of the *Industrial Relations Act* changed the position by providing that a collective agreement made in writing after the commencement of the Act should be conclusively presumed by the parties to have been intended to be a legally enforceable contract unless the agreement itself specifically stated otherwise.

The *Trade Union and Labour Relations Act*, 1974 provides that collective agreements made after the commencement of this Act shall be conclusively presumed by the parties *not* to have been intended to form legally enforceable contracts unless the agreement was made in writing and contained a provision to the contrary. Provision is made for the parties to agree that part only of the agreement should be legally enforceable. Although the 1974 Act has reversed the position as it existed during the preceding three years, its practical effects are not as significant since most collective agreements entered into during the 1971–4 period contained provisions excluding legal enforceability. ⟡ Collective Bargaining. W.F.F.

R. W. Rideout, *Principles of Labour Law* (Sweet & Maxwell, 1975).

Collective Bargaining Group, as opposed to individual, bargaining about wages and salaries and/or conditions of work in the widest sense. The parties are trade unions, groups within them, or federations of them on the one hand; and an employer, or his representatives, or an employers' association or federation on the other. ⟡ Employers' Association; Federation; Trade Union.

About 18 million out of 23 million employees are covered by voluntary collective bargaining and statutory wage-fixing arrangements, the latter providing for some 4 million employees. Three million non-manual and 2 million manual employees are not covered by collective arrangements but it is likely that their wages and salaries are greatly influenced by the level of remuneration of comparable workers who are covered. ⟡ Wage; Wage systems.

Collective bargaining takes place at a number of levels; at the level of the workplace, between ⟡ Shop Stewards and plant management (often called ⟡ 'Workplace Bargaining' or 'Plant Bargaining'); at the level of the company or other establishment, between union(s) and management ('company bargaining'); and at the level of the industry between a union or federation of unions and an employers' association or federation of employers' associations. International bargaining, as between an international trade union federation and a multinational company, exists in embryonic form.

Historically, collective bargaining in Britain has evolved from bargaining at the level of the workplace and small firm in the eighteenth and early nineteenth centuries, to district bargaining later in the nineteenth century; to so-called 'national' bargaining for the whole industry between the two world wars; and to a mix of industry-wide, company and workplace bargaining since 1945, with the last two types reasserting themselves strongly. Company and workplace bargaining are most typical of industries which operate substantially on piece-rates and financial incentives of various kinds; they may be characterized by 'effort bargaining', where the amount of work to be done for a given wage becomes as negotiable as the wage itself; and, irrespective of the wage system involved, they may include productivity bargaining. ⟡ Motivation; Productivity Bargaining; Wage Systems.

The Royal Commission on Trade Unions and Employers' Associations, 1968, indicated the declining effectiveness of industry-wide bargaining in determining actual pay levels and the significance of company and workplace bargaining in the following approximations shown in the table opposite.

The wide autonomy of managers in individual companies and work situations and the power of work groups comprises an informal industrial relations system in some industries substantially in conflict with the formal system of industry-wide organizations which assume capability of imposing their decisions on members. Often informal bargaining in the factory is of equal or greater importance than the matters in industry agreements. These latter tend to cover a narrow range of

Category	Industries	Collective Bargaining No. of employees U K June 1967
A	Where actual pay, excluding overtime, is thought to be in excess of nationally determined rates.	10·75 m.
B	Where there are substantial groups of workers whose pay, excluding overtime, is thought to be in excess of such rates, though these are not in the majority.	4·0 m.
C	Where industry-wide rates are generally followed but average overtime pay is high enough to add at least 50% to average earnings.	0·5 m.
D	Where industry-wide rates are generally followed.	4·5 m.
E	Insufficient evidence to relate nationally determined rates and actual pay.	4·0 m.
		23·75 m.

issues, such as basic wage rates and basic conditions of work, whereas the range in the informal system is much wider, including financial incentives, discipline, work practices, recruitment and redundancy. The informal system consists largely of tacit arrangements and understandings, in custom and practice, although written plant and company ⟨⟩ Procedure Agreements have tended to grow in number. The formal system assumes that collective bargaining is a matter of reaching written agreements. ⟨⟩ Group; Recruitment; Redundancy; Restrictive Labour Practices; Shop Steward; Wage; Wage Drift; Wage Systems.

Industry-wide collective bargaining, then, comprises a formal set of relationships and institutions. In many industries the collective bargaining committee composed of employer and trade union representatives, by whatever name it is known, has been developed on a voluntary basis and often by a process of collective bargaining. There is a statutory obligation laid on each of the nationalized industries to set up a collective bargaining system. In some industries the parties come together *ad hoc* to bargain, while in others there are standing arrangements. This last is true for those industries which adopt the ⟨⟩ Joint Industrial Council model.

For industries which the state has judged in need of support in the field of collective bargaining, ⟨⟩ Wages Councils or similar bodies, e.g. Agricultural Wages Boards, have been established by law as minimum wage-fixing bodies. These have some of the characteristics of voluntary collective bargaining in that they involve negotiations between representatives of managements and of unions in the industries concerned with a view to reaching agreement. The main differences are that statutory bodies also contain independent members whose votes can settle an issue in the event of a disagreement between the main parties, and their awards are legally binding and are enforced by an inspectorate on the staff of the ⟨⟩ Department of Employment.

Sometimes collective bargaining results in deadlock. The parties may then avail themselves of conciliation or arbitration. Conciliation (or 'mediation' as it should more properly be called) is the process of bringing the parties to a dispute together and of inducing them to bargain. An industry may provide conciliation services for itself on an *ad hoc* or permanent standby basis, but more usually an employers' association or a union or a company traditionally called on the services of the Department of Employment. Conciliation officers from the Department attended to thousands of cases at company level each year. ⟨⟩ Industrial Conciliation. Arbitration is a means of making an independent decision on the merits of the case put by both parties. An industry may set up its own arbitration system to provide for those cases where collective bargaining results in deadlock and this provision may be built into the national agreement. Alternatively the parties might avail themselves of the state provision of hearing by a single arbitrator, by a Board of Arbitration, or by the ⟨⟩ Industrial Arbitration Board, formerly the Industrial Court. As a result of the constraints of incomes policy, arbitration has fallen into disrepute with the trade unions in recent years and has therefore been little used. ⟨⟩ Prices and Incomes Policy. Disputes and other problems which do not lend themselves to treatment by conciliation or arbitration may be of sufficient public importance to merit an inquiry. ⟨⟩ Court of Inquiry. The DE's role in these matters and the officers and institutions concerned were all transferred to the ⟨⟩ Advisory, Conciliation and Arbitration Service in 1974.

The objective of all these devices ancillary to the original voluntary system of collective bargaining is to support the voluntary system and to make it work.

The ⟨⟩ *Industrial Relations Act*, 1971, made any written collective agreement a legally enforceable contract unless it contains an express provision to the contrary, but almost all agreements under this legislation did contain such disclaimers.

The law also intervenes in other ways in the voluntary collective bargaining system. Under the *Terms and Conditions of Employment Act*, 1959, trade unions or employers' associations may appeal to the Industrial Court, later the Industrial Arbitration Board, where it appears that an employer is not observing terms or conditions of employment established for the industry. An award by the Board requires the employer to observe the recognized terms or conditions of the industry and such award becomes an implied term of the employment contracts of the workers concerned. Additionally, the Fair Wages Resolution of the House of Commons, 1946, requires government contractors to observe recognized terms on conditions of employment in the industry concerned. ⟨⟩ Fair Wages Clause.

The British system of collective bargaining developed in a piecemeal and haphazard fashion but nevertheless came to contain certain principles:

(1) It took priority over other methods of external job regulation, for example tripartite regulation as in Wages Councils and state regulation.

(2) It has not been made the subject of much legal regulation compared with similar systems, for example in the USA, Australia and Sweden.

(3) It has accorded priority to voluntaryism and the minimization of third party intervention.

(4) The parties to collective bargaining have generally preferred to build their relations on procedural rules (i.e. the 'machinery' for joint negotiation, its constitution and its procedure) rather than on substantive rules about systematic structures for wages, rights and obligations attached to jobs.

Preference for procedural rules is exemplified by 'open-ended' agreements which are revised only under pressure from one of the parties and by a wide range of accepted but uncodified practices.

Further, British collective bargaining is dissimilar to that of most European countries in not distinguishing between 'conflicts of interest' (disputes over changes in the existing provisions of agreements), and 'conflicts of right' (concerning the application, interpretation or observance of these provisions).

The principles outlined above are now under some pressure, however, as a result of increasing state intervention in industrial relations, especially with the application of incomes policy and with the preoccupation with reform ⟡ Prices and Incomes Policy; Industrial Relations – Reform in Great Britain. Incomes policy has set standards and norms which constrain free collective bargaining at industry or local level and, in particular, has set ceilings to wage and salary agreements. Reform is concerned, *inter alia*, with producing more order and control at the levels of the company and the workplace and, particularly, with reducing the incidence of wage drift, restrictive labour practices, and unofficial strikes; and with producing positive industrial relations policies, rational wage structures and comprehensive, formal company agreements in place of chaotic wage structures and a shifting complex of tacit understandings and 'custom and practice'. ⟡ Productivity Bargaining; Restrictive Labour Practices; Shop Steward; Strike (sundry references); Wage; Wage Drift; Wage Systems.

The Conservative government's vehicle for reform, the ⟡ *Industrial Relations Act*, 1971, provided arrangements for ⟡ bargaining units; bargaining agents, esp. ⟡ sole bargaining agents; ⟡ procedure agreements; ⟡ disclosure of information; ⟡ approved closed shops; ⟡ agency shops, *inter alia*. The 'legal framework' approach embodied in the Act was however rejected by the trade union movement as inappropriate and the Act was replaced by the much slighter ⟡ *Trade Union and Labour Relations Act*, 1974. N.H.C.

A. Flanders, *Industrial Relations: What Is Wrong With The System?* (Faber, 1965); *Industrial Relations Handbook* (HMSO, revised edn., 1961); Royal Commission on Trade Unions and Employers' Associations, *Report* 1968, and *Written Evidence of the Ministry of Labour* (HMSO, 1965); W. E. J. McCarthy and M. D. Ellis, *Management by Agreement* (Hutchinson, 1973).

Colour The retina of the eye is made up of two types of receptors, rods and cones. The former, of which there are about 130 million, respond to light in the spectral range 400–650 millimicrons, but yield no sensation of colour. The cones, of which there are only about 7 million, require higher brightness intensities before they are activated but are sensitive to a wider portion of the spectrum, i.e. 400–750 millimicrons. They provide colour sensation. ⟡ Threshold.

Colour is described in terms of three dimensions. Hue is the subjective correlate of the predominant wavelength. Brightness corresponds to the intensity of stimulation. Saturation determines the degree of difference between a particular colour and a grey of the same level of brightness; a well saturated colour is far removed from grey.

Green, red and blue are the three primary colours. They may be added together to form others. If, for example, a red and a green patch are projected simultaneously on the same area, the result is yellow. If blue is added, the result is white. This notion of mixing *colours* should be distinguished from that of mixing *pigments*. The latter process, which is essentially a subtractive rather than an additive one, produces quite different effects.

Considerations of colour are relevant both to visual performance and comfort in addition to having certain special applications.

The luminance emitted by a surface is a function of the reflecting characteristics of that surface as well as of the illumination ⟡ Brightness. Thus the darker the colour of objects, the more incident light is required for detail to be clearly perceived. Contrast between figure and ground also facilitates visibility, and judicious use of colour can be put to good effect.

The general pleasantness of the visual environment depends a good deal upon the use of suitable colours. Hot work may be relieved by the use of 'cool' colours. Conversely in a cold environment the 'warm' colours produce a pleasing effect.

For purposes of certain types of sorting, matching and inspection processes, appropriate lighting may be of vital importance.

Colour is widely used for coding signal lights, pipes and cables. ⟡ Colour Blindness; Vision. E.E.

Colour Blindness Total colour blindness, in the sense that only brightness is present in the sensation of light, is extremely rare. This monochromatism may be due either to a congenital nonfunctioning of the retinal cones, or due to an acquired abnormality in the eye or optic nerve. In the latter case, reactions to brightness are fairly normal, whereas in the former case the patient can only tolerate lights of low brightness.

Far more common are the various forms of dichromatic vision. In both protanopia and deuteranopia there is confusion of red and green. In tritanopia and tetartanopia the confusion is between blue and yellow.

The table opposite compares the spectral colours seen by the normal person with those seen by the various types of dichromatics.

In addition to differences in perceived hue, there may also be brightness differences as a function of wavelength.

Numerous tests of colour vision are available, the best known being the Ishihara Isochromatic Plates.

There is a tendency for persons having colour anomaly to be reluctant to admit the defect. This reluctance seems absent in persons having such other visual defects as long-sightedness. E.E.

Colour Blindness. The table shows, in simplified form, the differences between normal colour sensation and that found in persons with anomalous colour vision.

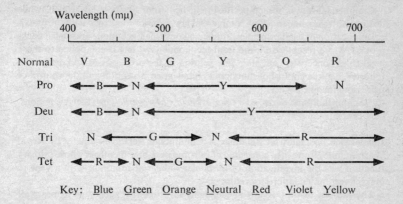

Key: <u>B</u>lue <u>G</u>reen <u>O</u>range <u>N</u>eutral <u>R</u>ed <u>V</u>iolet <u>Y</u>ellow

Commercial Law Also called mercantile law, this does not form a distinct part of English law, being an artificial combination of all those parts of English law which have relevance for commercial transactions. It has its foundations in the general law of contract and then branches out into those particular contracts which have special commercial significance, i.e. ⟨⟩ Sale of Goods; ⟨⟩ Agency; ⟨⟩ Partnership; ⟨⟩ Insurance Law; Transportation Method; Negotiable Instruments and Master and Servant (⟨⟩ Contracts of Employment). ⟨⟩ Bankruptcy Law and ⟨⟩Company Law are also frequently included under this umbrella.

Historically, commercial law originated in the customs of the foreign traders who in medieval days provided the trade links between England and the outside world. These traders, who came mainly from the eastern shores of the Mediterranean, brought their commercial customs with them and were allowed to operate these in their own courts in the so-called staple towns where they had established their English headquarters. Some of the customs were followed also by home traders who took them round the country while attending local fairs. Here again, special courts, known as *pie powder* courts, were available to administer instant justice in commercial disputes.

Lord Mansfield, Lord Chief Justice of the King's Bench Court in the late eighteenth century, is generally credited with having merged commercial customs into the Common Law of England, mainly by using special juries of merchants to settle the customs so that their nature had not to be proved in each case.

Similar developments have taken place in other countries and there exist probably fewer differences between the commercial laws of different legal systems than there do for any other branch of law. The original customs have been supplemented by international treaties on particular aspects of commercial law (e.g. air transport, protection of industrial property) and where these treaties have been received into the national laws of countries there exists a large measure of identity of law so necessary for healthy international trade. The next step will be for the customs of international trade to be given legal force within the legal systems of the main trading nations and agreement on this may not be far away.

Commission on Industrial Relations

Commercial law is sometimes distinguished from business law which, while dealing with the same topics as commercial law, is more concerned with the practical application of legal principles, studied against their economic and social background. More recently still, the term 'economic law' has been applied to those legal rules concerned with state intervention in the processes of commerce and industry, e.g. the control of monopolies, consumer protection and the control of prices and incomes. W.F.F.

Schmitthoff and Sarre, eds. *Charlesworth's Mercantile Law* (Stevens & Sons, 1972).

Commission on Industrial Relations A Commission set up originally by Royal Warrant in 1969 and then consisting of full- and part-time members whose primary function was the investigation of particular industrial situations with a view to making recommendations for reform.

The idea of instituting an independent, investigatory agency as a means of promoting change in industrial relations at company and plant level was originally sponsored by the late Mr Allan Flanders and was favourably received by the Royal Commission on Trade Unions and Employers' Associations ⟨⟩ Industrial Relations – Reform in GB.

The CIR's role was to lay the foundations for the long-term reform of ⟨⟩ Collective Bargaining, in accordance with the Royal Commission's emphasis on the necessity for individual companies to work out comprehensive industrial relations policies. On a reference from the Secretary of State the Commission was required to investigate and report on cases and problems arising out of the registration of collective agreements at the ⟨⟩ Department of Employment. The CIR's main concern was with ways of improving and extending procedural arrangements, for example, how to promote suitable company-wide procedures and how to develop acceptable rules governing disciplinary practices, dismissals, ⟨⟩ Redundancy, and the position of ⟨⟩ Shop Stewards within a plant or company framework.

To some extent the CIR was envisaged as taking over the functions of the *ad hoc* committees and courts of inquiry (⟨⟩ Court of Inquiry) which had previously been used to examine particularly troublesome situations in depth, for example the Devlin Committee on the Docks and the Scamp report on the Motor Industry. But the CIR was also required, by reporting on references by the Secretary of State, to tackle problems that hitherto had never been the direct responsibility of any public agency, for example, trade union demands for recognition and for more satisfactory negotiating procedures.

As originally constituted, the CIR was a purely advisory body with no power to enforce its recommendations on either company managements or trade unions. In his Note of Reservation to the Royal Commission Report, Mr Andrew Shonfield strongly argued that to be effective the CIR must be given quasi-judicial powers with which to enforce its recommendations and a much greater degree of latitude in the selection of cases for examination.

The cases originally referred to the CIR were determined by the ⟨⟩ DEP in consultation with the ⟨⟩ TUC and the appropriate ⟨⟩ Employers' Association, and all three parties had to agree on the desirability of a particular reference before the CIR was sent about its task. Thus constituted, therefore, the CIR was incapable of assuming the strategic role envisaged by its original sponsors. This lack of any initiating powers in practice confined the Commission to a purely 'fire-fighting' function. It was therefore not only extremely under-utilized but on the rare occasion when it was given some work to do it appeared to be acting as a mere extension of the DE's Conciliation Service ⟡ Department of Employment; Industrial Conciliation.

Under the ⟡ *Industrial Relations Act*, 1971, repealed in 1974, the CIR was reconstituted as a statutory body to investigate and report on matters referred to it by the ⟡ National Industrial Relations Court and by the Secretary of State for Employment. With respect to the latter, the CIR had a duty to advise on revisions in the ⟡ Industrial Relations Code of Practice and in the setting up, varying or abolition of ⟡ wages councils.

The Act also laid down that the CIR must include in its annual report a review of ⟡ collective bargaining in the previous year; handle procedural references made by employers or registered trade unions through the National Industrial Relations Court, or by the Secretary of State; handle references for the National Industrial Relations Court on recognition and similar issues within the provisions for ⟡ sole bargaining agencies, ⟡ agency shops and ⟡ approved closed shops; and handle references on ⟡ disclosure of information.

Failing voluntary settlement, the CIR's findings could be made legally binding in respect of some of these matters. The CIR thus became a body nearer to the kind Mr Shonfield recommended at the time of the Royal Commission. The CIR was abolished with the repeal of the Act and its function taken over by the ⟡ Advisory, Conciliation and Arbitration Service. N.H.C.

Industrial Relations Act, 1971, Ch. 72, H M S O, ss. 12, 17, 41, 45, 121, 123; Commission on Industrial Relations, General Reports, H M S O.

Committee of Investigation ⟡ Court of Inquiry.

Communication The process of transmitting or exchanging abstractions such as ideas or beliefs through the use of symbols; usually, but not necessarily, language.

Communication is an essential element in any cooperative activity and is of supreme importance in the large industrial organization for the motivation and coordination of those involved in its highly specialized and interdependent divisions and subdivisions. Furthermore, in the formal organization the need for good communications is particularly enhanced by the fact that those first perceiving the need for action are seldom those with the authority to initiate the action. Despite the fact that systems of communication may be carefully and elaborately prescribed, there must be very few large organizations in which communications are generally considered to be satisfactory. This is hardly surprising as the barriers to effective communication are formidable. These include the problems of selectivity and timing to ensure the transmission of an unambiguous message at the most appropriate moment, the possibility of distortion during transmission and the psycho-social context within which the communication takes place and which so influences the interpretation of the message.

Upward communication in an authority hierarchy and communication between persons of widely dissimilar status are both particularly liable to distortion. Recognition of the need to strengthen the channels of upward communication has led to the establishment of techniques such as suggestion schemes and joint consultative and negotiating bodies using a representative system. ⇨ Authority; Communication Networks; Coordination; Information Theory; Social Distance, Status. I.C.MCG.

> L. R. Sayles and G. Strauss, *Human Behaviour in Organisations*, Ch. 10 (Prentice-Hall, 1966).

Communication Networks Patterns of channels of communication. Communication networks have been the subject of a number of experiments designed to test the effectiveness of different networks in a variety of problem-solving situations. Typically, the experimental group consists of five persons confronted with a devised task, the successful completion of which requires communication amongst all five members. Various patterns of two-way communication are established (or, in some experiments, one-way communication) and it has been found that the pattern of communication employed by the group affects both the group's ability to perform its task and the morale of its members. Some examples of two-way communication networks are:

'The circle'   'The chain'   'The wheel'

Given a fairly simple task, the 'wheel' was consistently quicker and more accurate than either of the others. The person situated at position A, the hub of the communications system, almost invariably emerged as the leader. The 'circle', on the other hand, was slower and more erratic. No one position could be identified as providing a leader. The 'chain' was slowest and, on the whole, least effective. The person at position C, the most central, consistently emerged as leader. However, in terms of the satisfaction and interest of the group members, the 'circle' was much more effective than either of the other two patterns. Furthermore, when the groups were faced with more complicated tasks involving the transmission of ambiguous information, the 'circle' network enabled its group to adapt more readily so that they quickly achieved their previous level of performance. The 'wheel', with its pattern of centralized control, inhibited the adaptation of the group to its changed situation.

The different characteristics of the 'wheel' and 'circle' networks have been compared to the mechanistic and organic system of management. ⇨ Mechanistic and Organic Management. I.C.MCG.

H. J. Leavitt, *Managerial Psychology*, Ch. 15 (University of Chicago, 1967);
J. A. Litterer, *The Analysis of Organisations*, Ch. 14 (J. Wiley, 1965).

Communism and Trade Unions ⟡ Trade Union – Communism.

Company Bargaining ⟡ Collective Bargaining; Workplace Bargaining.

Company Law A company is in law a type of corporation, i.e. a collection of persons who have combined for some common purpose and who are treated by law as a person with rights and duties distinct from those of its individual members. Thus, a company differs from a ⟡ Partnership in that the company is a legal person which enjoys perpetual succession so that it does not come to an end through the death of any of its members.

Companies may be either chartered (established by royal charter), or statutory (created by Act of Parliament) or registered (formed under the *Companies Acts* 1948–67 or earlier Acts). Registered companies are by far the most important numerically. They are further subdivided into public and private companies. Private companies have a limited membership (up to 50) and there exist restrictions as to public appeals for share subscriptions. All other companies are public companies. Registered companies are also divided into limited and unlimited companies. In an unlimited company, which is very rare, members have unlimited liability for the debts of the company, while in a limited company the liability of members is limited either by shares or by guarantee. In the former, each member's liability is restricted to the amount, if any, unpaid on the shares he holds, while in the latter members have to contribute towards the assets of the company only when it is being wound up and only to the extent of the guarantee that they have accepted at the time of the company's formation.

A registered company is formed by its name being included on the register of companies kept by the Registrar of Companies. In order to secure registration the promoters of the company have to submit to the Registrar certain documents, the most important of which are the Memorandum and the Articles of Association. The Memorandum outlines the name, objects and capital of the company, while the Articles describe the proposed internal government of the company and the relationship between the company and its members.

It is generally agreed that company law is in need of reform and the Jenkins Committee made in 1962 certain suggestions for far-reaching changes in the law. A small proportion of these changes were embodied in the Bill which became the *Companies Act*, 1967 but other changes are still pending. Many of the provisions of the 1967 Act deal with technical accounting matters but the Act imposes on public companies certain additional duties of disclosure of information that, for reasons of public policy, should be made available to shareholders and the general public. This includes information about directors' emoluments paid and waived, salaries paid to employees in excess of £10,000 and the number of these employees, the number of shares and debentures in the company held by each director, the average number of employees of the company during the financial year, the amounts of money donated by the company for political or charitable purposes during the year and exceeding £50, the volume of the company's exports (in certain cases only). It is clear that much of the additional information that has to be provided under the Act is called for by considerations of economic policy or to assist in the compilation of national statistics, rather than for the benefit of shareholders. w.f.f.

R. R. Pennington, *Company Law* (Butterworth, 1973).

Company Models A logical or mathematical representation or analogue of some aspect of a Company that crosses all or several departmental boundaries.

Many management techniques are used to study one particular part or section of a company. There are an increasing number of techniques, however, that may be used to study the effect of possible decisions across the whole company (◊ Linear programming, Simulation Models). Many of these assist in strategic decision-making rather than tactical; thus a model may be devised to demonstrate the effect on the whole cost and financial structure of the company of a change in pricing policy, for example, or a change in the gearing. ◊ Capital Structure of the Equity Capital; Mathematical Programming; Simulation. A.J.A.A.

Company Union A company (or house) union is an organization of employees instituted or supported by their employer who thereby effectively controls the membership, representation, business and consequently the power of the organization. It is not a bona fide trade union.

Company unions violate the provisions of International Labour Convention No. 98 (◊ International Labour Organization) which has been ratified by the UK.

In Britain company unions were set up on a fairly large scale after the General Strike in 1926, often in the form of non-union Works Committees. There is also a strong link with the ◊ Joint Consultation stream of industrial relations, which has in the past been used by some firms as a means of preventing the development of independent trade unions. Company unions are now chiefly to be found in white collar employments. ◊ Trade Union Types – White-collar Union.

There are two basic strategies which may be employed by management to obstruct trade unionism, peaceful competition and forcible opposition. In the case of staff unionism, the latter is implemented by such tactics as overlooking union workers for promotion and pay rises, transferring active unionists from department to department, threatening to discontinue any 'extras', and dismissing leading union members. The tactics of peaceful competition includes a wide variety of activities; granting salary increases during a union recruitment campaign, establishing welfare and profit-sharing schemes, granting monthly staff status and establishing company unions.

Many employers sponsor staff associations or staff committees and these appear to have three common characteristics: they are established on the employers' initiative, in many cases after an approach from a staff union for recognition; in most cases they have consultative and advisory powers only, and cannot negotiate; and where negotiation is possible the company is the final court of appeal. Submission of disputes to independent arbitration is a rare phenomenon.

In Britain the most widespread use of company-sponsored staff associations to hinder the growth of unionism has occurred in banking, although over the years the bank staff associations have obtained a large measure of independence from employers. In 1967 they joined with the National Union of Bank Employees and all but two of the eleven London clearing banks are on a joint negotiating council for the banking industry.

The *Trade Union and Labour Relations Act*, 1974 affords advantages to members of an 'independent trade union', defined in such a way as to exclude company unions, house unions and staff associations. N.H.C.

Competition ⟡ Market Models. The idea of competition and the nature of an economy in which it is prevalent has exercised a powerful hold over economic and political theorists for many years. It finds its earliest expression in the writings of Adam Smith: 'Every individual endeavours to employ his capital so that its produce may be of greatest value. He generally neither intends to promote the public interest, nor knows how much he is promoting it. He intends only his own security, only his own gain. And he is in this led by an INVISIBLE HAND to promote an end which was no part of his intention. By pursuing his own interest he frequently promotes that of society more effectively than when he really intends to promote it.' Adam Smith, *Wealth of Nations*, 1776.

Later economists developed the thoughts of Adam Smith into the model of perfect competition ⟡ Market Models, whilst many politicians have craved for a society in which the good of society was promoted through the active pursuit of self-interest by its members. The competitive economy is usually seen as one in which there are few great concentrations of economic power, either in firms or trade unions, and in which the consumer is 'king'. Thus we find the following passage in the writings of the late Senator Estes Kefauver: 'At least up to now no better system has been devised to protect the public than the competitive system. . . . The distinct advantage of the market as the instrument of control is that, in its way, it constitutes a form of representative government. It allows the massive aggregate of the country's consumers to vote their preferences by extending or withholding their custom. And where there is a multitude of independent producers each vying for business, there need be no cause for concern.' Estes Kefauver, *In a Few Hands* (Penguin Books, 1966).

Within such an economy there may appear to be little room for the trade union, the large firm, and massive advertising. The practical benefits of such an economy are not so apparent, however, if we consider those industries in most countries which reproduce most closely the competitive conditions. Thus agriculture frequently needs government assistance and the same is true of the cotton industry and sections of the coal industry. Nor must we ignore the fact that resources are not fully mobile, that economies of large-scale production are available in many industries, and that trade unions give the individual worker power *vis-à-vis* his employer. All this is merely to suggest that we must not hold too rigid a conception of a competitive economy, for it is perfectly possible for there to be more effective competition in an industry of four producers than in one of forty. Equally well, of course, there could be less. Thus both the UK and the US can be called competitive economies for in both the dominant spirit is that of competition. Some industries have a large number of firms whilst some have only a handful; some industries are state-owned monopolies whilst others are heavily subsidized. In both countries the government through its anti-monopoly and anti-restrictive practices legislation (◇ Monopoly Policy, Restrictive Practices) tries to ensure that competition is not stifled and that large blocs of economic power are now allowed to be run in ways contrary to the national interest. Both governments also try to ensure that the pursuit of self-gain is moderated when it threatens the welfare of groups in society or geographical areas in the country ◇ Location of Industry; Regional Problems. These features will be found to be common to most competitive economies. L.T.S.

Competitive Problems Since the UK's economy is based on the ideal of private enterprise, it is platitudinous to note that in many business situations the outcome of a decision taken by a given company may be affected by a decision taken by its competitors. Examples of competitive situations are the bidding for a specific contract and the pricing and advertising of one's products in the open market. The Theory of Games has been developed to provide a useful conceptual framework for considering these problems but, unfortunately, its development has been too limited to solve any real life problems. An extension of this theory, known as statistical ◇ Decision Theory, has been of greater value.

A technique which has been of value both in the military and the business context is known as Operational Gaming. This is a variant on the simulation technique (◇ Simulation) and the nineteenth-century German *Krieg Spiel* (war game). Two or more teams play each other in a game. The structure of the competitive situation or rules of the game is built into a computer program. The interactions between the plays (that is, strategies pursued by the teams) are evaluated by the computer and reported back to the teams. As the game develops, using the experience built up, the teams try to improve their strategies in an effort to reach a winning position. Although the games lack psychological realism (e.g. a manager playing a game would know that a serious mistake will not really bankrupt his 'firm'), it is believed that they can be of value in determining the possible outcome in novel competitive situations. For example, this technique has been used to try to predict the introduction of a new product into a market. Two teams were formed, one representing the sponsors of the product and the other representing the competitors. The sponsors tried to pursue strategies which maximized the share of the market of the product and their competitors tried to prevent this. M.J.C.M.

Patrick Rivett and Russell L. Ackoff, *A Manager's Guide to Operational Research*, pp. 50–53 (Wiley, 1963).

Computer Program[1] A computer performs calculations on a set of data (◇ Computers). These calculations must be broken down into a sequence of arithmetic and logical operations, which the computer is instructed to perform. This sequence is known as a Computer Program. It is fed into the computer on one of the standard input media (◇ Input/Output Media). Before a program is written a flow chart which represents schematically the logic of the program is first drawn

1. The North American spelling is normally adopted as against the traditional 'programme', although some books still use the latter.

up. A person who writes programs is known as a computer programmer. Programs must be written in a language which the computer understands. Programming languages can be divided into two classes:

(1) Machine codes, or languages, which are directly meaningful to the computer, but which require specialist knowledge on the part of the programmer to write and which are unintelligible to a non-specialist reader.

(2) Autocodes which are not directly meaningful to the computer, but can be written by individuals after a relatively short training period (typically three days) and are usually understandable to a non-specialist reader. Programs in autocode are fed into the computer and then translated into the equivalent program in machine code by the computer itself. This operation is performed by a translation program known as a compiler.

The advantage of machine code over autocode is that it is more efficient, that is a calculation will be performed quicker if programmed in the former rather than the latter. The advantage of autocode over machine code is that it is easier to write. Therefore individuals who only use computers infrequently (e.g. engineers, scientists and managers) can write their own programs without excessive difficulty in autocode.

Each computer has its own unique machine code but there are a relatively small number of autocodes which can be used, with slight alteration, on a range of computers. These autocodes can be divided into two groups:

(1) Scientific Autocodes, which are designed to be used for scientific and engineering calculations. A commonly used scientific autocode is Fortran.

(2) Commercial Autocodes, which are designed to be used for commercial and business data-processing applications. A commonly used commercial autocode is Cobol.

An example of a program written in machine code and Fortran for an IBM 1020 computer is shown below. Its purpose is to read two numbers, add them together and punch out the sum. The flow chart is:

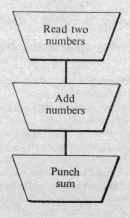

Machine Code Program

Operation Code	P Address	Q Address
36	04096	00400
32	04096	00000
32	04106	00000
21	04100	04110
26	04180	04100
33	04176	00000
38	04176	00400
48	00000	00000

This program is unintelligible to a reader who does not know the machine code. On the other hand, the Fortran program below is much easier to follow:

Fortran Program

READ 1, I, J   1 FORMAT (15, I10)
NUMB = I + J   2 FORMAT (I10)
PUNCH 2, NUMB   STOP

The operations performed by the computer on receiving each of the above instructions are as follows:

READ 1, I, J   This tells the computer to READ the numbers I and J and that this input layout or 'format' is described in the statement labelled 1.

NUMB = I + J   This instruction means set the value of NUMB equal to the sum of the numbers I and J.

PUNCH 2, NUMB   Similar to the READ instruction. It tells the computer to PUNCH a card with the value of NUMB, in the output layout or 'format' described in the statement labelled 2.

1 FORMAT (I5, I10)   A descriptive statement. It is used in this program to describe to the READ instruction where the two actual numbers represented by the symbols I and J are to be found on an input card.

2 FORMAT (I10)   As above. It is used in this program to describe to the PUNCH instruction where the value of NUMB is to be punched on an output card.

STOP   This tells the computer to stop processing. M.J.C.M.

John C. Cluley, *Electronic Computer*, pp. 120–47 (Oliver and Boyd, 1967).

Computer In a managerial context this term usually refers to an electronic digital stored program computer. Its characteristics are:

(1) It performs arithmetic operations (adds, subtracts, multiplies and divides) and a limited number of logical operations on a set of numerical (digital) data – that is, it performs computations and is hence known as a computer.

(2) It is ordered to perform these operations by a sequence of instructions or Program which is stored in the 'memory' of the computer.

(3) The operations are performed and the data and instructions stored by varying the electrical and magnetic configurations of a large aggregate of electronic circuits.

The computer is a very powerful management tool because, having an electronic structure, it can: (1) Perform operations very quickly (for example, it can add two numbers together in less than a millionth of a second); (2) Store data compactly and thus handle very large quantities of it.

These two properties mean that it can perform very effectively both the routine large-scale data processing tasks (for example, wages and salary calculations, customers' invoicing and billing, etc.) and the sophisticated mathematical tasks (for example, determining a production plan using linear programming) that arise in modern industry.

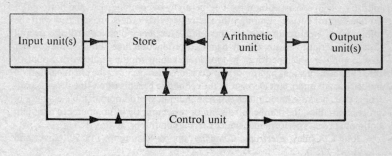

Data and instructions (the computer program) are fed in through an input unit to be stored. Instructions are then fed sequentially to the control unit which then 'orders' the arithmetic unit to perform these instructions on the data. The results are fed out through the output unit. The control unit, arithmetic unit and any core storage (◊ Storage Media) are also known collectively as the central processor unit (CPU). The remaining equipment – input/output units, backing store, remote access units etc. are known as Peripherals. Further details of the structure and method of operation of computers are given in entries elsewhere ◊ Binary Scale; Computer Program; Hardware; Input/Output; Off-line/On-line; Storage Media; Time Sharing.

Apart from their many scientific and engineering uses, computers have been used significantly in managerial applications. These applications can be crudely grouped into three types, although there is an appreciable overlap between them:

(1) Automation of clerical and routine administrative tasks. Typically, the calculation of wages and salaries, of sales invoices and billing, customer accounts (particularly in banking), and monitoring of stock-holding, etc., are examples of the earliest business applications of computers. They are relatively unsophisticated in concept and require a computer to take no decisions normally taken by managers.

(2) Rapid access to information. This type of application is represented by the airline or hotel reservation system. An airline has a central computer file which gives details of the seats available and all its flights for a given future period. Remote access equipment in all the airline booking offices can interrogate and amend this file, so that a customer's reservation may be made within a matter of seconds without fear of 'double booking'. Easier booking encourages customers

Conciliation

to use airlines and so increase seat utilization factors which critically affect profitability. Another application is in the provision of information to stock market investors. A remote access console may be rented which is connected to a computer installation which is continuously evaluating stocks, shares and market movement. It can provide immediate financial information to stockbrokers, banks and other large investors. ⟡ Information Retrieval.

(3) Production and process control. Installations are now exercising 'on-line' (⟡ Off-line/On-line) control of production processing. These can range from the numerical control of a single machine to a particular installation in the steel industry which consists of a three-tier hierarchy of computers. At the bottom tier on-line control ensures, among other activities, that orders are satisfied with the minimum of steel scrap loss. At the middle tier, computers control the overall flow of material to ensure evenly balanced production lines. Finally, the top tier has a computer which performs production planning for the whole work. Sophisticated applications making important decisions also occur in the chemical and oil industries. An important element in the economic benefits of on-line process control is that, because a computer can respond quickly to unpredictable changes in process variables, the plant controls can be re-set quickly by computer to maintain optimum process performance under varying conditions. M.J.C.M.

John C. Cluley, *Electronic Computer*, pp. 54–83 and pp. 148–70 (Oliver and Boyd, 1967).

Conciliation ⟡ Industrial Conciliation.

Confederation of British Industry A permanent association of British managements founded in 1965 as a result of the fusion of the National Association of British Manufacturers, the Federation of British Industries, the British Employers' Confederation and the Industrial Association of Wales and Monmouthshire.

The CBI was granted a Royal Charter in which its principal objects are laid down; to provide for British industry the means of formulating, making known, and influencing general policy in regard to industrial, economic, fiscal, commercial, labour, social, legal and technical questions; to develop the contribution of British industry to the national economy; and to encourage the efficiency and competitive power of British industry and provide services to that end. Financed from the subscriptions of members, it is an independent body and has no party political affiliations. To promote its aims, the CBI maintains a close relationship with the ministries and agencies of government and with the ⟡ Trades Union Congress.

Membership of the CBI at present embraces approximately 12,500 individual manufacturing and service-supplying companies; 220 trade associations and employers' organizations, including the National Farmers' Union; 10 nationalized industries; the major banking institutions; and 20 associations dealing with wholesaling, retailing and distributing.

The governing body of the CBI is the Council, with 430 members representative of all sections of the membership. It has some 30 standing committees, dealing with Economic Affairs, Taxation, Wages and Conditions, Overseas Policy, Fuel and Energy, Education and Training, Transport, etc. There are also 12 Regional

92

Councils with offices, 2 District Offices, and representatives and correspondents in more than 100 business centres overseas, together with a large permanent staff. At the head of the CBI is the Director-General, whose pronouncements are of major influence in projecting the policy of the CBI. N.H.C.

Confidence Level ◇ Hypothesis Testing.

Conflict Any perceived divergence of interests between groups or individuals, or lack of adjustment between an individual or group and the requirements of the job or the circumstances in which it is to be performed.

Many types of behaviour may indicate the existence of conflict, the most obvious being strike action. However, the emphasis placed on strikes, both official and unofficial, as the most dramatic manifestation of conflict, should not cause other manifestations to be overlooked: demarcation disputes, differing departmental viewpoints, inter-shift rivalries, absenteeism, sabotage, incompatible personalities, autocratic supervision, high labour turnover, poor timekeeping, etc. A certain level of conflict in an organization is not only inevitable but desirable, for conflict is both a cause and an effect of change. When conflict, or the possibility of conflict, exists, it is usually advantageous to secure its free expression so that conflicting viewpoints may be fully explored and resolved or compromised with a consequent improvement in the subsequent administrative decision and a greater degree of commitment to it. Accordingly, modern management practice emphasizes the encouragement of open communications, particularly between superiors and subordinates, and of habits of continuing consultation and negotiation.

However, different groups may differ in their ability to express conflict and a useful distinction may be made between 'organized' and 'unorganized' conflict. Organized conflict is normally expressed by positive action on a personal or group basis through recognized procedures or practices whilst unorganized conflict tends to be haphazard and personal, being expressed through negative action such as vague grumbles and dissatisfactions, poor timekeeping and indiscipline or withdrawals from the situation by apathy, absenteeism or labour turnover. It seems reasonable to suppose that unorganized conflict is associated with low morale and, as has been suggested elsewhere ◇ Morale, organized conflict may well be related to high morale. ◇ Authority; Group; Morale. I.C.MCG.

Robert Blake, Herbert A. Shepard and Jane Mouton, *Managing Intergroup Conflict in Industry* (Gulf, 1964); Alan Fox, *Industrial Sociology and Industrial Relations*, Royal Commission on Trade Unions and Employers' Associations, *Research papers, No. 3* (HMSO, 1966).

Conglomerates ◇ Diversification.

Consolidated Accounts Company law in England has since 1948 provided for financial statements which relate to the business entity as opposed to the legal entity (◇ Accounting Conventions) and this is the reason for the requirements for the publication of consolidated accounts relating to a group of companies under common control.

In the absence of special circumstances, as defined by the *Companies Acts*, consolidated accounts are required which reflect the underlying fact that the activities of the various companies are under a common control and represent the operations and interests of a central financial controlling interest. The controlling party is usually either the board of directors of the parent company or the shareholder with a controlling interest in the parent company.

In the preparation of group accounts, therefore, account balances of one company which are reciprocal account balances in the books of another company within the group, are eliminated as contra accounts when preparing the consolidated balance sheet and profit and loss account of the group of companies. Examples of such accounts are inter-company loans, sales and purchases within the group, the investment asset account in the parent company and the corresponding share capital, reserves and profit balance of the subsidiary companies. Another important part of group accounting is the inclusion within the consolidated balance sheet of an account representing the aggregate interests of shareholdings other than those of the controlling interest, usually referred to as 'Minority Shareholders' Accounts'. E.A.L.

Spicer and Pegler, *Book-keeping and Accounts* (16th edition by W. W. Bigg, H. A. R. J. Wilson and A. E. Langton, 1963).

Constraint A constraint is any action that a company's executives have decided they will not take even though they believe that it might help them to achieve an objective.

Two versions of this word are found: an executive may feel constrained from taking an action either (1) because it is not prudent or (2) because it is contrary to his personal convictions. In the first case the decision not to take action of some sort is likely to be because it would conflict with some other objective; thus it might be possible to improve profits in the short term (the first objective) by taking some action which might, however, also reduce profits in the longer term (the second objective) and hence the executive might feel constrained from taking it.

In the second case an executive may know that an action would certainly help to achieve the objective and that it would have no adverse effects on any other objective. Even so, he may not take this action if he believes it to be contrary to his own, or the company's, moral code. These are sometimes known as moral constraints.

All companies have their own moral code which is either developed by casehistory and tradition or, more rarely, is laid down as a conscious act of policy. Typical examples of moral constraints might be: 'This Company will manufacture and sell only products of the highest quality, even though it might be possible to make a larger profit by selling shoddy goods.' Or, 'This Company will treat its employees with humanity even if this results in a lower profit than enforcing strict discipline.'

To define a company's moral code completely requires statements as to its attitude to its shareholders, employees, customers, suppliers, the government and its officials, and to the local community. ⟡ Business Policy. A.J.A.A.

Consumer Panel A representative group of consumers who agree to provide data on a continuous basis about a particular product or service. It is in the continuous nature of the respondent's participation that the panel differs from the consumer survey ⟨⟩ Market survey method of data collection. A diary is normally left with the household or other participating unit, and is completed and returned on a weekly basis. Its particular value lies in the elimination of the need for respondents to think back to past behaviour; purchases are recorded as and when made, giving much greater accuracy. Data collected in this way is the major source for the analysis of brand loyalties and switching behaviour amongst consumers. By making the act of recording information such a conscious effort, however, it is often suggested that respondents are biased in their purchasing; to meet this problem many panels are self-renewing over a reasonably long period of time, e.g. every two years. In Britain the major panel companies are Attwoods Ltd and A.G.B. Ltd, but it is a service which any marketing research organization can provide. Although primarily used in consumer marketing, the panel method can be used amongst any group of users, and is occasionally used in research with distributors and manufacturers. G.S.C.W.

Consumer Protection Movement The general description given to a series of consumer organizations which emerged in strength during the 1950s. Their pressures led in 1959 to the establishment of the Moloney Committee which reported in 1962, *Final Report of the Committee on Consumer Protection*, HMSO, and recommended the establishment of the Consumer Council. This body was set up in 1963 to integrate consumer protection activities, but was abolished by the Conservative government in 1970. In 1973 a much more powerful agency, within the Department of Trade and Industry, was established under the *Fair Trading Act*. A Director General of Fair Trading was appointed with strong powers over a wide area and ministerial responsibility for the issues involved was formally confirmed. The major constituent parts of the movement have been the British Standards Institute, which in 1955 established the Consumer Advisory Council, which published *Shopper's Guide*, the first magazine to give comparative product test results. In 1957, the Consumers' Association was founded by private enthusiasts and began publishing *Which?*, a comparative testing magazine, with sales in 1967 of over 450,000 copies. Although readership of such publications is more substantial than the registered level of sales, research surveys have indicated that only a relatively small proportion of shoppers act directly on the findings. Businessmen whose products and services are examined, however, generally act quickly to meet any defects found in the tests, since the reports are frequently newsworthy and receive wide press coverage. The nationalized industries had had from their inception consumer consultative committees but the general experience with them proved to be disappointing. Other interested bodies are the Retail Trading Standards Association, Citizen's Advice Bureaux, Weights and Measures Inspectors, and the Cooperative Movement (particularly through its educational services). The major targets for action which the movement sets itself have been safety, labelling, honesty in advertising, guarantees and quality standards. The most thorough review of the subject is the Moloney Committee Report, which is referred to above. During its seven years' existence, the Consumer Council published numerous authoritative reports. G.S.C.W.

Consumption Function

Consumption Function The general name given by economists to the relationship between consumers' expenditure and income. The concept lies at the heart of Keynes's theoretical system and many would say it is at the centre of modern macro-economic theory. This is because of the importance of consumers' expenditure in the gross national product (⟡ National Income Accounts); any adequate explanation of the size of the gross national product of a country must grapple with the determination of expenditures by the consumers of that country.

The diagram below shows the simplest type of consumption function, the line $C_0 B$.

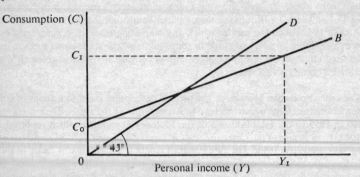

The functional form of the relationship would be:

$$C = a + bY$$

where a, b are parameters (or constants) of the equation as opposed to the variables C and Y.

This function indicates that if income is equal to OY_1 then consumers' expenditure will be OC_1. If income falls to zero then consumers' expenditure will be OC_0, indicating that consumers will dis-save rather than consume nothing. Two important concepts can also be shown from this diagram. The slope of the consumption function, b, is less than one and this means that only a proportion of any increase in income will be consumed. This proportion will be constant, irrespective of the income level from which the change is measured and it is referred to in the literature as the *marginal propensity to consume*. The other concept is the *average propensity to consume* which measures the proportion of total income that is consumed at any income level. This clearly falls as one proceeds along the function from a zero income level; at the point of the intersection of the two lines it is unity. Thus, in the above equation, if b was equal to 0·6, then this would mean that from any increase in income consumers would spend 60% and would save 40%. This means that if we knew the precise form of the function, a prediction of future income levels would enable us also to predict future consumption levels.

As befits its importance a great deal of empirical research work has been undertaken into the most appropriate form of the consumption function, none of which, however, has diminished the fundamental role of income. The variables that enter

96

into it have been refined and a division drawn between the short-period and the long-period consumption function.

The variables most frequently used are real (i.e. at constant prices) consumers' expenditure and real personal disposable (i.e. after taxes) income and the general evidence points towards a value of the marginal propensity to consume between 0·5 and 0·7. However, from time to time shifts appear to take place in the location of the consumption function and this means that regression lines fitted to observed yearly data often give values of the marginal propensity substantially higher than 0·7. Adequate explanations of these shifts are at present lacking but they could be caused by changes in income distribution or changes in the level of assets held by consumers. Such variables as net assets have been used in some studies but they do not seem to add much in the way of additional explanatory power to the basic income variable. The same is also true of attempts to modify the income variable. It has been variously suggested that consumers' expenditure is influenced by past income, by relative income, and by future income expectations, but none of these variables appears to be superior to current income in explaining consumers' expenditure.

The diagram below illustrates the derivation of an observed marginal propensity higher than the short-period values and this is called the long-period marginal propensity to consume.

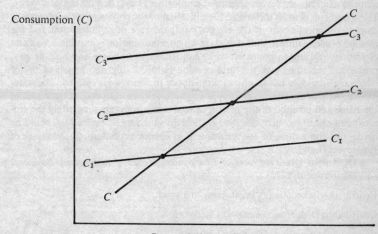

In the diagram $C_1 C_1$, etc., are short-period consumption functions whilst $C C$ is the estimated relationship from the observed yearly data X. It can be seen that the slope of $C C$, the long-period marginal propensity to consume, is greater than the slope of any of the functions $C_1 C_1$, etc., and it is in fact around 0·9. ⪢ National Income Accounts. L.T.S.

G. Ackley, *Macroeconomic Theory* (Macmillan, 1961).

Contribution Accounting

Contracts of Employment A contract of employment is one entered into between an employer (master) and an employee (servant) whereby the employee undertakes to render services to his employer in return for a remuneration. This contract differs from the similar relationship between an employer and an independent contractor in that while the employer is legally entitled to control the actions of an employee both in respect of what the employee is supposed to do and also in respect of his manner of performance, the employer does not enjoy the latter right in respect of the actions of an independent contractor. Another way of looking at the distinction between employees and contractors is by saying that the employee is part of the employer's organization, while an independent contractor stands outside the organization. It is important to distinguish between employees and contractors since the employer has certain duties in respect of the safety of his employees and is also responsible to third parties for wrongs committed by his employees while they were acting in the course of their employment. He is not in general liable for the wrongs of contractors, nor has he the same duties concerning their safety.

Contracts of employment need not be made in any particular form, e.g. in writing, but under the *Contracts of Employment Act*, 1963, as amended by the *Contracts of Employment Act*, 1972, an employer must give written particulars of the terms of a contract of employment (unless the contract itself was made in writing) to all his employees after their employment has lasted for thirteen weeks. These particulars must include an identification of the parties to the contract, the date of commencement of the employment, the rate of remuneration and the method of calculating it, the intervals at which remuneration is payable, terms and conditions relating to hours of work, entitlement to holidays and holiday pay, provisions regarding sick pay and pension rights, if any, the length of notice which the employee has to give and the notice to which he is entitled. The statement must also explain the employee's right to join an independent trade union, the name and position of the person to whom any grievances regarding the employment are to be submitted and manner in which such application should be made and the nature of the subsequent grievance procedure. ⟡ Dismissal of Employees (Law). W.F.F.

> D. Knight Dix, *Contracts of Employment Including Redundancy Payments* (Butterworth, 1972).

Contribution Accounting ⟡ Break-even Analysis.

Contribution Deduction Schemes ⟡ Check-off.

Control ⟡ Automation; Machine Controls.

Control as an accounting process The means by which a business organization attempts to ensure that its operations are in accordance with the plans formulated for achieving its objectives. Accounting systems provide *part of the basis* for control of a business in two ways: firstly by methods of custodial control and secondly by methods of efficiency control. Custodial control is facilitated mainly by means of financial accounting procedures (⟡ Stewardship Accounting), which are directed towards checking on the actual quantities of assets for which company officials are responsible (or accountable) and by means of the auditing procedures verifying the existence and ownership of assets ⟨⟩ Auditing.

The control of management efficiency is facilitated by budgeting, costing and managerial accounting procedures (⟨⟩ Budgeting; Costing Systems; Management Accounting) pertaining to the construction of budgets and analysis of cost data relating to the various divisions, departments, cost centres, manufacturing processes, contracts, capital projects, etc. The accountant assists the control of efficiency by isolating the differences between budgeted figures and actual costs (⟨⟩ Management by Exception). These differences (or variances) give management a point of departure in attempting to analyse the causes of deviations from plans. It is important to appreciate that most accounting control procedures assist control and are not complete controlling devices in, for instance, the sense of a system which incorporates formal adaptive control by means of feedback mechanisms. Neither do they pinpoint causes of variances. E.A.L.

R. N. Anthony, *Management Control Systems* (Irwin, 1965).

Control Charts A method of examining, and hence controlling the variation in, say, the weight, dimensions, composition of an item, or the number of defective items produced which may be the result of either chance variation or assignable causes, such as variation in material, wear on tools, etc.

A manufacturing process is said to be under control if the variables or attributes of the product conform to certain standards, i.e. are within certain predefined limits. Control charts are used in quality control to define such limits of acceptance and to indicate when items fall beyond such limits either because of chance variation or because of assignable variation.

Control charts for means (i.e. average value of a variable from a sample) variance or range (i.e. the variability about the mean) and percentage defective are common. ⟨⟩ Quality Control.

The figure on p. 100 shows control charts for mean and range for a certain item. Two limits are used, firstly the 'warning limits' to obtain advance warning of possible changes in mean or range, and 'action limits' beyond which the items are unacceptable. Warning limits are normally set such that, assuming a normal probability distribution, only 5% of items will by chance fall beyond the limits and the action limits such that only 0·2% fall beyond them. The process is under control if both mean and range are under control. R.W.

Cooling-off Order This new concept in English law was introduced by the *Industrial Relations Act*, 1971. It provided that when it appears to the Secretary of State for Employment and Productivity that in contemplation or furtherance of an industrial dispute a ⟨⟩ strike or other irregular industrial action or ⟨⟩ lock-out has begun or is likely to begin and has caused or would cause an interruption in the supply of goods or the provision of services of such a nature, or on such a scale, as to be gravely injurious to the national economy, to imperil national security or to create a serious risk of public disorder, or to endanger the lives of a substantial number of people or to expose them to serious risk of disease or personal injury, he may apply to the ⟨⟩ National Industrial Relations Court for a restraining order. He may do so, however, only if he is satisfied that the deferment

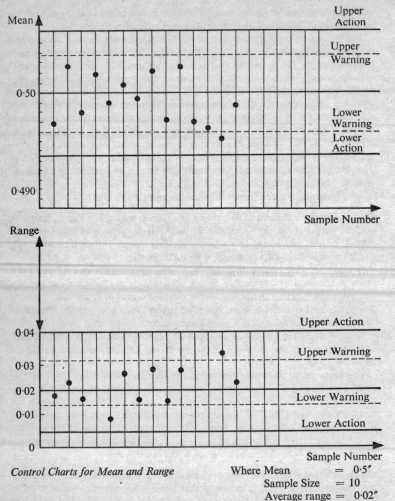

Cooperative Movement

Control Charts for Mean and Range   Where Mean   = 0·5″
                                       Sample Size   = 10
                                       Average range = 0·02″

of immediate industrial action would be conducive to a settlement of the dispute in one form or another. If the Court is satisfied that the above conditions have been fulfilled it will grant an order for a period not exceeding sixty days. The order must state clearly the persons to whom it applies and the dispute to which it refers. The *Trade Union and Labour Relations Act*, 1974 repealed the provisions dealing with cooling-off orders. W.F.F.

R. W. Rideout, *Principles of Labour Law* (Sweet & Maxwell, 1972).

Cooperative Movement A group of democratic trading organizations, where any profits available for disposal are allotted to members in proportion to the value of their purchases. Founded in 1834 in Rochdale, the movement is now world-wide, and in Britain accounts for approximately one tenth of all retail trade with over 10 million member-households. Its trade grew continuously until after the Second World War, when it was overtaken by the growth of powerful multiple selling, in particular through supermarkets in the food trade where cooperatives were formerly strongest (⟨⟩ Retailing). The movement is made up of over 300 retail societies which, in the nineteenth century, established two wholesale societies and a wide range of manufacturing units. The democratic structure, the independence of retail stores and the general dearth of good managerial ability, have all led to considerable difficulties since the mid-1950s for cooperatives. Average dividends on purchases had fallen from over 1s. 6d. to 6d. in the £ (see *Cooperative Independent Commission Report*, Cooperative Union, 1958). It was not, however, until 1966 that the central executive of the Wholesale Society was reorganized into product divisions in line with contemporary marketing ideas and a professional chief executive employed from outside the movement. Two further major decisions have been taken recently by the new management which will affect the future shape of the Cooperative Movement. The first rationalizes the more than 2,000 brand names under which the movement had traded to just one: Co-Op. This move is allied to a conscious effort to develop wholesale trade with the 'private sector' of the retail trade. The second major decision is to pursue a policy in the next decade of mergers amongst the local retail societies, with the end objective of 50 large retail societies covering the whole of England and Wales. The movement also has its own Bank and large Building and Insurance Societies. It is controlled overall by the Cooperative Union through an Annual Congress. A Cooperative political party exists and endorses candidates for election to Westminster in conjunction with the Labour Party. G.S.C.W.

Coordination Harmonious interaction. In that any organization involves the division of a total task into sub-tasks, it involves the reunification of the various divisions to form an integrated whole. The extent to which coordination will become a problem depends on many factors, notably the degree of subdivision which has taken place and the degree of interdependence of the various subdivisions which have been created. The mass production of a highly complicated product (e.g. an automobile) probably presents the greatest problems of coordination.

Attempts to achieve coordination take several forms. The most obvious lies in the design of the organization itself, in which each of the manifold subtasks is precisely defined both in content and in time, the entire schedule constituting a programme centrally administered and universally understood. Such a system depends for its success on, *inter alia*, near-perfect predictability. In practice, of course, perfect predictability is unattainable and the system must therefore be supported by the addition of controls, checks and feedback mechanisms. The resulting system, however carefully devised, remains vulnerable to the unexpected.

Particularly in situations in which the organization is required to function in unstable conditions – and to varying degrees, this applies to all organizations –

recourse must be had to the voluntary efforts of individuals to use their initiative to coordinate themselves as the situation of the moment may seem to require. Thus, increasingly, organizational provision is being made for horizontal communication at all levels through the use of coordinating committees, the encouragement of free interaction amongst peers and, as far as possible, the close social and geographical positioning of work groups whose activities are particularly interdependent. ⟡ Communication; Organization; Socio-technical System. I.C.MCG.

Copy ⟡ Advertising.

Copyright A copyright is the sole right to produce or reproduce any particular literary, artistic or musical work or any substantial part thereof in any material form whatsoever. A copyright protects only the work itself and not the ideas behind it. Thus, the author of a book has a copyright in the words that he has chosen in order to present his ideas but not in the ideas expressed as such.

Unlike ⟡ Patents and ⟡ Trade Marks, copyright does not require registration for its protection. An author of a literary work enjoys copyright in it for his lifetime and his estate owns the copyright for 50 years after his death. Copyright in photographs and records exists for 50 years from the end of the year of their making.

Copyright may be assigned by the author to another party in writing and the assignee will then enjoy all the author's rights for the remainder of the copyright period. W.F.F.

F. E. S. James and W. A. Copinger, *Law of Copyright* (Sweet & Maxwell, 1971).

Corporate Image ⟡ Branding; Public Relations.

Corporate Planner The official of a company responsible for introducing or maintaining a corporate planning system.

Two schools of thought exist as to his precise role. In the first the corporate planner takes over all the company's long-range planning himself, leaning upon the other executives for advice and only handing his plans over to them for action when they have been approved by the Board or a Planning Committee. This view is criticized on the grounds that it leads to excessively large planning departments, may result in 'ivory tower' plans that are impractical, and does not encourage enthusiastic participation by the executives who have to carry out the plans.

The second school suggests that the corporate planner should limit his activities to ensuring that long-range plans are drawn up by the line executives themselves, to helping them to do this and to ensuring that their plans are adequate to achieve the objectives and are in line with the company's policy.

Whichever school is correct, a corporate planner must be responsible to the Chief Executive and must have a broad and forward-looking attitude towards his company and its environment ⟡ Corporate Planning; Business Policy. A.J.A.A.

Corporate Planning An activity that probably started in USA in the mid-fifties, corporate planning is the systematic study of long-term company objectives and the strategy required to achieve them.

Correlation and Regression

It should be stressed that many companies do study these two problems but only those who do so systematically and methodically can be said to be using corporate planning.

This approach lays particular emphasis upon treating a company as a corporate whole rather than as a collection of departments, upon the long term rather than short, upon a careful study of the company within its environment past, present and future, and upon the precise definition of its objectives. It is probably the only 'Management Technique' that has yet been devised to study systematically the entire company (as opposed to parts of it) at the policy as well as the strategic levels. ⟡ Objectives; Business Policy; Strategy. A.J.A.A.

A.J.A. Argenti, *Corporate Planning – a practical guide* (Allen & Unwin, 1968).

Correlation and Regression Very often a statistician wishes to consider if and how variables are related. Correlation and regression techniques are used to estimate the relationship between one variable and one or more others. For example, if he works for an ice-cream manufacturer, the statistician may wish to know if daily ice-cream sales are related to the number of hours of sunshine on that day. Intuitively he may believe that ice-cream sales are larger on sunny as against dull days. To test his intuition he may compare the daily ice-cream sales with daily sunshine hours by correlation analysis. If the two sets of data are strongly correlated his judgement is vindicated. The degree of correlation is measured on a numerical scale between zero and one. Two variables that are strongly correlated will have a correlation coefficient 0·8–1, whilst that of two weakly correlated variables will be 0–0·2. The sign (+ or −) of the correlation coefficient will be dependent on the direction of variation between the variables. For example, if daily ice-cream sales increase with sunshine hours, the correlation coefficient will be positive. Conversely, if we examined the correlation between daily sales of raincoats and sunshine hours, we should expect the former to decrease as the latter increased. If this was so, the correlation coefficient would be negative.

If the variables daily sales and sunshine are correlated, the statistician may then wish to determine the exact form of the relationship between them. That is he may want to identify an algebraic equation which describes their relationship. He may do this by regression analysis. Positive and negative regression is defined similarly to correlation.

In performing correlation and regression analysis, statisticians must be wary of attaching too much weight to a high degree of correlation between two variables that, on other grounds, might not be considered to be associated in any way. A high degree of correlation does not necessarily imply a causal connection between the variables. Thus, there is a high degree of correlation between the increase in expectation of life of individuals in England and the increase in the annual numbers of registrar office marriages in successive years since 1900.[1] However, no one supposes that a registry office marriage will lengthen his life. It so happens that during this century there have been continual advances in medical science and improvements in living standard both increasing life expectancy and, at the same

1. Given in C. Mack, *Essentials of Statistics for Scientists and Technologists* (Heinemann, 1966).

time, an unconnected secularization of our society. A more dramatic example of spurious correlation is that which is claimed between the numbers of storks nesting in spring in Central Europe and the human birth rate later in the year! M.J.C.M.

P. G. Moore, *Statistics and the Manager* (Macdonald, 1966).

Cost, in accounting systems An accountant usually measures the resources acquired by a business in terms of their acquisition cost. Thus an accounting system will generally be a record in terms of historical costs of resources and the costings of outputs and finished goods will generally be fully-allocated unit costs (⟨⟩ Pricing, accounting information for). In contrast, the economist generally thinks of costs in terms of opportunity costs when considering the resources owned by the firm. Since the accounting system is the primary source of cost information for a business, it is essential to appreciate the significance of the differences and similarities in the approaches of the accountant and economist when using cost data for economic decision-making purposes (⟨⟩ Costs). E.A.L.

Joel Dean, *Managerial Economics* Ch. 5 (Prentice-Hall, 1951); M. H. Spencer, *Managerial Economics*, Chs. 7 and 9, 3rd ed. (Irwin, 1968).

Cost-Benefit Analysis This has been defined as: '. . . a practical way of assessing the desirability of projects, where it is important to take a long view (in the sense of looking at repercussions in the further, as well as the nearer, future) and a wide view (in the sense of allowing for side-effects of many kinds on many persons, industries, regions, etc.) i.e. it implies the enumeration and evaluation of all the relevant costs and benefits.'[1]

It is hardly surprising to find many cost-benefit studies carried out by teams composed of a variety of specialists. It is also clear, from the definition, that the value of cost-benefit analysis depends very largely on how completely the side-effects can be traced and the future repercussions forecasted. Equally important is the extent to which the costs and benefits can be expressed in comparable terms.

The fact that we are dealing with future benefits and costs means that we have to use discounted cash flow techniques (⟨⟩ Discounted Present Value), to take account of the incidence of the cash flows over the length of life of the project. This raises the problem of the appropriate rate of discount to use. Another problem is that in many cases the social costs and benefits have no prices attached to them and hence considerable judgement and ingenuity are called for in deciding upon the monetary values to use.

In recent years cost-benefit analyses have been carried out in fields as diverse as water-supply, education, and research and development, and considerable stimulus has come from government agencies as the share of the government in national investment expenditure has increased. L.T.S.

G. H. Peters, *Cost-benefit analysis and Public expenditure*, Institute of Economic Affairs, Eaton Papers, 1966.

Cost Functions ⟨⟩ Costs. A cost function expresses mathematically the relationship between costs and output. The purpose of obtaining cost functions is to test

1. A. R. Prest and R. Turvey, 'Cost-Benefit Analysis: A Survey', *The Economic Journal*, vol. LXXV, December 1965, p. 683.

the hypotheses with regard to short-run and long-run cost behaviour that are mentioned in the entry on 'Costs'.

The sort of function that would give rise to the U-shaped average cost curves of traditional short-run theory is as follows:

$$Y = a + bX - cX^2 + dX^3 \qquad (1)$$

where $Y =$ total costs
$X =$ output
$a, b, c, d =$ parameters (or constants) of the equation

Then $\dfrac{Y}{X} =$ average total cost $= \dfrac{a}{X} + b - cX + dX^2 \qquad (2)$

$\dfrac{dY}{dX} =$ marginal cost $= b - 2cX + 3dX^2 \qquad (3)$

Thus one test of the short-run hypothesis would be to fit an equation of the form in equation (1) to data on costs and output. If the estimates of the parameters are significant then this will add weight to the hypothesis. If they are not then another form, such as a quadratic or a straight line, can be tried.

The following points should be borne in mind in conducting such an investigation.

(1) The time-period chosen for the observations should be one during which the level of output was achieved by constant rather than variable production rates.

(2) Cost and output data should relate to each other.

(3) The period should be one of sufficient length to allow a wide variation in output and yet not too long to allow changes in capital stock to take place.

(4) The only variation in costs should be because of output changes. Thus changes in factor prices and changes in the fixed factors should not be allowed to contaminate the data.

As a general rule an approximation to such conditions is found in individual firms. The general findings are that quadratics or straight lines fit the data quite well rather than the cubic functions of equation (1). In the case of the straight line

e.g. (4) $\quad Y = a + bX$

e.g. (5) $\quad Y = a + bX + cX^2$

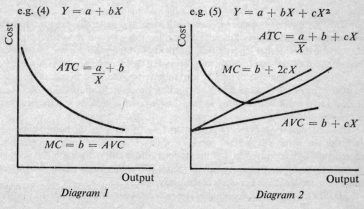

Diagram 1

Diagram 2

105

total cost function this would mean that the average variable cost curve and the marginal cost curve were the same, whilst average total cost falls as output increases (see diagram 1). In the case of the quadratic cost function, by contrast, the average variable cost curve and the marginal cost curve would be upward sloping straight lines whilst the average total cost curve would be U-shaped (see diagram 2).

The examination of long-run cost behaviour also requires some care in the sample data. The following points should be borne in mind in addition to those mentioned in connection with short-run cost functions ⇨ Costs.

(1) The requirement of a wide range of output observations is even more important because there is no capacity restriction.

(2) The state of technical knowledge must be assumed to be constant.

In this case it would appear that the best source of information would be a cross-section of firms in a particular industry, preferably one subject to slow technological change. Ideally, although the firms should be of different sizes, they should all have been open to the same state of technical knowledge. However, this is not always possible and ways must be found to cope with this feature of the sample data.

In general investigations have shown that average total costs fall from left to right, giving rise to the so-called L-shaped cost curve. Only occasionally is there evidence of an up-turn and hence of diseconomies of scale.

The evidence on short- and long-run cost curves conflicts with traditional economic theory. This is because the analysis of production has been too superficial. The evidence suggests that capital equipment is often not only adaptable to varying quantities of labour and raw materials but is divisible also. It also suggests that the managerial constraint on long-run costs is of little importance over most output ranges so far encountered ⇨ Costs. L.T.S.

J. Johnston, *Statistical Cost Analysis* (McGraw-Hill, 1960).

Cost of Living ⇨ Index Number of Retail Prices.

Costing Systems Traditionally, accounting systems have been divided into two separate parts, serving rather different purposes and generally kept in separate books of account; namely financial accounting (for external reporting) and cost accounting (for internal reporting). The attempt to integrate these two systems has been assisted by the development of a concept of ⇨ Management Accounting.

A cost accounting system may be said to have two main purposes: (a) to assist in cost control (⇨ Control as an accounting process; Responsibility Accounting), (b) to provide cost information for the purposes of making specific decisions and long-run plans.

The second purpose is served principally by an analysis of the nature of cost in terms of the various important concepts of cost (e.g. opportunity, marginal (or incremental), fixed, variable, full, joint, sunk, historical, etc.) combined with an appreciation of how this cost analysis relates to various kinds of short-term and long-term decisions (⇨ Costs; Accounting System). L.T.S.

G. Shillinglaw, *Cost Accounting: Analysis and Control* (Irwin, rev. ed., 1967).

Costs In order to make a profit a business must be able to sell its output at a greater price than the total cost of production. The margin between these two may be large or small and it may well vary with the size of output. Thus, if we assume that profits are to be as large as possible (⟡ Business Motivation) then in planning the output to achieve this goal a knowledge of cost/output variation is essential.

In the past economists have been interested in costs and their variation with output because they represent one step along the road towards the theory of price formation and resource allocation. Hypotheses based upon *a priori* reasoning have been put forward enabling one to produce the U-shaped cost curves shown in most elementary economics textbooks.

A distinction is drawn between variable costs and fixed costs, always with respect to some period of time, be it a week or a month. The distinction is based, in general, upon the possibility of variation in the utilization of the factors of production during the given period of time. Labour, raw materials and fuel are usually classified as variable costs, whilst rent, rates, depreciation, interest charges and supervisory management salaries are classified as fixed costs. However, it must be recognized that difficulties of classification occur. For example, depreciation contains both a wear and tear element and an obsolescence element. The former belongs properly to the variable side, the latter to the fixed side. In addition, a variation in the basic time period can also cause a classification change.

The variation of costs with output can be considered from two viewpoints, firstly when some factors are fixed in allocation to the firm and secondly when all the factors are variable and hence the firm can combine them in optimum proportions.

The basic hypothesis relating to the short-period is embodied in the so-called 'law' of diminishing returns or variable proportions. The 'law' states that as more and more of a variable factor is used in conjunction with a fixed factor then ultimately the increments to total production will fall off. The law gives rise to the familiar diagram on p. 108 relating various cost concepts to output. It is important to note the fundamental assumption that the fixed factor is in use all the time.

As will be seen average total costs decline until output *OA* is reached, at which point unit costs are a minimum and the fixed and variable factors are combined together most efficiently, for this level of fixed factors. Thereafter unit costs begin to rise as output increases.

There is no equivalent hypothesis relating to the long-period, when all factors become variable, but merely a collection of cases. The businessman can now consider the cost/ouput variation without any restrictions, and this means that for any output the most appropriate combination of all factors can be chosen.

As the scale of operation changes costs per unit of output can either rise, fall or remain constant. If we gradually increase output then initially unit costs might fall because of increased use of specialized machinery, increased opportunity for labour to specialize and because of administrative and managerial economies. The rise in unit costs is generally assumed to occur because ultimately managerial efficiency declines. In effect this means management itself is still a fixed factor in the long-period. ⟡ Cost (in accounting systems); Cost Functions. L.T.S.

R. G. Lipsey, *Introduction to Positive Economics* (Weidenfeld & Nicolson, 3rd ed., 1971).

Court of Inquiry

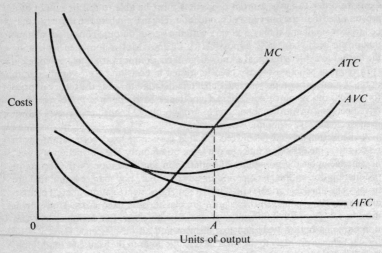

In the diagram:

ATC = Average Total Cost per unit of output.
AVC = Average Variable Cost per unit of output.
AFC = Average Fixed Cost per unit of output.
MC = Marginal Cost = Increment to Total Cost as Output changes by one
        unit.

Court of Inquiry The Secretary of State for Employment and Productivity is empowered under the *Conciliation Act*, 1896 (⟡ Industrial Conciliation) and the *Industrial Courts Act*, 1919 (⟡ Industrial Court), to inquire into industrial disputes (⟡ Industrial Dispute) and the consent of the parties is not necessary before such inquiries are made.

A Court of Inquiry set up under the *Industrial Courts Act* is generally appointed only as a last resort when no agreed settlement of a dispute seems possible, and when an unbiased and independent examination of the facts is considered to be in the public interest. A Court consists of one or more persons selected and appointed by the Secretary of State. The usual number is three, consisting of an independent chairman and one representative of employers and workers respectively, both representative members being chosen from an industry other than that under review. Proceedings are generally held in public and the Court may permit representation of the parties by counsel or solicitors and may sit with assessors.

A Court is not an instrument of conciliation or arbitration (⟡ Arbitration, Industrial), and it has no power to enforce a settlement or make an award, but it makes recommendations upon which a settlement of the dispute can be, and usually is, based. The report of a Court of Inquiry must be laid before Parliament.

Under the Conciliation Act the Secretary of State has power to inquire into the causes and circumstances of a dispute by appointing a single independent person sitting alone or a small committee, termed a Committee of Investigation, the latter constituted similarly to a Court of Inquiry. The Committee is used in cases where the public interest is not so wide and general as to call for a Court of Inquiry. Committee procedure is less formal and its report is not laid before Parliament.

In addition to inquiries set up under statutory powers, the Secretary of State may also set up inquiries under his general powers enjoyed by virtue of his position as Secretary of State. Such inquiries may also be set up by Ministers acting jointly, as in the case of those into the pay of London busmen and into London markets. Under general powers, inquiries have the additional advantage of the possibility of wider forms of reference: it may be desirable to inquire into matters which may not currently be in dispute between the parties. The Devlin Committee of Inquiry concerned with labour problems in the port transport industry examined long-term labour problems in addition to a current dispute. ⟡ Advisory, Conciliation and Arbitration Service. N.H.C.

> Royal Commission on Trade Unions and Employers' Associations, *Written Evidence of the Ministry of Labour* (HMSO, 1965); W. Wedderburn and P. L. Davies, *Employment Grievances and Disputes Procedures in Britain* (University of California, 1969), pp. 224–40.

Craft Union ⟡ Trade Union Types – Craft Union.

Critical Incidents Technique (in Accidents) One method of evaluating equipment and workplaces is to seek, by means of interviews or questionnaires, lists of errors, difficulties, near misses or other incidents which were experienced by operators. This method of elucidating information has the advantage, compared with accident investigations, that many more instances are likely to be available for classification and study. In addition to its application to the evaluation of hardware, the technique may also be used to obtain an index of job proficiency. ⟡ Accident Prevention. E.E.

Critical Path Method (CPM) ⟡ Network Analysis.

Culture The sum total of the beliefs, knowledge, attitudes of mind and customs to which a person is exposed during his social conditioning. Through contact with a particular culture the individual learns a language, acquires values and learns habits of behaviour and thought. The culture of his society will define objects and situations for the individual whereas other societies with other cultures may define the same objects or situations differently. For example, in some societies the tomato is regarded as a delicacy whilst in others it is believed to be poisonous; and some societies regard self-advancement in competition with one's fellows as meritorious whereas in others it is shameful.

Members of the same society will have a common culture to a considerable extent, but as societies become more complex, subgroups may be identified with distinctive subcultures which, although having much in common, will differ from each other in significant ways. In Britain for example, there are marked cultural differences between Merseyside, Tyneside, South Wales, the Scottish highlands and London, to mention only a few areas, and anyone familiar with the culture of one will face problems of adjustment when moving to another. Similarly, there are marked cultural differences between different social classes.

Organizations, too, have distinctive cultures and the newcomer must make the necessary adaptation before he can become fully effective: behaviour in one organizational context may be quite inappropriate in another. Culture may become modified over time and a number of industrial case studies show this process. ⟨⟩ Ideology; Institution; Norm; Role; Social System; Status; Values. I.C.MCG.

Cybernetics The term *Cybernetique* was first coined by A. M. Ampère to describe that area of the social sciences concerned with the art of government. About 100 years later, Norbert Wiener first used the anglicized form to describe the study of 'control and communication in the animal and the machine'.

Many workers in the 1940s, converging together from a variety of different starting-points, developed the view that a general theory of communication and control might well be equally applicable to a wide range of systems. That is to say, there is much in common between the brain and the computer; between problems of radar detection and inferential statistics; between diplomatic cyphers and the mechanisms of genetic transmission. In general, cybernetics is concerned with the theory of information flow in control systems. ⟨⟩ Automation; Information Theory.

There has been a good deal of controversy over the formal definition of Cybernetics; and a considerable degree of variety in the type of work carried out under its banner. Much of the work has been concerned with the mathematical basis of control theory; other parts have been directed more towards the theoretical foundations of telecommunications. Indeed, cybernetics might be described as the theoretical basis of automation's three Cs – Communication, Computation and Control. While cybernetics itself remains a formal rather than a practical subject, its results find application in such areas as automatic language translation, teaching machines, digital computation, machine-tool control and perhaps even politics. E.E.

N. Wiener, *Cybernetics* (M.I.T. Press and J. Wiley, 2nd ed., 1961).

Cyclegraph/Chronocyclegraph Records of the paths of movement obtained by attaching light sources to the moving objects and exposing to a photographic plate.

A cyclegraph uses continuous light sources to give continuous traces on the photograph. Alternatively, by pulsing the light sources a chronocyclegraph is obtained showing the path of movement as a broken line, the spacing of the pear-shaped spots of light giving the speed of movement and the shape the direction of movement.

The lights are normally attached to a worker's wrists, etc., to obtain a detailed record of the movement of limbs at the workplace, and hence facilitate detailed method study. ⟨⟩ Method Study. R.W.

A. G. Shaw, *The Purpose and Practice of Motion Study* (Columbine Press, 2nd ed., 1960).

D

Data Processing (in Accounting) The term 'data processing' refers to the continuous process of accumulation, classification and analysis of large quantities of facts and evidence in order to produce information reports. Hence data processing is basically concerned with the conversion of evidence and facts into information which, by reducing uncertainty, thereby has value for decision-making purposes.

Data processing has become more and more closely associated with the computer since the latter has the necessary capacities for classifying, adding, subtracting, storing and reporting a very large number of pieces of datum quickly. Thus accounting systems, being existing systems already precisely defined and operated, were from this viewpoint ideal for the earliest applications of the computer in matters such as order processing, invoicing, sales and purchases ledger compilation, purchasing routines, sales analysis, stores control, wages accounting and financial statement construction. However, it is likely that the use of computers will have farther-reaching consequences for accounting systems than the speeding-up and mechanizing of routine accounting functions. As computerized data processing develops, all-purpose single accounting systems will probably be replaced by several inter-related single-purpose accounting systems; 'correct' all-purpose practices will no doubt be replaced by those which give recognition to the specific purpose for which a particular accounting calculation is required. E.A.L.

T. W. McRae, *The Impact of Computers on Accounting* (J. Wiley, 1964).

Data Processing (Automatic/Electronic/Integrated) In an organization data must be gathered, processed, stored and reported for various reasons (e.g. to provide cost estimates, customer bills, wages and salaries etc.) Any arrangement for doing this can be described as a Data Processing System. Such systems have evolved historically as follows:

(a) Purely manual systems, based on pen and paper records of transactions.

(b) Mechanical and electro-mechanical systems, in which the data are partially processed by punched-card systems, calculating machines, accounting machines, etc.

(c) Electronic systems, in which the data are partially processed by electronic digital computers.

Systems (b) and (c) which incorporate some automatic elements are called Automatic Data Processing (ADP) Systems. Systems (c) which incorporate one or more electronic digital computing elements are called Electronic Data Processing (EDP) Systems.

Systems being developed to handle the data entirely by machine (from collection of the source data to the production of the final output data), are called Integrated Data Processing (IDP) Systems. ⟴ Computers. M.J.C.M.

Debentures ⟴ Claims.

Decentralization

Decentralization ⟡ Delegation.

Decision Theory Management is concerned with decision-making, therefore in efforts to help managers, statisticians and operations research scientists have developed a theoretical approach to decision-making known as Statistical Decision Theory – this consists of constructing a pay-off matrix or table in which:

(1) The rows list the alternative decisions that may be made.

(2) The columns list the alternative environments or 'states of nature' that may occur.

(3) The 'cells' at the intersection of a given pair of rows and columns represent the outcome of the given combination of decision and environment.

As a simple example, consider a manager who has a £100 unit to invest in the stock market. Suppose he has a choice of three alternative investments:

(1) Gilt edged stocks which will yield 5% regardless of the state of the market.

(2) Highly speculative stocks which will give a 20% yield if the market booms, 2% if it remains steady and -10% if there is a slump (i.e. the stocks will depreciate in value).

(3) Unit trusts which will give a 10% yield if the market booms, 5% if it remains steady and 0% if there is a slump.

A pay-off matrix incorporating this information may be constructed:

	Boom	Steady	Slump
Gilt edged	5	5	5
Speculative	20	0	−10
Unit trusts	10	5	0

Statisticians may then determine the best stock to buy, dependent on the probabilities of the market behaving in any one of the alternative ways and the criteria the manager wishes to use as the basis of his decision.

A similar pay-off matrix may be constructed when the outcome of the manager's decision is dependent on the decision made by a competitor. This approach is known as Game Theory. M.J.C.M.

Decision Trees Elsewhere is offered a conceptual approach to making 'one off' decisions ⟡ Decision Theory. However, very often a manager has to make a sequence of decisions in time in which, at any one decision-taking stage, the alternative decisions open are dependent on earlier ones taken and their outcomes. This situation may be viewed conceptually using Decision Trees.

For example, consider a manufacturer who is asked by a chain store owner to produce a product under a private label for sale in the latter's stores.[1] The manufacturer has the choice of agreeing to the request, ignoring it or offering a price reduction on the same product sold under his own brand label. If the manufacturer does not agree to the request, the store's owner can then make one of a set of alternative decisions which in turn may lead to a further decision by the manufacturer. The sequence of alternative decisions may be represented by the following decision tree:

1. This example is given by A. Mercer, ORQ *17*, September 1966.

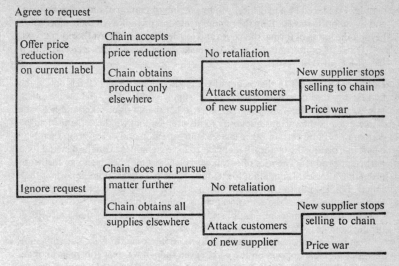

Once the decision tree has been constructed, from a knowledge of the probabilities of alternative decisions being made and the costs or profits associated with them, it may be possible to determine the best decision for the manufacturer to take. M.J.C.M.

J. F. Magee, 'Decision Trees for Decision Making', *HBR*, July–August 1964, p. 126.

Degrees of Freedom ⟡ Statistical Tests.

Delegation The act by which a person or group of persons possessing authority transfers part of that authority to a subordinate person or group. In all organizations there must be some delegation of authority although organizations differ in the extent to which delegation takes place. The terms 'centralization' and 'decentralization' refer to the extent to which authority is concentrated at high levels or is diffused throughout the organization. The present climate of organizational thinking encourages the belief that centralization should be avoided in favour of the maximum degree of delegation compatible with efficient decision making. By this means, the organization achieves greater flexibility, subordinates develop decision-making skills and, it is believed, organization members become more committed to the decisions which are taken.

To delegate effectively, a manager must define the limits of the authority delegated to his subordinate, satisfy himself that the subordinate is competent to exercise that authority and then discipline himself to permit the subordinate the full use of that authority without constant checks and interference. There is a paradox, however, in that although a manager may delegate authority to a subordinate he remains responsible for the subordinate's use of that authority; a state of affairs which does not encourage delegation. In practice, the effect of the

Demand

paradox is reduced by a realistically indulgent interpretation of such responsibility and by subordinates learning the requirements and prejudices of their supervisors beyond the limits of formal directives and job descriptions. ⟫ Authority. I.C.MCG.

H. D. Koontz and C. J. O'Donnell, *Principles of Management*, Ch. 4 (McGraw-Hill, 1964).

Demand (Theory of) In the theory of competitive markets, demand is one of the two factors that determine market price; supply is the other. The businessman, however, is most frequently a price-setter rather than a price-taker and hence he is interested in the various quantities of his product that will be demanded, given certain prices and certain other factors. Introspection and observation then play a part in isolating the factors that appear to have an influence on the demand for a particular product. Theories of consumer behaviour may be able to go further in providing a logical foundation for treating some factors as more important than others, but it is fair to say that they do not add much to the overall appreciation by the businessman of the demand situation facing his product.

The most familiar relationship is that between the quantity demanded for a product and its price and this is shown below.

Because economists have usually been more interested in price determination the price variable appears on the y-axis, even though we treat it here as an independent variable. As it stands, this demand curve indicates that if the price was set at OP_1 then quantity demanded would be OQ_1. If the price falls to OP_2 then quantity demanded will increase to OQ_2. The demand curve then gives a hypothetical schedule of prices and quantities, and it is drawn on the assumption that any other factor which might influence quantity demanded is for the moment held constant.

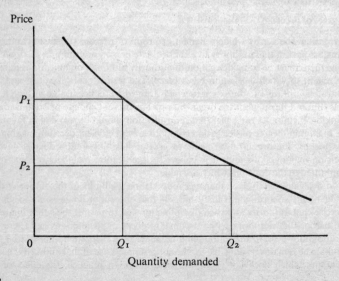

Price

P_1

P_2

0   Q_1 Q_2

Quantity demanded

114

What are these other factors and what will happen if they themselves are changed? Amongst other factors which may be important are consumers' income, prices of other products, tastes, advertising outlays, hire-purchase restrictions. When such factors are set down it is evident that changes in these factors are probably much more important to the businessman than changes in his prices in determining his sales. The diagrams below illustrate the likely relationships, using the basic concept of the demand curve.

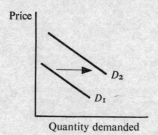
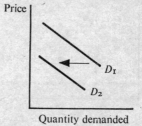

(a)
income increases
price of substitute increases
price of complement falls
advertising outlay increases
hire-purchase restrictions eased

(b)
income falls
price of substitute falls
price of complement increases
advertising outlay falls
hire-purchase restrictions tightened

In case (a) we say that demand has increased because the curve has shifted outwards. In case (b) demand has fallen because the curve has shifted inwards. Such moves are to be distinguished from movements along the demand curve which are solely brought about by price changes. ✧ Prices; Pricing (Market Pricing); Demand Functions; Elasticity. L.T.S.

R. G. Lipsey, *Introduction to Positive Economics* (Weidenfeld & Nicolson, 3rd ed., 1971).

Demand Functions (Theory of) A demand function shows mathematically the relationship between quantity demanded and the factors that influence consumers' spending decisions. With this information one can measure the effect of price changes upon quantity demanded and also the effect of such other factors as income and prices of competitive products.

The first task in any demand investigation is to examine the mechanism that has generated the data available. The simplest example of this is the data on quantities exchanged and prices that are yielded through the workings of a competitive market. The diagrams on p. 116 illustrate the way in which the three sets of data have been produced.

In case (1) the data is tracing out the shape of the demand curve and in this market the supply curve is much more variable than the demand curve. In case (2) it is the supply curve which is traced out because of the greater variability of the

Demand Functions

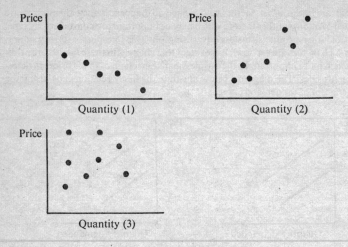

demand curve. In case (3) on the basis of the evidence so far neither relationship is traced out. The problem illustrated here is generally referred to as the *Identification Problem*.

Although we may be fortunate in finding that our data will enable us to identify either the demand curve or the supply curve, there is a second difficulty and that is how do we estimate the parameters of the demand or supply curve? Since the market involves two simultaneous relationships ordinary least squares is not appropriate because the parameter estimates are biased. Other estimation methods have been developed to overcome this problem such as limited information and two-stage least squares and details can be found in the references on p. 117.

In addition to the problem of which estimation method to use, the researcher must choose an appropriate mathematical form for the relationship to be estimated. The simplest of these is obviously a linear form and thus we might estimate the following relationship:

$$q_t^d = a + \beta p_t + \gamma y_t + u_t$$

where

q_t^d = Quantity demanded at time t

p_t = Price at time t

y_t = Income at time t

a, β, γ = Parameters (or constants) of the equation

u_t = Random variable or disturbance term at time t

If, however, the data exhibits some degree of curvature then the following transformation may be more appropriate for estimation purposes:

$$\log q_t^d = a + b \log p_t + c \log y_t + v_t$$

116

where
  a, b, c = parameters
  v_t = random variable
  logs to base e.

The great advantage of the second relationship is that the price and income elasticities of demand are constants, irrespective of price, income and quantity levels. They are, in fact, equal to the estimates of b and c respectively.

Although least squares is often inappropriate there are some models for which it is appropriate. The simplest example is the model underlying the so-called cobweb theorem of elementary economic theory.

$$p_t = a + \beta q_t^d + u_t \qquad (1)$$
$$q_t^s = \gamma + \delta p_{t-1} + u_t \qquad (2)$$
$$q_t^d = q_t^s + w_t \qquad (3)$$

In this model, in which the usual definitions apply, equation (1) is our demand relationship and we notice that the direction of causality is from quantity to price. Similarly, in our supply relationship, equation (2), we see that the direction of causality is from price of the previous period to current quantity. Hence the relationships are not simultaneous and least squares is quite appropriate.

Work in this field began in the USA in the 1920s and was particularly concentrated on the demand for agricultural produce. In recent years, however, the work has widened to include the study of consumer durables such as cars, televisions and washing machines. ⟡ Prices (Theory of); Demand; Elasticity. L.T.S.

  J. Johnston, *Econometric Methods* (McGraw-Hill, 2nd ed., 1972).

Demarcation ⟡ Trade Union – Demarcation.

Department A subdivision of an organization, commonly, although not necessarily, under the authority of a manager. The term is general and there is no agreement as to its precise usage. Such subdivision is necessitated by the problem of the span of control – the inability of an executive to direct the activities of more than a limited number of subordinates. The basis on which departments are formed varies but in the industrial organization the most common bases are function, product, customer, process and geographical location. Each basis has its attendant advantages and disadvantages and the designers of an organizational structure must evaluate each basis or mixture of bases in terms of the needs of the particular organization concerned. I.C.MCG.

  J. Woodward, *Industrial Organisation: theory and practice* (OUP, 1965); H. D. Koontz and C. J. O'Donnell, *Principles of Management* Ch. 13 (McGraw-Hill, 1964).

Department of Employment In April 1968 the Ministry of Labour was renamed the Department of Employment and Productivity, the Ministry having been formed in 1916 to take over the employment functions of the Board of Trade. The words 'and Productivity' were later dropped.

  The Department consists of a London headquarters and 10 regional offices, each headed by a controller responsible for the execution of DE policy in his area through employment exchanges, sub-offices, branch employment offices and local agencies. Regional offices ensure compliance with Orders made under the Wages Councils Acts. There are also 14 Factory Inspectorate divisions.

The Department's manpower policy is based on the maintenance of a high and stable level of employment and its basic objective is to make the best use of the labour and skills in the economy. The programme of its Manpower Research Unit includes analyses of trends in the distribution of manpower between different occupations and industries and more detailed studies of manpower development in the more important industries. It publishes statistical and other information in its monthly journal, the Department of Employment Gazette, and sponsors research into local labour markets. A National Joint Advisory Council consisting of representatives of the ☼ Confederation of British Industry and of the ☼ TUC meets periodically to advise the Secretary to the DE on broad policy questions. Present policy emphasizes the need to increase labour mobility.

The employment services of the Department include employment exchanges, transfer schemes, and a youth employment service. Nine hundred employment exchanges provide a free employment service for employers seeking labour and for employees, whether employed or not, seeking jobs. Vacancies which cannot be filled locally are circulated to exchanges over a wide area and if necessary over the whole country. Special services at many of the exchanges exist for ex-regular members of HMF; those seeking professional, managerial, executive or trainee posts; nurses and midwives; and disabled and blind persons. The Resettlement Transfer Scheme covers unemployed or redundant workers; the Key Workers' Scheme assists employees whose firms are moving to a development district; and the Nucleus Labour Force Scheme helps workers recruited in areas of high unemployment by firms setting up branches there to be trained in the parent establishment. The Youth Employment Service, in some areas run by the DE and in others by the local authority, gives advice to young people on choice of work and helps them to find suitable jobs.

The training function of the DE is dominated by its role under the ☼ *Industrial Training Act*, 1964, which empowered the Secretary to the Department to establish ☼ Industrial Training Boards, each responsible for training in a particular industry. A Central Training Council composed of representives of employers, trade unions, training boards, educationalists, and independent members advises the Secretary on training policy. Vocational training (☼ Industrial Training) in a number of trades of varying degrees of skill is provided in a growing number of Government Training Centres. Supervisory and instruction training is also provided. (☼ Training within Industry). Industrial Rehabilitation Units cater for those who, after long unemployment or illness, need gradual readjustment to the work environment.

On ☼ Safety, health, and ☼ Welfare at work, the DE is responsible via its Factory Inspectorate, for the administration and enforcement of the *Factories Act*, 1961 and associated legislation. (☼ Factory Inspector). (Under the *Offices Act*, 1960, offices may be inspected by Factory Inspectors or Local Authority Inspectors; the *Shops Act*, 1950, provides for inspection by officers of local authorities or sanitary authorities.)

118

The industrial relations function of the D E had a long history. When a settlement to an ⟨⟩ Industrial Dispute could be reached through an industry's own system the D E could render assistance under legislative authority derived from the *Conciliation Act*, 1896, and the *Industrial Courts Acts*, 1919, *et seq.* These services constitute conciliation (⟨⟩ Industrial Conciliation), arbitration (⟨⟩ Arbitration, Industrial), inquiry (⟨⟩ Court of Inquiry) and advice. The D E's services included assistance in the formation and maintenance of collective bargaining systems (⟨⟩ Collective Bargaining); assistance in the prevention and settlement of industrial disputes; administration of Wages Councils Orders (⟨⟩ Wages Councils) by a Wages Council Inspectorate; and advice on ⟨⟩ Personnel Management, including advice on ⟨⟩ Joint Consultation. The D E's industrial relations activity shifted from a negative, fire-fighting role to more positive work involving assistance in setting up coherent personnel and industrial relations policies in companies and other establishments. This industrial relations function passed to the ⟨⟩ Advisory, Conciliation and Arbitration Service on its foundation in 1974. ⟨⟩ Industrial Relations – Reform in Great Britain. N.H.C.

Royal Commission on Trade Unions and Employers' Associations, *Report* 1968, and *Written Evidence of the Ministry of Labour* (H M S O, 1965).

Depreciation Depreciation may be generally defined as the assessment of the change in value through use of an asset ⟨⟩ Assets.

In accountancy practice, the object of depreciation policy is to reduce the historical cost of fixed assets, at which figure they are initially entered in the books of account, to scrap or realizable value by the end of their expected lives. To this end an estimated amount for depreciation, according to some formula, is entered in the annual profit and loss account and deducted from the book value of the fixed assets. By this procedure the accountant maintains what he considers to be on the whole the most reasonable stated value for each fixed asset.

It is important to appreciate that this book-keeping procedure cannot, as is often supposed, result in the saving up of a fund of money with which to replace fixed assets. A mere entry in a book of account could hardly achieve this. What such an entry does ensure however is that recognition is given to the using up of assets when calculating the net profits of a business. Therefore in so far as owners or directors are guided in making drawings or dividend decisions, by their accounting net profits they will not draw more than they otherwise might but for the depreciation entry.

Accountants use certain formulas for calculating depreciation deductions the most usual of which are:

(1) The straight-line method, by which the asset value (less estimated scrap value) is written off by equal instalments over its estimated life.

(2) The reducing-balance method, by which depreciation for any year is a certain fixed percentage of the balance at the beginning of that year. Thus depreciation charge per period gradually diminishes throughout the asset's life.

Straight-line depreciation is generally considered to be better practice amongst accountants, yet it may well be that the latter more nearly reflects the actual loss in value of many industrial assets since obsolescence is often heavy during the first

119

few years where a significant rate of technological change is present. However, few are happy about present depreciation practice, especially those, including in their number many modern-minded accountants, who are concerned to use depreciation accounting as a means of maintaining the earning power of assets intact. ⟡ Changing Price Levels, accounting for. E.A.L.

> J. L. Meij (ed.), *Depreciation and Replacement Policy* (North Holland Pub. Co., 1961).

Depth Interview ⟡ Motivation Research.

Design The act of deciding into what form materials should be manipulated in order to have value added: hence not something which can be done at will by a manufacturing organization. In building, design is termed architecture, in machinery, engineering. The requirements of a product which the designer normally takes into account are: function, ⟡ Ergonomics, mechanism, structure, production, economics, brand presentation, aesthetics and motivation. Having isolated the relevant requirements for any particular product, their integration in an end-product becomes a problem-solving situation. The design of services, e.g. in advertising, print, letter-headings, is susceptible to the same analysis. A powerful school of thought contends that this integration of requirements in a design is a totally creative act, which cannot be reached by methodological analysis. An important influence in recent years has been the development of a new technique called 'value analysis'. This entails the systematic evaluation of products component by component, with the object of minimizing cost without impairing their specifically functional performance. However, an overall design methodology has also emerged along the lines of formal problem solving/optimization procedures. G.S.C.W.

> L. B. Archer, *Systematic Method for Designers* (Council of Industrial Design, 1965).

Desk Research (in marketing) The collation of relevant data, already collected for a different purpose, and its evaluation in terms of a given marketing situation. This form of research in relation to markets is most frequently conducted where extensive published data is available, and/or where the use of sample surveys (⟡ Market Survey) is not practicable for reasons of cost, urgency, or a lack of co-operation from the potential informants. Such collation of extant data is also entirely appropriate as a preliminary to any new investigation which is contemplated. Quite frequently, some data is only available on an informal basis, such as a comment over the telephone. The resulting report will often be fragmented and incomplete in certain details, particularly where commercial secrecy hinders data collection. (⟡ Industrial Espionage). G.S.C.W.

> M. Adler, 'The Use of the Telephone in Industrial Market Research', in *Marketing and Market Research* (Crosby Lockwood, 1967); G. Wills, *Sources of U K Information* (Benn Brothers, 1974).

Dials ⟡ Displays.

Dilution The relaxation of standards in the use of labour, in particular the relaxation of existing customs on the employment of skilled workers. This includes the

120

introduction of alternative classes of labour, or 'dilutees', on to jobs previously regarded as skilled; the use of semi-skilled or unskilled labour to assist skilled workers; and the employment of women on work hitherto performed by men. Alternatively, work itself may be diluted by increased mechanization or by the breaking up of jobs into smaller operations, some of which can be performed by semi-skilled or unskilled operatives.

Resistance to the dilution of labour is largely a function of trade union strength and policy. It is strongest where craft traditions are strongest. It can militate against the employment of workers who have taken courses at government training centres. Nevertheless dilution occurred on a large scale during both world wars to alleviate labour shortages. In the First World War dilution caused much labour unrest but in the Second World War there were a number of Relaxation Agreements between unions and employers or their federations. ♢ Employers' Associations. These were designed to last the duration of the war, but many have by common consent been continued into peacetime use. Apart from those under formal procedures, many cases of dilution take place by informal agreement at the workplace. Dilution may take place as a result of ♢ Productivity Bargaining.

Under some industry agreements, e.g. engineering, dilutees must be registered. N.H.C.

A. Marsh, *Industrial Relations in Engineering* (Pergamon, 1965); K. Hall and I. Miller, 'Industrial Attitudes to Skills Dilution', *British Journal of Industrial Relations*, vol. IX, No. 1, March 1971, pp. 1–20.

Direct Mail ♢ Advertising.

Disabled Persons' Employment The *Disabled Persons* (*Employment*) *Act*, 1944 provides that every employer of 20 or more persons must employ a quota of registered disabled persons. The size of the quota, expressed in percentage terms, is laid down by the Secretary for Employment. The Minister may, in addition, designate certain employments as being reserved entirely for disabled persons.

Employers have to maintain records showing the total number of their employees and the number and names of registered disabled persons. Failure to employ the requisite quota of disabled persons is an offence. For the purposes of the Act a disabled person is one who, on account of injury, disease or congenital deformity, is substantially handicapped in obtaining or keeping employment or in undertaking work on his own account of a kind which, apart from that injury, disease or deformity, would be suited to his age, experience and qualifications. w.F.F.

G. H. L. Fridman, *The Modern Law of Employment* (Stevens & Sons, 1963).

Discipline Control over behaviour. Any successful group activity requires each member of the group to understand what behaviour is expected of him and to be able and willing to produce that behaviour. It may be argued, therefore, that a necessary basis for a sound disciplinary policy is that each employee should understand the requirements of his own job, should possess the requisite skill and knowledge and should be convinced of the usefulness of his activities in relation to neighbouring activities and to the purposes of the organization as a whole.

121

Disclosure of Information

When company rules are seen clearly to arise out of necessity they are likely to command respect and disciplinary problems will be few. Where, however, there is no general confidence in the ability, reasonableness or integrity of management, good discipline will be exceedingly difficult to obtain.

Whenever possible rules should be positive rather than prohibitive, clear and well publicized. It is desirable that rules be formulated in collaboration with employee representatives. Penalties should be known in advance and applied without favouritism, although with due regard to particular circumstances. An impartial procedure for the investigation of the more serious infringements should be instituted together with an appeals procedure. Disciplinary action against an employee should be recorded in his personal file although it may be suggested that there should be a time limit after which the record of the offence be expunged. Finally, one may add that members of supervision and management must be scrupulous in their own observation of rules. ⟨⟩ Authority; Norm; Social Control. I.G.MCG.

Surprisingly little has been written on the specific subject of discipline although the subject is usually dealt with in any of the standard works on personnel management. For example: P. Pigors and C. A. Myers *Personnel Administration*, Ch. 19 (McGraw-Hill, 5th ed., 1965).

Disclosure of Information Under the ⟨⟩ *Industrial Relations Act*, 1971, repealed 1974, employers had a duty to make available to trade union representatives of a registered trade union information necessary for effective collective bargaining. Both the *Trade Union and Labour Relations Act*, 1974, and the Employment Protection Bill (at the time of going to press, September 1975) refer to a forthcoming Code of Practice to be drawn up by the Advisory, Conciliation and Arbitration Service relating to disclosure of information needed by trade union representatives for collective bargaining purposes. Under the Employment Protection Bill failure to provide such information could lead to binding arbitration over related terms and conditions of employment by a Central Arbitration Committee. The Bill also makes provision for the specific early disclosure of redundancies.

At date the Industry Bill gives power to the Secretary of State to order companies making 'a significant contribution' to a sector of manufacturing industry important to the national economy to divulge certain information both to unions and to the Government under penalty of heavy fines, while a Private Member's Industrial Democracy Bill lays down that workers' representatives on the supervisory board shall report on its activities to the trade union(s) concerned and that documentation distributed to shareholders shall also be distributed to the trade union(s), and thence, in both these cases, to the employees of the company.

The British approach to disclosure of information to employees began by being 'general' in nature as in the USA, where the parties are bound to bargain 'in good faith', but this approach seems likely to move nearer to the European continental mainland model of the 'shopping list'. For example, statutory requirements in Belgium include disclosure of lists of 'basic information', 'annual information', 'periodic information', and 'occasional information'. Despite proposed safeguards, British employers have anxieties about the security of information disclosed, particularly in relation to 'sensitive' information and to competitors. N.H.C.

Discounted Present Value The following illustration may help to explain the general idea of discounted present value. Suppose that P pounds are invested initially and that for each period of investment they earn at a rate i. Consider as an example a fixed interest investment of £100 in a Savings Bank at say 4% interest per annum. At the end of one period of investment we have our original sum (P) plus interest on that sum ($i \times P$), i.e.

$$P + iP = (1 + i), \tag{1}$$

(In terms of our example we have £100 + 0·04 (£100) = £100 (1 + 0·04) = £104.)

To consider the series in general terms and letting P_0 equal the initial investment at the beginning of the first investment period, P_1 the amount invested at the end of the first period, P_2 the amount invested at the end of the second period, ... P_n the amount invested at the end of the nth period then the investment series is:

$$P_1 = P_0 (1 + i) \tag{2}$$
$$P_2 = P_1 + i(P_1) \tag{3}$$
$$= P_0(1 + i) + i \cdot P_0(1 + i), \text{ substituting expression (2) in (3)} \tag{4}$$
$$= P_0(1 + i) (1 + i), \text{ [factorizing out } P_0 (1 + i) \text{ in (4)]} \tag{5}$$
$$= P_0 (1 + i)^2 \tag{6}$$
$$P_3 = P_2 + i \cdot P_2 \tag{7}$$
$$= P_0 (1 + i)^3, \text{ by similar steps as for } P_2 \text{ above} \tag{8}$$

The expression can be generalized for any number of periods to show the value of P_0 after n periods, i.e.

$$P_n = P_0(1 + i)^n \tag{9}$$

We now have a generalized expression for discounted present value which allows us to show the equivalent of any sum of money as between any two dates. For example, expression (9) gives us the present value of a sum of money to be received n periods hence, i.e.,

$$P_0 = \frac{P_n}{(1 + i)^n}, \text{ i.e. dividing both sides of (9) by } (1 + i)^n.$$

Moreover, having reduced sums received at different points in time to equivalent terms by the above procedures we can now add them up to give meaningful total sums. In order to do this more easily it is helpful to derive formulae for the total sum of such series. This is the purpose of annuity tables. ⇨ Capital Budgeting. E.A.L.

A. J. Merrett and A. Sykes. *The Finance and Analysis of Capital Projects*, Ch. 1 (Longmans, 1963).

Discretionary Income That proportion of the income of an individual or household which is not committed to regular, basic expenditure to maintain a prevailing style of living. As such, it is a continually changing concept both within and between social groups. The prevailing perception of an appropriate standard of living is basic to the classification of goods and services which at any time can expect to be purchased with such discretionary income. Many products and services can be expected as time passes in a developing society to move from being an object of discretionary expenditure to becoming a basic requirement, both socially and psychologically, e.g. the motorcar, holidays. Within any particular society, however, there will be differing perceptions of these classifications (◊ Market Segmentation) particularly between different income groups. Most new products or services are introduced into markets where their purchase must make a call on discretionary income. Hence the understanding of the determinants from time to time of such disbursements is vitally important to marketing management. Until such time as a product becomes a basic need, however, competition is not just between similar brands of a single product but also between one discretionary product group and all other product groups within a customer's current discretionary environment ◊ Consumption Function. G.S.C.W.

Dismissal of Employees (Law) An employer has the right to dismiss an employee, subject to the appropriate notice being given, without having to supply any particular reason for this action. When the dismissal has resulted from redundancy, the employee will, however, become entitled to certain payments under the ◊ *Redundancy Payments Act* 1965.

The proper period of notice is that agreed on in the relevant contract of employment and if none is mentioned there, it will be that customary for the particular trade or occupation. In the absence of a customary period of notice, reasonable notice would have to be given. The *Contracts of Employment Act* 1972 provides now that where an employee has been continuously employed by the employer for between 13 weeks and 2 years, 1 week's notice is the minimum; if his employment extended to between 2 and 5 years, 2 weeks' notice would have to be given, while an employee with over 5 years' employment is entitled to a minimum of 4 weeks' notice; employees with more than 10 years' continuous service are entitled to 6 weeks' notice while those whose employment lasted for more than 15 years may claim 8 weeks' notice. These periods are minima and they may be increased, but not reduced, by agreement of the parties. An employer may always ask his employee to leave at once by paying him the wages that the employee would have received during the appropriate period of notice.

An employer may also terminate summarily (i.e. without notice) the contract of one of his employees, but this has to be for a good reason which involves a breach of the duties which the employee owes to his employer, e.g. the employee's serious misconduct, serious negligence in carrying out his duties or his continued inability to perform his tasks. If an employer should dismiss an employee summarily without adequate justification, he will be liable in damages to the employee. The *Industrial Relations Act*, 1971, as amended by the *Trade Union and Labour Relations Act*, 1974, has added the new concept of an 'unfair dismissal', thus implying for the first time in English law that an employee can no longer be dismissed by his employer, even after proper notice has been given, without there being a legally acceptable reason for the dismissal. Such reason must be based on the capacity or conduct of the employee or the operational requirements of the employer's undertaking, i.e. redundancy, or that the employee's employment could not be continued without contravening some restrictions imposed by law. The burden of proof that a dismissal is not an unfair one rests on the employer. Dismissal for this purpose covers not only the situation where the employer gives notice to the employee, but also where the employer fails to renew a fixed term contract on its expiry and a so-called *constructive dismissal* where he acts in such a way as to compel the employee to hand in his notice. Dismissal will always be unfair if the principal reason for it was the exercise by the employee of his right to belong to an independent Trade Union, or his participation in union activities outside working hours or a breach of customary arrangements in selecting the employee for dismissal in a redundancy situation (e.g. by not following a customary 'last in first out' rule).

Dismissal of an employee with less than 26 weeks' service is excluded from the above provisions except where he was dismissed for exercising his trade union rights.

An employee who contends that he has been unfairly dismissed may complain to an ⟨⟩ Industrial Tribunal. Conciliation attempts may be made at this stage, but if they are unsuccessful the tribunal will have to pronounce on the complaint. If it is held to be well founded, the tribunal may recommend (but not order) the reinstatement of the employee provided that in the circumstances this is deemed to be practicable. Otherwise, the tribunal will make an award of compensation. If an employer unreasonably refuses to comply with a recommendation for reinstatement, the compensation to the employee will be increased. W.F.F.

B. Perrins, *Labour Relations Law Now* (Butterworths, 1975).

Dismissal Procedure An arrangement whereby an employer terminates his contract of employment with an employee whether on grounds of incompetence, misconduct or ⟨⟩ Redundancy. The dismissal procedure of a company defines the method of deciding that a person shall be dismissed, with whom the authority for dismissals rests, and what form an appeal against dismissal should take. As circumstances vary many employers object to compiling a list of offences with a penalty attached to each, although this is appropriate in some cases. Appeals against dismissal may be to the executive head of an establishment or to a works or company appeals committee on which there are representatives of employees as well as of employers and which may deal with all disciplinary questions. In most other industrialized countries there are independent labour courts to which an aggrieved worker can appeal against his dismissal. Under the ⟨⟩ *Redundancy Payments Act* there are tribunals which may have to form a judgement on the grounds for dismissing an employee, but this only arises when an employer alleges that the employee concerned has been dismissed for reasons of misconduct or incompetence rather than because he was redundant. ⟨⟩ Grievance Procedure; Dismissal of Employees (Law). L.S.

Dismissal Procedures United Kingdom (Overseas Employers' Federation, 1962).

Displays

Displays Any part of a machine which provides information to the controller is termed a 'display'. By far the most important displays for the purpose of controlling most machines are, of course, visual ones.

There are two complementary aspects to the design of good displays. The former is concerned with the basic form in which information is to be presented (e.g. Should it be pictorial or symbolic? Should it be continuous or intermittent?) and clearly it is necessary to relate these basic design features to the control decisions and actions which follow. The second aspect is concerned with the detail of design once the overall form has been established.

Displays may be used in many ways; they may provide precise quantitative values such as those obtained from odometers; they may provide approximate value indications such as those obtained from many motor vehicle thermometers; they may provide indications of current trend or signals of warning. On the basis of the information received, the human operator is required to make a decision and to act. Thus display design decisions should be based upon the operator's input requirements in relation to his consequent actions.

A good deal of published research describes detailed design recommendations concerning dials and other forms of visual display, and includes guidance concerning the size and shape of the whole display, pointers, graduation marks and numerals. ⟡ Machine Controls. E.E.

E. J. McCormick, *Human Factors Engineering* (McGraw-Hill, 1964).

Dispute ⟡ Industrial Dispute.

Distribution Mix The particular combination of channels or institutions through which a manufacturer distributes his product at any point of time. The more common are indicated in the diagram below.

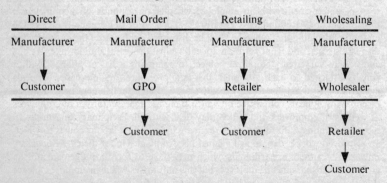

Direct	Mail Order	Retailing	Wholesaling
Manufacturer	Manufacturer	Manufacturer	Manufacturer
↓	↓	↓	↓
Customer	GPO	Retailer	Wholesaler
	↓	↓	↓
	Customer	Customer	Retailer
			↓
			Customer

It is normal for a manufacturer to use one sequence predominantly, although at times a combination may well be used where one does not exclude another. Extensive direct distribution and/or mail order (⟡ Selling, Mail Order) often generates resistance in other less direct channels. Marketing channels, once adopted, tend to become traditional; effective management requires their continual re-valuation.

⟨⟩ **Retail Audit.** The value of distribution secured in retail outlets and whole-saler's agreement to handle a product is an item of goodwill which can be very expensive to obtain, particularly in competitive markets. The particular channels chosen to distribute any product or service must take into account the other elements in the total ⟨⟩ Marketing Mix and in particular the image which it is desired to project (⟨⟩ Branding). It is unlikely that, e.g., *all* retail outlets will be permitted to offer a particular product or service. The appropriate outlets must be selected with the convenience of the eventual customer in mind. G.S.C.W.

B. Mallen, *The Marketing Channel* (J. Wiley, 1967).

Diversification A company is said to diversify when it extends its activities outside its existing field of business. This it can do in a number of ways: diversify; integrate; merge; acquire (take over).

Briefly considering the last two, a company may acquire (or take over) or merge with another company which may or may not be in the same line of business as itself; a take-over generally being of advantage to the company making the bid but not necessarily of advantage to the one being taken over, while a merger is a union which both companies see to their mutual advantage.

Integration can be 'forward' or 'backward'. A forward integration implies that the company is extending its activities down the natural route that is taken by its produce as it passes from the company to its eventual consumption – in other words the company goes into competition with some of its customers. A backward integration implies that the company is extending its activities up the product route into the raw materials or components from which it is made – in other words the company goes into competition with some of its suppliers. Thus a company making sulphuric acid could integrate forward into, for example, making fertilizers or could integrate backwards into mining or transporting raw sulphur.

Diversification, as well as having the meanings above, also implies extending beyond the existing field of business in three ways:

(a) Introducing new products into the same market (for example, a company selling soft drinks through public houses might start selling potato crisps through the same route).

(b) Introducing existing products into new markets (for example, a company selling soft drinks through public houses might start selling through cafés).

(c) Introducing new products into new markets (for example, a company selling soft drinks through public houses might start selling potato crisps through cafés).

As a general rule it is said that successful diversifications are those that involve a close relationship with the company's existing markets, as in (a) above, or its existing technology, as in (b) above. However some successful examples of type (c), sometimes known as conglomerates, do exist. Conglomerates are companies having a wide range of products, not necessarily related to each other in any way selling to a wide range of unrelated markets.

In the context of diversification it is worth noting 'divestment'. This means selling off a part of a company that is no longer considered appropriate; it is thus

Divestment

the opposite of diversification and is a disinvestment. ⟡ Patterns of Growth. A.J.A.A.

> Stanley S. Miller, *The Management Problems of Diversification* (J. Wiley, 1963); H. I. Ansoff, *Corporate Strategy*, Ch. 7 (McGraw-Hill, 1965).

Divestment ⟡ Diversification.

Dividend Policy Dividend policy is concerned with the division of net profits after taxes between payments to shareholders and retentions for reinvestment ostensibly on behalf of the shareholders.

From the legal viewpoint, dividends may generally be paid out of the balance of the past profits. It is not essential that profits should have been made in the company's accounting year to which the dividend relates.

Clearly there are a great number of factors which influence dividend policy, including the immediate cash position, the timing of capital repayments for redeemable debentures and preference shares, the financing requirements for growth of assets, profit expectations, future plans for capital raising and therefore the degree of need to please existing and potential investors.

A different, more analytical approach to the question of dividend policy is that of exploring the impact of dividend policy on shareholders' wealth in order to arrive at some optimal rate of dividend payment. The importance to the company of a consideration of this approach is evident since a high retention rate, although providing a source of financial merit, adversely affects the price of its shares and therefore its attractiveness for the investor. E.A.L.

> J. F. Weston and E. F. Brigham, *Managerial Finance*, Ch. 20 (Holt, Rinehart and Winston, 2nd ed., 1966).

Division of Labour ⟡ Specialization.

Double-entry ⟡ Accounting.

Dysfunctional ⟡ Functional (2).

E

Econometrics Suppose one was interested in explaining the demand for motor-cars in the UK over the last decade, perhaps because one wanted to forecast likely demand over the next decade. To do this one would need to isolate those factors, such as income and prices, etc., which have been important in explaining car demand in the past. The subject which deals with this sort of problem is called econometrics.

The subject matter of econometrics is the measurement of economic relationships that are produced from *a priori* reasoning. Such knowledge is useful for the testing of *a priori* reasoning and also for the opportunity that it gives of studying the implications of alternative courses of action. To take the example above, economic theory postulates a relationship between quantity demanded, price and income, one form of which is below:

$$q^d_{.} = a + b\,p_t + c\,y_t + u_t$$
where q^d_t = quantity demanded at time t
$\quad p_t$ = relative price at time t
$\quad y_t$ = real income at time t
$\quad u_t$ = disturbance term at time t
a, b, c = parameters (or constants) whose values are unknown

In this case the problem is to obtain estimates of a, b and c, given knowledge q^d_t, p_t and y_t.

According to economic theory the sign of the parameter attached to the price variable should be negative, whilst that attached to the income variable should be positive. An econometric analysis of such a relationship for a particular product will throw light on the theory and will also allow one to examine the consequences of alterations in the price and income variables. In particular, a forecast of future real income and prices will enable one to forecast car demand.

Econometrics as a subject in its own right builds upon several other disciplines. The relationships to be measured are derived from economic theory and expressed in the language of mathematics. Before measurement can occur data on the variables is needed and this is obtained from the field of economic statistics. Finally, mathematical statistics provides the tools of measurement and of testing the estimates for reliability.

The relationships to be measured may refer to a sector of the economy or the whole economy. Thus much early work was concentrated upon the measurement of demand functions, particularly in agriculture. However, in recent years, with the development of the high-speed computer, a great deal of effort has been devoted towards building models of the whole economy, particularly in the USA, Holland and the UK.

Any relationship involves parameters and variables and one must have data on the variables before one can obtain estimates of the parameters. This data may be

Economic Lot Sizes

available from government or trade sources but this is not always the case. The econometrician may have to compile his own data from primary sources. He may also have to adjust official data so that it refers to the same variables as the theoretical relationship.

Finally, the data used by the econometrician constitutes only a sample of human experience, whereas economic theories are formed quite generally. It is at this point, therefore, that statistical inference becomes necessary in order to ensure that the estimates of the parameters derived from the particular sample have a wider significance. ⟡ Forecasting (medium-term). L.T.S.

L. R. Klein, *An Introduction to Econometrics* (Prentice-Hall, 1962); J. Johnston, *Econometric Methods* (McGraw-Hill, 2nd ed., 1972).

Economic Lot Sizes ⟡ Batch Sizes.

Economics Academic literature abounds with definitions of economics. Rather than attempting another one we can say that economics is what economists do. In the main they have been concerned with three areas; firstly, the problem of resource allocation; secondly, the problems of unemployment and over-full employment; and thirdly, the problem of growth of output per head.

A still useful division is that between *economic theory* and *applied economics*. The role of economic theory is to explain the workings of the economic system, or parts of it, in a simplified manner (⟡ Model in Economic Analysis) whilst that of applied economics is to apply the theory to selected topics, e.g. the study of inflation or the control of monopoly. Clearly the development of economics as a body of knowledge depends heavily upon the interaction of these two branches of the subject, for theories are modified as they fail to explain reality and new theories are often called forth by a growing awareness of new facts which older theories cannot explain.

A division often found in the literature is that between *micro-economics*, or the economics of small units, and *macro-economics*, or the economics of aggregates ⟡ Macro-Economic Models.

Micro-economists study the way that resources in a country are allocated through the market system and this involves them in detailed studies of firms, industries, and the relationship of government and industry ⟡ Business Motivation, Costs, Cost Functions, Demand (theory of), Demand Functions, Elasticity, Forecasting (Medium-term), Growth of the Firm, Input/Output, Location of Industry, Market Models, Monopoly Policy, Patterns of Growth, Prices (theory of), Production Theory, Profits, Restrictive Practices.

Macro-economists look at the economic system in a different way, asking themselves the question 'Why is the level of gross national product what it is?' This means that they have to measure the production of the economic system (⟡ National Income Accounts) and then search for explanations of the level within the decisions of consumers, businessmen and the government ⟡ Balance of Payments, Consumption Function, Employment, Forecasting for the Economy, Fiscal Policy, Inflation, Investment in the Economy, Monetary Policy, Multiplier Planning.

130

The growth specialist is asking the question 'What makes the rate of growth in output per head of a country increase (or decrease)?' This means once again that one has to decide what is meant by growth ⟴ Growth: Measurement, before one can search for explanations of why it occurs (or fails to occur) ⟴ Growth in the Economy: Determinants.

As economics has developed we find that some areas of study have been transferred to other specialists whilst new areas of study have been developed. *Demography* is an example of the former whilst *growth* and *Cost-Benefit Analysis* are examples of the latter. The development of one subject, *econometrics*, deserves special mention, however.

The nature of economic theory is such that it can be translated into the language of mathematics, thus yielding significant benefits in terms of clarity and ease of argument. Side by side with this development came the urge to measure economic relationships and so subject the *a priori* theories to rigorous tests. Thus, from early work in the field of agricultural supply and demand functions, developed the subject of econometrics, fusing together economics, mathematics and statistics ⟴ Econometrics, Index Numbers.

One last development is worth noting. As management education has progressed so economics has appeared as one of the background subjects of study. This has caused economists engaged in the field to look closely at the subject through the eyes of the businessman and has to some extent paved the way for the development of a new subject ⟴ Managerial Economics.

The methods used in economics have changed over time, making it more akin to the physical sciences. As greater stress has been laid on the testing of hypotheses, measurements and predictions, so the use of mathematics and statistics has increased at the expense of more literary and qualitative methods. The quest for scientific detachment and rigour is perhaps most clearly seen in the work of academic economists, when they wear their academic 'hats'. The influence of political and social values and the exercise of qualitative methods, on the other hand, is most clearly seen in economic analysis when one considers the public pronouncements of economists.

All this has meant that the student of economics covers a different range of subjects than did his predecessor of 30 years ago. The course is likely to contain mathematics and statistics and accountancy to a considerable degree and there is likely to be less emphasis upon economic history and the historical development of economic analysis. L.T.S.

R. G. Lipsey, *An Introduction to Positive Economics* (Weidenfeld & Nicolson, 3rd ed., 1971).

Effort Bargaining ⟡ Collective Bargaining.

Elasticity As a general concept the elasticity between two variables, X and Y, measures the response in one variable to 1% change in the other. The two most common measures are the price elasticity of demand, measuring the response of quantity demanded to a change in price, and the income elasticity of demand, measuring the response of quantity demanded to an income change.

Algebraically the concept can be written as follows:

$$\frac{E}{XY} = \frac{\Delta Y}{\Delta X} \cdot \frac{X}{Y}$$

$\dfrac{E}{XY}$ = elasticity of Y with respect to X

$\Delta Y, \Delta X$ = change in Y and X

Y, X = values of Y and X

Because different values for the elasticity can occur, depending upon which values of Y and X the changes are measured from, some writers prefer to calculate using the arc elasticity concept.

Algebraically we have

$$\frac{E}{XY} = \frac{\Delta Y}{\Delta X} \cdot \frac{X_1 + X_2}{Y_1 + Y_2}$$

where

Y_1, X_1 = initial values of Y and X

Y_2, X_2 = value of Y and X after changes have occurred.

The following is the way the elasticity would be calculated for the data given below:

Variable	Y_1	X_1	Y_2	X_2	ΔY	ΔX
Value	100	10	150	8	+50	−2

$$\frac{E}{XY} = \frac{50}{-2} \cdot \frac{18}{250} = -1 \cdot 8$$

Elasticity can be either positive or negative, depending upon the fundamental relationship existing between the variables. Price elasticity of demand is always negative because price changes lead to changes of quantity demanded in the opposite direction (⟺ Demand), whilst income elasticity of demand is usually positive.

Many estimates have been obtained of the price elasticity of demand of goods, both durable and non-durable. Knowledge of this concept is extremely valuable to businessmen since it indicates the effect on their total receipts of a price change. Specifically, if the price elasticity is greater than unity, then total receipts will increase as price is reduced, whilst if elasticity is less than unity then total receipts will fall. Some typical values of the price elasticity of demand taken from recent studies are: flour −0·79, oranges −0·97 and butter −0·43. Thus, a 1 % fall in the price of flour would lead to a 0·79% increase in the quantity demanded; total receipts would fall, however.

The income-elasticity concept has also been extensively studied, data for such studies often being provided as a by-product of the construction of retail price index numbers. It is particularly useful in indicating to a manufacturer the effect of future income changes upon his sales. Some typical values of the income elasticity of demand are refrigerators 0·96, motor-cars 0·69 and butter 0·37. Thus, a 1 % increase in income would lead to almost the same increase in the quantity demanded of refrigerators. ⟡ Prices (Theory of); Demand (Theory of); Demand Function. L.T.S.

J. Bates and J. R. Parkinson, *Business Economics* (Blackwell, 2nd ed., 1969).

Electrophysiological Techniques Neural transmission within the body takes place by means of the conduction of electrical pulses along nerve fibres. By the suitable placing of electrodes and the use of high-grain amplifiers and recorders, it is possible to study this neural transmission at various places in the body. Numerous applications have been made of these electrophysiological recordings.

Electrocardiogram (ECG or EKG). Analysis of the wave shape is used in the diagnosis of cardiac dysfunction. The electrical impulses also provide a useful input into automatic pulse-rate counters, which may be used in assessments of physical work load or mental stress (⟡ Muscular Work; Pulse Rate).

Electrocorticogram Recordings made directly from the brain surface can obviously be made only under rather special circumstances. More usually brain activity is investigated by EEG.

Electroencephalogram (EEG). Electrodes placed upon the skull detect the activity in the brain. Under normal resting conditions, the predominant rhythm is a regular 10/sec. one. This is disturbed by the appearance of sensory stimulation, or by emotional arousal. Various patterns of activity are known to be characteristic of sleep or of neurological disorders.

Electromyogram (EMG). Muscle tension can be detected using either needle or surface electrodes. Applications of EMG include studies of posture, physical work load and emotional tension (⟡ Posture).

Electroretinogram (ERG). By placing one electrode on the cornea and one on the back of the eyeball it is possible to detect signals resulting from momentary stimulation of the retina. This technique makes possible studies of the sensitivity of the retina. E.E.

Employee Services ⟡ Welfare.

Employers' Association An organization of employers which seeks to assist, influence or control the industrial relations decisions of member-firms and/or which is engaged in trade activities on behalf of members.

Employers thus associate for two basic purposes, labour matters and trade matters. In some industries there are two associations, one dealing with labour matters and the other a 'trade association' which deals with technical matters; supplies; relations with government, public authorities, professional bodies and customers; and possibly cooperative research. Before anti-monopoly legislation, price-fixing was a key activity of many trade associations. In other industries both sets of activities are carried on in one association. In yet other cases a complex of associations has been simplified on the labour side by the formation of an overall federal body to deal with labour matters, whereas each section of the industry has its own 'trade association'.

Amongst employers, the distinction between 'association' and 'federation' is relatively unimportant, but it is common to find the term 'association' used for local organizations and 'federation' for national organizations. A firm outside

membership of the appropriate association or federation is generally known as
'non-federated'; a firm inside the organization as 'federated'. Non-federated
firms tend to be either very small ones or large ones which wish to manage their
affairs independently. In some industries firms have abandoned membership of
their association in order to take an independent line, e.g. in ⟡ Productivity
Bargaining.

Varieties of organization of employers' bodies include local organizations
affiliated to national federations; national associations with regional branches
and single organizations with a national coverage.

Employers' organizations are organized by industry for labour matters, but not
necessarily for trade matters. They are thus 'Industrial Unions' ⟡ Trade Union
Types – Industrial Unions on the employers' side. ⟡ Collective Bargaining.

Eligibility for membership is commonly based on 3 main factors: participation
in the appropriate industry; agreement to abide by policy decisions of the association; and satisfaction of the other members that the applicant has a 'reputable'
business. Discipline over members may be effected by using sanctions which can
include stigma in the society in which the employer moves, loss of the member's
share in the accumulated strike fund, loss of sundry services (usually the most
important loss) and expulsion from membership.

The range of services provided by employers' associations is very wide and the
amount and kind of service varies according to the attitudes of the association.
This in turn is a function of the prevailing view of member firms as to the role the
association should play. Some see the body as a forum where views and experiences may be exchanged; others as a means of attaining joint action to solve
common problems in the industry. Where labour relations in an industry are good,
the employers' association may run joint ventures with the trade union(s) concerned – for example, the shoe industry research centre.

The industrial relations activities of employers' organizations fall into two
categories: the representation of employers' interests in dealing with trade unions,
including the negotiation of wages and conditions of employment, and the handling of disputes between employers and workers (⟡ Collective Bargaining); and
assistance to members in dealing with their own management–labour problems.
All associations concerned with industrial relations negotiate a national wage
agreement, some as a means of establishing a pay structure for the whole industry,
others negotiating basic rates which may be supplemented by company and factory plus rates and bonuses of various kinds. ⟡ Wage; Wage Drift; Wage
Systems.

Other than industrial relations matters, the main activities of employers' organizations include representation of employers' interests to government and other
bodies; the provision of information services, including statistics; assistance in
manpower matters including its efficient use, labour supply and demand, recruitment and selection, education and training, and health, safety and welfare; and
assistance in trade and commercial matters.

Although they are not mass organizations like trade unions, employers' associations with industrial relations functions have many organizational similarities to
their counterparts on the employees' side. The final authority of a small national

association or of a local association can be a meeting of all the members, whereas in larger organizations some method of representation is adopted. Where local associations are grouped into regions, divisions or areas, election of representatives is normally through these bodies.

These representatives, together with a number of officials, form a General Council which elects committees to deal with particular aspects of the work of the organization. There is often an inner council or cabinet and the senior full-time officer of a large employers' body is normally known as the Director. Important decisions tend to be made by a few full-time senior officials together with one or two leading employers.

There is an immense number of trade associations and over 1500 district employers' associations concerned with collective bargaining, most being affiliated to about 270 national federations. Like trade unions, employers' associations as a whole would benefit from structural reform. Similarly, they employ too few full-time officers, many of whom have even less formal training for their tasks than do trade union officials. Local employers' association officials may be unpaid, or their function may be carried out part-time by a solicitor or accountant in private practice. N.H.C.

> A. Flanders and H. A. Clegg, eds., *The System of Industrial Relations in Great Britain* (Blackwell, 1956); Royal Commission on Trade Unions and Employers' Associations, *Research Papers 7, Employers' Associations* (HMSO, 1967).

Employers' Federation ◊ Employers' Association; Federation.

Employer's Liability According to English Common Law an employer has a duty to take all reasonable steps to protect the safety of the persons employed by him. This includes providing his employees with reasonably safe premises to work in, with reasonably safe tools, materials and appliances to work with and with a reasonably safe system of work. If an employer should be in breach of this duty and this breach were to lead to one of his employees sustaining injuries, the employer will be liable in damages to the employee concerned. The employer's duty is not, however, an absolute one: he is not responsible for all accidents but only for those which he should reasonably have anticipated and prevented by taking appropriate measures.

In addition, the employer is subject to certain statutory duties, e.g. those imposed on him by the ◊ Factory Law. These differ from the common law duties discussed above inasmuch as the employer has to carry out strictly the obligations imposed on him by statute and he is not able to claim that he has done all that can be reasonably expected of him.

The employee has also a duty to take reasonable precautions for his own safety and if he should fail to do so, the employer, who has also been in breach of his duties, may offer the defence of contributory negligence. If contributory negligence by the employee is proved, the court will divide the loss which the employee/plaintiff has suffered between him and the employer/defendant in proportion to their respective degrees of negligence. W.F.F.

> J. Munkman, *Employer's Liability at Common Law* (Butterworth, 1975).

135

Employment

Employment One of the central problems of macro-economics is the determination of the level of output in the economy and hence the level of employment. The prevailing climate of opinion before the publication in 1936 of Lord Keynes' *The General Theory of Employment, Interest and Money* was that there would be a tendency towards full employment in an economy because of wage–price flexibility. This was manifestly untrue in the 1930s and Keynes's book changed the approach of economists so that full employment was seen as a possible outcome for the economy, but not the only outcome.

The term 'employment' is capable of several definitions. The one most commonly used for statistical purposes includes 'employees in employment' and the 'wholly unemployed'. It is based upon mid-year estimates of the total number of employees and their industrial distribution, which are derived from counts of insurance cards.

The essence of the modern approach is a blending together of consumption demand and investment demand as determinants of the aggregate level of output, and hence employment. Consumption demand depends mainly upon the level of income, whilst investment demand depends upon profit expectations and the rate of change of output ▷ Consumption Function; Investment in the Economy. Thus the equilibrium level of output, and hence employment, will occur when the demands upon the economic system balance the supply of goods from the system. This need not occur at the level of output corresponding to full employment.

The diagram below illustrates the point for a simple economy having only a consumer sector and a business sector. The aggregate demand schedule, *CE*,

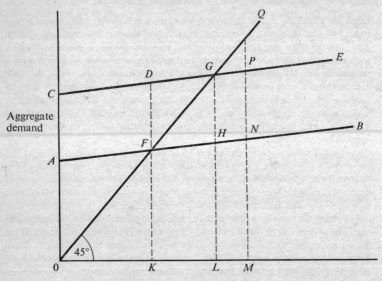

Aggregate output (income)

consists of a consumption schedule, AB, which shows how consumption varies with income, and an investment demand which is constant for all levels of income. At output OK aggregate demand will exceed aggregate output, $KD > FK$ $(= OK)$, and hence aggregate output will rise. Conversely, at output OM aggregate demand will be lower than aggregate output, $MP < MQ$ $(= OM)$, and hence aggregate output will fall. Only at output level OL is it the case that aggregate demand is equal to aggregate supply, $LG = LG (= OL)$.

In a simple economy this is how output and hence employment are determined. There is no guarantee, of course, that OL will correspond to the full-employment output level and if it does not then demand may have to be boosted in order to boost employment. We can complicate matters and introduce realism by introducing more sectors and a more realistic investment function, but the essence of the argument remains unchanged. ⟡ Consumption Function; Investment in the Economy; Multiplier. L.T.S.

F. Brooman, *Macro-Economics* (Allen & Unwin, 4th ed., 1970).

Entropy ⟡ Information Theory.

Environment An organism's environment comprises all those features of the surrounding world which in some way are detectable and which affect the organism's behaviour. The term 'internal environment' is used to describe a number of physiological states but is something of a misnomer (⟡ Homeostasis).

It is usual to distinguish between the physical environment and the social environment. The former includes such aspects as temperature, humidity, air pressure, vibration, gravitational loading, air pollution, noise, radiation and lighting, all of which affect human performance in a variety of ways (⟡ Heat; Illumination; Noise; Vibration). Of complementary importance in their effect on human behaviour are the aspects of the social environment (⟡ Incentives; Personnel Management).

In considering the effects of the environment upon behaviour it is essential to note that the effect of the total environmental pattern is not necessarily predictable from the separate effects of single variables. In many instances interaction effects are such that decrements resulting from simultaneous environmental stresses are a good deal in excess of the sum of the incremental values. It seems likely that many accidents and breakdowns are attributable to these large cumulative effects. E.E.

Equitable Payment ⟡ Time-span of Discretion; Job Analysis.

Equity (or Equities) in accounting ⟡ Claims.

Ergonomics The branch of technology concerned with the problems of the mutual adjustment between man and his work. Drawing upon the sciences of psychology, anatomy and physiology, ergonomics sets out to optimize the design of equipment, the environment and working procedures in respect of both the well-being of personnel and the effectiveness of the working unit.

Historically, ergonomics derives its origins from several relatively independent sources. Industrial medicine contributes some of the aspects of protection of the worker from the hazards of extreme environmental severities, such as the effects of heat or of toxic substances. The concept of protection may be broadened to encompass such items as the long-term effects of exposure to noise or of bad posture during lifting or even during prolonged periods of sitting. The complementary aspects of effectiveness owe much to pioneering studies in the rationalization of work methods (⟡ Taylor) and the introduction of the techniques of experimental psychology (⟡ Gilbreth).

Although the word 'ergonomics' was not coined until 1950, it is during the Second World War, in the face of a host of problems regarding human work, that the birth of ergonomics may best be located. Two features distinguish ergonomics from its antecedent disciplines. Firstly, it is based upon the scientific study of the capabilities and limitations of human performance. Secondly, it embraces all the facets of the study of men at work.

Human performance in industry may be classified under two broad categories, viz. that concerned with information and control and that concerned with physical energy. The relative importance of these two performance categories varies with the level of technological development achieved. The Table illustrates the trend of change in task allocation between man and machine consequent upon technological progress (⟡ Automation).

Level	Control	Energy
Pre-mechanization	Man	Man
Mechanization	Man	Machine
Automation	Man and machine	Machine

At the most primitive level, man provides both control and power. Such would be the situation in a task demanding, for example, the use of hand tools. Typical ergonomics problems here would include the study of the expenditure of energy, the forces necessary to manipulate the tools, the shape of the handles in relation to the anthropometry of the hand and the lay-out of the workplace ⟡ Anthropometry; Muscular Work; Posture.

It is probably at the level of mechanization that the contribution of ergonomics is best known. A schematic representation of the information flow in a man–machine system appears in the figure on p. 139.

The task of the human operator in such a system is to accept information from the displays, to interpret and process such information and convey the appropriate command signals by way of the machine control. This response generates a further signal from the machine and information passes in this way around the loop. The ergonomist is concerned to optimize the performance of the man–machine system by attending to the design characteristics of the ⟡ displays, the controls (⟡ Machine Controls), and of the machine's dynamics (⟡ Machine Dynamics; Tracking). The operator's performance is, in addition, affected by the properties of the physical ⟡ Environment in which he is working (⟡ Glare; Heat; Illumination; Noise; Vibration) and by the prevailing social and motivational conditions. (⟡ Socio-technical System; Organizational Theory.)

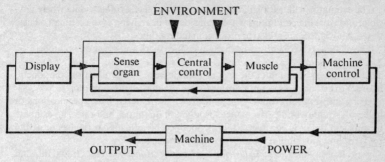

ENVIRONMENT

The human operator within an information loop in a mechanized man–machine system.

At a more sophisticated level of development, a different approach to the human factors problems is required. In recent years, the role of the human operator in complex computer-supported systems has been studied and has generated new problems for the ergonomist concerned in the design of such systems. At an early stage in the design process there arises the need for decisions to be made regarding the allocation of function between man and machine. Clearly such decisions demand the contribution of several experts including the ergonomist. Thereafter, at later stages in the development of the system, the ergonomist will be called upon to advise on matters of interface design, job analysis, operating procedures, training and system performance. Part of the change in emphasis in the ergonomics of automated systems is the shift of attention from hardware to software (⟡ Language). Swift and efficient communication media are essential ingredients of an effective man–machine dialogue.

Ergonomics has now become a fairly well established discipline in the UK. There exist the Ergonomics Research Society, the journals *Ergonomics* and *Applied Ergonomics*, university degree courses and research facilities, and several industrial units devoted to research and applications of ergonomics. E.E.

L. J. Fogel, *Biotechnology: Concepts and Applications* (Prentice-Hall, 1963); K. F. H. Murrell, *Ergonomics: Man in his Working Environment* (Chapman and Hall, 1965).

Errors (Types I and II) ⟡ Hypothesis Testing.

Estimating

1. *Analytical Estimating* (in Work Measurement)

A method used to determine basic times for jobs for which it has not been possible to compile sufficient data to obtain a synthetic timing. ⟡ Work Measurement; Synthetic Timing.

It is the most inaccurate and inconsistent work measurement technique, relying almost entirely on the ability, experience and knowledge of the estimator.

Once the job method has been established and agreed, basic times at standard rating are given to each job element. The same principles are used for breaking the job into elements as in direct Time Study but normally larger elements are used.

139

Executive Development

The estimator will use available, perhaps incomplete, synthetic data where possible, and working conditions will be considered in arriving at the estimated basic times. Allowances are added to produce standard times.

The method is frequently used in maintenance work and other one-off jobs.

2. *Cost Estimating*

This is necessary to predict the cost of manufacture of a product or component, in order to establish a sales price prior to manufacture, tendering, etc.

Using information from component drawings, material lists, specifications of materials, quality and performance, production quantities and rates, an estimate in sufficient detail is constructed, or is obtained by adjusting estimates or actual costs for previous similar jobs. ⟡ Costing Systems. R.W.

H. B. Maynard, ed., *Industrial Engineering Handbook* (McGraw-Hill, 2nd ed., 1963).

Executive Development ⟡ Management Development.

Expected Value ⟡ Measures of Location.

Exporting Problems ⟡ International Marketing.

Exports ⟡ Balance of Payments.

F

Factor Analysis (in Testing) This important and powerful statistical technique provides a method of examining a set of data in order to establish the underlying pattern of organization which brings about certain relations between groups of measurements.

An example is provided in the context of intelligence testing. Scores may be obtained on a battery of tests administered to a group of subjects. Inter-correlation coefficients (⟡ Correlation and Regression) indicate the degree of association between all pairs of tests in the total battery. Further analysis yields factor loadings, i.e. measures of the extent to which the observed degrees of association might be due to the existence of a fairly small number of causative factors.

This statistical technique has proved invaluable in the testing of hypotheses concerning the nature of human ⟡ Personality. E.E.

Factoring The provision of a range of services to an organization, including an optional financial facility. At its most highly developed extent, it will embrace the sub-contracting by a company of its sales ledger department to the factor who will carry out all transactions from raising an invoice to control and collection. Such agreement brings with it a range of financial advice and economies of scale, which would not normally be available to an organization. This pattern of activity was developed in Britain during the early 1960s but has a history in North America from the nineteenth century, where its annual turnover is currently estimated to be £4,000 m. It is an operation particularly suited to the needs of small and medium-sized businesses in manufacturing and wholesaling. G.S.C.W.

Factory Inspector HM Inspectors of Factories: first appointed in 1833 and now working in the Safety, Health and Welfare Department of the Department of Employment. Their principal duty is to see that the provisions of the ⟡ Factory Law and regulations are carried out. To achieve this they have wide powers, including the right of entry to industrial premises, the right to interview alone any-one found on the premises and the right to conduct proceedings in Magistrates Courts in cases of alleged breach of the law. The Factory Inspectorate, under the Chief Inspector of Factories, is organized in about a dozen divisions and 100 districts to which the majority of the staff (the general inspectorate) are attached. There are also specialist branches dealing with medical, electrical and engineering and chemical work. Much of the time of the general inspectorate is spent in inspecting places which come under the provisions of the *Factories Act* (these include docks, warehouses and building and engineering construction sites, as well as factories), and in investigating accidents. Although there is a policing element in their function (the *Factories Act* is part of the Criminal Law) much of the work is advisory, to help employers to adopt the best-known practices for the safety and ⟡ Welfare of employees. The Factory Inspectorate has published a number of pamphlets on ⟡ Accident Prevention, health and welfare. It staffs the Industrial

Health and Safety Centre in London. It works closely with government departments concerned with research, with voluntary bodies such as the Royal Society for the Prevention of Accidents, and deals with problems in its field arising from the work of the ⟡ International Labour Organization. L.S.

> T. K. Djang, *Factory Inspection in Great Britain* (Allen & Unwin, 1942); Sir G. Ince, *The Ministry of Labour and National Service* (Allen & Unwin, 1960).

Factory Law A factory for the purposes of the *Factories Act*, 1961 means any premises in which or within which persons are employed in manual labour in any process for, or incidental to, the following: (a) the making of any article; (b) the altering, repairing, finishing, washing or demolition of any article; (c) the adapting for sale of any article or (d) the slaughtering of certain animals; being premises in which the above work is carried on by way of trade or for purposes of gain and to or over which the employer of the persons employed therein has the right of access or control.

The main purpose of factory legislation is to protect the safety, health and welfare of the persons employed or working in factories and detailed provisions are contained in the 1961 Act which have to be complied with by the occupier of the factory. In the event of any breach of these provisions, the occupier will be liable criminally in a prosecution and may also be liable civilly in damages to an employee who has been injured as a result of the breach. The enforcement of the Act is the responsibility of the factory inspectorate. Factory inspectors may enter and inspect factories, interrogate employees and examine records so as to satisfy themselves that the provisions of the Act have been complied with. They have the right of prosecuting any person whom they suspect of having broken one of these provisions.

The duties imposed by the Act are additional to the ⟡ Employer's Liability at common law. Generally speaking they are more demanding in that the employer has to do what the Act requires irrespective of whether it is reasonable or practicable, unless the Act itself specifically provides otherwise.

Legislation concerning health and safety in employment was spread over some thirty-one statutes, of which the *Factories Act* was by far the most important one. The Robens Report commented in 1972 on the fragmented nature of this legislation and as a result of this Report the *Health and Safety at Work Act*, 1974 was passed. The new Act is primarily an enabling statute which came into force on 1 April 1975. In order to enforce the provisions of the Act and the orders that will be made under it, the Health and Safety Executive was set up which works under the general supervision of a Health and Safety Commission. For the time being existing statutory provisions under the Factories and similar Acts will continue until replaced by regulations to be made under the Act. The existing supervising officials, e.g. factory inspectors, will join the staff of the Executive. W.F.F.

> A. Redgrave, *Factory Acts*, ed. I. Fife and E. H. Machin (Butterworth, 1972).

Fair Wages Clause In accordance with a resolution passed by the House of Commons for the first time in 1891 and reaffirmed since on a number of occasions, most recently in 1946, government departments are expected to include in con-

...otiating bodies and more formal federations is an uncertain one. A ...mber of ⟡ Joint Industrial Councils have multiple union representa-...ederal principle has also been at work on the internal structure of ...ere the basis for arriving at amalgamation has involved a degree of ...tonomy and continued identity to the original unions, or where the ...o large that separate 'trade groups' are established, as in the Transport ...ral Workers' Union.

...ajor federal organization representing British trade unions is the ⟡ ...ut there is a small body of a somewhat similar kind, the General Federa-...Trade Unions, formed in 1899 because of dissatisfaction with TUC policy. ...iginal intention was to create an organization which would draw all unions ...er for joint industrial action and to build up a central strike fund. Its origi-... wanted the General Federation to have authority to direct the industrial ...of its affiliated unions, an authority lacking in the TUC. In the event only ...ber of smaller unions joined the new body, which retains its support from ...which feel lost among the big battalions.

...ere are a number of international federations of trade unions which have come together in each case to exchange information and ideas on common prob-lems within an industry. Some of these are developing policies for dealing with the multi-national company. N.H.C.

Royal Commission on Trade Unions and Employers' Associations, Research Papers 5, Part 1, John Hughes, *Trade Union Structure and Government* (HMSO, 1967).

Feedback A controllable system may be regulated (i.e. its output may be brought to any desired value) by the provision of an adjustment to the input. In Figure 1, an input I_1 produces a corresponding output O_1. This output may differ from the ... ...ired output, O_R, by an amount of error, e, where

$$e = O_R - O_1.$$

A human observer might note this error and adjust the input value in such a way ...t the system output corresponds to the required value.

$$I_1 \blacktriangleright \boxed{\text{Machine}} \blacktriangleright O_1$$

...ystem illustrated in Figure 1 is termed 'open loop' since the input is not ...affected by the output. The addition of the human operator 'closes the ...providing at the input some information about the output. The closed ...ustrated below.

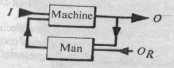

tracts made with private contractors a fair wages clause. Although the resolution does not cover contracts made by local and other public authorities, many of these voluntarily embody such a clause in their contracts as well.

The fair wages clause in government contracts provides that the contractor should pay his workers wages and observe in respect of them working conditions which are not less favourable than those established for the industry by collective agreement or, in the absence of such agreements, are not less favourable than those applied by other employers in the trade or industry whose general circum-stances are similar to those of the contractor. The contractor must observe these terms in respect of all his employees and not only those who are directly engaged on the government contract. He must also recognize the freedom of his work-people to be members of trade unions and accept responsibility for the observance of all the above terms by any subcontractor whom he may be using on the con-tract.

If any question arises as to whether a contractor has observed the requirements of the clause, the question will, if not otherwise disposed of, be referred by the Secretary of State for Employment to an independent tribunal for decision. This tribunal is usually the ⟡ Industrial Arbitration Board (to be replaced shortly by the Central Arbitration Committee). ⟡ Collective Bargaining. W.F.F.

Industrial Relations Handbook (HMSO, 1964).

Fatigue Used to describe an observable decrement in performance resulting from a repetition of behavioural activity, fatigue serves as a useful label to group to-gether a wide variety of well-known phenomena. Its use as a causal explanation of these decrements is, however, questionable. It is unlikely that a single causative factor brings about the numerous observable effects which are probably due to a wide variety of mechanisms including loss of sleep, the accumulation of metabolic waste products, boredom, neural inhibition, and loss of sensory acuity (⟡ Adap-tation).

Concepts of fatigue include reference to subjective feelings of tiredness and to certain physiological states in addition to performance decrements. Experimental studies have usually failed to establish any clear relationship between these three aspects. Subjective feelings of tiredness are difficult to separate from those of boredom; a professional man may well describe himself as 'very tired' at the end of a working day but is then able to indulge in quite strenuous recreational pastimes. None of the numerous physiological indices proposed as an index of fatigue has yet shown itself to be closely related to the individual's work achieve-ment, or to serve as a reliable predictor of work potential.

Various attempts have been made to establish the ideal length of a work period between rest pauses. Only a very limited amount of success has resulted as a good deal depends not only upon the particular tasks but also upon the individual. For certain types of task, where a high standard of attention is required from the worker, half-hour periods interspersed with short rest pauses appear to be suit-able.

There is no doubt that a very significant practical problem exists in attempting to consider the problems of fatigue in relation to working periods and conditions, particularly where safety is involved. Such examples as the working hours of bus drivers and aircraft pilots are obvious. Unfortunately, there is very little scientific evidence available at the moment to assist in the provision of guiding rules. E.E.

Fayol, Henri (1841–1925) One of the pioneers of management thought and ⟨⟩ Classical Organization Theory.

Born in France in 1841, Fayol became a mining engineer and eventually managing director of a metallurgical and coal combine. From his experience as a chief executive, he developed a framework for a unifying doctrine of administration that he believed would hold good for business, for public service, and wherever the art of management had to be exercised. He believed there were basic principles of management which could and should be taught.

In attempting to set up efficient business procedures, Fayol produced a theoretical model which appears mechanistic, but he noted that personal qualities could be of enormous significance and seems to have been aware of an informal structure existing alongside the formal one. ⟨⟩ Formal Organization. He compared the ⟨⟩ Organization to the animal, using the expression *corps social* (or body corporate) to mean all those engaged in any given corporate activity. This mode of thinking in biological terms continues and forms one of the sources of the modern study of ⟨⟩ Cybernetics.

Fayol declared that in conducting an undertaking towards an objective, technical activities needed to be supplemented by managerial activity, and 'to manage is to forecast and plan, to organize, to command, to coordinate and to control'. Here he clearly influenced Lyndall F. Urwick in Britain.

'*Gouverner c'est prevoir*': 'To govern is to foresee.' In giving prominence to foresight as the first characteristic of sound administration, Fayol laid stress on that judgement and intelligent anticipation which is prerequisite to the success of the whole management process. Observing that long-term planning and development studies were often neglected by the busy executive, Fayol proposed a staff of specialized assistants to senior management.

Fayol's central theme in his discussion of organization is the *hiérarchie*. This was translated into English as 'scalar chain', an expression which has taken root in management writings. To indicate that a formal plan could and should be constructed, Fayol emphasized his concept of the organization chart, suggesting that each position on the chart be accompanied by a job description (⟨⟩ Job Analysis) and that lists be prepared showing the 'value' of each employee. Here lay the foundation for his scheme of ⟨⟩ Management Development. Fayol indicated that each superior should normally have a 'span of control' comprising no more than four or five immediate subordinates, a concept which has sometimes been attributed to his compatriot, Graicunas.

Managers, he alleged, should develop initiative by allowing subordinates 'the maximum share of activity consistent with their position and capability, even at the cost of some mistakes . . .' Freedom to use initiative was a source of job satisfaction. General control could be maintained by a periodic 'management audit'. In dealing with subordinates Fayol emphasized the need to be fair and equitable. Union agreements must be clear and as fair as possible. He deprecated national

bargaining and frequent state interventi[on] plant agreements. ⟨⟩ Collective Bargaining.

Preparation was necessary for those posts ized expertise in engineering or accounting was even be a hindrance. Though there was a dearth gerial ability could be developed in the same wa educational institutions, later in the workshop or oth

Fayol's work in France, a country with a long tradit complementary to that of ⟨⟩ Taylor in the USA, a na notion of 'coming up the hard way'. Taylor worked prima level, from the bottom of the hierarchy upwards, while Fayol c senior manager and worked downwards. While Fayol was less Weber, his principles of management are akin to the characteristics organization, or ⟨⟩ Bureaucracy, laid down by the latter, although it is unlikely that Weber's work was known to him. N.H.C.

H. Fayol, trans. C. Storrs, *General and Industrial Management* (Pi[tman] 1949); N. H. Cuthbert, 'Fayol and the Principles of Organization', i[n] Tillett, T. Kempner and G. Wills, eds., *Management Thinkers* (Penguin, 1970).

Federation The banding together of organizations to form a unity for some common object while remaining independent in internal affairs.

Federated groupings are typical of employers and of trade unions in Britain. Employers' federations may be associations of employers in an industry formed to manage ⟨⟩ Collective Bargaining with trade unions; or formed to deal with trade matters on behalf of members; or may be multi-functional. ⟨⟩ Employers' Associations. The major federation formed to represent British employers as a whole is the ⟨⟩ Confederation of British Industry.

Among trade unions, federations are one of a number of devices for achieving inter-union decision-making which also include the Bridlington Rules (⟨⟩ Trade Union – Jurisdiction); agreements on 'closer working'; and amalgamation (⟨⟩ Trade Union – Structure).

The Webbs, in *Industrial Democracy*, envisaged the development of a [network] of trade union federations within each of which it would be difficul[t] where sovereignty lay. In practice the retention of sovereignty by of a federation has been marked, with few exceptions. Such a case of the National Federation of Building Trades Opera unions in the building industry, which has a Central Council sions binding on affiliated unions without the need for further ally there are difficulties in communication with affili larly when joint negotiations run into difficulties. T connection with policy-formulation, finance and union federation is the Confederation of Shipbui which in 1965 consisted of 35 unions.

In their external relations, particularly when th industrial one, trade unions pursue varying degr borderline between regular meetings of union

In many cases, this human function may be automated. The error is measured by a comparator which provides a feedback signal which is combined with the input to the system. In this way, the output of the system will be adjusted automatically so that it remains at O_R in spite of input fluctuations. Figure 3 below illustrates the system with automatic feedback.

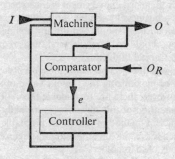

Feedback.   Figure 1   The open loop system.
                   Figure 2   Closing the control loop by means of the Human Operator.
                   Figure 3   The basis of automatic control.

The governor used in James Watt's steam engine provides an early example of the provision of automatic control by means of feedback. If, as a result of a down gradient on the track, the speed of the engine increases, the centrifugal force on the weights in the governor causes these weights to rise. A mechanical linkage then causes the regulator to adopt a lower setting which in turn causes the speed to fall. Thus an automatic feedback loop, comprising the essential stages Detect, Compare, Communicate, Adjust, keeps the locomotive running at constant speed.

Ideally, a feedback loop will satisfy completely the required output conditions. In practice, however, there are two classes of constraint. Firstly, there will be certain limits within which the input may vary and a satisfactory output achieved; beyond these limits, the feedback loop will fail to cope. There will be limits, for example, in the range of gradients upon which the locomotive governor may bring about constant running speeds. Secondly, there may be time lags between the detection of an error and the corresponding adjustment of the input value. If the independent input is itself varying at a fast rate, the system may fail to respond with sufficient speed. The extent to which a system is capable of keeping pace with change in input values is termed its 'frequency response'. Associated both with feedback magnitude and frequency response is the notion of stability. A system is said to be stable when input disturbances are met with effective corrective tendencies, such that the output values from the system still remain within definable limits. ⟡ Automation; Cybernetics. E.E.

Financial Institutions ⟡ Capital Market.

Financial Management The practical tasks of financial management are those of capital raising; determining the mixture of debt and ordinary capital for a business; deciding upon alternative investment opportunities; valuing shares and businesses, as going concerns; considering the financial basis for amalgamations; calculating the basis for reconstructions, take-over bids; recommending the basis of dividend policy, etc.

As a subject of study, financial management is concerned with achieving a given financial objective for a business by solving three interdependent problems: what total volume of assets a business should acquire and maintain; what their composition in kinds of assets should be; how the total funds required for this purpose should be financed (⊘ Capital Budgeting).

The financial management objective which most accords with legal and economic principles is that of maximizing the present value of existing shareholders' financial interests. However, there are formidable theoretical and practical difficulties to the implementation of this objective; principally they are those of the requirements of an efficient method of search for profitable and feasible business projects and of the need for reconciling the differing circumstances and individual values of any given body of shareholders.

The management of a business may therefore adopt other objectives, both financial and non-financial, especially where management is wholly or partially divorced from the ownership of a business. For instance, a more operational objective might be that of maintaining a certain minimum return to shareholders judged to be essential for an adequate flow of capital from the stock market to the particular business. In taking account of shareholder interests for purposes of the setting of financial objectives, dividends and the price of a firm's shares can generally be the only indicator of their economic value to shareholders and of shareholders' reactions which a company management can take note of.

Once the relevance of stock and share price to financial management has been established, then the scope of its subject-matter is accordingly increased to include empirical studies of the capital market and other financial institutions as well as theories of investor behaviour. The answers to questions such as 'how should a maximum return from a portfolio of investments be obtained for a given degree of riskiness (i.e. variability of expected future investment income)?' and 'how do individuals make share investment decisions?' become as important as answers to company policy questions such as 'what, if any, is the optimal capital structure of a firm?' and 'what is the cost of capital to the company?'

The consensus of opinion concerning the kinds of methods necessary for a 'proper' financial management function within an enterprise has broadened in its outlook during the last decade or so. A discussion of these methods may be divided into three main parts, as follows: (1) Antecedents to financial analysis. (2) Components of an analytic approach. (3) Institutional and descriptive aspects.

1. *Antecedents*

Financial analysis has its roots in accounting. Consequently an appreciation of accounting methods at least is a first necessity in order to understand the three flow concepts basic to financial analysis; namely the flow of income, the flow of funds (or economic resources) and cash flow (⟡ Accounting, Accounting System).

Some understanding of both macro- and micro-economic theory is also a pre-requisite to a study of financial management. Keynesian national income analysis has been used extensively by business economists to forecast the level of business activity and thus give a basis for the construction of enterprise budgets, both short- and long-term. Equally important is an understanding of the theory of money and interest rates as well as the general body of the economist's theory of the firm in order to construct budgets for an enterprise. Of central importance also is capital theory as the basis for realistic capital budgeting rules (⟡ Capital Budgeting; Capital, Cost of).

In general it is reasonable to suggest that the relatively greater emphasis on the economic theory relevant to financial analysis has turned the focus of attention to the future and to methods of prediction and away from purely historical accounting approaches to financial analysis and from forecasting techniques based upon mere extrapolation of past data.

This trend has been evidenced by the introduction of a number of analytical models. Whilst it is necessary to have a general understanding of statistics, calculus, matrix algebra, etc., to appreciate their contributions, the 'pay-offs' for the subject of financial management of using such analytical models are becoming clear in terms of the replacement of intuitive thinking by explicit and logical statements.

2. *Components*

A brief consideration of the analytic approach to financial management should consider financial objectives and long-term and short-term financing decisions.

The analytic models of finance tend, like the bulk of those of economic theory, to be prescriptive (what 'ought' to be done) rather than descriptive. Such models remain important as opportunity cost approaches to the evaluation of alternative policies. However, more empirically-based work of an imaginative kind, as illustrated by that of G. P. E. Clarkson and O. E. Williamson,[1] requires to be done in order to make such models more relevant to financial management decision-making in practice.

In relation to the long-term financing decision, the traditional financial attitude has been that shareholders' worth, per share held, can be increased by the use of debt up to some point of optional leverage (⟡ Capital Structure). In contrast, Modigliani and Miller ('The Cost of Capital, Corporation Finance and the Theory of Investment', *American Economic Review*, June 1958) have shown that the expected value of the future returns from a set of assets cannot be changed by juggling with the status and relative rights of the legal claims (i.e. the share capital and loans) relating to those assets. The as yet unresolved controversy as to the realism of their hypothesis centres around whether the workings of financial institutions in Western economies are sufficiently 'perfect' in the economic sense for the purposes of their arguments.

1. G. P. E. Clarkson, *Portfolio Selection: A Simulation of Trust Investment* (Prentice-Hall, 1962); O. E. Williamson, *The Economics of Discretionary Behaviour* (Prentice-Hall, 1964).

In relation to the shorter term the financial manager needs to specify the cash requirements for the firm's operations over, say, one year and for this purpose to be able to understand the accounting budgeting procedures which can identify fairly precisely the needs for liquid resources in the shorter term.

In order to carry out his function properly a financial manager must also have an understanding and working knowledge of the relevant financial institutions and the legal framework of finance. Indeed the descriptive and analytical approaches must be viewed as complementary; neither can do without the other ⟨⟩ Capital Market. E.A.L.

S. H. Archer and C. A. D'Ambrosio, *The Theory of Business Finance: A book of readings* (Macmillan, 1967); B. V. Carsberg and H. C. Edey (eds.) *Modern Financial Management* (Penguin, 1969); E. Solomon, *The Theory of Financial Management* (Columbia University Press, 1963); J. F. Weston and D. H. Woods, *Theory of Business Finance; advanced readings* (Wadsworth, 1967).

Fiscal Policy The fiscal policy of a government is the name given to the taxation and expenditure policies by which it seeks to influence the workings of the economy. Such a policy can obviously affect all the main components of expenditure and income in the country (⟨⟩ National Income Accounts). The objectives of fiscal policy may be many. Initially fiscal policy was largely determined by the government's budget, the aim being to ensure that sufficient income was raised to meet expenditure in the same financial year. However, in the modern economy there are additional objectives such as the desire to preserve a balance between demand and utilization of resources, the desire for a reasonable rate of growth and the desire to improve the balance of payments (⟨⟩ Forecasting for the Economy; Growth: Determinants). Fiscal policy can play a part in the realization of all these objectives.

The main sectors of the economy are the personal sector, business sector, government sector and foreign sector ⟨⟩ National Income Accounts. Dealing firstly with the personal sector, the various fiscal measures available are changes in income tax rates and allowances, changes in value added tax and revenue duties and, lastly, changes in social security contributions and payments. In the UK value added tax can be varied by up to 20% of its existing level between budgets, subject to parliamentary approval. This is known as the regulator power.

The business sector of the economy is affected by investment incentives and also taxation changes and to some extent these spill over to affect the personal sector. With regard to investment incentives, countrywide taxation allowances are available on capital expenditure and in the assisted areas these basic investment incentives are supplemented under the Industry Act by a new system of cash grants. On the taxation side, company taxation has been reorganized and the structure of Corporation Tax altered so that it no longer discriminates against distributed profits. Other government aims, such as the employment of more labour in the Development Areas, have been furthered by the Regional Employment Premium which pays cash grants for each worker employed in manufacturing establishments.

If fiscal policy is the responsibility of the government, what can the government do about its own income and expenditure flows? The key areas on the income side have already been mentioned but on the expenditure side we find that capital investment programmes are often an item to be considered. In the 1950s a cut in the investment programmes of the nationalized boards was a favourite way of controlling the economy but, in recent years, the emphasis has moved towards the control of personal expenditure. Another item of government current expenditure which has been cut in recent years to satisfy other objectives is military and defence spending.

Fiscal policy, along with monetary policy, is important in the government's attempts to control the cyclical fluctuations in the economy. The available evidence so far, for the UK, suggests that of all the fiscal measures that could be used, only tax changes that affect personal consumption have been really effective. ⟡ Forecasting for the Economy: Short-term; Monetary Policy. L.T.S.

Flow Lines ⟡ Assembly Lines.

Flow Process Charts ⟡ Process Charts.

FOB Contracts The free on board contract for the sale of goods differs from a CIF contract in that the agreed price covers, apart from the cost of the goods only, the cost of having them placed on board ship. The remaining costs, including freight and insurance charges, will have to be borne by the buyer. The goods are treated as having been delivered to the buyer as soon as they are placed on board ship and the buyer has been informed. It is then the buyer's responsibility to arrange insurance cover since the goods will be at his risk once they are on board. If the seller has, however, failed to inform the buyer of the goods being shipped, the risk of loss or damage will remain with the seller.

C. M. Schmitthoff, *The Export Trade* (Stevens & Sons, 1975).

Follett, Mary Parker (1868–1933) ⟡ Authority.

Forecasting for the Economy: Short-term Since the Second World War the British Government, in common with many others, has accepted considerable responsibility for the running and performance of the economy. This stems from a desire to avoid the waste of resources and potential output and misery of the 1930s. This responsibility means that the modern government must ascertain the direction in which the economy is moving and take appropriate action if it appears that difficulties might arise. Thus it is necessary for the government to know if demand is likely to outstrip production overall or in certain sectors, for then appropriate action can be taken before price rises begin or wage demands are made. Similarly, corrective action can be taken if it appears that resources will be under-utilized. The purpose of short-term forecasting procedures is to ensure that this knowledge is available so that corrective action may be introduced through fiscal or monetary measures.

Whilst such procedures are still in their infancy certain common features appear for many countries, in particular the widespread use of the National Accounts as a framework for the forecasts. The major categories of demand are forecast and compared with the forecasts of available supplies. The two sets of forecasts are not entirely independent, however, for some items of demand are dependent upon the income generated in producing goods to satisfy aggregate demand and thus either a simultaneous procedure or a trial and error procedure must be introduced in order that the demand and supply forecasts are consistent.

If we take the categories of aggregate demand such as consumers' expenditure and public expenditure (both current and capital), then a crucial distinction is introduced by the method of forecasting. This can be either functional or autonomous. Consumers' expenditure, for example, is functionally derived from a knowledge of its previous relationship with personal disposable income. Public expenditure, on the other hand, is autonomous because it is deduced from the plans and programmes laid down by the government. Considering the five main categories of demand – consumers' expenditure, public expenditure, private fixed investment, investment in stocks and foreign trade, three are regarded as functional from the viewpoint of the forecaster. These three are consumers' expenditure, stock investment and imports.

Taking these five categories in turn, the following appear to be the generally accepted methods of forecasting. Public expenditure depends largely upon the plans and programmes already laid down. Exports are closely dependent upon activity abroad and this must be translated into demand for a particular country's products. Business fixed investment is at present derived from anticipations data. House building data is obtained from data on housing starts and permits or licences plus the average time taken to build. Investment in stocks in principle is determined by the concept of a normal relationship between stocks and total sales. If each of these categories is forecast for the next period (be it a quarter or year) then we would almost have total final demand. However, the last category, consumers' expenditure, is closely related to personal disposable income (⟨⟩ Consumption Function), and this cannot be known until total demand is known. One way of proceeding from this point is to take a plausible figure for consumption, thus obtaining total final demand, from which we can derive a figure of personal disposable income. This, in turn, will yield a consumption figure which can be compared with the original and the process must be repeated if differences are apparent until the forecasts are self-consistent.

Forecasting on the supply side is necessary in order to derive personal disposable income from our forecasts of total final demand. Imports and indirect taxes minus subsidies must be forecast and then deducted from total final demand to give Gross Domestic Product (GDP). From this one must now work out the implications that the future level of GDP has for employment, given the general expectations about labour productivity. When this is combined with a forecast of average earnings, transfers, salaries and dividends and taxation, we have arrived at our required figure of personal disposable income which will yield a figure for consumers' expenditure. If this fails to agree with our initial plausible assumption then the process is repeated until consistency is achieved.

This is a general picture of forecasting procedures and it should be stressed that individual variations abound. The greatest stress on formal models is laid by Holland whilst until recently the UK laid little stress on a formal model. Similarly some countries forecast ahead for a period of three months whilst the basic period for others is one year. ⟨⟩ Fiscal Policy; Monetary Policy; National Income Accounts. L.T.S.

Techniques of Economic Forecasting (OECD, 1965); M. J. C. Surrey, *The Analysis and Forecasting of the British Economy* (Cambridge, 1971); C. Robinson, *Business Forecasting* (Nelson, 1971).

Forecasting: Medium-term The environment of modern business is characterized by uncertainty. This being so it is hardly surprising that businessmen have sought to forecast future demand for their product(s) as an aid to better decision-making now. Such forecasts are necessary for the correct planning of capital expenditure, otherwise demand may have to remain unsatisfied because capacity is unavailable or capacity may be under-utilized because demand has been overestimated. Although uncertainty characterizes our world, the forecaster believes that there are regular patterns of behaviour and knowledge of them will be helpful in looking into the future. Even at its lowest a forecast based upon previous patterns of behaviour can be instructive and aid the learning process whilst one based upon 'judgement' is almost immune from constructive criticism. A useful framework for forecasting for the individual firm was suggested in an article in the *Journal of Industrial Economics*, November 1965, by C. Robinson. This envisages a three-stage procedure for the forecasting of future demand for a firm's product(s). Firstly, one should forecast future movements of the economy; secondly, future movements of the industry and product group; and thirdly, future market shares and demand for the individual product(s).

A considerable amount of work has been undertaken by government statisticians and economists and also by private organizations such as the National Institute of Economic and Social Research into forecasting the future of the economy. Whilst it is true that forecasting is both an art and a science, nevertheless such forecasts are based upon quantitative relationships and are, therefore, open to modification as they are compared with actual events.

The second stage of forecasting future demand for the industry or product group depends upon the existence of stable relationships between, for example, industry demand and personal disposable income. Such relationships can be estimated (⟨⟩ Econometrics) from past data and then projected into the future, given a forecast of personal disposable income from the first stage of the procedure. Two industries which have been exhaustively studied along these lines are the car industry and the steel industry.

The final stage is to forecast the market share of the individual firm and this is probably the most difficult stage of the procedure as one enters the realm of interdependent decision making. It is a crucial stage, however, for on it depend future capital and labour requirements.

Although forecasting has been treated here exclusively in terms of demand for a product, interest is growing in the application of forecasting techniques in other areas of business. The whole area is known as corporate or long-range planning and it encompasses not only demand forecasting but also manpower planning and forecasting and the forecasting of changes in technology. The linking factor in

153

these diverse fields is the growing utilization of models, mathematically expressed and statistically estimated. ◊> Decision Theory; Plans; Corporate Planning; Demand Functions; Econometrics. L.T.S.

A. J. Merrett and G. Bannock, *Business Economics and Statistics* (Hutchinson, 1962); H. D. Wolfe, *Business Forecasting Methods* (Holt, Rinehart & Winston, 1966).

Forecasting Techniques: Short-term Short-term forecasting, that is for periods up to six months, is needed throughout industry and commerce, especially within the context of sales forecasting and production planning/stock control. This entry discusses some statistical techniques, but it should be remembered that forecasts produced by these techniques should always be complemented by management judgement.

If we consider the monthly demand for a product, there are usually three components about the general level or mean:

(a) A trend which may be up, down, or zero dependent on whether the demand is expanding, contracting or stationary.

(b) A seasonal variation which reflects varying demand throughout the year (e.g. ice-cream or heating fuel).

(c) A residual random variation.

Techniques consist of analysing past data to identify (a) and (b) to provide as accurate a forecast as possible. The most common ones used are:

(1) Moving Average. This is one of the simplest and takes the average of the last 'n' months as the forecast for the next month. For example, with $n = 5$ and the following past demands:

January	February	March	April	May
11	9	10	8	12

Then the forecast for June is:

$$\frac{11 + 9 + 10 + 8 + 12}{5} = 10$$

(2) Weighted Moving Average. If the above individual demands had occurred in a different sequence (say 8, 9, 10, 11, 12) the same moving average forecast of '10' would have been obtained and an opposite trend would have been ignored. This follows because the demand five months ago carries equal weight with the demand last month. To overcome this weighting factors can be attached to monthly figures to give increased weight to the most recent demands:

Month	Weighting (%)	Demand	Weighted Demand
January	10	11	1·1
February	15	9	1·4
March	20	10	2·0
April	25	8	2·0
May	30	12	3·6
June Forecast	100		10·1 or 10 to the nearest whole number

(3) Exponentially Weighted Moving Average. The above technique is cumbersome and it is better to attach a constant weighting factor (less than one) to each successive month working backwards. Thus in the above example the forecast would be:

$$0.2 [12 + 8 (0.8) + 10 (0.8)^2 + 9 (0.8)^3 + 11 (0.8)^4 + \ldots]^1$$

This technique too looks cumbersome, but it may be shown algebraically that if '$1 - a$' is the weighting factor (so in the above case $a = 0.2$):

$$\begin{array}{c}\text{FORECAST} \\ \text{(for this month)}\end{array} = \begin{array}{c}\text{FORECAST} \\ \text{(for last month)}\end{array} + a \left[\begin{array}{c}(\text{ACTUAL} - \text{FORECAST}) \\ \text{(for last month)}\end{array}\right]$$

(4) Seasonality. If demand for a product is seasonal it is relatively easy to calculate a seasonality factor which can be incorporated into the forecast. M.J.C.M.

P. G. Moore, *Statistics and the Manager*, pp. 110–24 (Macdonald, 1966).

Formal Organization 'The patterns of human interrelations, as defined by the systems, rules, policies and regulations of the company' (F. J. Roethlisberger and W. J. Dickson, *Management and the Worker*, Harvard U.P., 1939). The formal organization is deliberately and rationally designed to achieve the objectives of the enterprise both directly and indirectly. It is manifest in organization charts, rule books, manuals, rules of procedure, negotiating machinery, etc., and is implicit in a general understanding of officially expected behaviour.

The classical theorists focused exclusively on the formal aspects of organization but after the publication of the report on the ⟨⟩ Hawthorne Investigations attention was directed to the tendency for employees to form small social groups with their own status systems, behavioural patterns, beliefs and objectives, different from, and often opposed to, the requirements and expectations of the formal organization. These social groups and their associated behaviour have been called the informal organization, presumably in order to emphasize the contrast with formal organization.

Much research work has centred on the informal group and on the relationship between it and the industrial supervisor. The findings suggest that membership of such groups provides satisfactions that the formal organization cannot or does not supply. For example, the impersonality of the formal system may be counterbalanced by the opportunities for personal friendships and personality expression which the informal group provides; necessary information may be communicated more effectively via informal contacts; and the security of the group provides its members with psychological support and enables the members to protect or to further their collective interests. The ability of the group to take action is dependent, *inter alia*, on its solidarity and to this end the group will tend to exert some measure of control over its members' attitudes and behaviour. The term informal organization, however, is no longer applied exclusively to social groups but refers to all relationships in the organization which are not officially prescribed or expected. Such relations may further the personal interests of the people con-

1. The factor of 0.2, or '$1 - 0.8$', outside the bracket is required to ensure that a true weighted average is obtained.

cerned or, perhaps more frequently, may be highly relevant to the achievement of organizational objectives, for such informal practices often develop to counter bureaucratic tendencies and other deficiencies in the formal. The modern organizational theorist is not concerned exclusively with either formal or informal elements of organization but recognizes that neither can usefully be considered in isolation. His concern is, therefore, with both formal and informal aspects of organizational structure and behaviour and with the interaction between the two. ⟡ Bureaucracy; Classical Organization Theory; Hawthorne Investigations; Human Relations; Organizational Theory; Social System. I.C.MCG.

J. A. Litterer, *The Analysis of Organizations* (J. Wiley, 1965).

Frequency Distribution ⟡ Statistics.

Frequency Distributions Elsewhere (⟡ Statistics) it is indicated that the concept of frequency distribution curves is fundamental to statistics. The shape of such curves, that is, the pattern of variability they display, can vary widely, but some distributions occur very often. Three commonly occurring distributions are:

(1) Normal Distribution. Many present-day goods are manufactured by mass production methods on machines which repetitively produce almost identical items. However, owing to uncontrollable variations in the quality of the processed materials and the settings of the processing machines, no two units are exactly identical. Thus, if we operate a manufacturing process which produces one-inch diameter ball bearings, we cannot expect every bearing to have a diameter of exactly one inch. Rather, we can expect to produce quantities of the bearings of mean (⟡ Measures of Location) diameter one inch, but although some individual bearings will have one inch diameters, others will have diameters slightly below or above this value. If we plot a histogram (with sufficiently small-class intervals) of the diameters of the bearings, we shall generate a distribution curve of diameters with mean values of one inch and the variation about this mean. Such a curve would be a Normal Distribution.

A Normal Distribution curve is produced when we plot measures which are subject to variation, for a variety of causes, about some mean value. Another example is the distribution curves for the heights of Cup Final attendance discussed in the entry on 'Statistics', since men's heights are determined by numerous factors in their heredity and environment.

(2) Binomial Distribution. Suppose that instead of manufacturing ball bearings we are making transistors. Our manufacturing process is a very inefficient one and each transistor has a 30% chance of being defective and therefore a 'reject'. Suppose that the transistors are made in batches of 10, so that on average 3 in each batch are rejects. However, just as the diameters of ball bearings discussed above varied about an average diameter of one inch, similarly the number of rejects in successive batches of transistors will vary about an average of 3. This follows because, since each transistor has a 30% chance of being defective then, purely by chance, some batches will contain 0, 1, 2 up to 10 rejects. Using the laws of probability, we can calculate the probabilities of obtaining 0, 1, 2, etc., up to 10 rejects in a batch. These probabilities are shown as follows:

Number of rejects in a batch	0	1	2	3	4	5	6	7	8	9	10
Probability %		2·82	12·11	23·35	26·68	20·01	10·29	3·68	0·90	0·14	0·01	0·00

These probabilities could be plotted as a histogram with unit class intervals, which would represent the pattern of variation of the number of rejects per batch.

Suppose that, instead of making transistors in batches of 10, we make them in batches of 10,000. Then the average number of rejects per batch would be 3000 and, again using the laws of probability, we could calculate the probabilities of a batch containing 0, 1, 2, etc., up to 10,000 rejects. These probabilities could be plotted as a distribution curve which again would represent the pattern of variation of the number of rejects per batch. Because the underlying probability theory is based on a mathematical theorem known as the binomial theorem, such a curve is known as a Binomial Distribution.

(3) Poisson Distribution. In the above example, the event of interest, the manufacture of a defective transistor, occurred quite frequently (30% of the time). Managers are often concerned with the pattern of variations of events that occur quite rarely – for example, the pattern of variation of the occurrence of industrial accidents in a company. Such patterns often form a distribution known as a Poisson Distribution.

For example, in the nineteenth century, Bortkewitch performed an analysis of the pattern of variation of deaths from horse kicks of cavalry men in the Prussian army. He analysed the records of 10 cavalry corps over 20 years, thus obtaining 200 corps-years of observations. From these records he was able to construct a table showing the number of corps-years in which 0, 1, 2, etc. deaths occurred. The total number of deaths was 122, so the average number of deaths were 122/200 or 0·61 per corps-year. However, as the Table below shows, this average is spread over sets of years in which 0, 1, 2, etc. deaths occur because of all the chance influences that are present. Since there were a large number of men in a cavalry corps and on average only 0·61 men were killed per year, the probability of a fatality per man at risk was small. Therefore, Bortkewitch predicted the pattern number of years in which 0, 1, 2, 3 and 4 deaths should occur using a Poisson Distribution. These predicted values are compared with the observed values in the table below:

Number of deaths/year/corps	0	1	2	3	4
Actual number of corps-years	109	65	22	3	1
Predicted number of corps-years	109	66·3	20·2	4·1	0·6

It can be seen that the agreement between prediction based on the Poisson Distribution and the observed values is very good.

Data that is subjected to variability following a Poisson Distribution occurs quite often in organizations. M.J.C.M.

M. J. Moroney, *Facts from Figures*, pp. 82–119 (Penguin Books, 1951).

Fringe Benefits The supplements to wages and salaries which are part of total labour costs but do not constitute a direct reward geared to the output, effort and merit of an employee.

Functional

Strictly speaking a labour cost is a fringe benefit only when it is an avoidable factor, i.e. when it could be replaced by money wages without detriment to productive efficiency. But in practice the borderline between avoidable and unavoidable labour costs cannot be drawn with any precision and consequently the size and scope of fringe benefits may vary quite substantially from one firm to another and from one industry to another. A survey of 350 companies in 1960 showed that there were wide variations in fringe benefits paid to manual workers. Two-thirds of the companies spent between $7\frac{1}{2}\%$ and 15% of the payroll on fringe benefits and one-fifth spent between 15% and 25%. Fringe benefits for salaried employees tended to be higher than those for wage-earners.

Normally, however, fringe benefits include most of the following items: (1) Pay for time not worked, such as sickness, accidents and holidays. (2) Awards for special status, such as long service. (3) Social Security payments by employers, such as those under statutory and voluntary social insurance arrangements like unemployment, sickness and pensions. (4) The cost of services provided for the benefit of employees, often by means of subsidies or loans, such as canteen and sports facilities, employee discounts and mortgages. (5) Other payments not directly related to work done such as profit sharing, severance pay over and above payments necessary under the Redundancy Payments Act (◊ Redundancy) and payments made for attendance on training courses.

Fringe benefits, therefore, exert an equalizing tendency in so far as they are conferred on the diligent and the indolent alike. Critics regard the piecemeal extension of these benefits as inimical to increased effort and higher productivity in so far as they appear to be moulding the factory environment into a comfortable welfare state in miniature. But in the absence of any conclusive evidence one way or the other it can be argued with equal plausibility that fringe benefits contribute directly to the creation of a working environment conducive to good human relations and indirectly therefore to higher productivity.

In recent years the rigours of ◊ Prices and Incomes Policy have compelled some trade unionists to look upon fringe benefits as at least a partial alternative to conventional wage increases. This awakened interest on the part of the unions has met with a favourable response from those employers who regard the concession of more fringe benefits as the least expensive way of obtaining increased productivity from their work force. For this reason fringe benefits have played a prominent part in the negotiation of a number of productivity bargains (◊ Productivity Bargaining) in recent years, most notably in the Electricity Supply Industry and their future role in ◊ Collective Bargaining seems assured. It would certainly appear that many British firms have a good deal of ground to make up on their West European competitors in the size and scope of the fringe benefits they provide. N.H.C.

G. L. Reid and D. J. Robertson, eds., *Fringe Benefits, Labour Costs and Social Security* (Allen & Unwin, 1968).

Functional (1) Specialized in terms of a general purpose. Thus functional organization is that which is based on administrative units each representing a specialist activity: for example, a multi-product company may have as its basic divisions

Production, Marketing, Accounting, Purchasing and Personnel with further subdivision following the lines of these basic divisions. Functional organization has certain advantages: it enables the maximum attainment of the advantages accruing from specialization; it facilitates centralized direction and control; special equipment can be economically utilized; professional expertise is more readily built up. On the other hand, an overenthusiastic adherence to functional principles has its attendant disadvantages: decentralization of decision-making is more difficult to achieve: there is a tendency for subunits to develop too narrow a specialist viewpoint and to perceive their own activities as ends in themselves with consequent problems of communication and coordination; and particularly at the lowest levels in the organization, too much specialization may result in monotonous, repetitive work with reduced job satisfaction and motivation.

Organization along functional lines raises problems of authority relationships and concomitant responsibility. F. W. Taylor (*Shop Management*, 1911) was the first writer to draw attention to the need for specialists to exercise authority within the area of their specialist expertise for by this means the organization would be enabled to make best use of specialist knowledge and skills and to achieve a consistent application of company policy. Such authority is called functional authority and occurs wherever a manager is empowered to prescribe processes, methods, policies or actions for personnel who are not his own subordinates. Functional authority violates the principle of unity of command and makes it difficult to equate authority with responsibility. ⇨ Authority; Department; Responsibility; Specialization; Line and Staff; Unity of Command. I.C.MCG.

W. Brown, *Exploration in Management* (Penguin Books, 1965).

Functional (2) The extent to which a social phenomenon facilitates the achievement of a given objective. The phenomenon is *dysfunctional* to the extent that it militates against the achievement of the objective. The terms, commonly encountered in sociological writings, should not be used unless the objective in respect of which the phenomenon is functional or dysfunctional is clearly stated or understood. It is frequently the case that a phenomenon may be functional in regard to one objective, whilst, at the same time, it is dysfunctional in regard to another. I.C.MCG.

Funds Flow Analysis The term 'funds' has several meanings. In its widest accounting meaning it refers to purchasing power and the flow of funds refers to the flow of purchasing power into and out of a business or other organization. The chief sources of such funds flows are:

Funds Flows into the Firm
Gross revenues from product; Sales of fixed assets; Sales of investments; Issues of debentures, loans and shares.

Funds Flows out of the Firm
Outlay costs, i.e. costs incurred in earning revenues from product requiring payments to creditors (depreciation and cost is therefore excluded); Purchases of fixed assets and investments for credit or cash; Repayment of capital or long-term debt; Payment, or the recognition as owing, of dividends and taxes on profits.

Further Education

The most widely used method of showing funds flow movements is to consider the effect of changes in working capital. All transactions which result in an increase in working capital are shown as sources of funds, e.g. gross revenues are sources since they result in increase in debtors or cash. All transactions that result in a decrease in working capital are applications (or dispositions), e.g. incurring the outlay cost of production, such as purchases of materials for cash or credit. Thus the objective of this form of analysis is to show the net change in working capital for a particular period.[1] Although funds flows are sometimes defined merely as cash flows, this is not a reasonable definition.

The accounting status of the funds flow statement has gradually increased and it is now widely recognized as being as important a document as the balance sheet or profit and loss account. E.A.L.

Hector R. Anton, *Accounting for the Flow of Funds* (Boston; Houghton Mifflin, 1962); R. A. Rayman, *Journal of Accounting Research* (Spring, 1969).

Further Education That part of the national system of education which is concerned with the full-time and part-time education of those who have left secondary school, but have not moved into higher education at universities and colleges of education for the training of teachers and schools of art. The major responsibility for further education rests with county councils and county boroughs as the local education authorities. Most of it takes place in technical and commercial colleges and is primarily vocational in the sense of preparing students for recognized technical and professional or quasi-professional qualifications. A considerable amount of further education also takes place in evening institutes in which evening classes are given, usually of a non-technical kind in a large range of subjects, some of which are academic or artistic, others dealing with crafts and hobbies. Many of these students are adults whose more academic demands are also catered for by University Extra-Mural Departments and bodies like the Workers' Educational Association. These bodies also provide works-based courses in industrial and social subjects for apprentices, shop stewards and managers. An increasing number of employers send young people under 18 to County Colleges which provide non-vocational education on a day-release basis. At the technical colleges, in addition to the training related to particular trades and industries, increasing provision is being made for first-year, full-time courses for engineering and other craftsmen and technicians as required by the Training Boards under the *Industrial Training Act*, 1964. At the other end of the spectrum students at many technical colleges are taking full-time, sandwich and part-time courses leading to degrees, as well as courses in management studies. In 1964–5, 10% of public expenditure on education was on further education; this proportion is increasing. ⟫ Industrial Training Act; Industrial Training; Industrial Training Board. L.S.

A. J. Peters, *British Further Education* (Pergamon Press, 1967).

1. However, since current asset valuations are affected by profit calculations this definition of funds is a less objective one than other possible definitions.

G

Games, Operational and Business ◇ Competitive Problems; Simulation; Decision Theory.

Gantt Charts The Gantt chart, developed by Henry L. Gantt around 1900, is a graphical method of depicting work schedules or work loads. Each job or activity is represented as a block or bar drawn on a time-scale, e.g.

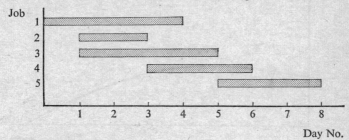

Such charts are used extensively in production planning and control and also appear as multiple activity charts in method study. ◈ Production Planning and Control; Multiple Activity Charts. R.W.

Gantt, H. L. ◇ Gantt Charts.

Gap Analysis Gap Analysis is the mathematical calculation made to investigate the difference between two curves.

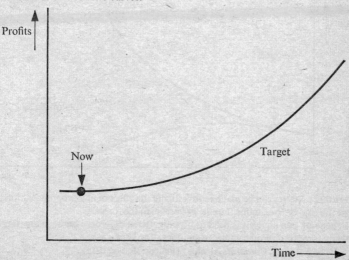

Gap Analysis

A typical example is the difference between a profit target curve and a profit forecast curve: a company may have decided that a suitable target to aim for is a 10% growth in profits each year starting at the current year's profit of £100,000. The target will appear as illustrated.

The company may also calculate that, if it continues to trade in the existing manner, its profits will probably turn out as below:

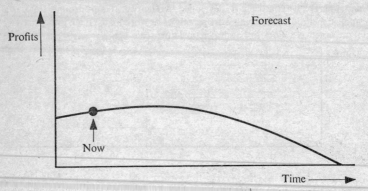

By superimposing one graph on the other it is possible to observe the widening gap between what the company wishes to achieve (its target) and what it will probably achieve if no special action is taken (its forecast): the size of the gap indicates how much extra profit this special action will have to yield if the company is to achieve its target rate of growth.

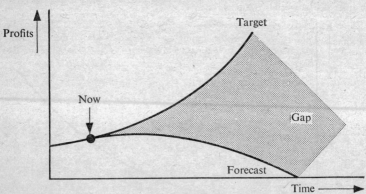

Further analyses can be made to investigate the effect of any proposed action to close the gap, or to examine the effect of errors in the forecast.

In general, gap analysis is used to investigate the difference between any target and any forecast ⟐ Forecasting Techniques; Target. A.J.A.A.

H. Igor Ansoff, *Corporate Strategy* (Pelican Books, 1973).

Gearing ◇ Capital Structure.

General Union ◇ Trade Union Types – General Union.

Gilbreth, Frank B. and Lillian M. The combination of engineer and psychologist in this famous pioneering team seemed ideal for tackling the numerous problems associated with the description, measurement and improvement of manual work.

Frank B. Gilbreth's earliest studies were carried out in the building industry where he was able, by means of careful observation and ingenious invention, to bring about enormous improvements in the work output of bricklayers. The Gilbreths' approach, involving the development of numerous techniques of Motion Study, was later brought to bear upon problems in a wide variety of industrial settings. In 1912 the Gilbreths described the technique of micro-motion study, using movie film and an accurate clock. Other ◇ Photographic techniques included the Cyclegraph in which movement patterns are recorded on a photographic plate and the Chronocyclegraph which incorporates a time marking system. Other innovations included the SIMO (Simultaneous Motion) Chart for recording activity and the famous analytic notation of 'Therbligs'. ◇ Motion Study. E.E.

Glare Three deleterious effects result from glare: reduction in visual performance, discomfort and increase in visual fatigue. Glare may be induced directly from a light source, or by reflection.

Several methods of glare reduction are available: (1) Removal of light source from direct line of sight. (2) Reduction of brightness of source, e.g. by using large numbers of low-intensity sources rather than fewer, brighter ones. (3) Use of screens and visors. (4) Avoidance of surfaces having high reflectances, e.g. high-gloss paint, polished metal.

The extent of existing glare may be assessed using the glare index. This may be calculated from data describing the luminances of a light source and of the background, the angle subtended at the eye by the source, and the position of the source in relation to the viewer (◇ Brightness; Illumination; Vision). E.E.

Goodwill (in accounting) That part of the value of a business attributable to its reputations and connections. In accounting theory it may be considered to be that part of a firm's capital value arising through an ability to earn more than a normal rate of return on its assets. A firm may have exceptional earnings because of monopolistic market position, quality of management, ability to innovate, etc.

Conceptually goodwill can be measured by reference to an assessment of the present value of expected future earnings (◇ Present Value). Goodwill is then the difference between that figure of present value and the aggregate total of the individual economic values of the tangible assets less liabilities. However, the measurement difficulties are quite formidable since they include the forecasting of expected total earnings and the basis for a 'normal' rate of return on businesses of a similar kind. For these kinds of reasons it is accountancy convention to record goodwill in books of account only when it has been paid for as, for example, on the purchase of a business. It is then normally recorded as the difference between the market or realizable values of tangible assets less liabilities and the total purchase price. It is considered not necessary, although 'prudent', to write goodwill off, but essential not to write it up. ⟡ Capital (Cost of). E.A.L.

H. C. Edey, 'The Super Profit Method', *Accountancy*, Jan.–Feb. 1957; J. C. Bonbright, *Valuation of Property* (McGraw-Hill, 1937; reprinted by the Michie Company, Charlottesville, Virginia, 1965).

Goodwill (in Law) Goodwill has been defined as 'the benefit arising from connection or reputation' of an existing business. While it clearly has a monetary value it is not at all easy to quantify this. Lawyers have distinguished between 'cat goodwill' and 'dog goodwill'. The former is goodwill attached to premises which occupy a convenient and valuable site for particular business purposes, while the latter is goodwill which is based on the special knowledge or skill of the people running a business. The difference is important when it comes to disposing of the goodwill. Cat goodwill can only be sold with the premises, while dog goodwill is either not saleable at all or, if saleable, implies that some know-how or other information is being sold with the tangible assets of a business.

A new partner admitted to a ⟡ Partnership will be required to make a payment to the existing partners for a share in the goodwill. When a partnership is dissolved and the assets of the firm are sold, goodwill is generally disposed of as one of the assets and the purchaser of it will have a sole right to it. If, however, no provision is made for the sale of the goodwill, any of the former partners could use the goodwill of the firm's business (e.g., to the extent of using the former firm's name) provided always that in doing so he does not imply that his former co-partners are associated with him in his new enterprise. W.F.F.

C. D. Drake, *Law of Partnership* (Stevens, 1972).

Grievance Procedure The arrangements for settling disputes arising on the shop floor between trade-union members and management.

In most other industrial countries these arrangements tend to be formal, written agreements, often enforceable at law. Under the continental and American systems of ⟡ Collective Bargaining most substantive agreements, i.e. those dealing with terms and conditions of employment, tend to carry their own negotiating procedures for the settlement of disputes. In Britain, however, there has traditionally been a clear distinction between substantive and procedural agreements with, in both cases, much less emphasis on formality and enforceability. Almost all industries have some kind of dispute procedure, including arbitration (⟡ Arbitration, Industrial), though there are considerable differences with regard to complexity, speed and general effectiveness. Historically most industry-wide procedures have developed piecemeal, often as a result of ⟡ Strike action, and may therefore still reflect an anachronistic balance of bargaining power as between management and trade unions.

Under the provisions for avoiding disputes in the engineering industry any worker concerned was first required to raise any question in person with his foreman. If he was not satisfied he went with the ⟡ Shop Steward to the departmental manager. Subsequent stages might take the form of a works committee (if one exists), or a works conference with official representatives of the appropriate ⟡ Trade Union and ⟡ Employers' Association and then a local conference at which a panel of *employers* not directly involved in the question at issue met to hear the two sides of the case from the union and the firm concerned. If no agreement was reached the final stage was a Central Conference at which a panel of National Representatives of the Engineering Employers' Federation formed 'Courts' which heard the case of the firm and of the workers. Only when this procedure was exhausted and no agreement reached did strike action become constitutional.

Not surprisingly the engineering procedure and several other industry-wide arrangements were attacked on the grounds that they were cumbersome, outdated, biased in favour of delay rather than settlement, and totally at variance with the current trend towards decentralized collective bargaining. By and large both managements and trade unions prefer to settle a dispute within the confines of the establishment in which it originated and for this reason, and in the absence of any effective reform of industry-wide procedures, more and more companies are paying attention to their own domestic conciliation (⟡ Industrial Conciliation) machinery. The Royal Commission urged that Boards of Directors should, with the help of the CIR and the DE, take a long look at their own procedural arrangements with a view to clarifying and formalizing them, thereby making a resort to national procedures less necessary (⟡ Industrial Relations – Reform in Great Britain). One school of thought sees procedural reform as the *sine qua non* of a better system of industrial relations, believing that most grievances can be redressed to the satisfaction of both parties if only they use the right methods. But a grievance procedure, no matter how enlightened and efficient it may appear on paper, is only effective if both parties operate it in good faith. It is perhaps rather naïve to expect 'model' procedures to smooth over all or even most of the real conflicts of interest which do arise from time to time in many industrial situations ⟡ Industrial Relations Code of Practice. N.H.C.

Royal Commission on Trade Unions and Employers' Associations, Research Paper No. 2, A. I. Marsh; A. I. Marsh, *Industrial Relations in Engineering*, Ch. 4 and 5 (Pergamon, 1965).

Gross Domestic Product (GDP) ⟡ National Income Accounts.

Gross National Product (GNP) ⟡ National Income Accounts.

Group A number of persons viewed as a collectivity.

The literature commonly distinguishes primary groups from secondary groups. Primary groups are groups sufficiently small to enable the members to interact on an informal face-to-face basis as, for example, in the family or small friendship clique. Secondary groups are those too large to be classed as primary and which, therefore, require a formal structure as, for example, a trade union or a factory community. In practice it is often impossible to draw precise boundaries round groups or to designate them firmly as primary or secondary. In another usage of the term, 'group' is applied to any aggregate of persons who share a given characteristic such as the same income (income group), the same age (age group), the same occupation (occupational group), etc.

The type of group most relevant to an understanding of organizational behavi-

Group Discussion/Interview

our is probably the interest group, composed of those persons who consider themselves to have socio-economic interests in common. These interests are usually believed to be different from, and in varying degrees to be in conflict with, the interests of other groups. There are many possible bases for interest groups but in the industrial organization the most important are probably common occupation, similarity of function and face-to-face or primary group membership. Recognition that they possess interests in common will frequently lead the members of the group to develop practices designed to defend or to promote their interests or to establish formal organizations for that purpose. ⟡ Conflict; Formal Organization; Hawthorne Investigations; Socio-Technical System. I.C.MCG.

The literature on group phenomena is enormous but for an excellent, if slightly dated, summary of research findings see: D. Cartwright and A. Zander, *Group Dynamics* (Tavistock Publications, 1968). Also: A. Fox, *Industrial Sociology and Industrial Relations*, Royal Commission on Trade Unions and Employers' Associations, Research Paper No. 3 (HMSO, 1966).

Group Discussion/Interview ⟡ Motivation Research.

Group Incentives ⟡ Wage; Wage Systems; Motivation.

Group Methods of Training An educational innovation in which the members of a group learn about group structures and processes by studying their own interactions as they experience them.

The activities in which the group engages vary considerably according to the training goal set but in all cases the emphasis is on learning through personal experience.

Probably the best known of such learning situations is the T Group which made its appearance in the United States just after the Second World War. The T Group consists of about a dozen individuals who meet in the presence of a tutor for a number of sessions each of about an hour and a half or two hours' duration. The group is relatively unstructured and learning occurs as the members try to mould themselves into a competent and emotionally satisfying working unit. During this process members develop an increased awareness of their own motives and emotional needs and of the reactive feelings their behaviour produces in others. In the T Group and in later developments of laboratory training, personal experience precedes the theoretical conceptualization which is provided by the tutor as and when he perceives that the group is ready for it.

More recent developments of laboratory training have made use of more or less structured group activities carefully designed to achieve specific learning objectives or to give practice in particular skills. These activities vary from the comparatively highly structured and standardized ERGOM exercises and Blake's Managerial Grid to role-playing sessions and syndicate discussions. Particularly in this country, the T Group is still the subject of controversy but the more structured group exercises are being used increasingly and the further development of group methods of training seems certain. I.C.MCG.

E. H. Schein and W. G. Bennis, *Personal and Organisational Change through Group Methods* (J. Wiley, 1965); L. P. Bradford, *et al.*, *T. Group Theory and*

Laboratory Method (J. Wiley, 1964); G. Whitaker (Ed.), *T. Group Training*, A.T.M. Occasional Papers, No. 2 (Blackwell, 1965).

Group Selection Methods ⟡ Selection.

Group Technology A production method, involving the manufacture of parts in 'families' or groups of related parts, rather than in small numbers, hence achieving the improved resource utilization inherent in quantity production.

The basis of a group technology production system is in defining and describing groups or families of parts. Similarity of shape (design classification) and/or similarity of manufacturing requirement (production classification) may exist. Although the two classifications are usually related, only a detailed investigation within a company will indicate whether this relationship exists and whether sufficient suitable parts exist to merit this type of production.

Several proprietary systems exist (e.g. the Opitz and Brisch systems), their main difference being the method of classification and coding. Two techniques – 'Production Flow Analysis' and 'Component Flow Analysis' – take account of the sequence of operations required in the manufacture of items, whilst the formation of production 'cells' is a common consequence of the adoption of Group Technology in batch production (⟡ Cell Production). R.W.

> G. A. B. Edwards, *Readings in Group Technology* (Machinery Publishing Company, 1971); J. Gombinski, 'Group Technology – An Introduction', *The Production Engineer*, Vol. 46, No. 9. 1967, pp. 557–64.

Group Working Recently, prompted largely by the behavioural problems commonly thought to be associated with repetitive assembly-line work, efforts have been made to redesign production systems in order to facilitate the provision of more satisfying jobs. One approach concentrates upon the design of the individual's job, (⟡ Job Restructuring) whilst an alternative approach, which often leads to job restructuring, concentrates on the organization of workers in the production group. This approach aims to increase the degree of autonomy and responsibility exercised by the worker through the delegation of certain responsibilities to the work group. Thus group working involves the creation of formal functional work groups able to exercise some degree of self-organization and possessing delegated autonomy and responsibility beyond the area of the immediate task. Group working is often mistakenly seen as an alternative to assembly or flow line working, i.e. as an alternative production system. However, this type of semi-autonomous and responsible functional work group can be created within the constraints imposed by the production system and thus this form of work organization is appropriate in mass, jobbing and batch production (⟡ Cell Production). R.W.

> R. Wild, *Mass Production Systems*, Vol. 1 (Administrative Staff College, Henley-on-Thames).

Growth in the Economy: Determinants What are the factors that determine the rate of growth in a country's productive potential? This question is invited by tables which show Britain's poor rate of growth compared to many of her competitors. Two sets of arguments have been advanced, one from the supply side and

Example: Coding and Classification by the Opitz System

FORM CODE

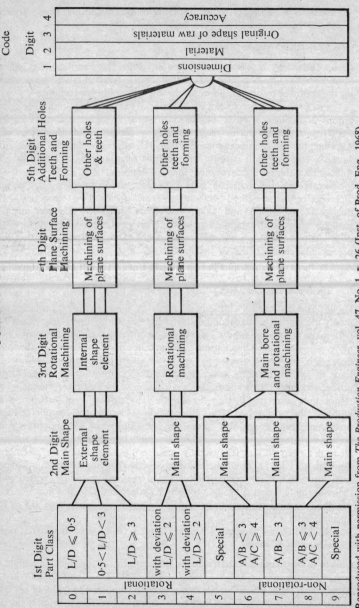

	1st Digit Part Class		2nd Digit Main Shape	3rd Digit Rotational Machining	4th Digit Plane Surface Machining	5th Digit Additional Holes Teeth and Forming
0	$L/D \leqslant 0.5$	Rotational	External shape element	Internal shape element	Machining of plane surfaces	Other holes & teeth
1	$0.5 < L/D < 3$					
2	$L/D \geqslant 3$					
3	with deviation $L/D \leqslant 2$		Main shape	Rotational machining	Machining of plane surfaces	Other holes teeth and forming
4	with deviation $L/D > 2$					
5	Special	Non-rotational	Main shape	Main bore and rotational machining	Machining of plane surfaces	Other holes teeth and forming
6	$A/B < 3$ $A/C \geqslant 4$		Main shape			
7	$A/B > 3$					
8	$A/B \leqslant 3$ $A/C < 4$		Main shape			
9	Special					

Supplementary Code

Digit	1	2	3	4
	Dimensions	Material	Original shape of raw materials	Accuracy

Reproduced with permission from *The Production Engineer*, vol. 47, No. 1, p. 26 (Inst. of Prod. Eng., 1968).

one from the demand side. From the supply side some or all of the following factors have been blamed: poor management, restrictive trade unions, rigid educational structure, social attitude to competition, laziness, insufficient investment, too much government interference and crippling taxes. On the demand side it has been suggested that stop-go policies have created such an unsettled climate that businessmen have been reluctant to plan too far ahead and have been reluctant to invest, thus reducing the growth of productive potential.

It is interesting in this context to consider the main findings of an authoritative study of the sources of economic growth in the United States.[1] During the period 1929–57 the following factors accounted for the growth in real National Income that took place: changes in the quality and quantity of labour 54%, increases in capital input 15%, and advances of productivity 31% (of which 20% related to advances in knowledge). Whilst one must stress the pioneering and tentative aspects of this work, it is quite surprising to note the importance given to labour in all its aspects.

The following table shows the international comparison of growth rates and investment rates, since this is the factor that has dominated discussions in recent years.

Output, Employment, Output per head and Investment rates 1955–64

Country	Output (a)	Output per head	Employment	Investment ratio (c)
Japan	10·4	8·8	1·4	21·5 (d)
West Germany	6·3	5·0	1·3	18·4
Italy (b)	5·7	5·6	0·1	15·6
Sweden	5·4	3·9	1·5	17·4
France	5·2	4·9	0·3	14·3
Denmark	5·0	3·8	1·2	15·4
Belgium	3·6	3·0	0·6	13·7
UK	3·1	2·6	0·5	12·2
USA	3·1	2·0	0·1	12·7

Source: DEA progress report No. 21, Oct. 1966.

(a) The definition of output used is gross national product (GNP) at constant market prices.

(b) 1960–64 Source: OECD

(c) Gross fixed capital formation excluding dwellings as percentage of GNP (☼ National Income Accounts).

(d) NEDO estimate 1955–63.

The figures in the table do suggest some positive association between growth in output and output per head and the percentage of GNP devoted to investment. This is strengthened by a breakdown of recent British experience which shows that the increase in the proportion of investment (including dwellings) from about

1. E. F. Denison, *The Sources of Economic Growth in the United States* (Committee for Economic Development, 1962).

14% in the 5 years up to 1952 to 19% in 1964 has helped to raise the growth of output per head from about $1\frac{1}{2}$% a year to nearly $2\frac{3}{4}$% between 1960 and 1964.[1] Quantity by itself, however, is not enough and it is equally important that the investment is of the right quality and that it is undertaken in the right industries. For the UK in the future particular stress will have to be laid on labour-saving machinery in view of the slight increases to be expected in the labour force.

In recent years a considerable number of measures have been taken to increase our growth of productivity such as the introduction of new investment incentives, the selective employment tax, introduction of new business schools, and the attempt to plan ahead and so break out of the stop–go cycle. In the long run these factors should both create the right climate for and aid the growth of productivity. To this, in order to raise the growth rate of productive potential, we must couple increases in the quality and quantity of the labour force. In the coming years the rate of growth in the labour force will be 50% less than in the period 1955–64. To counteract this an active attempt is being made to use 'hidden' reserves of labour in the Development areas and to increase job mobility through redundancy and retraining schemes ⧁ Growth: Measurement. L.T.S.

A. Maddison, *Economic Growth in the West* (Allen & Unwin, 1965).

Growth: Measurement One of the most familiar sights in recent years to men of affairs has been the international league tables of rates of growth. Generally they show the poor progress of the UK compared with her major competitors. A growing economy as opposed to a static economy is clearly desirable if living standards are to be improved and commitments abroad maintained. But what exactly is growth and how do we measure it?

Growth is most conveniently measured by the gross domestic product (GDP) at factor cost ⧁ National Income Accounts. This gives us the total value of the goods and services produced as a result of economic activity in the UK before providing for depreciation or capital consumption. However, a glance at the year-to-year changes in the GDP between 1955 and 1964 shows that the highest change was $+5\cdot8$% between 1959 and 1960 and the lowest was $-0\cdot2$% between 1957 and 1958. Changes such as these occur very largely because of the year-to-year changes in the pressure of demand upon resources. This factor can clearly affect our calculations, for the resources of the country may well have increased but the increase failed to be utilized because of a shortfall in demand. What we therefore measure, or want to measure, is the growth in the nation's capacity to produce or the growth of its productive potential. This is best measured by comparing years in which the pressures on resources of labour and capital are broadly similar, for then the change in GDP will be a real reflection of the change in capacity to produce. The rate of growth in productive potential is then calculated as the compound growth rate which will make the two GDPs equal.

Further refinements are possible and they derive from a consideration of the factors that make for growth in productive potential. One factor is the growth in the labour force and the other is the growth in productivity, sometimes referred to as the underlying trend in productivity or GDP per man. The latter can be re-

1. Sir Robert Shone, *Investment and Economic Growth*, Stamp Memorial Lecture.

fined still further by taking account of changes in hours worked, thus leaving us with GDP per man-hour.

Once having obtained the growth rate of a country it is a short step to comparing it with other countries and then trying to account for the differences. One has to be even more careful about ensuring that the demand pressures are roughly similar in the relevant years. However, such comparisons have been made.

The two tables below illustrate the calculation of the growth in productive potential for the UK and also present an international comparison. The years 1953, 1960 and 1964 were all years of similar demand pressure as revealed by the unemployment percentage. In the international table the comparison is biased in favour of Germany, Italy and the Netherlands because their unemployment rates were lower in 1960 than in 1950.

UK Growth 1953–64[1]

	Per cent per annum	
	1953–60	1960–64
Gross domestic product	2·7	3·4
Employment	0·9	0·9
GDP per employee	1·8	2·5
Actual hours worked by manual workers	nil	−0·2
GDP per man-hour	1·8	2·7

1. *The UK Economy: A Manual of Applied Economics*, 1st Edition, ed. A. R. Prest, p. 37 (Weidenfeld & Nicolson, 1966).

International Growth Rates 1950–60[2]

	GDP	GDP per man	GDP per man-hour
Belgium	2·9	2·5	2·5
Canada	3·9	2·0	2·5
Denmark	3·3	2·3	2·9
France	4·4	3·8	3·9
Germany	7·6	5·3	6·0
Italy	5·9	4·1	4·1
Netherlands	4·9	3·7	3·7
Norway	3·5	3·2	3·9
Sweden	3·3	2·7	3·5
Switzerland	5·1	3·8	4·2
United Kingdom	2·6	1·9	2·0
United States	3·2	2·1	2·4

2. *Economic Growth in the West*, A. Maddison (Allen & Unwin, 1965).

▷ National Income Accounts; Growth: Determinants. L.T.S.

Growth of the Firm The reasons for the growth of a firm can be divided into two categories: impersonal and personal.

It has been customary to play down the role of business leadership, or entrepreneurial ability, in contributing to the growth of firms. This accords with the approach to history that deals with political and economic forces rather than the great statesmen and monarchs. However, students of the past growth of firms detect at least some qualities or skills that must be present for growth to take place, although their presence does not guarantee it. Sheer physical strength appears necessary and this must be coupled with an ability to work hard and concentrate entirely upon the business if needs be. Since uncertainty is part of the framework of life there must be present a willingness, almost a desire, to take risks. To this must be coupled a determination which can amount to ruthlessness, if necessary. Finally one notes that in the past technical or commercial training have not always been present in the successful businessmen. However, the growth of knowledge in the field of management plus the general raising of educational standards means that this will be much less so in the future and we would expect to see the successful businessman having a training in science, engineering, accountancy or perhaps one of the newer areas such as marketing or corporate planning.

The impersonal forces that create the conditions for growth can range from the possibility of government financial aid to the threat of competition in established markets. The existence of unexploited technical economies of scale will obviously favour growth as will the possibility of marketing or managerial economies. Finally one should not neglect the internal pressures from research and product improvement departments.

To classify the growth patterns that emerge from a combination of these two sets of forces, economists have talked about three types of integration. They are horizontal, vertical and lateral integration. ✧ Patterns of Growth. One should note, however, that although integration tends to imply takeover or amalgamation, expansion may also come purely from within the firm itself.

The parameters used to determine growth of a company are varied. Turnover is often used as are value of assets, number of employees, profits or share of the market. More recently a further criterion has been used, namely net present value to shareholders and this may well be the most all-embracing criterion of growth for a company. ✧ Present Value; Financial Management; Patterns of Growth.
L.T.S.

> C. I. Savage and J. R. Small, *Introduction to Managerial Economics* (Hutchinson, 1967).

Guarantees A guarantee is a collateral promise by a person to be answerable for the debt or wrongful act of another party. A collateral promise means that there must exist a primary liability by another person and that the guarantor has merely indicated his undertaking to be liable if the main debtor should be unable or unwilling to discharge his obligation. Where a person promises to be responsible for the debt of another party and it is not made clear that this promise is merely a collateral one, in the sense of depending on the existence and validity of the main debt, this would constitute an indemnity and not a guarantee. The difference between them is important, since a guarantee is not legally enforceable against the guarantor unless there exists written evidence of it, while an indemnity could be proved by any form of evidence.

The creditor to whom the guarantee has been given is legally bound to inform the guarantor of any change in the circumstances affecting the transaction or the person of the debtor so as to enable the guarantor to reconsider his position if there has been a serious change in circumstances. If the guarantor is obliged to honour his guarantee, he is entitled as against the creditor to be handed all securities supplied by the debtor and generally speaking the guarantor steps into the creditor's shoes taking over from him all legal rights which the creditor enjoyed against the debtor whose debt the guarantor has now discharged. w.f.f.

G. Borrie, *Commercial Law* (Butterworth, 1975).

H

Hardware/Liveware/Software These are slang terms used to describe the three parts of a computer installation:

(1) Hardware describes the electronic and mechanical equipment (central processer and peripheral equipment) that constitutes the physical installation.

(2) Liveware describes the specialist staff (programmers, systems analysts, data preparation clerks, etc.) who are responsible for operating the installation.

(3) Software describes the library and general support services that are available for use on the computer. Library describes the collection of standard programs that are available for use on a computer. Since it is expensive to develop programs, the range of programs, or library, that a manufacturer can offer with a computer can be an important selling point.

It is important to note that the costs of developing adequate software and providing sufficient liveware often exceed the capital cost of the hardware. ⇨ Computers. M.J.C.M.

Hawthorne Investigations A programme of research conducted at the Hawthorne plant (Chicago) of the Western Electric Co. into various aspects of individual and group behaviour. The main research took place during the period 1927–32 and must be the best known and most widely quoted investigation in the history of social research.

In November 1924, the Western Electric Co. commenced a series of short experiments to determine the relationship between different intensities of illumination and productive efficiency. The experiments were inconclusive and prompted the consideration that relevant variables of a psychological nature had been inadequately controlled. Accordingly advice was sought from academics, notably Professor Elton Mayo of the Industrial Research Department, Harvard Graduate School of Business Administration, and in April 1927 six female workers were isolated in a room where output could be measured whilst various conditions relating to rest pauses and hours of work could be varied, and the effects noted by an observer. This stage of the investigation, the Relay Assembly Test Room, lasted for approximately five years. The experimenters were surprised to discover that, although output increased fairly steadily throughout the first two years of the Test Room, the variables with which they were primarily concerned apparently had little effect on production. Instead, what seemed of particular importance was the change in social climate created by the experimental conditions, including the development of personal friendships amongst the girls and their freedom from supervisory pressures. This change in the social environment was associated with a marked change in the girls' attitudes towards their work.

Subsequent stages in the investigations overlapped with, and arose out of, the first. The apparent importance of employee attitudes to work and to supervision suggested the advisability of discovering more about the attitudes of employees generally. In September 1928, therefore, a programme of formal interviews was started, first in the Inspection Branch and later extended to other branches, so that by the end of 1930 well over 20,000 employees had been given the opportunity to talk confidentially with a member of the interviewing team. The data from the interviews revealed, *inter alia*, that there might be a connection between worker attitudes and productivity and that worker attitudes were considerably influenced by the other members of the work group to which the worker belonged: in other words, that attitudes were less personal than social phenomena.

The final stage in the research was the systematic observation of such a work group. It consisted of 14 men engaged in wiring, soldering and inspecting a 'bank' of telephone terminals. The Bank Wiring Observation Room was set up in November 1931 and continued until May 1932 when it was abandoned because of the economic depression. The investigators discovered that the operators adhered to a more or less fixed standard of output regardless of the existence of individual and group incentive payments and that they maintained output at that level consistently, this being achieved partly by exaggerating in the records the amount of work actually done and by claiming 'allowances' for work stoppages which, in fact, had not occurred. These breaches of company regulations were condoned by the men's immediate superior. The investigators noted the difficulty of the supervisor's position as he tried to satisfy the demands of his superiors without losing the essential goodwill of his workforce. This stage of the investigation with its emphasis on workgroup and supervisory behaviour, was particularly important for its theoretical implications.

The value of the Hawthorne studies is inestimable. Industrial psychology was transformed as an academic discipline. Prior to the investigations the individual was viewed and treated as an isolated unit; after the investigations this view was no longer tenable. For the next 30 years research workers utilized the theoretical concepts generated by the investigations and directed their research along lines suggested by the Hawthorne findings. As a seminal work it is virtually without equal. Unfortunately the work contained too much that was new for it to be readily assimilated, even by its authors, and a grossly oversimplified interpretation of its contents helped to give rise to the Human Relations School. ⟡ Human Relations; Organizational Theory. I.C.MCG.

F. J. Roethlisberger and W. J. Dickson, *Management and the Worker* (Harvard U.P., 1939); H. A. Landsberger, *Hawthorne Revisited* (Cornell University, 1958).

Hearing Sound is produced by vibration and transmitted, usually through the air, by means of pressure waves. A 'pure' tone is produced by a sinusoidal pressure wave, the amplitude of which determines the loudness of the sound, and the frequency of which determines the pitch. Differences in timbre or quality of sounds are brought about by differences in complexity of waves, which can be regarded as consisting of a number of individual sinusoidal components.

The speed of sound in air is approximately 750 mph; in liquids and solids it is considerably increased.

In the human ear the tympanic membrane vibrates in response to pressure waves. The vibration is transmitted via the three bony ossicles of the middle ear into the cochlea, the spiral tube of the inner ear, wherein the mechanical vibrations are converted into hydraulic form and ultimately transduced into nerve impulses.

The frequency range of human auditory sensitivity is around 20–20 kHz, there being considerable differences between individuals. Subjective loudness of sounds depends upon frequency as well as amplitude, the maximum sensitivity occurring between 4 and 5 kHz. In this frequency range perception of sound occurs at a sound pressure of about 0·0002 dynes/sq. cm. Sound intensity levels are usually measured in decibels above this basal value ($\diamondsuit$ Threshold). The overall intensity level of normal speech, for example, is about 66 dbs. ($\diamondsuit$ Speech).

Hearing is generally dichotic, that is, each ear gets a slightly different signal. Localization in the horizontal plane is brought about by the interpretation of differences in phase and intensity of signals arriving at each ear. It is necessary, however, for the listener to move his head in order to identify the elevation of the source.

Loss of hearing ability occurs as part of the normal ageing process and takes the form of a steady decline from age 20 onwards. High frequency sounds are subject to greater loss with age than low frequency ones ($\diamondsuit$ Ageing). E.E.

J. O. Stevens *Handbook of Experimental Psychology* (J. Wiley, 1951).

Heat Various automatic physiological mechanisms, notably rate of blood flow and sweat rate, contribute to the maintenance of body temperature at a constant value near to 37° C. Only small (about 4° C) increases can be survived, although cooling to temperatures below 20° C are sometimes possible. In order to achieve thermal equilibrium, the following equation involving Metabolism (M), Evaporation (E), Conduction and Convention (C) and Radiation (R) must be satisfied:

$$M - E \pm C \pm R = 0$$

Sensations of thermal comfort are affected by air temperature, humidity, rate of air movement and amount of radiant heat. Numerous attempts have been made to derive a single index to combine these atmospheric variables. The corrected effective temperature is probably the most useful of these indices and is derived from radiant temperature, wet-bulb temperature and rate of air flow. It is defined as the numerical value of the temperature of still saturated air which would induce an identical sensation. Comfort zones have been established empirically.

Decrements in both physical and mental work output result from high temperatures. Most work tasks become almost impossible to perform at corrected effective temperatures in excess of about 34° C. Temperature differences of only about 5° C at constant relative humidity separate 'impossible' from 'relatively easy' performance. A similar difference in judgements results from changes in relative humidity of about 15 % at constant temperature.

Several studies have demonstrated decrements in physical work performance at low temperatures. There is no evidence of corresponding mental work deterioration. E.E.

Heuristic Programming Elsewhere (↻ Simulation) it has been explained that OR scientists sometimes use simulation to tackle problems on which a rigorous mathematical analysis is not feasible. Simulation is a particularly useful approach to representing the behaviour in time of complex systems incorporating a large degree of uncertainty. Other problems may be complex because there are a large number of factors and constraints involved, which may be combined in an astronomical number of ways to produce feasible solutions. These problems are often not amenable to rigorous analysis or particularly suited to simulation and Heuristic programming provides an alternative non-rigorous approach which has proved to be most useful. Such problems are typically managerial and a large measure of a manager's ability lies in his skill in distinguishing the relatively few good approaches to the problem from the many feasible alternatives available. He may do this by developing 'rules of thumb' in which he tries to account either consciously or subconsciously (that is, by 'hunch') for all the factors or constraints involved. Owing to the limitations on the human brain's ability consciously to store and manipulate information and/or the manager's lack of time, he may not be able to evaluate all promising alternatives, so 'solutions' better than the actual ones he obtains may escape his attention. Typically, the man responsible for production scheduling in a large jobbing shop faces this situation.

A computer, on the other hand, can store and manipulate large amounts of information quickly and, if it can be programmed to use similar 'rules of thumb' to the manager, it is likely to produce better solutions. The term 'Heuristic' means a procedure or 'rule of thumb' used to solve a particular problem and so Heuristic Programs have been written for computers which solve the problem by this method.

Heuristic programming is proving very useful and has been used with success on problems of assembly-line balancing and job-shop scheduling, plant layout, warehouse location, stock control, resource allocation to large projects, and portfolio selection. M.J.C.M.

Jerome C. Wiest, 'Heuristic Programs for Decision Making', *Harvard Business Review* Sept./Oct. 1966, p. 129.

Hire Purchase Law A contract whereby a person hires goods from their owner on the basis that on completing the agreed hire payments the hirer will become entitled, if he so wishes, to buy the goods for a final, generally somewhat nominal, payment. This type of contract differs therefore from one for the ↻ Sale of Goods in that the hirer has not *agreed* to buy but has merely an *option* to buy.

Since the people obtaining goods on hire-purchase terms generally belong to the poorer sections of the community, legislation has been passed to protect their interests, the latest measure being the *Hire Purchase Act*, 1965, but the legislation applies to those hire-purchase transactions only where the hire-purchase price does not exceed £2,000. The main provisions aimed at protecting hirers are:

(1) The owner cannot enforce the agreement against the hirer unless it is in writing and has been signed by the hirer. The agreement, a copy of which must be given to the hirer, must contain a statement of the hirer's legal rights.

(2) Where the hirer has signed the agreement in a place other than the owner's

place of business (e.g. at his own doorstep) he may withdraw from the agreement within four days, thus giving the hirer a chance of having second thoughts.

(3) The hirer may terminate the agreement at any time by written notice and would then become liable to pay to the owner the difference between one half of the hire-purchase price and the payments already made or due.

(4) The owner has no right to enter the hirer's premises for the purpose of recovering possession of the goods. Once the hirer has paid one third of the hire-purchase price the owner can recover possession by court order only. Any attempt at self-help on his part will mean that all monies paid will have to be returned to the hirer.

The existing legislation on hire purchase and allied contracts will, over the next few years, be replaced by the *Consumer Credit Act*, 1974 which has broadly enacted the recommendations of the Crowther Committee on Consumer Credit. The Act will be brought into effect gradually by means of orders to be made in stages, though it is hoped that the whole Act will be effective by the first half of 1976. The Act covers of course more than hire purchase contracts; it deals with the whole spectrum of credit transactions affecting consumers. Supervision over the implementation of the Act and the licensing of various credit-giving agencies is placed in the hands of the Director-General of Fair Trading. W.F.F.

A. L. Diamond, *Introduction to Hire-Purchase Law* (Butterworth, 1971).

Histogram ⟡ Statistics.

Homeostasis The significance of a number of physiological control mechanisms in maintaining constancy of the internal bodily variables was first recognized by W. B. Cannon who coined 'homeostasis' to designate these states of equilibrium. In respect of many bodily variables, it is necessary to control values within quite narrow tolerances in order to avoid severe damage or death. Examples of variables which are maintained by automatic physiological control systems include body temperature, blood sugar level, and blood pH. The concept of homeostasis may be enlarged beyond such autonomic activities and may include gross somatic activity including, for example, the hungry animal's search for food.

Numerous symptoms of disease involve the breakdown of the usual homeostatic mechanisms, so that the individual is unable to make the usual effective adjustments to cope with environmental stresses. The ageing process is characterized by a slow decline in the efficiency of homeostatic mechanisms (⟡ Ageing; Environment). E.E.

Horizontal Integration ⟡ Patterns of Growth.

House Union ⟡ Company Union.

Human Engineering ⟡ Ergonomics; Psychology.

Human Relations An approach to organization theory which places heavy emphasis on the importance of morale and informal social relationships as determinants of organizational effectiveness.

The human relations approach drew much of its inspiration from the ⟡ Hawthorne Investigations and subsequent research work and had an immediate appeal for those welfare workers and others who deplored the dehumanization of the workplace implicit in the scientific management approach or who were disturbed by the phenomena of industrial conflict. That both approaches had something valid to offer was immediately apparent to the classical theorists who found little difficulty in synthesizing them. The proponents of each, however, regarded the others with hostility, each claiming that the other ignored the most important variables. Whilst much in the human relations approach remains valid, several of its basic assumptions have been challenged. In particular, its critics claim that there was a tendency to make generalizations about social relationships *in vacuo*, without regard to their cultural, economic and technological environments; that the beneficial effects of sympathetic, supportive supervision were not universal but depended on a complex of factors; that harmony in relationships and job satisfaction were too readily equated with productive efficiency; and that explanations for the various phenomena of conflict were too facile. The criticisms were well founded, and the number of empirical studies of organizational behaviour has increased the body of knowledge available, so that the human relations school, preoccupied with too narrow a range of variables, has been superseded by the social systems approach. ⟨⟩ Hawthorne Investigations; Morale; Organization Theory. I.C.MCG.

A. Etzioni, *Modern Organisations*, Ch. 4 (Prentice-Hall, 1964).

Hypothesis Testing Many investigations are performed by statisticians to determine whether a certain belief is true or false. A frequently used procedure is to set-up the Nul Hypothesis that the belief is false and then perform experiments to see if the observed results agree with the proposed hypothesis. Details of the types of experiment or tests that may be performed are described elsewhere (⟨⟩ Statistical Tests).

For example, a statistician may possess a penny which he suspects is biased towards heads and he may wish to determine whether this belief is true. He sets up the Nul Hypothesis that the coin is unbiased. That is, that there is an equal chance (or 50% probability) of obtaining a 'head' or 'tail' each time it is tossed. He then performs the 'experiment' of tossing the coin 10 times and recording the number of 'heads' occurring. Using the laws of probability, he calculates the chances of obtaining 0, 1, 2, etc., to 10 'heads' in the experiment. If the coin is unbiased, these chances are given below:

No. of 'heads'	0	1	2	3	4	5	6	7	8	9	10
Probability %	0·10	0·98	4·39	11·72	20·51	23·73	20·51	11·72	4·39	0·98	0·10

The observed number of 'heads' can be compared with these figures to test the Nul Hypothesis.

Suppose 7 'heads' are observed. The chance of 7 or more heads with an unbiased coin is 17·2%. This is reasonably high, so he cannot say that the evidence suggests that the coin is biased. Therefore he says that the results are 'not significant' and he does not reject the Nul Hypothesis.

Suppose 8 'heads' are observed. The chance of 8 or more with an unbiased coin is 5·5%. This result is less likely to occur by chance and he says that the results are 'probably significant', and unless he wants very convincing evidence before doing so, he will reject the Nul Hypothesis.

Similarly, the chance of 9 'heads' or 10 'heads' alone occurring with unbiased coins are 1·1% and 0·1% or 1 in 100 or 1 in 1000 respectively. Clearly these results are very unlikely to occur by chance and they are said to be significant and highly significant respectively. If either of these results occur he will reject the Nul Hypothesis.

The level of truth that the statistician requires for accepting or rejecting a hypothesis is sometimes known as the significance or confidence level. If the statistician requires to be reasonably convinced, he will set the significance level at 5%, then, if the observed results have less chance than 1 in 20 of occurring (that is less than 5% probability) if the hypothesis were true, he will reject the hypothesis. If he requires more convincing evidence he will set the significance level at 1%. Then, if the observed results had less than 1 in 100 chance of occurring (that is less than 1% probability) if the hypothesis were true he will reject the hypothesis. If he requires very convincing evidence before rejecting the hypothesis, he will set the level at 0·1% and require that the observed result should have less than 1 in 1000 chance of occurring if the hypothesis were true.

When accepting or rejecting a hypothesis, the statistician usually states the significance level at which he has done so. Thus, in the coin tossing example, if he were working at the 5% significance level, suppose that 9 'heads' were observed then he would state that the Nul Hypothesis that the coin is unbiased is rejected at the 5% level. Conversely, if he were working at the 1% significance level, he would state the Nul Hypothesis that the coin is unbiased and cannot be rejected at the 1% level.

In performing tests of significance statisticians are comparing two sets of data (say the means in a 't' test) to see if they are different.

Because of the nature of variability, there is a small probability that although the test indicates a significant difference, the two sets of data do come from populations with the same mean. This is known as a Type I Error.

Conversely, the test may indicate no significant difference, when there is a difference in the population means. This is known as a Type II Error. M.J.C.M.

M. J. Moroney, *Facts from Figures*, pp. 216–37 (Penguin Books, 1951).

I

Ideology A system of beliefs which provides for the members of a group a moral justification for their individual and collective behaviour and which offers satisfying, although often grossly oversimplified, explanations of various social phenomena. All social groups develop ideologies, although it is seldom that any ideology is capable of precise definition or that all members of the group subscribe equally to all elements of it. An ideology will reflect the ⟨⟩ Values of the group members and serves to unite the group. The adherents of a given ideology have an emotional commitment to it and will tend to select supportive facts and to ignore or deny contradictory facts. The racist, for example, whose ideology stresses the inherent superiority of one racial group over another, will be strongly inclined to repudiate genetic evidence to the contrary. Where an ideology is patently demonstrated to be inadequate, its adherents may have recourse to the identification of scapegoats whose malevolent activities may then be claimed to have prevented the manifestation of phenomena consistent with the ideology: the ideology can thus be vindicated. For example, a manager whose ideology embraces the concept of the essential unity of interests of management and men, may attribute recurrent industrial disputes to the activities of agitators. I.C.MCG.

R. Bendix, *Work and Authority in Industry* (J. Wiley, 1956).

Illumination Good lighting serves to promote safety, working efficiency and comfort. The appropriate levels of illumination for a large number of occupational tasks have been determined empirically on the basis of studies of visual performance and user preference. Some typical recommended levels of illumination are indicated below (⟨⟩ Brightness).

Location	Lumens/sq. ft.
Halls, lifts, stairways	10
Offices and laboratories	30
Hand tailoring workshop	100
Inspection bench for minute objects	300

In addition to levels applying to task areas, recommendations are available for surrounding areas and general backgrounds. In general, it is desirable that areas surrounding objects being viewed should not vary substantially in luminance from that of the viewed object. The difference in luminance levels is measured by the brightness ratio.

Lighting installations should take account of the avoidance of glare, the control of flicker effects and the proper rendering of colour (⟨⟩ Colour; Glare).

If daylight is to be used, careful attention should be paid to the fenestration of buildings to achieve satisfactory levels of illumination and to avoid poor distribution of light. If large windows are used, excessive penetration of sunlight may

Imports

be troublesome. It is important to ensure that the glazing is regularly cleaned, and the windows kept clear of large obstructions.

Artificial light fittings vary in terms of their characteristics and their initial and maintenance costs. Tungsten filament lamps have a life expectancy of about 1,000 hours and an average light output of about 15 lumens/watt. Fluorescent tubes involve increased capital cost but lower maintenance charges, due to an increase by a factor of ×5 in life expectancy and about ×2 in output efficiency. Regular cleaning of light fittings is of the utmost importance.

When mixed artificial and daylighting is to be employed, it is usually found necessary for the artificially lit sections of an area to have about 100 lumens/sq. ft. to avoid comparative gloominess on bright days. It is important too that the bluer coloured light fittings are used to produce satisfactory colour blending. E.E.

> Illuminating Engineering Society. *The I.E.S. Code: Recommendations for Good Interior Lighting* (I.E.S., 1961).

Imports ⇨ Balance of Payments.

Incentives ⇨ Motivation; entries on Wage.

Income ⇨ Profit (in accounting).

Incomes Policy ⇨ Prices and Incomes Policy.

Index Number of Industrial Production This is another key indicator of the overall state of the economy, showing the level of industrial production each month compared with 1963 = 100.

The object of the index number is to reflect changes in the volume of industrial production in the UK and it is calculated as a weighted average of quantity relatives, according to the Laspeyres form.

For purposes of calculation the algebraic form of the index number is as below.

$$I_{MAR.\ 1973/1963} = \frac{\Sigma p_{63}\, q_{63} \left(\frac{q_{MAR.\ 1973}}{q_{63}} \right)}{\Sigma p_{63}\, q_{63}} \times 100$$

where $q_{MAR.\ 1973}$, q_{1963} are quantities in March 1973 and 1963 (monthly average),
p_{1963} is the 'price' in 1963,
Σ indicates summation over all industries concerned.

The term in brackets is the quantity relative whilst the term $q_{63}\, p_{63}$ is referred to as the weight.

Two problems present themselves in the compilation of any index number, one being the problem of the weights, the other being the problem of the indicators.

The data most frequently used to indicate changes in the volume of industrial production are output data. For some industries, however, input data must be used and even, as a last resort, data relating to employment or man-hours worked. In the case of industries whose products take a long time to complete, direct measures of work done are compiled.

The weights, which combine together the quantity relatives, are proportional to

182

the value of work done in each industry as shown by the Census of Production for 1963, adjusted to take account of incomplete information in the census records.

Since the purpose of the index is to compare the level of production in different months, corrections must be made for the fact that the number of working days varies from month to month. In effect, therefore, the published index compares the average weekly rate of production in different months. In addition, seasonally adjusted figures are produced which take account of regular holiday periods in different industries and other normal seasonal influences.

The present index number, which is published monthly in *Trade and Industry*, replaces one based upon 1958. In general, revisions seem to take place as the results of full Censuses of Production become known, for these enable a revision of the weights to take place.

Full details are given for all industries and for mining and quarrying, manufacturing, construction, gas, water and electricity. The manufacturing section is broken down into major industry groups. Both seasonally adjusted and unadjusted figures are provided.

The provisional level of the index for March 1973 (seasonally adjusted) was 137·0 compared to 1963 = 100 (⟡ Index Numbers).

The Index of Industrial Production and other Output Measures, Studies in Official Statistics, No. 17 (H M S O, 1970).L.T.S.

Index Number of Retail Prices Interest in the movement of this index number has assumed considerable importance in recent years. The government has been compelled to explain and justify rises, whilst these same rises form the spring-board for wage and salary claims. In the 'popular' press it is often called 'the cost of living' index number.

The present index number is best described as a modified Laspeyres one and one can think of it as measuring the change in cost from month to month of a very large and representative 'basket' of goods. Although the 'basket' is changed each year to keep it up to date, the results for each year are linked together in order to produce a continuous series of percentage changes from January 1962.

For purposes of calculation the algebraic form of the index number is as below.

$$I_{\text{MAY 1973/JAN. 1973}} = \frac{\Sigma p_{\text{JAN. 73}} \, q_{70, \, 71, \, 72} \left(\dfrac{p_{\text{MAY 73}}}{p_{\text{JAN. 73}}} \right)}{\Sigma p_{\text{JAN. 73}} \, q_{70, \, 71, \, 72}} \times 100$$

where $p_{\text{JAN. 73}}$, $p_{\text{MAY 73}}$ are prices in January and May 1973.

$q_{70, \, 71, \, 72}$ is the average quantity purchased in 1970, 1971 and 1972.

Σ indicates summation over all goods and services that are priced.

Each monthly figure obtained is then linked back to the base period, January 1962.

Two problems arise in dealing with index numbers. The first of these is the selection of the goods whose prices will 'indicate' the movement in prices of the groups and sections for which they stand. The second is the choice of weights to combine the price changes together.

The present index number covers 11 main groups of items and these are subdivided into approximately 90 sections. After careful consideration price information on nearly 350 items is regularly obtained and this information is representative of the movement of prices as a whole. Where regional and area variations are thought to be important (e.g. Food group) information is collected by local offices of the Department of Employment. Similarly, where the type of retailer varies, data is collected from as wide a selection as possible.

The importance of the sections and groups in consumers' budgets varies considerably and thus the items priced must be weighted accordingly. For example, the Food group receives approximately three times the weight accorded to the Clothing and Footwear group. To ensure that the weights reflect up-to-date consumption patterns they are based upon data derived from an average of the three previous Family Expenditure Surveys. Such a survey covers a sample of households of every kind throughout the UK, and the weights so derived are representative of the expenditure pattern of practically all wage earners' households and of most households of small and medium salary earners.

The index is published each month in the *Department of Employment and Productivity Gazette*, details being given of the 'All Items' index and also 11 major groups. For example, at 22 May 1973, the 'All Items' index stood at 178·0 compared with 16 January 1962 = 100. In addition two special indices are produced for pensioner households. ◊◊ Index Numbers. L.T.S.

Method of Construction and Calculation of the Index of Retail Prices (HMSO, 1964).

Index Numbers A convenient way of comparing the level of a set of data at a particular point of time with its level at some base period. Thus it is useful to know, for example, that the level of retail prices in a certain period is 10% greater than it was in some base period. Similar useful statements can be made about the level of production and the level of import and export prices, to take the more obvious examples.

Suppose we want to calculate an index number of retail prices. Then the easiest way of regarding such an index number is as a weighted average of price relatives. This follows because to measure the level of prices requires that we link together the changes in prices of a diverse selection of goods whose importance in consumers' budgets varies considerably. The weights used reflect the importance in consumers' budgets of the product concerned.

The following example illustrates the algebraic construction of a simple price index number involving only two products. Because the weights used refer to the base period it is called a Laspeyres price index number.

Let p_1^1, p_1^2 be the price of products 1 and 2 in period 1.

p_2^1, p_2^2 be the price of products 1 and 2 in period 2.

q_1^1, q_1^2 be the quantity produced of products 1 and 2 in period 1.

q_2^1, q_2^2 be the quantity purchased of products 1 and 2 in period 2.

Σ indicates summation over all products.

$I_{2,1}$ is the Laspeyres index number for period 2 compared to period 1.

Then

$$\underset{I_{2,1}}{LA} = \frac{p_1^1 q_1^1 \left(\frac{p_2^1}{p_1^1}\right) + p_1^2 q_1^2 \left(\frac{p_2^2}{p_1^2}\right)}{p_1^1 q_1^1 + p_1^2 q_1^2} \times 100$$

$$= \frac{\Sigma p_2 q_1}{\Sigma p_1 q_1} \times 100.$$

Using the same symbols we can form another index number, known as a Paasche price index number. In this case the weights used refer to the current time period.

$$\underset{I_{2,1}}{PA} = \frac{p_2^1 q_2^1 + p_2^2 q_2^2}{p_2^1 q_2^1 \left(\frac{p_1^1}{p_2^1}\right) + p_2^2 q_2^2 \left(\frac{p_1^2}{p_2^2}\right)} \times 100$$

$$= \frac{\Sigma p_2 q_2}{\Sigma p_1 q_2} \times 100.$$

In theory, in comparing any two periods one has the choice of using either form. For this reason, since, for the same set of data the answers will usually differ, Fisher's ideal index number is sometimes used. This is obtained by taking the geometric mean of the two index numbers above.

$$\underset{I_{2,1}}{FI} = \sqrt{\underset{I_{2,1}}{LA} \times \underset{I_{2,1}}{PA}}$$

However, in practice base-period weighting is nearly always chosen for regularly published indices because the weights of the current period are usually unavailable and the Laspeyres index is easier to calculate. ⟡ Index Number of Industrial Production; Index Number of Retail Prices. L.T.S.

P. H. Karmel, *Applied Statistics for Economists*, Ch. 12 (Pitman, 1963).

Induction The introduction of new members to the objectives, policies and practices of an enterprise and to their place and tasks as workers in it. The aim of induction is to make clear the relationship which should exist between a man and his work, i.e. his job, his workmates and his firm. Induction is a matter of telling and showing – explaining about the works rules, the products, the organization; showing the welfare facilities, the processes, the workplace, the safety devices. In many firms induction includes a tour of the works, films about the products and talks by senior managers. It may last for two or three days for school leavers, or half a day or a day for adult employees. A second induction course is sometimes held after six months, when new employees have settled in and are ready for further knowledge and information. Induction on the job or in the workplace may include a period in a training department but will be largely the responsibility of the foreman under whom the new employee is to work. It starts at the engagement interview and ends when the employee has settled down to his job and has achieved a normal output. L.S.

Induction (Institute of Personnel Management, 1950).

Industrial Arbitration Board The Industrial Arbitration Board was set up by the *Industrial Courts Act*, 1919 under the name of the Industrial Court which was in fact a misnomer since this body never operated as a court of law to which parties might apply as of right but was always a permanent arbitration body, a fact recognized by the *Industrial Relations Act*, 1971 which gave it its present title. The name Industrial Court is now used as an abbreviation for the ⟡ National Industrial Relations Court. The members of the Board consist of a President, who has the status of a High Court judge, a number of independent members and some persons representing respectively employers and workpeople. The Board generally sits in divisions, presided over by the President or one of the independent members together with one employer and one employee member.

The parties to a ⟡ Collective Agreement may specify that any disputes not otherwise resolved shall be submitted to the Board. The Board is also mentioned in a number of Acts of Parliament as the proper tribunal for hearing disputes, e.g. in connection with the application of ⟡ Fair Wage clauses. The awards of the Board are not legally binding on the parties to the dispute, but in practice they are rarely disobeyed. In one case, however, an award of the Board will be legally binding, namely where the Secretary of State for Employment has asked the Board to ascertain whether a particular employer is paying wages or observing conditions of employment equal at least to those settled by collective agreement for his industry. In this instance the award of the Board will be legally binding on the employer who may thus be compelled to adjust the wage-rates that he pays to those prevailing in his industry.

The Employment Protection Bill, which is likely to reach the Statute Book in 1975, replaces the Board with a Central Arbitration Committee to be set up as part of the new Conciliation and Arbitration Service. W.F.F.

Wedderburn and Davies, *Employment Grievances and Disputes Procedures in Britain* (California U.P., 1969).

Industrial Conciliation – in Law Differs from ⟡ Arbitration in that an arbitrator's task is that of resolving a dispute for the parties who have been unable or unwilling to do so themselves, while a conciliator's aim is the more modest one of bringing the parties together with a view to persuading them to settle their differences themselves.

In many industries there exist permanent conciliation procedures so that a dispute between trade unions and employers may be dealt with peacefully before industrial action is even contemplated. Where the procedure has broken down or where a dispute has arisen in an industry lacking such procedural arrangements, the Secretary of State for Employment may intervene and make available to the parties the assistance of highly experienced officers within the Manpower Advisory Service of the Department of Employment. Arbitration facilities would not be offered unless requested by both sides, but conciliation facilities may be made available at the request of one of the parties only. Some types of dispute lend themselves more readily to conciliation than to arbitration since it is difficult at times to find any generally agreed principles on which an arbitration award could be based. It is much easier to arbitrate in a dispute where the interpretation of an existing agreement is at stake than in one where the parties have for instance failed to agree on a wage claim. It is here that conciliation is particularly useful. Under the Protection of Employment Bill, likely to be enacted in 1975, the Conciliation and Arbitration Service, set up in September 1974, will be placed on a statutory basis. This will make available conciliation and arbitration facilities either on its own initiative or at the request of the parties or of the Secretary of State. ⟡ Arbitration, Industrial; Collective Bargaining; Manpower Adviser. W.F.F.

R. W. Rideout, *Principles of Labour Law* (Sweet & Maxwell, 1975).

Industrial Court ⟡ National Industrial Relations Court.

Industrial Democracy A term used to describe a number of theories about the government of industry and a number of schemes for reorganizing industrial management.

Stable political democracies, for example Britain, are characterized by certain institutions, such as political opposition, adult franchise, freedom of speech and assembly. In such stable democracies there is a system of industrial relations which approximates to an industrial parallel of political democracy promoting the interests of employees by means of ⟡ Collective Bargaining between employers and managers on the one hand and, on the other, free trade unions independent of management and government. This could be called *industrial democracy by consent*, or *pressure group industrial democracy*, or *industrial democracy through collective bargaining*.

Early theories of industrial democracy advocated workers' control of industry and were developed from the controversy about the means to socialism between Marx and Bakunin in the second half of the nineteenth century. There followed a syndicalist movement in French trade unions, the rise of the Industrial Workers of the World in opposition to the American Federation of Labour and the First World War shop stewards' movement in Britain. These movements were casualties of postwar depression.

A link between these early revolutionaries, who wished to replace existing industrial management, and later reformist theorists, was provided in Britain by the Guild Socialists, who kept workers' control of industry as their objective but recognized industry's need for technical skills and managerial ability. The guilds which would control industry would include workers both by hand and by brain. The Guild Socialists also recognized the roles of the consumer and of the state and their suggestion for gradually encroaching workers' control was parallel to that of the Fabians' gradual extension of public ownership.

Reformists after the First World War took the view that under capitalism the role of the employer should be taken into account. The Whitley Committee, appointed in 1916 to consider the future shape of industrial relations, suggested not only model national ⟡ Joint Industrial Councils on which representatives of employers and employees in an industry should settle wages and basic conditions of work, but also Works Committees and District Councils. Whitley (Joint Industrial) Councils were set up in a number of industries, but interwar depression emasculated the movement.

During the Second World War there developed a movement intended to harness the energies and ideas of employees to increasing output by Joint Production Consultative and Advisory Committees; that is, workplace committees jointly staffed by representatives of management and of workers. These were set up to deal with any matters which affected production other than wages and basic conditions of work. ⟨⟩ Joint consultation systems were set up in the newly-nationalized industries and, furthermore, trade union officials were appointed to the boards of these industries. Both here and in the private sector of the economy, however, joint consultation has often failed. Prominent among the many reasons has been the refusal of workers' representatives and especially ⟨⟩ Shop Stewards, to interest themselves in committees with management wherein no ⟨⟩ Collective Bargaining could take place. Significantly, successful ⟨⟩ Productivity Bargaining and other plant level negotiations often ensure that joint consultation and collective bargaining become fused into one activity.

Under the British joint consultation system workers' representatives can only suggest and discuss, whereas under the German codetermination system of industrial democracy they share directly in decisions. Yugoslavia is not a democracy in the western sense, either politically or industrially, but its workers' councils provide a continuing experiment in which Western socialist observers are interested. The Private Member's Industrial Democracy Bill at date (May 1975) is drafted in part on the German model and provides for worker directors.

In Britain it may be that many unofficial ⟨⟩ Strikes reflect an implicit pressure for more democracy and individual rights in industry. Encroachment by shop stewards on areas often regarded as appropriate to the 'managerial prerogative' may realistically be viewed as developing *industrial democracy through collective bargaining*. ⟨⟩ Participation. N.H.C.

H. A. Clegg, *A New Approach to Industrial Democracy* (Blackwell, 1960); K. Coates and A. Topham, *Industrial Democracy in Great Britain* (MacGibbon & Kee, 1968).

Industrial Disease A disease which is caused by exposure to harmful or poisonous substances or rays at work. The diseases range from toxic conditions such as poisoning by lead, phosphorus, arsenic or mercury, to fibrosis of the lungs caused by silica or asbestos, skin ailments such as dermatitis and ulceration caused by chromic acid, pitch or tar. Under the ⟨⟩ Factory Laws the more serious diseases have to be notified to the district Inspector of Factories by the occupier of the factory in which they occur, and to the Chief Inspector of Factories by the doctor who attends the case. In 1967 a total of 368 cases were notified to HM Factory Inspectorate, including 144 of chrome ulceration and 97 of lead poisoning. Two fatal cases, one of mercurial poisoning and one of anthrax, were also reported. There are numerous regulations under the *Factories Act* which require employers to take certain steps to reduce the risks. There are three lines of attack: (1) the removal or reduction of risk of exposure to the dangerous substance, e.g. by enclosing plant or removing fumes or dust by localized exhaust ventilation; (2) the protection of employees working on the dangerous process by masks and protective clothing; (3) regular medical examinations. The regulations under the *Factories Act* include sections on the 'duties of persons employed' which require them to make use of the protective devices, to wear the protective clothing and to submit to medical examination. ⟡ Industrial Injuries. L.S.

D. Hunter, *Health in Industry* (Penguin, 1959).

Industrial Dispute Under the ⟡ *Industrial Relations Act*, 1971, repealed 1974, an industrial dispute was defined as a dispute between one or more employers or organizations of employers and one or more workers or organizations of workers, where the dispute relates wholly or mainly to any one or more of the following: (1) terms and conditions of employment or the physical conditions in which any workers are required to work; (2) engagement or non-engagement, or termination or suspension of employment, of one or more workers; (3) allocation of work as between workers or groups of workers; (4) a procedure agreement, or any matter to which a ⟡ procedure agreement can relate.

The *Industrial Relations Act* repealed the *Trades Disputes Act*, 1906, which defined a 'trade dispute' as any dispute between employers and workmen, or between workmen and workmen, which is connected with the employment or non-employment, or the terms of the employment, or the conditions of labour of any person. The *Industrial Relations Act* is thus more restrictive of definition, excluding disputes between 'workmen and workmen' except where an employer is a party concerned.

The *Industrial Courts Act*, 1919, contains the same definition as in the *Trades Disputes Act*, 1906. This definition still remains, therefore, in respect of the work of the Industrial Arbitration Board, subsequently abolished and known prior to the passing of the Industrial Relations Act as the Industrial Court. ⟡ Collective Bargaining; Industrial Conciliation; Lock-out; Strike (sundry references).

The ⟡ *Trade Union and Labour Relations Act*, 1974 restores the pre-1971 protection against legal action which was given to people involved in strikes and reverts to the original term 'trade dispute'. N.H.C.

Industrial Engineering The American Institute of Industrial Engineers defines industrial engineering as being 'concerned with the design, improvement and installation of integrated systems of men, materials and equipment. It draws upon specialized knowledge and skill in the mathematical, physical and social sciences together with the principles and methods of engineering analysis and design, to specify, predict and evaluate the results to be obtained from such systems.'

A common misapprehension in the UK, where the term industrial engineering is not in general use, is that it is a function equivalent to work study. The emphasis, however, is on the total production system and there is a continuing trend to draw upon and use all relevant branches of science, e.g. Operational Research, Industrial Psychology, etc.

The emphasis on the production system suggests the equivalence of industrial engineering to what is normally called production management in the UK. Notice, however, that like the components of production management, e.g. Work

Study, Inventory Control, Facilities Layout, etc., industrial engineering is not restricted to the manufacturing industries, and is widely practised in government public services, etc. R.W.

H. B. Maynard (ed.), *Handbook of Industrial Engineering* (McGraw-Hill, 2nd ed., 1963).

Industrial Espionage Espionage undertaken with the object of obtaining information which will be of economic or political advantage. It can usually be anticipated that its major rewards will be in terms of personal and/or corporate profit and political subversion. There is little indication as to the extent of industrial espionage in Britain, and it is not a criminal offence to steal trade secrets. In McPherson *v.* Downey, 1965, the defendant received a 3-month prison sentence for stealing £3 worth of paper from his employers on which company secrets were recorded. Had he merely made a photocopy, presumably no theft would have been involved and no sentence at all incurred. The use of espionage for political subversion, for example to foster unofficial strikes when grievances are detected, is again unmeasured but thought to be present. Counter-espionage is most effectively achieved by maintaining the secret that there is a secret, by concentrating the risk, and by ensuring that a maximum of complicity is required to break security. G.S.C.W.

P. Hamilton, *Espionage and Subversion in an Industrial Society* (Hutchinson, 1967).

Industrial Injuries An employee who is injured in the course of his employment may claim damages from his employer if he can prove ⟡ Employer's liability. Independently of such an action he may, however, be entitled to benefits under the *National Insurance (Industrial Injuries) Act*, 1965. In order to substantiate his claim under this Act, the employee must be employed in insurable employment and must have sustained an injury 'by accident arising out of and in the course of his employment'. The injury may be physical or mental. Industrial diseases are also covered by the insurance scheme, but the claimant must have been employed in an occupation for which by Ministerial regulations this disease has been scheduled as a special occupational risk. Injuries sustained by the claimant on his way to or from work entitle him to benefit only if he was using transport specifically provided for the sole use of the employees of his employer.

Injury benefit is payable at standard rates, irrespective of the claimant's normal wage. It is not payable for the first 3 days of incapacity, except where the incapacity extends over 12 working days. When incapacity has ceased or after 6 months of receiving injury benefit, the claimant may apply for disablement benefit which is intended to compensate him for the lasting effects of his injury. The rate of disablement benefit payable depends on an assessment of the degree of 'loss of capacity', i.e. the lasting effects of the injury and the benefit is payable either as a lump sum (in the case of insignificant losses) or as a disablement pension. Certain supplements are payable in prescribed cases in addition to the pension. W.F.F.

J. Bell, *How to get Industrial Injuries Benefits* (Sweet & Maxwell, 1966).

Industrial Law In Britain the term Industrial Law is used for that branch of law which deals with ⟡ Contracts of Employment, the special provisions concerning

190

particular forms of employment (e.g. ⟡ Factory Law) and the law dealing with collective labour relations, such as ⟡ Trade Union Law and the law of ⟡ Collective Bargaining. In some other countries this branch of the law is referred to as labour law.

British industrial law has come into existence by accident rather than by design. Part of it is represented by the common law rules dealing with the master–servant relationship as modified over the centuries by statute as and when parliament found it necessary to deal with particular abuses. Trade unions in Britain have by and large preferred to deal with their problems by direct negotiation with employers rather than by invoking legal sanctions since they have had little confidence in the impartiality of the law when faced with industrial problems. Academically, the subject has been somewhat neglected as shown by the fact that there exists in Britain only one chair of industrial law unlike the position on the continent where such chairs have been founded in most universities.

British writers on industrial law are divided into those who feel that the scope of the subject should not be enlarged, except where necessary to reinforce voluntary agreements between managements and employees. Others, however, feel equally strongly that in a planned or semi-planned economy the law should exercise more control over wages and conditions of employment, not necessarily in order to protect employees, but more in order to protect the interests of the community as a whole. w.f.f.

O. Kahn-Freund, *Labour and the Law* (Stevens & Sons, 1972).

Industrial Marketing ⟡ Marketing.

Industrial Relations Also known as Labour Relations. These concern the complex of relationships between employees, managements and government, together with their respective organizations, trade unions, employers' associations and governmental agencies.

Strictly, the term 'industrial relations' is a misnomer. Not all the relationships associated with the organization of industry are relevant, for example the term does not include relationships between firms as to their price policy or market share, or between firms and their customers. At the same time the expression 'industrial' is conceived in the broadest possible terms. It includes all environments where paid work is carried out, for example shops, banks, hospitals, etc., as well as manufacturing industry. The study of industrial relations is the study of job regulation.

The term is used in two different senses, one all-inclusive, the other restricted to collective relations. Industrial relations in the all-inclusive sense may be defined as all the relationships between management and employees in the community. In this sense industrial relations cover relations between individuals at work, such as the individual employer and employee, together with relationships within and between work groups, sometimes known as ⟡ 'human relations'; and also interaction between organized groups such as ⟡ Trade Unions and ⟡ Employers' Associations. The term covers formal relations, as evidenced in collective agreements and written works rules; and informal relations as characterized by informal agreements on the allocation of overtime, discipline and the distribution of work loads and by the ⟨⟩ Norms imposed by work groups on their own performance.

In the restricted sense industrial relations denote only collective relations between trade unions, or sections of them, and employers.

In either event, relationships are constrained by the interests of, and rules set up by, the agencies of government, for example the ⟨⟩ Department of Employment and the Pay Board. ⟨⟩ Prices and Incomes Policy.

Industrial relations problems may arise at the level of the plant or workplace, as in the case of disputes over piece-rates or discipline; at the level of the firm, as in the case of trade union recognition; at the level of the industry, as in the case of 'national' wage rates in dispute between unions and an employer (or employers' association); and at the level of the economy, as where a government attempts to implement some form of incomes policy.

Industrial relations discussion may centre on human efficiency at the workplace; or on employee-management cooperation, as (allegedly) in ⟨⟩ Joint Consultation; or on employee-management ⟨⟩ Conflict, as in ⟨⟩ Collective Bargaining. Studies may concentrate on the industrial relations system of the workplace, the plant, the firm, the industry, or the economy; or on institutions operating at one or more of these levels, for example the trade union or the employers' association.

Initially much investigation in the industrial relations field took the form of historical and descriptive studies of institutions, particularly of trade unions, their battles, leadership, and growth. Many of these studies were made by practitioners or historians. They were soon followed by economists, initially descriptive of institutions but latterly analytical in their approach, examining the economic environment in which industrial relations operate and also analysing labour markets, collective bargaining, wage levels (⟨⟩ Wage), productivity (⟨⟩ Productivity Bargaining), and incomes policies (⟨⟩ Prices and Incomes Policy). Lawyers came to examine the legal environment and to survey ⟨⟩ industrial law, ⟨⟩ trade union law and the law of strikes (⟨⟩ Strike and the Law). The contribution of political science has lain in studies of the political climate in which industrial relations operate with detailed work on trade union organization and government ⟨⟩ Trade Union – Government and Administration. Behavioural scientists and statisticians have come most recently to study the industrial relations scene. Industrial sociology has contributed work on ideological differences between management and employees (⟨⟩ Ideology), on complementary and competitive goals in the work situation and on conflict and its resolution; psychologists have discussed motivation, incentives (⟨⟩ Motivation; Wage Systems) and adaptation to work; while group formation, attitudes and functions and formal and informal group structures and behaviour have been investigated by social psychologists (⟨⟩ Formal Organization; Group). Statisticians have, *inter alia*, analysed ⟨⟩ Strikes and ⟨⟩ Wage Drift.

Only recently have there developed attempts to offer an integrated view over the whole complex of activity in this field and to produce theories of industrial relations; to set up industrial relations models; and to explain industrial relations in a company, an industry, or a country in terms of systems. Such an attempt, explaining industrial relations as a system involving three groups of actors:

workers and their organizations, managers and their organizations, and governmental agencies concerned with the work environment – creating and operating a system of rules of many kinds within an environment comprised of three inter-related contexts (the technology, the market or budgetary constraints, and the power relations and statuses of all the actors, bound together by understandings shared by the actors), is set out by John T. Dunlop (see references below).

It remains true, however, that there is as yet no generally accepted theory of industrial relations, although 'the problems are interconnected and held together by a particular logic', in the words of Hilde Behrend (see below). So far 'each separate discipline has approached the subject with its own emphasis and bias, using its specific tools, methods and jargon . . . [which] has resulted in poor communication across boundaries and has often hidden considerable overlaps in the problems studied'. This has on the whole made it difficult for practising managers to obtain guidance in day-to-day problems from the literature, unless the investigation has been of the case study type exemplified by Allan Flanders's *Fawley Productivity Agreements*.

Within the firm industrial relations management may form only a part of the total responsibility of ⟡ Personnel Management, irrespective of the size and influence of the personnel department; or it may be so significant for the enterprise that the industrial relations manager has a seat on the board of directors but not the personnel manager, although this latter case is so far relatively rare in Britain. In practice there are dangers that differing industrial relations policies are carried out by operational managers, by personnel managers, and by other service managers, e.g. industrial engineers. Increasingly, however, British management is moving towards more coherent, more rational and more positive industrial relations policies, although most firms fall below the standards of the best in this respect.

Institutional studies, particularly of trade unions, still tend to dominate the literature of industrial relations, perhaps because unions are convinced of the rightness of their cause and are at the same time more open and less security-minded than managements and government, although the attitudes of these last are beginning to change. Union studies, too, are becoming less descriptive and more analytical. There are so far few studies of employers' associations and even fewer of government agencies. There are many studies of the industrial relations systems of industries and of countries, but the growth areas seem to be in the micro-study of workplaces, plants and firms; and in the macro-study of the development of the national industrial relations system in relation to governmental policy.

If British performance in industrial relations is to be improved, more study is required, particularly of workplace and enterprise environments. Additionally, much more industrial relations training is necessary to bring all boards of directors, managers, supervisors and trade-union officers and members to the standards of the best.

Many of the key features of the British industrial relations system are cross-referenced above. For others ⟡ Business Unionism; Check-off; Closed Shop; Confederation of British Industry; Demarcation; Dilution; Federation; Indus-

trial Democracy; Industrial Relations – Reform in Great Britain; Industrial
Relations Act; Lock-out; Manpower Adviser; Restrictive Labour Practices; Shop
Steward; Strike (sundry references); Trade Union (sundry references); Trade
Union Types (sundry references); Trades Council; Trades Union Congress;
Wage (sundry references); Workplace Bargaining. N.H.C.

Hilde Behrend, 'The Field of Industrial Relations', *British Journal of Indus-
trial Relations*, Vol. I, No. 3, Oct. 1963; B. C. Roberts (ed.) *British Journal of
Industrial Relations*, 3 issues p.a. (for a sample of the latest work and a
chronicle of recent events); J. T. Dunlop, *Industrial Relations Systems* (Holt-
Dryden, 1958); A. Flanders, *The Fawley Productivity Agreements* (Faber &
Faber, 1964); *Industrial Relations Journal*, quarterly; T. Lupton, *On the Shop
Floor* (Pergamon, 1963); National Board for Prices and Incomes, *Reports*,
HMSO; Royal Commission on Trade Unions and Employers' Associations,
Report 1968; *Research Papers and Evidence* (HMSO); *Industrial Relations
Law Reports*; *Industrial Relations Review and Report*, fortnightly (for up-to-
date news and commentary).

Industrial Relations Act The objective of the *Industrial Relations Act*, 1971, was to
provide for the first time in the British industrial relations system a legal framework for the conduct of industrial relations in contrast to the pre-existing volun-
tarist system.

The Act contained four broad categories of provision: (1) The rights of employees; (2) The registration and conduct of trade unions and employee associations; (3) Strikes and lockouts; (4) The reform of collective bargaining. Allied
with these provisions were arrangements for investigation by the ◊ Commission on
Industrial Relations and for legal processes through the ◊ Industrial Tribunal and
the ◊ National Industrial Relations Court. The Act was backed by an ◊ Industrial
Relations Code of Practice.

The rights of employees included a right to a written statement of terms of
employment which must contain entitlement to holidays and holiday pay; an
explanation of the employee's rights to join and not to join a trade union, the
latter subject to ◊ agency shop or ◊ approved closed shop agreements; the way
in which grievances can be taken up (◊ Contract of Employment); and the right
not to be dismissed unfairly (◊ Dismissal).

Union registration (◊ Trade Union – legal definition; Trade Union – registration) was conditional on the acceptance of minimum standards as to rules and
members' rights, and it conferred privileges on the registered organization. Registration was possible only for an independent organization of employees which
had power to alter its own rules and control the use of its own property and
funds. Requirements for registration directly affected the position of ◊ shop
stewards and their equivalents; not only must their powers and duties be specified
in the union rules, but the circumstances in which they could call strikes or
impose other sanctions must be spelled out.

The Act distinguished between the freedom of the individual to strike (◊ Strike
and the Law) and his freedom to organize a strike, restrictions being imposed on
the strike leaders, the main one arising out of ◊ unfair industrial practices.

194

Employers could also commit unfair industrial practices. The Act made a minor amendment to the law of ⟡ picketing. Where a strike was likely to endanger the national economy or security, or public health or order, provision was made for a cooling-off period and a ballot of the employees involved.

The Act provided new machinery for determining bargaining structure and recognition rights when these could be solved by voluntary methods. In cases of dispute the ⟡ Commission on Industrial Relations could be brought in to recommend an appropriate ⟡ bargaining unit for a particular group of employees and whether there should be a ⟡ sole bargaining agent for that unit.

All pre-entry ⟡ closed-shop agreements were made illegal. Provision was, however, made for ⟡ 'approved closed-shops' and ⟡ 'agency shops'.

The Act concentrated on measures to be taken in the absence or defectiveness of ⟡ procedure agreements (⟡ Industrial Relations Code of Practice). It also laid down that collective agreements made after enactment of this legislation would be legally enforceable unless containing an express provision to the contrary. ⟡ Collective Agreements in Law. Provision was made also for ⟡ disclosure of information by the employer in order to ensure effective ⟡ collective bargaining.

Unions affiliated to the ⟡ T U C opposed this legislation before and subsequent to its enactment and adopted a policy of non-cooperation in the implementation of the Act. In particular, they refused to register and to cooperate with the institutions established under the Act, except in self-defence. Any affiliated unions not complying were expelled from the T U C. The T U C unions were particularly incensed by the making of their former legal immunities conditional on registration; by the constraint on the powers of trade union officers; by the outlawing of the traditional pre-entry closed shop; by the new right of employees not to join a trade union or other workers' organization, by the provision for making collective agreements legally binding unless specifically provided otherwise by the parties; and by the arrangements for the use of the ⟡ National Industrial Relations Court and the ⟡ Commission on Industrial Relations to determine disputed bargaining rights.

In practice the Act was particularly effective in two areas, those of unfair dismissal and of procedures. With respect to procedures, many companies have been stimulated to improve their industrial relations systems with the aid of the Industrial Relations Code of Practice which remained in force on the Act's repeal and replacement by the ⟡ *Trade Union and Labour Relations Act*, 1974. N.H.C.

> Industrial Relations Act, 1971, Ch. 72, HMSO; W. E. J. McCarthy and N. D. Ellis, *Management by Agreement* (Hutchinson, 1973).

Industrial Relations Code of Practice Sometimes said to be the Industrial Relations equivalent of the 'Highway Code', the Industrial Relations Code of Practice was set up under the provisions of sections 2–4 of the ⟡ *Industrial Relations Act*, 1971. Its objects were to provide for companies and other employing organizations industrial relations standards which, though not legally enforceable, would be admissible in evidence before an ⟡ Industrial Tribunal or the ⟡ National Industrial Relations Court. The Code remains in force despite repeal of the Act in 1974.

The Code provides standards for the responsibilities of managements, trade unions, (◊ Trade Union at Law), ◊ employers' associations, and the individual employee; for employment policies (◊ Industrial Training, Manpower Planning; Recruitment, Redundancy, Selection, Wage Systems); for ◊ communication and ◊ joint consultation; for ◊ collective bargaining; for employee representation (◊ Shop Steward); and for grievance, disputes, and disciplinary procedures. ◊ Discipline; Grievance Procedure. N.H.C.

Industrial Relations Code of Practice, HMSO, 28 February 1972.

Industrial Relations Commission ◊ Commission on Industrial Relations; Industrial Relations – Reform in Great Britain.

Industrial Relations Officer (Ministry of Labour) ◊ Manpower Adviser (Department of Employment).

Industrial Relations – Reform in Great Britain The Royal Commission on ◊ Trade Unions and ◊ Employers' Associations emphasized the dual system of British industrial relations, one formal and embodied in official institutions, the other informal and produced by the behaviour at the workplace of managers, ◊ Shop Stewards and workers, with the resulting competitive sectional wage adjustments, chaotic pay structures, ◊ Wage Drift, Unofficial ◊ Strikes and other forms of workshop pressure.

The Royal Commission's suggested remedy was the development of positive, company industrial relations policies, specifically to include such matters as the setting up of formal company collective bargaining systems, disciplinary and ◊ Grievance Procedures, rules regulating the position of shop stewards, ◊ Redundancy Agreements, and ◊ Joint Consultation on safety; and deliberate attempts by companies to control incentive schemes, to regulate working hours and to introduce rational ◊ Wage Systems, including those based on ◊ Job Evaluation. The Commission also recommended that ◊ Wages Councils would be better replaced by a national minimum ◊ Wage.

Since it was not confident that voluntary action alone would be speedy enough, the Commission proposed an Industrial Relations Act under which companies, initially those with more than 5000 employees, would be required to register their collective agreements (◊ Collective Bargaining) with the ◊ Department of Employment; and an Industrial Relations Commission, which would in effect monitor company industrial relations systems for smooth working ◊ Commission on Industrial Relations.

A majority of the Commission rejected as a remedy for strikes (◊ Strike – sundry references) the making of all agreements into legally enforceable contracts (◊ Collective Agreements in Law) although Mr Andrew Schonfield dissented and pressed also for a Restrictive Practices Office for control of work practices (◊ Restrictive Labour Practices). The Conservative Party Policy pamphlet, *Fair Deal at Work* went further, urging that sympathetic strikes, secondary boycotts and inter-union strikes become illegal (◊ Strike – Forms).

One of the Commission's most far-reaching proposals was to recommend transformation of the present Industrial Tribunals (◊ Redundancy Payments Act) into Labour Tribunals to cover all disputes between employer and employee arising out of ⟨⟩ Contracts of Employment or from statutory claims they might have on each other as employer and employee. Labour Tribunals would thus deal with allegations of unfair dismissal, including dismissal as a result of the introduction of a ⟨⟩ Closed Shop, although the Commission did not advocate the abolition of the closed shop. Complaints of unfair expulsion from a union and of union electoral malpractice could also be dealt with by Labour Tribunals.

The Commission rejected industrial unionism (⟨⟩ Trade Union Types – Industrial Union) as a solution to multi-unionism, recommending more union mergers and 'one union for one grade of work within one factory' ⟨⟩ Trade Union Structure. It also advocated properly organized shop stewards' committees; a revision of union rules on shop stewards to define their role, authority and functions; more full-time officers (⟨⟩ Trade Union – Officers) and better salaries for them; and further extension of the ⟨⟩ Check-off. The Commission recommended compulsory registration for unions with a new Registrar of Trade Unions and Employers' Associations which would have close supervision over union rules.

Despite dissentients, the proposal of the ⟨⟩ TUC for worker-directors was rejected by a majority of the Commission, although this principle is being applied in the renationalized steel industry.

The Royal Commission concentrated on suggestions for making the voluntary system of ⟨⟩ Collective Bargaining work by persuasion and publicity rather than by radical changes in the law and took the view that the unions needed strengthening if they were to be more 'responsible'. Some members of the Commission doubted the efficacy of any reform attempted without constraining the freedom of trade unionists to break agreements, and in this they were nearer the harder line suggested in the Conservative Party's statement, *Fair Deal at Work*, which proposed a legal framework to industrial relations somewhat similar to that in the USA.

The Labour government's White Paper, *In Place of Strife*, endorsed many of the Commission's suggestions in its proposals for an Industrial Relations Act, including the establishment of the Industrial Relations Commission. It further introduced notions of government financial aid for rational trade-union development, including the costs of training; of a cooling-off period ('conciliation pause') for unconstitutional strikes and strikes where inadequate joint discussions have taken place; and of an Industrial Board to deal with conflicts of recognition between rival unions ⟨⟩ Trade Union – Jurisdiction. It was also suggested that employers might be ordered to recognize a particular trade union and might be required to bargain in good faith against financial penalties. This White Paper provided much of the foundation for the Labour government's abortive Industrial Relations Bill.

The eventual legislation enacted by the subsequent Conservative government, the ⟨⟩ *Industrial Relations Act*, 1971, now repealed, was based on the Conservative Party's policy statement, *Fair Deal at Work*, and the Inns of Court Conservative and Unionist Society's study, *A Giant's Strength*.

The decision of most unions to deregister and to oppose the Act's provisions resulted in its repeal and replacement by the much slighter *Trade Union and Labour Relations Act* in 1974. The voluntary nature of the UK industrial relations system thus continues but legislation increasingly intervenes, e.g. the *Health and Safety at Work Act*, 1974, and at date (May 1975) the Trade Union and Labour Relations (Amendment) Bill, the Employment Protection Bill, the Industry Bill, the Sex Discrimination Bill, and a Private Member's Industrial Decmocracy Bill, all have implications for industrial relations. N.H.C.

Industrial Sociology ◊ Social Sciences.

Industrial Training That part of ◊ Personnel Management which is directed to helping people acquire the knowledge, skills and capacities necessary to do their work well, to prepare them for transfer to other jobs and for promotion, and to help them to fit into the working group, department and enterprise in which they work. Some knowledge and skill is gained before work starts; industry builds on this by more specialized training. Industrial training is relevant to all levels of employment from the 'unskilled worker' who needs skill to lift, carry, move and assemble with ease and efficiency, to the senior manager, who may need to understand the use of computers and of operational research as well as those aspects of human behaviour which affect performance at work and relations between groups. Training starts with ◊ Induction, i.e. introductory courses and on-the-job instruction for new employees. It includes intensive training for unskilled and semi-skilled workers, who by means of tailor-made, works-based courses may be able to achieve a normal output in half the time possible if operators are left to pick up a job by watching others. Training in craft skills is normally associated with systems of apprenticeship and is increasingly started with a year's general training off the job. For training foremen and supervisors it is as important that the content of outside courses should be related to the actual work they will be doing as it is for operators, process workers and apprentices. A large variety of courses are combined with experience for training professional and technical staff, many of them provided in colleges of technology or commerce. They also provide a growing volume of courses in business and management studies which at higher levels are available at a number of universities and at independent establishments such as the Administrative Staff College at Henley and the Management College at Ashridge. 'Training' is often considered to be narrowly vocational in contrast to 'education' which is liberal and concerned with the whole man. This may be broadly true, but an employer is interested in the responsibility, capacity for leadership and foresight of his managers and supervisors, so that experiences, including training courses, which demand initiative, test stamina or broaden people's understanding of social and economic processes, are as important at some stages and at certain levels as those which increase technical knowledge or improve manual skills. Furthermore the young operator, clerk or apprentice brings the whole of himself to his training, and awareness of this makes the teacher, however technical his subject, more 'liberal' in his approach.

Training policies, to be effective, have to be related both to ◊ Manpower Planning, which indicates the future requirements of different categories of employee, and to ◊ Job Analysis which gives a clear and accurate description of the job which people do and for which they need training. It is necessary to keep these job descriptions up to date to allow for changes in technology and organization.

With these guides it is possible to estimate the numbers and types of trained personnel required and to decide which parts of the training are best given on the job, in a training department or on outside courses. Many industries now have Training Boards (⟡ Industrial Training Boards) which have been established under the ⟡ *Industrial Training Act*, 1964. These are having an increasing impact on industrial training especially that of craftsmen and technicians. ⟡ Further Education; Group Methods of Training; Management Development; Training within Industry (T W I). L.S.

A. Tegla Davies, *Industrial Training* (Institute of Personnel Management, 1962); W. Douglas Seymour, *Operator Training* (Institute of Personnel Management, 1959); J. R. Armstrong, *Supervisory Training* (Institute of Personnel Management, 1961); E. G. Sterling and S. Crawford, *Apprentice Training* (Institute of Personnel Management, 1963).

Industrial Training Act 1964. Industrial training has been hindered in the past by the fact that the less enterprising firms devoting little time and money to the training of their employees were in fact being subsidized by the more enterprising companies. The purpose of the Act is to rectify the position. It provides for the setting up by the Minister of Labour, now Secretary of State for Employment, of Industrial Training Boards for the major industries. A board, once set up, may approve suitable training courses for persons employed in the industry and may make recommendations about suitable training programmes for these persons. In order to raise money for its functions, the board may recommend to the Secretary that a levy be imposed on the firms in the industry. The Secretary may then make a levy order which will specify the method of assessment of the levy. This is generally done by a percentage charge on the firms' payrolls. The main way of utilizing the money thus collected is by paying grants to firms providing approved training facilities for their employees, but the board may also pay maintenance, tuition fees and travelling allowances to persons attending courses provided or approved by the Board. W.F.F.

B A C I E, *Industrial Training Boards* (a series of progress reports giving information about levies, grants, etc., for the various boards).

Industrial Training Boards Boards established by the Secretary of State for Employment and Productivity under the ⟡ *Industrial Training Act* to see that the provision of training (⟡ Industrial Training) is adequate to meet the needs of the industries for which they are instituted. Boards may be set up for any branch of industry and commerce; those now existing include Agriculture and Horticulture, Hotels and Catering, and Retail Distribution as well as Engineering, Construction, Wool, and Iron and Steel. Boards are appointed by the Minister of Labour and have to consist of a Chairman with industrial or commercial experience; an equal number of persons appointed from the two sides of industry after consultation with the appropriate Employers' Association and Trade Unions; and people with educational or training experience appointed after consultation with the Minister of Education. A board has two main duties: to ensure that sufficient training is provided in its industry, and to publish information on such matters as the nature, content and length of training for different occupations. A board's authority extends to all forms of training and to any further education which should be associated with the training. It can approve training facilities and courses, lay down standards, impose tests, inspect and advise, and undertake research. It must impose on employers in its industry a financial levy, which is normally a percentage of the total wages and salary bill, and it must make grants to employers in accordance with its assessment of the quantity and quality of the training provided. The only legal obligation on employers is to pay the levy and to give to the board information about its training arrangements A board may exempt from its operations employers of a particular class, e.g. those with few employees. L.S.

Industrial Tribunals Industrial tribunals were originally set up by the Industrial Training Act, 1964 to deal with certain disputed matters under the Act. Their functions have since been widely extended. They deal now also with disputes under the ⬧ *Redundancy Payments Act*, 1965; the *Contracts of Employment Acts*; the *Equal Pay Act*, 1970; unfair dismissal under the *Trade Union and Labour Relations Act*, 1974 and various other matters laid down by this Act. Each tribunal consists of a legally qualified chairman together with two lay members. Parties appearing before a tribunal may be represented by a solicitor or counsel, a representative of a trade union or an employers' association or by any other person of their choice. Appeals from the decisions of an industrial tribunal would be heard by the High Court. W.F.F.

   B. Perrins, *Labour Relations Law Now* (Butterworths, 1975).

Industrial Union ⬧ Trade Union Types – Industrial Union.

Industrialization The process of change in a society from a predominantly agrarian economy to one based on manufacturing techniques involving modern technology, mass production and standardization, and a pronounced division of labour.

   Whilst the purpose of industrialization is ostensibly to improve the standard of living of the general population of the society, its introduction leads inevitably to far-reaching social changes, many of which are unforeseen (although often foreseeable). The changes are too complex to be discussed fully here and the details will vary from one society to another. In general terms, however, it may be suggested that changes are likely in the power structure and hence, perhaps, in the political system; that economic activity previously traditional and often involving ritual will become rational and purposive; that there will be an increase in the importance of science and technology at the expense of religion and magic; that there will be a rapid growth in the size of towns and an increase in geographical and social mobility; that there will occur a need for widespread educational opportunity, particularly at the secondary level; that there will be a reduction in the power and influence of the wider kinship system in favour of the nuclear family and a need for the development of social services to replace the supportive functions previously undertaken by the extended family or tribal units.

   These substantial changes in social organization and traditional habits, customs and beliefs create strains and tensions both social and personal. Indeed, even after the transitional period, industrialization imposes social change of an apparently ever-increasing rate with its concomitant problems of adaptation. I.C.MCG.

Wilbert E. Moore, *The Impact of Industry* (Prentice-Hall, 1965).

Inflation A situation in which prices are rising. The table below gives some idea of the course of prices since the First World War in the U K.

Average Annual Changes in the Retail Price Index[1]

	Per cent per Annum
1919–29	−2·1
1929–39	−0·4
1939–44	6·9
1944–54	−4·9
1954–64	3·1

1. Source: A. R. Prest, *The UK Economy: A Manual of Applied Economics*, 2nd ed., 1968, p. 31, Weidenfeld & Nicolson.

The word inflation is to some extent an emotive one, the general feeling being that inflation is a bad thing because of the ill effects it forces upon people unable to protect themselves, e.g. people on fixed incomes and creditors. However, price increases are only the symptom of inflation and we must now look at the process of inflation itself. It is customary to argue that an inflationary process can be either demand-induced or cost-induced. Such a dichotomy is useful as a starting point although it is doubtful if the distinction can be held in advanced analysis.

The usual phrase of 'too much money chasing too few goods' aptly describes demand-induced inflation. Such a statement implies that money demand in the economy runs ahead of physical supplies, thus leading to price rises which, to some extent, choke off the demand. However, prices of products in the economic system do not appear to be as flexible as this approach suggests; in addition, one should remember that inter-connections appear on the macro scene which are absent on the micro scene and thus if prices increase this will feed back to increased incomes. Most industrial prices are 'administered' prices that respond only slowly to changes in demand conditions. On the other hand they do seem to respond to general changes in cost conditions. This, therefore, means that whilst a rise in money demand may not lead to price increases because firms fear to spoil the market and invite retaliation, prices may well rise when all the firms are experiencing cost increases due to changes in raw material or labour prices. This situation may then develop as price rises are reflected in the retail price index and hence lead to renewed wage demands. Whilst excess demand appears to have little direct effect on prices of products it does appear to have an indirect effect on the labour market. Excess demand for products can easily lead to bidding among manufacturers for scarce labour with a consequent upward twist given to wage-rates and earnings and, later, prices.

The general consensus of opinion about postwar inflation in Britain is that it is the result of both demand and cost factors. In the early 1950s the rise in import prices during the Korean War was an important causal factor and several studies have established a link between the pressure of demand and wage and salary earnings. To this must be added the power of Trade Unions to exert an upward pressure on wage rates and the 'cost of living' clause in many national wage agreements. ⟡ Index Number of Retail Prices. L.T.S.

F. Brooman, *Macro-Economics* (Allen & Unwin, 4th ed., 1970).

Informal Organization ⟡ Formal Organization.

Information Retrieval This term is often used in the context of a computer-based management information system. Such a system would incorporate a data bank held on appropriate ⟡ Storage Media (Computer), consisting of files of company data which are being continually up-dated. Information retrieval is a term used to describe the organization of the storage of data in the files and the procedures for the selection and extraction of any particular item from the files, so that relevant data are easily accessible when required. For example, in the airline reservation system referred to elsewhere (⟡ Computers, Rapid Access to Information), it must be possible for a booking clerk to check for vacant seats on flights quickly.

The term is also used to describe document retrieval, in the context of manually or computer-based library or abstracting services.

Information retrieval in an airline reservation system is comparatively straightforward, but more sophisticated applications are difficult to design. The design of a retrieval system can pose complex logical and semantic problems and considerable effort is being put into solving these problems. Indeed, what data to store and how to store and retrieve it is the basic problem in the design of computer-based management information systems. M.J.C.M.

Information Theory The mathematical theory of information sets out to provide a measure of the amount of information which exists in a message, and to provide a formal basis for the study of information flow in systems of communication and control.

The amount of information (referred to as 'entropy' or 'uncertainty') associated with a source of signals is related to the unexpectedness of the signals. Thus a signal with a high prior probability has a low information value, and a rare or unexpected signal has a high value.

It is a requirement of such a system of measurement that all possible signals must be definable in advance, and that their respective prior probabilities must be known. Messages (i.e. sequences of signals) may form an infinite set. In the case, for example, of a teleprinter communication system, the number of possible signal elements may number only 27 (i.e. capital letters and space) and the relative frequency of occurrence of each element may be known for a given class of messages (e.g. those in the English Language). Thus the average rate of information transmission through such a system may be calculated, although there is no upper limit to the number of possible transmittable messages.

The unit of such selective information is the 'bit', which is the amount of uncertainty associated with the choice between two equally likely outcomes. Probabilities of occurrence of signal elements usually depend not only upon relative frequencies, but also upon the sequential relationships between elements which exist within most language structures. E.E.

E. Edwards, *Information Transmission* (Chapman and Hall, 1964).

Input/Output Analysis Input/output analysis is an attempt to reveal the structural interdependence of the economic system. An input/output table shows the purchases by a particular sector from all the other sectors and sales by the sector to the other sectors. The table below shows a simple hypothetical input/output table:

Table 1

Purchases by Sales by	X	Y	Z	Final Demand	£ Total Output
X	—	60	40	100	200
Y	40	—	100	260	400
Z	50	100	—	50	200
Labour	110	240	60	—	410
Total input	200	400	200	410	1210

If we consider the output of industry X, £200, we find that £60 was purchased by industry Y, £40 by industry Z and £100 by final consumers. Similarly, to produce this output, industry X purchased £40 of output from industry Y, £50 from industry Z and £110 of labour services.

From the above table we can easily obtain the table of input coefficients given below:

Table 2

	User of output		
Producer of input	X	Y	Z
X	—	0·15	0·2
Y	0·2	—	0·5
Z	0·25	0·25	—
L	0·55	0·6	0·3

What this table shows is the amount of output that needs to be purchased from the various sectors to produce one unit of output for a particular sector. Thus the first column shows that to obtain £1 of output from industry X requires purchases of £0·2 of output from Y, £0·25 from Z and £0·55 of labour services.

Clearly this type of information is only available for years in which a detailed Census of Production has been taken. In the UK the most detailed information refers to 1963 and the breakdown is into 70 industry/commodity groups. In America the Department of Commerce has produced an input–ouput table for 1958 which contains 86 producing and 6 final demand sectors. Larger breakdowns have been undertaken in some of Professor Leontieff's earlier work – obviously computational problems increase as the number of separate industries increases.

Provided some simplifying assumptions are made, the uses of this type of analysis are considerable, although argument remains as to whether or not the simplifying assumptions are too restrictive. For example, we may wish to know what the effect would be of an increase in final demand for the product of industry X to

£120, other final demands remaining constant. Thus an assumption is made about consumer demand. We also assume that prices remain unchanged and that the input coefficients remain unchanged. This latter assumption is a special case of constant returns to scale, the important point being that factor substitution due to either changes in the relative prices of inputs or changes in technology is ruled out.

The answers to our question can be obtained by solution of the three simultaneous equations given below where x, y, z, are the outputs in £s from industries X, Y and Z. Clearly all three outputs will change because of structural interdependence.

$$x = 0.15y + 0.2z + 120 \tag{1}$$
$$y = 0.2x + 0.5z + 260 \tag{2}$$
$$z = 0.25x + 0.25y + 50 \tag{3}$$

Equation (1), for example, tells us the demands that are made upon the output of industry X by industries Y, Z and final consumers. The solution to the equations are:

$$x = £222 \qquad y = £408 \qquad z = £208$$

This indicates the amount of new output required to satisfy intermediate and final demands.

A final step would be to work out the new demand for labour services to see if this is feasible in view of known resources.

The full potential of this type of work has only been realized with the advent of high speed computers – to solve a three-equation system is feasible by hand, but this quickly ceases to be true and many of the large tables have 100 or more sectors. The computer does mean that some relaxation of the restrictions on the input coefficients may be made. However, restrictions notwithstanding, this approach has already proved useful in examining the implications of growth in the British Economy into the 1970s. L.T.S.

W. Leontieff, *Input–Output Economics* (OUP, 1966).

Input/Output Devices and Media (of Computers) A computer must communicate with the outside world so some form(s) of input/output facilities are required.

The data given to the computer are manipulated within it by electrical pulses. Initially they are hand- or typewritten on paper, so input facilities are required to convert them into electrical forms. Since computers operate very quickly input facilities must be designed to operate as fast as possible. Similar considerations apply to output facilities.

There are several types of input facilities available and the type most suitable is dependent upon the particular application. Computer installations usually have two or more alternatives present to provide flexibility.

We shall consider the more common types in turn:

1. *Punch Cards*

These are basically the punched cards used in data processing since 1890. Information is coded by punching holes in alternative positions (usually 12) in a vertical column. Cards are usually '80 column' or '40 column' in size.

The cards are 'read', that is the positions of the holes are 'sensed' by a card reader. Sensing is performed in a number of ways:

(a) Electrically – by passing the card between an electrically energized roller and a set of wire bushes. Where holes are present electric circuits are completed.

(b) Mechanically – a set of steel pins, each coincident with a punching position, is pushed down on the card face. Where a hole is present, the pin passes through, activating a mechanism.

(c) Photo-electrically – light is focused on the card, which is supported over a set of photo-cells, each coincident with a punching position. The presence of a hole activates the appropriate photo-cell.

Card readers to perform this operation can 'read' at 1000 or more cards a minute.

2. *Punched Paper Tape*

This consists of a continuous strip of paper, or plastic, tape $\frac{3}{4}$–1 in. wide. Data are recorded by punching holes laterally across the tape. There are 5–8 punching positions, giving 5–8 track tape.

Data from the tape is read serially by a tape reader operating photoelectrically. Tape readers can read at 1000 or more characters per second.

3. *Magnetic Tape*

This is analogous to the material used with domestic tape recorders and consists of a magnetically sensitive deposit on a plastic tape substrate $\frac{1}{4}$–1 in. wide. The spots of sensitive material can be magnetized in either of two directions corresponding to a 'hole' or 'no hole'. Magnetization is performed by small electro-magnets ('writing heads') and similar electro-magnets recognize the polarity of the magnetic spots ('reading heads').

Data from magnetic tape can be read serially 20 or more times as fast as from paper tape, but such tape is more expensive and is difficult to edit and correct. It is more commonly used for transferring data from one unit to another and for backing storage ($\Diamond$ Storage Media).

Handwritten data are usually transferred to punched cards or paper tape by manual keyboard operators. To produce paper tape, operators 'copy type' the data using a typewriter-style keyboard which automatically translates and punches the data. Some units automatically produce typescript copies of the data. Similar equipment exists for producing punched cards and magnetic tape.

Similar data can be used for output as for input. The computer records output directly on to cards or paper tape by card or paper tape punches. Output punches are slower than card and paper tape readers. Magnetic tape input/output may also be recorded directly on to magnetic tape. Card or tape output is converted to a conventional typescript by appropriate type printers.

The output can be printed directly using a line printer connected directly to the computer. This produces a typed script a line at a time (hence the name) as against each character serially as a conventional typewriter. This mode of printing is adopted to obtain maximum data output speed. Speeds of over 1000 lines per minute are obtained. M.J.C.M.

Inspection Every firm is concerned with the quality of its output, also that its products meet certain minimum standards. This involves two aspects: (1) the quality of past production – i.e. the inspection of articles already produced; (2) the quality of future production – i.e. action, usually resulting from inspection, taken to ensure that future production is acceptable (i.e. change in material, machine settings, etc.). Inspection therefore is one aspect of ⟡ Quality Control.

Inspection is not restricted to the end product, but is also applied to purchased material, components, etc., and at intermediate stages of manufacture. Intermediate inspection should be located to provide maximum economic benefit:

$$\text{i.e. Cost of Inspection} < \text{Expected Saving}$$
$$< \frac{\text{No. of new rejects}}{\text{produced at stage}} \times \frac{\text{Subsequent}}{\text{Production costs}}$$

A 100% inspection of items is rarely possible or economically practical, e.g. the time required may be excessive or inspection may be of a destructive nature. This gives rise to the practice of acceptance sampling by which the overall quality of production is measured from a random sample. This method of inspection reduces cost and handling. ⟡ Acceptance Sampling.

Eternal vigilance is the key to efficient inspection. Wartime studies of watchkeeping on radar and other apparatus laid the foundation of our knowledge of the characteristics of human performance in inspection tasks. The variables which affect inspection efficiency include the number of possible faults, their frequency of occurrence, the length of the work and period, the action required following upon fault detection, in addition, of course, to the numerous aspects of the worker's environment. R.W. & E.E.

Institution A more or less permanent complex of related behavioural expectations which have a positive social value. A social institution is thus an aspect of culture which relates to the satisfaction of specific basic human needs. The family, for example, is a social institution in that there exist generally held expectations about the behaviour required of the family members and of the nature of the relationships amongst them. The expectations in question may be formally prescribed in legal enactments, in constitutions, rule books, etc., or may simply be generally understood. Social institutions both reflect and determine the values of the society and determine the roles that the persons act and comprise the norms to which they should conform. ⟡ Culture; Norm; Role; Values. I.C.McG.

Insurance ⟡ National Insurance; Insurance Law.

Insurance Law A contract of insurance is one whereby the insurer (generally an insurance company) undertakes in return for a premium to indemnify the insured against the financial consequences of the contingency insured against, up to the maximum amount stated in the insurance policy. The term 'assurance' is sometimes used for those contracts where the contingency (e.g. death) is one that is bound to occur at some time.

Contracts of insurance have three general features:

(1) They are contracts of utmost good faith. This means that the insured must volunteer to the insurer all information about the risk which might influence the

insurer's decision whether, and if so at what premium, to insure. Failure to do so would entitle the insurer to disclaim his liability under the contract.

(2) The insured must have an 'insurable interest' in the subject matter of the policy. This means that the insured faces a financial loss in the event of the contingency materializing. If the insured lacks an insurable interest, the transaction would be treated as void being by nature of a gamble.

(3) All contracts of insurance, except for life and accident insurance, are treated as contracts of indemnity and the insured may, irrespective of the amount of the policy, recover no more than the loss which he has actually suffered. If this loss exceeds the amount of the policy, no more than the sum insured for could be claimed. W.F.F.

R. P. Colinvaux, *Law of Insurance* (Sweet & Maxwell, 1970).

Integration (Vertical and Horizontal) ⟡ Diversification; Patterns of Growth.

Intelligence Sometimes defined as overall mental ability, a safer, but somewhat uninformative, definition is the operational one: 'that which intelligence tests measure'. Interest in the differences between individual human abilities led J. McKern Cattell to construct batteries of tests at the end of the nineteenth century. Later work carried out on French schoolchildren by Alfred Binet led to the construction of the first set of standardized test items.

Early thinking was centred around the concept of mental age, which is defined as the mean chronological age of children having comparable ability. The ratio of mental age to chronological yields the mental quotient which, if multiplied by 100 produces the familiar intelligence quotient, i.e.

$$IQ = \frac{MA}{CA} \times 100$$

Thus, if, for example, a child of eight years of age produces test scores comparable with those of the average child of nine years, we have

$$IQ = \frac{9}{8} \times 100 = 112\frac{1}{2}$$

More recently, the concept of mental age has been abandoned and intelligence is measured in terms of percentile ranks for persons within a given age range (⟡ Percentiles).

Factor studies (⟡ Factor Analysis) indicate the existence of such aspects of test ability as Numerical Ability, Spatial Relations, Verbal Fluency and Abstract Reasoning. Test scores are known to be dependent upon age, sex, racial and national origin, geographical background, and socio-economic level.

The chief application of the technology of intelligence testing lies in the prediction of scholastic and occupational success (⟡ Personality; Psychology). E.E.

Interference (Machines) ⟡ Machine Assignment and Interference.

Internal Rate of Return (Marginal Efficiency of Capital) This measure of the profitability of an investment project was made prominent by the economist J. M. Keynes, who called it the marginal efficiency of capital.

International Labour Organization

It may be defined as that rate of discount (interest or return) which would make the initial investment outlay exactly equal to the discounted present value of the expected net flows of funds (or cash) from that project. More concisely it is the value for r in the following equation:

$$I_0 = \frac{Y_1}{(1 + r)} + \frac{Y_2}{(1 + r)_2} + \ldots + \frac{Y_n}{(1 + r)^n},$$

where I_0 = the initial investment outlay, made now,
Y_j = the net cash flow in year j ($j = 1, 2, 3, \ldots n$),
$\quad n$ = the number of periods over which the cash flows are expected to continue,
$\quad r$ = the internal rate of return (I R R).

Given that expected values can be placed on I_0 and $Y_1, Y_2, \ldots, Y_n$, then the expression can be solved for the value of r. The I R R can be interpreted as the rate of profit implicit in the project's expected cash flows. That is to say it is the rate of profit earned on the capital initially invested after providing for the depreciation of that capital. However, it should be noted that there may, in some cases, be more than one value for r ($\diamondsuit$ Present Value versus $\diamondsuit$ Internal Rate of Return).

Thus according to this criterion of capital investment, projects are ranked in descending order of profitability according to the value of r the higher the value of r, the greater the profitability. In principle, all projects should be accepted which have a higher value for r than the company's cost of capital.

In principle and sometimes in practice, this method will not give the 'correct' ranking of projects and is generally inferior to the present value method when capital is 'rationed'. $\diamondsuit$ Present Value; Capital Budgeting. E.A.L.

A. A. Alchian, 'The Rate of Interest, Fisher's Rate of Return over Cost, and Keynes' Internal Rate of Return', *American Economic Review*, XLV (Dec. 1955), pp. 938–43.

International Labour Organization Set up in 1919 under the Treaty of Versailles, the basic aim of the International Labour Organization was the promotion of social justice by ensuring minimum standards of employment in all member states. The two main organs of the Organization are the International Labour Conference and the International Labour Office.

The Conference is the policy-making body. Each member state is represented by four persons, two of whom represent the government, one the employers and one the employees. The Conference makes its policy decisions in three forms, namely by *resolutions*, *recommendations* and *conventions*. Resolutions may be passed by a simple majority of the delegates and represent some statement of collective opinion not calling for any particular action by member states. Recommendations and conventions have to be passed by a two-thirds majority of votes and must then be submitted by the governments of member states to their respective parliaments. The difference between them is that a convention, if ratified by a member state, becomes directly binding on it and the national law will have to be altered accordingly. A recommendation calls for certain changes in national laws without (as with conventions) laying down the exact terms of the proposed change.

The International Labour Office, situated in Geneva, is the fact-finding, research and administrative section of the Organization. w.f.f.

> B. E. Lowe, *International Protection of Labour: International Labour Organisation – History and Law* (Interscience, 1935).

International Marketing The marketing of goods and services across national boundaries. Such activity gives rise to all or some of the following additional obstacles in the marketing process: language, tariffs, foreign exchange arrangements, international credit, political disturbances and cultural differences. The term is synonymous with export marketing. Although it has been traditional in most British companies to institutionalize international marketing within a separate organization framework, the development of product-oriented structures, frequently based on segmentation analysis (↺ Market Segmentation) has also led to an integration with domestic marketing. The two common patterns of organization are currently geographical areas and products. Although language and trading aspects have always received detailed attention, the contribution particularly of anthropology and sociology in different nations to the development of international marketing is of growing significance. The indigenous population is generally employed in order that localized cultural and social factors are not overlooked, and in order to avoid the cost of acquiring knowledge of, e.g. local distribution and media facilities, by expatriates. g.s.c.w.

> J. Fayerweather, *International Marketing* (Prentice-Hall, 1966).

Interviewing The interview is the most widely used technique for assessing human ability. Its popularity derives from the ease with which it can be carried out, its flexibility and enormous face validity.

There is no doubt that the interview is also the most widely misused technique. Interviewers are frequently untrained, inexperienced, stereotyped in their approach and unaware of the lack of validity in their conclusions.

Good interviewing demands skill, patience, careful planning and preparation and, above all, an appreciation of the limitations of the method. The interviewer should be quite clear about the data he is attempting to elicit, he should have a flexible, yet systematic plan of procedure; he should make the most of the opportunity to observe all aspects of the subject's behaviour; and he must have the ability of establishing swiftly the type of personal relationship which is appropriate to the particular situation.

The evidence on the validity of interviewing as a means of assessment and selection is far from encouraging. Several studies suggest that interviewing is of no value, or is even detrimental to judgements which may depend, in part, on more objective evidence. In spite of the evidence, most interviewers feel that they themselves are able to make successful use of the method. This important fact is, in itself, a cause of further problems. e.e.

> S. A. Richardson *et al.*, *Interviewing: its forms and functions* (Basic Books, 1965).

Inventories or Stocks

Inventories or Stocks Three basic types of inventory or stock exist in manufacturing systems. Their main purposes are:

1. Stocks of finished items:
   (a) To act as a buffer against fluctuations in demand for a product. Even if such fluctuations in demand could be predicted, it is often undesirable or inconvenient to accommodate them by corresponding fluctuations in the level of production. Consequently stocks of finished items are often maintained in order to permit a reasonably level production rate in the face of a fluctuating demand. (b) To provide a quick service to the customer. (c) To reduce the risk associated with stoppages or reductions in production caused by breakdowns, strikes, shortages of materials etc.

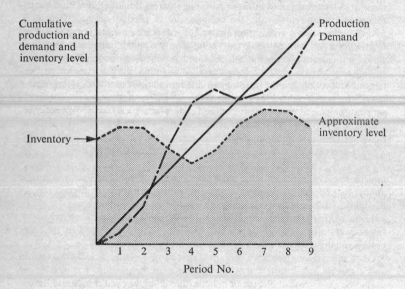

2. Work in progress:
To disconnect or decouple the various stages of production thus facilitating production planning and enabling fluctuation in output at successive stages to occur without immediately affecting other stages. This decoupling process might also enable the production rates at successive stages to be stabilized (⇦ Buffer stocks). The use of inventory to permit level production rate in face of fluctuating demand.

3. Raw materials and purchased items:
   (a) To enable advantages to be taken of bulk or other favourable purchasing terms. (b) To reduce the risk associated with delays in deliveries for other reasons. (⇦ Inventory or Stock Control Problems). R.W.

   R. Wild, *Management and Production* (Penguin Books, 1972).

210

Inventory or Stock Control Problems In this context inventory is defined as idle resources. The company usually needs to maintain some of its resources, e.g. raw materials or finished good stocks, men or money, in reserve and therefore idle stock. The function of inventory control is to determine the best level for these reserves. Taking raw material stock as an example, we may say that some costs increase and some decrease as the level of stock is increased: (a) Tied up capital, storage space, taxes and insurance costs, together with risks of obsolescence and spoilage all increase as stockholding increases. (b) Shortage, ordering and purchasing costs generally all decrease as stockholding increases.

An accurate assessment of how demand for stock items varies, using the mathematics of probability, can identify the stock level or the policy required to keep stockholding costs minimal. The minimum cost may be as much as 40% lower than that obtained by 'rule of thumb' methods and so substantial cash savings can be made.

Problems of similar logical structure arise when deciding on: (a) how many items to make in a production run, so as to minimize the total of production and finished goods stockholding costs; (b) how often to hold training courses for airline stewardesses and how large the classes should be, to ensure that an airline has adequate but not excessive supplies of trained stewardesses; (c) how much operating capital a company should carry. M.J.C.M.

Patrick Rivett and Russell L. Ackoff, *A Manager's Guide to Operational Research*, pp. 35–8 (J. Wiley, 1963).

Investment in the Economy The proportion of the Gross National Product (⟨⟩ National Income Accounts) devoted to investment is an important determinant of a country's rate of growth in productive potential. The level of investment demand is also important in determining how much of the country's productive potential is being utilized (⟨⟩ Multiplier). It is, therefore, of some importance to investigate the factors that determine investment demand; specifically we look at the factors that can influence spending on plant and machinery.

The table below gives some indication of the course of this spending since 1957; in particular we notice its variable nature compared to consumers' expenditure.

	1957	1958	1959	1960	1961	£m. 1962
All Sectors' expenditure on plant and machinery[1]	1,288	1,328	1,388	1,502	1,763	1,766
Consumers' expenditure[1]	14,582	15,362	16,175	16,990	17,903	18,991
	1963	1964	1965	1966	1967	
	1,873	2,163	2,420	2,681	2,767	
	20,195	21,577	22,956	24,296	25,323	

1. Both at current prices.

Source: National Income Blue Book, 1968.

One of the most famous explanations of investment demand is known as the acceleration principle and although it has serious deficiencies it still provides a useful starting-point. The example below is for an individual firm and for our purposes we assume that behaviour for the whole economy is an aggregation of individual behaviour patterns.

(*Years*) Time Period	*Output per period*	*Capital Required*	*Replacement*	*Net Investment*	£000 *Gross Investment*
1	50	100	10	0	10
2	50	100	10	0	10
3	60	120	10	20	30
4	70	140	10	20	30
5	85	170	10	30	40
6	85	170	10	0	10

In this example we assume that the optimum capital output ratio is 2:1, meaning by this term that two units of capital are necessary to produce one unit of output without involving either strain or under-utilization of capacity. Then an output rate of £50,000 per year would require £100,000 of capital and we assume £10,000 of this would require replacing each year. From period 3, however, the output rate moves as shown. As output increases new capital is required and the effect is that whilst output increases by 20% between periods 2 and 3, gross investment demand increases by 200%. Similarly between periods 5 and 6, there is no increase in output, whilst gross investment demand falls by 75%. The name 'acceleration principle' is given because net investment depends upon the acceleration or deceleration of output. Clearly when aggregation takes place over all firms this would lead to severe fluctuations in investment demand, certainly far more severe than appears to happen in practice. Why is this? The fundamental answer is that the acceleration principle, whilst beautiful in its simplicity, cannot stand by itself as an explanation of investment demand. It needs qualifications and we must also introduce other factors. To take the qualifications first, it is unlikely that a rigid capital output ratio is adhered to as output expands or contracts. Much depends upon the existence of unused capacity and businessmen's estimates of the likely permanence of increases and decreases in demand. We must also take account of businessmen's expectations about the future and the time scale on which investment projects are planned.

All this suggests that the acceleration principle will only provide a partial explanation of investment demand. This is so when one thinks of one factor which has been omitted from consideration: present and future profits. In recent years companies appear to have provided between 50% and 60% of the funds needed for investment projects from their retained profits and this points to the influence of present profits as a source of funds. On the other hand, future profits are anyway the main rationale for investment and they figure extensively in the evaluation of investment projects. It therefore seems that any analysis of investment demand must include both profits and the acceleration principle, or some variant of it. ⟨⟩ Growth; The Multiplier. L.T.S.

C. Schultze, *National Income Analysis* (Prentice-Hall, 1964).

J

Jaques, Elliot ⟡ Time-span of Discretion.

Job Analysis The method or technique of obtaining all the facts about a job in such a way that they can be used for various purposes in ⟡ Personnel Management. The process starts with a detailed study and description of the tasks that make up a job; this is then analysed under headings such as job requirements (skill, knowledge, physical and mental effort), responsibility (for people, materials, to customers), and working conditions (physical environment and hazards). The job analysis forms the basis of a job specification which is a description of the individual qualifications and disqualifications (age, sex, education history, experience, etc.) required of a person who is to do the job. A job analysis can be used for the ⟡ Selection, placement, ⟡ Industrial Training and promotion of employees. It can also be used for job evaluation, i.e. the rating of jobs against each other according to comparative skills, responsibilities, etc. Job evaluation is used to determine wage and salary differentials. It may be described as a rational method of doing this, but it is not scientific, as it is not possible to quantify accurately the relative importance in a job of aspects as different as are, for example, skill and effort. In practice, at the basis of most systems of job evaluation there is a reference to traditional views of grading jobs; nevertheless it is a technique which brings to light inconsistencies and is more objective than the alternatives. ⟡ Job Evaluation. L.S.

J. L. Otis and R. H. Leukart, *Job Evaluation* (Prentice-Hall, 1954); H. E. Roff and T. E. Watson, *Job Analysis* (I P M, 1961)

Job Description ⟡ Job Analysis.

Job Enlargement To build up the content of jobs so as to increase the skill, interest, initiative and responsibility required of employees. It aims to reduce the frustration and monotony associated with much routine factory and office work and it challenges the view that higher productivity is inevitably associated with an extension of the division of labour. If, it is argued, more use is made of human capacities, stronger ⟡ Motivation can lead to levels of labour productivity which are higher than those associated with a narrow specialization of tasks. An example occurred in a factory making typewriters. Men had only been responsible for fitting parts of typewriters to a frame on an assembly belt. They were given the additional tasks of aligning the parts, of inspecting the completed task and of some maintenance work. Job enlargement meant increased scope for initiative and skill; it up-graded the job and increased both the earnings of the workers and the productivity of the process. Job enlargement is an aspect of policies for the improved use of manpower (⟡ Manpower Planning) and is closely associated with ⟡ Selection and training (⟡ Industrial Training). L.S.

Georges Friedman, *The Anatomy of Work* (Heinemann, 1961).

Job Evaluation

Job Evaluation The comparison of jobs by the use of formal and systematic procedures in order to determine the relative position of one job to another in a wage or salary hierarchy.

Job evaluation is essentially concerned with relationships and not absolutes. It provides data for developing basic pay structures but cannot determine what the pay levels should be. It is the job that is evaluated, not the job's current occupant. Job evaluation methods do, however, depend to some extent on a series of subjective judgements made in the light of concepts like logic, justice and equity and the progressive refinement of job evaluation techniques is in large measure an attempt to minimize the subjective personal element.

Before embarking on job evaluation it is advisable to apply ⟴ Job Analysis in order to gain detailed knowledge of the requirements and specifications of the jobs under review. Once this has been done it will then be possible to decide which particular job evaluation scheme is most suitable. The size and complexity of the graded job hierarchy which emerges, and ultimately of the revised pay structure (⟴ Wage Systems) which is the end-product of the whole exercise, depends upon the type of job evaluation adopted.

There are four main types of job evaluation in common use:

(1) *Ranking*. This method is simple and non-quantitative. It aims to determine the importance of a job by descriptive comparison with another. Under this approach a few 'key' jobs tend to determine the rank of all the others. The advantages are that it is easily understood and administered but, on the other hand, it has no defined standards of judgement, it becomes increasingly difficult to apply as the range of jobs widens (i.e. as the firm grows) and leaves the assessors more open to influence by the current occupants of the jobs under review.

(2) *Grading*. Basically the same as (1) except that whilst with the latter the number of grades and their pay levels are determined *after* the jobs have been evaluated and ranked, under the grading system the order is reversed.

(3) *Factor Comparison*. Examines jobs in terms of selected factors such as mental, physical and skill requirements, responsibility and working conditions. 'Key' jobs are examined factor by factor and a rank order produced for each factor used. An attempt is then made to establish how much of the current wage rate of each key job is being paid for each factor. The total rate for all the other jobs is similarly determined by the sum of the individual factor values. The criteria employed under this method are more objective but it is complex, difficult to explain to those affected, and is arbitrary in the way in which existing wage rates are ascribed to different factors.

(4) *Points Rating*. Also analyses jobs in terms of a number of components but here the results are expressed in numerical rather than monetary rank-order. This method utilizes a wider and more flexible range of factors, each of which is allocated a set of points. A total points' score then determines the position of each job in a hierarchy, at the same time indicating numerically the relationship between one job and another. One big advantage here is that the processes of money wage fixing and job evaluation are clearly separated, since the translation of points into money values is a distinct process.

Analytical methods like (3) and (4) obviously allow a finer distinction to be drawn between jobs and so provide a more acceptable basis for showing whether jobs which have changed in content should also change in pay. Control over the wage structure is thus made easier. One of the basic causes of wage inflation (⟡ Wage Drift) is that ⟡ Workplace Bargaining so often takes place on a piecemeal, fragmented basis giving rise to anomalies and compensatory counter-claims from individual work groups. Job evaluation means the comparison of jobs, not men, by systematic analysis, to determine their place in a hierarchy and thus offers a basis for a structure of pay which can at least be presented as rational. Job evaluation, therefore, forces on management the same disciplined approach to personnel problems as is required in other spheres. Conversely, for the employee. job evaluation means that increase in skills and responsibility can be rewarded and recognized.

From the evidence gathered by the Ministry of Labour in a survey (June 1967) it is clear that job evaluation is used predominantly by large firms. Some 23 % of the 6,431,100 employees covered had their pay grade determined by job evaluation, but these were employed in only 9 % of all establishments. Only 6·4 % of firms with less than 500 employees used job evaluation, compared with 32·2 % for firms with over 500. Industries like timber, construction, printing, shipbuilding and leather goods, where job relationships seem deeply rooted in tradition and craftsmen are numerous, are those which are least affected by job evaluation. The NBPI *Report No. 83* found that job evaluation is applied most widely to the 'managerial' occupational group (30 % of the workers covered in the survey) followed by staff (27 %) and non-craft workers (26 %). The smallest coverage was of craftsmen (11 %). Coal-mining, a single-employer industry, and tobacco manufacture, an industry dominated by a few large companies, are the two industries in which job evaluation is most widespread. N.H.C.

NBPI *Report No. 83*, and Statistical Supplement, '*Job Evaluation*', Cmnd. 3772 (H M S O, Sept. 1968).

Job Enlargement ⟡ Job Restructuring.

Job Enrichment ⟡ Job Restructuring.

Job Restructuring Job restructuring is concerned with job and work changes, i.e. the modification of the tasks and involvement of individuals. Restructuring which leads to the addition of further similar tasks is often referred to as job enlargement and can be seen as a horizontal change. Vertical changes involve increased individual involvement through perhaps the addition of different tasks and duties – such changes are generally referred to as job enrichment.

Job restructuring, i.e. individual work and job changes, should be distinguished from organizational changes which generally concentrate on groups of workers (⟡ Group Working) or aim to provide increased job variety for individuals without the modification of jobs, e.g. job rotation. Such organizational changes will often give rise to some form of job restructuring – indeed, in many cases job restructuring is possible only as a consequence of organizational change. R.W.

Job Rotation ⟡ Job Restructuring.

Job Specification ⟡ Job Analysis.

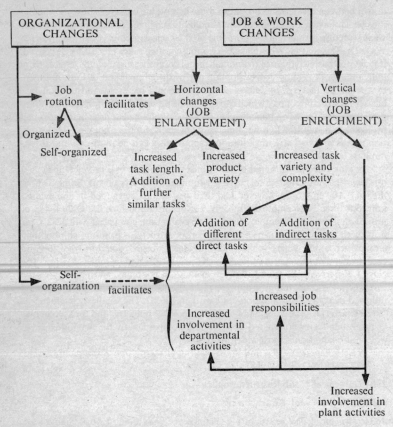

Types of Job Restructuring

Jobbing Production Jobbing type production is concerned with the simultaneous manufacture of a series of different products in very small or unit batch sizes to customer orders.

Because of the differing and often unique nature of the products, a jobbing shop is normally characterized by the following:

(1) General purpose production equipment.

(2) Equipment arranged according to the type of work performed (Layout by process). ⟢ Plant Layout.

(3) Differing sequence of operations for each product.

(4) Large range of operation times for different operations and jobs and inaccurate prediction of individual operation times.

Items 3 and 4 above give rise to considerable planning and control problems.

Production control in jobbing type production is more difficult than in any other type of production. Accurate scheduling is almost impossible, and the sequencing or despatching problem is considerable (⟡ Sequencing and Despatching Problems).

Because of the difficulty in planning and control a situation normally exists where high work-in-progress stock is accompanied by under-utilization of equipment, and products require a total production time (i.e. processing and waiting) far greater than the processing time (often as high as 10:1).

Items 1 and 2 above facilitate ⟡ Plant Layout, supervisions, provision of services, etc. but complicate materials handling. R.W.

Joint Consultation The process of discussion of the common problems of an enterprise between employers and employees, usually through representatives. It takes place at all levels of an undertaking; but the term is most commonly applied to meetings between the representatives of senior management and of workers on the shop floor in Joint Consultative Committees or Works Councils. These committees deal with questions of health, training, discipline, welfare and safety and, sometimes, changes in methods of production. They are not usually concerned with questions of wages and conditions of employment which are negotiated with trade unions. ⟡ Collective Bargaining, Wages. The committee's functions are normally advisory rather than executive, but the distinction may be blurred, for example, a Joint Consultative Committee may have authority over some welfare and social activities. As trade unions become concerned to negotiate over ⟡ Fringe Benefits it is argued, especially by trade unionists, that most of the matters dealt with by Joint Consultative Committees might well be transferred to Joint Negotiating Committees. This would enlarge the authority of the workers' representatives and, by relating the discussions to decisions, increase the importance of the consultative process. The critics of joint consultation consider that the meetings of committees are an unnecessary intrusion on the normal lines of authority from managers, through foremen to shop-floor workers, and from ⟡ Shop Stewards and trade union officials to employees. But these criticisms can be met, at least in part, by ensuring the representation of foremen on the committees and by requiring that the workers' representatives shall be members of trade unions. It is important to consider and evaluate joint consultation for its contribution to the whole system of ⟡ Communication in an enterprise. ⟡ Joint Industrial Council. L.S.

National Institute of Industrial Psychology, *Joint Consultation in British Industry* (Staples Press, 1952); H. A. Clegg, *A new approach to industrial democracy* (Blackwell, 1960).

Joint Consultative Committee ⟡ Joint Consultation.

Joint Industrial Council A collective bargaining and/or consultative committee for an industry or public service with a constitution based on the model laid down by the Whitley Committee set up by the government in 1916. Hence some Joint Industrial Councils are known as Whitley Councils (⟡ Collective Bargaining; Joint Consultation).

During the First World War the government became concerned about industrial unrest, much of which seemed to stem from the unofficial Shop Stewards' Movement (⟡ Industrial Democracy; Trade Union Types – Industrial Union; Shop Steward). It therefore set up the Whitley Committee to make suggestions for improving relations between employers and employees. The Committee proposed the formation of Joint Industrial Councils at industry level and Works Committees at the workplace, both representative of managements and employees; the extension of statutory wage regulation in industries badly organized in terms of trade unions and employers' associations (⟡ Wages Councils); the setting up of a permanent court of arbitration (⟡ Industrial Court); and the authorization of governmental inquiry into disputes (⟡ Court of Inquiry, Industrial Dispute). The policy suggested was adopted, although Joint Industrial Councils were not set up in industries where adequate collective bargaining arrangements existed. There are today some 200 Joint Industrial Councils or bodies of a similar character.

Although largely based on a model constitution, Joint Industrial Councils present considerable variety in structure, in their degree of authority in the industry, and in the nature and extent of their activities. While a few Councils deal only with the negotiation of wages and conditions, most have at some time dealt with other matters. Conversely, there are examples of Councils which do not negotiate wages. Among the matters dealt with are research, welfare, health and safety, and training, including apprenticeship. In some Joint Industrial Council Industries there are District Councils which may have a limited amount of local autonomy.

Joint Industrial Councils with District Councils have been established for local authorities in England and Wales, one each for white collar and for manual workers. There is a National Whitley Council together with Departmental Councils for the administrative and legal department of the Civil Service and, for government industrial employees, a Council for each of the main employing departments. Food manufacture provides a private sector example. N.H.C.

Industrial Relations Handbook (H M S O, revised edn., 1961).

Joint Stock Company ⟡ Company Law.

L

Laboratory Training A method of training in interpersonal and intergroup relationships which consists of a temporary (and often residential) community of persons who undergo a series of planned experiences in a social atmosphere which supports personal experiment and learning. A frequent feature of laboratory training is the T group but other more structured activities may also be used. ⟡ Group Methods of Training. I.C.MCG.

Labour Relations ⟡ Industrial Relations.

Labour Stability ⟡ Labour Turnover.

Labour Turnover An index of the number of people who leave an enterprise in a given period as a percentage of the average number of people employed during that period. The standard formula for calculating labour turnover is:

$$\frac{\text{Number of separations during the period}}{\text{Average number employed during period}} \times \frac{100}{1} \times \frac{12}{X}$$

In certain circumstances labour turnover may be an index of the effectiveness of company policy in personnel matters. If there is a high *overall* figure in an establishment, with all departments and categories of workers affected in similar degree, then some fundamental defects in the pay, recruitment, training and promotion situations are highly likely. But this situation is almost hypothetical and it is far more common for a particular department or a particular class of employee within a firm to display a significantly higher rate of turnover than elsewhere, and here the nature of the work undertaken is the key factor.

In the vast majority of firms unskilled workers have an annual rate of turnover markedly in advance of their skilled colleagues, female workers have a higher rate than male, and young workers higher than their seniors. Departments like the foundry and the canteen may always, by their very nature, be unable to retain more than a relatively low percentage of their work force for any length of time. In these circumstances personnel policies can have little more than a purely marginal effect on labour turnover. Because of social and family preoccupations female labour is notoriously unstable, so that industries employing relatively large proportions of women, such as textiles and the distributive trades, tend to have relatively high average rates of turnover irrespective of the quality of individual personnel management. This high turnover tends to keep wages down and often prevents trade unions from achieving a sufficient level of organization in an establishment to achieve much in the way of improved conditions, all of which in turn promotes labour instability. In the four weeks ending 17 May 1969, for example, the following labour turnover figures were recorded:

Language

Industry	Number of engagements per 100 employed at beginning of period			Number of discharges per 100 employed at beginning of period		
	Males	*Females*	*Total*	*Males*	*Females*	*Total*
Food, drink, tobacco	3·9	5·6	4·6	4·0	5·0	4·4
Chemical and allied	2·1	4·0	2·6	2·2	4·2	2·7
Metal manufacture	2·4	3·2	2·5	2·7	2·9	2·7
Engineering and electrical	2·4	4·0	2·8	2·7	4·1	3·0
Vehicles	1·7	3·4	1·9	1·9	3·1	2·0
Textiles	3·9	4·1	4·0	4·0	4·1	4·0
Clothing/footwear	2·6	3·7	3·4	3·4	4·2	4·0
Paper/printing	2·1	3·7	2·6	2·1	3·8	2·6

Source: *D EP Gazette*, August 1969

High labour turnover and low stability indices bring to light the number and kind of replacements which a company is having to make. Replacement, which means finding, selecting and training new employees, is expensive and adds appreciably to labour costs. Thus in order to discover the causes of wastage many firms have systematic interviews with all leavers. An analysis of the results provides evidence which may lead to changes in personnel policy. In other words more and more personnel managers are approaching the problem of labour turnover with the object in mind of maximizing retention rates. The one sure way to reduce high rates of turnover is to strengthen the incentives for employees to keep their current jobs.

High turnover can have a bad effect on the morale of the remainder of the work force, especially that of supervisory staff. It is important, therefore, to distinguish between the loss of newly-hired workers and of long-serving employees. The key index is the proportion of workers who stay with the firm for an appreciable time.

One of the most common reasons for high turnover is the division of responsibility between those who engage labour and those who manage it. Foremen and supervisors, for example, frequently complain that they are sent unsuitable people. One way of tackling turnover in the larger firms, therefore, would appear to be the appointment of a manager with specific responsibilities for the 'nursing' of new labour. N.H.C.

British Institute of Management, *The Cost of Labour Turnover* (1959).

Language Efficient communication depends largely upon the existence and use of an appropriate language, whether the communication is between human beings or between men and machines. Such natural languages as English or German exhibit an enormous complexity; their vocabularies are large, and the rules by which words can be assembled into meaningful utterances are many. Over and above the questions of literal meaning are the further complications associated with emotive overtones of statements, and the aesthetic value of certain word juxtapositions.

Apart from the natural languages, extensive use is made of other information sources during man–man communication such as the interpretation of posture and gesture. Other indirect means of communication between men involve such special purpose symbol systems as those used in mathematics, musical notation, maps and engineering drawings. Very little research has yet been done in an attempt to study the efficiency of such language systems or to produce superior ones.

The study of language in the context of man–machine communication is still in its infancy, but will certainly occupy an ever-increasing role in human factors studies as technological innovation proceeds. Obvious examples of areas where some progress has already been made include telephone dialling codes, aircraft instrumentation and computer autocodes.

The existence of an appropriate language facilitates not only efficient man–man or man–machine communication but also contributes a good deal to the way in which a single individual can handle problems. Mathematics provides a ready example. It is a simple matter to evaluate the sum $134 + 69$ using the familiar Arabic notation, but extremely difficult to solve the same problem translated into Roman notation, CXXXIV + LXIX. E.E.

Lateral Integration ⇧ Patterns of Growth.

Leadership The process whereby an individual exerts a positive influence over the behaviour of others without the use of coercion.

Leadership is important for the success of any group activity although the nature or style of the leadership needed in one situation may differ substantially from that required in another. Traditionally, leadership has tended to be equated with autocratic command and there are still many who see leadership mainly in terms of the issuing of orders which are eagerly obeyed by followers whose loyalty is largely determined by the ⇧ Charisma of the leader. An earlier generation of social psychologists devoted much time to an endeavour to identify those specific traits of character or personality which distinguished leaders from followers. The attempt was unsuccessful and attention has since been directed towards the conception of leadership as a process rather than as a particular pattern of personality traits. The current view, therefore, is that the leader cannot usefully be considered apart from the situation in which he exercises his leadership and that his personal characteristics and abilities are seen as only one variable amongst others: (1) the personality of the leader; (2) the expectations and needs of the followers; (3) the structure of the group and the immediate situation which confronts it; and (4) the wider cultural environment within which the group is located. ⇧ Authority. I.C.MCG.

D. McGregor, *The Human Side of Enterprise* (McGraw-Hill, 1960).

Learning and Training In view of the variety of different occupational skills which personnel are called upon to acquire, it is impossible to lay down a set of simple and comprehensive rules by which training programmes should be devised. Nonetheless, there are some general principles of human learning which require to be observed in the development of any training programme.

Little or no improvement will result from unmotivated trainees. Appropriate incentives such as cash rewards, promotion prospects or the attainment of status and reputation, may serve as methods for producing an adequate motivational level.

Generally speaking, learning will be facilitated by short periods of instruction followed by rest or at least a relief from novelty. As skill is acquired, the length of the training session may be increased.

It is essential that the trainee should be provided with information about his achievement. This should be accurate and comprehensive and should be given as soon as possible after each trial. One of the advantages of the use of automatic machines as trainers is the speed and precision with which they may display results of trials.

In many cases it is advisable to present the trainee with an overall view of the total task before detailed instruction is provided in the performance of the individual task elements. In this way, the trainee is able to build up a correct view of the whole skill, and bring about an appropriate synthesis of the elements when these have been learned. In certain types of skilled activity this synthesis (involving perhaps elements of timing) is the essence of successful performance.

Habit interference occurs when practice at one activity brings about a decrement in another. This may be minimized by making as different as possible both inputs and outputs which might be confused. Consistency in training procedures similarly minimizes interference. Thus meticulous standardization is required when, for example, several different instructors contribute to a training programme.

There is a good deal of evidence to contradict the widely-held misconception that older people cannot benefit from training. It is, however, usually the case that more time is required by an older man to acquire new knowledge and skills. ⟡ Industrial Training. E.E.

    S. S. Stevens, *Handbook of Experimental Psychology* (J. Wiley, 1960).

Leverage ⟡ Capital Structure.

Liability ⟡ Claims.

Library (computer) ⟡ Hardware/Liveware/Software.

Lighting ⟡ Illumination.

Line and Staff (1) Line functions are those which are specifically charged with the responsibility for directly achieving the objectives of the organization. Staff functions are those responsible for assisting the line. This classification by function seems gradually to be losing favour as the closely interdependent nature of the various functions in the organization is increasingly recognized. With such interdependence it seems neither logical nor useful to attempt to classify departments according to their implied importance in the attainment of organizational objectives. Accordingly, many writers now regard the description of some functions as primary, with the relegation of others to secondary status, as more likely to lead to confusion than to clarity in the analysis of organizational relationships. I.C.MCG.

Line and Staff (2) A line relationship is the authority relationship between superior and subordinate in the chain of command. A staff relationship is a service or advisory relationship. These usages derive from a (mistaken) analogy with military organization. The concept of a line relationship is reasonably unambiguous but in military, as well as in industrial, organization non-line relationships are too complex to permit the use of a single classificatory term. A production department, for example, is likely to interact with maintenance department, production scheduling, progress department, budget control, personnel department and so on. It would seem very probable that each relationship so established would differ significantly from each of the others. Organization theory, however, has not yet developed a terminology which gives recognition to these differences. The existence of staff relationships violates the principle of unity of command although this violation has been obscured by the insistence that, in theory, such relationships are advisory. Recently, however, there has been a greater willingness to recognize that many 'advisory' relationships involve functional authority and that organizational difficulties frequently resulted from the failure to make this explicit. ⟡ Authority; Chain of Command; Functional. I.C.MCG.

D. McGregor, *The Human Side of Enterprise* (McGraw-Hill, 1960); W. Brown, *Exploration in Management* (Heinemann, 1960).

Linear Programming ⟡ Mathematical Programming.

Liveware ⟡ Hardware/Liveware/Software.

Location of Industry and Regional Problems The depressed economic conditions of the 1930s in the UK drew attention to the plight of several areas dependent upon old established industries such as coal, iron and steel, textiles and shipbuilding. The problem of these areas was that the population was heavily dependent upon these industries, alternative employment opportunities being rare. Although the problem has not recurred on such a scale in the postwar world, nonetheless the following table illustrates its presence.

Wholly Unemployed 1959–66[1]
Annual Averages – percentages

	Great Britain	Development Areas	Rest of Great Britain
1959	2·0	3·8	1·6
1961	1·3	2·8	0·9
1963	2·2	4·4	1·6
1965	1·3	2·8	0·9

1. Extracted from *DEA Progress Report*, No, 28, May 1967.

The location of an industrial enterprise depends upon two sets of costs, these being transport costs and processing costs. Transport costs cover the cost of transporting materials and fuel to the point of manufacture and transporting the finished product to the market. Processing costs depend upon the cost of raw materials, labour, capital equipment and managerial expertise. On the whole there is little evidence of regional variation in processing costs and thus location has been determined in the past by the incidence of transport costs. The majority of our old-established industries are materials-dominated and hence were located close to coal, iron ore and adequate water supplies. On the other hand the new and growing industries have been freed from the coalfields by the development of new fuels and since, on the whole, transport costs to the market have dominated, they have settled close to the large centres of population in the Midlands and the South-East. Thus, we have the present situation of the Development Areas with too little diversification, too much labour and too few jobs. This has meant that when the rest of the economy is booming, the Development Areas are just beginning really to move and hence they suffer when brakes to the economy are imposed.

Over the years from the 1930s government policy has varied both in the amount of aid and the areas to which it has been applied. After moving through a period in the late 1950s when aid was channelled to small Development Districts, attention focused again on larger areas. Under the *Industry Act*, 1970 there are now three different categories of assisted area: Special Development Areas, Development Areas and Intermediate Areas and, broadly, they cover Scotland, Wales, the Northern Region, the North West Region, Yorkshire and Humberside, Cornwall, and parts of Devon, Derbyshire and Nottinghamshire. In these areas basic investment incentives available countrywide are supplemented by a new system of regional development grants. These grants are cash grants towards the cost of plant, machinery and buildings and currently are valued around 20% of cost. In general it may be said that the incentive system is now more profit centred, proportionately more weight being given to tax allowances and less to cash grants. In addition the Department of Trade and Industry can still provide modern factories for sale or rent on favourable terms, and loans on preferential terms for projects providing employment. Finally, other government departments can help with labour difficulties such as retraining and rehousing. One final inducement for firms to move to these areas has been the Regional Employment Premium and although it was phased out in 1974 it represented a cash subsidy for each employee in a manufacturing establishment.

In addition to these inducements, several checks on expansion are available ranging from Industrial Development Certificates and local planning machinery to the controls over new office building in the London area.

One other positive measure has been the creation of new towns throughout the country. These have helped to disperse industry from congested urban areas and there are now over 22 new towns in Britain.

The interest in wider areas is also seen in the creation of regional economic planning machinery. In each of the eight regions there is an Economic Planning Council and a Board. The former consists of part-time members and has advisory functions, whilst the latter consists of senior civil servants. Their role is to transmit the regional viewpoint into national planning and all have now produced studies and/or plans of their region's past and future development. L.T.S.

H. G. Hunt, *Industrial Economics* (Pergamon Press, 1965).

Lock-out Defined by the ⟐ *Industrial Relations Act*, 1971, repealed 1974, as 'action which, in contemplation or furtherance of an ⟐ industrial dispute, is taken by one or more employers, whether parties to the dispute or not, and which consists of the exclusion of workers from one or more factories, offices or other places of work in one or more such places or of the collective, simultaneous or otherwise connected termination or suspension of employment of a group of workers.'

The Act laid down that dismissal by way of a lock-out was fair, and not an ⟡ unfair industrial practice as long as the person concerned was offered re-engagement. The ⟡ *Trade Union and Labour Relations Act*, 1974 contains a provision similiar in principle.

In practice it may be difficult to distinguish a lock-out from a strike, trade unionists claiming that they are locked out of work and employers claiming that their employees are not entitled to be on the work premises since they have taken strike or other action in attempt to settle an ⟡ industrial dispute.

The incidence of lock-outs varies by industry, by country, and by time. Britain experienced a high incidence in the nineteenth century, especially in those industries with a tough industrial relations environment, like coal-mining. ⟡ Strike – causes; forms; remedies; statistics. N.H.C.

Lot Sizes ⟡ Batch Sizes.

Loudness ⟡ Hearing; Noise.

M

McGregor, Douglas ◊ Line and Staff (2).

Machine Assignment and Interference If, when several machines are assigned to the care of one operator, two or more of the machines require his attention at the same time, machine interference occurs, and waiting time results.

i.e. If a = Combined work time per cycle for operator and machine
(e.g. working together, setting, loading, etc.),
b = Operator independent work time per cycle,
t = Machine independent work time per cycle,
n = Number of machines; n^1 = Ideal n.

If a, b and t are constant then ideally $n^1 = \dfrac{a + t}{a + b}$ machines must be assigned to the operator. However, where any or all of these values are not stable and/or where n^1 is not an integer, interference is usually unavoidable.

The effect of such interferences, as with any other delay, is to reduce or limit output and, consequently, some measure of interference must be available for: (1) inclusion as an allowance in the calculation of standard times in Work Measurement. (◊ Allowances) (2) use in production planning.

Given certain assumptions about the nature of variables a, b and t, analytical methods may be used to determine working time, least cost assignment, etc. Alternatively, direct time studies and/or work sampling can be used to determine machine interference, which often accounts for from 10% to 35% of total time required. R.W.

> H. B. Maynard, (ed.), *Handbook of Industrial Engineering* (McGraw-Hill, 2nd ed., 1963).

Machine Controls A control is a device by which a man provides information or energy for a machine. Typical controls include pedals, joy-sticks, switches, hand-wheels and knobs.

The ideal control for any specific application is a function of its purpose and conditions of use. The relevant variables to be considered include the speed, range, direction, frequency, duration, precision and force for which control movements are called. Thus, for example, cranks are suitable for high rates of rotation and where a wide range of adjustment is required with a fairly heavy load. If, however, the load is light, the extent of the range is fairly small and accurate adjustment is called for, then a knob is probably more suitable. Relative merits of various control devices, together with detailed design recommendations, are well documented in the literature.

The correct grouping of machine controls in a cab is of utmost importance in order to ensure that an operator is able to use the controls either simultaneously or in swift succession as required. In such a situation a proper system of coding,

226

based upon position, size, colour or shape, will assist in the avoidance of mistaken operation. In certain cases, a device to avoid inadvertant operation of certain controls is desirable.

Certain associations are generally expected between directions of control movement and the corresponding machine response. An upwards control movement, for example, is usually associated with an upward, forward or increasing response. These expected relationships should, as far as possible, be maintained.

Similarly, there are expected relationships between control movements and resulting display changes. Both qualitative and quantitative aspects require careful attention (⟡ Machine Dynamics; Stereotypes).

Frequently the same physical component serves as both display and control. In this case, special problems arise from competing requirements of the two uses. Design decisions should only be made with full knowledge of the limitations imposed by a compromise solution. E.E.

E. J. McCormick, *Human Factors Engineering* (McGraw-Hill, 1964).

Machine Dynamics Effective ergonomics design of a man–machine system demands attention being paid to three areas of the system, viz. the interface which serves as an input to the human operator (⟡ Displays); the interface at the machine input (⟡ Machine Controls); the properties of the hardware system which determine the relationship between its inputs and displayed outputs. In order that man–machine effectiveness may be facilitated, both the qualitative (⟡ Stereotypes) and the quantitative aspects of machine dynamics should be engineered to suit the relevant characteristics of the human controller.

In the case of a simple linear relationship between control and display movements, the critical design factor is the ratio between control displacement and corresponding display movement. Optimization of this ratio may reduce positioning time by several seconds.

The introduction of more sophisticated control mechanisms brings about the need to satisfy numerous design criteria dictated by the characteristics of human performance. Time lags in human response of the order of half a second or so are typical, and are dependent upon the sensory modality of the signal input, its intensity, its uncertainty (⟡ Information Theory), its duration, its complexity and several other factors.

The functional relationship between machine input and displayed output requires careful design attention. In many tracking tasks, such as those associated with vehicle guidance or process control, the relation between control movement and corresponding display movement may be non-linear. An example of one such system is illustrated in Figure 1. Here the machine output comprises a summation of three functions which are related to the input signals by amplification factors (K_1, K_2, K_3) and/or time integrals. The ratio of the amplification factors in such a system (in this case it is an acceleration-aided control system) must be established empirically, being dependent upon the type of signal input, the properties of the control elements etc.

Should there of necessity be three or more stages of integration relating the movement of a control element and the consequent system response, control performance is greatly enhanced by the application of quickening, i.e. the production of a contrived display fed from a number of sources within the system, suitably combined. A quickened fourth-order system is illustrated in Figure 2. E.E.

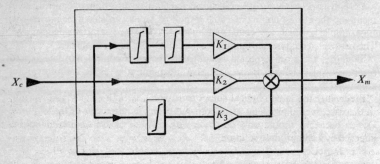

Figure 1. The dynamics of an acceleration aided system. The relation beteeen the control output, X_c, and the machine output, X_m, is given by the equation

$$X_m = k_2 X_c + k_3 \int X_c \ dt + k_1 \iint X_c \ dt$$

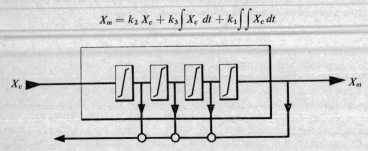

Figure 2. A fourth-order control system in which four signals are mixed to provide the feedback to the display. This 'quickening' makes much easier the operator's control task.

Macro-economic Models (in Economic Analysis) Macro-economic models, as their name implies, are the formal representation of economists' notions about the determination of such macro variables as consumption expenditures, investment expenditures and total employment. As such they are relevant to government policy-making, quite apart from their role in economics. Whilst a considerable number of models have now been built for various countries, only one country, Holland, has incorporated a full model into its planning procedure. In other countries one sometimes finds part of a model in use, although this does not always imply the existence of a full model.

The purpose of such models is twofold. On the one hand they tell us about the behaviour of groups in the economy such as consumers and producers who are simultaneously acting together. On the other hand they can tell us something about the likely path of certain key variables in the future.

The simplest type of model which will serve for illustrative purposes is given below. It consists of a consumption function, equation (1), and the national income identity, equation (2), there being no government or foreign trade sector:

$$C_t = a + B Y_t \tag{1}$$
$$Y_t = C_t + I_t \tag{2}$$

where C_t = purchases of consumption goods
I_t = purchases of investment goods
Y_t = aggregate output (= income), all at time t.

These two equations are called the structural equations of the model because they explain the structure of all or part of the economy. As it stands, however, knowledge of a and B will not enable us to determine C_t, I_t and Y_t because we have too many variables and too few equations. Suppose, however, we assume that investment decisions are given by some process unrelated to economic conditions. Then we say that investment is an exogenous variable, because it is determined outside our model. Now we are left with two variables to be determined by the model, C_t and Y_t, and we term these variables endogenous variables. Solution of (1) and (2) will yield values for C_t and Y_t, determined by a, B and I_t.

$$C_t = \frac{a}{1-B} + \frac{B}{1-B} I_t \tag{3}$$

$$Y_t = \frac{a}{1-B} + \frac{1}{1-B} I_t \tag{4}$$

For obvious reasons these two equations are called the *reduced-form* equations.

This model has only been used for illustrative purposes. If we are interested in the behaviour of consumers then we need the structural version of the model. If, however, we are interested in tracing the impact of a change in I_t, then we must use the reduced-form version.

Realistic models of advanced economies may require anything from 10 to 50 equations depending upon the degree of disaggregation. In addition, many endogenous variables in equations such as (1) will be found to depend upon lagged variables as well as current variables. In all cases, however, their purpose is to show the structural and reduced form relationships. Problems of data collection and estimation abound but this is no argument against the models themselves, but rather a stimulus to improvement, for thereby will the government and other users of these models see more clearly the implications of alternative policies. ⟨⟩ Model (in Economic Analysis); Economics. L.T.S.

M. R. Fisher, *Macro-Economic Models*, Eaton Paper No. 2 (Institute of Economic Affairs, 1964).

Mail Order The process by which manufacturers or wholesalers sell to their customers, using postal or delivery services to effect distribution (⟨⟩ Distribution Mix). In Britain, this business is most commonly conducted through female, part-time agents who pass catalogues amongst potential customers, and act as a distribution point. The method more common in North America, and which is growing in Britain, involves the use of small keyed advertisements in newspapers, etc. The telephone is also increasingly being used in addition to letter post for the placing of orders. In 1967 it was estimated that there were some $2\frac{1}{2}$ million agents, who received commission at approximately 10% on sales made. The average sales per agent were £150 p.a. The trade is predominantly with the lower social classes and, although it showed dramatic growth in the 1950s and early 1960s, it still accounts for less than 5% of total retail sales volume. ⟡ Retailing. G.S.C.W.

Maintenance The various activities involved in keeping equipment or a system in working order, or in returning equipment or a system to working order.

In practice equipment is expected to break down and/or require attention; consequently an operational definition of maintenance must involve the concept of reliability, i.e. to ensure at minimum cost that equipment operates at a certain level of reliability or to increase the reliability of equipment.

Reliability of equipment can be retained or improved by:

(1) Improvements in equipment design.

(2) Use of a sufficiently large repair department to minimize breakdown time.

(3) The use of preventive maintenance to minimize breakdowns.

In addition reliability of a production system can be improved by:

(4) Sufficient work in progress between production stages to minimize the probability that the breakdown of equipment at one stage will affect production at successive stages.

(5) Provision of duplicate equipment or excess capacity.

Only (2) and (3) above are direct approaches to ensuring or improving reliability. There will always be a need for a repair or breakdown function since, even with ⟡ Preventive Maintenance, breakdowns will still occur.

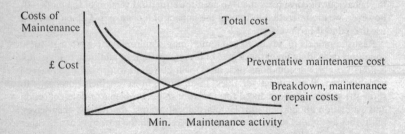

The object is to minimize total maintenance cost by (1) determining, often for each piece of equipment, the optimum relationship between breakdown and preventive maintenance, from (a) a distribution of breakdowns obtained either from records, other users or manufacturers, (b) the relative total costs of preventive and breakdown maintenance for the equipment or system; (2) determining the optimum amount of replacement or repair work to undertake as a result of, or to prevent, a breakdown. When failure occurs or is expected in a com-

230

ponent the following alternatives are available: (a) replace that component only; (b) replace that and all similar components; (c) replace that component and selected others (e.g. those exceeding mean life). Optimum policy may after be determined by means of simulation, from cost and life data. (3) Determining optimum staff requirements, i.e. balance the cost of staff with the cost of waiting for maintenance, either from records or perhaps by using simulation or queueing theory. R.W.

L. J. Garrett and M. Silver. *Production Management Analysis* (Harcourt, Brace & World, 1964).

Man–Machine Chart ◇ Multiple Activity Chart.

Man–Machine System ◇ Ergonomics.

Management Accounting As a function within an organization, management accounting may be defined as the use of the output from the *accounting system* for planning and controlling the activities of that organization primarily from a financial viewpoint (◇ Accounting).

The accounting system consists of the store of information derived from the application of *accounting method* (◇ Accounting System) to the analysis of financial data from past *transactions and events* relating to that organization and its exchange and production activities.

A more comprehensive definition of the nature of management accounting which will serve also as a foundation for developing an efficient accounting function within enterprises, may be based upon the five following complementary aspects:

(1) Regarded as a method of processing financial information to satisfy the needs of a decision maker who is concerned with the achievement of organizational objectives, in the context of an uncertain situation.

(2) Regarded as a kind of statistical technique in which data relating to transactions and events is observed, tabulated, analysed and presented for purposes of decision and control.

(3) Considered in its relationship to other disciplines and techniques required for the construction of effective accounting systems and functions.

(4) In relation to the practices and conventions of the accountancy profession, at any given time, and their relevance to organizational purposes.

(5) Considered as an application of the 'duality principle' to the construction of accounting systems and statements.

In a historical context, the term *management* accounting has originated from the need to distinguish its requirements from those of traditional financial accounting with its emphasis upon reporting parties external to enterprises. This traditional approach with its preoccupation with 'stewardship' accounting has resulted in a conventional accountancy which consists of a rather haphazard and partly conflicting collection of conventions, definitions and principles often having little relevance to the needs of enterprise management (◇ Accountancy Conventions).

In contrast, the motivating ideas of management accounting are (1) that accounting measurements only make sense in the light of the stated objectives and purposes for that particular calculation; (2) that accounting figures can only be justified in terms of the insight which they give to the present situation and to future action; (3) that accounting analyses must serve principally for decision and control purposes.

For decision purposes, flexibility is an essential requirement of accounting analyses since the concept of costs and revenues required varies with the kind of decision, whether it be for make or buy, pricing, advertising programmes, capital additions, methods of financing, etc. (⟡ Costs; Costing system.) Generally the concept required depends upon the economic analysis relevant for each alternative under consideration. Also the estimates must be in terms of forecasts and expectations of the future, supported rather than determined wholly by historical accounting data (⟡ Cost, in accounting systems).

For control purposes, in contrast, it can be argued that the emphasis should be on uniformity of standards especially where the accounting information is required for *more routine* business operations. But perhaps more notably the information for control should be relevant to the control *of people by people* rather than of (impersonal) 'factors of production'. Therefore the accounting control data should be seen as communications intended to *influence the behaviour of people*. Put in this way, behavioural considerations tending to modify technologically-derived standards and budgets become of primary importance (⟡ Control).

With regard to the development of management accounting, it may well be necessary to reconsider the structuring and breadth of its contents. In principle, it is necessary that accounting should be seen as a scarcely-separable part of a management science and that the quantitative, behavioural and economic aspects of that science which relate to an effective accounting function should be considered as part of the body of accounting as a discipline, in addition to much of its present substances. E.A.L.

R. Mattessich, *Accounting and Analytical Methods* (Irwin, 1964); R. I. Tricker, *The Accountant in Management* (Batsford, 1967); C. L. Moore and R. K. Jaedicke, *Managerial Accounting* (South Western Publishing Co., (1963)).

Management Development Finding, training and developing men and women for positions of responsibility in an enterprise, sometimes described as management succession. Management in this context usually excludes supervisors and chargehands, but includes those in staff positions with important advisory or 'decision-making' duties as well as 'line' managers who have considerable responsibility for the work of others. Management development is a systematic and continuous process which starts with an analysis of present managerial resources, estimates future needs, and operates policies of recruitment, training, transfer and promotion to secure and to make the most of these resources. There are three main aspects of management development: (1) the role of the senior manager in developing those under him, possibly through a system of ⟡ Management by Objectives; (2) the experience of jobs of different kinds and different levels of responsibility which are given to potential managers; (3) the opportunities for increasing their knowledge of different aspects of business by attending training courses, either inside or outside the particular enterprise. L.S.

F. I. De La P. Garforth, *Management Development* (Institute of Personnel Management, 1959); NEDC, *Management Recruitment and Development* (HMSO, 1965); T. J. Roberts, *Developing Effective Managers* (Institute of Personnel Management, 1967).

Management by Exception ⇨ Standard Costing; Budgeting (Short-term).

Management by Objectives This is the name given to the systematic setting of targets for each employee.

There is little difficulty in setting a target for most machine operators or salesmen, judging their performance by this criterion and arranging some form of payment by results for them. It is much more difficult to do this for managerial tasks, however, and a great deal of study has lately been given to procedures whereby a similar system could be applied to this type of work.

Job descriptions can readily be drawn up for any job, including those that consist entirely of managing, but these descriptions merely indicate the general area in which each employee is to work, what are his duties and responsibilities. They do not set out what results are required of him over the following weeks or months or years. Management by objectives is concerned with results.

The procedure consists of identifying the key areas of each job and then deciding what level of achievement in each of these areas would represent a satisfactory result. This decision is often made during a discussion between the employee who is being set the target and his superior. The question, 'what are the conditions we would expect to see if this job was being done well?' is often used during these discussions to help in identifying what key results the employee should be aiming to achieve.

Progressively more companies are adopting this technique and progressively more types of job are being analysed so that the key results can be identified. There is also a trend towards linking part of the manager's remuneration to the attainment of key results and promotion and dismissal are often so linked.

Experts in this field emphasize the need to dovetail the objectives set to each manager with the objectives set to the department in which he works and in turn to dovetail these with the overall objectives of the company. They also emphasize the desirability of participation between each manager and his superior when setting these targets. Considerable skill is often required, however, not only to identify the key results for some managerial jobs but also in selecting a challenging but attainable level of achievement. ⇨ Objectives. A.J.A.A.

J. W. Humble, *Improving Business Results* (McGraw-Hill, 1968).

Management Sciences In the singular management science is used as a synonym for the application of quantitative methods in management or for ⇨ Operational Research; Quantitative Methods.

In the plural management sciences is used as a synonym for the application of quantitative methods and the social sciences (economics, psychology and sociology) in management. M.J.C.M.

Managerial Economics With the growth of management education in the UK the basic social sciences of economics, psychology and sociology have appeared in another guise – as core subjects in the budding business manager's curriculum. Whilst for undergraduates, and possibly post-graduates, a traditional course in economics is reasonably satisfactory, this has not proved true when the students are middle and senior managers. If this is coupled with the complaint of many industrial economists that much of their previous education has proved irrelevant to their work in industry, then it is not surprising that a new course has emerged. There is, of course, ample precedent for this in the USA, but one may still ask in what sense is managerial economics different from traditional Economics?

A cynic may reply that there is no difference and a glance at the contents of any managerial economics textbook will soon show why. The mixture – demand, costs, profits, investment, etc., is as before, only the name and order vary. A more positive attitude can be taken, however, when the contents are examined more closely. The various sections are geared more closely to the individual firm; moreover it is the firm of reality and not of arid theory. In addition there is a willingness to use the work of operations researchers, marketing men, management accountants and econometricians. Thus a recent writer[1] in the field has sub-titled his book *Analysis for Business Decisions* and a glance at the contents page reveals a considerable reliance upon the methods of operations research and accounting. The sub-title reminds us that this is what managers are paid for and that the stress must be upon theory which is operational; in this way managers can be aided to take better decisions.

It is a point of some debate whether one can make a case for a separate discipline known as 'managerial economics'. Wouldn't it be better to admit that it is just the relevant parts of economics, accounting, marketing and operations research? This argument can be countered in two ways. On the one hand it is possible to argue that the separate pieces are welded together by the common use of mathematical and statistical techniques. On the other hand it is also possible to argue that they are welded together by having their roots in economics. Economics is concerned with the optimum use of resources and this is exactly what the accountant is trying to do in his analysis of capital projects and the operations researcher in his use of programming methods and analysis of inventory systems. Perhaps the best solution is to incorporate both ideas into the subject matter and we then have a discipline which finds its roots in economics and its methods from mathematics and statistics. The cynic may feel that this is another example of economists, rather late in the day, attempting to recapture ground previously developed by specialists. In this they may well be correct, but one can only wish that the pace was quicker. ⟡ Economics. L.T.S.

J. Dean, *Managerial Economics* (Prentice-Hall, 1951); D. C. Hague, *Managerial Economics: Analysis for Business Decisions* (Longmans, 1969).

Managerial Grid, The The focus of much current training activity is the actual process of managing. This kind of training aims to give managers greater insight

---

1. D. C. Hague, *Managerial Economics: Analysis for Business Decisions*.

into the methods used for getting results through people and how people react to different management methods. The Managerial Grid, which has been developed by Drs Blake and Mouton, concentrates specifically on managerial behaviour. The Managerial Grid Seminar is the first step of Grid Organization Development, which is a systems approach to increasing managerial and organizational effectiveness.

Prework for a Managerial Grid Seminar

Those attending a Managerial Grid Seminar are required to do some 30 hours prework during which they learn the grid as a framework for thinking about management. At this stage Grid participants answer a series of questions concerned with their own managerial behaviour and the climate or culture of their organization.

The Managerial Grid

The grid is based on the traditional dichotomy of concern for people and concern for production or results. The horizontal scale from 1 to 9 depicts degrees of concern for results, whilst the vertical scale depicts degrees of concern for people, also from 1 to 9. Since concern is neither all present nor all absent 1 denotes low and 9 high concern for people and results respectively. Five basic styles of management, which are amplified in *The Managerial Grid* by Blake and Mouton, can now be identified on the grid:

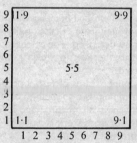

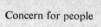

Concern for results

9.1 *Management (Scientific Management)*
Efficiency in operations results from arranging conditions of work in such a way that human elements interfere to a minimum degree.

1.9 *Management (Country Club Management)*
Thoughtful attention to needs of people for satisfying relationships leads to a comfortable friendly organization atmosphere and work tempo.

1.1 *Management (Impoverished)*
Exertion of minimum effort to get required work done is appropriate to sustain organization membership.

5.5 *Management (Middle of the Road)*
Adequate organization performance is possible through balancing the necessity to get out work with maintaining morale of people at a satisfactory level.

9.9 *Management* (*Team Management*)

Work accomplishment is from committed people. Interdependence through a 'common stake' in organization purpose leads to relationships of trust and respect.

This framework can be used as a framework for thinking and talking about individual and company management practices.

The Managerial Grid Seminar

The one-week seminar which has been developed over a period of 10 years, is run by Scientific Methods Inc. (Blake and Mouton's organization) as a public seminar, with representatives from different companies, or by line managers as an in-company programme. The objectives for the seminar are:

1. *Personal Learning*. Learning the grid as a framework for thinking and talking about management, learning about one's own managerial style and the managerial values on which this style is based.

2. *Developing Effective Team Work*. A series of team tasks provide an opportunity to learn how candid communication, commitment to objectives and the constructive handling of conflict contribute to effective team work.

3. *Group Dynamics*. When representatives from different teams meet to resolve issues of mutual interest, objectivity can be impaired by personal managerial styles and team loyalties. These issues are closely examined in a problem-solving situation.

4. *Organization*. Established practices and traditions constitute the culture of an organization. Through team discussion based on a multiple choice questionnaire an Ideal Culture is described. The extent to which this ideal differs from existing practice represents the task to which a Grid Organization Development programme is directed.

During the seminar teams of 6 to 9 people work on complex problems, with each team determining its own method of working. At the conclusion of each task team effectiveness is compared and is followed by a critique session during which the quality of team work is assessed by team members and specific plans prepared to improve performance.

In tackling these tasks grid participants develop understanding of each other's approach to problems and decision making. This experience forms the basis for aiding each person to recognize his own managerial style and how others react to it. This proves to be a most stimulating task during which each person gains considerable insight into his own strengths and weaknesses as a manager.

Grid Organization Development

Improved performance at work is often difficult to accomplish and part of the problem lies in transferring newly gained knowledge to sound application at work. This is true of almost any training course including the Grid Seminar. Effective follow-up is needed in order to derive maximum benefit and this is the aim of Grid Organization Development.

Phase I: The Managerial Grid Seminar with emphasis on personal learning constitutes the first phase.

Phase II: Work Team Development is a self-administering phase where people who are jointly responsible for specific tasks or work areas define the action needed to improve their own and their unit's effectiveness.

Phase III: Where intergroup coordination is ineffective or inadequate progress towards organizational goals is impaired. The problems which may exist in the relationships between departments, or headquarters and branch offices, or management and union are examined during Phase III, to develop improved coordination.

Phase IV: Phases I, II and III concentrate on creating the conditions needed for effective development of long-range plans. During Phase IV corporate objectives are set and an Organization Blueprint drawn up.

Phases V and VI: These phases are concerned with implementing the plans, consolidation and review.

It is intended that these six phases should be used as a guide for Grid Organization Development rather than as a fixed programme. Successful implementation is more adequately assured when top management is directly involved and line managers undertake full responsibility for each phase.

Conclusion: The Managerial Grid contains concepts which can be closely compared with the work of many authorities on management and organization, including Mary Parker Follett, Elton Mayo, Kurt Lewin, Peter Drucker, Douglas McGregor and Rensis Likert. Its principal value is the structured learning about successful management derived from the work materials used during all phases, together with the follow-through from personal learning to the achievement of improved organizational effectiveness. ⟨⟩ Group Methods of Training. C.M.H.H.

R. R. Blake and J. S. Mouton, *The Managerial Grid* (Gulf Publishing Co. 1964); R. R. Blake, H. A. Shepard, J. S. Mouton, *Managing Intergroup Conflict in Industry* (Gulf Publishing Co., 1964); R. R. Blake and J. S. Mouton, *Corporate Excellence through Grid Organization Development, A Systems Approach* (March 1968); R. R. Blake and J. S. Mouton, 'Initiating Organisation Development', *Training Directors Journal*, October 1965.

Manpower Adviser An official of the ⟨⟩ Department of Employment, formerly known as an Industrial Relations Officer, whose main duties were concerned with the settlement of industrial disputes and the prevention of future trouble through advising companies on the formulation of positive employment policies.

Manpower Advisers also advised employers on personnel management questions, including ⟨⟩ Joint Consultation and communication. In their conciliation (⟨⟩ Industrial Conciliation) work they relied on persuasion rather than authority and had no legal sanctions. They could only do their work as trouble-shooters and peace-makers on the invitation of both the employers and the unions concerned. Their task then was to discover the precise nature of the differences which existed, to see that any established negotiating procedure was followed and to try to secure an adjustment of the differences by mutual agreement. They also assisted employers and workers to establish or improve their ⟨⟩ collective bargaining arrangements and it was this positive, forward-looking aspect of their work which became so important in recent years. As industrial relations at company level become less and less an *ad hoc* exercise in trouble-shooting and are regarded as being on a par with other branches of corporate strategy, requiring forward planning and detailed supervision, so it was expected the advisory role of the DE official would expand. The Manpower Adviser was of particular value to small and medium-sized firms who had little or no specialist staff to deal with personnel questions.

On the formation of the ⟡ Advisory, Conciliation and Arbitration Service in 1974, this role was transferred from the DE to the Service and the job title reverted to that of 'Industrial Relations Officer'. N.H.C.

Manpower Planning The name given to the drawing up of a schedule showing the number of employees of different types that the company will require over a period of years.

Once a company has developed a long range strategy (⟡ Corporate Planning) it becomes possible to estimate the number of people of all types and categories that may be required over the following years. At the time that these estimates are made, some companies take the opportunity to review their staffing criteria as well as the mere numbers required in each category. Thus it may be desirable to evaluate the performance of men with different qualifications who have been doing the same job – for example, a company having a large sales force may discover as a result of analysing the records that the salesmen with the best records are those with a third-class science degree while those with the worst record have first-class arts degrees. Any such conclusion would, of course, be taken into account when preparing a long-term manpower plan.

The function of the manpower plan is to indicate how many employees will need to be selected, trained, promoted, retired, dismissed and so on over the following years and hence an estimate of the personnel facilities that will be required can also be made. The factors that are usually taken into account in making up a manpower plan include (a) the changing nature of the business, (b) the rate of retirement and other causes of staff losses, (c) changes in social and employment conditions, (d) changes in education, (e) changes in job content, (f) changes in the company's organization structure and promotion pattern. A.J.A.A.

Marginal Costing ⟡ Break-even Analysis; Overheads.

Marginal Efficiency of Capital ⟡ Internal Rate of Return.

Market Models and Competition Whilst the models of markets used by economists often seem to have little value as direct aids to decision-making, nevertheless they provide a useful way of classifying actual firms and suggest the types of competition that may occur. The table on p. 239 shows the major models, classified according to number of producers, type of product and ease of entry.

The firm in pure competition must accept the price that is set by the market. Conditions of entry restrict the opportunity for large profits whilst the number of firms rules out concerted action. Such industries are usually producing raw materials or agricultural produce. They often tend towards chronic overcapacity and wide swings in prices, production and incomes. Hence one often sees governments intervening to introduce orderly marketing and raise productivity.

Market Model	Number of Producers	Product	Entry
Pure (Perfect) Competition	Large	Homogeneous	Unrestricted
Monopolistic Competition	Large	Differentiated	Unrestricted
Pure Oligopoly	Small	Homogeneous	Restricted
Differentiated Oligopoly	Small	Differentiated	Restricted
Monopoly	One	—	Restricted

The situation in monopolistic competition is identical apart from the fact of differentiated products. Thus producers have some slight control over price, and competition can be undertaken through advertising, packaging, and service, as well as price. The retail trade exhibits many of these characteristics.

Pure oligopoly often develops from pure competition as the benefits of economies of scale are realized. Producers can exercise price control, although this is limited by the homogeneity of products. Since prices are interdependent one frequently finds price leadership and price agreements in such industries. The production of raw materials is again a source for this type of market model.

Differentiated oligopoly is a model in which price and non-price competition flourish, although experience suggests that price wars are purely destructive. Producers have control over price but usually the main competition comes from brand advertising, product improvements and innovations. Price wars cannot be ruled out, however, particularly if competitors threaten the market leader. Industries such as cars, cigarettes, soap and detergents conform closely to this model.

Monopoly is now closely associated with the nationalized industries such as coal, gas, electricity and railways. Producers, in theory, have complete control over price or output and hence over profit levels. This is one reason for the government control. Competition can still occur, however, as witness the competition in domestic fuel supply for central heating. ⟨⟩ Competition. L.T.S.

A. W. Stonier and D. C. Hague, *A Textbook of Economic Theory* (Longman, 1964).

Market Segmentation Seeks to differentiate between buyers/users of an identical product or service in terms of relevant marketing characteristics. Until the recent development of attitude analysis in marketing (⟨⟩ Motivation Research), it was common to segment markets in terms of age, socio-economic groupings based on occupation and gross income, ethnic groups or geographical location. Numerous occasions have been found on which these are not prime determinants of purchase, nor relevant dimensions for different marketing strategies. Two new categories have been added, in terms of personality, e.g. gregariousness, conservatism, ambitiousness; and buyer behaviour, e.g. usage rate, end use, brand or channel loyalty (⟨⟩ Branding) and price sensitivity. With segmentation analysis marketing management can more effectively develop its total sales by the use of alternate approaches to each segment. The cold remedy market has been shown to be segmented in terms of: users who believe that the remedy will be effective; users who do not believe it will help but wish to feel that they are doing something; non-users who feel that the remedies are useless and do not wish to do anything. To consolidate or develop marketing to each segment calls for a different approach. A wide range of research techniques can be employed both to analyse a market for relevant segments, and measure the effectiveness of marketing approaches to them (⟡ Marketing Research). G.S.C.W.

> P. Kotler, *Marketing Management: Analysis, planning and control*, Ch. 3 (Prentice-Hall, 1967).

Market Survey An overall appraisal for a product or service which an organization offers or proposes to offer to a market. It will normally indicate not only the market situation for the commissioning organization but also the position of competitive forces and future trends. The investigation will frequently be made by the collection of previously unknown data, but may be made by the collation of existing information (⟡ Desk Research). The former pattern is most common in consumer markets where few official or trade statistics are available; the latter is more common in industrial and agricultural markets. The original investigation, although occasionally conducted via a census of a total relevant population, will generally involve the selection of representative respondents (⟡ Sampling) by either quota or random sampling procedures. A uniform, structured questionnaire may be used to gather the relevant information and the findings will be published as a report. Where the survey examines a market of considerable complexity, or involves interviews amongst a well-informed population concerning the product or service, e.g. architects, computer technologists, a less structured approach may be used in the questioning. A wide variety of other research methods are available, and sometimes used, either in conjunction with or in place of the questionnaire survey or desk research investigation (⟡ Marketing Research).

Some controversy centres around the correct method of report presentation in order that the findings in such a survey can be most effectively communicated. The Market Research Society lays down a code for its members, insisting that they provide sample, time and methodological details, etc. G.S.C.W.

> *Standards in Market Research* (1954, revised 1965 and 1973).

Marketing Marketing can usefully be defined as 'the process in a society by which the demand for economic goods and services is anticipated or enlarged, and satisfied through the conception, physical distribution and exchange of such goods and services'. Hence, within any individual company satisfying demands of this nature, there must always be a marketing process. The success of an enterprise, however, will depend on the skill with which its management is able to give satisfaction and obtain the appropriate net profit. Two of the most significant factors affecting the relative ease with which this state of affairs can be achieved will be the nature of demand in a market and the nature of the forces competing for the incomes which can be allocated to any particular product or service. The ever-increasing consciousness in companies of the need to look closely at the marketing process has largely come about as a result of dramatic shifts in these factors in recent decades.

Three key ideas dominate the pattern of marketing in all advanced market economies: marketing orientation, marketing research and marketing management.

Marketing orientation is the philosophy of business management which derives from the acceptance of the need to plan and control the marketing process consciously within a company. It can only affect the character of policy decisions if it is effectively embraced by top management. Once paramount, however, its ramifications for the development of new products and services and for diversification programmes are extremely important. It involves a definition of a company's purpose beyond the offering of this and that product or service; the company exists to satisfy a need, e.g. to travel from Glasgow to London. Whether this is most effectively accomplished by stagecoach, canal barge, train, aeroplane or hovercraft is a subsidiary consideration.

Once a company has consciously embraced this concept, two functions must be established to facilitate its implementation. (1) Contact must be made with the customers who have the needs to be satisfied. (2) The customers must effectively receive the offering the company seeks to make. These are the roles of marketing research and marketing management respectively.

Marketing research is charged with the continuous task of monitoring the marketing itself and any extra-market factors liable to influence customer behaviour in the given market, e.g. economic trends, the political situation (especially in export markets). The data which is collected will be in the form of regular surveys and analyses of economic goods and services currently available (a company's own and its competitors'), and *ad hoc* studies from time to time.

The launch of a new product illustrates well the nature of such *ad hoc* work. It could involve the testing of the concept of the product, expressed in verbal terms, with potential users before a prototype was prepared. The next stage would be to build a few prototypes for testing by customers. Finally, if all has gone favourably, a limited launch on to the market will often be made. The optimum combination of promotional activity, distribution and price elements will be sought and customer's purchases and reactions measured.

A second major field of marketing research is in the measurement of the effectiveness of the activities of marketing management.

Marketing management is the engineering function in the marketing process. The marketing manager is responsible for the totality of a company's market offering – the range of products and their packaging, the prices charged, the discount structures offered, the communications media employed (be they television, press, outdoor hoardings, cinema, personal salesmen, direct mail circulars, etc.), and the channels through which the product or service is made available (retailers, mail order, automatic vending, door-to-door selling, etc.). His activity determines whether or not the company meets its financial objectives. The sale of products and services is normally the sole revenue generator in a company; most of the remaining personnel are engaged solely in incurring costs. Hence, marketing management must maintain continuous contact with those colleagues in the company responsible for manufacturing the products or providing the service for sale, and with those financial colleagues responsible for controlling budgets, raising capital and distributing profits. The marketing manager is concerned with

241

market opportunities based on his interpretation of the continuous monitoring implicit in marketing research; his colleagues are concerned with technical and financial possibilities.

Professional marketing education developed in Britain in the early 1960s, through the large professional organization, the Institute of Marketing (13,000 members in 1973). It offers a 3-year diploma course on a part-time basis, taught in many Polytechnics and Colleges of Technology. In the mid-1960s the universities began to develop marketing as a subject for study either for higher degrees alone, or as a major part of an advanced education for management.

Teachers of marketing at an advanced level established an Annual Conference in 1965, and shortly afterwards the *European Journal of Marketing*, reporting current research, theory and development, was founded (1967). In 1966, the British Productivity Council established a National Marketing Council to promote the subject and to develop research and teaching in Britain. The EDC for the Distributive Trades also implicitly assumed a general responsibility for marketing in Britain at the time of the Prime Minister's 2nd Productivity Conference in 1967, which was devoted to marketing and distribution. G.S.C.W.

> Substantial literature in Europe is only now emerging. See particularly G. Wills, *Contemporary Marketing* (Pitman, 1971).

Marketing Audit The process by which a marketing organization attempts to develop an independent judgement of the quality and direction of its effort. It examines the entire marketing effort of a company (⟡ Marketing Mix), or a specific aspect of it, covering its objectives, programme, implementation, and organization, for the triple purpose of determining what is being done, appraising what is being done, and recommending what ought to be done in the future. Such audits are conducted on a periodic basis with greatest effect rather than *ad hoc* in the face of a crisis. They may be conducted either internally – through the cross-transfer of company personnel, by the individuals involved, by superiors, through a formalized audit office or task force or by external consultants. The important criteria in choice of auditors are objectivity, breadth of experience, and familiarity with company operations. G.S.C.W.

> A. Schuchman, 'The Marketing Audit: its nature, purposes, and problems', in *Analysing and Improving Marketing Performance* (American Management Association, 1959).

Marketing Channel ⟡ Distribution Mix.

Marketing Communications Mix The combination of methods chosen from time to time by a marketing organization to communicate about, and thereby promote, goods or services which are offered. It is seen as essentially an integral part of the total ⟡ Marketing Mix, and consequently communications mix management whilst aiming to optimize resource allocation avoids doing so at the expense of the total activity. The principal media of communication available are ⟡ Advertising in the general and trade press (⟡ Audience Measurement), commercial TV, direct mailings, outdoor sites and posters, cinemas, ⟡ Packaging, Point-of-Sale and ⟡ Merchandising, Promotion, Public Relations and personal salesmanship

(⟡ Selling). The marketing communications mix within any particular industry often tends to inertia and a breakaway becomes difficult for any individual organization both psychologically within, and in relation to, distribution channels and end-users, e.g. a particular industry may devote a very high proportion of its expenditure to TV advertising and to point-of-sale display materials, with a relatively passive role for personal salesmanship. Another may use keyed press advertising and mail order catalogues (⟡ Mail Order). To change from one style of mix to another has implications for the total employment status of the marketing activity in an organization, and its structure, as well as the financial investment of goodwill implicit in an extant mix. G.S.C.W.

E. Crane, *Marketing Communications* (J. Wiley, 1965).

Marketing Concept The philosophy of management which postulates that in all consideration given to the marketing of a product or service the needs of the customer must be paramount, subject to the governing factor of an organization's profit objective (see Figure). Although widely accepted as commonsense, only since the Second World War have mass market demand conditions (⟡ Discretionary Income) and organization structures within companies (⟡ Marketing) made its effective implementation possible. The main problem of implementation is to be found in the distortion which occurs in securing details of customer needs and/or reactions to any market offering. Mass markets have presented the major problems. The development of marketing research methods (⟡ Marketing Research) largely based on modern sampling methods (⟡ Sampling) has overcome this in many ways. The philosophy has always been implicit in jobbing or custombuilt production, with their direct channels of communication. Prior to the present substantial growth of discretionary incomes, management philosophies

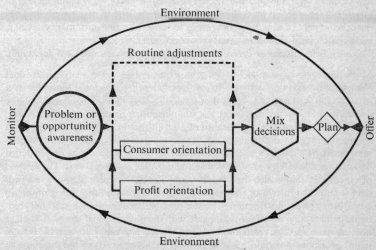

The marketing concept

tended to be dominated first by production objectives and then by sales objectives, as ends in themselves (⟡ Selling). The phrase is thought to have been first adopted in the General Electric Company (USA) *circa* 1952. In that company it meant that marketing established for the engineer, the designer and the production controller what the customer wanted, what price he was willing to pay, and where and when it would be wanted (⟡ Marketing Mix). G.S.C.W.

G. Schwartz, *Science in Marketing*, Chs. 4 and 5 (J. Wiley, 1965).

Marketing Environment The amalgam of those factors affecting the market which are external to the company's sphere of direct influence but which act as constraints on company behaviour (⟡ Marketing). The most significant are generally identified as. (1) the legal system within which marketing takes place; (2) the ethical/moral values as institutionalized in any particular society at any point in time; (3) the economic system and level of individual and national income (⟡ Discretionary Income); (4) the psychological mechanisms of the individual which condition behaviour and the interpretation of messages (⟡ Branding, Motivation Research); (5) the group influences which condition the behaviour of the individual, especially as described in sociology; (6) cultural factors, such as are demonstrated in social anthropology and linguistics, of importance particularly in cross-cultural or export marketing (⟡ International Marketing); (7) spatial aspects of human settlement, as influencing, e.g. location of trading centres, depots and gravitation of custom, as particularly considered in economic geography, human ecology and social physics (⟡ Retail Gravitation); (8) institutionalized channels for the distribution of goods and services (⟡ Distribution Mix) and organization structures within companies and market agencies. The relative importance of any of these factors will vary according to the product or service under offer, the time and place. The development of study in this field as an integrated approach in marketing is of recent origin, and in many areas involves the development of new theoretical bases for understanding customer behaviour, e.g. psychological and sociological economics. G.S.C.W.

S. H. Britt, *Consumer Behaviour and the Behavioural Sciences* (J. Wiley, 1966).

Marketing Experimentation The use of experimental design to analyse individual elements in marketing activity. It involves balancing unwanted variables in a situation, by such means as control or randomization, in order to ensure that any resultant variations are due to the test stimulus rather than some spurious effect; in addition the statistical significance of a result should be assessable. The most common form of experimental design in marketing research is the split or matched sample. At its simplest level, say in the test of two new products, one matched half of a sample will try product A first and the other product B first. The method of experimentation is also used in test marketing (⟡ New Product) where a product is launched in two or more areas, with different total marketing mixes; in advertising; price; distribution. The use of experimentation as a research technique in marketing is still rare compared with the observational methods, such as questionnaire surveys, retail audits and panels (⟡ Marketing Research). It faces major problems in certain areas, such as test marketing where the matching of samples both initially, and sustaining the match over time, is still not completely feasible. However, its use is greatly increasing in those areas where matching is practicable, and where the time for the conduct of an experiment can be kept relatively short, e.g. product placement, pre-testing of advertisements. G.S.C.W.

Marketing Logistics ⟡ Physical Distribution Management.

Marketing Mix The combination of procedures and policies adopted from time to time by an organization in its marketing programme. The various elements may combine in a wide variety of ways in order to achieve marketing objectives, and management normally seeks to minimize the cost overall. This approach to marketing management was first formulated by Neil Borden at Harvard University in 1948. The twelve variables he lists in his model are: product planning (⟡ New Product, Product Mix), pricing (⟡ Market Pricing, Prices), ⟡ Branding, channels of distribution (⟡ Distribution Mix), personal selling (⟡ Selling), ⟡ Advertising, promotion (⟡ Marketing Communications Mix), ⟡ packaging, display (⟡ Merchandising), servicing, physical handling (⟡ Physical Distribution Management), fact finding and analysis (⟡ Marketing Research). The formulation of an optimum mix (⟡ Marketing Experimentation) has to be undertaken in the framework of market forces beyond the direct control of the marketing manager in the short term. These include buyer behaviour, trade behaviour, competitor's behaviour and position and government restraint (⟡ Marketing Environment). Finally, in the short term, mix alternatives can only be effectively selected in the context of a company's existing resources. The model emphasizes not only the interdependence of the action variables, the market forces and company resources, but also the interaction of each constituent variable on one another (⟡ Operational Research). G.S.C.W.

G. Schwartz, *Science in Marketing*, Ch. 13 (J. Wiley, 1965).

Marketing Plan ⟡ Sales Forecast.

Marketing Research That function in a business which is specifically charged with providing information to facilitate the making of marketing decisions. These decisions can be classified as either operational, i.e. relating to problems encountered in the continuous process of marketing a range of products or services; or *ad hoc*, i.e. arising out of particular problems or developments. The stages of the problem solving process are matched with a variety of techniques, of which the most popular are shown in the following table (⟡ Market Survey; Retail Audit; Consumer Panel).

The Sequential Process of Research

Stage	Techniques
1. Problem-awareness and conceptualization	Monitor trade press. Appraise current practice. Marketing feedback. 'Related-area' reading.

2. Hypothesizing and problem-refinement (qualitative stage)	Group discussions. Motivational research. Unstructured interviews. Memo-motion cameras and photographic observation. Laboratory experimentation. Consumer 'clinics'.
3. Validation and quantification	Surveys. Retail audits. Panels. Mass-observation. Marketing experimentation.

The first marketing research department is thought to have been established in North America by Charles Parlin in 1923 and the first formal commercial investigation was his classification of department store shopping habits. The massive growth of marketing research began in Britain after the Second World War as many markets became more competitive and in the face of rising consumer discretionary incomes. The Market Research Society, the largest professional association, was established in 1947 and 20 years later had over 2000 members. A smaller organization also exists. the Industrial Market Research Association, some 400 companies were estimated in 1969 to have marketing research departments of their own, and their total annual expenditure was estimated at £26 m. Most market research, however, is sub-contracted to consulting agencies of which there are currently more than 100 in Britain. Board of Trade grants are available for 50% of the cost of marketing research conducted in overseas markets. G.S.C.W.

C. R. Wasson, *Research Analysis for Marketing Decisions* (Appleton · Century-Crofts, 1966); and *Organisations Providing Market Research Services in Great Britain* (Market Research Society, published annually).

Mass Production Mass production has been adopted as a generic rather than specific term. Although the term was born around 50 years ago, the type of systems which it now describes are considerably older. Large-quantity production is as old as large-quantity demand. The concept is not new; only the manner in which the concept is translated into practice has any claim to be of recent origin. Historically the stimulus for mass production derived largely from the invention and increasing availability of mechanized methods of production. Tools such as lathes, drilling machines, forges, etc. were important, their development giving rise to perhaps the simplest aspect of mass production, namely the quantity production of single piece items from single machines.

A second aspect of mass production deals with the manufacture of more complex items, such as domestic appliances, motor vehicles, etc., which depend on a different type of mass-production technology, the central feature of which is product flow and hence usually referred to as flow-production. Such items, because of their complexity or composite nature, cannot usually be manufactured by one

246

tool or piece of equipment. They normally require the services of several facilities. The mass production of such items, a more recent development than quantity production, is dependent on the use of the flow principle, i.e. the continuous flow of the products through or past a series of production facilities.

Flow production is most easily achieved for products which flow naturally. For example, in petroleum refining, the product and the raw material have a propensity to flow and the design of the flow process is facilitated. Similarly, many foodstuffs, drinks and other products, because of their natural properties, lend themselves to this type of production. In contrast, 'hard' discrete items such as engine cylinder blocks, motor vehicles and domestic appliances do not possess this characteristic. Hence considerable effort must be made to design flow systems for their manufacture. The mass production of complex discrete items using the flow principle is one of the most important achievements in manufacturing technology and one of the most important aspects of mass production. Indeed, the importance of this method of manufacture is such that, for many people, the term mass production is synonymous with flow or assembly line production (⇨ Assembly Lines).

Thus the term 'mass production' embraces two technologies. Flow-production consists basically of two subsections, namely, flow processes designed for the manufacture of large quantities of bulk, fluid or semi-fluid products, and flow lines, which use the same principle of efficient material and product flow in the manufacture of large quantities of complex, discrete items. Flow lines in which

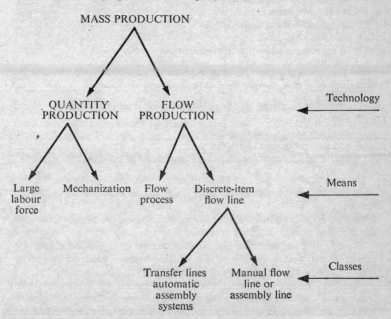

manual labour is used essentially for product assembly are often referred to as manual-flow or assembly lines, whilst those using automatic material transfer between automatic machining 'stations' are normally referred to as transfer lines or machines or, in the case of assembly work, automatic assembly systems.

Recently, prompted largely by behavioural problems such as high labour turn-over, absenteeism, etc., some companies have in part replaced manual flow line work by systems of individual or group manual working (⟡ Group Working). In such cases, work – normally assembly work – which would normally have been undertaken on an assembly line is executed by people working individually or in groups. In such cases, the work flow characteristic does not predominate and individual tasks are usually enlarged or enriched in comparison with the tasks of workers at stations on flow lines (⟡ Job Restructuring). R.W.

R. Wild, *Mass Production Management* (J. Wiley, 1972).

Materials Handling The need to move and otherwise handle materials, components, products, etc., is a basic process in manufacture and often accounts for a large proportion of total manufacturing cost.

The primary factor in materials handling is movement, the objective of which should be, to move material:

(1) towards completion,
(2) on or by the same device,
(3) smoothly, safely and quickly,
(4) the shortest distance,
(5) easily and without undue effort,
(6) economically,
(7) to coordinate with other activities, processes, etc.

The practice of materials handling is primarily concerned with methods and equipment. The type of equipment to be used depends upon:

(1) objects to be moved – size, weight, quantity, condition, mobility,
(2) routing and sequence,
(3) production rates and quantities,
(4) speed of movement required,
(5) special requirements or limitations (e.g. shape of buildings, etc.).

The relation of materials handling with other functions is important. Efficient plant layout may eliminate, reduce or facilitate materials handling. ⟡ Plant Layout.

Storage is an important associate function and, where possible, materials handling and storage should be combined.

The recording and analytical techniques of method study are particularly useful in the study and design of materials handling systems, Memomotion photography and flow process charts being frequently used. ⟡ Method Study.

The need for effective materials handling is self-evident. Handling can account for up to 40% of total manufacturing costs. Approximately 25% of all industrial accidents are associated with faulty handling and inadequate materials handling may result in high work in progress, deterioration and damage, increase in labour costs, underutilization of space, etc. R.W.

> J. M. Apple, *Plant Layout and Materials Handling* (Ronald Press, 1960).

Mathematical Programming This is a generic term used to describe a set of related mathematical techniques used in operational research to solve resource ⟡ Allocation Problems.

The most commonly used member of the family is known as Linear Programming (LP). The adjective 'linear' describes a straight line relationship between the variables in the problem. This is a concise way of saying that, for example, the total cost of producing a batch of an item is directly proportional to the batch size. That is, if it costs £10 to produce 100 items, it costs £20 to produce 200, £30 to produce 300, etc. If all the variables present in an allocation problem are related in this simple way, it may well be appropriate to use LP. Surprisingly, many problems have been found to fulfil these requirements and the technique is used extensively. There are a number of sub-techniques of LP which are each appropriate for particular problems. The most generally usable is the Simplex Method, whilst others are the Transportation Method (so called because, among other applications, it can be used to find the cheapest way of transporting goods from factories to warehouses) and the Assignment Method (so called because it can be used to find the best way of assigning workers to jobs).

In some problems, all the variables do not have linear relationships and non-linear programming techniques have been developed. Among these are Quadratic Programming (where there is a 'squared' relationship between some of the variables), and Stochastic Programming (where the exact relationships between some variables are uncertain). Techniques which can be used when the relationships between variables are both linear and non-linear are Integer Programming where some or all of the variables must have whole number or 'integer values' and dynamic programming (which is particularly useful when resources are required to be allocated sequentially). M.J.C.M.

> M. J. Sargeaunt, *Operational Research for Management*, pp. 30–49 (Heinemann, 1965).

Mayo, Elton ⟡ Hawthorne Investigations.

Mean ⟡ Measures of Location.

Means A means is any action that an executive takes in order to achieve an objective.

Means are often confused with ends or objectives partly because the means of a senior executive can also be one of the objectives of his junior. Thus the objective of a Sales Director may be to increase sales and to achieve this end he may have chosen several means – one of which might be to take on more salesmen. The task of taking on these men might fall to a junior manager and this becomes his objective; he in his turn decides that one means by which this can be achieved is to advertise these vacancies and this may become the objective of his assistant. There may thus be a hierarchy of means and objectives.

Measures of Dispersion

The only criterion by which the efficacy of a means may be judged is whether it results in the objective being achieved – provided that it does not run counter to any moral code in force within the company. ⟡ Constraints; Objectives (in planning); Business Policy. A.J.A.A.

Measures of Dispersion The variability of a given measure, or statistic (e.g. heights of Englishmen or diameters of ball bearings) can be represented visually by a histogram or frequency distribution (⟡ Statistics). This visual representation is not suitable for the algebraic manipulations used by statisticians and a *quantitative representation* is required. This is achieved by using one or more of a number of measures of location and dispersion of the distribution. The two most commonly used measures of dispersion are as follows (⟡ Measures of Location, for discussion of these):

(a) *Range*. This is the simplest measure of dispersion and is the difference in value between the items of lowest and highest value, e.g. the manager's suits referred to elsewhere (⟡ Measures of Location) cost £23, £34, £16, £52, £25, so the range of the cost of his suits is £52 − £16 = £36.

Although this provides the easiest and most obvious measurement of dispersion, because it gives equal attention to all the items, it may give a misleading impression of the pattern of the dispersion. If the salaries of nine managers in an organization are £2,000, £2,100, £2,400, £2,900, £3,000, £3,400, £3,500, £4,000, £100,000, the range of salaries is £100,000 − £2,000 = £98,000, although the salary range of the first eight managers is only £4,000 − £2,000 = £2,000. Thus when all nine are included, the range of £98,000 gives an inaccurate picture of the pattern of remuneration of the managers. Furthermore if the dispersion of a distribution is being obtained from taking a sample (⟡ Sampling) the range of the sample is likely to increase progressively as the sample size increases. This follows as any increase in the number of items in the sample cannot possibly decrease the range of the sample already obtained but can only maintain or increase it.

(b) *Standard Deviation and Variance*. The extent of the dispersion of a given value is reflected in the extent of its deviation from the mean value of all the items. Thus the mean cost of the suits in the first example above is £30, so the first deviates by − £7, the second by + £4, etc. (see column 2 of the table opposite). By virtue of the definition of the mean, the sum of these deviations from it will be zero but, if we square the terms (as in column 3 of the Table below), because all the squared terms will be positive, the sum will be non-zero. If this sum is divided by one less than the number of items[1] a representative measure of dispersion is obtained. This measure is known as the variance and its square root is known as the standard deviation. The detailed calculation for the above example is given in the table opposite.

To summarize, the variance and standard deviation are calculated as follows:
  (i) Calculate the mean value of group of items.
  (ii) Calculate the deviation of each value from the mean of the group.

1. For technical reasons that cannot be discussed here, the sum of the squares of the deviations is divided by one less than the number of items rather than the number of items (that is four rather than five in the above example).

(iii) Square each deviation and calculate the sum of these 'squared deviations'.
(iv) Divide by one less than the number of items in the group to obtain the variance.
(v) Extract the square root of the variance to obtain the standard deviation.
M.J.C.M.

P. G. Moore, *Statistics and the Manager*, pp. 27–31 (Macdonald, 1966).

Column 1 Value	Column 2 Deviation from Mean	Column 3 Squared Deviation
23	− 7	49
34	+ 4	16
16	−14	196
52	+22	484
25	− 5	25

Total = 150 Total = 0 Total = 770

Mean = $\frac{150}{5}$ Variance = $\frac{770}{4}$ Standard Deviation = $\sqrt{192 \cdot 5}$

= 30 = 192·5 = 13·9

Measures of Location The variability of a given measure or statistic (e.g. heights of Englishmen or diameters of ball bearings) can be represented visually by a histogram or frequency distribution (⟡ Statistics). This visual representation is not suitable for the algebraic manipulations used by statisticians and a *quantitative representation* is required. This is achieved by using one or more of a number of measures of location and dispersion of the distribution. The three most commonly used measures of location are as follows (⟡ Measures of Dispersion for discussion of these):

(a) *Arithmetic Mean*, which is more usually called mean or expected value. This is the sum of the total value of all the items (e.g. the sum total of heights of all Englishmen) divided by the total number of items (e.g. the total population of Englishmen).

E.g. a manager might buy five suits in two years paying the following prices for each of them, £23, £34, £16, £52, £25. His total expenditure on suits is:

$23 + 34 + 16 + 52 + 25 = £150$. The mean price he pays is $\frac{150}{5} = £30$.

It can be seen that the mean is in fact the same as the layman's average. Statisticians prefer to use the term 'mean' since 'average' is sometimes confused with the second measure of location.

(b) *Median*. If we arrange all the items in order of value (which is usually done in a histogram), then if there are an odd number of items the middle item is the median item and its value is the median. If there are an even number of items, the median value is taken as the arithmetic mean of the two middle items. Thus the median item has as many items below it as above it. When plotting a histogram each class interval has a height proportional to the number of items in it. It follows geometrically that the area below the median class interval equals the area above it. Similarly in a frequency distribution, a vertical line drawn through the median value divides the distribution into two halves of equal area.

The mean is much more suitable for algebraic manipulation but the median represents the location of the centre of the distribution. If a distribution has a small number of items with very low or very high values, these values will deflate or inflate the mean considerably. They will not unduly affect the median, however, since this identifies the middle item, not the middle value.

E.g. suppose the salaries of nine managers are as follows: in order of increasing salary: £2,000, £2,100, £2,400, £2,900, £3,000, £3,500, £4,000, £100,000.

Eight are 'middle managers' whilst the ninth is the chief executive of a large company (whose managers are well paid!). The Median salary is the fifth and is £3,000, which is fairly representative of eight of the managers' pay. On the other hand, the Mean is $\frac{123,300}{9}$ (that is the sum of all their salaries divided by the total number of managers) or £13,700 and represents no one's pay!

Because a small group earning relatively high pay compared direct with the rest can inflate the mean figure, median salaries are invariably quoted in executive salary surveys.

(c) *Mode.* Many distributions occurring in real life are roughly bell shaped, with the frequency of items of given value rising to a maximum and falling off again. The mode or modal value is the value of the most frequently occurring items. It therefore corresponds to the maximum height in the distribution and the term is derived from the French 'à la mode' or most fashionable item. The advantage of the mode is that it can often be located quickly visually, however, as two grossly dissimilar distributions can have the same mode, it is only of value as a quick comparison between two distributions that can be expected to be of similar shape. M.J.C.M.

M. J. Moroney, *Facts from Figures*, p. 34 ff. (Penguin Books, 1951).

Mechanistic and Organic Management Terms used by T. Burns and G. M. Stalker to differentiate two contrasting systems of management. The mechanistic system is characterized by a precise subdivision of the total organization into sections each with its own semi-discrete objectives. Coordination is achieved by superiors in the hierarchy and by formal procedures. Individual tasks and responsibilities are precisely specified and the majority of interactions are between superior and subordinate. There is, in other words, a heavy emphasis on formal organization. On the other hand, an organic system places considerable reliance on the members of management forsaking their specialist preoccupations and adapting their behaviour in voluntary and spontaneous cooperation with colleagues in pursuit of common objectives as the situation may require. Rights and responsibilities are assumed or conceded with changing circumstances. Very little use is made of formal authority; most interactions, even those between supervisor and subordinate, are or resemble consultations between colleagues.

Burns and Stalker do not suggest that either system of management exists in its pure form to the total exclusion of any elements of the other, but their research indicated a clear division between those managements who emphasized the mechanistic system and those who emphasized the organic. The mechanistic seemed to work when the organization was operating in comparatively stable conditions so that events could be foreseen and anticipated by the devising of appropriate procedures. The organic was most suited to situations of rapid change and uncertainty when fluid organizational practices were necessary to achieve the swift responses required. ⟡ Bureaucracy; Formal Organization. I.C.MCG.

T. Burns and G. M. Stalker, *The Management of Innovation* (Tavistock Publications, 1961).

Media ⟡ Marketing Communications Mix.

Median ⟡ Measures of Location.

Medical Services Arrangements made for the supervision of the health of employees and for their treatment at the place of employment. Under the ⟡ Factory Law minimum standards are laid down for the provision of First Aid, and for the medical examination of young people under 16 and of employees working in certain processes which are dangerous to health (⟡ Industrial Disease). A comprehensive concept of a firm's industrial medical service includes measures taken to prevent illness such as the provision of good lighting, heating and ventilation, washing facilities and canteens at the workplace, as well as arrangements for medical supervision and for quick and competent first-aid treatment. Some larger establishments provide services for the care of the teeth, the feet, for regular medical checks, including X-ray examinations and even, in a few cases, for the care of mental health. It is sometimes maintained that an industrial medical service should be established as part of the National Health Service, with increased responsibilities for appointed Factory Doctors and with industrial medical officers as agents of the Health Service rather than as employees of Companies. Defenders of the present system point to improvements in the health of industrial workers in the last 50 years, including the almost complete elimination of the more serious industrial diseases. L.S.

Ministry of Labour, *Health at Work* (HMSO, 1960).

Memomotion Photography A method of recording activities using a cine camera designed to take pictures at longer intervals than normal. The time interval available is normally from one frame/sec. to one frame/30 seconds.

This method of recording is particularly suitable for: (1) Studies of work involving a group of workers. (2) Long cycle and irregular cycle work. ⟡ Method Study.

Memomotion photography is a method of activity sampling and should be treated as such. Since the sampling interval is fixed and regular it is less suitable for recording repetitive constant cycle work than either continuous recording or random sampling. ⟡ Work Sampling.

As well as being a useful means of recording activities during a method study investigation, memomotion photography is often used to record movement patterns for ◊ Plant Layout purposes. R.W.

Maynard (ed.), *Handbook of Industrial Engineering* (McGraw-Hill, 2nd ed., 1963).

Mental Age ◊ Intelligence.

Merchandising The use of display and promotional devices, specifically at the point of sale, for goods and services (◊ Marketing Communications Mix). The term sometimes includes ◊ Packaging, and in North America was formerly used as a synonym for ◊ Marketing. Point-of-sale promotion and display are most common in consumer markets, particularly for products selling through self-service/supermarket outlets (◊ Supermarket). The growth of such retailing activity has led to an increased use of such promotion and display. The most frequently used devices are the giving away of free samples and gifts, self-liqui-dating, i.e. cost covering, premium promotions, cut-price offers, and the use of window and interior display, special dump bins and racks. Expenditure in 1965 on window and interior displays alone was £36 m., free samples cost £20 m. and other premium offers to the order of a further £20 m. The specific marketing objectives of the dominant incentive schemes are as follows: (1) sample give aways/free send-ins – to secure customer trial, (2) self-liquidators – to gain display in a store and catch the eye, (3) consumer clubs and voucher schemes – to develop brand loyalty (◊ Branding), (4) trading stamps – to develop store loyalty. Such incentive ideas are also used in relation to retailers and wholesalers in order to secure distribution. Variations of discount structures etc. are termed 'dealer loaders' and have become increasingly frequent as competition for shelf-space in self-service has increased. This latter type of merchandising can also be found in industrial markets. The Institute of Point of Sale Advertising was established in 1967. G.S.C.W.

Mergers A merger by acquisition occurs when one firm absorbs another so that the latter ceases to exist. A merger by combination generally occurs when two or more firms join together to form a new firm. Examples of the general objectives of mergers are: quick growth; reduction of overall risk by diversifying products; control of markets; access to finance or cheaper finance; large-scale research (where this is important as in industries subject to rapid technological change); pooling of managerial talent; economies of scale in production etc.

In arriving at the terms of a merger a number of factors are important, for example: earnings, dividends, market values, going-concern values (or book values), sufficiency of working capital. One rule-of-thumb method for arriving at the relative values of shares in the various companies to be merged is to derive a per share ratio for each of the factors considered important in the situation and to take an average of these ratios as the basis. However, it is unlikely that such quantitative factors alone will generally be an acceptable basis, especially as the measures are likely to be based upon mainly historical data. The exchange ratio will also be influenced by the bargaining powers of the parties to the merger and the generally recognized weaknesses and strengths of the companies concerned, e.g. their relative images as regards technology, management calibre, business leadership, product image, etc. E.A.L.

    A. J. Merrett and A. Sykes, *The Finance and Analysis of Capital Projects*, Chs. 10, 11 and 12 (Longmans, 1964); J. F. Weston and E. F. Brigham, *Managerial Finance*, Chs. 26 and 27 (Holt, Rinehart & Winston, 2nd ed., 1966).

Merit Rating A method of rewarding a worker according to his merit or worth to the enterprise over and above the normal or acceptable performance of a job. It may be described as a form of ✧ Performance Appraisal – which is used for the purpose of pay. Whereas ✧ Job Analysis is used as a method of arriving at fair comparative rates for different jobs, merit rating is used as a method of rating or ranking workers. Different workers doing the same jobs will perform differently; they will vary in cooperativeness, time-keeping, quality of workmanship and length of service. Even if pay is related to individual output, these other factors also have their importance. Merit rating starts by listing the factors to be taken into account and then rates workers under the different heads. There are a number of ways of making these comparisons, from simple rankings and 'paired comparisons' to more sophisticated methods such as the 'forced choice' method and the 'critical incident' approach. The aim is to reduce the subjective element in the judgement of the merit of an employee, and to arrive at standards which are consistent and which can be explained and justified to those to whom they are applied. L.S.

    British Institute of Management, *Merit Rating* (1954).

Method Study Method study is the systematic recording and critical examination of existing and proposed ways of doing work, as a means of developing and applying easier and more effective methods and reducing costs (British Standard 3138). ✧ Work Study.

    Method study is the creative aspect of work study. By means of a defined procedure either improved methods of doing existing jobs or efficient methods of doing new jobs are developed in order to achieve near optimum use of men, materials and machines. Frequently work measurement may be necessary in order to compare alternative work methods.

    The basic method study procedure consists of the following steps.

1. *Select the Job to be Studied*
Work study and hence method study should be applied in those circumstances where maximum or useful economic returns will be obtained, i.e. factors to be considered: (a) Anticipated life of Job; (b) Labour content – Cost of Labour; Ratio Man/Machine Time; (c) Extent of Job – Output; Man-hours involved; (d) Investment in equipment, tools, etc.

2. *Record Job Method*
Memomotion Photography; Multiple Activity Chart; Outline Process Chart; Flow process chart; S I M O chart: Cyclegraph/Chronocyclegraph.

3. *Examine critically*
Primary questions, to establish the fundamental need, i.e. the purpose of the

255

activities, the place at which they are done, the sequence, the person performing the activity and the means. Secondary questions, to establish alternative place, sequence, person and means and suggest improvements.

4. *Develop improved Method*
(a) Attempt to eliminate activities; (b) Attempt to combine activities; (c) Attempt to change sequence; (d) Attempt to simplify remaining activities.

Utilize principles of Motion economy, i.e. (a) Minimum movements; (b) Simultaneous movements; (c) Symmetrical movements; (d) Natural movements; (e) Rhythmical movements; (f) Habitual movements; (g) Continuous movement.

Consider the working environment, workplace layout and tool and machine design.

5. *Define Method*
E.g. Written standard practice; Job descriptions; Operating instructions.

6. *Install and Maintain*
Prepare Layouts; Demonstrate method; Train workers; Modify records, payment systems, etc.; Rehearse; Review progress; Modify, if necessary. R.W.

R. M. Barnes, *Motion and Time Study* (J. Wiley, 5th ed., 1963).

Mode ↻ Measures of Location.

Model ↻ Operational Research; Model (in Economic Analysis).

Model (in Economic Analysis) A model has been defined as 'the formal representation of the notions that we have about a phenomenon'. Thus whilst the notions may be familiar ones about the workings of a market or an economy, the formal representation of this in an abstract model is relatively new. The 'formal representation' is a simplified version of reality containing only those aspects of reality that are thought to be important by the model-builder. However, the model-builder is free to change the model if other factors omitted are later found to be important. From this there would appear to follow at least two advantages. In the first place the assumptions and implications of the model can be seen more clearly in the language of mathematics than in that of everyday speech. Secondly, the model becomes more amenable to statistical estimation.

A useful distinction is that drawn between *exact* and *stochastic* models, the former belonging to the province of economic theory, the latter to that of econometrics. Below we present the same basic model in an exact and stochastic form. In both cases the purpose is to explain economists' notions about the determination of equilibrium price and quantity in a market.

Exact		*Stochastic*	
$q_t^d = f(p_t)$	(1)	$q_t^d = f(p_t, u_t)$	(1)
$q_t^s = g(p_t)$	(2)	$q_t^s = g(p_t, v_t)$	(2)
$q_t^s = q_t^d$	(3)	$q_t^s = q^d + w_t$	(3)

where q_t^d = quantity demanded at time t,
$\quad q_t^s$ = quantity supplied at time t,
$\quad p_t$ = price at time t,
$\quad u_t, v_t, w_t$ = random normal disturbance terms at time t.

Both models contain a demand function, supply function and an equilibrium condition Consider, however, the two demand functions, equation (1). Knowledge of p_t and the functional form will be sufficient to determine q_t^d in the exact model. The corresponding equation in the stochastic model tells us that even if we know the functional form and p_t, other influences are at work on q_t^d, some of them known, others unknown. All we can assume is that the influences when combined follow the normal law, are random and have a zero mean.

This, therefore, means that whereas, given the equilibrium condition and knowledge of the functional form, we can determine the equilibrium price and quantity in the exact model, in the stochastic model these two values also depend upon the disturbance variables.

Does this, therefore, mean that the exact model is to be preferred? The answer to this is no, since the two models serve different purposes. A knowledge of f and g will enable one to calculate the equilibrium price and quantity for the exact model as has been stated already. On the other hand, if we have price/quantity data obtained from a market in the real world, the sketching out of the stochastic model is an essential prelude to obtaining estimates of the demand and supply functions, f and g.

Although our example has been taken from a particular market, the concept of a model obviously has applications in macro-economics, in addition to its use in other subjects such as operations research and marketing. Even though one may not wish to (or cannot) obtain knowledge of the functions because of the lack of data, the concept is still useful as an aid to understanding the causal mechanism at work. ⟐ Economics; Econometrics. L.T.S.

E. Malinvaud, *Statistical Methods of Econometrics* (North Holland, 1966).

Monetary Policy The general objectives of monetary policy in Britain were clearly laid down by the then Chancellor of the Exchequer in 1957 when he announced the formation of the Radcliffe Committee: 'This country stands determined to maintain a fixed and stable exchange rate. The primary requisite for this is that we shall be able and determined to avoid inflation at home. Equally it is also agreed policy to avoid slumps and severe unemployment, if these perils should again confront us.'

To these one should perhaps add: a speedy and steady rate of growth. Monetary Policy and ⟐ Fiscal Policy are used by the government to try and achieve these objectives. So far, however, it has not managed to attain all these objectives simultaneously and the notion of a fixed exchange rate has been temporarily abandoned as the major currencies of the world float in accordance with demand and supply pressures.

In 1971 in a consultative document 'Competition and Credit Control', the Bank of England made new proposals for regulating the extension of credit by the banks and deposit-taking finance houses and the aim of the proposals was to make for a more competitive banking system and a more flexible method of influencing monetary conditions. Many of these proposals came into effect in September 1971.

The main weapons of monetary policy now consist of: changing the minimum lending rate offered by the Bank of England to the discount market, and hence the often short-term rates linked to it; open-market operations to affect all banks' policies through their $12\frac{1}{2}\%$ reserve asset ratio; and requests for Special Deposits to be lodged by all the banks with the Bank of England.

It will therefore be observed that all banks and finance houses are covered by the new policies, rather than just the clearing banks. In addition, quantitative restrictions on bank lending have been abolished and instead more emphasis will be placed on the control of money supply as a whole with the help of a more vigorous interest-rate policy.

One purpose of changing interest rates is to affect the purchase of goods in which interest costs are important such as plant and machinery. However, available evidence suggests that interest costs are neither an incentive nor a deterrent to purchases of such goods. Changes in interest rates also have an effect on the liquidity position of financial institutions and individuals that reinforces fiscal measures and thus helps to control the general level of demand in the economy. The generally accepted view is that it is the whole liquidity position of financial institutions and individuals that is relevant to their spending decisions and willingness to lend and interest-rate changes, by their effect on the value of financial assets, play an important role in determining this liquidity position. L.T.S.

Committee on the Working of the Monetary System, Cmnd. 827 (HMSO, 1959). 'Competition and Credit Control', Bank of England Quarterly Bulletin, June 1971.

Monopoly Policy The British approach to monopoly power is to examine cases individually and judge each on its own merits. This reflects the fact that few, if any, conclusive statements can be made about the effects of monopoly power, either from theoretical reasoning or empirical research.

A monopoly was defined by the *Monopolies and Restrictive Practices Act*, 1948 as existing where at least one third of the supply of a good came from a single firm or group of firms, and if such a situation was thought to exist then the President of the Board of Trade could request the Monopolies Commission to verify its existence and pronounce upon its effects on the public interest. This latter phrase is open to considerable interpretation: where does the public interest lie if large profits are ploughed back to finance new capital expenditure or research and development? The framers of the Act were concerned that consumer preferences for goods should be met and that efficient methods of production and distribution should obtain and these objectives occur in various guises through subsequent reports of the Commission.

The Monopolies Commission has been reorganized several times in order to carry out its duties of reporting and recommending on a given situation. Until 1953 the Commission of 10 members considered each case together, but from then until 1956 its size was increased to 25 and several cases could be considered simultaneously by the use of smaller groups. The passing of the *Restrictive Practices Act*, 1956 took away from the Commission what was at the time considered to be a significant part of its work, i.e. its work on restrictive trade practices. Thus the Commission was returned to its pre-1953 size and mode of operation. In 1965, however, with the passing of the *Monopolies and Mergers Act* its size was increased again but, in addition, its sphere of interest was widened to cover investigations of the possible effects of proposed mergers. The latest change has occurred with the passing of the *Fair Trading Act*, 1973, for under this legislation the post of Director General of Fair Trading has been established with the power, amongst others, to gather detailed preliminary information before deciding whether to refer a 'monopoly' situation to the newly named Monopolies and Mergers Commission. Amongst other important developments introduced by this Act are the lowering of the monopoly criterion to one quarter from one third and the widening of the area of application of the Act to cover nationalized bodies.

Amongst the results of monopoly power that have cause for concern are the failure to develop research and development expertise (Supply of Industrial Gases), the restriction of competition (Supply of Wallpaper), and the use of price, advertising and promotion policies specifically designed to support monopoly power (Supply of Household Detergents). The 1973 Act gives the Director General power to negotiate with companies subsequent to the Commission's proposals as an alternative to the imposition of statutory orders but, so far, the general feeling about all monopoly legislation is that the initiative lies with the companies rather than the law makers. In addition, it is probably the case that the general evidence so far is more favourable to single-firm and group monopolies than the original drafters of the 1948 Act anticipated. It was upon trade associations and their restrictive agreements that the Commission were particularly severe in their *Report on Collective Discrimination 1955*.

The function of looking into proposed mergers was only introduced in 1965 and under the 1973 legislation the Director General will keep mergers under review, but the final decision to make a reference lies with the Secretary of State for Trade and Industry. As before a merger may be referred if a monopoly situation would result or if it would involve the taking over of gross assets exceeding £5 million.

Since the 1965 Act there have been over 7000 mergers and nearly all have been cleared without a reference to the Commission. Only 22 cases have actually been referred to the Commission whilst well over 700 have been specially considered by the mergers panel of the Department of Trade and Industry. Recently the record shows that references to the Commission have resulted in the collapse of bids before any public airing of their industrial logic, e.g. Glynwed–Armitage Shanks, and the evidence from 17 cases before 1973 shows a mixture of results. Seven suffered objections from the Commission (including British Sidac–Transparent Paper and Rank–De La Rue) whilst four went forward after a report (i.e. BMC–Pressed Steel, GKN–Birfield, BICC–Pyrotenax and Thorn–Radio Rentals). Of the remaining six cases, at least three were withdrawn before the Commission began its work and the others abandoned at a later stage.

There is no doubt that this side of the Commission's work has already aroused considerable controversy. Initially this was because the presumptions against mergers clashed with the general attitude of other government bodies such as the Industrial Reorganization Corporation and the Ministry of Technology. But of late many have detected an absence of underlying principle about references to the Commission and this pragmatic approach was recently defended at a conference by the Deputy Secretary at the D T I in charge of merger work. 'I frankly doubt whether a cut-and-dried set of criteria or guidelines is going to emerge against which firms and their financial and legal advisers will be able to say, with any more certainty than they can now, that such and such will be the Government's attitude in any particular case.'

Whether such criteria can be found now lies with the Director General of Fair Trading who will conduct the crucial preliminary examination. ⟨⟩ Restrictive Practices. L.T.S.

A. Hunter, *Competition and the Law* (Allen & Unwin, 1966).

Morale The extent to which the members of a group identify with the aims and activities of the group. Earlier usage of the term included its application to the emotional state of individual persons divorced from a group context but current usage is in accordance with the definition given.

If the interests of different groups are occasionally, or in some respects, conflicting – and this is certainly the case in an industrial organization – it is quite possible for morale in each of the conflicting groups to be high whilst that in the total organization would be comparatively low. Indeed, the ability of a group to engage successfully in conflict from time to time may be a condition of high morale. There is evidence to support that this is in fact the case and that an inability to exert a positive influence over its situation is likely to lead to low morale in a group. It follows from the foregoing that low morale cannot be inferred from the existence of occasional disputes even if some of these result in strike action. The degree of interest and involvement in group activities and the levels of absenteeism and labour turnover are more valid indications of the state of morale and even here absence and turnover are both affected by other variables.

High morale is not necessarily related to high productivity although it may be suggested that the failure of research to identify any consistent correlation between the two may be due to the adoption of too narrow a definition of productivity. It is difficult to resist the common-sense conclusion that high morale must be reflected in productivity *at least in the long run*. ⟨⟩ Alienation. Conflict. I.C.MCG.

W. H. Scott *et al.*, *Coal and Conflict*, Ch. 2 (Liverpool U P, 1963).

Motion Study The term Motion Study was first used by Frank and Lilian Gilbreth to describe their contribution to what was afterwards called 'scientific management'. They described motion study as consisting of 'dividing the work into fundamental elements; analysing these elements separately and in relation to one another; and from these studied elements, when timed, building methods of least waste'.[1] ⟨⟩ Gilbreth.

In the U K, motion study is often taken as synonymous with method study. However, motion study is only a part of method study, i.e. the study of the various *movements* which together constitute the work *method*.

Because of the wider implications the term method study is recommended by British Standard 3138 in preference to motion study.

In the U S A, motion study and method study (as well as methods research,

1. R. M. Currie, *Work Study* p. 6 (BIM, 2nd ed., 1963).

methods analysis and methods engineering) are often used interchangeably although the American Society of Mechanical Engineers' definitions distinguish between motion study – a study of movements; and method study – a study of the sequence of motions.

Micromotion Study

Motion Study utilizing ⇨ S I M O charts or Cyclegraphs, i.e. the most detailed type of motion study is usually referred to as micromotion study. ⇨ Method Study; Predetermined Motion Time Study. R.W.

British Standard 3138 (1959) A. G. Shaw, *Purpose and Practice of Motion Study* (Columbine Press, 2nd ed., 1960).

Motivation (of individuals and groups) The process of initiating and directing behaviour. An individual produces and sustains behaviour when he finds it rewarding to do so; that is, when the behaviour accomplishes an objective which satisfies a need. As far as the industrial organization is concerned, an employee will be motivated to carry out the duties assigned to him to the extent that to do so satisfies his personal needs. Whilst it has long been recognized that individual needs are complex and unstable, considerable reliance has been placed on financial incentives as a motivating device. Undoubtedly, financial rewards are extremely important not only for the material needs they indirectly satisfy but also for their symbolic significance as indicators of social and personal worth and status. In recent years, however, there has been an increasing disillusionment with the effectiveness of financial incentives and, following the theoretical assumptions of A. H. Maslow, attention has been directed to the need to place greater emphasis on rewards intrinsic to the work itself as a necessary supplement to the traditional extrinsic rewards. Accordingly, once provision has been made for adequate earnings and satisfactory general working conditions, attempts are made to structure the work situation so as to provide opportunities for increased independence and personal accomplishment. On the whole, research data appear to support the general validity of this approach but it must be borne in mind that motivation is highly complex and that personal needs differ greatly from one person to another and within the same person over time. ⇨ Alienation; Job Enlargement; Morale. I.C.MCG.

V. Vroom, *Work and Motivation* (J. Wiley, 1964); D. McGregor, *The Human Side of Enterprise* (McGraw-Hill, 1960).

Motivation Research (in Marketing) The process of seeking to identify the attitudes, habits and motives which trigger behaviour most particularly in the purchase of goods. Findings are used to make more effective promotional appeals and product formulations. The techniques involved, of which the most common are the small group discussion/interview (perhaps six to eight respondents) and the depth/unstructured interview, cannot always look for a direct revelation of motives but rather for comments which by interpretation can indicate the factors determining behaviour. Such interpretation relies heavily on the insights developed through psychoanalysis and many of the leading practitioners are psychologists and sociologists. The most famous pioneer of the technique was Ernest Dichter who still practices in North America, although the standard work on the subject was written in Britain: H. Henry, *Motivation Research* (Crosby-Lockwood, 1957). The technique caused a controversy when first introduced into ⟨⟩ Marketing Research since it was considered by many to be unethical, but was defended on the grounds that participants were volunteers in any event. Large samples are not normally taken with depth/unstructured interviews since it is contended that the relatively small variety of attitudes in a population will normally be present in a small group. However, the extent to which any particular attitude, habit or motive is held in any population must be quantified in a structured interview (⟨⟩ Market Survey). An extensive group of tools has been developed to facilitate this (⟨⟩ Attitude Scales). G.S.C.W.

Multiple Activity Chart (Also called: Man – Machine Chart; Work Planning Chart) A chart on which the activities of two or more subjects (men or machines) are recorded on a common time scale.

The activities and their duration are represented by blocks drawn against a time scale. Since it is difficult to include much detail on such diagrams, multiple activity charts constitute a less detailed method of recording work methods than proven charts. (⟨⟩ Gantt Chart; Method Study; Process Charts.)

Although there are many different conventions, depending on the purpose of the chart, the following is usual.

Independent Work ▮

Man working independently of machine, e.g. Preparing material, reading drawings.

Machine working independently of man, i.e. Operation not requiring either physical or mental attention of operator.

Combined Work □

Man working with machine or vice versa. Hand operation, e.g. hand feed.

Waiting ⊐⫙

by either man or machine, one for the other, or both for something else. R.W.

The Multiplier During the depression of the 1930s the theoretical approach of economists to the problems of the economy was changed by the publication of *The General Theory of Employment, Interest and Money* by J. M. Keynes. One important development was the idea of the multiplier, developed by Lord Keynes from earlier ideas of R. F. Khan. In essence the multiplier process shows how sustained changes in the level of components of final expenditure in the economy (⟨⟩ National Income Accounts), can produce multiplied effects on the level of gross national product. The importance of this development of thought for an economy in the grips of a depression is hard to exaggerate, because it showed, for example, that increases in investment demand if sustained would lead to increased levels of GNP and hence of employment. However, the idea is also useful for conditions of full utilization of resources. In addition, in conjunction with the acceleration principle (⟨⟩ Investment in the Economy) it offers some insights into the fluctuations in GNP (⟨⟩ National Income Accounts) that occur in most economies from time to time.

The multiplier, in its simplest form, shows the effect on a simple economy of a change in investment demand. Such a simple economy is usually postulated to have no foreign trade sector or government sector, but the multiplier can be modified to take account of these moves to reality. Traditionally macro-economists have been as much interested in the equilibrium of the whole economy as micro-economists have been in the equilibrium of particular markets. Thus the multiplier was originally developed as a static concept from a comparison of two equilibrium positions, but later work has focused attention upon its essentially dynamic character.

The following diagram shows the static multiplier as the simple economy moves from one equilibrium position to the next. Equilibrium here means that aggregate demand, the total demands upon the system, balance aggregate supply, the total output of the system.

In this case we imagine an economy with only two sectors, a consumer sector and a business sector. The demands that they make upon the system at any given level of income (= output) are shown by the schedule AB. Therefore, the economy will be in equilibrium at output (= income) level OK because at this level of output aggregate demand is also equal to OK (since $FK = OK$). Suppose now that investment demands increase, causing the aggregate demand schedule to rise vertically by amount GH. Then we have a new aggregate demand schedule CE and hence a new equilibrium level of output (= income) OL. A comparison of these two equilibrium positions using simple geometry shows that whilst investment demand has increased by GH, the equilibrium level of output (= income) has increased by $GJ (= FJ = KL)$ which is greater than GH. The multiplying factor is referred to as The Multiplier.

The following numerical example conveys exactly the same principle as before

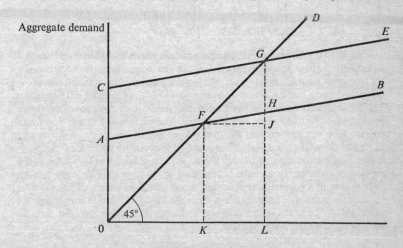

Aggregate supply (income)

but the actual process of change from one equilibrium position to the other is made clear. The assumptions that are made are as follows:

(1) The consumption function is of the form $C_t = 0.6\ Y_t + 150$.

(2) Investment demand is 50 initially and then rises in period 2 to 100. It does not vary with income levels.

(3) Output in the current period is equal to the previous period's aggregate demand.

The following symbols are used:

$O_t = Y_t =$ current output (Income)

$O_i =$ current production of investment goods

$I_t =$ current demand for investment goods.

$O_o =$ current production of consumer goods.

$C_t =$ current demand for consumption goods.

Then starting from the initial equilibrium position in period 1, with investment demand equal to 50, when investment rises to 100 the following happens in subsequent time periods.

Period	$O_t = Y_t$	O_c	O_i	C_t	I_t	Aggregate Demand ($C_t + I_t$)
1	500	450	50	450	50	500
2	500	450	50	450	100	550
3	550	450	100	480	100	580
4	580	480	100	498	100	598
5	598	498	100	508·8	100	608·8
|	|	|	|	|	|	|
|	625	525	100	525	100	625

In period 2 the demand for investment goods increases by 50 but output cannot adjust until the next period. In period 3 output and income increase to 550 because the new investment demand is satisfied. However, because consumption demand is dependent upon income it now increases to 480 ($C_t = 0.6\ (550) + 150 = 480$). This consumption demand cannot be met until period 4 when output of consumer goods rises to 480. However, this means that income is now 580 and thus again consumption demand exceeds the available supply of consumption goods and aggregate demand exceeds aggregate supply. However, we notice that the increments to aggregate demand in each period are diminishing and each is 0·6 of the previous increment. In fact the progression of the aggregate demand column follows that of a geometric progression, reaching 625 ultimately. Thus the final increase in output (= income) is 2·5 times the initial increase in investment demand. At this point the system is in equilibrium again because aggregate demand and aggregate supply are in balance.

$$125 = 2.5 \times 50 = \frac{1}{1 - 0.6} \times 50$$

In general then one can say that

$$\Delta Y = k\Delta I = \frac{1}{1-c}\Delta I$$

where ΔY = increment to total income (output)
ΔI = increment to investment
k = multiplier
c = marginal propensity to consume.

Whilst this is only true for a simple economy the principle is widely applicable. Thus the introduction of a government sector and a foreign trade sector means that increases in government spending and export demand set off multiplier processes of their own. Against this, however, not all the additional income reaches the final consumer because some disappears into undistributed profits, taxes or into the purchase of imports. Such 'leakages', as they are termed, act to reduce the value of the multiplier, which for this country has been put around 1 to 1·5. This compares with estimated marginal propensities of 0·5 to 0·7 which would give multipliers ranging from 2 to 3·3 ⟡ Consumption Function; Growth in the Economy; Employment. L.T.S.

F. S. Brooman, *Macro-Economics* (Allen & Unwin, 4th ed., 1970).

Muscular Work Movement is achieved by muscular contraction. The energy required for contraction is stored in the muscles within the large Glycogen molecules which disintegrate to produce glucose, the breakdown of which liberates energy and produces lactic acid as a waste product. No immediate supply of oxygen is required for this series of reactions, but an 'oxygen debt' is created in that oxygen is required for the further breakdown and removal of the lactic acid. Thus, in the long term, the amount of oxygen consumed is proportional to the amount of physiological work performed. It must be noted that a certain expenditure of energy takes place without obvious movement, since work is done by such muscles as the heart, in addition to those involved in the maintenance of posture.

Numerous equipments and techniques are available to measure the rate of oxygen consumption and hence the physiological energy cost of any activity of human performance. This energy cost provides one index for evaluating different methods of performing a particular task. E.E.

Myers, Charles Samuel (1873–1946) It is probably to C. S. Myers that the greatest debt is owed for the establishment of Industrial Psychology in the UK.

Following a distinguished undergraduate career in the natural sciences and later qualifying in medicine, Myers achieved eminence as an experimental psychologist in the first British laboratory at Cambridge. His interests were directed largely towards the establishment of applications of psychological principles in the fields of medicine, education and industry. In 1922, being disillusioned by the lack of support at Cambridge, Myers resigned his Readership to devote his full time attention to the National Institute of Industrial Psychology which he, along with H. J. Welch, had founded two years previously. Myers was elected as the first President of the British Psychological Society in 1920 and served as Editor of the *British Journal of Psychology* between 1913–24. E.E.

265

N

National Income Accounts Fundamentally the National Income Accounts (or Social Accounts) show the results and interconnections of economic activity in the country during a particular calendar year. The economic activity of the country is viewed in three logically distinct ways: (1) it can be viewed as the result of expenditure decisions; (2) as the result of production decisions and (3) since production necessitates factors of production, it can be regarded as giving rise to factor payments.

In August of each year the Central Statistical Office produces the National Income Blue Book which provides full statistical detail on the three ways of measuring economic activity. It is now an international convention that the aggregate measure of economic activity for a country is its Gross National Product, but the term National Income also has a special meaning besides being the general term used for such studies. Another widely used term is Gross Domestic Product (GDP) which is equal to the Gross National Product minus net property income from abroad. This is a measure of the goods and services produced as a result of economic activity in the UK. In addition the Blue Book contains a wealth of subsidiary material, known as the Social Accounts, which are useful in examining the progress and interconnections of different sectors of the economy such as the personal sector and the government sector.

Although the August publication refers to the previous calendar year, quarterly estimates of the National Income are also produced in *Economic Trends*, but of necessity they are lacking in the detail of the Blue Book. Nevertheless they are important for forecasting purposes.

The table opposite illustrates the three methods of measuring the economic activity of the country:

On the expenditure side we see that the decision-makers are individuals, firms, government agencies and overseas consumers. These demands are satisfied by the industries and services that make up the 'Value added' section of the table. Lastly, we note that the proceeds of economic activity go to wage and salary earners, self-employed people, firms as their profits and the holders of overseas property (net).

The initial impetus to the development of systems of National Accounts came from the publication in 1936 of Lord Keynes's book *The General Theory of Employment, Interest and Money*. This was reinforced by the Second World War, during which use was made of National Income Accounts for the overall control of the economic system. Today, in many developed and developing countries, the basic structure of the national accounts lies at the heart of government economic planning and forecasting. This is because the accounts provide the size of the key variables that influence the level of gross national product and from them one can work out rates of growth in these variables and their interconnections, e.g. consumer expenditure is a key variable and one can work out the relationship be-

266

Gross National Product (UK) 1967 £m.[1]

Expenditure	£m	Income	£m	Value Added	£m
Consumer Expenditure	25,323	Income from employment	23,471	Agriculture, Fishing, Forestry	1,121
Public Authorities' current expenditure on goods and services	7,063	Income from self-employment[2]	2,623	Mining and Quarrying	713
Gross domestic fixed capital formation	7,145	Gross Trading Profits of Companies[2]	4,694	Manufacturing	11,385
				Construction	2,394
Value of physical increase in stocks and work in progress	130	Gross Trading Surplus of Public Corporations[2]	1,111	Gas, Water, Electricity	1,110
				Transport and communication	2,807
Exports and property income from abroad	8,736	Gross Trading Surplus of other public enterprises[3]	92	Distribution	3,759
				Insurance, Finance, Banking	1,078
Less imports and property income paid abroad	—8,894	Rent[3]	2,142	Ownership of dwellings	1,610
		Less stock appreciation	— 200		
Less taxes on expenditure	—6,001	Residual error	— 51	Public Administration and Defence	2,101
Subsidies	790			Public Health and Education	1,703
				Other Services	4,352
				Less stock appreciation	— 200
				Residual error	— 51
		Gross Domestic Product at Factor Cost	33,882	Gross Domestic Product at Factor Cost	33,882
		Net Property Income from Abroad	371	Net Property Income from Abroad	371
Gross National Product at Factor Cost	34,292	Gross National Product at Factor Cost	34,292	Gross National Product at Factor Cost	34,292

1. National Income Blue Book 1960.
2. Before providing for depreciation and stock appreciation.
3. Before providing for depreciation.

tween growth of consumer expenditure and growth of personal disposable income. ⟪⟫ Forecasting for the Economy. L.T.S.

The National Income Blue Book (HMSO, 1968).

National Industrial Relations Court This court, also known for short as the Industrial Court, though in no way related to the Industrial Court set up in 1919 and now renamed ⟪⟫ Industrial Arbitration Board, was set up by the *Industrial Relations Act*, 1971. The court, which was treated as a branch of the High Court, consisted of judges of the High Court and the Court of Appeal appointed by the Lord Chancellor and of at least one judge of the Court of Session of Scotland appointed by the Lord President. One of these judges was appointed President of the National Industrial Relations Court. In addition, the court had also a number of non-legal members who were selected because of their special knowledge of industrial relations problems. The court could sit anywhere in Great Britain and sit in any number of divisions. Cases were heard in general by one of the judges assisted by between two and four of the lay members. Procedure before the court

267

was informal and while parties might be legally represented they might, if they wished, appear in person or be represented by a layman.

The court dealt with all complaints of ⟨⟩ unfair industrial practices arising under the *Industrial Relations Act*, 1971, with the exception of complaints about ⟨⟩ unfair dismissal which were tried in the first place by an ⟨⟩ industrial tribunal. The court also heard applications for the establishment of an ⟨⟩ agency shop, a permitted ⟨⟩ closed shop or a ⟨⟩ sole bargaining agency. The court also dealt with the interpretation and enforcement of contractually binding ⟨⟩ collective agreements. At the request of the Secretary of State the court could order a compulsory ballot in connection with a threatened industrial dispute. The court heard appeals from decisions of ⟨⟩ industrial tribunals while appeals on points of law from its own decisions went to the Court of Appeal (in England) or the Court of Session (in Scotland). The *Trade Union and Labour Relations Act*, 1974 abolished the National Industrial Relations Court. Most of its functions were transferred to the High Court. W.F.F.

A. Campbell, *The Industrial Relations Act* (Longmans, 1971).

National Insurance The aim of national insurance is to provide a measure of financial security for all citizens of this country. For purposes of national insurance all persons over school-leaving age and under retirement age are covered and have to pay weekly contributions, either as employed, or self-employed or non-employed contributors. The contributions and the types of benefit vary as between the different classes of contributors. Married women are excepted from insurance, but if employed they pay contributions unless they choose to opt out from the insurance scheme and to rely on their husbands' benefits.

The main benefits available under the National Insurance scheme are sickness benefit, unemployment benefit, retirement pensions, widows' and orphans' benefits and death benefits. Family allowances do not form part of the National Insurance scheme, since they are paid out of tax revenue and are not related to contributions paid.

National Insurance benefits differ from those paid under the ⟨⟩ Industrial Injuries scheme in that entitlement to benefits depends on the claimant having satisfied certain contribution conditions. Those who have not satisfied these conditions in full may be entitled to reduced rates of benefit. Details of current rates of contributions, benefit rates and contribution conditions are to be found in leaflets obtainable from any office of the Department of Health and Social Security which administers the scheme. W.F.F.

G. H. L. Fridman, *The Modern Law of Employment* (Stevens & Sons, 1963).

Negotiable Instruments A negotiable instrument is a document embodying a debt of a sum of money, where the document enjoys the quality of negotiability. Normally, a debt of money may be transferred (assigned) by the creditor to a third party, but this assignment must be made in writing, written notice of it must be given to the debtor and the third-party assignee acquires no better title to the debt than was possessed by the assignor. With a negotiable instrument, however, the transfer may be effected by mere delivery of the instrument without the necessity of either a written assignment or written notice to the debtor, and the third party who receives such an instrument in good faith acquires a good title to it, irrespective of the title of the transferor. The only exception to the rules about transfer apply to bills of exchange and promissory notes which require a written endorsement for purposes of transfer.

Whether or not an instrument enjoys the quality of negotiability depends largely upon commercial custom. Negotiable instruments embrace bank notes, bills of exchange, cheques, promissory notes, Treasury Bills and dividend warrants. It is unlikely that further instruments will be added to this list by commercial custom, but statute law could be used to create further negotiable instruments w.f.f.

D. Richardson, *Guide to Negotiable Instruments* (Butterworth, 1970).

Network Analysis This is a generic term which describes a number of techniques used to plan and control complex projects consisting of a set of interrelated activities. The essence is to represent the sequential relationships between the activities by a network of lines and circles.

For example, the pattern of activities required to complete the move of a machine in a production line to a new site is shown below.[1] The time to complete the move is kept to the minimum to minimize production losses.

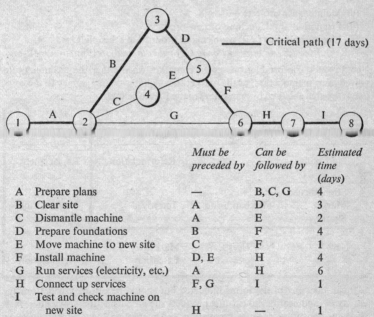

		Must be preceded by	Can be followed by	Estimated time (days)
A	Prepare plans	—	B, C, G	4
B	Clear site	A	D	3
C	Dismantle machine	A	E	2
D	Prepare foundations	B	F	4
E	Move machine to new site	C	F	1
F	Install machine	D, E	H	4
G	Run services (electricity, etc.)	A	H	6
H	Connect up services	F, G	I	1
I	Test and check machine on new site	H	—	1

Note that an individual activity is defined by a line between two circles, and its position in the sequence is defined by the other lines (activities) which are also

1. This example is taken from G. R. Gedye, *Scientific Method in Production in Management* (OUP, 1965).

linked to these two circles. Knowing the time, money, or other resources required to complete an activity, a schedule or dove-tailing of the activities can be derived which minimizes the total resources utilized in completing the project. In most common applications (including the above example) time is the resource that is minimized and the sequence or path of activities which must be completed on time to achieve this is known as the critical path. Network analysis techniques can be roughly grouped under two headings:

(a) Critical Path Method (CPM) assumes that the time required to complete an activity can be predicted exactly, identifies the critical path and calculates the total time along it.

(b) Program Evaluation Review Technique (PERT) recognizes that the time required to complete an activity cannot usually be predicted exactly and allows for this in evaluating the critical path.

Both methods may be extended to evaluate the utilization of costs and other resources.

Typical applications of network analysis techniques are:

(a) Construction projects.

(b) R and D projects.

(c) Maintenance projects.

(d) Promotion and launching of new products.

(e) Line of Balance (LoB) problems in production scheduling. M.J.C.M.

K. G. Lockyer, *An Introduction to Critical Path Analysis* (Pitman, 1964).

New Product The product offered to a market when either the technology involved in its manufacture, or the market to which it is offered, is new to the company (the area enclosed by heavy lines in the Figure below).

	Technology		
Markets	No Change	Improved	New
No Change	—	Reformulation	Replacement
Strengthened Market Share	Re-merchandising	Improved	Product Line Extension
New	New Uses	Market Extension	Diversification

It can take any of the forms indicated but should be distinguished from the variety of modifications to existing products shown outside the heavy lines. New products constitute product innovation and marketing management normally subjects such innovation to a rigorous series of tests as indicated on page 271. (⟡ Marketing Experimentation.)

G. Wills, D. Midgley and R. Hayhurst, *Creating and Marketing New Products* (Staples, 1973).

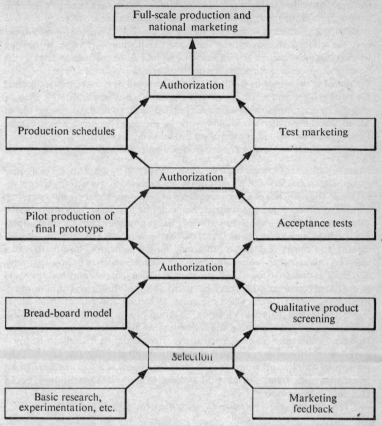

A sequence of new product development

Noise In the sense of sound without identifiable pitch, noise consists of a complex of vibrations which are not in harmonic ratio. In another sense 'noise' describes any sound which is unwanted by the listener. This latter sense of the word has been enlarged to encompass any signal, either auditory or otherwise, which occurs in a communication system but contains no intelligence for the recipient (⟨⟩ Information Theory).

Acoustical noise has three deleterious effects: it may produce reductions in work output; it is annoying and produces discomfort; it may bring about temporary or permanent hearing loss.

Noise levels are assessed in decibels above a standard basal level of 0·0002 dynes/sq.cm. (⟨⟩ Hearing). Since the various effects of noise are dependent upon frequency as well as amplitude, it is usual to measure the sound energy present in various parts of the spectrum by means of an octave band analyser.

Hearing loss is measured by establishing the absolute threshold for pure tones over the whole frequency range. The typical audiogram (i.e. the plot showing hearing loss as a function of frequency) of persons suffering from damage as the result of exposure to noise displays a marked dip in the region of 4 kHz.

Control of noise may be facilitated in numerous ways. It may be introduced at the source by attention to design and maintenance of machinery; it may be assisted by the introduction of screens and enclosures and the proper use of sound-absorbing materials. Should work be necessary in noise which cannot be adequately attenuated, the use of ear defenders is advocated. E.E.

C. M. Harris (ed.), *Handbook of Noise Control* (McGraw-Hill, 1957).

Norm A standard of specific behaviour expected of and by the members of a social group. The term refers to the actual behaviour expected and not to some theoretical ideal. The existence of agreed standards of behaviour greatly facilitates group action and enhances group solidarity. Some norms (e.g. those concerning social manners) may simply serve the purpose of making group life more pleasant, others (e.g. perhaps, those concerning dress) may serve to increase the group's sense of identity and others (e.g. those concerning output standards, loyalty to other members) may serve to protect the group from other competing or hostile groups. Some norms may be so loosely or erratically enforced that they may barely be said to exist at all, whereas others may be strictly enforced. Enforcement of norms is likely to be most rigorous when the group feels itself under threat from either internal or external forces. Violation of group norms by a new member will probably be treated charitably and the newcomer may receive gentle correction. However, deliberate violation, particularly if ostentatious, is likely to be interpreted as an act of hostility and the group members will react accordingly, perhaps by withdrawing from the violator the privileges of group membership or, in extreme cases, by acts of physical violence ⟡ Informal Organization; Social Control; Values. I.C.MCG.

J. A. Litterer, *The Analysis of Organisations*, Ch. 6. (J. Wiley, 1965).

Normal Distribution ⟡ Frequency Distributions.

O

Objectives (in Planning) An objective may be defined (1) as any aim or goal. This definition, which is by far the most common in use, causes some confusion partly because it can be confused with ⟡ Means and partly because, on this definition, an aim or goal can be any result that any manager wishes to achieve over any period of time, however trivial.

Thus it would be valid, on this definition, for an executive to have as his objective 'complete this report by lunch-time today'. While it may not be incorrect to define objective in this way it does cause further confusion to have to distinguish between such ephemeral short-term objectives and what are sometimes known as long-term objectives, especially since agreement is seldom obtainable on what is long term and what is short.

Much of the confusion disappears if a more fundamental interpretation of the word is made: (2) an objective is the *raison d'être* of an organization, that is to say it is its purpose, the reason for its existence. An objective thus becomes fundamental to the very existence of the organization such that if it fails to achieve it, it can be said to have failed as an organization. It thus becomes possible to judge whether an organization is succeeding or not by observing the extent to which it is achieving its stated objective, so that if it is decided that a company exists in order to make a satisfactory profit, then it can clearly be seen whether or not the company is succeeding or failing *as a company* by observing whether its profits are satisfactory or not.

In the same way it is possible to state the objective of a department by referring to its fundamental purpose within the organization: thus a research department may have the objective of 'preparing the products and processes that the company will need in the next few years'. Its success can be judged by the extent to which these products and processes have been prepared when they are required.

In the same way, also, the objective of any manager may be determined by reference to the fundamental purpose of the job he is doing.

The objective is, on this second definition, the answer to the question 'What is it for?' The more clearly and unequivocally the answer is stated the more readily can it be seen how the organization, department or person is progressing towards the objective. In general the objective of any organization can be defined as its *raison d'être* and all that is required to determine the objective for any organization is to ask what it is for. Invariably the answer will be that the organization exists to bring some benefit to a person or group of persons: all organizations exist to benefit someone and if they fail to produce that benefit they fail as an organization. However, it should be noted that to define an objective completely it is necessary to state both what the intended benefit is and who are the beneficiaries. Thus merely to state that an organization exists 'to make a profit' or 'to give aid' is only a partial answer. One needs to know also for whom the profit is to be made and to whom the aid is intended to be given. ⟡ Business Policy. A.J.A.A.

Objectives, Financial ⟡ Financial Management; Capital, Cost of.

Obstacles and Opportunities An obstacle is any event in the environment of the company which, if it occurred, might make the achievement of the objective more difficult. An opportunity is any such event which might make it less difficult.

While obstacles and opportunities are said to occur in the environment, ⟡ Strengths and Weaknesses which also affect the company's ability to achieve its objective occur within the company.

In general the larger the company the more obstacles can it overcome: a large company might even be able to bring such pressure to bear upon a government as to force them to remove a tariff or quota that was restricting its overseas market or to overcome the objections of a Preservation Society to a proposed factory extension – a small company might have less success against such obstacles. Obstacles to profit are usually fairly readily identified. Opportunities, however, usually need to be sought out with diligence before they can be identified and exploited: companies need to study changes in their markets closely before being able to discern a new corner of it to exploit and to study their competitors' weaknesses with some care before turning these to their own advantage.

The point has been made that overcoming an obstacle cannot increase profits, it can only prevent them falling. Increased profits can only come from exploiting new opportunities. A.J.A.A.

P. Drucker, *Managing for Results* (Heinemann, 1964).

Occupational Training ⟡ Industrial Training.

Off-Line/On-Line The term 'on-line' describes computer installations which are controlling industrial or commercial operations while they are occurring. Data on the operations are observed, calculations performed and results obtained quickly enough to enable the outcome of operations to be controlled. For this reason a computer can be said to be working in Real Time. Examples of on-line installations are process control applications in the chemicals, oil and steel industries and ticket reservation systems in commercial airlines.

The term 'off-line' describes computer installations which, although controlling a process, are not directly linked to the process and are only required to produce the results of calculations at relatively infrequent intervals. Examples of off-line installations are gas or electricity billing and customer accounting in banks. A customer's gas or electricity bill is computed on a monthly or quarterly basis whilst individual customers' bank accounts are usually checked at the end of each day. M.J.C.M.

Office Employment Working conditions in offices are governed by the *Offices, Shops and Railway Premises Act*, 1963. The Act defines an office as a building, or part of a building, used solely or mainly for office purposes, i.e. one of the following: administration, handling money, telephone or telegraph operating and clerical work in general including writing, book-keeping, sorting papers, filing, typing, duplicating, machine calculating, drawing and the editorial preparation of matter for publication.

The provisions of the Act dealing with health, safety and welfare largely repeat the corresponding provisions of the *Factories Act*, adapted to meet the special needs of office employment. The provisions of the Act are being enforced by the factory inspectorate as far as offices situated in factory buildings are concerned, while other offices are supervised by district and borough councils. Like the *Factories Act*, the 1963 Act will be replaced eventually by the new machinery set up under the *Health and Safety at Work Act*, 1974 ⟡ Factory Law. w.f.f.

I. Fife and E. A. Machin, *The Offices, Shops and Railway Premises Act, 1963* (Butterworth, 1963).

Oligopoly ⟡ Market Models and Competition.

Operational Analysis ⟡ Operational Research.

Operational Planning ⟡ Tactics.

Operational Research O R, known in the U S A as Operations Research or Operational Analysis, is defined by the U K O R Society as: '. . . the application of the methods of science to complex problems arising in the direction and management of large systems of men, machines, materials and money in industry, business, government and defence. The distinctive approach is to develop a scientific model of the system, incorporating measurements of factors, such as chance and risk, with which to predict and compare the outcomes of alternative decisions, strategies or controls. The purpose is to help management determine its policy and action scientifically.'

Put briefly it is the scientific approach to the analysis and solution of management problems to provide a quantitative basis for management decision-taking. The approach has the following characteristics:

(1) When presented with a management problem, the O R scientist will adopt a 'systems' viewpoint. Since any business organization is a complex system of the interacting parts, actions taken in one part of the organization are likely to produce effects elsewhere, so the systems orientation is logical. However, it is contrary to the natural inclinations of managers who, to make analysis by common sense principles and experience practicable, prefer to simplify a problem and amputate it from its environment. Because of their differences in outlook, the O R scientist will differ, at least slightly, with management in his formulation of the problem.

(2) Given a formulation of the problem, the O R scientist next develops a model. This term is usually associated with the physical replicas built during the prototype development of new ships, aircraft, buildings, etc. These models can be manipulated and used for experimentation at far less cost and risk than the 'real thing'. Furthermore, they are a useful means of communication, since, say. a physical replica of a proposed new building provides a far better vehicle for an architect to display his ideas than a verbal description. The problems examined by O R scientists (e.g. a production planning problem) are abstract in form and, by analogy, abstract replicas or models of these problems may be constructed. These models consist of mathematical and to a lesser extent verbal description of the problem studied. In using the word 'model' O R scientists are conforming to the terminology used by other scientists. Nowadays, most scientists use the term

model rather than law or theory to describe the conceptual framework they have erected to describe a particular aspect of reality. Thus Newton's so-called Law of Gravitation is a mathematical model which describes the gravitational interactions of bodies.

The accuracy with which the model represents the reality of the problem depends on the skill of the O R scientist and the techniques he has available. Given that his model is representative of the problem, he can use it to identify the alternative decisions that management has available, compare the outcomes of these alternatives and so discover which decision is best. Considering the production planning example, using the model, the effect on profitability of different production plans may be examined. Having identified the best policy, management may then implement it. It is interesting to note that the term 'model' may be applied to any conceptual framework for representing a problem. Managers use simple 'models' whenever they think about their problems, just as they use 'prose' whenever they write a letter, memorandum or report. The difference between an O R scientist's and a manager's model is that the former is mathematical and quantitative rather than intuitive (see (3) below).

The scientific approach manifests itself in O R in three ways:

(1) The emphasis is placed on objective observation and recording of quantitative data during the model-building period. Realistic model-building in O R requires similar skills to those required in the traditional sciences and, as an activity, can be accurately described as 'scientific'.

(2) An element of the scientific method is the confirmation of hypothesis by experiment. If management implements a policy recommended by O R men based on a model, later the latter observe the effects of the policy to see if it conforms to the prediction of the model.

(3) The physical, and to a lesser extent the other, sciences, are concerned with quantitative model building which, because of the apparent complexity of reality, require the use of sophisticated mathematics. Many management problems are complex and must be defined by accurate quantitative models, e.g. if the policy which maximizes profit is to be discovered. This need for quantification further identifies the O R scientist with the traditional scientist and is also responsible for one of the important benefits of O R, namely, that with a quantitative model it may be possible to identify the 'best' policy as against the 'good' one which would be obtained by traditional management intuition. For a problem which involves large sums of money the difference between the 'best' and the 'good' policy could be a large increase in profits or saving in costs.

Despite the similarities there are significant differences between O R and traditional science. The traditional science, for example physics, is made up of two parts:

(a) The activities of physicists engaged in investigating various phenomena of the physical universe, establishing theories, and building models of the phenomena under study, and the experimental and analytical techniques they use. (b) The body of knowledge known as physics which is (in principle anyway) a synthesis of the individual models for the various phenomena, to form a conceptual unity which embraces the whole physical universe.

At present O R is not attempting to build a unified body of knowledge like physics. The O R scientist is concerned with solving immediate problems and employing the techniques, mainly mathematical, at his disposal. Work on new, and the improvement of the existing, techniques is continuous and constitutes an important area of development of the discipline. Nevertheless, O R has discovered that, however varied their business or industrial context, operational problems can be reduced to an individual one of simple conceptual structure, or combination of a few. It has been suggested that at present only eight types of problem structure have been discovered and these are described elsewhere (⋄ Allocation; Competitive; Queuing; Replacement; Routing; Search; Sequencing; Inventory or Stock Control Problems).

The techniques employed depend on the nature of the problem. For example, whether it is static and deterministic (i.e. independent of time with quantities that are fixed) or dynamic and probabilistic (i.e. varies in time with quantities that are subject to variability or uncertainty). Some of the more useful techniques are discussed elsewhere (⋄ Decision Theory; Decision Trees; Heuristic Programming; Mathematical Programming; Network Analysis; Risk Analysis; Simulation (Computer)). M.J.C.M.

> Patrick Rivett and Russell L. Ackoff, *A Manager's Guide to Operational Research* (J. Wiley, 1963).

Operations Management Systems for the provision of goods or services are often referred to as operating systems, hence Operations Management concerns the management of both manufacturing systems (provision of goods) and service systems. Operations management is not only related to, but includes Production Management (⋄ Production Management), and whilst, in many cases, reference to operations management is synonymous with manufacture, sufficient similarity exists between goods-producing and service systems to justify a common approach to their study and management. R.W.

> H. L. Timms, *Introduction to Operations Management* (Irwin, 1967).

Operator Training ⋄ Industrial Training.

Opportunities ⋄ Obstacles and Opportunities.

Organization A social group deliberately created and maintained for the purpose of achieving specific objectives. This definition distinguishes organizations of the formal or bureaucratic type from other forms of social system.

The objectives of the organization are usually made explicit and their achievement involves the division of labour, often to a considerable degree, procedures for the coordination of effort, a hierarchical authority structure and, particularly in the business organization, economic measures of performance. The basic units of the organization are roles, not persons, so that, at least in theory, the organization may continue in unchanged existence despite frequent changes in personnel. The importance of organizations in modern society has been increasing at an accelerating pace but they have become the subject of systematic study only during the last two or three decades.

The term organization is also used to refer to the process of determining the activities necessary to achieve the objectives most economically, structuring the relationships among the roles thus created and ensuring the effective operation of the total system. ⟡ Authority; Bureaucracy; Formal Organization; Organization Theory; Role; Specialization. I.C.MCG.

> J. A. Litterer, *The Analysis of Organisations* (J. Wiley, 1965); A. Etzioni, *Modern Organisations* (Prentice-Hall, 1964).

Organization Development Planned and integrated effort to improve the effectiveness of an organization through the restructuring of its processes on the basis of behavioural science knowledge.

The application of an organization development programme involves a careful diagnosis of the organization's shortcomings, the preparation of a strategy for change and the marshalling of the physical and intellectual resources which the programme is seen to require. Typically, organizational development, as the term implies, seeks improvement in the total organization, or in a quasi-autonomous sub-organization, recognizing that, to be effective, change in any one part of the system requires supportive change in other parts.

Organization development conceives the ideal organization as one which is characterized by comparative clarity in the objectives established at all levels, a high degree of commitment to those objectives, open and honest communications throughout the system, open expression of disagreements and a constructive approach to conflict resolution and a culture that supports personal integrity and growth. I.C.MCG.

> R. Beckhard, *Organisation Development: Strategies and Models* (Addison-Wesley, 1969).

Organization and Methods O and M may be defined, from a techniques viewpoint, as the application of work study to the detailed administrative, clerical and office operations of an organization in order to improve the methods and procedures in use. It is therefore a study of the problems affecting the development, management and operations of offices. Other names given to this kind of activity are systems and procedures, clerical work study and systems analysis although the scope of the latter term has considerably widened in recent years to cover activities outside offices.

Generally the methods of O and M consist (1) of questioning the need for the procedures relating to a given area of activity and (2) if the activity can be justified of examining the effectiveness of the individual operations involved.

The scope of O and M, like work study, is perhaps limited mainly by lack of a general and well-developed conceptual framework as to criteria of efficiency and methodology of working. From this viewpoint an O and M approach compares unfavourably with that of ⟡ Operational Research, another approach to business problem-solving. E.A.L.

> H M Treasury, *The Practice of O & M* (H M S O, 2nd ed., 1965).

Organizational Theory 'The study of the structure and functioning of organizations and the behaviour of groups and individuals within them' (D. S. Pugh).

Despite the importance of formal organizations to modern societies, they have been objects of systematic study for little more than one generation. During the nineteenth century, various industrialists published their own personal philosophies of management, either describing the organization of their own factories or explaining the enlightened nature of their treatment of their labour force. However, it was not until the early days of the present century that attempts were made to formulate general propositions concerning organizational structure and processes. Early contributions to an understanding of organizations came from three main sources: the scientific management movement, industrial psychologists and the classical theorists. The primary concern of all three was to increase managerial efficiency.

The scientific management approach, pioneered by F. W. Taylor, concentrated on shop floor organization and developed techniques for studying, analysing and measuring the work of the operative, and for scheduling and recording work in progress. It may be argued that the 'scientific managers' were more concerned with the problems of analysing and improving performance at shop floor level than with the creation of general theories of administration, although Taylor's determination to maximize managerial expertise led him to advocate the use of functional authority and to suggest an appropriate structure. Their work also did much to stimulate interest in management as a rewarding subject for intellectual application.

The First World War further focused attention on industrial problems and the academic behavioural scientist became increasingly involved. Psychologists, both in Britain and in the USA, studied the problems of personal adjustment experienced by the newcomer to factory work and sought to systematize the hitherto haphazard process of selection, placement and training. Research was conducted to ascertain the effect on the operative of various elements in the organizational environment such as heat, light, ventilation, hours of work and the number and distribution of rest pauses.

Between the two world wars, the classical organization theorist sought to develop principles of management which would guide the general manager in his task of structuring and administering the business organization. The contributions came almost entirely from practising managers and reflected their concern with practical problems such as departmentalization, coordination and control and the distribution of authority.

The shop floor approach of the scientific management school and the industrial psychologists and the general management approach of the classical theorists were complementary yet they remained distinct. It may even be suggested that the development of general theory was retarded by the activities of the scientific managers whose methods promised quick and dramatic improvements in efficiency and so possessed a greater appeal than the more abstract general principles of the classicists. The two approaches were linked by the report on the Hawthorne Investigations when attention was drawn to the contrast between actual employee behaviour and the expectations of management. The Hawthorne studies emphasized the importance of studying the industrial worker, not in isolation, but in relation to the wider organizational context in which he was located. This context, it was suggested, should be viewed as a social system.

Overheads

Since the Second World War behavioural scientists – psychologists, social psychologists and sociologists – have been increasingly attracted by organizations as fields of study and, being mainly academic in orientation, they have been concerned primarily to develop theory rather than to seek specific solutions to *ad hoc* problems.

Accordingly there is gradually emerging a coherent body of knowledge to which has been given the name organization theory. However, organization theory is not yet as coherent as it needs to be if it is to reach a mature development. The representatives of many academic disciplines have turned their attention to the study of organizations and have contributed to the growing understanding of their functioning. Mathematicians, economists, biologists, engineers and others have all examined organizational behaviour from the standpoint of their respective disciplines. It is therefore not surprising that an all-embracing theory has not emerged. Instead, a number of 'organizational theories' grounded in different disciplines are being developed and this process will presumably continue. Common to nearly all the approaches, however, is the concept of an open system: a theoretical construct representing the interdependence of a number of variables interacting with each other and with the environment. The range of relevant variables is extremely large, perhaps infinite, so that each discipline must select those variables most relevant to its own considerations, recognizing that by so doing, it is inevitably presenting a very incomplete view of reality. The least esoteric of these developments and therefore, perhaps, the most likely to be of use to the industrial manager is the *social system model* of the behavioural scientist. As psychologists and sociologists begin to abandon their interdisciplinary demarcation lines, the prospects for the advancement of organizational theory seem bright. ⟡ Classical Organization Theory; Human Relations; Scientific Management. I.C.MCG.

D. S. Pugh, 'Modern Organization Theory', *Psychological Bulletin* Vol. 66, No. 4, Oct. 1966, pp. 235–51; M. Haire, *Modern Organisation Theory* (J. Wiley, 1959); T. Lupton, *Management and the Social Sciences* (Hutchinson, 1966).

Overheads Overhead, as an accounting term, is generally defined as the sum of all business costs which cannot be traced to specific units of output or are not traced because it is *inconvenient* or *too costly* to do so. Traceability in this context refers to identification with the unit of output in a physical sense of being 'embodied' in that output. Two essential characteristics of the accountant's overhead cost classification are, firstly, that such costs are common costs with respect to specific individual units or batches of output and, secondly, that they contain both fixed and variable cost elements. Alternatively overheads are sometimes defined as being synonymous with indirect costs to distinguish them from the three categories of direct costs; namely direct raw materials, direct wages and direct expenses. Overhead costs are usually classified for purposes of accountability into a number of categories reflecting the organization of the business. For example they may be classified into factory, warehouse, packing and distribution, selling, research and development, general administration, financial, non-operating, etc.

The most important aspect of overhead cost accounting is the question of an allocation or attribution of overheads to the costs of units of output and to the costs of alternative courses of action when making business decisions. Advocates of absorption costing procedures emphasize the need to allocate all costs (whether fixed or variable) to outputs and decision-alternatives on the perhaps misguided notion that 'one must allocate all costs on some convenient basis in order to recover them'. In contrast, marginal (or direct) costing advocates suggest that attempts to allocate the unallocable, namely fixed and common overhead costs, merely misinform the decision-maker and that only costs which vary with the volume of output or the implementation of a particular decision alternative can be (and should be) attributed to that output or alternative.

It is important to distinguish the traditional accountant's use of the term overhead, as defined above, from that of the economist's; the economist generally defines overhead costs as fixed costs and would generally be in sympathy with marginal costing procedures (⟡ Costs). E.A.L.

G. Shillinglaw, *Cost Accounting: Analysis and Control*, Chs. 4 and 8 (Irwin, 1967); J. M. Clark, *Studies in the Economics of Overhead Costs* (University of Chicago Press, 1938).

Overtime A variable amount of time, usually measured weekly, worked by an individual over and above the agreed minimum of standard hours for his industry and for which he is paid at a rate in excess of the agreed basic wage.

There has been an increasing amount of criticism of the level of overtime worked in British industry in recent years but this has not prevented it from rising to an average of about seven hours a week for adult males. Virtually every industry has some overtime and over a third of industries work an average in excess of five hours a week. The week ended 14 June 1969, provides a typical example of the overtime spread (Source: *DEP Gazette*, August 1969):

Industry	Operatives working over as a percentage of all operatives	Average hours worked over in the week
Food, drink, tobacco	34·2	9·8
Chemicals and Allied Inds.	29·1	10·3
Metal goods	31·2	9·5
Engineering and Electrical	46·1	8·4
Vehicles	43·3	7·5
Textiles	25·2	8·4
Clothing/Footwear	11·3	5·0
Paper/Printing	40·6	8·9

Overtime patterns tend to be regular and permanent: they are the same industries, firms and individuals who work high overtime. This regularity in itself casts doubt on the validity of the argument that overtime, the level and distribution of which is determined almost entirely by ⟡ Workplace Bargaining, is a necessary auxiliary in the struggle to meet production deadlines and heavy short-term work

Overtime

loads. In no other country, with the exception of France, is so much overtime worked, and yet the indices of overall production and productivity have risen more slowly here than elsewhere over the past two decades. The highest levels of overtime tend to occur in those industries with the lowest basic rates. This suggests that overtime, far from being at the discretion of management, is in fact an indispensable component of many weekly wage packets – indispensable because the low basic rates paid in many industries are insufficient to meet the needs of those workers with only average financial commitments. Far from facilitating essential additional output, much of the overtime worked seems to arise out of a desire to waste time at work in order to obtain an adequate wage. There are some conspicuous examples of firms which have managed to effect drastic cuts in overtime through the implementation of productivity agreements without any loss of output, e.g. Esso, Fawley. ⟰ Productivity Bargaining. N.H.C.

Royal Commission on Trade Unions and Employers' Associations, Research Paper No. 9; *Overtime working in Britain*, E. G. Whybrew (H M S O, 1968).

P

Pacing (in Assembly or Flow Line Work) Two forms of work pacing are evident on assembly or flow lines. Mechanical work-pacing occurs on moving belt type lines, whilst operator-pacing predominates on non-mechanical lines (◊ Assembly Lines). Mechanical pacing exists when workers are constrained to complete their operations within a certain allowed time. Rigid pacing occurs when workers are given an absolute time, neither more nor less, to complete their operation. Pacing with margin exists where a tolerance about the allowed time exists.

Rigid pacing rarely occurs, but pacing with margin is normal in this type of work, e.g. workers on an automobile assembly line give themselves margin by riding along the line whilst completing their operations.

Too little margin can lead to System Loss, i.e. in the diagram the curve represents the time required by the worker to complete the operation (between 20 and 140 seconds but usually about 60 seconds). If the allowed times are 50–70 seconds, there will be frequent occasions on which the worker will not be able to complete the operation and similarly occasions on which too much time is allowed. ◊ System Loss. Whilst mechanical pacing is absent on non-mechanical lines, a similar effect may occur, since although short-term variation in operation times is generally accommodated by the existence of buffer stocks between stations (◊ Buffer Stocks), longer-term balance must be maintained and hence workers are to some degree constrained by their colleagues.

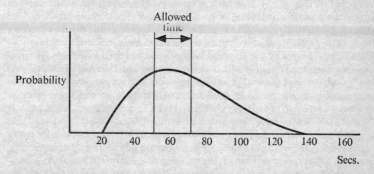

To reduce or eliminate these losses, the pacing effect must be reduced by one of the following methods, each allowing the worker to offset unusually long cycle times with unusually short ones. (1) Make the job available to the worker for as long as possible, e.g. where workers on an assembly line are fed with jobs placed on a moving belt, closer spacing increases the time available. *Example:* For a worker who can reach 2 feet up and 2 feet down the belt, job spacing of 4 feet on a 4 feet/min. belt makes the job available for 1 minute, 2 feet spacing on a 2 feet/min.

283

Packaging

belt, whilst providing for the same line output, makes the job available for 2 minutes. (2) By providing larger buffer stocks between the stations on non-mechanical lines, thus effectively 'disconnecting' workers at adjacent stations on the assembly line. R.W.

Packaging (in Marketing). The wrapper or container in which a product is enclosed to facilitate distribution and use. The marketing approach towards design of packaging has undergone substantial change in recent decades. Protection of the contents, the original purpose, is now deemed only one of many functions performed by the packaging; it is seen as a vitally important part of communications in consumer markets (⟡ Marketing Communications Mix). In industrial markets particular attention is paid to the problems of handling, storage and shipment, especially through the use of bulk packaging which breaks out into smaller packs (⟡ Design). This latter pattern is familiar also in consumer markets. Eight general principles have been evinced for good packaging: (1) it should be integrated in design, particularly in colour and typographically, with the other communications media of the organization; (2) it should be designed to be eye-catching; (3) it should establish its own identity; (4) it should be appropriate to the product contained in terms of users' subjective expectations; (5) it should be aesthetically pleasing; (6) it should invite handling; (7) it should be well constructed, as durable as necessary for its purpose and convenient in use, paying particular attention to pack size for, e.g. storing, table use; (8) it should be designed specifically to communicate with its market segment. ⟡ Market Segmentation. G.S.C.W.

J. Pilditch, *The Silent Salesman* (Business Publications, 1964); The Journal of Packaging, 1965.

Participation The act of taking part. A major problem confronting the leaders of large-scale organizations is that of how best to maximize the commitment of the rank and file to their own specific tasks and to the goals of the organization as a whole. The problem has been particularly acute in large industrial organizations and since the advent of a widespread factory system of production various remedies have been tried or advocated. There were some who believed, like Marx, that the ⟡ Alienation of the worker was due principally, if not entirely, to the pattern of ownership of the means of production. Accordingly, it was urged that the system of ownership be radically changed – Guild Socialism, Syndicalism or State ('Public') ownership have been proposed as alternatives. Others considered that it would be sufficient if the pattern of ownership were modified through the use of profit sharing, employee shareholding or co-partnership schemes. More recently, attention has concentrated less on the question of the ownership of the organization than on the administrative processes which characterize it, and formal systems of joint consultation or, in some cases, joint decision-making have been advocated. The success of any of these measures is difficult to gauge with any accuracy but it seems safe to observe that none seems to have led to a very marked increase in commitment.

There is, however, a gradual accumulation of research data which appears to support the contention that commitment is likely to be enhanced if the persons concerned participate in the making of decisions which affect them personally,

284

particularly those which affect them directly. It may be, of course, that in some cases a change of ownership pattern may be a necessary preliminary to the requisite change in administrative structure and practice but in general a solution is increasingly being sought in a modification of the day-to-day practices of managers and supervisors. The formal machinery of joint consultation enables the participation of only a small minority of the labour force and the involvement of the majority requires that a participative style of supervision and management be adopted throughout the organization. Additionally, provision is made for increased participation by the restructuring of tasks so as to permit a much greater degree of individual initiative and judgement in their performance ⟡ Alienation; Authority; Job Enlargement; Joint Consultation; Motivation; Specialization. I.C.MCG.

W. H. Scott, *Industrial Leadership and Joint Consultation* (Liverpool University Press, 1952); C. Argyris, *Integrating the Individual and the Organisation* (J. Wiley, 1964); F. Herzberg, *Work and the Nature of Man* (Staples, 1968); P. Blumberg, *Industrial Democracy: The Sociology of Participation* (Constable, 1968).

Partnership A partnership is defined by the *Partnership Act*, 1890 as 'the relation which subsists between persons carrying on a business in common with a view of profit'. The relationship which gives rise to a partnership may be based on an express agreement (generally embodied in a partnership deed) but it may also be implied from the conduct of the parties. Thus, whenever a person shares in the profits of a business conducted by another, he will be deemed to be his partner. A partnership must have at least two members and not have more than twenty. A business association of more than twenty persons, not registered as a joint stock company, would be treated as an illegal association. The partners in a partnership are jointly liable for all contractual commitments entered into on behalf of the partnership and are jointly and severally liable for all wrongs (torts) committed by or on behalf of the partnership.

The partners are collectively referred to as a firm. The firm, unlike a company, is not a separate legal entity and legal actions will have to be brought against the partners and not against the firm. The partners may select the firm name and have a free choice in doing so, except that they may not select one which is similar to that of another firm so as to be likely to mislead the general public. Unless the firm name includes the full names of all the partners, the name has to be registered with the Registrar of Business Names in London. ⟡ Company Law. W.F.F.

C. D. Drake, *The Law of Partnership* (Sweet & Maxwell, 1972).

Patents A patent is a monopoly right granted by the Crown to the inventor of an invention. The true and first inventor, or his assignee, may apply to the Patent Office for a patent which, if granted to him, will entitle him to prevent others from exploiting the invention while the patent lasts. A patent is granted in the first place for four years and may subsequently be renewed annually by the payment of renewal fees at a rising scale, up to a maximum of sixteen years in all.

The subject-matter of a patent must be a 'manner of manufacture', i.e. the patent must specify how a particular article can be made and patents cannot be granted for basic scientific ideas which are not related to the manufacture of a particular object.

While the patent is in existence the patentee may stop by court proceedings any infringements of his monopoly rights but, if he should fail to use the invention commercially, any other interested party may obtain a compulsory licence enabling him to use the invention against the payment of royalties to the inventor. Once the patent has expired, the patented process is free and may be used by anyone. W.F.F.

> T. Terrell, *Law and Practice relating to Letters Patent for Inventions* (Sweet & Maxwell, 1971).

Patterns of Growth By horizontal integration one refers to a situation in which the firm grows by extending the production of its existing products. This may be because the firm has unexploited technical and marketing economies of scale and thus grows from within. However, the firm may recognize deficiencies in its own organization and see in a rival a way of remedying them: e.g. such motives appeared in the inquiry into the proposed merger of Montague Burton and United Drapery Stores in 1966.

Vertical integration refers to growth by a firm either forwards into retailing and additional production processes or backwards into the ownership and manufacture of raw materials. Both moves may occur, the end result being to bring more operations under the control of the firm. Clearly a frequent way of accomplishing this end is to acquire other firms but it need not necessarily be so. The motives for vertical integration are usually fear of curtailment of supplies or outlets and the desire, with modern manufacturing methods, to maintain even flows of production. A desire to safeguard their supply of good quality tube steel was one reason why Tube Investments Ltd purchased the Round Oak Steel Works in 1953. Similar fears prompted the purchases in the 1950s of Briggs Motor Bodies Ltd and Fisher and Ludlow by Fords and BMC respectively. A movement in the other direction is well illustrated by the purchase of retail outlets by The Wallpaper Manufacturing Co. Ltd.

Lateral integration refers to growth in the direction of different products which may have a common technical base or use existing marketing facilities. The uncertainties of economic life are one reason for this growth for it ensures that all one's resources are not tied to one product or market segment. Another reason may be that whilst technical economies in the existing product range are exhausted there are still marketing and managerial economies unexploited. A good example of this type of development is Hoover Ltd with its move from the original vacuum cleaner into a general range of household electrical durables and now into gas heaters. ⬦ Corporate Planning; Business Policy; Growth of the Firm. L.T.S.

> R. S. Edwards and H. Townsend, *Business Enterprise* (Macmillan, 1962).

Pay Board ⬦ Prices and Income Policy.

Payback Period This is a measure of the worth of an investment project widely used in practice (⬦ Capital Budgeting). However, since payback defines a period of time it is not as such a measure of return. Payback in fact measures the time-period by the end of which the initial investment outlay is expected to be returned by the funds flow resulting from the initial outlay. For example, if investment projects A and B both require an initial outlay ($= I$) of £1,000 and A returns £250 per annum and B £200 per annum in additional net cash flows ($\diamond$ Funds Flow Analysis) and the number of years over which the flows are expected to continue (n) are 4 and 16 respectively then the payback period measure (P) is:

$$P \qquad = I/Y \text{ Years}$$
$$\text{For } A, P_a = 1000/250 = 4 \text{ years}$$
$$\text{for } B, P_b = 1000/200 = 5 \text{ years}$$

Since A returns the investment outlay more quickly it is, according to a payback criterion, a more desirable project. Yet 'common sense' tells us that B must be more worthwhile. In fact A, taking interest into account, gives a negative return, since it returns only just the initial investment whereas B returns considerably more. It is therefore clear that where Payback is used in practice the businessman cannot use it literally without taking other aspects of the investments into account.

The principal defects of this method are therefore that: (1) No account is taken of what happens after the end of the payback period nor of the timing of the receipts. A £ received now is valued as highly as a £ received one, two or any years hence. (2) Depreciation of the investment outlay is ignored. (3) The time-value of money is ignored.

Justifications made for the use of the payback measure relate to the ease of its measurement and, in so far as the uncertainty of cash flows increases with distance in time, its ability to take account of uncertainty in a crude fashion.

The reciprocal of the payback period, i.e. Y/I, provides a means of expressing the payback measure as an estimate of the rate of return. For example, for projects A and B above, the estimates would be 25% and 20% respectively. It is interesting to note that given the simplest pattern of flows, i.e. the investment outlay is made at the beginning of the project and returns are constant per period, then as the life of the project increases the payback reciprocal quickly becomes a closer and closer approximation to the 'true' rate of return (i.e. net present value); so that for an important class of projects (generally those with a life of more than 15 years) the payback reciprocal becomes a reasonable measure. E.A.L.

M. J. Gordon, 'The Payoff Period and the Rate of Profits', reprinted in E. Solomon (ed.), *The Management of Corporate Capital* (The Free Press of Glencoe, 1959).

Payment by Results $\diamond$ entries on Wage.

Payroll Deductions $\diamond$ Check-off.

Pedal $\diamond$ Machine Controls.

Percentiles It is often convenient to express a frequency distribution of values in terms of the percentage of the whole population of values which occurs at or below a particular value. Such a method of expression is in general use, for example, to describe the range of anthropometric dimensions in a given group of people. Thus the 50th percentile (or median) is the value below which half the population appears and the 10th percentile is that below which a proportion of 0·1 of the population appears.

A typical extract from an anthropometric table appears below.

Measurement	Percentiles (inches)				
	1st	5th	50th	95th	99th
Male Stature	62·7	64·6	69·0	73·4	75·2
Female Stature	56·5	58·4	62·8	67·3	69·2

From such a table, it can be concluded that, for example, the stature of 99% of the whole population falls within the range 56·5″–75·2″. ⟡ Measures of Dispersion and Location. E.E.

Perfect Competition ⟡ Market Models and Competition.

Performance Appraisal A systematic method of assessing the performance of employees in their jobs with a view to helping management decisions on promotions, transfers, training or changes in pay (⟡ Merit Rating). This is a process which is undertaken, more or less informally, whenever an employee's future is being considered. Modern methods involve a regular and systematic procedure whereby an employee's immediate superior is required to assess his subordinate's performance over a period of time and under given heads. Present practice sometimes includes an initial self-appraisal by the individual employee followed by an interview with his manager, at which an agreed appraisal may be reached. This process may result in an agreement on targets relative both to individual performance and work to be done for the period ahead. Appraisals of this kind are one aspect of a system of ⟡ Management by Objectives – which is operated at all levels of an enterprise. The purpose of this approach is to reduce the 'sitting in judgement' aspect of superior/subordinate relationships and to increase the sense of shared responsibility and involvement among employees, in the lower as well as the higher ranks of management. L.S.

Douglas McGregor, *The Human Side of Enterprise* (McGraw-Hill, 1960); E. Anstey, *Staff Reporting and Staff Development* (Allen & Unwin, 1961).

Performance Rating (in Time Study) The comparison of an actual rate of working against a defined concept of a standard rate of working.

The standard rating is defined as 'corresponding to the average rate at which qualified workers will naturally work at a job, provided they know and adhere to the specified method and provided they are motivated to apply themselves to their work'. (BS 3138)

During a ⟡ Time Study a worker's observed performance is 'rated' in order to convert observed times to basic times,

$$\text{i.e. Basic Time} = \frac{\text{Observed Time} \times \text{Observed Rating}}{\text{Standard Rating}}$$

On the British Standard Performance Scale, standard rating is equal to 100, i.e. an observed rating of 50 is equal to half the standard rate of working.

British Standard Scales and terminology are by no means exclusively adopted. Several other performance scales are in use, and often two points are defined, a higher one equivalent to 100 on the BS scale, corresponding to the rating and performance of piece-workers (but *not* always called Standard Rate or Performance), and a lower one corresponding to the rating and performance of time-workers, i.e.

British Standard Scale	60/80 Scale	75/100 Scale	100/133 Scale
100	80	100	133
	60	75	100
0	0	0	0

Methods of Rating

Although Standard Rating is defined (above), in practice the concept of a standard rate of working is a function of the situation, e.g. physical conditions, company policy, etc. The time study observer is trained by the use of training films and exercises to recognize a standard rate for different jobs and in different conditions. e.g. effort required; skill used; pace of work; physical conditions; difficulty of job, etc.

Various methods of performance rating have been devised, ranging from entirely subjective procedures to more quantitative approaches in which numerical values are allocated to certain different conditions affecting the work, e.g. the physical or mental effort involved.

Nevertheless it is impossible, using direct time study, to guarantee absolute uniformity of rating within a company and even less between companies. R.W.

R. M. Currie, *The Measurement of Work* (BIM, 1965).

Peripheral Equipment (Computers) ⟡ Computers.

Personality In common usage, the meaning of 'personality' can vary between eccentricity and sex appeal. To the psychologist the term signifies that integrated organization which determines each individual's pattern of behavioural responses to the environment. Thus the study of personality is essentially the study of differences between people. The fact that particular human responses are seldom completely predictable is an indication of the complexity of organization involved; the study of psychology is possible because human behaviour is not completely random.

There have been numerous theories of personality structure, each of which tends to be associated with a set of techniques for measuring differences between individuals. Questionnaires and inventories, for example, are used to assess attitudes and interests. The projective techniques rely upon an interpretation of a person's response to a minimal stimulus, such as an incomplete sentence. Psycho-analytic techniques involve the interpretation of data from free association, the analysis of dreams and perhaps responses evoked under hypnosis.

During the last 20 years or so, the introduction of powerful statistical methods has made possible the handling of large amounts of data on human responses and has facilitated the classification of some of the most important dimensions of human personality (⟡ Factor Analysis). E.E.

C. S. Hall and G. Lindzey, *Theories of Personality* (J. Wiley, 1958).

Personnel Management That part of the process of managing which is concerned with the policies, procedures and practices governing the recruitment, selection, training, promotion, remuneration and working conditions of the people employed by an enterprise. Personnel management is thus part of the job of anyone who manages other people, as well as the description given to the function of specialists called personnel managers or personnel officers.

As enterprises have grown in size, the tendency has been for the work of management to be subdivided, initially into such primary functions as manufacturing, selling and purchasing, and later into functional areas like accounting and personnel management concerned with the resources of money and people. Since work generally has become more specialized, greater knowledge is now required by those choosing employees for jobs. In addition, scarcities of certain types of human resource in countries using complex technologies, allied to the growth in membership and bargaining power of ⟡ trade unions, have further encouraged the development of personnel management as a separate function staffed by specialists knowledgeable in such areas as industrial ⟡ psychology, industrial sociology and ⟡ organization theory.

Social scientists in these fields have extended the knowledge of human behaviour within organizations and have helped to devise more reliable techniques and procedures for the ⟡ selection and ⟡ motivation of individuals and for influencing performance in working ⟡ groups. Personnel management today therefore goes far beyond a concern for the ⟡ welfare of employees which characterized the policies and practices of some businessmen in the nineteenth and early twentieth centuries who felt that they had a responsibility to ensure good working conditions for women and young employees considered unable to protect themselves from exploitation by the employer. Today, in the face of strong trade unions and a greater understanding of motivation, employers not only aim to provide fair conditions of employment, but also seek to make work more satisfying for employees. To this end, employees are being enabled to make fuller use of their abilities and interests at work by the redesign of jobs and a recognition of the satisfactions to be derived from membership of a working group.

In implementing the policies of an enterprise that concern employees and their relationships with each other, personnel management thus becomes involved with employment, remuneration, training, working conditions, employee services and industrial relations, as well as questions of organization development and ⟡ communication.

Employment includes all those tasks which are performed in order to secure the efficient and flexible manning of an undertaking; that is to say, recruitment, selection, placement, appraisal, transfers, promotion and dismissals. Hours of work, holidays, overtime, rest pauses are also included under this heading. As a means to this, personnel records have to be kept and be kept up to date, giving the necessary information about all employees including relevant facts in their personal histories. Remuneration is concerned with the rates of pay and earnings of wage- and salary-earners and may be based on trade union agreements and on job evaluation, which form the basis for a wage and salary structure for the whole enterprise. It also covers the actual payment of ✩ Wages and salaries (✩ Salary Structure), whether weekly or monthly, and whether in cash or by cheque. ✩ Industrial Training is undertaken to equip employees to carry out efficiently the tasks they have to do. It is the employer's responsibility to provide a safe and healthy working environment. Certain standards, in most cases minima, are pre-scribed by the *Factories Act* and the *Offices, Shops and Railway Premises Act*. (✩ Welfare and ✩ Accident Prevention.) Employee services cover pensions, sick pay, holiday fund and similar schemes, to many of which employees make a financial contribution; other services are the provision of canteens and rest-rooms.

✩ Industrial Relations is the whole field of relationships between employer and employees, although it is sometimes used in a restricted sense to apply to those between trade unions and employers. In the context of personnel management it includes arrangements for ✩ Joint Consultation through Committees or Works Councils, face-to-face dealings between foreman and shop steward or between works manager and trade union official. It is concerned with the agreements between the two sides of industry and the disputes and conflicts which arise both before and after such agreements are made. (✩ Collective Bargaining; Dispute; Productivity Bargaining; Shop Steward; Strikes.)

The growing body of research in ✩ Cybernetics and ✩ Organization Theory is producing a body of knowledge which is demonstrating the relation of the struc-ture of organizations and of systems of communication to behaviour and perform-ance at work. The relevance of this knowledge to effective management makes it an integral part of the personnel function. What responsibilities and authority are given to specialists working in the personnel function will depend upon the nature of the enterprise and the context within which it operates, and what is con-sidered to be the most effective way of organizing its resources to achieve its objectives. L.S.

P. Pigors and C. A. Myers, *Personnel Administration* (McGraw-Hill, 1961).

Personnel Management Adviser ✩ Manpower Adviser.

Personnel Manager ✩ Personnel Management.

Personnel Officer ✩ Personnel Management.

Personnel Policy ✩ Personnel Management.

PERT ✩ Network Analysis.

Physical Distribution Management That activity which treats all decisions relating to the physical movement of output as a unified total system. The system consists of eleven cogs, which centre on inventory management as illustrated in the figure. The system objective is to maximize the total profit potential. This concept is of

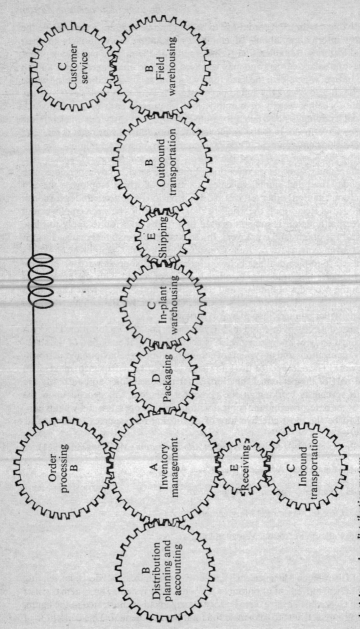

Activity cogs in a distribution system
Redrawn from Wendell M. Stewart, 'Physical Distribution: Key to Improved Volume and Profits', *Journal of Marketing*, XXIX (January 1965), 66.

recent origin and many organizations do not yet embrace it. They treat the cogs separately and a substantial degree of suboptimization is encountered in terms of, e.g. stock levels, warehouse location, channel selection (◊ Distribution Mix). It does, however, provide the managerial framework for optimization and offers an opportunity for employment of more capable executives than hitherto in this sector of business. The concept is attributed to Wendell Stewart as recounted in 'Physical Distribution: Key to Improved Volume and Profits', *Journal of Marketing*, XXIX, January 1965. G.S.C.W.

See particularly M. Christopher and G. Wills, *Marketing Logistics and Distribution Planning* (Allen & Unwin, 1972).

Picketing There does not exist any precise definition of picketing, but the term includes all methods used by strikers to cut off the employer with whom they are in dispute from contact with the outside world. Under English law picketing is legal provided that the persons engaged in it:

(1) Act in contemplation or furtherance of an ◊ Industrial Dispute;

(2) Act peacefully;

(3) Restrict their actions to obtaining or communicating information or to persuading persons to work or to abstain from working.

If picketing is unlawful, such as where the pickets obstruct access to private premises, they will be guilty of a public nuisance. An employer is of course not obliged to tolerate the presence of pickets on private property, even if the pickets behave quite peacefully, and he may treat pickets who enter his property as trespassers. If pickets cease to behave peacefully, they will become individually liable to prosecution for assault or public nuisance depending on the nature of their actions. W.F.F.

R. W. Rideout, *Principles of Labour Law* (Sweet & Maxwell, 1975).

Piece Rates ◊ Wage Drift; Wage; Wage Systems.

Planned Maintenance ◊ Preventive Maintenance.

Planning (in the Economy) The idea of planning arouses strong feelings in people – to some it is a dirty word, whilst to others it conjures up visions of the promised land. This dichotomy of attitude stems in part from the different meanings of the word. A clear difference between a planned system and a non-planned system is provided by Sir Robert Shone in an article in the *Economic Journal*, March 1965. He says that planning: 'contrasts directly with the classical approach summed up in the phrase of Adam Smith that the individual "is brought as by an invisible hand by seeking his own advantage to secure that of the community at large".'

Thus planning indicates for each individual: 'what is the expected contribution of his own work and that of his fellows to the life of the community'.

Starting from this viewpoint the old idea of planning conjures up visions of central direction of the economy such as the country became accustomed to during the period 1939–45. Resource allocation was accomplished by the physical requirements needed to produce the final goods for the war effort, rather than by the interplay of market forces. The government decided upon the structure of final demand and resources of land, labour and capital were allocated accordingly.

Planning

Such an exercise would appear to be dependent for its success largely upon the degree to which all members of the community believe in the major national objective. Obviously in wartime, planning of this variety has a good chance of success. The keynote of this overall planning is physical control backed up by authority to discipline if targets and schedules are not met. Clearly, to maintain such control would be difficult in peacetime because national objectives are then by no means so clearly defined. This explains to some extent the growing dissatisfaction with the controls that were carried on by the Labour Government after the war.

The formation of the National Economic Development Council (NEDC) in 1961 marks the beginning of the new type of planning in the UK. The initial desire for it stemmed from a belief that short-term considerations were weakening the basic economic strength of the country and that benefits would flow from the setting of a new national objective – in this case growth. The basic standpoint from which NEDC and later the Department of Economic Affairs (DEA 1964) worked is that it is a useful exercise to indicate where the economy is going in the next five years. Hence this type of planning is known as 'indicative planning'. The plan for the years ahead, however, is based partly upon industrialists' expectations of the future and partly upon government desires for the future. By the publication of a target rate of growth, industry, trade unions and the government are at least aware of the implications for each of them if this target rate is to be achieved. However, in the end there are no compulsory powers that can be used to ensure that the targets are reached. Rather is it the belief that the published forecasts will have a compulsive power of their own.

No doubt it can be argued that this is not really planning. But the government has implemented a number of measures and formed a number of new bodies to aid the realization of the objective of faster growth. The crucial problem to solve at the moment is the link between long-term objectives and short-term problems and when this is solved one may expect to see a resurgence of 'indicative planning'. Recent experience suggests, however, that future plans will be based much more closely upon feasible rates of growth rather than target rates of growth. In essence this follows recent steps to shift from broad aggregative policy to micro policy affecting sections and sectors in the community.

A survey[1] of recent experience in the UK and Europe suggests that one could say, justifiably, that an economy is planned if there exists a quantitative programme and if economic policy is so used as to bring about the objectives of the plan. The quantitative programme would indicate the growth of the main industries and economic aggregates over a medium-term period (say five years) and would also indicate the obstacles and bottlenecks to growth, which could be both quantitative and qualitative in nature. The instruments of economic policy, e.g. ♢ Fiscal Policy, Monetary Policy, would be used so as to remove the obstacles and bottlenecks and thus aid the achievement of the objectives of the plan. For example, changes in fiscal policy could be used to stimulate investment in industry

1. Based upon PEP, *Economic Planning and Policies in Britain, France and Germany*, p. 25 (Allen & Unwin, 1968).

and to direct more output towards exports and away from home consumption.
L.T.S.

G. Polanyi, *Planning in Britain: The experience of the 1960s* (IEA, 1967).

Plans Although some plans by their nature are clearly long term and some are clearly short term there is no hard and fast rule to distinguish between them, nor does there appear to be any difference in kind, only in degree. Two features that are common to both are the number of variables and the extent of uncertainty.

Short-term plans are, by their nature, more concerned with the efficient use of existing resources while long-term plans may embrace the provision of new physical resources as well as the efficient use of existing ones. Since it usually takes time to provide new physical resources they cannot be considered in short term planning. So long as the plan is limited to manipulating existing resources the number of variables to be considered is limited; as soon as the time horizon of the plan is extended to include the possibility of altering the existing resources or adding to them, the number of variables to be considered in the plan increases. The longer the range of the plan the greater is the number of variables that may have to be taken into account.

The second feature that increases as the range of planning extends is uncertainty. All forecasts are inaccurate. Since plans are based on forecasts and since plans must be prepared with these possible errors in mind, the greater the range of the plan the more seriously will these errors have to be considered by the planner.

These two features increase in severity as the range of the plan increases. Both are present in all plans, short and long range, but they become of overwhelming importance in long-range planning ⇨ Forecasting; Strategy; Tactics. A.J.A.A.

Plans, Contingency A contingency plan is a prepared response to an event that may occur.

Normally such plans are not prepared in great detail and they are often not prepared at all unless the event is likely to be of such importance as severely to affect the company's ability to achieve its objectives.

Typical of such planning is the company which recognizes that sooner or later its plant may be put out of action by some catastrophe and that no insurance can cover it for loss of customer good-will. Accordingly it may make arrangements with its competitors, its suppliers, its transport contractors and so on to maintain deliveries on its behalf in that event. The thoroughness with which contingency plans are prepared will depend upon the probability of the event occurring, in the opinion of the management, and the likely severity of its effects. A.J.A.A.

Plant Bargaining ⇨ Workplace Bargaining.

Plant Layout Layout problems occur at four levels, i.e. in an industrial context:
(1) Factory Location ⇨ Location of Industry.
(2) Layout of Departments within the Plant.
(3) Layout of Facilities within the Departments.
(4) Workplace Layout ⇨ Work Study; Ergonomics.
Items (2) and (3) above can be considered as the macro and micro version of a

similar problem, which is to obtain a relative location of departments and facilities to achieve most efficient operation.

The arrangement of production facilities is determined in the main by the type of production and three types of facilities layout exist:

1. *Layout by Process* (Layout by Function) All facilities for performing the same or similar functions are grouped together: i.e lathes, milling machines, etc., are found in separate areas.

Layout by process is associated with jobbing in small batch production and has the following characteristics: (1) allows specialized supervision; (2) facilitates provision of services; (3) failure of machines or absence of workers does not disrupt production excessively; (4) good machine utilization; (5) operations may be missed and 'bad' jobs delayed because of the necessary flexibility of control; (6) high work in progress.

It is appropriate in the following circumstances: (1) variety of products; (2) small batch sizes; (3) intermittent demand for products.

2. *Layout by Product* (Flow or Line Production). One product or component is produced in one area on the necessary facilities. Layout by product is associated with mass and large batch production and has the following characteristics: (1) little material handling necessary; (2) good machine utilization; (3) low work in progress; (4) production control facilitated; (5) minimum floor space required; (6) machine breakdown disrupts production; (7) production is geared to fastest machine; (8) effective use of labour, i.e. minimum training, job specialization, etc. ◊ Job Analysis.

It is appropriate in the following circumstances: (1) large batch sizes or continuous production; (2) standardized design; (3) stable demand; (4) continuous supply of material.

3. *Layout by Fixed Position*, i.e. where the material or principal component is fixed or must remain in one position, i.e. building of aircraft, shipbuilding, civil engineering. Unlike the previous layouts the facilities move to and from the product: (1) poor facility utilization (particularly on remote work, e.g. civil engineering); (2) can accommodate variety in product, changes in design, etc.; (3) satisfaction for intermittent demand.

The product, and hence parts to be manufactured, and the method of manufacture will determine machinery requirements. Storage, inspection, etc. will be required, and total space requirements for each area or department can be calculated, making allowance for movement, development, etc.

The criterion used for layout planning is normally materials handling or transport cost, consequently an investigation of the pattern of interdepartment or interfacility movement is required before a layout may be developed using one of the many techniques. ◊ Plant Layout Techniques. R.W.

J. M. Moore, *Plant Layout and Design* (Macmillan, 1962).

Plant Layout Techniques Irrespective of the technique adopted, the criteria normally used in developing plant layouts are total material handling or transport cost.

Two approaches exist: (1) consideration of dominant parts only, i.e. to

Example — Cross Chart

From Dept. \ To Dept.	1	2	3	4	5
1	14	13			
2			29	18	
3	4		7		
4		8		1	
5	5			9	
6		26			

Loads/Week

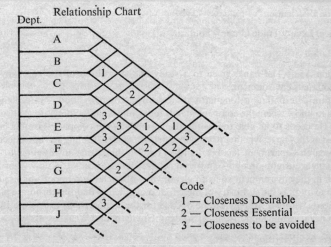

Relationship Chart

Dept. A B C D E F G H J

Code
1 — Closeness Desirable
2 — Closeness Essential
3 — Closeness to be avoided

simplify the problem consider only the products or parts which constitute the majority of production in terms of quantity or value; (2) methods considering the complete range of products.

Cross charts and relationship charts may be used to record the pattern of material handling or transports and indicate the desirable relative location of departments (see example, p. 297).

Given the size of departments and the desirable relative locations, two methods exist for developing a layout.

(1) Graphical Methods, using templates, diagrams, etc., to develop a layout meeting the above requirements and filling the requirements of existing buildings, etc.

(2) Analytical Methods, using heuristic algorithms to minimize total material handling cost.

Several computer programs exist, e.g.

'CRAFT' (Computerized Relative Allocation of Facilities Technique).

Input – (1) Initial or arbitrary layout configuration showing department areas.

(2) Load Flow Matrix between all departments.

(3) Inderdepartmental Material Handling Cost Matrix.

Output – (1) Best Layout configuration developed after a series of interchanges of departments.

(2) Total Material Handling Cost.

Other computer programs exist, using as input a statement of department size, limitation of existing buildings, and a statement of desirable relative locations (e.g. Relationship Chart). R.W.

E. S. Buffa, *Modern Production Management* (J. Wiley, 1965).

Point-of-Sale Promotion ◊ Merchandising.

Poisson Distribution ◊ Frequency Distributions.

Political Levy ◊ Trade Union – Politics.

Population ◊ Statistics.

Position Audit The name given to a study of the position of the company in relation to its environment.

Before determining a long-term strategy for a company a corporate planner needs to know where the company stands today and what factors have shaped its past. He needs to be able to identify the reason why the company's profits have moved as they have, whether it has gained or lost a share of the market, how effective its research department has been and so on. He thus gains an insight into the company's current strengths and weaknesses. He also needs to know what lies ahead in the environment so as to identify any obstacles and opportunities. The position audit is the summary of these four main factors that the corporate planner needs before a strategy can be devised for the company. ◊ Corporate Planner; Obstacles and Opportunities; Strategy; Strengths and Weaknesses. A.J.A.A.

Posters ◊ Advertising.

Posture Correct posture is essential in order that maximum working efficiency may be attained and if discomfort and the risk of injury are to be minimized. Two complementary programmes are necessary to achieve these goals: equipment of all types must be properly designed for the people using it and training schemes are necessary in order to teach the safe and efficient ways of deploying the body. The latter programme is usually confined to the lifting and handling of heavy articles, but might well be extended to include such simple postures as those of standing and sitting.

Occupational studies of the design of equipment in relation to posture have included examinations of motor vehicle cabs, aircraft and space vehicle cockpits, computer consoles and crane cabs.

Fairly extensive studies have been carried out into the nature of seated posture and the design of chairs. The main weight of the body, when seated, should be upon the bony ischial tuberosities and very little pressure should be exerted on the underside of the thighs. Nothing should press behind the knees, and it should be possible for both feet to be placed upon the floor or upon a foot-rest. Backrests should provide proper support in the small of the back and should be shaped to accommodate the natural curvature of the spine. ⟡ Ergonomics. E.E.

Power The ability to exert a positive influence over objects, persons or situations. This ability may derive from many sources: for example, it may be based on superior physical strength, superior or specialized knowledge, an ability to inspire by personal example, charisma, the use of material rewards or punishments, the creation of social obligations through demonstrations of affection or friendship, skilled oratory, influence or control over resources. It is unfortunate that the concept of power has pejorative connotations for this has limited not only the rational discussion of the concept but also the recognition of its importance.

Every organization attempts to define the powers of its various members and the right to exercise such power is called authority and tends to be limited to the minimum considered necessary for the efficient discharge of the members' duties and responsibilities. Not all power, however, is legitimate and in any organization there are members who are generally perceived to possess power which the organization does not formally recognize: for example, persons who have privileged access to information, who are in close social contact with those who possess legitimate power, or who are believed to be able to influence decisions, particularly decisions affecting rewards. There tends to be competition among the members of an organization for power and for those roles which are associated with power, not only for the sake of the power itself but also for the higher rewards and status which such roles usually carry. An understanding of the distribution of power in an organization is essential for an understanding of the social relationships among the members. ⟡ Authority; Charisma; Status. I.C.McG.

J. Pfiffner and F. Sherwood, Ch. 17, *Administrative Organisation* (Prentice-Hall, 1960); D. McGregor, *The Human Side of Enterprise* (McGraw-Hill, 1960).

Predetermined Motion Time Study (PMTS) 'A work measurement technique whereby times established for basic human motions (classified according to the

Distance Moved Inches	Time TMU				Wt Allowance			Case and Description
	A	B	C	Hand in Motion B	Wt (lb.) Up to	Factor	Con-stant T	
¾ or less	2·0	2·0	2·0	1·7	2·5	1·00	0·0	
1	2·5	2·9	3·4	2·3				
2	3·6	4·6	5·2	2·9	7·5	1·06	2·2	A Move object to other hand or against stop
3	4·9	5·7	6·7	3·6				
4	6·1	6·9	8·0	4·3	12·5	1·11	3·9	
5	7·3	8·0	9·2	5·0				
6	8·1	8·9	10·3	5·7	17·5	1·17	5·6	
7	8·9	9·7	11·1	6·5				
8	9·7	10·6	11·6	7·2				
9	10·5	11·5	12·7	7·9	22·5	1·22	7·4	B Move object to approxi-mate or indefinite location
10	11·3	12·2	13·5	8·6				
12	12·9	13·4	15·2	10·0	27·5	1·28	9·1	
14	14·4	14·6	16·9	11·4				
16	16·0	15·8	18·7	12·8	32·5	1·33	10·8	
18	17·6	17·0	20·4	14·2				
20	19·2	18·2	22·1	15·6	37·5	1·39	12·5	
22	20·8	19·4	23·8	17·0				C Move object to exact location
24	22·4	20·6	25·5	18·4	42·5	1·44	14·3	
26	24·0	21·8	27·3	19·8				
28	25·5	23·1	29·0	21·2	47·5	1·50	16·0	
30	27·1	24·3	30·7	22·7				

Reproduced with permission from *Methods Time Measurement* by H. B. Maynard, G. J. Stegemerten and J. L. Schwab (McGraw-Hill, 1948). N.B. 1 TMU = 00001 hr.

nature of the motion and the conditions under which it is made) are used to build up the time for a job at a defined level of performance.' (British Standard 3138.) ⟡ Work Measurement (sometimes called Basic Data). PMTS differs from ⟡ Time Study because it is an indirect method of obtaining basic times for jobs.

PMTS systems at least originally relate to fundamental motions, and conse-quently it is possible to obtain basic times for all jobs (fundamental motions being by definition the lowest common denominators of human work). In this respect PMTS differs from ⟡ Synthetic Timing which is concerned with job elements. Many systems are available, e.g. Work Factor; Master Standard Data; Basic Motion Time Study; Methods Time Measurement (MTM).

MTM is perhaps the best known and is the only non-proprietary PMTS system. Because the PMTS data is derived from an extensive analysis of man jobs (usually from motion films) greater accuracy and consistency results.

There has been a tendency recently to develop systems concerned with larger units of work (e.g. MTM 2). This has resulted because the systems based on fundamental motions (e.g. MTM 1) were often time-consuming and expensive to apply.

Example: MTM 1

Seven basic hand motions are defined and times under different conditions are provided: e.g. Reach – the basic motion used when the purpose is to transport an object to a destination. R.W.

> H. B. Maynard (ed.), *Industrial Engineering Handbook* (McGraw-Hill, 2nd ed., 1963).

Present Value The present value concept can be used to measure the value of an investment project. The net present value (*NPV*) of a project is the difference between the present value of revenues (or benefits) and the present value of costs (or sacrifices) when all revenues and costs are discounted back to the present time by reference to the cost of capital (⟨⟩ Capital, Cost of).

Assuming that the whole of the investment outlay is made immediately then the *NPV* is usually defined as follows:

$NPV = P - I$, where $P =$ the present value of periodic future flows of revenues and costs, as defined below, and

$I =$ the investment outlay assumed to be paid out entirely at the commencement of the project's life.

$$P = \frac{Y^1}{(1+i)} + \frac{Y^2}{(1+i)^2} + \ldots + \frac{Y_n + S_n}{(1+i)^n}$$

where $Y =$ the net cash flow, i.e. revenues less costs, in time period $j (j = 1, 2, 3, \ldots, n)$,

$S_n =$ the scrap or realizable value from the project, received in year n,

$n =$ the life of the project in number of time periods, e.g. one year.

and $i =$ the cost of capital to the firm.

If the *NPV* is positive then the project in question is, according to present value theory, acceptable since in present value terms a profit after earning a sufficient rate of return is shown. A negative value for *NPV* indicates that the project is expected to earn less than a sufficient rate of return and is therefore unacceptable.

It can be shown that the present value and internal rate of return criteria are generally equivalent (although in some specific situations the latter may be misleading).

For example, consider a project which has an initial investment of £1,000 and a net cash flow for the following 50 years of £100. The *NPV* of such a project will vary with the firm's cost of capital. As this increases and therefore as the rate at which the future receipts are discounted also increases, the *NPV* will fall. The relationship can be shown by the following figure, in which the curve VV' shows the NPV of this project as the cost of capital increases.

The curve VV' shows the present value of the project, continuously, as the cost of capital varies. As the latter increases the present value falls indefinitely. For example, the NPV is given by point A on VV', i.e. £500 approx. when the cost of capital is 2%. Likewise when the cost of capital is 4%, NPV is £200 approx. At C,

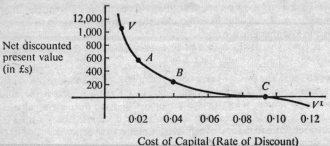

Cost of Capital (Rate of Discount)

the intercept between VV' and the cost of capital axis, the NPV is zero. Since the ◊ Internal Rate of Return is defined as that rate of interest (or discount) at which the NPV equals zero, the value for i at this point defines the Internal Rate of Return. ◊ Discounted Present Value; Internal Rate of Return. E.A.L.

Press Relations ◊ Public Relations.

Prestige The degree of esteem in which a person is popularly held. This definition, which seeks to maintain a careful distinction between *prestige* and *status*, is regarded by many to be rather pedantic. Accordingly, the distinction is frequently not made and the terms may be regarded as interchangeable. ◊ Status. I.C.MCG.

Preventive Maintenance Two direct methods are used to ensure or increase reliability of equipment or production processes – preventive maintenance and breakdown maintenance or repair. ◊ Maintenance.

There are two facets of preventive maintenance:

(1) Regular inspection to detect the need for repairs or replacement to prevent breakdown.

(2) A regular maintenance routine, determined by experience or from manufacturers' recommendations to avoid or reduce wear, etc.

Preventive maintenance is more suitable and particularly beneficial where:

(1) Breakdown-time distributions are known and accurate, and have low variability (i.e. if the operating life is known and constant, preventive maintenance can be arranged just prior to 'breakdown'). (See figure, p. 303.)

(2) Where the cost of preventive maintenance is less than that for breakdown maintenance. Often cost of preventive maintenance is less than breakdown maintenance even when the down time is greater for preventive maintenance. For example, in an automated process, preventive maintenance can be scheduled to

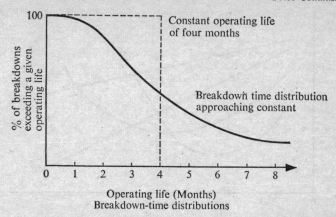

Operating life (Months)
Breakdown-time distributions

take place during inoperative periods, whereas breakdown even for short periods will stop the whole plant. The cost of preventive maintenance is often offset by providing operating stability. R.W.

Price Commission ⇨ Prices and Incomes Policy.

Prices (Theory of) A firm's pricing policy is an important element of its competitive strategy but it must be considered in relation to product and promotional policies. As far as traditional microeconomics is concerned, the interest in prices stems from their role in allocating scarce resources rather than their determination within the firm. This partly explains the many controversies over methods of pricing by economists and businessmen.

If the firm is selling in a perfectly competitive market (⇨ Market Models) then it has no pricing policy because price is determined by the market. Demand and supply forces interact to determine the price that will clear the market and the individual firm strives to sell as much as it can at this price. In practice the system does not work perfectly, shortages and excess supplies occurring because of imperfect foresight or poor weather conditions. This means that either the government enters the market, or producers attempt to organize themselves, in order to stabilize prices and incomes. Such a pattern applies to many agricultural commodities and industrial raw materials

For the firm selling in other than a perfect market (⇨ Market Models), the appropriate price to set is that which satisfies its objectives. If profit maximization is the objective then this leads to the well-known condition that the profit maximizing output occurs where marginal receipts and marginal costs are equal (this is the first-order condition). The price of this output can then be read off the demand curve.

The diagram on p. 304 illustrates the point using demand and cost curves. Output *OP* is the profit maximizing output, because at this output marginal receipts and marginal costs are equal. The price at which this output can be sold is *PR*.

From this basic model several variants have been developed to explain observed

Prices

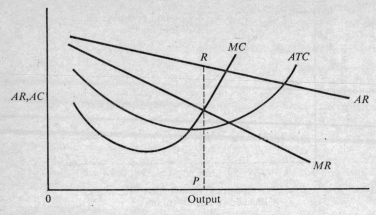

AR = Average receipts (price) for different levels of output
ATC = Average total cost for different levels of output
MR = The change in total receipts caused by changing output by one unit
MC = The change in total costs caused by changing output by one unit.

behaviour of firms in different structures. Thus the existence of price discrimination leads to a price discrimination model, whilst the suggested stability of prices in oligopolies has given rise to the kinked demand curve which enables stability and profit maximization to be preserved in the model ⟨⟩ Market Models.

For a variety of reasons the general approach outlined above has been criticized. The following are among the most important points:

(1) Firms do not have such a detailed knowledge of demand and cost data.
(2) Firms do not seek to maximize profits.

Empirical research into pricing policies has tended to reveal the prevalence of full-cost pricing or some variant of it. In its simplest form this would require the estimation of unit variable costs at some standard level of output and then the addition of percentages to cover overheads and selling expenses with a final, say 10%, profit margin. However, this basic approach appears subject to considerable variation depending upon market conditions, whilst there are still problems involved in the correct measurement of costs. If mark-ups are rigid then prices are entirely cost-determined but evidence does suggest that considerable variation in mark-up occurs in response to various competitive pressures. One of the reasons most often given for adhering to full-cost procedures is that such prices are thought to be 'fair' prices and consistent with objectives such as earning a 'reasonable' rate of return on capital. Perhaps this indicates that they may serve as bench mark figures.

Finally, mention should be made of what has been termed going-rate pricing. In this case the price of the product is taken from those of its near competitors and the product is then produced in such a way as to match the price with a 'reasonable' profit rate. There is evidence that such a procedure is followed in oligopolies such as the car industry. ⟨⟩ Business Motivation; Costs; Demand Functions; Economics; Market Models; Pricing (Market Pricing); Transfer Pricing. L.T.S.

M. Spencer, *Managerial Economics* (Irwin, 3rd ed., 1968).

Price–Earnings Ratio Measured by market price per share divided by earnings per share, the price–earnings ratio is often referred to as the P/E ratio. It may be said to represent the price which an investor is willing to pay for each £ of current earnings from a particular investment in a company. It is therefore a useful basis of comparison between investments; but a low ratio does not necessarily indicate a desirable investment since any difference between alternative investments may be more than compensated for by additional risk ⟨⟩ Risk and Uncertainty (in Financial Management).

The reciprocal of the P/E ratio, i.e. earnings-to-price ratio, is known as the capitalization rate. It is sometimes used to arrive at a notional value for ordinary shares, using an estimated rate of return figure for businesses of that kind, much in the same manner as is done for debentures and fixed interest securities. But in the case of ordinary share valuation such a procedure is most unsound since the current capitalization rate for an ordinary share is most unlikely to reflect its value.

Closely connected with the P/E ratio as a share valuation concept for comparative purposes is the measure of dividend yield, which may be defined as dividend per share divided by market price (as a percentage). The use of earnings and dividends in this connection raises the question of whether it is dividends or earnings which are appropriate for valuation purposes. On this question the reader is referred to the references given below. E.A.L.

Ezra Solomon, *The Theory of Financial Management* (Columbia UP, 1963); J. F. Weston and E. F. Brigham, *Managerial Finance*, Ch. 20 (Holt, Rinehart & Winston, 2nd ed. 1966).

Prices and Incomes Policy A policy for the control of prices and incomes laid down by government in its role as manager of the economy.

No government can avoid having a prices and incomes policy. It may be a policy which involves no direct interference with market forces, including those involved in ⟨⟩ Collective Bargaining over wages and salaries, but even *laissez faire* is a policy. Governments are concerned about the general level of economic activity, and therefore about the general level of incomes. They seek to exercise influence over incomes by means of ⟨⟩ Monetary and ⟨⟩ Fiscal policies. Additionally they may employ administrative controls: to a greater or a lesser degree the governments of Britain, the USA, Australia, Sweden, Holland and other countries have interfered with the freedom of collective bargaining in this fashion.

Since the end of the Second World War successive British governments have been concerned both with attempts to control ⟨⟩ Inflation in a high employment economy and to deal with successive ⟨⟩ Balance of Payments crises, those in 1949 and in 1967 leading to a devaluation of the pound. Governments have sought to contain the level of domestic expenditure, thereby stabilizing domestic and export prices and to divert more resources for export production. They have relied mainly on a policy of wage stabilization to hold back domestic consumption, although the changing terminology of administrative control reflects some change in attitude: 'wage restraint' has given way in turn to 'wages policy', 'incomes policy' and 'prices and incomes policy'.

The beginning of the Labour government's prices and incomes policy of the 1960s was marked by the Joint Statement of Intent on Productivity, Prices and Incomes, signed in 1964 by representatives of government, ⟡ TUC and those employers' associations which were forerunners of the ⟡ Confederation of British Industry. The purpose was to raise productivity; to keep increases in money incomes in line with real national output; and to maintain a stable price level.

In 1965 the National Board for Prices and Incomes was set up to examine cases of price and income behaviour referred to it by the government and to advise whether or not they were in the national interest. A White Paper set out the criteria for determining prices and incomes, indicating that the average rate of annual increase in money incomes per head should be kept in line with an underlying productivity rise of $3-3\frac{1}{2}\%$. Faced with the threat of further government intervention and a compulsory 'early warning system', the TUC set up its own wage-vetting committee to deal with the flood of claims from its affiliated members.

The next step was taken in 1966 when the government called for a breathing space of 12 months in which productivity could catch up with the excessive increases in incomes which had taken place. This took the form of a 6 months' voluntary standstill on price and incomes increases, followed by a further 6 months of severe restraint. Since special treatment was allowable in cases of increased efficiency, of the lowest paid, and of acute labour shortage, a tremendous stimulus was given to ⟡ Productivity Bargaining. The criteria for employment incomes were also made applicable to all other forms of personal income, for example there were to be no dividend increases. Most trade unions remained ambivalent in their attitude towards the prices and incomes policy, however, and the Draughtsmen's and Supervisors' Unions fought the freeze in the courts.

The Prices and Incomes Act, 1966 established the National Board for Prices and Incomes as a statutory body, replacing its original status as a Royal Commission; in 1967 its scope was widened, for example price increases in nationalized industries could in future be referred to it. In 1968 responsibility for incomes policy was transferred from the Department of Economic Affairs to the ⟡ Department of Employment.

A further *Prices and Incomes Act* in 1968 endorsed the government's power to require notification of proposed increases in prices, incomes and dividends; restricted increases in rents and dividends; allowed standstills to be imposed for up to 12 months and ⟡ Wages Councils orders to be postponed; and introduced the power to impose price reductions. Wage and salary increases below the ceiling of $3\frac{1}{2}\%$ p.a. now needed justification by productivity, comparability, low pay or manpower shortage, although such evidence did not inevitably justify increases. Increases above the ceiling could be achieved only by genuine productivity agreements.

The Conservative Government from 1970 disbanded the Prices and Incomes

Board and revived the concept of a voluntary incomes policy operated jointly by the government, the TUC and the CBI. When talks broke down, however, it imposed a standstill on incomes by the *Counter-Inflation (Temporary Provisions) Act*, 1972. This was followed by a second stage in a programme for controlling inflation to last from March to Autumn 1973, providing for the most comprehensive set of economic controls used since the Second World War years. Pay increases for any group of employees were limited to £1 plus 4% of the total wage bill (excluding overtime) in the previous year, with an upper limit of £250 per annum.

Further legislation, the *Counter-Inflation Act*, 1973, established a Pay Board and a Price Commission to operate for three years with the power to restrict pay and prices in accordance with a Prices and Pay Code. Stage Three of the counter-inflation programme came into operation in the late Autumn of 1973 against a background of rapidly rising world and import prices. It aimed to restrain domestic prices and secure price reductions where possible by strict controls and, on the side of remuneration, to limit pay increases to 7% with a flexibility margin of 1% and additions for genuine efficiency schemes, together with provisions for 'unsocial' hours, anomalies and threshold safeguards.

The Labour Government of late 1974 abolished this statutory policy, substituting a reliance on the voluntary measures involved in the Social Contract with the TUC. By May 1975, however, inflation was running at more than 30%. N.H.C.

John Corina, *The Development of Incomes Policy* (Institute of Personnel Management, 1965); Reports of the National Board for Prices and Incomes; H. A. Clegg, *How to Run an Incomes Policy* (Heinemann, 1971).

Pricing (Accounting information for) There has been considerable controversy as to what are the appropriate accounting data for the making of pricing decisions. In particular some accountants contend that fully allocated unit costs are appropriate whilst others have suggested that they should consist of marginal or variable unit costs. The argument between the two schools suggests that some contenders do not always appreciate that in any case realistic pricing policy requires attention to both demand and competitive factors. The marginalists suggest that if price is above the marginal or variable cost of the product then the firm will be better off whereas the fully-allocated costs school contends that all costs must be covered if the firm is to make a profit in the long run. A proper perspective is perhaps that marginal cost sets a *lower limit* on price, otherwise demand and competitive factors should be paramount in arriving at a price which is likely to be in accord with the achievement of a long-run profit objective. Moreover an unimaginative application of fully-allocated unit cost to pricing could result in economic disaster for a firm. If, for instance, sales volume is falling, then the addition of a share of fixed overhead costs to each unit for pricing purposes will increase price further, causing sales volume to fall even more. E.A.L.

W. Brown and E. Jaques, *Product Analysis Pricing* (Heinemann, 1964); B. V. Carsberg and H. C. Edey (eds.), *Modern Financial Management*, Pt. 2 (Penguin, 1969).

Pricing

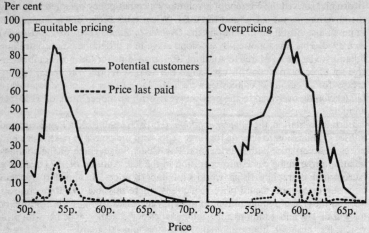

Figure 1. Market Price Profile

Pricing (Market Pricing) The setting of prices at a level that the market expects or countenances, ignoring company cost considerations. This approach is most closely associated with work since the Second World War at the Sorbonne, Nottingham University, and the Glacier Metal Company, and has led to two specific techniques, Price Profiles (Figure 1) and Product Analysis Pricing (Figure 2). The first offers the opportunity for price levels to be set in the context of the total marketing strategy the company wishes to employ and is based on marketing

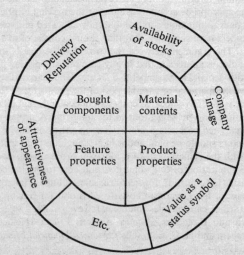

Figure 2. Product Analysis Pricing

research interviews. The interviews elicit customers' price expectations for any given product grouping, and these are plotted as a curve of price willingness (see Figure 1). When this data is available to marketing management, and is compared with the extant structure of brand pricing, specific price strategy and the role of price in the total marketing strategy can be formulated. Product Analysis Pricing makes possible delegated pricing decisions in a company where hundreds of price decisions are taken each week (⟡ Prices). This approach must be held in contra-distinction to the development of new techniques of costing (⟡ Costing System) which seek to compute the contribution of products after the recovery of direct costs, and to the total cost recovery approach to pricing. ⟡ Changing Price Levels (Accounting for).

Neither approach can provide for short-term adjustments made necessary by competitor's pricing behaviour. Discount structures, deals, etc. are used as short-term tools since they provide greater flexibility. G.S.C.W.

A. Gabor and C. W. J. Granger, 'Foundations of Market-Oriented Pricing', in *Pricing Strategy* (Staples, 1968); W. Brown and E. Jaques, *Product Analysis Pricing* (Heinemann, 1965).

Priority Rules ⟡ Sequencing and Dispatching Problems.

Probability Elsewhere (⟡ Statistics) it is indicated that, because of the variability inherent in much of the data used in business, many management problems must be analysed and solved using the science of probability and statistics.

The theories of probability and statistics have been developed mainly since the seventeenth century when mathematicians like Fermat and Pascal were invited by gambler friends to determine the odds in various games of chance. Probability theory is concerned with events in which the outcome is determined by chance, or when enormous numbers of causes combine to produce the final outcome so that it cannot be predicted with certainty. A simple example is the outcome from tossing a coin. If a coin is unweighted, then the outcome of the toss (that is, whether it lands 'heads' or 'tails') will depend on a number of factors such as the degree of force and spin imparted to the toss, air movement, position of the hand when the coin is caught, etc. However, if we toss the coin many times we find that an approximately equal number of 'heads' and 'tails' appear. Because, in the long-run, heads occur in half the tosses, we can say that the probability of a head occurring is a half. We measure the probability of the outcome of events on a scale ranging from 0 to 1, where a probability of 0 means that an outcome is certain not to occur and a probability of 1 that it is absolutely certain to occur. For example, if we tossed a double-headed penny the probability of a tail occurring would be 0 since the coin can never land tails, and of a head occurring would be 1 since the coin must always land heads.

Obviously, in many situations there are more than two possible outcomes to an event. For example, if we throw an unweighted dice there are 6 possible outcomes $(1, 2, \ldots 6$ spots on the upper-most face), but we can say that the probability of a particular number (say, 4) being thrown is $\frac{1}{6}$.

Using the example of the dice we can also show how the probability of combinations of events can be evaluated. Suppose we wish to know the probability observing a 3 or a 4 in the single throw of a dice:

Probability of outcome being '3' $= \frac{1}{6}$

Probability of outcome being '4' $= \frac{1}{6}$

Probability of outcome being either '3' or '4'

is the sum of the constituent probabilities $= \frac{1}{6} + \frac{1}{6} = \frac{1}{3}$

Similarly suppose we wish to know the probability of obtaining a 4 in two successive throws:

Probability of outcome being 4 on the first throw $= \frac{1}{6}$

Probability of outcome being 4 on the second throw $= \frac{1}{6}$

Probability of outcome being 4 on both throws $= \frac{1}{6} \times \frac{1}{6} = \frac{1}{36}$

These addition and multiplication theorems of probability are two of the basic bricks on which the theories of probability and of statistics are built. M.J.C.M.

M. J. Moroney, *Facts from Figures*, p. 4 *et seq*. (Penguin, 1951).

Procedure Agreement An agreement which sets up a procedure to regulate conflict between the parties concerned.

The procedure agreement has always existed in the British system of industrial relations but the ◊ *Industrial Relations Act*, 1971, repealed 1974, defined the term to include that collective agreement, or part of it, which relates to consultation, negotiation or arbitration machinery for dealing with terms and conditions of employment or other questions arising between employer(s) and worker(s) or their organizations; negotiating rights; facilities for officials of trade unions or other workers' organizations; and grievance, discipline and dismissal procedures.

The Act afforded the Secretary of State power to make regulations requiring employers to notify him of existing procedure agreements and to supply him with particulars and provided legal remedies where procedure agreements were nonexistent, defective or widely broken in the case of a group of undertakings or all or part of a single undertaking.

The ◊ Industrial Relations Code of Practice stresses the need for clarity in procedure agreements and lists their desirable contents.

Procedure agreements can theoretically be distinguished from 'substantive agreements', which concern the substance of agreements on remuneration, conditions of work, fringe benefits, etc. In practice, however, the two often overlap. ◊ Collective Bargaining; Shop Stewards. N.H.C.

Process Charts A graphical method of recording the sequence of activities which occur during a work process, along with any other information necessary for analysis. Process charts are the main method of recording existing work procedures and describing proposed procedures, during a ◊ Method Study investigation.

The following types of chart are frequently used.

(1) Outline Process Chart: a record of the main parts of a process only (i.e. the operations and inspections). Normally used as a preliminary step prior to a more detailed investigation.

(2) Material Flow Process Chart: presents a detailed record of the sequence of operations, transportations, inspections, delays and storages, which occur to the material during a work process.

SYMBOLS	OUTLINE	MAN	MATERIAL	TWO HANDED
○	Operation	Operation	Operation	Operation
⇨	Transportation	Transportation	Transportation	Transportation
□	—	Inspection	Inspection	—
▽	—	—	Storage	Hold
D	—	Delay	Delay	Delay

Example   Two handed process chart

Date:

Charted by:

Proposed ⎤
                ⎬ method
Present ⎦

Operation

Assemble bolt and nut

Summary per 1 pieces	Present		Proposed	
	L.H.	R.H.	L.H.	R.H.
○	2	5		
⇨	2	4		
▽	2	0		
D	2	0		
Total	8			
Distance	36″	56″		

Layout

B — Bolts
N — Nuts
O — Operator
A — Assembly

Parts

2½″

Nut   Bolt

Left Hand								Right Hand
Reach for bolt 18″	○	⇨	▽	D	○	⇨	▽	D	Reach for nut 18″
Grasp bolt head	○	⇨	▽	D	○	⇨	▽	D	Grasp nut
Carry to central position 18″	○	⇨	▽	D	○	⇨	▽	D	Carry to central position 18″
Hold bolt	○	⇨	▽	D	○	⇨	▽	D	Place nut on bolt
Hold bolt	○	⇨	▽	D	○	⇨	▽	D	Screw nut onto bolt
Release assembly to R.H.	○	⇨	▽	D	○	⇨	▽	D	Grasp assembly
Idle	○	⇨	▽	D	○	⇨	▽	D	Carry to box 10″
Idle	○	⇨	▽	D	○	⇨	▽	D	Release
Idle	○	⇨	▽	D	○	⇨	▽	D	Return hand to central position 10″

Product Innovation

(3) Man Flow Process Chart: presents a detailed record of what the worker does during a process in terms of operations, transportations, inspections and delays.

(4) Two-Handed Flow Process Chart (*or* Operator Process Chart): a graphical record of the coordinated activities of an operator's two hands in terms of operations, transportations, holds, and delays. R.W.

R. M. Barnes, *Motion and Time Study* (J. Wiley, 5th ed., 1963).

Product Innovation ⟡ New Product.

Product Mix The range of products offered by an organization. Income from the sale of products is normally a company's major if not sole revenue-earning activity, hence the combination on offer is subject to continuous examination entailing new introductions (⟡ New Product) and deletions. The demand for any one pro-

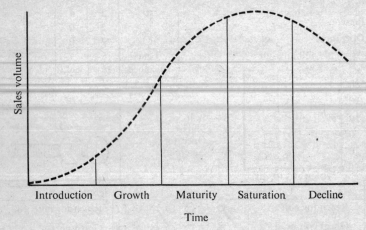

duct in a range may sometimes be a function of others in the range but, in general, managements treat each product separately for taxonomic and life-cycle analysis. Substantial economies are available in marketing a wide range of products provided they are compatible in terms of promotion and distributive channels (⟡ Branding). The figure illustrates the different phases in the market life of a product; the time scale differs e.g. between product groups. Different styles of marketing activity will be associated with each phase in order most effectively to meet the objectives set. A taxonomy of products within a range has been suggested as follows: (1) today's breadwinners, (2) tomorrow's breadwinners, (3) productive specials, (4) development products, (5) failures, (6) yesterday's breadwinners, (7) repair jobs, (8) unnecessary specialities, (9) investment in managerial ego, (10) cinderellas. Effective product management is dependent on identifying such categories and ensuring that managerial and financial resources are optimally allocated. Product cost data is fundamental to such control, and marginal analysis of profit contribution will indicate the time at which resources should be switched.

The time scale over which returns are calculated is of great significance in governing allocation. G.S.C.W.

T. Berg and A. Schuchman, *Product Strategy and Management* (Holt, Rinehart & Winston, 1963).

Production Lines ⊳ Assembly Lines.

Production Management According to economists, the purpose of production is the satisfaction of 'wants'. Of course human 'wants' are not restricted to the acquisition and use of goods, but also extend to the use of certain services, for example the services of professionals such as lawyers, architects, entertainers, or the use of libraries, transport or retailing systems. Production, according to the economists' definition, is concerned with the provision of both goods and services but, in practice, production is usually identified with *goods* and not services. Production is associated with the creation or *manufacture* of goods, in fact, an adequate definition of the function is: 'The fabrication or assembly of a physical object by means of equipment, "men" and materials.'

Production is one of the two principal functions of business, the other – marketing – is concerned with the *demand* side of business whilst production is concerned with the *supply* side. Production management is concerned with the organization and control of the production function or, more specifically, it is concerned with the decision-making necessary to ensure that goods are made in accordance with the requisite quality standards in the requisite quantities, at the requisite times and at minimum cost.

Production management is concerned with the design and operation of production systems, hence the scope and nature of the production manager's job is influenced primarily by the nature of the production system.

There are three basic types of production: jobbing or unique production, batch production and mass production. Each system has its own principles and applications and each makes specific demands on management. Jobbing production is concerned with the manufacture of small, often single, quantities of a large range of different products. The products are normally made to the customer's order rather than for stock and general-purpose machinery and equipment is used. Because of the difficulty, often impossibility, of accurate production planning in this type of manufacture, the principal management problem is one of control. Mass production is, basically, the opposite of jobbing production, in that a small range of products are manufactured in very large quantities. The product(s) are manufactured on special-purpose equipment, for stock rather than to customer order. Because this type of production is comparatively inflexible, and because a very large capital investment is involved, it is essential to ensure that an adequate and stable demand for the product(s) exists and that equipment is fully utilized; hence the principal management problem is one of planning. Process production is similar to mass production, the emphasis being upon the same management problems, but production is normally in bulk, rather than in discrete items, and chemical rather than mechanical processes are usually involved. Batch production falls between mass and jobbing production, in that products are manufactured neither singly nor continually, nor usually are products manufactured entirely for

313

stock nor entirely to customer orders. Many firms in the engineering industries are involved in this type of production, and the principal problem areas for management concern the size of production batches, the timing of production and the requisite stock levels. Rarely do these types of production exist in isolation, indeed many companies are involved in several types of production and consequently the task of production management is often complex and varied.

Because production is one of the central aspects of business, it has many frontiers with other functions, particularly marketing, personnel and product research and development. Many of the techniques used in production, for example the techniques used in production planning, stock control, quality control, etc., were amongst the first analytical management techniques to be developed. Statistical methods of stock and quality control were first developed almost 40 years ago: consequently a large number of those techniques have subsequently been absorbed into such disciplines as operational research. Because of this overlapping of both responsibility and technique, categorical definition of the scope of production management is hazardous. Consequently the following should be considered only as an outline of the principal areas of responsibility of production management:

1. Responsibilities during the *pre-production* stage:
   (a) Production Engineering (i.e. the design of tools and jigs, the selection of plant, the design, development and installation of equipment) is often within the field of responsibility of the production manager.
   (b) Plant Layout and Materials handling, i.e. the design and layout of factories and departments and the design of materials handling systems.
   (c) Production Planning, i.e. demand forecasting, material ordering, production scheduling, workforce balancing and machine loading.
   (d) Work Study (an activity which is also conducted 'during production'), i.e. the design of work methods and workplaces, the establishment of time standards, and the measurement of production.

2. Responsibilities occurring during production:
   (a) Production Control, i.e. the sequencing of jobs, processing of jobs, and the updating and correction of production schedules.
   (b) Stock Control, i.e. stock ordering, stock keeping and stock handling.
   (c) Quality, i.e. inspection, acceptance testing and the control of quality.
   (d) Maintenance and Replacement, i.e. the repair, preventive maintenance and replacement of items of production equipment.

In addition to the areas outlined above, production management is also concerned with the following functions:
   (a) Product Design – the design of products to facilitate production.
   (b) Payment Systems – the design and administration of incentive payment systems based on work measurement.
   (c) Purchasing – the acquisition of raw materials, parts, sub-assemblies, indirect materials and equipment.

Although production engineering is shown above to be part of the production manager's field of responsibility, this branch of engineering is a well-established profession, taught separately or as part of mechanical engineering, and is not therefore covered by the entries of this handbook. With this exception all of the above subjects are covered by entries provided by the various contributors to this handbook. R.W.

E. S. Buffa, *Modern Production Management* (J. Wiley, 1967); H. L. Timms, *The Production Function in Business* (Irwin, 1966).

Production Planning and Control Production planning is concerned with the determination, acquisition and arrangement of all facilities necessary for the future production of products, to satisfy either expected or expressed demand. It is concerned with the design of the framework within which functions, e.g. production control, inventory control, etc., will eventually operate.

The extent and details of this function depend largely upon the type and nature of production. In jobbing production, production planning is a continuous function, mainly involving the scheduling of customer orders against the capacity of existing equipment and to satisfy required delivery dates. Because the nature and extent of production facilities are fixed, except for replacement, improvement and expansion, production planning in jobbing production is primarily a routine resource allocation problem. ◊ Jobbing Production.

In mass or large-scale production, production planning is principally concerned with the future provision of all facilities necessary for the manufacture of a standard product(s). This is the most comprehensive and complex application, and necessarily involves not only forecasting, design of production layouts and procedures, acquisition of equipment, etc., but also manpower planning and the provision of services, stores, dispatching, etc. (◊ Assembly Lines).

Production control is concerned with the implementation of a predetermined production plan or policy and the control of all aspects of production according to such plan or policy.

Like production planning, the extent and the details of the production control function depend mainly upon the type of production system. In mass production on flow lines, the production control problem is trivial, since the production system once designed for a given performance is self-operating, and it remains only to provide the necessary materials and components and remove the finished product. In jobbing production, the emphasis is reversed. Here production planning is a routine operation: however, because precise scheduling is impossible, work in progress levels are normally high, throughput time is high, and a considerable amount of expediting and 'progressing' of production is necessary. Here the production control may involve 'breaking down' a general production plan into individual operations, allocating operations to machines, acquiring of raw materials, progressing jobs through the operations, storage, rectification, transport dispatching, etc.

The terms production planning and control are often used interchangeably. Production control is often considered to include the planning function, particularly in small-scale production and is frequently considered to incorporate responsibility for stock control, quality control, purchasing, etc.

The two functions are complementary and consecutive, their relative importance and complexity depending primarily on the type of production involved. Mass production necessitates complex and comprehensive production planning followed by routine simple production control. Small-scale production results in a routine planning function and a complex control function. R.W.

S. Eilon, *Elements of Production Planning and Control* (Macmillan, 1962).

Production Theory Economists have devoted a considerable amount of effort to the problem of what determines the allocation of resources in a country. They have also been interested in resource allocation within the individual firm. For a businessman just about to set up or extend a plant there may be a variety of ways of producing the product. Likewise a firm with a plant already in existence may still be able to exercise some control over the factor combinations used in production. What advice can be offered to aid these decisions?

The starting-point for such decisions is the concept of a process, which may be defined as the way of performing a task. Thus wheat can be produced from a given amount of land with varying combinations of labour and fertilizer. Many industrial goods can be produced with varying quantities of labour and raw materials. Finally, if we are not tied to a particular type of machinery then the same product may be produced using different machines that demand different quantities of labour. In all these cases the different ways of doing things are referred to as processes. At one extreme there may be many processes to choose from, at the other extreme very few.

The simplest assumption that can be made about a process is that the inputs must always be used in fixed proportions and output varies directly with inputs. Hence, if for a particular process 4 units of factor Y and 2 units of factor X produce 16 units of output, then 8 units of Y and 8 units of X will produce 32 units of output.

Suppose then that two processes are available for producing a given product. The process vectors are shown below:

$$P_A = \begin{pmatrix} 1 \\ 0.5 \end{pmatrix} \qquad P_B = \begin{pmatrix} 0.5 \\ 1 \end{pmatrix}$$

Thus process A requires one unit of factor Y and half a unit of factor X to produce one unit of output, and similar reasoning applies for process B. If one unit of Y can be purchased for £2 and one unit of X for £4, which process should one employ in order to maximize production for a given expenditure of £32? Although this example seems and is trivial, nevertheless the general formulation of the problem is akin to that facing manufacturers with given resources wishing to maximize production, or alternatively minimize costs of production of a given output. The major difference is that the number of factor inputs and processes will be considerably larger.

The problem can be put formally as follows:

maximize $P = A + B$
subject to $4A + 5B \leqslant 32$

where A = level of output from process *A*

     B = level of output from process *B*

    £4 = cost of producing one unit from process *A*

    £5 = cost of producing one unit from process *B*

The problem can easily be solved by trial and error. For example, if *B* is zero then *A* is 8 units. If *A* is zero then *B* is $6\frac{2}{5}$ units. Finally it is easily verified that intermediate positions using both *A* and *B* and costing £32 will yield less than 8 units of output. Thus process *A* should be chosen and operated at 8 units of output.

The fact that this choice of process is determined by the relative prices of factors *Y*, *X* is more clearly shown in the graphical solution to this problem below:

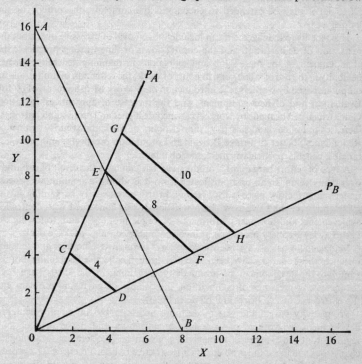

The process ray OP_A shows combinations of *Y* and *X* that yield given levels of output. The same applies to the ray OP_B, hence we can obtain points such as *EF*, *GH* and *CD* which indicate positions of equal output. The line *AB* is a budget line whose slope is given by the price of *X* divided by the price of *Y* and whose location is determined by the budget limit £32.

Clearly maximum output of 8 units can only be produced by process *A*. The total cost at point *F* is too great, reaching £40. As we can see, however, the choice of process would be reversed if the prices of the inputs were interchanged, thus illustrating the point that it is relative costs that are important in determining which productive methods to employ and this proposition is applicable to both the short- and long-run situation and irrespective of the number of processes and inputs available. L.T.S.

W. Baumol, *Economic Theory and Operations Analysis* (Prentice-Hall, 3rd ed., 1972).

Productivity Bargaining A process enabling employers to reduce or at least stabilize unit labour costs by getting more effective work done and enabling employees to obtain greater rewards for doing it.

Productivity bargaining usually takes place at the level of the workplace or plant but it may be extended to encompass the company, the group, or the industry.

The benefits to management can include the removal of excessive overtime; the relaxation of demarcation and the cutting-down of time-wasting practices; the abandonment of the mate's job and reductions in manning generally; greater flexibility in the use of labour and in hours of work; the reduction of limitations on output imposed by workers; the introduction of ⟨⟩ Work Measurement, of ⟨⟩ Job Evaluation and of new equipment; and the increase of apprenticeship ratios. Gains which can be made by workers can include higher and more stable earnings; increases in holiday and sick pay; shorter hours of work and security against ⟨⟩ Redundancy; better ⟨⟩ Fringe Benefits and promotion prospects; and other less tangible benefits, particularly increased job interest.

A type of 'effort bargaining', productivity bargaining is the result of evolution over many years. In an unsophisticated form it is almost a continuous process under many factory piece-work systems. British productivity bargaining in the 1960s, however, had two new characteristics. It was concerned with controlled achievements and not past performance or vague promises; and, following the Esso Fawley Refinery prototype, it involved highly complex package deals.

Management has always been seeking ways to improve efficiency and in some instances these changes have been executed through collective bargaining, but the stimuli to the development of productivity bargaining in the 1960s have been the increasing pressures of competition, the balance of payments problem and the emergence of a ⟨⟩ Prices and Incomes Policy.

Productivity bargaining was made more necessary by full employment, the development by workers of workshop organization, and the growth of joint regulation at the expense of managerial prerogative. Accelerating technological change has enhanced the problem of ⟨⟩ Restrictive Labour Practices. The process of productivity bargaining can result in the elimination of the old distinction between ⟨⟩ Joint Consultation and ⟨⟩ Collective Bargaining.

Practical problems of implementation are a function of the activities of the specific employers' organization and the level at which bargaining can usefully be carried on, and whether plant bargaining can be reconciled with national bargaining in the industry concerned. It was envisaged in the 1960s that future national

Profession

agreements could be permissive or enabling agreements, setting standards and providing a frame for plant agreements; and in certain circumstances they might embody specific 'pieces' of productivity bargaining, for example, where aspects of the industry were common to most plants, or where the existing national agreements contained restrictive practices on manning, loading and the like. ⟨⟩ Restrictive Labour Practices.

Possible dangers in productivity bargaining include attitudinal limitations on the part of management and the workforce; the saving up by the workforce of inefficiencies in order to raise the price of jobs; and the disruption of differentials within firms and between firms.

The National Board for Prices and Incomes (⟨⟩ Prices and Incomes Policy) laid down rules for model productivity agreements and new schemes of payment by results in its Report 23. In the late 1960s and early 1970s, however, managements became disillusioned with productivity bargaining, while trade unions lost interest during the wage–price explosion.

By no means a panacea for all labour–management ills, productivity bargaining does however provide an opportunity for management to take the initiative in ⟨⟩ Industrial Relations, to reduce unit labour costs, to reform the social structure of the plant, and to set the scene for future changes. N.H.C.

A. Flanders, *The Fawley Productivity Agreements* (Faber, 1964); R. B. McKersie, 'Productivity Bargaining – Deliverance or Delusion?', *Personnel Management* (Sept. 1966).

Profession An occupation possessing high social status and characterized by considerable skill and knowledge much of which is theoretical and intellectual in nature. The possession of such skill and knowledge is usually tested by formal examination approved by an authoritative body. The members of a profession subscribe to a code of ethics governing their professional behaviour and define the area of their professional competence, preserving their status by confining the right to practice within the area so defined, to those who possess the appropriate formal qualifications Many occupations are nowadays described as professions although they may not meet all the criteria enumerated above. Traditionally, the professional worked independently, placing his skills at the disposal of clients who were not competent to evaluate the services for which they were paying. In these circumstances, the professional claimed to be accountable for his performance only to the judgement of his fellow professionals. With the growth of large-scale organizations many professionals have surrendered their independence and have become employees, a development which has served to blur the distinction between professions and non-professions. As an employee, the 'professional' is accountable to his superiors in the organizational hierarchy and, in those circumstances, is unlikely to be held legally liable for his own negligence. Further, as an employee, the 'professional' will often need to make a choice between pursuing his career within the organization or within the profession. If the former, he may need to acquire skills and knowledge outside his professional specialism so as to fit himself for promotion into administrative duties and, if the latter, he may wish

Profit, in accounting

to move from one organization to another in order to broaden his professional experience. In the former he will seek to impress his employers with his competence as an employee and in the latter he will seek to impress his fellow professionals with his competence as a professional. He will be described as a professional to the extent that he identifies with his profession rather than with his employing organization. Particularly in recent years, some professional associations have become considerably involved in the negotiation of conditions of employment for their members, and in the determination of scales of fees. In this respect, many are virtually indistinguishable from trade unions. The most prominent example, despite their indignant disclaimers, is the British Medical Association. ⟡ Norm; Role; Values. I.C.MCG.

> P. M. Blau and W. R. Scott, *Formal Organisations*, Ch. 3 (Routledge & Kegan Paul, 1963).

Profit, in accounting (⟡ Profits) An accounting profit (or loss) is conventionally defined in terms of the increase (or decrease) in a firm's net assets resulting from its *ordinary business activities*. Thus items such as profits from the sale of assets other than output of products and capital contributions from investors are excluded from the calculation of the change in the value of net assets. An alternative but equivalent definition of accounting profit, for any given time period, is in terms of the difference between the total amount of revenue from sales of products (or services) for that time period and the amount of assets and resources consumed in earning those revenues.

The principal defects of the traditional method of business profits measurement may be said to be the accounting conventions relating to the valuation of assets used in arriving at the change in the value of net assets (⟡ Valuation of Assets). E.A.C.

Profit Sharing An arrangement by which employees receive, in addition to their wages or salaries, a share in the profits of an undertaking. It usually takes the form of an agreement to pay annually (or in instalments) a fixed proportion of the profits made by the firm during the preceding year. The case for profit sharing is based on three points:

(1) Equity: employees have contributed to the profits by their labour (just as investors have contributed their capital) and are therefore entitled to a share of the profits.

(2) Involvement: if employees benefit directly from the success of the enterprise, measured by its profitability, they can be expected to be concerned for its success.

(3) Incentive: employees will be likely to work harder for the profitability of a firm if they are to have a share of the profits.

It is generally recognized that profit sharing provides little direct incentive to most employees because payments are too far removed from today's work to have any influence on it. When profit sharing is associated with arrangements giving employees financial information about the company there is evidence that it increases the sense of involvement of some employees. The argument for equity seems sound, but implies a sharing of losses in a bad year as well as profits in a good one. There is a body of opinion that opposes all forms of profit sharing as an attempt to paper over the conflict of interest that exists between employers and workers and as a threat to trade unionism. L.S.

William Wallace, *Prescription for Partnership* (Pitman, 1959); Allan Flanders, Ruth Pomeranz and Joan Woodward, *Experiment in Industrial Democracy – A Study of the John Lewis Partnership* (Faber, 1968).

Profits Profit is a term capable of several definitions according to the purpose in hand. As seen by the economist profits are a reward to that factor of production known as enterprise. But in the modern corporation whilst most people are clear about the traditional factors of production, land, labour and capital, what is enterprise?

As a starting-point we take the term as used by earlier economists in considering the typical business unit of developing economies – the one-man business. Then the owner provided at least several services from the following list: organization and control, risk-bearing, provision of capital, introduction of product and manufacturing innovations, land and buildings.

However, whilst the return to enterprise was called 'profit' it is quite clear from the list of services rendered that part of what has been called 'profit' could be more properly ascribed to labour, capital and land. Thus in the modern corporation we find that salaries are paid to managers, rent to the owners of land and buildings and interest to the owners of capital. These payments cease, therefore, to be counted as profit and even if payments are not made to third parties for services because the firm owns its own buildings and land, for example, an imputed payment ought properly to be deducted in order to arrive at profit.

At this point one is left with a residual figure for profit which is the payment for risk-bearing and introducing innovations and also may reflect the market position of the firm. The shareholders of a corporation clearly bear some risk but it could hardly be claimed that they act as innovators. At this point, therefore, one can either argue that some salaried managers receive extra payments for their services as innovators or, alternatively, that the rewards to this service pass to the shareholders by default, or finally one may believe that both events take place.

One final point should be noted since it is important in determining profits as defined above. This is the problem of setting a figure to imputed costs. The economist would say that the opportunity cost figure is the relevant one, i.e. the return available for the service in the next best alternative employment. However, it should be clearly recognized that the calculation of such payments is difficult in the absence of market-transactions data and this is why recourse is usually made to historic cost data, or alternatively, why no deduction is made at all.

As defined above there are three replies to the question 'Why do profits arise?'

Uncertainty. The human environment is always uncertain, in spite of modern aids to managerial decision-making. Profits are therefore seen as a reward to those who take non-insurable risks.

Innovation. This approach is closely aligned with the first. The role of the businessman or manager in successfully exploiting inventions is stressed. The introduction of a new product or production process is fraught with uncertainty as to success or failure, but successful innovators steal a march on their competitors and for some time earn extra profits. Ultimately these may be competed away by imitators and hence the innovator must always be on the look-out for new inventions to exploit.

Monopoly Power. In the event of the successful innovator protecting his position in the market by trademarks, advertising, low production costs, brand names, etc., he acquires monopoly power. As this power is maintained so the profits obtained may be ascribed to monopoly power or 'imperfections and rigidities in the system'.

It is by no means easy to disentangle these strands of thought. Taken together they provide the nucleus of a theory of profit. L.T.S.

D. Lamberton, *The Theory of Profit* (Blackwell, 1965).

Programmed Instruction Recent attempts to apply certain principles regarding the ideal characteristics of material to be learned have given rise to a group of techniques loosely classified together as Programmed Instruction. The principle characteristics of these techniques are that material is presented to the learner systematically, progressively and in manageable-sized chunks, and that his progress is regularly checked. Frequently use is made of some special teaching equipment. Three basic types of programme are in use.

(a) The Linear Programme (first advocated and developed by Professor B. F. Skinner) emphasizes the need to break down a subject-matter into units which can be presented one by one to a student who proceeds methodically through the whole programme.

(b) The Branching Programme is designed to cope with individual differences in rate of learning. At the end of each presentation, the student is obliged to select one of a number of offered solutions to a set problem. The subsequent presentation is a function of the student's selection. A correct answer will lead him progressively on; a faulty answer leads to recapitulation or further explanation. The method of progression through the programme is facilitated by the use of a teaching machine or by use of a 'scrambled' textbook.

(c) The Adaptive Programme is one which alters its own level of difficulty according to the student's level of performance. Such programmes are normally incorporated into the control mechanisms of machines which teach manual or other skills. The learner's speed or error-rate are detected by the machine, the parameters of which are altered as appropriate.

Numerous published studies have indicated that in certain circumstances considerable benefits can result from the use of programmed learning. E.E.

D. Crane, *Explaining Teaching Machines and Programming* (Fearon Publishing, 1961).

Programmers ⬦ Computer Program.

Promotion (in Marketing) ⬦ Marketing Communications Mix.

Psychiatry ⬦ Psychology.

Psychology The word 'psychology' was coined early in the nineteenth century to mean, literally, 'the science of mind'. Naturally enough, attitudes and philosophies have changed a good deal during the passage of 150 years and most psychologists today would prefer to describe their subject as 'the science of behaviour'.

Both the nouns are important. 'Science' emphasizes the systematic empirical studies which characterize the psychologist and distinguish his approach from the intuitive methods of the novelist or political leader. 'Behaviour' implies an observable event involving the complete intact organism and distinguishes the psychologist from the anatomist or physiologist who are concerned with the structure and functioning of the individual parts of the body.

Experiments and methodical observations of real-life behaviour have yielded a considerable body of knowledge concerning man's nature. Early studies were centred largely around the problems of sensation (↻ Hearing; Threshold; Vision) and attempts were made to obtain quantitative relationships between the properties of subjective sensations and the physical characteristics of the signals (↻ Brightness; Colour; Noise). Much of the information so obtained is of practical as well as theoretical significance (↻ Colour Blindness; Displays; Illumination). Other lines of investigation have been directed at the clarification of the abilities of people to process information (↻ Intelligence) and to perform skilled tasks (↻ Reaction Time; Skill; Tracking).

Man is essentially a dynamic, changing being and part of psychology is concerned with the developmental processes from infancy through adolescence to adulthood and decline (↻ Ageing). On a shorter time-scale, people also alter their states either spontaneously or in response to environmental influences (↻ Adaptation; Fatigue; Learning and Training).

It is convenient to classify the influences of the outside world upon the individual as aspects of the physical environment (↻ Environment; Heat; Glare; Vibration) or of the social environment (↻ Attitude Scales; Incentives; Stereotypes). As a consequence of environmental influences overlaid upon an individual's hereditary background, each human being is unique in his patterns of adjustment. This uniqueness of individual personality forms an important area of research in psychology which is complementary with the study of typical or universal features of human nature (↻ Personality).

Applied psychology falls into three main technologies. Each of these parts has become something of a professional specialization in its own right.

(a) Clinical Psychology. The study of abnormalities in behaviour has always commanded a good deal of human interest. The removal of superstitious elements from the description of such behaviour paved the way towards a rational study and classification of disorders. The clinical psychologist is concerned firstly with diagnosis, by the use of a variety of testing techniques and, subsequently, with therapeutic treatment in an attempt to bring about an improved adjustment between the patient and his environment. Psychiatry, which is a branch of medicine, shares this goal of the removal of behaviour disorders, but unfortunately it usually lacks a sound scientific basis.

(b) Educational Psychology. The study of the developmental processes together with the general psychology of teaching and learning provide the background material for educational psychology. The specialists in this area are concerned to make recommendations concerning normal teaching techniques (↻ Programmed Instruction; Training), to diagnose the sources of backwardness or other individual difficulty, and to provide special remedial facilities.

(c) Occupational (or Industrial) Psychology. Psychological methods and data have been applied to such problems as vocational guidance, personnel selection, training, equipment design, motivation, accidents and job analysis. The industrial psychologist is concerned with all the aspects of contact between man and his occupational environment. In view of the enormous breadth of coverage in this area, there is a tendency towards further specialization. Consequently, Engineering psychology, which is concerned particularly with the design of equipment and man-machine systems, has emerged as a relatively independent discipline. This subject is sometimes labelled 'human engineering' or 'human factors'. It also forms a substantial part of ergonomics. ⟨⟩ Ergonomics; Personality. E.E.

S. S. Stevens, *Handbook of Experimental Psychology* (J. Wiley, 1951).

Public Relations The conscious effort on the part of an organization to communicate relevant information to its publics which will be to its advantage. An organization's publics may be existing or potential customers, shareholders and other sources of capital, employees, or perhaps legislators where decisions affecting an industry, etc., are imminent. It is one grouping of media used as part of an organization's total communications process, and is often used in a complementary manner to advertising (⟨⟩ Media; Marketing Communications Mix; Advertising). Perhaps the most common form of external public relations activity is the continuing effort to secure editorial coverage and favourable comment in the main news media, i.e. TV and Press. The main media used for securing such coverage are the 'press release', and personal briefings of leading journalists and TV editors. Internally, good relations with the organization's work force are often maintained by house journals which can range from lavish colour magazines to mimeographed newsheets. Their purpose is to foster identification with the organization and to ensure that relevant information is effectively disseminated. The Institute of Public Relations is the official professional body and publishes a quarterly journal, *Public Relations*. G.S.C.W.

Pulse Rate The measurement of pulse rate, usually expressed in beats per minute, has long been used in clinical diagnosis. It has value too in the assessment of work loads, since both physical work and mental stress produce increases in pulse rate. A similar effect is also brought about by increases in ambient temperature.

Considerable variation exists between the resting pulse rates of different individuals, and it is consequently necessary to use an index of work based upon proportional increase in pulse rate above the basal value for any particular individual. Heavy muscular work (such as running or cycling) will produce maximal values in the region of 200 beats per minute.

Studies on motor vehicle drivers and aircraft pilots have suggested a close relation between variations in pulse rate and the stress brought about by the performance of certain critical manoeuvres in the performance of a skill. ⟨⟩ Ergonomics; Muscular Work. E.E.

Purchasing The acquisition of raw materials, components, goods and services for conversion, consumption or resale. The term is more specifically used within business to describe the work of the industrial buyer who purchases primarily for conversion and consumption in the manufacturing process. The role of purchasing officer includes advising on make or buy decisions for components (◇ Design), integrating deliveries with sales and production schedules, selecting and appraising the vendors from whom purchases are to be made and minimizing the costs incurred in carrying out these activities. Within the company it also involves responsibility for the receiving and storing of purchased items and the disposal of surplus materials. The control of stock levels held, balancing holding costs against economies of large order quantities, has been subjected to detailed mathematical treatment (◇ Stock Control). The professional organization is the Institute of Purchasing and Supply. G.S.C.W.

L. Lee and D. W. Dobler, *Purchasing and Materials Management* (McGraw-Hill, 1965).

Q

Quality Control Most present-day goods are manufactured by mass production methods on machines which repetitively produce *almost* identical units. However, owing to uncontrollable variations in the quality of the processed material and in the settings of the processing machines, no two units are exactly identical. A customer accepts this as the price to be paid for the economies of mass production, but usually he specifies limits within which the dimensions of a unit must lie (e.g. engineers' 'tolerances'). The manufacturer, if he wishes to stay in business, must ensure that most of the units lie within these limits.

However, although any units which do not fulfil the specification will usually be scrapped and will therefore incur a loss to the producer, in general it is usually cheaper to design a production system which tolerates a proportion of 'defective' items to be produced, rather than to design one which produces one hundred per cent 'good' units. Since the properties of successively produced units are subject to variability which can be expressed using the concepts of statistics, procedures for monitoring and controlling the variability of these properties have been developed under the term Statistical Quality Control. These procedures can be roughly grouped under two headings:

(a) Process control, which evaluates properties of the units in an 'on-going' process to ensure that they are keeping within the specified limits. This object is usually achieved by means of control charts, in which measures of the required property or properties of successive units are plotted in a form which reveals quickly the random fluctuations and trends present in the measure. If the measures display excessive fluctuations about, or trends away from, the required limits, corrective action can be taken before a larger number of 'rejects' have been produced.

Clearly Process Control must be performed by the manufacturers, whereas

(b) Acceptance sampling is usually performed by the customer. In this case, the customer evaluates a number of units by choosing an appropriately designed sample of the units in the lot (✧ Sampling) and determining the number of 'defects'. If this number exceeds a given value, the lot is rejected, otherwise it is accepted. M.J.C.M.

M. J. Moroney, *Facts from Figures*, pp. 173–215 (Penguin, 1951).

Quantitative Methods It can be argued that there are four academic disciplines underlying management. These are the social sciences (economics, psychology, sociology) and mathematics; and that other disciplines relevant to management are derived from a combination of two or more of these. The term Quantitative Methods is often used to describe those branches of mathematics that are relevant to management. These are: (1) those branches of probability and statistics that are relevant to management (✧ Probability, Statistics); (2) Operational Research techniques (✧ Operational Research); (3) those branches of mathematics that have been employed in the development of the social sciences.

Because mathematics now plays an important role in management, courses entitled 'Quantitative Methods' are often included in management education programmes. M.J.C.M.

Queueing Problems When a situation exists whereby there are more customers requiring a service than there are service facilities to serve them, a queue of customers waiting for service forms. Such situations are common in ordinary life (e.g. queues at bus stops, supermarkets, doctors' waiting rooms, etc.) but also occur very frequently in industry. For example, partially processed parts may queue before the machine which will process them further, lorries may queue to be loaded at a dispatch bay, or aeroplanes may queue to land or take off at an airport.

In these situations it is required to balance conflicting sets of costs. If 'customers' are made to wait a long time in the queue increased direct or indirect costs will be incurred (for example, stockholding costs of work in progress stock, slower turnround of delivery lorries and slower delivery service to customers, slower turnround of aircraft and increased fuel costs). The queue lengths and hence the waiting costs can be reduced by providing increased service facilities (more machines, dispatch bays and runways) but introducing these will incur increased capital and running costs. A careful analysis needs to be made, to balance the costs associated in generating a queue and those associated with increasing the service facilities. Because the patterns of arrival of customers for service and the service times are subject to variability from a number of causes, such an analysis is performed using mathematical techniques based on probability theory and statistics which have become known as 'queueing theory'.

Quite often analysis of queueing problems using queueing theory produces answers which are unexpected from a commonsense viewpoint. For example, it may be cheaper to provide an extra service facility which is only used for 50% of the time in order to ensure that very 'expensive' customers are not kept waiting too long. M.J.C.M.

Patrick Rivett and Russell L. Ackoff, *A Manager's Guide to Operational Research*, pp. 41–3 (J. Wiley, 1963).

Quickening ◊ Machine Dynamics.

R

Range ◊ Measures of Dispersion.

Rate of Return (Accounting) The accounting rate of return is generally measured by reference to the net income accruing to shareholders, divided by shareholders' capital invested. This percentage will give a measure of the overall effectiveness of management from an ex-post viewpoint and also of the return to ordinary shareholders.

An alternative calculation relates the net income, accruing to all long-term investors, to the long-term investment in the company (that is the total of shareholders' net worth plus non-current liabilities). The measure then relates to all permanent capital and is used with a view to eliminating considerations concerning capital structure (◊ Capital Structure; Risk and Uncertainty in Financial Management).

Sometimes operating profits before and after tax are related to an average of total claims (= total assets) since it can be argued that the efficiency of management is more properly measured by its use of all assets under its control.

Clearly in making comparisons through time a consistent basis for measurement must be maintained.

The accounting rate of return should be used to estimate the firm's long-run average rate of return and clearly differs in purpose from the rate used for assessing capital projects which is designed to measure the marginal efficiency of capital (◊ Capital Budgeting; Present Value; Internal Rate of Return). Nevertheless, the use of the former rate for capital budgeting is sometimes advocated, quite erroneously. E.A.L.

Ratefixing The establishment of piecework rates by Time Study, Synthetic Timing, Estimating, etc. It is an infrequently used term having a similar meaning and covering precisely the same area as ◊ Work Measurement. R.W.

Ratio Delay Study ◊ Work Sampling.

Ratios, Financial Financial ratios are relationships, usually measured in percentages, between accounting figures. Their usefulness lies in the fact that they add further to the information content and meaning of single, absolute figures. However, ratios themselves require standards of comparison and without these it is almost impossible to conclude exactly how good or bad is a given ratio figure for a particular business. Such standards *still* require to be developed. It is reasonable to say that whilst financial ratios give a helpful point of departure for financial analysis they raise questions rather than provide answers.

Financial ratios may be grouped into the following categories:

(1) Tests of profitability, for example: (a) Rate of return, i.e. net profits to capital employed. (b) Net profit to sales (or gross income). (c) Gross profit to sales (or gross income).

(2) Tests of liquidity, for example: (a) Current ratio, i.e. current assets to current liabilities. (b) Acid test, i.e. quick assets (cash and easily realized investments) to current liabilities. (c) Average debtors to credit sales. (d) Average period of collection of trade debts.

(3) Tests of solvency, for example: (a) Capital to liabilities. (b) Number of times interest payable is covered.

(4) Stock Exchange tests, for example: (a) Earnings per share. (b) Market price – earnings per share ration. (c) Capitalization Rate, i.e. earnings per share to market price (or 4(b) inverted). (d) Dividend yield. E.A.L.

K. W. Bevan, *The Use of Ratios in the Study of Business Fluctuations and Trends* (Institute of Chartered Accountants in England and Wales, 1966); W. Beaver, *Empirical Research in Accounting – Selected Studies: Accounting ratios as predictors of failures* (Institute of Professional Accounting, University of Chicago, 1966).

Reaction Time The time interval between the arrival of a stimulus and the initiation of the appropriate response is one of the fundamental lags in human control mechanisms, and has formed the subject of many psychological experiments over the last hundred years.

With practice, subjects are able to reduce this lag to less than $\frac{1}{5}$ second. Accurate measurement reveals that the reaction time is a function of numerous variables. The sensory modality, for example, is one such variable; reactions to sounds are swifter than those to lights. Again, faster reactions will follow from intense signals than from weak ones.

There is considerable variation between different individuals in their speed of reaction, and in any one individual such factors as the level of motivation play an important part.

Reaction times increase when a subject is faced with choice; this increase is logarithmic. The practical significance of this result is that operators' decision times must be allowed for, and that the amount of variety of both input and response should be kept as low as possible in order to achieve fast reactions. E.E.

Readership ⟡ Audience Measurement.

Real Time ⟡ Off-Line/On-Line.

Recruitment Securing a supply of possible candidates for jobs in an enterprise. It is the first stage in the process which continues with ⟡ Selection and ends with the placement of an individual man or woman in a job. Recruitment begins with information about and contact with the sources of supply of the different kinds of recruit required to fill vacancies in a company. In the case of young recruits these will be schools, colleges, universities and the Youth Employment Service. For older people it will be employment exchanges, trade unions, private employment agencies and a variety of local groups with whom the management and the personnel department have contact. In practice existing employees may be the most useful 'recruiting officers', telling the people they know and meet of possible vacancies in their own firms. Effective recruitment is not just a question of a requisition from a manager or foreman followed by the advertisement of a vacancy or an application to an employment exchange. It should be related both to forward estimates of requirements as part of a policy of ⟨⟩ Manpower Planning, to careful ⟨⟩ Job Analysis and to a consideration of the ethos and organizational health of a particular business. It is in relation to all these factors that the sources of supply will be selected and cultivated, but success in securing the right quality and kind of recruits, though conditioned by the state of the labour market, depends a great deal on the reputation of a firm as an employer and the outside assessment of its standards of ⟨⟩ Personnel Management. This is particularly evident in the recruitment of university graduates and of qualified professional staff. L.S.

P. Pigors and C. A. Myers, *Personnel Administration* (McGraw-Hill, 1961).

Redundancy Dismissal of an employee or group of employees as a result of a readjustment of the operational manpower requirements of an undertaking.

Such a readjustment may arise from the closure of all or part of the business, or from a reorganization of work so that a particular job is no longer required. Before the ⟨⟩ *Redundancy Payments Act* of 1965 there was no effective legal limitation on an employer's right to give notice as and when he wished. The Act requires him either to show that a dismissal is not due to redundancy or to pay compensation to the employee if it is. Under the Act a Redundancy Fund was established, financed by flat-rate contributions from employers, from which not less than two thirds of each redundancy payment made was drawn. In 1968, for example, a total of £61,836,000 in redundancy payments was made under the Act, of which £46,377,000 was borne by the Fund and £15,460,000 paid directly by employers. During the year the total number of payments made was 264,500 of which 46,200 were in the engineering and electrical industries, 32,400 in building and construction, 24,300 in the distributive trades, 19,800 in mining and quarrying and 15,000 in miscellaneous services.

Though many employers were hostile to these payments when the system was introduced in 1965, both the ⟨⟩ Confederation of British Industries and the government appear to agree now that they have significantly reduced shop-floor opposition to redundancy and have contributed to easier redeployment of labour. The decision taken in January 1969 to raise the maximum liability of the individual employer from one third to one half of each payment has not dissipated goodwill in this respect. In any case less than a third of the 800,000 to one million workers made redundant each year qualify for compensation, mainly because of the high proportion with less than the statutory minimum of two years' service.

Many companies, however, in conjunction with the trade unions, seek to work out a redundancy policy for themselves over and above the minimum provisions made by the Act. Once trade unionists have agreed in principle to a measure of redundancy their bargaining position is that the claims of seniority, the 'last in, first out' principle must be given priority – though, in practice, these may be modified by the company's manpower requirements and particular individual circumstances. Disputes (⟨⟩ Trade Dispute) over redundancy may arise as a result of opposition by employees or trade unions to all or part of a firm's redundancy policy, or in the case of an individual who may disagree with the reason given by the employer for his dismissal and claim entitlement to redundancy pay when he was allegedly dismissed for misconduct. In this way the Act constitutes a deterrent to victimization by the employer and all disputes over payment are heard by tribunals which operate under the Act. Appeals to these tribunals by workers to establish entitlement to redundancy payments or the correct amount payable numbered 8,229 in 1968. L.S. & N.H.C.

Hilda R. Kahn, *Repercussions of Redundancy* (Allen & Unwin, 1962); Alan Fox, *The Milton Plan* (Institute of Personnel Management, 1965).

Redundancy (of Information) A sequence of signals may contain more information than the minimum required to convey a given amount of meaning. The excess information within the message is called redundancy. Simple repetition serves as an example. In a system which is free from sources of information loss or error, redundancy might be regarded as completely wasteful and undesirable. In less perfect systems, however, redundancy facilitates the detection and correction of errors.

If there were no redundancy in our normal use of a 26-letter alphabet, then at each point in a printed English text, any one of the 26 letters would be equally likely to appear next in sequence. Clearly such is not the case; Q must be followed by U, J cannot follow Z, a J is almost certain to be followed by a vowel. Because of such redundancy, it is possible to tolerate a certain amount of error without losing any part of the intended message. In certain artificial coding systems redundancy is intentionally incorporated in the structure of the symbols as a means of detecting errors (◇ Information Theory). E.E.

Redundancy Payments Act The *Redundancy Payments Act*, 1965 was passed in order to provide some financial compensation for employees who lose their jobs through redundancy. Redundancy is defined for this purpose as arising when an employer has either ceased to carry on his business altogether, or has ceased to operate in a particular place, or where his requirements for employees of a particular skill or craft have ceased or diminished. An employee who has in this way lost his job is entitled to receive from his employer a redundancy payment, the amount of which depends on the number of years of continuous employment of the employee and the employee's weekly rate of pay (subject to a maximum of £80). Only employment above the age of 18 and below retirement age is taken into account and the employee is to be paid at the rate of half a week's pay for every year of employment between 18 and 21, one week's pay for every year between 21 and 40 and one and a half weeks' pay for employment above 40, subject to no more than 20 years of employment being countable.

The employer may recover part of the payments made by him from the Redundancy Fund, which is financed by a weekly surcharge on the employer's share of national insurance contributions. If an employer is unable to make the appropriate redundancy payment, the Redundancy Fund will see to it that the employee is paid. Disputes as to whether redundancy has occurred and how much is payable are heard in the first place by the Industrial Tribunals set up by the ⬦ *Industrial Training Act*, 1964. W.F.F.

> D. Knight Dix, *Contracts of Employment including Redundancy Payments* (Butterworth, 1972).

Regional Problems ⬦ Location of Industry and Regional Problems.

Registered Trade Unions ⬦ Trade Union (at Law).

Regression ⬦ Correlation and Regression.

Replacement Cost Accounting ⬦ Changing Price Levels.

Replacement Problems Many firms have planned maintenance schemes for machinery on the floor, but only some know when is the right time to replace it. Basically it is the same problem as deciding when to buy new cars. A machine deteriorates and its second-hand value depreciates with the passing of time. As it deteriorates, the machine falls off in efficiency and requires increased expenditure on repairs and maintenance. The time comes, before the machine is worn out, when the increased capital investment required to buy a new one less the second-hand value of the old one is more than offset by the savings in maintenance and repair costs.

An alternative replacement problem is that with a part (such as an electric light bulb) with an efficiency which remains constant throughout its life, but which fails unpredictably. Again analysis may show a pattern of group replacement which is cheaper than replacing each item as it fails.

Replacement problems can be examined using probability theory and statistical analysis and have led to the development of a branch of statistics known as renewal theory.

An interesting replacement problem is that concerned with the planning of labour recruitment to balance wastage. One of the UK's largest industrial operational research groups has developed a replacement model to determine the pattern of recruitment of new graduates into the group to offset the loss of trained operational research scientists to other firms. M.J.C.M.

> Patrick Rivett and Russell L. Ackoff, *A Manager's Guide to Operational Research*, pp. 47–50 (J. Wiley, 1963).

Resale Price Maintenance Law Resale price maintenance implies that a manufacturer of goods wishes to enforce that his goods should be retailed at a price laid down by him. At common law, the position depended on whether or not the retailer had obtained the goods directly from the manufacturer. If he had done so and had agreed to observe the manufacturer's price, the manufacturer was able to enforce this promise, but if the retailer had obtained the goods from a third party (e.g. a wholesaler) the manufacturer was unable to force the retailer to observe price conditions since in this case there did not exist a direct contractual link between manufacturer and retailer.

The *Restrictive Trade Practices Act*, 1956, while prohibiting collective resale price maintenance (price maintenance through a trade association), made it possible for a manufacturer to compel a retailer to observe the manufacturer's prices, if the retailer had acquired the goods, even from a third party, with knowledge of the existence of resale conditions.

The *Resale Prices Act*, 1964 now provides that the manufacturer may always fix a maximum retail price for his goods, but the fixing by him of minimum prices is void, except where the goods in question have been exempted from this restriction by the Restrictive Practices Court on certain specified grounds, mainly concerning damage to the public interest that might result from unrestricted competition. If the manufacturer gives notice to the Registrar of his intention to apply for exemption, he may continue enforcing minimum prices until the Restrictive Practices Court has pronounced on his application. w.f.f.

Wilberforce, Campbell and Elles, *The Law of Restrictive Trade Practices and Monopolies* (Sweet & Maxwell, 1969).

Reserves ⟡ Claims.

Responsibility The obligation to use delegated powers for the purposes for which they were delegated. In this usage, the term is virtually synonymous with *accountability*. The term is also used, however, to mean a duty or activity assigned to a given position or (in the plural) the aggregate of such duties.

It is axiomatic in organizational processes that responsibility should be equal to authority, for power without corresponding responsibility is likely to lead to behaviour uncontrolled by the organization and hence to unintended and probably undesirable consequences. Also such power is particularly resented by those subjected to it. Conversely, it is considered to be unreasonable to hold a person responsible for events caused by factors which he is powerless to control: the delegated powers must be adequate for the purposes for which they were delegated.

Although it is possible to delegate both duties and the necessary authority, it is not possible to delegate responsibility. That is to say, a superior is always responsible for the actions of his subordinates and cannot escape this responsibility by delegation. In practice, however, a strict and literal adherence to this precept is liable to lead to inadequate delegation and too close supervision with a consequent stifling of initiative. ⟡ Authority; Delegation; Power. I.C.MCG.

H. D. Koontz and C. J. O'Donnell, *Principles of Management*, Ch. 4 (McGraw-Hill, 1955).

Responsibility Accounting A system of cost reporting by which costs are accumulated and analysed according to the departmental or divisional responsibilities of individual managers. These costs are then compared with the budgeted or standard costs over which the manager can be said to have effective control.

The basic principles of responsibility accounting require an ordered and logical approach to the formal organization of the business. (1) First requirement is that each departmental head or cost centre manager should be assigned the general responsibility, as well as given the necessary authority, for the carrying out of clearly specified tasks or activities (⟡ Management by Objectives). He in his turn must be accountable to a superior and his subordinates accountable to him in clear authority lines. (2) A proper understanding must be developed concerning the factors affecting his area of activity over which a manager can be fairly said to have control. (3) The quality of his administration and management must be periodically reviewed.

Once these organizational aspects of responsibility have been settled, it is then essential to consider the cost accounting implications; principally the question of which costs, of those attributable or allocable to a department or cost centre, it can be fairly be said to have control over. As responsibility reports reflect only those costs over which the manager has control, they are useful to superiors for evaluating his past performance and to the manager himself for improving his future performance. E.A.L.

> D. Solomons, *Divisional Performance; Measurement and Control* (Financial Executives Research Foundation, New York, 1965); E. Jaques, *Measurement of Responsibility* (Tavistock Institute, London, 1956).

Rest Pauses ◊ Fatigue.

Restraint of Trade An agreement in restraint of trade is one whereby a person's freedom of action regarding his employment, trade or business is being curtailed. This agreement forms generally part of a bigger contract, either one of employment, or one for the sale of a business or one made between suppliers and buyers of goods. Originally, all contracts in restraint of trade were treated as illegal by the courts, but over the years it came to be accepted that certain restraints might be enforced after all in the courts. These enforceable restraints are those which are deemed by the court to be reasonable both from the point of view of the parties directly affected and also from the wider point of view of the general public interest. The courts are generally less ready to treat a restraint attached to a contract of employment as reasonable than they are in respect of restraints in contracts where the bargaining power of the parties is rather more equal. In deciding whether a restraint of trade is reasonable, the court will wish to be satisfied that the party who accepted the restraint has received in return some benefit or that it would be grossly unfair on the part of the person to be restrained to take advantage of the situation for his own benefit. Thus a restraint in a contract of employment will be deemed reasonable if its purpose is to protect the employer's proprietary interest in trade secrets or trade connections. It would not be reasonable, however, to prevent an employee from engaging in competition with his former employer where no such proprietary considerations are involved. If a restraint is bad in part even the court will treat it as totally void except where, without having to redraft the contract, it is possible to separate the good parts from the bad ones, in which case the good parts will be enforced. W.F.F.

> G. H. L. Fridman, *The Modern Law of Employment* (Stevens & Sons, 1972).

Restrictive Labour Practices Arrangements imposed by employees under which labour is not used efficiently, there being no social or economic justification as far as society as a whole is concerned.

Many restrictions on the use of labour are now generally regarded as desirable. On economic grounds it may, for example, be more efficient to prevent excessive hours of work, since people when tired tend to produce poorer performances. A normal working week of 60 hours might not in some cases be excessive in terms of efficiency but would now be unacceptable on social grounds. Many such restrictions are incorporated in the safety, health and welfare provisions of the *Factories Acts*.

Some restrictive labour practices which are the product of management decisions may or may not be justified, according to circumstances. Overmanning seems indefensible at times of high employment, but the retention of labour during a temporary recession may make both economic and social sense if it prevents the dispersal of a trained and experienced workforce.

Restrictive practices may be formal and agreed as between trade unions and management, even subject to a written agreement after collective bargaining, as in various types of apprenticeship regulations. They may be informal and by no means 'agreed', for example where work groups set their own standards of performance. Trade unions may or may not be involved. In any event, they are acquiesced in by management, and management shares the responsibility for their existence.

Restrictive labour practices may occur by ⟪⟫ Demarcation, low effective performance resulting from employment of craftsmen's mates, overmanning, restrictions on output, unnecessary overtime, excessive tea breaks and bad timekeeping practices.

Restrictive labour practices are most marked in industries where there is little security of employment, e.g. shipbuilding, docks. They are also marked where trade unions have considerable bargaining strength, e.g. in the printing industry where unions have extensive control over entry to employment as well as over jobs. Management weakness is another facilitating factor, e.g. in the newspaper industry where the product is perishable, where there is considerable competition between employers, and where there is no external pressure such as foreign com petition. Tradition and convention, e.g. among crafts, can be significant, although many restrictive labour practices are new, having sprung up with new work situations.

It is primarily management's job to eliminate or reduce restrictive labour practices by improving its handling of industrial relations generally. Unions can help by improving their structure and education programmes. Governments can assist in the last resort, e.g. the Devlin Enquiry into the docks. N.H.C.

> Royal Commission on Trade Unions and Employers' Associations, Research Papers 4 (HMSO, 1967). *Productivity Bargaining and Restrictive Labour Practices.*

Restrictive Practices Restrictive Practices Legislation developed from the early Reports of the Monopolies Commission between 1948 and 1955. Many of these reports contained strong criticisms of Trade Associations rather than the single-firm monopoly and these criticisms were drawn together in the *Report on Collective Discrimination*, 1955 which formed the evidence for the *Restrictive Trade Practices Act*, 1956. Amongst the practices criticized were price rings, cartels, market sharing agreements, resale price maintenance and collective discrimination against outsiders. Fundamentally they were criticized because they encouraged inefficiency and a quiet life rather than efficiency and innovations.

The 1956 Act outlawed collective resale price maintenance and made it clear that trade agreements were *prima facie* against the public interest. The onus of proof to the contrary was to rest with the parties to an agreement who would have an opportunity to prove their case before the Restrictive Practices Court. The case against an agreement was to be presented by the Registrar of Restrictive Practices with whom all such agreements should first be registered. The composition of the Restrictive Practices Court is such that it marries legal experts and industrial and commercial experts and the procedure before it is similar to that in any court of law, in that expert witnesses can be called for prosecution and defence.

The types of agreements to be registered were those between at least two persons whereby restrictions were accepted in respect of prices to be charged, conditions of sale, quantities and types to be produced, persons or areas to be supplied and persons or areas from whom supplies may be obtained. Even though, as we have said, such restrictions were deemed to be against the public interest, nevertheless the Court could uphold any restriction which satisfied certain conditions, provided that the Court was also satisfied that the advantages to the public outweighed the disadvantages. These conditions were all designed to encourage serious discussion about the agreement; the one which has been pleaded most often is section 21(1)b: that the agreement confers specific and substantial benefits upon the consuming public.

Application of the Act seems to have changed over time. In the period up to 1960 11 cases had been considered and 3 agreements had been upheld but, since then, the number of cases upheld has increased considerably as defence experts have worked away at the interpretation of section 21(1)b. However, it is undoubtedly the case that many agreements were abandoned without ever being registered.

In 1964 the Registrar was given the further task of presenting for judgment individual resale price maintenance agreements. Again the presumption was that such practices were against the public interest, but 5 conditions were provided for possible escape with an overall survey of benefits and disadvantages if one of the conditions was thought to be fulfilled. The general effect appears to be that many agreements have been abandoned without going to court, but that fought by the chocolate manufacturers was particularly long and drawn out. In this case the judgment went against the manufacturers.

As one restrictive practice is abandoned so manufacturers find other loopholes in the legislation and in 1968 the Registrar was given further powers to deal with 'information' agreements. Such agreements may provide for the parties to exchange information about prices, costs and allocation of contracts, etc. and in this way the same results as before can be achieved. The 1968 Act, however, weakened restrictive practices legislation in two important ways. Probably concerned with information agreements, an additional gateway was introduced so that a restriction could be defended on the grounds that 'it does not directly or indirectly restrict or discourage competition to any material degree in any relevant trade or industry and is not likely to do so'. The second way in which legislation was weakened arose out of an attempt to clarify certain apparent conflicts on policy between various government bodies. For example the Economic Development Committee (EDC) for an industry might encourage agreements which were, however, registrable under the Act. Thus the 1968 Act also provides exemption from registration of certain agreements of importance to the national economy, where the object is to promote efficiency or create or improve productive capacity, and where that object cannot be achieved within a reasonable time except by means of an agreement.

The latest moves in this area have been connected with the *Fair Trading Act*, 1973 which abolishes the office of Registrar of Restrictive Practices and transfers his functions to the Director General of Fair Trading. Two important points from the new legislation are as follows: Firstly, the Court is now empowered to make interim orders in relation to agreements which it does not think can be shown to be defensible by reference to any of the so-called 'gateways'. Secondly, the Act brings under the surveillance of the Court agreements between suppliers of services, other than those of a professional nature, because these agreements are also to be registered. Both these moves should strengthen the general attack upon restrictive practices. L.T.S.

C. Brock, *The Control of Restrictive Practices from 1956* (McGraw-Hill, 1966).

Retail Audit The regular measurement of retail trading activity in a sample of retail outlets for purposes of marketing research. The technique involves the selection of a representative sample of outlets, to which visits are made, normally monthly, to count current stock levels in selected product categories, and to examine deliveries of goods to the outlet and inter-branch transfers. This data provides sales per outlet by the following calculation:

Stock at start + Net deliveries inwards
− Stock at close = Sales

In addition to providing total sales, stock-cover in terms of 'week's supply' at the current rate of sale can be computed. The percentage of outlets which have any particular product and/or brand in stock provides a measure of distribution and when total sales values of a product through outlets stocking it are expressed as a percentage of total sales value of the product, the *sterling* distribution is obtained. This latter measure of distribution provides a measure of the quality of distribution held as well as quantity, a matter of importance when the size of the outlets stocking varies widely. The technique was pioneered in North America in the 1920s by A. C. Nielsen, and in Britain this company is the largest retail audit organization. G.S.C.W.

Retail Gravitation The movement of customers to retail outlets (⟨⟩ Retailing). The problem has attracted considerable attention in order both to assess the potential for the development of existing trade and to facilitate the effective location of new shopping centres. The earliest attempts to establish relationships between retail trading centres and their hinterland were made by William Reilly (*Methods for*

Study of Retail Relationships, University of Texas, 1929) and took account of population mass (P) and distance (D):

$$\frac{Ba}{Bb} = \left(\frac{Pa}{Pb}\right)\left(\frac{Db}{Da}\right)^2$$

where Ba and Bb represent the proportion of trade going to towns a and b. This gives a breaking point (Db) in miles from town b, for trade between the two towns of:

$$Db = \frac{Dab}{1 + \sqrt{\dfrac{Pa}{Pb}}}$$

Where the population of town a is 200,000 and of town b, 50,000, and the two towns are 10 miles apart, this gives a breaking point for trade $6\frac{2}{3}$ miles from town a and $3\frac{1}{3}$ miles from town b. A number of more recent models of a deterministic nature have been developed, incorporating modifications for the attractiveness of a shopping centre. Huff has recently developed a probabilistic model, which can be based on either empirical ascription of probabilities by interview or deductive procedures. Deductive methods are still the most common in use. The contribution of economic geographers through central place theory, and from social physics, in developing an explanation of patterns of gravitation is increasingly apparent. G.S.C.W.

> R. L. Nelson, *The Selection of Retail Locations* (F. W. Dodge Corporation, 1958).

Retailing The ultimate sale of any goods in small quantities. Normally it will be the final stage in the distribution of a product or service which transfers ownership to the person who will control where it will be used (◊ Distribution Mix). It is commonplace these days to find retailing as a separate institution in the marketing process, but the time is not so long since the producer/retailer, and there are signs that many multiple retailers, e.g. Marks and Spencer, are seeking to influence and control their suppliers. The retailer offers ready access to a wide range of related goods which he has broken out (*retailler*) from a larger supply purchased at a discount known as the retail margin. ◊ Mail Order is a special case where the goods offered are seen in a catalogue and requested by post; this sector of retailing is the fastest growth area in Britain today, probably due to the congestion encountered in many shopping centres and the increasing importance of time in a society with many working wives. The abolition of rpm (◊ Resale Price Maintenance Law) in 1964 has led to an undermining of retail margins which, when added to the trends to self-service (◊ Supermarket), larger units, and multiple chains with volume advantages in buying from suppliers, has meant swift changes in the structure of British retailing. Smaller units, particularly in the food trade, have formed voluntary groups with wholesalers in order to secure buying economies, of which the most important are Wavy Line and Mace. Cooperative retail outlets already had this opportunity through the Cooperative Wholesale Society (◊ Cooperative Movement) but have been unable to maintain their share of the market. Parallel with the loss of personal influence over customers implicit in the change-over to self-service has been an increasing tendency for manufacturers to appeal over the retailer's head direct to the customer, using mass advertising and ⟨⟩ Branding to create insistence for a product or service and therefore ensure distribution. The pattern and value of distribution in Britain is given in the Censuses of Distributors, conducted by the Board of Trade in 1950, 1957 and 1961. In 1961, retail trade through over half a million outlets was valued at over £9,000 m. G.S.C.W.

W. G. McClelland, *Costs and Competition in Retailing* (Macmillan, 1966).

Retirement Policy The arrangements made by an undertaking in connection with the cessation of work by its older employees. These may include courses in preparation for retirement, changes in work and holidays as retirement approaches (gradual retirement), provisions for contributory or non-contributory pensions, special medical, welfare and social facilities both for those nearing retirement and for those who have retired. Any policy must include a decision about the age of retirement, whether this shall be fixed to avoid charges of discrimination and for the sake of administrative convenience, or flexible to allow for the differences between psychological and chronological age, i.e. the wide variation in individual capabilities of people of the same age which are common knowledge and have been studied scientifically by research into the process of ⟨⟩ Ageing. From the point of view of national manpower policy and of making the best use of human resources, more attention is likely to be paid in the future to flexible retirement policies with associated changes in work load, and provisions for the health and welfare of older workers. L.S.

Retirement. A Study of Current Attitudes and Practices (Acton Society Trust, 1960).

Reward The total return, tangible and intangible, which accrues to an individual as a consequence of his behaviour. A reward may be negative, in the sense that it may consist of the avoidance of an unpleasant consequence, but more usually is positive in that it wholly or partially satisfies a need. The extent to which an individual will be motivated by a potential reward will be greatly influenced by his need for the reward, by his assessment of the likelihood that he will receive it, and by what he has to do to get it. In the industrial organization, the most obvious rewards are monetary and take the form of wages or salaries with or without additional bonuses. Yet other rewards are common: for example; fringe benefits such as sick pay, pension rights, holiday pay, subsidized canteens; perquisites ('perks') such as a company car, an expense account, assistance with school fees, privileged access to company products; security of pay and employment; desirable hours and working conditions; social satisfactions including satisfactions intrinsic in the job; the approval of those whose opinions are valued; the prospects of better rewards in the future; and status.

These various elements are not always consistent and to some extent more of one may compensate for less of another; security may make up for low job satisfaction, or prospects compensate for immediate income. The different elements cannot validly be quantified and totalled, yet it seems clear that in practice some such crude summation does take place and a given pay differential may be considered justified because of awkward hours of work, dirty conditions, etc.

Rewards are not distributed randomly throughout an organization but are arranged in an orderly relationship, known as the reward system. Generally the reward system correlates fairly closely with the status system. Not only does this happen but it is widely considered to be morally right that it should happen, and where, for whatever reasons, there should develop a disjunction between the two systems, there will be dissatisfaction, particularly on the part of the individual or group whose rewards are below those implied by their status. If the rewards are not adjusted, the status of the group will decline until the two systems are again in conjunction. ⟡ Motivation; Status. I.C.MCG.

J. A. Litterer, *The Analysis of Organisations*, Ch. 15 (J. Wiley, 1965).

Right to Work The term 'right to work' may be used in a number of meanings. The written constitutions of some countries include this 'right' among the constitutional rights of their citizens. In this context it merely implies that the government of the country should follow an economic policy which will achieve a state of full employment. In the USA and in some other countries the term 'right to work legislation' has been used to describe measures intended to prevent trade unions from insisting on a ⟡ Closed Shop, thus debarring non-unionists from securing employment. A third meaning that has been given to this term is that of implying that an employee has a kind of property right to his job so that in the event of his dismissal for some reason other than misconduct, his employer should have to compensate him for the loss of his 'property'. The ⟡ *Redundancy Payments Act*, 1965, has introduced this principle, though in a somewhat limited form, into British law. In some continental countries a dismissed employee has a right to appeal to an independent tribunal which may order his reinstatement. In Britain this principle operated only in respect of employees who had to leave their jobs because of call-up for the Armed Forces. Under the provisions of the *Trade Union and Labour Relations Act*, 1974 in connection with the ⟡ Unfair Dismissal of Employees, an ⟡ Industrial Tribunal may recommend, though not order, the reinstatement or re-engagement of an unfairly dismissed employee. By providing for the payment of compensation to employees who have been unfairly dismissed the Act has brought English law more into line with continental practice.

A final meaning of the right to work is the right of every citizen to follow his chosen calling or profession without being denied entry by unreasonable restrictions, such as those based on considerations of colour, creed or sex. W.F.F.

F. Meyers, *Ownership of Jobs* (Berkeley, 1964).

Risk Analysis This approach has been developed in OR particularly to evaluate capital investment opportunities. The actual future cash flows and/or other benefits generated by a given financial investment are likely to be dependent on the combination of at least a number of factors which are individually subject to variability and uncertainty. Current methods of evaluation assume fixed values for cash flows in each year and calculate the return on investment using a standard technique such as discounted cash flow. Because factors which are each subject to variability and uncertainty will combine according to the laws of probability, it is more accurate to express the return as a frequency distribution (⧫ Statistics) of possible returns such as is shown in the diagram below.

This shows that the probability of obtaining a return of 0% is small and the probabilities increase until 10% then tail off slowly, so that the probability of obtaining more than 23% is zero. This is a better approach to evaluating investment opportunities and can provide a more refined comparison between alternative investment proposals.

Because the mathematical analysis of the interactions of the factors involved is complex, the above yield curve is often obtained by simulating these interactions by computer simulation. ⧫ Capital Budgeting; Discounted Present Value; Simulation. M.J.C.M.

Risk and Uncertainty (in Financial Management) Several distinctions have to be made in discussing financial risk and uncertainty. Modern decision theory generally follows the distinction made by F. H. Knight between risk and uncertainty. Risk is said to refer to matters against which one can be protected by applying ordinary insurance principles. That is to say, it applies to situations, the outcomes of which are not certain but the probabilities of the alternative possible outcomes of which are known or can be accurately estimated by practicable experimentation or the use of statistical data. Uncertainty is said to be present where the outcomes cannot be predicted even in some probabilistic sense.

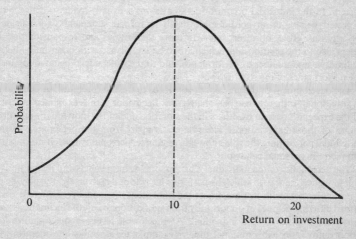

Business risk should be distinguished from financial risk. The latter arises when the firm's capital contains fixed interest securities (or debts), e.g. debentures or loans. The former refers to the general risks underlying the cost, revenues and profits of the firm, i.e. all business risks other than financial risks and uncertainties.

Borrowing (which for some purposes includes preference share issues also) increases the shareholder's risk and uncertainty. It does so by imposing a fixed charge which must be met if the firm is not to be made bankrupt and also that according to the extent that borrowing is used so the variability of profits accruing to ordinary (equity)-shareholders is increased by the imposition of a fixed charge (⟡ Capital Structure). Since the expected average return to all investors in the company is generally expected to exceed the rate of interest payable on the debentures and loans, the expected return to ordinary shareholders must increase to the extent that the firm is debt financed. However, when the rate of profit falls below that of the rate of debt capital, the return to equity holders falls further because of the existence of debt. Thus equity holders gain the possibility of higher incomes but at the cost of wider expected variability of income because of debt capital. Since investors are generally said to be averse to risk the question for financial management is what is the rate of compensation, in terms of increased expected rate of income (or dividends), for given additional amounts of financial risk; much of the discussion of 'gearing' revolves around this question. For both the valuation of investment and the cost of capital issues this is a central question. E.A.L.

> A. A. Robichek and S. C. Myers, *Optimal Financing Decisions* (Prentice-Hall, 1965); K. N. Borch, *The Economics of Uncertainty* (Princeton University Press, 1968).

Role The behaviour expected of the occupant of a given position in a social system. In the industrial organization an attempt is usually made to define such expected behaviour in considerable detail in formal statements, such as job descriptions. Role, however, refers to more than duties and responsibilities. It refers also to the relationships which are to be established with other individuals, to the style and manner of performance, and to the wider social behaviour which the performance of the role involves.

The development of the concept of role leads to the interpretation of behaviour in situational, rather than in personal, terms. Behaviour is thus explained in terms of the expectations held by others in the situation and of the individual's interpretation of those expectations. The role exists apart from the personality of the individual performing the role although, of course, personality is itself an important factor in personal behaviour.

The personality of the individual – his personal values, beliefs and inclinations – will influence the way in which he performs his role and conversely, the playing of a particular role will, in time, affect the individual's personality. Different roles afford differing degrees of opportunity for modification to suit the inclinations and particular abilities of the individual. At the lowest levels in the organization opportunity is probably minimal and, for example, the assembly line operator will have his role closely prescribed. At the higher levels, the executive is able to modify his role substantially in order to make the greatest use of his particular abilities and interests. This partially explains why executives tend to achieve a greater degree of job satisfaction than do manual workers and why it is more difficult for the organization to accommodate a change in executive personnel. ⟡ Social System; Status. I.C.MCG.

> J. A. Litterer, *The Analysis of Organisations* (J. Wiley, 1965).

Role Conflict A situation in which the individual is subjected to stress due to the fact that the performance of his role or roles seems to require incompatible or impossible behaviour.

Role conflict can arise from several sources. It may be due to a lack of compatibility between role and personality, in which the individual is unable or unwilling to perform the role although wishing to do so, or, at least, to avoid the consequences of *not* doing so. It may be caused by lack of clarity in the role so that the individual is unable to perform because he does not know what behaviour is expected of him. Or the expectations may themselves be conflicting, as with the industrial foreman whose subordinates expect behaviour from him which is incompatible with that expected by his superiors. Again, the demands of different roles may conflict; for example, the young executive seeking to establish himself in his career may be required to work long hours and to travel frequently on company business, activities which conflict with the behavioural requirements of his roles of husband and father.

Reactions to role conflict will vary with the individual and the situation but may include the rejection of one of the conflicting roles, deception of one of the groups or persons that their expectations are being fulfilled when in fact they are not, escape from the situation by resignation, transfer or illness, or increasing anxiety and emotional tension. ⇨ Role. I.C.MCG.

Robert L. Kahn *et al.*, *Organisational Stress* (J. Wiley, 1964).

Routing Problems Large sums of money are spent on the physical distribution of goods from producers to customers and on the routing of collection and inspection services (for example postmen, meter readers, refuse collectors and on school bus routes). If delivery, collection and inspection routes can be designed at minimum mileage or cost, large sums of money will be saved nationally, and routing problems have received considerable attention. Although such problems can quite often be formulated using ⇨ Linear Programming it is often very difficult to obtain a rigorous mathematical solution which minimizes costs. However, substantial reductions over common-sense methods in routing vehicles, etc., may be obtained by using operational research techniques and most computer manufacturers have available standard programs for tackling this type of problem. (⇨ Library [computer]). M.J.C.M.

Patrick Rivett and Russell L. Ackoff, *A Manager's Guide to Operational Research*, pp. 46–7 (J. Wiley, 1963).

Royal Commission on Trade Unions and Employers' Associations ⇨ Industrial Relations – Reform in Great Britain.

S

Safety The safety of personnel and equipment is a problem which has a bearing upon many aspects of industrial management including design engineering, production engineering, medical services, factory supervision, maintenance services and training.

Two aspects of safety are distinguishable in as far as they relate to the well-being of personnel. Firstly accidents (i.e. specific traumatic incidents) must be avoided and secondly, persons must be protected from damage or discomfort resulting from long-term exposure to hazards.

A great deal of research has been carried out into the causes of accidents, and a great deal can be done by way of the design of equipment and environments, the establishment of procedures and the training of personnel to minimize the occurrence of such accidents (⟡ Accident Prevention).

Damage to personnel can also result without the occurrence of specific incidents. Noise, for example, can produce hearing loss in a worker who has been subjected to high noise levels for a prolonged period of time. Similarly dusts may produce long-term effects, and spinal damage may result from prolonged periods of bad posture. In almost all such cases, remedial measures are available for the protection of personnel. E.E.

Salary Structure The organization of salaries according to a systematic comparison of the similarities and differences in occupations. These comparisons can be made by job evaluation (⟡ Job Analysis), which normally takes into account skills, qualifications, experience, responsibilities and seniority. A salary structure will be divided into a number of grades and will include scales, usually in the form of annual increases up to a maximum for each grade. These increments may be related to seniority or length of service in the grade, or to merit (⟡ Merit Rating) or to both. In practice there is often a large element of tradition in the actual grading of jobs, if only because of the impossibility of grading jobs in terms of money with scientific accuracy. Actual salaries paid are also influenced by the state of the labour market, so that when there is a shortage of people qualified for particular jobs these salaries will be higher than a job evaluation would suggest. Some grading of salaries exists in any enterprise; the concept of a salary structure leads to a rational approach to the decision about grading and about the relationship between grades, and to the removal, where possible, of inconsistencies and inequities. L.S.

J. E. Genders and N. J. Urwin, *Wages and Salaries* (Institute of Personnel Management, 1962).

Sale of Goods A contract for the sale of goods is a contract whereby the property of goods is transferred by the seller to the buyer for a money consideration, called the price. These contracts are governed in the U K by the *Sale of Goods Act*, 1893.

Goods are tangible, movable things and do not therefore include land or things permanently attached to land.

It is important to ascertain when the property in goods passes from the seller to the buyer since the risk of loss or damage passes with the property. The Act states that the property passes at such time as the parties want it to pass and certain rules are laid down to indicate the position where the parties have not clearly expressed their intention.

The parties may attach certain terms to the contract and if these terms are vital to the very existence of the contract they are known as conditions, while if they are merely subordinate terms they are called warranties. Both conditions and warranties may be either expressly stated in the contract or may be implied into the contract by law. A breach of a condition entitles the buyer to treat the contract as discharged and to claim damages, while a breach of warranty entitles him to damages only.

Where goods are sold by description there exists an implied condition that the goods supplied will correspond with the description and that they will be of merchantable quality. Where the buyer has indicated to a seller, who is selling goods in the course of a business, the particular purpose for which the goods are being bought, there is an implied condition that the goods supplied will be reasonably fit for this purpose except where it can be shown that the buyer did not rely on the seller's skill and judgment in advising him. The protection granted to the buyer has been substantially increased by the *Supply of Goods (Implied Terms) Act*, 1973. W.F.F.

D. W. Greig, *The Sale of Goods* (Butterworth, 1974).

Sales Forecast The estimate of likely sales which an organization can achieve during a future period. It will normally be broken down in terms of individual products or services offered, and expressed in terms of unit and value sales. Such forecasts most frequently cover a 12-month period, with weekly and monthly targets by, e.g. area representative. They are derived in general from the statistical evaluation and projection of past sales data, modified in the light of factors thought likely to influence any trend found to be present in past data (⟡ Forecasting). The sales forecast is the lynch-pin of much company planning. Within the marketing plan it is the basis of profit forecasts and of control as variances from forecast emerge. It enables effective action to be taken early on if an unsatisfactory situation emerges. The sales forecast also acts as the basis for production planning within a manufacturing organization, and for the purchasing of raw materials and components. The profit plan implicit in given levels of sales forecast acts as the basis for cash flow analysis by the financial management of an organization. G.S.C.W.

Business Forecasting (Market Research Society, 1958).

Sampling It has been stated elsewhere (⟡ Statistics) that it is often impossible or prohibitively expensive to measure given characteristics of each member of a statistical population, and a statistician examines a sub-group or sample from it. The accuracy with which the properties of the sample represent the properties of the population from which it is drawn is primarily dependent on the care taken in sampling.

Samples are taken by attribute or variable. The former are concerned with whether an individual selected by sampling has a specified attribute or characteristic. For example, in sampling births we may only wish to know if a baby is male or female. The latter are concerned with the measure or quantity of a particular characteristic or variable. For example, in sampling births we may wish to know the baby's birth weight or height, that is we are sampling the variable weight or height.

Although each sample must be designed with its specific purpose in mind there are a number of general approaches:

1. *Random Sampling* occurs when each member of the population has an equal chance of being selected. Thus if a sample of size 1000 of the heights of Englishmen over 20 years is taken, then if 18 million is the total number of Englishmen over 20 years, each has a 1 in 18 thousand chance of being selected.

2. *Systematic Sampling* occurs when a sample of fraction $1/n$ of the population is required. Then if every nth member of the population is selected, the required fraction is obtained. This may work well when no cyclical patterns are expected to occur in a population, such as in an alphabetical list of electors or a file of stock cards. However, if cycle patterns are present, it can introduce a bias. For example, if an electoral role is listed by streets (as in the normal case) and a sample is chosen by selecting a number of every fifth household then, if the houses are built in groups of five, either one end house or one terraced house will be selected every time, depending on which was chosen initially. Since it is likely that the occupants of end houses will be more prosperous than those in terraced ones (as the former houses normally cost more money), bias will have been introduced.

3. *Stratified Sampling*. It may be known that there are, or may be, differences between different parts or 'strata' of a population. For example, annual income groups or geographical areas can form strata for a national population of industrial workers. If the percentage of the total population in each strata is known, then the sample may be designed or stratified to be made up of similar percentages from each strata. Within a given stratum, the required selections may be made by (1) or (2) above. Quota sampling is a technique commonly used by market researchers which is really a form of stratified sampling. A market research interviewer is given a quota or number to interview from each strata and can stop sampling once he or she has obtained the required quota in every strata.

4. *Cluster Sampling* is used particularly in market research and is best illustrated by an example. To obtain a sample of approximately 200 housewives in England, a county may be chosen, then a town or village within it, and finally a street within that, all by successive random selections. Once the street has been chosen all housewives in it may be interviewed. Thus a sample consists of a cluster of individuals. This method is popular because it is relatively cheap. M.J.C.M.

P. G. Moore, *Statistics and the Manager* (Macdonald, 1966).

Scanlon Plan A method, American in origin, of sharing with employees the monetary gains derived from increased productivity.

The object is to concentrate attention on the productivity of a company, factory or department by giving to the employees on a monthly basis a proportion (usually 50–75%) of the savings from the reductions in labour costs which are made in the unit concerned. But labour costs are to be reduced and productivity increased by suffusing the whole establishment with a realization that workers and management have a common interest in greater efficiency and a more cooperative atmosphere. Thus the Scanlon Plan is not so much a formula for sharing productivity bonuses as a whole concept of union–management cooperation, of which increased monetary rewards for the workers are just one side-effect.

Found mainly in small and medium-sized companies in the USA, the plan is normally implemented through a system of committees on which representatives of every work-group and managerial function serve and which operate at all levels of the organization. The plan combines the practices of profit-sharing, ⟡ Joint Consultation and suggestion schemes, though its exponents claim that *in toto* it represents something of greater significance than the mere sum of its component parts. The plan is supposed to implicate employees in the success of an enterprise by giving each one an opportunity to use his own intelligence and ideas to increase productivity. Clearly schemes of this kind are likely to be effective only when the business itself is expanding, when the technology is new enough and transitory enough to permit useful suggestions from the shop floor, and when worker and management attitudes are dynamic enough to permit new departures in this direction. For these reasons the plan has made few appearances in Britain. The Rootes group, for example, employed a variation of the plan at its Linwood 'Imp' Factory in the form of a factory bonus geared to the level of car sales. But when 'Imp' sales began to fall the bonus pool began to shrink, with predictably adverse effects on industrial relations within the factory, and eventually the whole scheme had to be abandoned. L.S. & N.H.C.

F. G. Lesieur (ed.), *The Scanlon Plan* (M.I.T. Press and J. Wiley, 1958); Douglas McGregor, *The Human Side of Enterprise* (McGraw-Hill, 1960).

Scheduling Problems ⟡ Sequencing Problems.

Scientific Management That approach to problems of organization based upon, and following the same basic premises as, the work of Frederick Winslow Taylor. Taylor was deeply concerned about the quality of the relationships that existed between management and men in the factories around him and about the inefficiency and work dodging that were a feature of the industrial life he experienced. He came quickly to the belief that these troubles were due to managerial laxity. There was a universal tendency to leave the details of work performance to the discretion of the workmen and work was therefore performed inefficiently; there was only the crudest understanding of how much work could reasonably be expected of a workman and this led to constant disagreements and bitterness between management and men; and workmen were inadequately motivated to give of their best. Taylor accordingly devoted his life to the development of techniques for the study of work and the determination of the most efficient way for each task to be performed. By careful observation and timing by stopwatch, 'objective' standards of performance could be determined and an incentive system devised which would reward above-standard and penalize sub-standard performance.

Taylor thus believed that managers must accept full responsibility for planning, organizing and supervising work. The skill and experience of the better workmen and craftsmen were to be analysed and classified so that they might be reduced to rules, laws and formulae. Therefore, once the best way to do a job had been ascertained by trained observation, the worker should be scientifically selected and instructed in the proper method. In this way managers would assume the duties for which they were better fitted than the workmen and the latter would be free from responsibilities they were not fit to discharge. Taylor was of the opinion that every employee had two needs: high wages and the opportunity for personal advancement. The worker was thus viewed, and treated, as an individual 'workhorse' in social isolation. It was a fundamental tenet that managers should never deal with workers in groups.

The Taylor approach attracted many disciples, most notably F. B. Gilbreth, and exerted considerable influence on management thought and behaviour. Despite the naïvity of the assumptions concerning motivation and the patent exaggeration of the claim to scientific objectivity, scientific management spread rapidly to virtually all industrial countries, including the Soviet Union. It is manifest not only in the growth of departments of work study, production engineering, production scheduling, etc., but also in the attitude of mind which seeks the collection and analysis of data as the basis for decision-making and the increasing rationalization of production processes. ⟡ Classical Organization Theory. I.C.MCG.

F. W. Taylor, *Scientific Management* (Harper and Brothers, 1947).

Search Problems These problems were first identified during the war when tactics for searching the oceans for hostile submarines were developed. An oil company faces similar problems in searching an area of desert for oil deposits. In both cases with the resources available (aircraft or money) a decision must be made on what search tactics to use A large area can be searched quickly, thereby increasing the chances of passing over a submarine, say, but reducing the chances of spotting it should the searcher pass over it. Alternatively a smaller area can be searched slowly, thereby reducing the chances of passing over a submarine, but increasing the chances of spotting it should the searcher pass over it. Probability theory and statistical analysis have been applied to this problem to determine the optimum search policy.

Account auditing is a similar type of search problem and these techniques have been applied to a very limited extent to auditing in large organizations. M.J.C.M.

Patrick Rivett and Russell L. Ackoff, *A Manager's Guide to Operational Research*, pp. 53–5 (J. Wiley, 1963).

Seating ⟡ Posture.

Selection Choosing from a number of candidates the one most likely to be suited to a particular job. The process of selection starts with ⟡ Recruitment on the one hand and, on the other, with a ⟡ Job Analysis which enables the selectors to identify the qualities, qualifications and experience required in the post to be filled and to list these in a job specification. In practice, particularly for management positions, the selectors are also interested in the overall potential of a future employee and with the way in which he will contribute to and develop in the organization. In these cases the specification will be wider than that derived from the job analysis of one occupation. The task of selection is to assess the candidate against the job specification however widely conceived. In doing this information is required about the candidate's physique and health, general ⟡ Intelligence, special aptitudes, achievements, temperament and personality. Some of these qualities can be measured by tests, e.g. ⟡ Aptitude Tests for specific skills, or by medical examination; others, such as academic or professional qualifications, can be given on application forms. But others are left to a personal ⟡ Interview which serves the purpose of being both an element in the selection procedure and an opportunity for candidates to learn about the job they may be offered and the firm for which they may be working. Some employers supplement interviews with group selection procedures, especially in the recruitment of university graduates. By putting a small number of candidates together and giving them a problem to solve or a subject to discuss, it is possible to compare the performance of the candidates in relation to each other and to discover qualities and intelligence and ⟡ Personality in action which a face-to-face interview may not reveal. Interviews are often the most decisive part of selection, but research findings have exposed their fallibility. Bodies such as the Institute of Industrial Psychology have developed methods which increase the reliability of interviewing. L.S.

M. D. Dunnette, *Personnel Selection and Placement* (Tavistock Publications, 1967); E. Sidney and M. Brown, *The Skills of Interviewing* (Tavistock Publications, 1961).

Selection Tests ⟡ Selection; Aptitude Tests.

Selling Exchanging the right to goods or a service with another in return for an agreed sum of money. The function within a company of organizing the distribution and sale of its products or services was formerly described as selling, but this usage is much less common (⟡ Marketing). Selling is currently associated predominantly with the act of personal communication which is an important part of the total concept of marketing communications ⟡ Marketing Communications Mix. Controversy exists over precisely which aspects of selling are an art and which subject to scientific treatment. The social sciences, particularly psychology, have been applied extensively in achieving effective and persuasive communication. Rigid analysis of potential sales in geographical areas, and the optimization of salesman's journeys, are also employed. The most significant use of salesmen, in terms of securing orders from retail traders throughout the country, has undergone change since the development of mass advertising. Increasingly, such salesmen have taken on the additional role of merchandisers (⟡ Merchandising), and the soliciting of orders has frequently been made much simpler by brand insistence by customers ⟡ Branding. In industrial and technical markets, however, the role of the salesman has traditionally incorporated that of technical advisor. As technical complexity increases this is increasingly so. The salesman's task here has been encompassed by the development of mathematical methods of control for stocks, etc., and an increasing degree of critical assessment in ⟡ Purchasing. G.S.C.W.

D. W. Smallbone, *Control of the Field Sales Force* (Staples, 1966).

Sensitivity Training ⟡ Group Methods of Training.

Sequencing and Dispatching Problems Both sequencing and dispatching are used as terms describing the process by which the order in which items are to be passed through one or more locations is determined. Within the context of production, we are normally concerned with jobs and machines, hence the problem is concerned with the ordering of jobs through one or more machines. The term sequencing is normally used when the problem concerns the order of jobs on *several* machines, i.e. determining the sequence of jobs on the machines. The term dispatching is normally used to describe the process by which jobs are placed in order for *one* machine.

Both the sequencing and dispatching problems, particularly the latter, occur to a large extent and are particularly important in jobbing production. In mass production where a homogeneous set of jobs are to be manufactured by passage through a set of machines in a given order, precise scheduling is possible, i.e. it is possible to predict with some accuracy the time at which any job will arrive at any machine. Quite the opposite situation exists in jobbing production where, because many different products are to be manufactured, and because manufacturing information is imprecise, accurate scheduling is impossible. As a result, a large amount of work-in-progress stock usually exists and queues of jobs form at departments and machines. Such a situation gives rise to sequencing and dispatching problems. ⟡ Production Planning and Control.

Sequencing Even in comparatively simple situations involving few jobs and machines, the number of possible sequences of jobs through the machines is so large that rigorous solution of the problem is often impractical. Simple algorithms have been produced for solving highly abstract and simple sequencing problems. Techniques such as linear programming, the branch and bound method and simulation have been used but frequently the amount of computation, or the simplifying assumptions made, discount their use in practical situations. ⟡ Mathematical Programming; Branch and Bound method; Simulation (computer).

One method of overcoming this situation is to consider the problem in terms of single machines only, i.e. to determine in which order available jobs will be processed on one machine at a time, rather than attempt to determine the sequence of jobs for several machines. This is the dispatching problem.

Dispatching An essential part of production control. In practice both manual and computer-based production control procedures normally rely upon priority rule dispatching. The use of priority rules enables decisions to be made as and when required, i.e. when machines become vacant.

Examples of Priority Rules: 1. *Job slack* (S) This is the amount of contingency

350

or free time, over and above the expected processing time, available before the job is completed at a predetermined date (t_0).

i.e. $S = t_0 - t_1 - \Sigma a_i$
where t_1 = present date
and Σa_i = sum of remaining processing times.

Where delays are associated with each operation, e.g. delays caused by inter-machine transport, this rule is not suitable, hence the following rule may be used.
2. *Job slack per operation* i.e. S/N where N = no. of remaining operations. Therefore where S is the same for two or more jobs, the job having the most remaining operations is processed first.
3. *Job slack ratio*, or the ratio of the total remaining time to the remaining slack time, i.e.

$$\frac{S}{t_0 - t_1}$$

In all the above cases, where the priority index is negative, the job cannot be completed by the requisite date. The rule will therefore be to process first those jobs having negative indices.
4. *Shortest imminent operation* (SIO) i.e. process first the job with the shortest processing times.
5. *Longest imminent operation* (LIO). This is the converse of (4).
6. *Scheduled start date*. This is perhaps the most frequently used rule. The date at which operations must be started in order that a job will meet a required completion date is calculated, usually by employing reverse scheduling from the completion date.

e.g. $x_i = t_0 - \Sigma a_i$
or $x_i = t_0 - \Sigma(a_i + f_i)$
where x_i = scheduled start date for an operation
and f_i = delay or contingency allowance.

Usually some other rule is also used, e.g. first come, first served, to decide priorities between jobs having equal x_i values.
7. *Earliest due date*, i.e. process first the job required first.
8. *Subsequent processing times*. Process first the job that has the longest remaining process times, i.e. Σa_i or in modified form $\Sigma(a_i + f_i)$.
9. *Value*. To reduce work in progress inventory cost, process first the job which has the highest value.
10. *Minimum total float*. This rule is the one usually adopted when scheduling by network techniques.
11. *Subsequent operation*. Look ahead to see where the job will go after this operation has been completed and process first the job which goes to a 'critical' queue, that is a machine having a small queue of available work, thus minimizing the possibility of machine idle time.
12. *First come, first served* (FCFS).
13. *Random* (e.g. in order of Job No. etc.). Rules 12 and 13 are random since,

unlike the others, neither one depends directly on job characteristics such as length of operation, value etc. R.W.

R. Wild, 'Jobbing Shop Sequencing', *Chartered Mechanical Engineer*, Jan. 1967; R. Wild, *Techniques of Production Management* (Holt, Rinehart and Winston, London, 1971).

Severance Pay ◊ Redundancy.

Severity Rate ◊ Accident Prevention.

Sex Differences The superiority in occupational achievement of men over women, even in such 'female' areas as cooking, is overwhelming. The question of whether these differences are due mainly to the social pattern of our society, or whether they have a more innate cause is still an open one. It seems reasonable to suppose that sex differences are brought about principally by the sex chromosomes. But conclusive evidence is lacking.

Some anthropometric sex differences are obvious. Mean male stature, for example, exceeds that of females by about 4 in. Strength measurements indicate male superiority of the order of 70%. In reaction times, men are slightly swifter than women. Comparison of school achievements of boys and girls indicate superior attainments by age for the girls; this may be associated with an earlier physical development to puberty. Arguments from intelligence test scores are usually impossible due to the systematic balancing of sex differences in the standardization procedure (◊ Intelligence). E.E.

Shares ◊ Claims.

Shift Work An arrangement of working hours whereby different groups of workers are employed for periods of work during different times during any 24 hours.

There are five main types of shift system: (1) fixed or alternating double-day shifts, usually two eight-hour periods between 6 a.m. and 10 p.m. when it is legal under certain conditions to employ women and young people aged 16 or over; (2) double-day shifts combined with a permanent night-shift; (3) three-shift non-continuous working with breaks at weekends; (4) continuous three- or four-shift systems in which the plant is manned for the full 168 hours in each week; (5) evening shifts for part-time employees and staggered daywork, used in industries such as food preserving which, with different starting and finishing times for different groups of workers, make possible a longer working day without employing individual workers for excessive hours.

With advancing technology and the ever-present need to raise productivity, British Industry has been turning more and more to the use of shift work. The number of manual workers engaged on shifts has risen by over 50% in the past 10 years and this trend is expected to continue. In a survey (Dec. 1967) by the Ministry of Labour of 19 firms in various industries, the following salient points about shift working emerged: (1) In every firm the system had brought about a reduction in hours worked through either the elimination of overtime or a reduction in the length of basic time worked. (2) Shift work can provide a means of making the best use of machinery, attracting extra labour, reducing overtime or meeting peaks in demand. In two out of three firms it had been introduced as a result of the installation of expensive new machinery: here it enabled management to obtain much higher production and hence a higher rate of return on capital invested. This is of particular importance where a particular technology is subject to rapid change. (3) In two thirds of these firms extra labour was required, so the state of the local labour market is a very important factor in the introduction of a shift system. Most firms had difficulty recruiting for the afternoon and night shifts. In some cases part-time and double day shifts had been introduced to attract women not available for normal day working. (4) Shift-working does, however, increase the work load on management and supervision, demands prior consultations (◊ Joint Consultation) in detail not only with full-time trade union officials (◊ Trade Union Officers) but also with ◊ Shop Stewards and workers, and entails higher machinery maintenance costs. The need for comprehensive forward planning can hardly be overstressed. (5) It is frequently argued that shift-working tends to be inflexible and makes it difficult to cope with production peaks, but all these firms in the survey stressed that it had increased their capacity to spread additional work loads and made it easier to deal with urgent orders. L.S. & N.H.C.

F. P. Cook, *Shift Work* (Institute of Personnel Management, 1954); *D.E.P. Gazette*, 1968.

Shop Steward A trade union representative in the (work)shop or other workplace Normally lay, rather than full-time officials, shop stewards have other names in some industries, e.g. 'fathers of the chapel' in printing, 'works representatives' in iron and steel, 'staff representatives' in the Clerical and Administrative Workers' Union, but the term shop steward is the one most commonly employed. There are over 100,000 formally appointed shop stewards in Britain.

To be classified as a shop steward the worker concerned will have to be recognized by his union as having some representative function at the place of work, i.e. it must be part of his job to raise grievances and make claims arising out of the system of wage payment on behalf of a group of members. He is most powerful in firms where some form of piecework as an incentive bonus system exists.

In a few industries, such as mining, where union branch organization is based on the place of work, workplace representation is the formal responsibility of branch officials, e.g. the branch secretary, but this is unusual. In other cases, stewards are mere collectors of union dues and not shop stewards proper with rights of representation and negotiation.

Shop stewards are mostly to be found in the larger work units and in the largest of all there are often formally recognized leaders of the shop stewards' group known as 'convenors' or 'chief', 'leading' or 'senior' stewards. A very few such convenors are full-time paid shop stewards. Most stewards' work is voluntary, part-time and unpaid.

The methods employed by shop stewards in shopfloor bargaining include comparisons with other individuals or groups, pressure for informal arrangements and unwritten agreements, and various types of sanctions, including the withdrawal of cooperation, insistence on formal rights and customs, limitations on output and restrictions on overtime, and withdrawals of labour. The strike (⟨⟩ Strike) is only the most extreme form of sanction and many are mainly 'demonstrative', to indicate to management that something should be done quickly. Many bring to light genuine misunderstandings and muddles. Most are neither started nor led by politically-motivated shop stewards.

A 69% sample of personnel managers has been discovered by Clegg *et al.* to prefer dealing with shop stewards than with local full-time trade union officials, most of all because of their intimate knowledge of the circumstances of the case. Other reasons included a preference for keeping issues within the factory and the need for speedy decisions. This and other evidence suggests that the power of shop stewards has been fostered by management. When the growth of the labour force in a plant makes it difficult for managers to retain individual and personal relations with groups of workers, some form of internal representation is required and the shop steward system provides it.

Four-fifths of stewards are subject to regular re-election and the turnover of stewards' jobs is high. Almost half leave the job because of promotion by management, most no doubt on merit, but some in order to render them innocuous.

Although shop stewards are often linked in the popular press with unofficial strikes and ⟨⟩ Wage Drift (⟨⟩ Wage), there is no doubt that the great majority of them perform an arduous and thankless task responsibly and well. As part of this they occupy a considerable 'helper role' to personnel and to line management. Nevertheless, sustained high employment has produced an increase in domestic negotiation and in unconstitutional action in a small percentage of firms. In the extreme case a shop stewards' committee can become a 'union within a union', as at Briggs Motor Bodies in 1957. Shop stewards' committees, whether company or industry-wide, can provide, as do ⟨⟩ Trades Councils, platforms for militant criticism of official union policy. From such platforms would-be rivals to established leaders can advertise themselves.

The ⟨⟩ *Industrial Relations Act*, 1971, repealed 1974, imposed legal duties on unions for the conduct of their shop stewards. Under the Act any strike or other irregular industrial action was illegal if it was an ⟨⟩ Unfair Industrial Practice or in support of such a practice, although a *registered* union or its *authorized* officials could call a strike without notice provided it was connected with an ⟨⟩ Industrial Dispute. A shop steward or other person in an unregistered union, or in a registered union but with no authority to call a strike, had to give appropriate notice of a strike. ⟨⟩ Strike – and the Law; Trade Union – registration.

The ⟨⟩ Industrial Relations Code of Practice, 1972, provides guidelines on the functions, appointment, status, coordination, facilities, and training of shop stewards. N.H.C.

H. A. Clegg, A. J. Killick and R. Adams, *Trade Union Officers* (Blackwell, 1961); W. E. J. McCarthy, Royal Commission on Trade Unions and Employers' Associations, Research Paper 1, *The Role of Shop Stewards in British Industrial Relations* (HMSO, 1966); W. E. J. McCarthy and S. R. Parker, Research Paper 10, *Shop Stewards and Workshop Relations* (HMSO, 1968); B. Hepple, 'Union Responsibility for Shop Stewards', *Industrial Law Journal* Vol. 1, No. 4, December 1972.

Simo Chart (Simultaneous Motion Cycle Chart) A SIMO chart is used to record the coordinated movements of the limbs of one or more workers, the movements being described in terms of fundamental motions on a common time scale.

The SIMO chart is used under similar conditions as the Two Handed Process Chart, but normally results from the analyses of a motion film, and utilizes Therbligs to describe the movements taking place. Because of the detailed analysis possible from frame by frame examination of a film, and the detailed description of the Therbligs, SIMO charts are associated with micromotion study and represent one of the most detailed recording techniques available in method study. ⟡ Method Study; Therbligs; Process Charts. R.W.

R. M. Barnes, *Motion and Time Study* (J. Wiley, 5th ed., 1963).

Simplex Method ⟡ Mathematical Programming.

Simulation (Computer) OR scientists often use very sophisticated mathematical analysis to obtain solutions to management's problems. However, in many cases, although the logical structure of, and the numbers involved in, the problems or situations studied are known, because of the complexity of the problem it is impossible to develop a mathematical analysis and solution. In such circumstances an approach known as Computer Simulation may be adopted.

This means that a computer program is written which simulates the logical ·structure of the situation studied. When this program, together with the numbers involved, is fed into the computer, the behaviour of the 'real life' situation can be imitated or simulated by the computer and represented by the computer output. Because computers operate very quickly many 'years' of simulated behaviour or 'history' may be generated within an hour of computing time.

If, in a given situation, management has (e.g.) three alternative decisions to make or policies to pursue, the outcomes of each can be determined quickly by performing three simulations assuming each policy in turn. The policy that gives the best outcome, in terms of maximum profit, minimum cost or whatever measure is chosen, can then be identified. Thus simulation is essentially a 'trial and error' or 'suck it and see' approach where the experience is generated synthetically by computer. In many situations, the numbers involved vary in a random manner and this randomness must also be simulated. In simulations 'random numbers' are generated by special Monte Carlo Methods, so called because they were first used in the examination of gambling problems.

Simulation has been applied extensively to problems at all levels in business and industry. Indeed, attempts are being made to simulate the behaviour of a firm as a whole in its environment by Forrester in an approach known as industrial dynamics.

Although simulation provides a trial and error approach that is cheaper than applying it to the real life situation, it is important to note that large sums can be spent in this way. The cost of performing a simulation often limits the extent to which it is applied. M.J.C.M.

M. J. Sargeaunt, *Operational Research for Management*, pp. 125–39 (Heinemann, 1965).

Sinking Fund

Sinking Fund A sinking fund is a means of gradually accumulating a relatively large amount of funds for a specific purpose. The fund is usually invested outside the organization in interest (or dividend) bearing investments. Although the creation of such a fund might be termed 'prudent accounting' yet, from the viewpoint of 'good' business economics, it may be questioned when such a procedure involves outside investment in a 'safe security'. Clearly there may be a good case for having a certain amount of money fairly readily available for business emergencies but the investment of large amounts of funds at possibly low rates of return is highly questionable in terms of the opportunity costs of inside investment in the case of a profitable business.

In the case of sinking funds for the replacement of assets, a distinction requires to be made between such a fund and the annuity method of depreciation. The annuity method is based upon the notion that any asset represents a store of future earning power and should therefore be valued at the present value of the expected future net fund flows attributable to that asset. The annuity method does not imply outside investment for replacement purposes, and the rate of interest used is the estimated rate at which that asset is expected to earn revenue.

In business practice, sinking funds are in fact rarely used. Instead firms prefer to budget for investment in fixed assets globally rather than for particular assets in isolation and to provide for the necessary funds by incorporating their requirements into two- or three-year 'cash forecast and requirements budgets' prepared for the business as a whole. E.A.L.

Skill Much of human behaviour comprises learned responses which enable a person to achieve some particular goal. The criteria of the level of acquisition of any skill are the speed, accuracy and economy with which the goal is approached.

Skills vary a good deal in their complexity, from walking or running to flying an aircraft or directing a large commercial enterprise. They vary too in their demands upon different parts of the organism. At one end of this continuum we have the 'knacks', i.e. those skills in which the muscular movements are of paramount importance (as, for example, in the golf swing) and at the other end those skills which demand integration of information and the making of decisions.

The rate of skill development depends upon the nature of the skill itself, and also upon the individual, his age, level of motivation, state of fatigue, etc. Most skills require regular repetition if they are to be maintained at their optimal level, although few skills, once acquired, are ever completely lost. E.E.

R. M. Gagné and E. A. Fleishman, *Psychology and Human Performance* (Henry Holt, 1959).

Skills Analysis ⟡ Job Analysis.

Social Control The processes by which a group influences the behaviour of its members in the direction of conformity to the group's standards. The most obvious example of such a process is the legal system, involving the publication of precise codes of conduct, the establishment of a system of checks to detect violation of the codes, and a scale of formalized punishments. In the industrial organization, appropriate behaviour may be defined in statements of duties and

356

responsibilities, job descriptions, rule books, etc., and emphasized by formal training: conformity is rewarded by financial bonuses, increments or promotion, or the increased expectation of such rewards, and nonconformity is punished by the witholding of rewards or by reprimand, suspension or dismissal. In general, it would seem that the more coercion is practised and the more emphasis placed on punishments, the more hostility and resentment are generated and the greater the social tensions in the organization.

The more common forms of social control, however, are continuous and are more subtle than the use of formal rewards and punishments. The appropriate behaviour and concomitant attitudes are acquired mainly by imitation, often unconsciously, of the behaviour and attitudes of the members of that social group with which the individual is in most close social contact and whose approval he most values. Indeed, the strength of the primary group identification may be considerably more important as a determinant of behaviour than are the rewards and punishments of the formal organization. The problem of how best to achieve compliant behaviour on the part of organizational members is one which currently exercises industrial managers. ⟡ Authority; Discipline; Group; Norm; Role; Role Conflict. I.C.McG.

J. A. Litterer, *The Analysis of Organisations* (J. Wiley, 1965).

Social Distance The degree of stiffness or formality in a social relationship. Such formality is a recognition of a difference in status between the persons concerned as, for example, between members of different social classes or between superior and subordinate in formal organizations. Social distance in superior/subordinate relationships is associated with the use of authority. It is, therefore, particularly a feature of authoritarian organizations, and is commonly manifest in formal rules constraining social interaction: army officers may be forbidden to fraternize with 'other ranks', the captain of a civil aircraft may be required to stay overnight at a hotel different from that used by his crew members. Social distance does not necessarily imply any hostility in the relationship; on the contrary, where the status difference is fully accepted by both persons, the maintenance of social distance will be regarded with mutual satisfaction. However, the existence of social distance militates against the development of free communication between the persons concerned. ⟡ Authority; Communication; Status. I.C.McG.

P. M. Blau and W. R. Scott, *Formal Organisations* (Routledge & Kegan Paul, 1964).

Social Institution ⟡ Institution.

Social Sciences The social sciences are those branches of learning which are concerned with the study of man and society. The precise delineation of the boundaries of academic disciplines is not possible but it may be suggested that, by convention, the social sciences are held to include economics, political science, psychology, social psychology, social anthropology and sociology. The claim to scientific status, less disputed now than formerly, rests on the fact that each discipline involves the collation and analysis of data derived from a systematic collection and observation of phenomena or controlled experimentation and the formulation and constant refinement of general principles.

The subject-matter of the different disciplines overlaps and each is distinguished mainly by the nature of the concepts it employs and only partly by the range of phenomena studied. The nature of economics and psychology, including social psychology, is discussed in the appropriate sections in this handbook. Political science is concerned with the forms of power in society, the various bases of power, the manner in which power is exercised institutionally, and the ordering of power relationships. In so far as the study has increasingly developed an empirical basis, it has virtually become a branch of sociology (political sociology). Social anthropology, as distinct from physical anthropology, studies approximately the same range of phenomena as sociology but has tended to concentrate on small tribal or village communities in pre-industrial societies and to make almost exclusive use of direct observation and questioning as research techniques.

Sociology seeks to study all those aspects of human behaviour which are socially determined. Including within its focus society as a whole, it necessarily embraces the subject-matter of each of the other disciplines discussed above as well as those features of society which have not yet become the subject of specialist concern. Central to the sociological approach is the concept of the ⟨⟩ Social System: a complex of interrelated parts. At the societal level, the most basic of these parts are social ⟨⟩ institutions which arise in response to the need to regulate the means to satisfy fundamental human requirements. Thus sociologists study the culture and institutions of specific societies, the structure and processes of the organizations to which the institutions give rise and the nature of the relationships between institutions. Such a study encompasses an enormous range of phenomena and it is not surprising that, in common with other sciences, sociology has been subject to a considerable degree of division into subspecialisms. Such subdivisions tend to follow, in the first place, the main social institutions and there are thus sociologists specializing in the study of the family, education, work and industry, government, science, religion, etc. All these areas, and many more, have received attention from social scientists other than sociologists. The feature that characterizes the *sociological* approach is the study of each area in its relationship to other areas in the total system. For example, the industrial sociologist will study not only the structure and functioning of specific industrial organizations with a view to the formulation and testing of general principles, but also the relationship between various features of industrial organizations and relevant aspects of the wider society such as the educational system, social class and social status, and societal values.

However, the term industrial sociology is used by some writers more narrowly to refer to organizational studies at the factory or plant level in the study of particular groups such as managers, various categories of professional employee and white-collar workers. Empirical studies of organizational behaviour date from the ⟨⟩ Hawthorne Investigations and continued with a strong emphasis on factory organization. More recently, however, the sociological analysis of organizations has been advanced by a broadening of research interest to embrace a wide variety of organizations with greatly differing structures and functions.

Hospitals, schools, universities, prisons, government departments, trade unions, collieries, docks, churches and many others have been studied and the resulting accumulation of case material has considerably aided the development of organizational theory. Such comparitive studies are likely to continue and already there are signs that a new academic specialism is emerging, organizational sociology. Such a title, however, gives scant recognition to the work of the social psychologists who have contributed substantially to the development of organization theory. Conversely, the use of the term organizational psychology fails to indicate the essential social systems approach of the developing theory. Perhaps suitable recognition of the interdisciplinary nature of organizational studies will be given by the adoption of the compromise title, organizational behaviour. ⟨⟩ Economics; Hawthorne Investigations; Organizational Theory; Psychology. I.C.MCG.

N. Mackenzie (ed.), *A Guide to the Social Sciences* (Weidenfeld & Nicolson, 1966); S. F. Cotgrove, *The Science of Society* (Allen & Unwin, 1967); D. C. Miller and W. H. Form, *Industrial Sociology* (Harper, 1964); T. Lupton, *Management and the Social Sciences* (Hutchinson, 1966).

Social System A network of interrelated roles. There is no limit to the size of a social system; two persons may constitute one (e.g. husband and wife) or, at the other extreme, the entire population of the earth is a social system. All social systems are open; that is to say, every social system interacts with other social systems and every social system is a part of some larger social system. The industrial organization, the factory, may be regarded as a social system and taking this point of view, the sociologist will endeavour to identify the various constituent elements in the system and to ascertain their relationships to each other and to the organization as a whole, their interaction with the wider society and their functions and dysfunctions. Every social system has certain needs: (1) each occupant of a status must understand the behaviour expected of him (⟨⟩ Role) and must be motivated to produce that behaviour (⟨⟩ Reward System); conversely undesirable behaviour must be discouraged (⟨⟩ Social Control): (2) there must be some provision for communication amongst the various parts of the system: (3) the system must develop means of protecting itself from, or adapting to, other external systems so as to ensure its own continuity: and, (4) there must be sufficient consensus in attitudes, values and interests among the members of the system to form a basis for their continued interaction. The business organization is distinguished from other types of social system mainly by its highly differentiated role structure in which the roles and their interrelationships are rigorously defined, by its elaborate control systems and by its preoccupation with the economic attainment of precise objectives. ⟨⟩ Culture; Institution; Organization Theory; Role; Social Control; Status. I.C.MCG.

J. A. Litterer, *The Analysis of Organisations* (J. Wiley, 1965).

Socio-Technical System A conceptual recognition of the interdependence of technical and social factors in organization. A socio-technical system is considered to comprise three elements: (1) *technical factors*; mechanical equipment, technical processes and the physical environment; (2) *social factors*; the relationships amongst the people required to carry out the work and their individual and collective attitudes to it and to each other; and (3) *economic factors*; the measures by which the efficiency of the technical and social 'mix' is evaluated.

The concept has been developed mainly by members of the Tavistock Institute of Human Relations and originated from their work in the coal industry. Attention was attracted, particularly, to the organizational problems apparently inherent in the longwall method of coal-mining. Analysis of the situation revealed that the essential cooperation required amongst the three groups performing the main tasks in the work cycle – cutting, filling and conveyor moving – was considerably hampered by the mode of organization conventionally adopted. Despite the interdependent nature of the main tasks, each of the three groups was organized as a discrete unit, occupationally homogeneous, on its own group bonus for payment purposes and separated from the other two groups by the shift system. Thus there were created three groups, each intensely aware of its own identity and of its own socio-economic interests. The resultant rivalry and intergroup hostility destroyed any hope of cooperation and productivity was generally low. When the interdependent nature of the tasks was recognized, an alternative form of social organization was seen to be necessary. The occupational differentiation of the three shift groups was abandoned in favour of a total task force of all-round faceworkers each of whom was capable of cutting, filling or conveyor moving, as the situation required. Bonus payment was earned by the entire face group and shared equally amongst them. The effect of the changed social organization was to break down the intergroup, intershift hostility in favour of a group consciousness extending to all who worked on the face, and the cooperation required by the technical factors now became possible. The socio-technical systems approach to organizational design has led to many improvements in productivity. The approach requires an awareness that productive efficiency requires the optimization of the technical and social mix and not simply the maximization of the technical factors. (The foregoing discussion of the longwall method has been grossly simplified so as to improve the clarity of the discussion of the organizational principle concerned. For a full account of the Tavistock research into coal-mining methods, see E. L. Trist *et al.*) ⟡ Conflict; Coordination; Formal Organization; Group. I.C.MCG.

E. L. Trist *et al.*, *Organisational Choice* (Tavistock Publications, 1963).

Sociology ⟡ Social Sciences.

Software ⟡ Hardware/Liveware/Software.

Sole Bargaining Agent Under the ⟡ *Industrial Relations Act*, 1971, repealed 1974, a sole bargaining agent was the organization of workers or joint negotiating panel (not necessarily a registered trade union or unions) which had exclusive bargaining rights for a ⟡ bargaining unit, except for matters dealt with under more extensive bargaining arrangements.

If procedures could not be reached voluntarily, the Act laid down that a registered trade union(s), an employer(s), or the Secretary of State might ask the ⟡ National Industrial Relations Court to refer to the ⟡ Commission on Industrial Relations the questions whether a particular group of employees constituted a bargaining unit; whether a sole bargaining agent should be recognized by the employer(s) concerned; and which organization of workers or joint negotiating panel (not necessarily a registered trade union or unions) should be the sole bargaining agent if such an agent was deemed appropriate.

Where the Commission on Industrial Relations recommended the recognition of a sole bargaining agent, either of the parties could apply within six months for this to be legally enforced. Application could not, however, be made by an unregistered union, nor was legal enforcement possible where the recommended bargaining agent was not a registered union. A majority of employees voting in secret ballot could ensure that the recommendations be made legally binding by order of the National Industrial Relations Court. Where it was claimed that a union with sole bargaining rights was not adequately representing its members, there was a somewhat similar procedure for depriving it of those rights.

In connection with the provisions on sole bargaining rights the Act specified a number of ⟨⟩ Unfair Industrial Practices. N.H.C.

Industrial Relations Act, 1971, Ch. 72, H M S O ss. 44 *et seq.*

Somatotype Observations upon the relationship between personality characteristics and physique have been made over many centuries. Numerous classifications of physique types have resulted from attempts to systematize this relationship. The most comprehensive study in this field is that of W. H. Sheldon and his co-workers who developed techniques of assessing the physique either from standardized photographs or from a series of anthropometric measurements. An individual's Somatotype is expressed by three numerals which represent respectively a rating on a 7-point scale for each of the primary components endomorphy, mesomorphy and ectomorphy. Thus, for example, an individual of Somatotype 4–7–1 is about average in endomorphy, high in mesomorphy and low in ectomorphy. Endomorphy is characterized by a soft and rounded surface, indicating deficient development of bone and muscle. The Mesomorph shows high bone and muscle development and is hard and rectangular in appearance. Linearity, fragility and delicacy are the characteristics of the Ectomorph. Of the 343 possible Somatotypes, less than 100 appear to exist in the human population.

By means of the statistical analysis of data describing individual differences in temperament, Sheldon isolated three primary components of personality which he named Viscerotonia, Somatotonia and Cerebrotonia. An individual with a high score in Viscerotonia is characterized by a love of comfort, of food and of people, and is generally easy-going. High Somatotonia scores resulted from a love of adventure and of exercise and from aggressiveness. A high score on the third component implies a lack of sociability, fast reactions and a love of privacy and secrecy.

High correlations have been demonstrated to exist between individuals' personality ratings and Somatotypes, relating the components in the following way:

> Endomorphy – Viscerotonia
> Mesomorphy – Somatotonia
> Ectomorphy – Cerebrotonia. E.E.

W. H. Sheldon, *The Varieties of Human Physique* (Harper, 1940).

Sound ⬦ Hearing; Noise.

Span of Control The number of subordinates over whom a given superior exercises direct authority. A management consultant, V. A. Graicunas, first formulated the concept in a paper published in 1933 and appeared to demonstrate mathematically the impossibility of maintaining efficient control if the number of such subordinates exceeded six. Other writers in the classical tradition have broadly concurred. Empirical studies, however, have shown that the span of control of chief executives varies widely and spans as large as twenty have been recorded. It would seem that, in practice, many factors may influence the span of control and inefficiency should not be inferred solely from the shape of the organization chart. The personality of the chief executive, the competence of the subordinates, the use of coordinating committees, the desired location of decision-making and the technical complexity of the production processes are all among the influences which affect the determination of a given span of control and attempts to define an optimum span regardless of the specific circumstances in which it is to be located would seem to be inappropriate. ⬦ Authority; Classical Organization Theory. I.C.MCG.

> J. A. Litterer, *The Analysis of Organisations* (J. Wiley, 1965); H. D. Koontz and C. J. O'Donnell, *Principles of Management* (McGraw-Hill, 1964).

Specialization The fine division of a total task into its component sub-tasks each of which is then performed by a separate individual.

Adam Smith was one of the earliest writers to draw attention to the economic advantages of specialization in his celebrated account of pin making in the eighteenth century and subsequently the division of labour and specialization have been carried to an advanced stage in most industries. The process is apparent not only in the minute subdivision of tasks in mass production industry but also in the increasing differentiation of managerial functions. However, specialization introduces the concomitant problem of coordination. Each sub-unit is highly dependent on the correct functioning of other sub-units and much organizational energy must be devoted to the standardization of operations, the precise planning of production sequences and the development and maintenance of production and quality control systems. In the resulting administrative complex it becomes difficult for the individual, particularly at the lowest levels in the organization, to understand the importance of his own minimal contribution. Furthermore, the careful and systematic removal from jobs of any opportunity for human error removes, at the same time, opportunity for the exercise of judgement and any element of intrinsic job interest. This process has heightened problems of employee motivation and introduced a tendency towards inflexibility. As a result there is a gradual realization that the benefits of specialization are subject to the law of diminishing returns and a number of managements are considering the possibilities of job enlargement. ⬦ Alienation; Coordination; Function (1); Job Enlargement; Profession; Socio-Technical System. I.C.MCG.

> J. A. Litterer, *The Analysis of Organisations*, Chs. 9 and 10 (J. Wiley, 1965).

Speech Speech sounds are produced by the expulsion of air from the lungs past the larynx which provides the basic sound-producing process, phonation. This primary sound tone is then modulated by means of the vocal organs in the throat, mouth and nose to produce a wide range of possible speech sounds. The comparatively small number of different symbols used in the written form of a language gives a misleading impression of simplicity compared with the rich variety of the spoken word.

Individual speakers exhibit different characteristics in their speech habits. Some of the most important of these characteristics include intensity, pitch, speed and the frequency and duration of pauses. Intensities of speech vary not only between different speakers, but between different elements of the language. The amount of sound energy in certain vowel sounds, for example, may be 700 times greater than the energy in a soft 'th' sound in the same word. Different pitches are attained by the utilization of frequencies ranging between about 300 and 6000 Hz. Speeds much below 100 words/minute are slow; fast talkers can more than double this speed.

The proportion of spoken language which can be understood by a listener depends upon the type of material and upon its context, as well as upon the quality of the received signal. This latter is usually measured in terms of the Articulation Index which is derived from measurements of both speech and noise levels in each of a number of frequency bands. The extent to which noise will affect reliable speech communication may be expressed in terms of the Speech Interference Level, an Index which provides a measure of the required intensity level of speech to overcome noise of a given intensity.

Many communication systems, such as the telephone, bring about selective filtering of speech such that the very high and very low frequency elements are attenuated severely. Intelligibility of speech can survive a good deal of such distortion, particularly in the absence of noise.

Experiments upon the characteristics of good talkers indicate that the most intelligible speech results from long average syllable duration, high syllable intensity, the absence of pauses and some variation in pitch. E.E.

E. J. McCormick, *Human Engineering* (McGraw-Hill, 1957).

Stability ◊ Feedback.

Stabilized Accounting ◊ Changing Price Levels (Accounting for).

Staff (1) ◊ Line and Staff.

Staff (2) The collectivity of clerical, secretarial, technical and, perhaps, managerial personnel in an organization as distinct from the wage earning, manual workers. Traditionally, staff have enjoyed working conditions and benefits superior to those of manual workers. Amongst these benefits have been longer holiday entitlements, greater security of employment, a more pleasant working environment, higher pay and better prospects of promotion. In recent years, a number of factors, principally associated with technology and changes in the social class structure, have caused a critical examination of the privileged position of the 'white-collar' group and many firms have adopted the policy of eliminating or reducing the differences between the two groups. I.C.MCG.

Staff Appraisal

Staff Appraisal ⇨ Performance Appraisal.

Staff Assessment ⇨ Performance Appraisal.

Staff Association ⇨ Company Union.

Staff Management That part of ⇨ Personnel Management which is concerned with 'staff' rather than 'labour', i.e. with those whose work is primarily mental or social rather than manual. Shop, office and laboratory workers are normally included in this category, as well as managers, technicians, salesmen and supervisors. In retail stores and large offices, e.g. in banks and insurance companies, the personnel manager is often called staff manager. In industrial undertakings there may be a specialist staff manager in a personnel department whose head is a personnel director and which includes a labour manager who deals with manual workers. Although the tasks of staff and labour management are similar, the emphasis of staff work is more with individuals than with groups; for example in selection procedures (⇨ Selection) especially for managerial and specialist posts, in fixing salaries and in career development. A staff manager is less likely than a labour manager to be concerned with ⇨ Trade Union negotiations except in the Civil Service, local government and nationalized industries; he will be more concerned with ⇨ Fringe Benefits and with other questions relating to status, security and amenities. There is a tendency for these two sides of personnel management to be assimilated with the growth of trade unionism among office workers and improvements in the conditions and ⇨ Status of manual workers. ⇨ Trade Union Types – White-collar Union. L.S.

    Elizabeth Barling, *Staff Management* (Institute of Personnel Management, 1959).

Staff Status Indicates the advantages in conditions of employment which are given to the members of the staff in a firm in comparison with those of 'hourly paid workers', e.g. the 'staff' usually work shorter hours, have longer periods of notice, better pension and sick-pay benefits and separate canteens; they may have longer holidays and be paid monthly by cheque instead of weekly in cash. All these things combine to give staff employees a higher standing, or ⇨ Status. Changes in social outlook and in technology have led to questions about the validity of these distinctions in status and some firms have removed or reduced them by giving staff status to all or some of those employed in the factory. L.S.

    Status and Benefits in Industry (Industrial Society, 1966).

Standard Costing Standard costs may be defined as 'predetermined costs related to carefully planned methods of making and selling a product or, in the case of services, rendering a service. In principle, there is no difference between standard costs and budgeted costs: both are based on the principle of predetermination of cost. But there is a difference in scope between a budget system and a system of standard costs. Budgeting includes objectives for all activities of a business during a certain period whereas standard costs relate to detailed costs of operation.' (*Cost Accounting and Productivity*, OEEC Report, 1952.)

    A standard costing system serves as a method of feedback in which deviations

between actual and predetermined costs for a given period are isolated and reported. Costs are accumulated by departments and cost centres, covering the
direct and overhead costs allocated to them which are considered to be the direct
responsibility of the individual managers (⟡ Responsibility Accounting). Each
managerial unit is charged with actual costs and credited with output measured
in standard cost terms. The difference between actual and standard cost is known
as a variance and represents the discrepancy between actual and standard performance. This total variance is generally analysed into component parts:
variances for materials and wages are analysed into price (wage rate) and usage
variances; overheads into volume, budget and efficiency variances. A cross-
classification in terms of controllability and non-controllability is also attempted.
The analysis of standard costing variances gives a point of departure for the
investigation of costs but since the analysis is not in terms of causation, it cannot
settle all issues about control and efficiency.

In so far as standard costs are target costs they implicitly contain assumptions
about how people are motivated. It is therefore important that the basis for the
setting of standards be investigated from a behavioural viewpoint and to ask
whether the particular standards set motivate people in the way which best helps
achievement of the firm's objectives regarding production efficiency and cost
minimization. However, from a human relations viewpoint such economic ends
are by no means the only 'values' present when considering a control system such
as a standard costing system. E.A.L.

C. T. Horngren, *Cost Accounting: A managerial emphasis*, Chs., 5, 7, 9 and 11
(2nd ed., Prentice-Hall, 1966).

Standard Deviation ⟡ Measures of Dispersion.

Statistical Tests It is often necessary to compare sets of data to determine if they
have certain statistical properties in common. Statisticians have a number of tests
that perform these tasks. The most commonly used ones are as follows:

1. *Student's 't' test*. This test may be used when we wish to compare the means of
sets of data. For example, it may be used to determine: (a) whether the mean of a
sample of observation differs significantly from the mean of the normal population from which it is drawn; (b) given two independent samples with different
means, whether their means differ significantly or whether the two samples may
be regarded as drawn from the same normal population.

2. *'F' test*. This may be used when we wish to compare the variability or variance
of sets of data. For example, given two independent samples of different variances,
it may be used to determine whether their variances differ significantly or whether
the two samples may be regarded as drawn from the same normal population.

3. x^2 (*Chi-Squared*) *test*. This may be used when we wish to establish whether an
observed frequency distribution conforms to or fits a particular theoretical distribution. When used in this way it is known as the Chi-Squared test of 'goodness
of fit'. For example, a personnel director may possess three years of records of
the industrial accidents occurring in all the factories in his organization. He may
express these records in the form of a histogram or frequency distribution showing

Statistics

the number of shifts in the three years that 0, 1, 2, etc. occurred. The frequency of industrial accidents often follows a well-known theoretical distribution known as a ⟨⟩ Poisson distribution. Using the Chi-Squared test, the personnel director will be able to establish the measure of the probability that the observed frequency distribution of accidents is significantly different from a Poisson distribution, or whether the latter provides a 'good fit' to the data. M.J.C.M.

M. J. Moroney, *Facts from Figures*, pp. 216–70 (Penguin, 1951).

Statistics Much of the data that the manager uses in performing his job is subject to a variability which prevents it being estimated with certainty. For example, the dimensions of successive units of a product, the weekly running costs of a particular stage of a production process or the monthly sales of a product, may vary due to a number of causes which are individually unpredictable. However, a manager may have to make decisions based on a knowledge of the pattern of variation of these quantities. In fact, he is in a similar position to an actuary, who must use his knowledge of the pattern of life spans of individuals to fix life insurance premiums. Both the life spans of individuals and the dimensions, costs, sales figures, etc., arising in industry are subject to variability from a large number of causes. Fortunately for the actuary and the manager, the science of probability and statistics has been developed specifically to handle such problems.

Statistics can be defined as the science of collecting and analysing data. To be analysed, data must be presented in a convenient form such as a histogram which can be illustrated by means of an example:

Suppose that a personnel manager wishes to represent the weekly overtime hours worked in a department of 60 operatives whose individual overtime hours are given below:

3·75	1·50	1·00	5·00	1·38	6·00	4·50	6·00	7·00	6·00
5·50	6·00	3·00	2·63	4·37	1·75	9·25	7·25	6·50	2·75
3·13	5·87	4·87	8·25	2·13	6·13	9·75	6·87	9·63	6·25
6·00	5·50	6·00	3·25	9·00	7·87	5·13	8·13	5·63	7·50
4·50	6·00	5·87	6·00	4·50	5·50	3·75	4·50	7·00	6·00
2·75	7·25	7·63	6·63	8·75	5·83	6·00	4·87	8·00	8·25

The lowest is 1·00 hours and the highest is 9·75 hours and the variations in hours can be divided into 9 class intervals, 1·00–1·99, 2·00–2·99, etc., to 9·00–9·99. If this is done, the number of operatives in each class can be obtained. Then a diagram is constructed as shown opposite.

In this diagram the class intervals are represented on a horizontal scale whilst the vertical height of the columns correspond to the number of operatives in that class interval. Since each class interval is of equal width, it follows that the area in each class interval also corresponds to the number of operatives. This histogram provides a very convenient visual representation of the spread of operatives' earnings and the concentration of earnings in each class.

We can extend the idea of plotting a histogram to introduce another important concept in statistics – the distribution curve.

Suppose instead of the earnings of 60 operatives, we wish to represent the

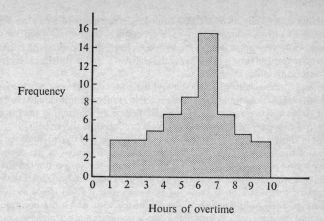

Frequency

Hours of overtime

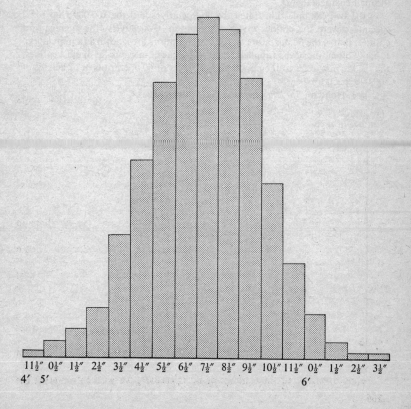

$11\frac{1}{2}''$ $0\frac{1}{2}''$ $1\frac{1}{2}''$ $2\frac{1}{2}''$ $3\frac{1}{2}''$ $4\frac{1}{2}''$ $5\frac{1}{2}''$ $6\frac{1}{2}''$ $7\frac{1}{2}''$ $8\frac{1}{2}''$ $9\frac{1}{2}''$ $10\frac{1}{2}''$ $11\frac{1}{2}''$ $0\frac{1}{2}''$ $1\frac{1}{2}''$ $2\frac{1}{2}''$ $3\frac{1}{2}''$

4' 5'   6'

variability of the heights of 100,000 adult Englishmen attending a Cup Final at Wembley. Further, suppose that each spectator's height had been measured automatically very accurately as he passed through the turnstiles, he could then plot a histogram as shown in the lower diagram on p. 367 with 1-in. class intervals and many individuals in each class.

However, since we have 100,000 individuals we could choose much narrower class intervals which would each contain a fair number of individuals. In fact we could go on making our intervals finer and finer until the steps in the histogram virtually disappear and a continuous curve is produced, as shown below.

This is known as the distribution curve since it describes the extent of the distribution of the heights of the Cup Final attendants. The area of the curve lying between two points, say *A* and *B*, still represents the proportion of the total attendants whose heights lie between H_1 and H_2 along the horizontal scale. The concept of this distribution curve or frequency distribution (since the vertical measure of each point represents the frequency with which the corresponding horizontal measure occurs) is fundamental to statistics since it underlies much of the mathematical theory.

In the two examples illustrated the 60 operatives and the 100,000 Cup Final spectators were the entities under examination. Collectively, the aggregate of entities, that is the 60 operators or 100,000 spectators are known as a population. Equally often, the term is applied to the aggregate of measures as against entities, that is, we may refer to the population of wages of 60 operatives or of heights of 100,000 spectators.

L. J. Holman, *Statistics for Business* (Pitman, 1966).

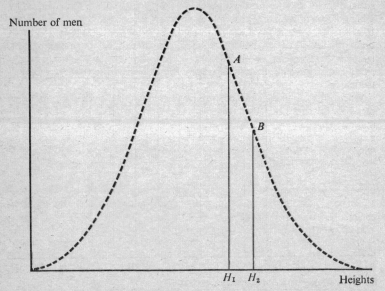

Often the statistician wishes to analyse characteristics of very large populations; for example, if he wishes to establish the viewing figures for particular national TV programmes, his population consists of all the people in the UK who watch television. In such cases it is either impossible or prohibitively expensive to measure the characteristic of each member of the population and the statistician examines a chosen group or a sample of the population.

The histogram and frequency distribution discussed above, although useful visual representations of the variability of a measure, are most unsuited to algebraic manipulation. Therefore, statisticians use other algebraic measures to represent the extent of the variability of the population. Collectively these are known as ⬧ Measures of Location and of Dispersion. M.J.C.M.

P. G. Moore, *Statistics and the Manager* (Macdonald, 1955); M. J. Moroney, *Facts from Figures* (Penguin, 1951).

Status (a) A position in a social system, or more commonly (b) the evaluation of such a position, person or group on a scale of relative esteem.

Technically a distinction is sometimes made between status (the degree of esteem in which a *position* is held) and prestige (the degree of esteem in which a *person* is held). In practice, however, the distinction is often extremely difficult to maintain and even in academic sociological writing, the term 'status' commonly refers to the evaluation of a person.

Status is based on many factors. It is closely associated with authority and the reward system: those positions with most authority receive the highest rewards and are accorded the highest status. Status is enhanced by the maintenance of social distance and the more status-conscious organizations are characterized by a high degree of formality in social relationships, persons addressing each other by status (Matron, Sergeant, etc.) rather than by name. Status may also be based on the skill or educational level that the role requires. It may be influenced, too, by the status system of the wider society: if persons of low status are consistently recruited to certain positions in the organization, those positions will be accorded low status.

Where there is uncertainty concerning the status of a given position, other members of the organization are likely to resent showing deference to, or submitting to the authority of, the occupant of the position in question. For example, a chargehand required to undertake the duties of foreman for an extended period whilst retaining the title and privileges of chargehand, may encounter the resentment of others in the organization when he tries to act like a foreman. The efficient discharge of his duties requires that others should treat him as a foreman whilst the organization's formal definition implies that he should be treated as a chargehand. Such status ambiguity can give rise to difficulties in relationships and to personal irritation or anxiety.

Status may also be derived from association with other positions. The most obvious example is that of wives, who tend to be accorded the status of their husbands. The wife of a senior manager will expect, and will usually be given, a status higher than that of the wife of a junior clerk. A similar phenomenon is often observed among personal secretaries.

Status Symbol

Social interaction, including the exchange of information, is most free among persons of similar status. Where groups consist of persons of widely differing status there is likely to be some element of tension and guardedness in interpersonal relationships.

The wider differences in status are recognized formally in the organization but there are many ramifications and nuances of status which are less well recognized. Subtle distinctions may exist among those of ostensibly similar status and these distinctions may have important behavioural consequences. A high proportion of pay disputes are concerned with differential rather than absolute payment. Many seemingly lateral transfers are resisted because to the employees concerned the move is to a lower status group and is thus viewed as a demotion despite managerial assurance to the contrary. ⟨⟩ Authority; Role; Status Symbol. I.C.MCG.

J. A. Litterer, *The Analysis of Organisations*, Ch. 4 (J. Wiley, 1965).

Status Symbol Anything from the possession of which a person's status may be inferred. In organizations in which status is particularly important (e.g. authoritarian organizations such as the military, hospitals), badges of rank may be worn expressly for that purpose. In the industrial organization status differences are not usually proclaimed by badges although different styles of dress, such as the wearing of white coats or different coloured overalls, are commonly associated with different occupational grades. Most status symbols arise because of their incidental association with status and not because they are intended to signify status. The range of possible symbols is almost infinite and the identification of a new and unusual symbol is always a source of joy to the industrial sociologist. Office furnishings constitute an almost universal category and in the larger organizations one's entitlement to office furniture is likely to be formally prescribed in meticulous detail and promotion to a higher status grade may be heralded by the arrival of furniture removers. Size and location of office, title of the position, frequency of pay (hourly-paid, weekly staff, monthly staff) and rights and privileges appropriate to the position all help to signify status and to confirm that status in the eyes of the other members of the organization. Conversely, the absence of appropriate symbols can create uncertainty concerning status and give rise to status ambiguity. I.C.MCG.

J. A. Litterer, *The Analysis of Organisations*, pp. 73–7 (J. Wiley, 1965).

Stereotypes Although the processes of classification and generalization are fundamental operations in any system of logical development, these same processes without proper control can easily lead to unwarranted judgements based upon inadequate information and insufficient differentiation. Thus we may develop coarse representations of classes such as 'Big Business', 'Jews' or 'Drugs' in such a way that the stereotyped concept is a completely inadequate representation of the real world. Not only concepts themselves, but the thought processes by which they are manipulated can equally become stereotyped and hence lead to indefensible conclusions.

In the context of human engineering, the term 'population stereotypes' refers to expectations which are found to exist between the relative directions of move-

370

ment of controls and displays. Violation of these stereotypes in machine design leads to errors in the use of equipment. Some well-known examples are illustrated in the diagram. ⇔ Machine Controls. E.E.

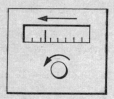 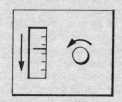 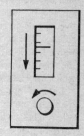

Stereotypes.
The diagrams illustrate the most commonly expected relationship between the direction of movement of a control knob and the corresponding movement produced upon the dial.

Stewardship Accounting ⇔ Accountancy Conventions.

Stock Control ⇔ Inventory or Stock Control Problems.

Storage Media (Computer) One of the principal distinctions between an electronic digital computer and a conventional calculating machine is that the former can store large quantities of data. This storage, or memory, can be used to hold the data and instructions required to perform a calculation, and the intermediate and cumulative data that may be produced and required later in the processing before the final output data are generated

The two interrelated criteria which determine the utility of a storage media are access time and size. Firstly, in performing a calculation, data are continuously being recalled from storage, operated on and returned to storage. Therefore the time taken for the whole calculation will depend markedly on the access time to data in store. Secondly, since many commercial and scientific applications of computers require the manipulation of large quantities of data and, by implication, provision of large quantities of storage, it is important that a storage medium be as compact as possible. Fortunately since, at a naïve level, it can be argued that the speed of operation of an electronic circuit is ultimately limited by speed of light, reductions in the physical dimensions of a circuit should increase the speed of response.

In many calculations data can be divided into two groups. Firstly, data that are being manipulated at the current state of the calculations and need to be readily available in storage. Secondly, data which are not currently required, but will be wanted later, can be held until required in less accessible storage. Most computer installations reflect these needs by having two levels of storage: (1) Internal Storage – where data is readily accessible; (2) External or Backing Storage – where data can be held when not in immediate use. Data are transferred between the two levels as and when appropriate.

The most common storage media will be discussed under the above headings:

1. *Internal Storage.* The first computers used magnetic drums. One of these consists of a non-magnetic metal cylinder with a magnetic coating on its curved outer surface. It rotates about its axis at 3,000–17,000 rpm. Read/write heads are placed over the drum so they can read and write data at specific locations as the drum rotates. The access time of an item of data depends upon whether, when it is wanted, its location is just above or has just passed the head. If the latter applies then the drum must complete a full revolution before the data becomes accessible, which may take up to 20 milliseconds.[1]

Later computers used core storage internally. These consist of a network or matrix in one plane of two parallel sets of wires, each set at right angles to the other. These wires are threaded through small rings about 0·1 in. diameter or cores of magnetic material such that a core is placed at the intersection between two wires. Either of two magnetic states (representing '1' or '0') of a core is both imposed and measured by the voltage present on the pair of wires defining its location, which together act as read/write heads. Access time to each core is the same and varies between a fraction of a micro-second[1] and two hundred microseconds. Because access time is independent of location, core stores can be described as random access stores.

2. *External or Backing Storage.* Magnetic tape is used to store intermittently required data not currently in use. When required it can be fed into the internal store of the computer (⟨⟩ Input/Output).

Magnetic disc devices are in common use. They have a short access time compared to tape and have a large storage capacity. They consist of a stack of metal circular discs coated on both sides with magnetic material. Data is represented by alternative magnetic configurations. The discs rotate at about 1200 rpm. The data is written on or read off by a read/write head for each disc face. The read/write heads move in unison and interleave between the discs. A typical six-disc pack can store 22 million characters. Access times are in the range 20–200 milliseconds dependent on how far the head has to move. M.J.C.M.

Strategy A proposed action or sequence of actions intended to have a far-reaching effect on the company's ability to achieve its objective.

Strategy is often confused with policy and with tactics. Policy decisions are wider than strategic which in turn are wider than tactical decisions. Policy

---

1. The speed of operation of computers is usually quoted in units that are small fractions of a second (cf. the engineer's use of 'thou's' which are thousandths of an inch). Thus:

1 millisecond $= \dfrac{1}{1,000}$ second and is written 1 m sec.

1 microsecond $= \dfrac{1}{1,000,000}$ second and is written 1μ sec.

1 nanosecond $= \dfrac{1}{1,000,000,000}$ second and is written 1μn sec or 1n sec.

decisions often remain valid for a decade or more. Strategic decisions may remain valid for a period of several months to several years. Tactical decisions usually refer to a period of less than one year: these time-spans can only be an approximate guide. While policy decisions can include the setting of overall company objectives and constraints as well as means, strategic decisions usually refer only to means.

Once a policy decision has determined the long-term objectives for the company as a whole, it becomes the task of the senior managers to decide the best way in which to achieve these over the following few years. Unless a policy decision has been made that severely limits the field of study for the strategists, their task will be complex for the time-span they will be considering may be long enough to allow the complete reorientation of the entire company and its physical resources. They will certainly need to consider the desirability of some of the types of diversification, the changes required in the organizational structure of the company (◊ Manpower Planning), the need for introducing new product lines (◊ Marketing), the research effort and facilities required, the building of new, or rebuilding of existing, factories, the location of warehouses and sales offices and many other complex and far-reaching factors. The range of choice facing strategists is always wide and the element of uncertainty associated with the long-range forecasts upon which they must rely is also large (◊ Forecasting).

It is usual, once the final choices between these many alternatives have been decided, for a long-range plan, or strategy, to be submitted in writing to the board. Once approved, each part of the plan becomes the responsibility of an executive who may then take a series of tactical decisions in order to implement or, within the limits of his authority, modify the strategy. ◊ Business Policy; Tactics. A.J.A.A.

H. Igor Ansoff, *Corporate Strategy* (McGraw-Hill, 1965).

Strengths and Weaknesses A strength is any activity at which a company is unusually efficient. A weakness is any activity that it carries out with less than normal efficiency. The definition is often extended to include the physical reason for such efficiency or inefficiency.

Thus a company may be one of the acknowledged leaders in the field of welding titanium – this activity would be one of its strengths. The definition can be extended to include the physical reason for this supremacy and it may therefore be said that among its strengths are its 'special welding equipment' or the 'long experience and knowledge of its technical director'.

Strengths and weaknesses may be present in a firm through historical accident or due to years of careful cultivation but, whatever the reason, they are crucial to the continued health of the company. In order to be successful or even to remain in business at all, every company has to be good at a certain minimum number of activities: precisely what these must be is a subject of continuing controversy. Some experts believe that all companies must be strong in marketing if nothing else, others believe that management is the prime requirement of any firm or that it is research or finance. It seems probable that no hard and fast rule exists and that a more satisfactory answer can be obtained by each individual firm asking itself what it has to be good at in order to be successful in its current line of business and checking these desiderata against its own strengths and weaknesses as the executives see them. Such an inquiry can highlight areas where improvement is essential.

It is essential to make an inquiry such as this before any diversification is undertaken. Many firms have launched out into new fields of business only to find that they do not have the strengths necessary to succeed in this new area or that it calls for efficiency in some activity in which they are weak. ⟡ Synergy. A.J.A.A.

Strike – and other Industrial Action ⟡ Conflict is inherent in any society with different interest groups, each with its own attitudes, expectations and objectives. Conflict is thus inherent in an industrial society as between employees and managers. The strike is an extreme form of industrial conflict.

Conflict at the workplace may also be evidenced by an abnormally high sickness rate, or accident rate (⟡ Accident Prevention); or by abnormally high voluntary ⟡ Absenteeism or ⟡ Labour Turnover; or by 'go-slow', overtime ban, 'work-to-rule', or 'blacking' of goods. Industrial disharmony manifests itself in overt action on the shopfloor more frequently than the official ⟡ Strike Statistics imply. The strike, however, is regarded as the ultimate sanction which gives reality to ⟡ Collective Bargaining in a free society, the right to strike being one of the basic freedoms enjoyed by employees in a democratic country. Occasionally non-unionists have resorted to strike action, and there are examples of such activity by women, though women, even as trade unionists, tend to be more reluctant than men to strike.

Historically the strike has been the weapon of the manual worker in attempts to maintain and raise his standards. Some professions exercise an effective pressure to maintain members' standards by defining minimal terms on which they should accept employment. Some groups have control over entry to their occupations which is sufficient almost by itself to ensure relatively high rewards to those admitted (⟡ Profession). Strikes are not commonly resorted to by those who have a substantial prospect of competitive individual advancement, rather than advancement by identification with a group, and this is why salaried employees have been comparatively exempt from strike action. Many white-collar employees, however, are now suffering a crisis of ⟡ Status, e.g. bank clerks, teachers. They wish to retain or recover their social status while accepting the fact that they now have much the same economic status as manual workers. They have, therefore, come to accept the institutions and methods of manual workers, trade unions and strikes ⟡ Trade Union Types – White-collar Union.

The effects of strike action are difficult to measure in economic terms. A strike by a key group in a long chain of production and distribution can put many people out of work in the same firm, in other firms, and even in other industries. Cost may be indicated by lost output, lost customers, and lost management confidence. There may be offsetting factors. Lost output resulting from strikes by dockers and engineering pieceworkers is often quickly made up by extra effort and overtime. The size and duration of car industry strikes tend to rise in recessions when some of the output lost would not have been readily saleable. In coal-mining an occasional strike appears to increase productivity.

Such devices as the 'go-slow' and 'work to rule' can in some cases be economically more damaging than strike action. ⟡ Strike – Causes; Forms; Remedies; Statistics. N.H.C.

K. G. J. C. Knowles, *Strikes* (Blackwell, 1952).

Strike – and the Law A strike has been judicially defined as a 'simultaneous cessation of work on the part of workmen'. The general principle of English law concerning strikes is that workers are free to withdraw their labour without thereby incurring criminal liability, except when a person wilfully breaks his contract of employment knowing or having reasonable cause to believe that the probable consequence of his so doing will be to endanger human life or cause serious bodily injury or expose valuable property to destruction.

A strike generally, but by no means always, represents a breach of contract on the part of the strikers since they are withholding their labour while their contracts of employment are still in existence. Where, however, the strikers have handed in advance strike notices of a length equal to that necessary to terminate their contracts of employment, it is now generally held that the contracts of employment are not discharged but are in suspense until such time as the strike is settled or definite notices to terminate the employment are given either by the employer or by the employees.

Although a strike is likely to cause severe financial loss to an employer, the strikers, strike organizers and the union funds are to some extent protected against actions for damages except where the means used by them in pursuance of the strike were illegal ones. What is 'illegal' in this context is a complicated question which cannot be fully discussed here. ⟡ Industrial Disputes. W.F.F.

R. W. Rideout, *Principles of Labour Law* (Sweet & Maxwell, 1975).

Strike – Causes Strikes are not the outcome of a single cause. Immediate reasons may be 'basic', i.e. about ⟡ Wages and hours; 'frictional', i.e. about working arrangements, rules and discipline; or 'solidarity', as in the case of sympathetic strikes. Underlying these, however, are more fundamental causes to do with the economic situation, e.g. changes in money or real wages, differentials, the position in the business cycle and the level of employment; governmental policy on such matters as prices and incomes and intervention in disputes; management action in such areas as discipline, redundancy and technological and organizational change; and union activity in the areas of demarcation, jurisdiction, the demand for recognition and for the ⟡ Closed Shop. (⟡ Trade Union – Demarcation; Jurisdiction.)

This list is not exhaustive. On the union side alone strikes due to ignorance of the employers' bargaining strength; to the felt need of keeping the union in training; to lack of confidence in the official union leadership; to the failure of communications; to specific personalities; all these have been noted. In very few cases are strikes engineered by communist or other agitators. (⟡ Trade Union – Communism.) It is competition for leadership which produces militancy in union leaders rather than their political views. As for ⟡ Shop Stewards, most managements prefer to deal with them rather than with full-time union officials (⟡ Trade

375

Union – Officials), and the most common reason for their surrendering office is promotion by management.

On the management side it is less frequently the tools of management action like work study and automation which produce strikes than autocratic decision-making and inflexible attitudes. However, 'management prerogatives' are now being matched by the notion of a worker's 'rights' in his job. Analysis by Turner of workplace demands other than those on wage matters has revealed three basic types: for an effort bargain (◊ Collective Bargaining); for changes in working arrangements, methods and the use of labour to be subject to agreement; and for fair treatment of individuals or groups by managers and supervisors. These demands all involve attempts to limit the 'managerial prerogative' or submit it to agreed rules. Alternatively they reflect an implicit pressure for more democracy and individual rights in the work situation (◊ Industrial Democracy).

The Royal Commission noted that unofficial strikes were caused by disputes over:

	per cent
Wages	50
Working arrangements, rules and discipline	29
Redundancy, dismissal, suspension	15
Demarcation	2·6
House of work, closed shop, union recognition, etc.	3·4
	100·0

Since the Royal Commission reported, the percentage of strikes attributable to wages issues has risen.

Though not so in other countries, the motor industry is strike-bound in Britain. While some shop stewards are politically motivated and some are troublemakers, most are responsible and often cast in the role of mediators trying to prevent strikes from taking place while grievances are examined. Neither are strikes in the industry caused by the dull and repetitive nature of the work, in that the men do not complain. Nor is green labour the cause, labour turnover being lower than in engineering and manufacturing generally. Strikes in the British car industry are caused by chaotic plant and company wage structures with their inequalities and unfairnesses; by pay subject to variable fluctuations outside the workers' control; by fragmented bargaining; by slow disputes procedures; by the failure of employers to develop adequate industrial relations policies; and by union rivalry in a multi-union situation; in short, by the failure of institutions.

Most major strikes are official and result from a breakdown of negotiations at industry level about a claim by the union(s) concerned for improved rates of pay and conditions of employment. Official strikes account for approximately five per cent of all strikes, but they have tended to increase in number in recent years.

⟡ Industrial Relations – Reform in Great Britain; Strikes – Forms, Remedies, Statistics; Wage Systems; Workplace Bargaining. N.H.C.

K. G. J. C. Knowles, *Strikes: A Study of Industrial Conflict* (Blackwell, 1952); Royal Commission on Trade Unions and Employers' Associations *Report* (HMSO, 1968); H. A. Turner, G. Clack and G. Roberts, *Labour Relations in the Motor Industry* (Allen & Unwin, 1967); W. E. J. McCarthy, 'The Nature of Britain's Strike Problem', *British Journal of Industrial Relations*, Vol. 8, No. 2, July 1970; M. Silver, 'Recent British Strike Trends: A Factual Analysis,' *British Journal of Industrial Relations*, vol. xi, No. 1, March 1973.

Strike – Forms
These include

Constitutional: A strike called only after the procedure for dealing with ⟡ Industrial Disputes agreed by the union(s) and the employer or his ⟡ Employers' Association has been exhausted (⟡ Grievance Procedure).

General: A strike supported by all or most of the trade union movement of a country. The only British case is that of the 1926 General Strike in support of the miners. There is some doubt about its legality. In many countries general strikes for political purposes are a feature of, e.g. emergent nationhood, opposition to single party government.

Lightning: A sudden stoppage of work at the workplace which may be spontaneous, as when tempers flare (USA terminology: 'wildcat'); or planned as part of a strategy to harass a specific employer or employers in an industry.

Local: A strike involving union members in a small geographical area, usually a workplace, plant, or company but occasionally a town or district. Most workplace and plant strikes are short, unofficial and unconstitutional.

National: A strike involving the whole of a union's membership wherever it may be found, *or* involving a whole industry and thus all the unions with members employed in it, e.g. a 'national engineering strike'.

Official: A strike sanctioned or ratified by the union(s) whose members are on strike in accordance with the appropriate union rules. National strikes are official, but most local strikes are not. There is no legal distinction between official and unofficial strikes.

Sit-down: A strike where the employees in question do not walk off the premises but stop work and remain at their workplace. Such strikes are unofficial, unconstitutional and illegal.

Sympathetic: A strike by a group of trade unionists not in dispute with their employer(s) in support of and in sympathy for strikers in a trade dispute.

Token: A short stoppage, e.g. a one-day strike, which may be official or unofficial, national or local, to indicate the attitude and strength of trade union members in an industrial dispute. If official, this is an economical form, producing a limited call only on union funds.

Unconstitutional: A strike called without using or exhausting disputes procedure. *See* Constitutional.

Strike – Remedies

Unofficial: A strike not sanctioned or ratified by the union(s) concerned. *See* Official. ⟨⟩ Strike – and the Law. N.H.C.

Strike – Remedies Some strikes may be justified. Some, indeed, may be useful to senior management in pointing up weaknesses in the social structure of the firm, or inadequacies in junior management or supervision. But many strikes are avoidable, and the problem is one of matching treatment to diagnosis, of providing an 'early warning' system of conflict, and then channelling, reducing and resolving it.

In democratic countries the right to strike is one of the basic freedoms. The extent to which the exercise of this right is legally regulated varies from country to country, but evidence from countries like the USA and Australia, which impose fairly severe legal restrictions on strike action, as well as from Britain itself, does not suggest that such regulation reduces, much less controls, strike incidence.

The Royal Commission, 1968 and subsequent White Paper, 1969, have suggested that the contribution by government should include speedier and less formal investigation and conciliation (⟨⟩ Industrial Conciliation); the possibility of strike ballots and a cooling-off period or 'conciliation pause'; investigations by a Commission on Industrial Relations; and the facilitating of trade union recognition and negotiation rights, of speedier resolution of inter-union disputes, and of protection by government agency against unfair dismissal. The now defunct *Industrial Relations Act*, 1971, contained some of these concepts within its 'legal framework' for industrial relations.

On the union side structural rationalization would be of great help, particularly in respect of demarcation and jurisdiction issues. So would training and the development of research facilities. This is true also for employers' associations if they are to improve their services to member firms.

The system of ⟨⟩ Collective Bargaining in Britain requires restructuring where it is disordered and defective, but since most strikes are at the level of the workplace, plant, or company, management has the key role in improving the situation. Boards of directors would benefit from positive industrial relations policies and comprehensive plant and company agreements. Rational company pay structures are needed, together with speedy disputes procedures and company negotiation systems which regularize the role of the ⟨⟩ Shop Steward. ⟨⟩ The Industrial Relations Code of Practice, 1972. Not least, and without the implication of 'kid-glove management', many organizations need to think less in terms of unilateral action and more in terms of participative management, recognizing the organization as a plural society rather than a unitary one where every member has common interests on all occasions. ⟨⟩ Employers' Associations; Industrial Relations – Reform in Great Britain; Strikes – Forms, Statistics; Trade Union – Demarcation, Jurisdiction, Officers, Structure. N.H.C.

B. C. Roberts, *Trade Unions in a Free Society* (Hutchinson, 1962); Royal Commission on Trade Unions and Employers' Associations, *Report* 1968, and A. Fox, Research Papers 3: *Industrial Sociology and Industrial Relations* (HMSO, 1966).

Strike – Statistics
Stoppages in the years 1963–73

Year	Number of stoppages beginning in year	Numbers of workers* involved in stoppages			Aggregate number of working days lost in stoppages		
		Beginning in year		In progress in year	Beginning in year		In progress in year
		Directly	Indirectly		(a)	(b)	
		000s	000s	000s	000s	000s	000s
1963	2,068	455	135	593	1,731	1,997	1,755
1964	2,524	700†	172	883†	2,011	2,030	2,277
1965	2,354	673	195	876	2,906	2,932	2,925
1966	1,937	414†	116	544†	2,372	2,395	2,398
1967	2,116	551†	180	734†	2,765	2,783	2,787
1968	2,378	2,073†	182	2,258†	4,672	4,719	4,690§
1969	3,116	1,426	228†	1,665†	6,799	6 925	6,846
1970	3,906	1,460	333	1,801	10,854	10,908	10,980
1971	2,228	863†	308†	1,178†	13,497	13,589	13,551
1972	2,497	1,448†	274†	1,734†	23,816	23,9236	23,909
1973	2,854	1,097	407	1,519	7,066	7,145	7,173
1974	2,882	1,145	456	1,605	14,684	‡	14,740

(a) The figures in this column only include days lost in the year in which the stoppages began.

(b) The figures in this column include days lost both in the year in which the stoppages began and also in the following year.

* Workers involved in more than one stoppage in any year are counted more than once in the year's total. Workers involved in a stoppage beginning in the year and continuing into another are counted in both years in the column showing the number of workers involved in stoppages in progress.

† Figures exclude workers becoming involved after the end of the year in which the stoppage began.

‡ As some stoppages were still in progress at the end of the year this figure is not yet available.

§ In 1968 about 1½ million days were lost as a result of a one-day national stoppage in the engineering industry.

Source: *Department of Employment Gazette*, HMSO, January 1974, p. 62.

A study by Mr Michael Silver (see p. 380) has produced some new findings on British strikes, in particular –

'1. The incidence of strikes in the UK relative to that of other countries has risen significantly in recent years.

2. In stark contrast to the broad industrial base over which *changes* in Britain's overall strike-proneness have been evenly spread, strike-proneness itself appears

to be a highly localized phenomenon which is exceptionally uneven in its distribution throughout the economy.

3. In recent years not only the frequency of strikes (outside of coal-mining) but also the number of workers involved in strikes and, most of all, the amount of working time foregone, have shown strong upward tendencies.

4. The rise in strike activity has been caused above all by discontent over wage rates.

5. Unofficial stoppages, while constituting the vast majority of the total number of strikes, have been increasing in frequency to an extent similar to that of official stoppages.

6. The degree both of authorization and of observance of procedure are aspects of strike behaviour which have been subject to variability over time.

7. The statistical importance of unofficial and unconstitutional strikes is less than it is conventionally assumed.'

In the last few years a different pattern of strike activity has emerged. Strike frequency, the number of strikers, and especially the number of days lost through strike action, have risen considerably compared with the pattern typical of the mid-sixties. The industrial composition of strike activity has also changed, with the new-found militancy of public employees dominating the scene, e g in the coal, railway, electricity supply, local authority, and post office industries. The large scale of recent official strikes is perhaps the most significant change of all, indicating a re-emergence of the 'major confrontation as a central focus of industrial conflict'. ⟨⟩ Strikes – Causes; Forms; Remedies. N.H.C.

Michael Silver, 'Recent British Strike Trends: A Factual Analysis', *British Journal of Industrial Relations*, Vol. XI, No. 1, March 1973.

Suggestion Schemes Organized arrangements to encourage employees to put forward their ideas for improving the efficiency, safety or working conditions in a firm. The idea behind these schemes is that any employee, from his technical knowledge and experience, may have ideas about reducing costs or changing methods of work, guarding machines etc., which will be of advantage to the business but which may remain undisclosed if no special encouragement is given. The encouragement usually takes the form of a cash payment related to the value of the suggestion. L.S.

Successful Suggestion Schemes (Industrial Society, 1958).

Supermarket Officially defined in Britain as a retail establishment of not less than 2000 square feet of sales area, operated on a self-service basis with three or more check-outs. In common parlance the term tends to embrace any type of self-service store using the check-out method of payment for goods selected. Self-service initially appeared in Britain in 1942 as a war-time expedient in the face of staff shortages. Although self-service leads to increased pilferage, costs are reduced and it gives a much increased flexibility for display and in-store promotion of products (⟨⟩ Merchandising). The Cooperative Societies (⟨⟩ Cooperative Movement) led in the introduction of self-service into food trading, but not into the broadening of their stocking policies. The conversion by many multiple chains of traditional food stores into supermarkets carrying a wide selection of dry goods led to a major managerial crisis. The much larger units involved in the trend to one-stop-shopping were unable to find capable managers from the conventional source of recruits. Discount houses are a special case of predominantly non-food supermarketing where the overhead costs and service offered to customers are kept to an absolute minimum. The first such store was opened in Southend-on-Sea in 1962. Their growth has been slow compared with that of the conventional supermarket which offers a congenial shopping environment and service whilst obtaining major economies from saved labour costs and high stock turn-round.

R. J. Markin, *The Supermarket* (Washington State University, 1963). G.S.C.W.

Supervisory Training ⬥ Industrial Training.

Synergy Synergy is said to have taken place when the combined return on the firm's resources is greater than the sum of its parts. It is sometimes known as the '2 + 2 = 5 Effect'.

When a company adds to its existing activities the new activity will make use of the company's existing resources to a greater or lesser extent: the extent to which it does so is the extent of the synergy arising from this new activity. Where there is no relation at all between the new and existing activities there will be no synergy – i.e. the return on investment of the company as a whole will simply be the return on the existing activities plus that of the new activities. But where the new activity makes use of existing resources the return for the company as a whole will be greater than the simple weighted average of the new and existing activities (2 + 2 = 5).

Synergy can arise from the commonality of resources required by the new and existing activities and 'resources' includes not only such physical resources as factories, transport facilities, etc. but also management competence, know-how, research, marketing, operations and starting up economies. In estimating the extent of synergy likely to be obtained from a project, it is possible to prepare a 'capability profile' for the company to determine how far the new activity might mesh in with the existing activities. This profile is similar to a list of ⬥ Strengths and Weaknesses. A.J.A.A.

H. Igor Ansoff, *Corporate Strategy* (McGraw-Hill, 1965).

Synthetic Timing An alternative to direct Time Study, i.e. a technique for indirectly obtaining basic times for jobs by using:
(1) Element times from previous Time Studies.
(2) Element times from previous studies of other jobs containing the same elements.
(3) Data derived from an analysis of suitable accumulated data. ⬥ Time Study.
(Also called elemental or standard data.)

Synthetic Timing is of particular value where direct Time Study would be uneconomical or impractical, e.g. on a new job, on short-run jobs, etc. Furthermore, it is a more reliable and consistent method since data from several studies are normally used and the use of a stop-watch on the shop-floor is avoided.

System Loss

Synthetic timing normally produces basic times, to which appropriate allowances must be added. The procedure normally involves analysing data accumulated from previous time studies and data obtained specifically for the purpose of developing synthetic data (see 3 above).

Three types of job elements exist:

(1) Machine elements, controlled entirely by the machine, e.g. speed, feed, etc.

(2) Constant elements.

(3) Variable elements which, whilst of a similar motion pattern, vary with changes in (say) weight, distance, etc.

Machine and constant elements usually present no problems. Variable elements are examined to determine the influence of the various factors and possible element basic times under varying conditions are expressed as equations, tables or curves. R.W.

M. E. Mundel, *Motion and Time Study* (Prentice-Hall, 3rd ed., 1960).

System Loss Although, usually as a result of work measurement, a fixed standard time is allowed for a job operation, the worker does not complete every cycle in the same time. An individual's operation cycle time varies, usually forming a positively skewed unimodal distribution.

i.e.

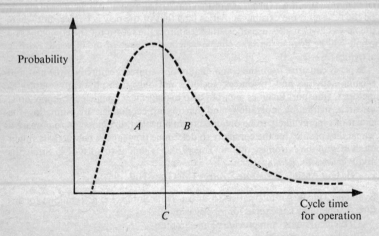

If a fixed time is allowed for the operation, say C, then on some occasions the worker will be able to complete the operation in less than the allowed time (Area A) and on other occasions will be unable to complete the operation (Area B).

Such a situation results in System Loss which has two components:

A – Corresponding to Area A

The worker will be able to complete the operation in less than the allowed time, and hence either waiting time will result, or the worker will work more slowly. In either case an underutilization of labour results.

B – Corresponding to Area *B*

The worker will be unable to complete the operation and the job will pass on to the next operation incomplete, and defectives will be produced.

Increasing the allowed time for the operation does not reduce total system loss (merely reducing area *B* and increasing area *A*).

Only one satisfactory solution exists to reduce the pacing effect, i.e. to provide a tolerance about the allowed time as, for example, in the diagram below. ⟡ Pacing. R.W.

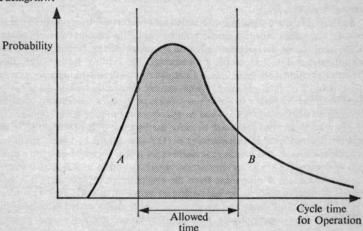

Systems Analysis and Design Before a computer can be installed in a business application a number of investigations must be performed. These can usefully be grouped under three stages:

(1) Feasibility study which determines whether it is feasible on economic and/ or technological grounds for a computer to perform the desired task. If it is feasible, then:

(2) The System Analysis stage which determines the structure of the existing system into which it is proposed to introduce the computer installation.

(3) The System Design stage which is the complete design of the new computer based system.

The individuals who perform the systems investigations as distinct from the detailed computer programming are known as systems analysts. However, in some companies the distinction between the two roles is not clear-cut and an individual may perform both tasks in a given project.

The term Systems Analysis is also used to a limited extent to describe two other activities not necessarily associated with computers:

(1) As a synonym for ⟡ Operational Research, since OR workers analyse man/ machine systems.

(2) As a synonym for systems engineering. This latter is a term sometimes used to describe the engineering of new large-scale complex man/machine systems (e.g. a new weapons system, or intercontinental microwave system). M.J.C.M.

T

Tactics Short-term decisions made in response to changing circumstances so as to make the best use of existing resources, sometimes known as operational planning. Tactical decisions are also those taken to put into effect the details of a strategic decision.

Strategic plans are usually broad statements concerning the continued use of existing resources or the introduction of new ones. This leads to two types of tactical planning, one dealing essentially with the use of existing resources, the other with the detailed implementation of a strategy. The cardinal feature of the first type, or operational planning, is that it consists more of re-planning or revision of plans than of original planning. Circumstances change so rapidly – a surge of demand, a breakdown, a strike at a supplier's premises, a snowstorm – that an operational planner's function must be mainly to revise previously laid plans in response to these events in order to make the best use of the then available resources. The sequence of such planning is: (1) A plan for the best use of resources is made for a week or a month or sometimes for a year ahead based upon a forecast of demand, of stocks, of production capacities and so on. (2) Actual results are monitored. (3) A divergence from the original plan is observed. (4) A new plan is devised, monitored, revised again and so on, often with a very short timecycle. Thus tactical planning consists largely of frequent revisions of plans in response to changing conditions and is normally limited to making use of existing resources only.

Tactics can also refer to the detailed implementation of a strategy and in this sense it may be distinguished from operational planning in that it can involve the introduction of new resources. Thus a strategic plan may call for 'the opening of 10 new branches in important city centres'. Such a plan may legitimately contain no further details than this and in such a case it is left to the discretion of an executive to decide when and where such branches are to be opened.

Each of these is a tactical decision: precisely which street in which city, the best shopping day on which the opening ceremony should be held, and so on, are tactical considerations. ⟺ Strategy. A.J.A.A.

Target A target is the precise restatement of an objective, often given in figures.

Objectives are often stated in rather general, broad terms. Targets are usually precise and unequivocal translations of these. Thus it may be an objective of a company 'to improve its return on capital': restated as a target this might be 'to raise return on capital to 15% by 1980' – an aim that is of such precision that there can be little doubt whether the company has actually achieved it or not. In the same way an executive may be given the objective of improving labour efficiency: his target may be 'improve output per head by 4% every year until further notice'.

As a general rule a target set to a company or an individual should be pitched

384

at a level that is challenging but attainable and it is said to be advisable to discuss the appropriateness of any target with an individual before he is officially given it to achieve as part of his duties. It is important that the target figure should be verifiable – i.e. that it is possible to determine unequivocally that the target figure has or has not been achieved by the target date. ⍧ Management by Objectives.

A.J.A.A.

The Manager's Guide to Setting Targets (The Industrial Society, 1966).

Taxation (Accounting Treatment of) Profits chargeable to taxation for a period often bear little relationship to the profits stated in the accounts for the same period. There are two main reasons for this. First, profits for tax purposes may exclude certain income included for accounting purposes, or may be struck after disallowing certain expenses included in the profit and loss account; these are 'permanent differences' between taxable and accounting profits. Second, there are the 'timing differences' when income or expenditure is taken into account in a period for tax purposes different from that for accounting purposes. Examples of 'timing differences' are the disallowance for tax purposes of certain reserves and provisions; the use of a receipts or payments basis in certain cases for tax purposes compared with an accruals basis used for accounting purposes; and the writing off of certain capital expenditures more quickly for tax purposes than for accounting purposes.

Accounting follows the accruals concept and requires that revenues and costs are accrued, matched and dealt with in the profit and loss account of the period to which they relate. For accounting purposes, taxation should follow the same rule and the taxation expense shown in the profit and loss account should be based on the profits stated in the accounts rather than on the profits chargeable to taxation. Where taxation is deferred (e.g. because tax allowances for capital expenditure exceed the depreciation charged in the accounts) the benefit of the deferment should be disregarded and the full amount of taxation ultimately due on the accounting profits should be charged as an expense of the period to which the accounting profits relate. The deferred taxation is then recorded separately on the balance sheet. This treatment took effect from 1 January 1974.

A different problem concerns the treatment of taxation on dividends and certain other distributions. After 1 April 1973, when a company pays a dividend it is required to account to the tax authorities for advanced corporation tax (ACT) within 14 days of the end of the quarter in which the dividend was paid. The ACT is subsequently allowable as a credit (subject to certain restrictions) against the 'mainstream' corporation tax liability of the company. For accounting purposes dividends paid should be shown net and the related ACT should be included in the charge for taxation. Where dividends are proposed, but not declared, at the accounting date (e.g. the final dividend) the ACT relating to the dividend should be treated as included in the charge for taxation unless the circumstances are such that the credit is *not* reasonably certain and foreseeable; in this case the ACT should be written off. In the presentation of the profit and loss account, ACT written off should be treated as a charge in arriving at profits after tax (and should therefore be separately disclosed) and not shown as an appropriation of profit. It should be charged in arriving at profits before extraordinary items.

Taylor, Frederick Winslow (1856–1915) His contribution towards the establishment of the very notion of scientific management is but one of the achievements for which F. W. Taylor is remembered.

Taylor was born in Philadelphia: medical problems and the prevailing American labour situation forced him to accept employment as a labourer with the Midvale Steel Company but, following a phenomenal series of promotions, became Chief Engineer at the age of 31. His later studies of work rationalization at the Bethlehem Steel Company are probably the most frequently cited examples in the area of management. Taylor developed a comprehensive policy for the study of human work, stressing the importance of such aspects as the need to analyse and investigate each separate element of a task; the importance of selection and training procedures; the role of proper communication and cooperation between the two sides of industry and the need for equality in the divisions of labour and responsibility.

Four years before his death in 1915, Taylor founded the Society to Promote the Science of Management, later renamed in his honour the Taylor Society. ⟡ Scientific Management. E.E.

Taylorism ⟡ Scientific Management.

Technological Forecasting The process of identifying and assessing future threats and opportunities arising from the development of relevant technology. As such it is a positive rather than a passive process, which can lead to management action designed to change any forecast probabilities. It is a new technique which has emerged with the accelerating rate of change in technology, and is an important tool in effective long-range planning (⟡ Corporate Planning). It will not necessarily predict the precise form in which a technology will evolve, nor the exact timing. As in any forecast, however, it must evaluate the probabilities of future technological changes and their concomitant significance. The rate at which any innovation diffuses through the economy is an important element in the forecast, as well as the development within companies of pressures for innovation as extant products reach a mature stage in their life cycle (⟡ New Product). Certain aspects of technological development appear to be beyond the scope of such forecasting, e.g. unpredictable interactions, termed 'spin-off', unprecedented demand, major new discoveries. A major problem exists for management in the task of integrating forecasts into current decisions. A journal deals exclusively with the subject, *Technological Forecasting*, American Elsevier Publishing Co. G.S.C.W.

> J. B. Quinn, 'Technological Forecasting', *Harvard Business Review*, 45, 2, 1967; G. S. C. Wills, *Technological Forecasting* (Penguin, 1971).

Technology and Organization The system of machines, equipment and technical methods fundamental to economic performance, together with their associated knowledge, beliefs and values.

Technology, surprisingly neglected for so long by students of organizational behaviour, has been recognized in the last decade or so as an extremely important variable. Joan Woodward showed a relationship between technology (in terms of unit, batch, mass or process production) and organizational structure. By so doing, she demonstrated that many of the principles of management formulated by the classical theorists were of specific and not universal application. In the USA, Leonard Sayles reported research which indicated that different technological circumstances typically give rise to different patterns of work group behaviour. He identified four categories of such behaviour to which he gave the names Apathetic, Erratic, Strategic and Conservative, each implying a different pattern of relationship with supervision and management.

It is now known, therefore, that a relationship exists between technology and organizational (and hence social) structure and process. However, this is not to say that organizational structure is determined solely by technology: the work of the Tavistock Institute drew attention to the possibility of basing different organizational arrangements on the same technology. Nevertheless, similar technologies are likely to give rise to *broadly* similar organizational structures and behaviour by limiting the range of structure and behavioural alternatives from which choice can be made. ⟡ Socio-Technical System. I.C.MCG.

J. Woodward, *Industrial Organisation: Theory and Practice* (OUP, 1965); L. R. Sayles, *Behaviour of Industrial Work Groups: Prediction and Control* (J. Wiley, 1958); Alan Fox, *Industrial Sociology and Industrial Relations*, Commission on Trade Unions and Employers' Associations, Research Papers, No. 3 (HMSO, 1966).

Temperature ⟡ Heat.

Test Marketing ⟡ Marketing Experimentation.

T-Group ⟡ Group Methods of Training.

Therbligs The activities of a worker can be described in terms of 18 fundamental elements. Each of these elements is called a Therblig, after Frank B. Gilbreth, who was initially responsible for defining fundamental work elements.

The classification is based on an analysis of the purpose for which a movement is made, rather than on physiological definitions.

Because of the precise nature of Therblig descriptions, their use facilitates very detailed method study. Therbligs are normally used in conjunction with SIMO (Simultaneous Motion) Charts and normally involve the use of motion photography to record the movement. These, together, constitute the basic technique of micromotion study. (⟡ Method Study: SIMO Charts.)

Each Therblig is identified by a symbol and colour, see chart on page 388.

N.B. The Therblig 'Find' is sometimes omitted since it is considered as equivalent to select. R.W.

J. Barnes, *Motion and Time Study* (J. Wiley, 5th ed., 1963).

Threshold One of the most intensively investigated of human functions is that of sensitivity to incoming sensory stimulation. Two types of threshold may be described for each sensory modality. The absolute threshold defines the minimum strength of signal which is detectable. The differential threshold defines the

SYMBOL	NAME	COLOUR
⊂	Search	Black
⊂⊃	Find	Grey
→	Select	Light Grey
∩	Grasp	Red
⌒	Hold	Gold Ochre
⌣	Transport Load	Green
9	Position	Blue
#	Assemble	Violet
∪	Use	Purple
#	Disassemble	Light Violet
0	Inspect	Burnt Ochre
⦵	Pre-position	Pale Blue
⌒	Release Load	Carmine Red
⌣	Transport Empty	Olive Green
ℓ	Rest for overcoming fatigue	Orange
∧	Unavoidable Delay	Yellow
⌐ᵒ	Avoidable Delay	Lemon Yellow
ρ	Plan	Brown

minimum change in the signal which gives rise to a detectable subjective difference.

No single threshold value can be quoted for any sensory channel, since the detectability of signals depends upon a large number of factors. In the case of light, for example, the absolute threshold is dependent upon such factors as wavelength, duration of signal, state of adaptation of the eye, and part of the retina receiving the signal (◇ Adaptation; Colour). There is a further complication in that an individual's threshold will fluctuate from moment to moment. The convention is to define the threshold as the amplitude of the signal perceived 50% of the time.

Differential thresholds are governed largely by Weber's Law which states that subjective differences in signal amplitudes depend upon *proportional* increases in signal strength. ⟨⟩ Ergonomics. E.E.

Time Sharing Since a ⟨⟩ Computer is a number of specialist units which can work partially independently of each other, it is desirable to coordinate their operations so as to obtain the most efficient overall working.

When a computer performs a calculation, the sequence of units through which the program and data pass are input unit, processor, and output unit. For most of the duration of the calculation, two of the three units will be idle and clearly such an arrangement is inefficient. If a way can be found for the computer to handle several calculations simultaneously by performing the different stages of the calculations on the different units simultaneously (e.g. the input for one calculation fed in simultaneously with the output from another being fed out), higher equipment utilization would be obtained. Such an arrangement is known as time sharing.

Time sharing may be achieved by having special electronic equipment (hardware) or special programs (software) providing control routines which enable peripheral units to work simultaneously, that is in parallel. Also, arrangements can be made for a number of programs to be processed simultaneously on the computer as a whole. Interchange of the programs between individual units is arranged according to a set of priority rules so as to make maximal use of facilities. The manipulations of the programs are under the control of a master or executive program. This facility is also known as parallel or multi-programming.

A development of growing importance is the provision of units which give remote access to a computer operating on a time sharing basis. A teletypewriter unit in, say, Yorkshire can be linked directly by telephone line to a computer in London. The user in Yorkshire dials a telephone number and his unit is immediately connected to the computer, which he may then use, just as if it were in the same room. A number of companies in the UK and USA offer such computing facilities and it is a mode of operation that will grow rapidly. Details of two current uses of remote access terminals are described elsewhere (⟨⟩ Computers (Rapid Access to Information)). M.J.C.M.

Time-Span of Discretion 'The longest period which can elapse in a role before the manager can be sure that his subordinate has not been exercising marginally substandard discretion continuously in balancing the pace and the quality of his work' (Elliott Jaques, *Time-Span Handbook*). The concept was developed by Jaques in the course of his work with the Glacier Metal Company and arose out of an attempt to establish salary levels and differentials which would be regarded universally as equitable. Although it was appreciated that length of service might be accorded some recognition through a system of increments, it was considered that basic salary should be closely related to the level of work performed. Existing systems of job evaluation seemed to be inadequate in that they included elements not directly related to work content and failed to identify the factor or factors in the work itself which might meaningfully be measured for payment purposes. There was, Jaques claimed, a discernible consensus as to the appropriate payment, whether expressed in hourly, weekly, monthly, or annual rates, for a given level of

389

work. Analysis of the nature of work suggested the existence of two elements: a prescribed content and a discretionary content. The prescribed content consists of that aspect of the task which is subject to detailed instructions so that the performer has simply to obey: there is no feeling of responsibility. The discretionary content consists of that aspect of the task in which the performer must exercise personal judgement: here a weight of responsibility is felt. The notion of equitable pay was considered to be related to the discretionary content and the attempt to measure this element led to the development of the Time-Span of Discretion. Time-span theory is a useful addition to the growing body of knowledge of work measurement, yet it has been strongly criticized from several quarters. Economists complain that the theory ignores both the effect and the legitimacy of economic forces influencing payment structures, and sociologists reject the basic thesis that time-span is the only factor influencing subjective judgements about the fairness of pay.

Like Frederick W. Taylor, half a century before him, Jaques believed that the universal application of his system would eliminate the chief cause of conflict between management and employee in that objective measurement would replace collective bargaining. However, as might be expected, few trade unionists have been prepared to concede to management control of wage differentials based on time-span analysis and its main application has been in salary as distinct from wage administration. I.C.McG.

Elliott Jaques, *Time-Span Handbook* (Heinemann, 1964); Elliott Jaques, *Equitable Payment* (Heinemann, 1961); Alan Fox, *The Time-Span of Discretion Theory: an appraisal* (IPM 1966).

Time Study 'A work measurement technique for recording the times and rates of working for the elements of a specified job carried out under specified conditions and for analysing the data so as to obtain the time necessary for carrying out the job at a defined level of performance.' (British Standard 3138.) ⟡ Work Measurement.

Time study is now normally considered as that part of work measurement concerned with the direct timing of job elements by means of a suitable time device (e.g. stop-watch). This distinguishes it from indirect time-study methods, such as synthetic timing, predetermined motion time study and analytical estimating. ⟡ Synthetic Timing; Predetermined Motion Time Study; Estimating.

The object of time study is to establish the time which should be required by a worker to do a job in a prescribed manner, under standard conditions and at a defined level of performance.

Such data is of value: (1) To calculate work schedules; (2) To assist in Method Study; (3) For incentive schemes; (4) To determine Standard Costs; (5) To determine labour requirements; (6) To measure operating efficiency; (7) For machine allocation; etc.

Direct time study normally involves the following steps:
(1) Divide the job into elements for convenience of study.
(2) Time a sufficient number of elements to obtain the observed time.

(3) Rate the worker's performance for each of the timed elements in order to convert the observed time to the basic time.

$$\text{Basic Time} = \frac{\text{Observed Time} \times \text{Observed Rating}}{\text{Standard Rating}}$$

N.B. Standard Rating = 100 on the British Standard Scale. Standard Rating corresponds to the 'average rate at which qualified workers will naturally work at a job, provided they know and adhere to the specified method and provided they are motivated to apply themselves to their work'. (BS 3138.) ⟡ Performance Rating.

(4) Add allowances to the basic time to obtain the standard time. ⟡ Allowances. R.W.

R. M. Currie, *The Measurement of Work* (BIM, 1963).

Tracking Much of the study of human control performance has taken the form of experiments on tracking; that is, the subject is faced with a moving display and is required to carry out appropriate movements in an attempt to minimize an error function.

There are two basic designs of tracking task. In pursuit tracking, the subject sees both a target, over which he has no control, and a follower, whose position is determined by him. His task is to keep the follower upon the target. Such a task might be performed by an anti-aircraft gunner. In compensatory tracking, there is but one moving part on the display, the position of which is determined partly by the tracker's control movements and partly by external circumstances. The compensatory task is carried out by a motorist attempting to drive at constant speed over undulating country.

Tracking accuracy is a function of such variables as the shape and speed of the independent track, the type of display and control used, in addition to the skill of the individual tracker. ⟡ Ergonomics. E.E.

Trade Association ⟡ Employers' Association.

Trade Marks A trade mark is some distinguishing mark which is used on or in connection with goods with a view to indicating that these goods are those of the owner of the trade mark. The owner of the trade mark may be a manufacturer or a retailer.

In order to acquire property rights to a trade mark it is necessary to register it with the Controller of Patents. The registration is valid for seven years but may be renewed for up to another fourteen years. A trade mark may be assigned by its owner, generally in connection with the sale of a business. W.F.F.

Sir D. M. Kerly, *Trade Marks and Trade Names* (Sweet & Maxwell, 1972).

Trade Union – Communism Most British trade unions have rules which forbid, within the union, party political activity of the kind which is normal in national and local authority elections. Yet union elections in practice are often conducted on political lines. While Conservatives, Liberals and Roman Catholics pursue their political ends through organized group participation in union elections, it is in the main Communist Party members who seek to win control over the unions.

Communists accept rigid discipline: they do not miss meetings. They can thus succeed at the expense of the apathetic member.

When Communists lose positions of power they may be prepared to violate democratic practices. This was demonstrated in the Electrical Trades Union ballot-rigging case heard in the High Court in 1961, as a result of which Frank Foulkes, President of the Union, and Frank Haxell, General Secretary, were removed from office. It was successfully claimed that elections for the Union's chief posts had for three years been fraudulently conducted by means of unlawful conspiracies to substitute, miscount, destroy or invalidate ballot papers. The case led to suggestions that Britain should follow the example of Australia and adopt legislation to enable official inquiries to be made into allegations of ballot-rigging without the necessity of expensive legal action. Where internal union politics produce industrial unrest, the Minister of Labour may set up a Court of Enquiry to investigate, as was done in the case of Briggs Motor Bodies in 1957. In the USA the *Labour Management Reporting and Disclosure Act* 1959, prohibits, *inter alia*, Communists from serving as union officers, labour consultants and employers' association officers for five years after termination of Communist Party membership.

Because Communist union members are so active and vocal, they can often make an impact at local level. Their zeal makes them good shop stewards and success on the members' behalf with management breeds loyalty from the members and a feeling that they are trade unionists first and Communist Party members second. They are most successful in traditionally militant trade unions; for example, in the engineering, mining, docks and construction industries.

Partly because many political extremists are active trade unionists, few unions discriminate against them on political grounds, although Communists have been debarred from full-time union office in the General and Municipal Workers' Union since 1926, and (together with Fascists) in the Transport and General Workers' Union from 1949 and, after the notorious trial, the Electrical Trades Union. In 1934 ⟨⟩ Trades Councils were instructed by the TUC to exclude Communists from office. At the international level the Communist unions' endeavour to use the World Federation of Trade Unions for propaganda purposes caused the ⟨⟩ TUC and other non-Communist delegations to withdraw in 1949 and form the International Confederation of Free Trade Unions.

Individual Communists, Trotskyists, and members of other extreme left-wing groups, generally much more militant, are active from time to time in strikes; sometimes, though rarely, they may work together. But there appears no evidence of a 'Red Plot' to disrupt the economy. ⟨⟩ Strike. N.H.C.

Trade Union – Demarcation Demarcation is the marking out of a given job or set of jobs as appropriate to be carried out by the members of a given trade union. Demarcation disputes between unions are disputes about which union should have what job (⟨⟩ Trade Dispute).

Demarcation disputes should be distinguished from jurisdiction disputes about which unions should have what members.

The demarcation dispute is typical of unions of the closed, craft type. When confronted by changes in technology, they wish to extend or prevent a decline in their membership and so claim exclusive rights to a new job which has a fringe relationship to a job previously done solely by their members. Demarcation problems are most common in situations involving unions facing a long-run decline in membership.

Demarcation disputes can be and are prevented by resolute and efficient trade union leadership together with resolute and efficient management. Foresight and early consultation are important. Where disputes of this type develop, managements prefer to leave them to be settled by the unions concerned, who work through them without the aid of the TUC Disputes Committee, which has only an advisory role. In a few industries, however, (e.g. shipbuilding, building, civil engineering) employers have been parties to demarcation agreements as their interests are clearly affected when a conflict over the allocation of work leads to a ⟨⟩ Strike.

Demarcation disputes can be reduced by the amalgamation of rival craft or ex-craft unions, for example that of the shipwrights and the boilermakers in the shipbuilding industry. They may be prevented by productivity bargaining, not so much by the agreed introduction of multi-craftsmen as by the agreement that work on fringe jobs, usually done by one craft, may be carried out by a member of another craft if he could do them equally well. Even where historical justifications for present day demarcation practices no longer apply, they are so bound up with concepts of job security that productivity bargains aimed, *inter alia*, at their elimination may need to include guarantees by management against redundancy.

The fact that, historically, women were employed generally at lower rates of pay than men has resulted in a fairly clear and well-established demarcation between men's work and women's work throughout the greater part of manufacturing industry. N.H.C.

H. A. Clegg, *The System of Industrial Relations in Great Britain* (Blackwell, 1970).

Trade Union – Government and Administration Trade Unions each have their individual character. A union's internal organization is a function of the aims, size, and diversity of its membership, but a general picture can be drawn which does not do too much injustice to the realities of each separate situation. Typically the union has a pyramidal structure and the main lines of formal communication are expected to extend from the individual member through the Branch, possibly via a District Committee, to a National Executive Committee, and periodically to a National Delegate Conference.

The branch (known in some unions by other names, e.g. lodge, club, chapel) is the basic organizational unit. Branches in their size, form and content of meetings should encourage the active cooperation of the membership, but their policy-making power varies from union to union. The branch is usually based on a geographical area and varies greatly in size; the Amalgamated Union of Engineering Workers has set a maximum of 300 members while the Transport and General Workers' Union has had a branch of 9000 members. The branch deals with applications for membership and provides for the collection of contributions and distribution of benefits. In a study of a branch in 1952, Joseph Goldstein emphasized membership apathy and showed that attendance at branch meetings could often be as low as 3%. Clearly, resolutions in the branch meetings need not necessarily represent the views of branch membership. It is often suggested that where numbers permit unions should base their branches on the workplace, rather than on some wider geographical area in order to stimulate greater interest and attendance and to tighten the link between the ⟡ Shop Steward, the local leader at the workplace, and his branch officials, who are responsible for formal two-way communication between the branch and the main body of the union. This can work well, as in the Steelworkers' Union, but in other cases, e.g. the National Union of Mineworkers, it has made no apparent contribution towards reducing independent, unofficial action.

District organizations are concerned with the proper functioning of branches in the district and with local negotiations. They are composed of delegates from branches and the secretary may be a lay member or a full-time official. Some have a wide measure of autonomy. The Transport and General Workers' Union has also Regional Committees, Regional Trade Group (or 'Industrial') Committees, and National Trade Group Committees.

The National Executive Committee is the governing body or top leadership of the union, responsible for its day-to-day operation and subject only to the National Delegate Conference. It can influence the Conference, containing as it does the principal national officers, of whom the General Secretary (⟡ Trade Union Officers) is normally the most important and who, except in the very small unions, is always a full-time official.

The National Delegate Conference, which meets annually, or at longer intervals, is the supreme authority of the union and is usually composed of delegates from branches or other, larger, units together with the National Executive Committee. The Committee normally presents to the Conference a report on its work over the previous period and this is discussed. Motions and amendments are submitted by branches or district organizations. The Conference is sometimes responsible for electing the principal lay officers, the full-time officials, the Executive Committee or part of it.

It is apparent that the study of a trade union as an organization cannot be effected solely by examination of its rule book. Both its formal and informal organization structures are products of more than its personal legal rules. Nevertheless, rule books could often be clearer, and many might be redrafted with advantage, for example with regard to the rights of members. N.H.C.

B. C. Roberts, *Trade Union Government and Administration in Great Britain* (Bell, 1956); J. Goldstein, *Government of British Trade Unions* (Allen & Unwin, 1952).

Trade Union – Jurisdiction The jurisdiction of a trade union is, in effect, its sphere of influence in terms of membership and potential membership. Jurisdiction disputes between unions are about which unions should have what members. ⟡ Trade Dispute.

Jurisdiction disputes should be distinguished from demarcation disputes (⟡ Trade Unions – Demarcation) about which union's members should have what jobs.

The strategy of a trade union determines the nature of its membership, the kinds of workers it will organize. Thus in Britain the recruitment area of the original, closed craft unions (☼ Trade Union Types – Craft Union) was clearly marked. This was not so for the newer, open unions, operating over a broad front (☼ Trade Union – Structure). Jurisdiction disputes, involving rivalry for the same potential membership, could thus arise. Rivalry can also clearly occur between two open unions.

Many British unions have developed agreements with rival organizations establishing methods of resolving jurisdictional conflict, but the key code of behaviour for settling such disputes has been laid down by the ☼ TUC. This is based on the recognition of established 'organizing rights' and was developed by the TUC Disputes Committee set up specifically to summon unions in conflict, to hear evidence, and to issue an award in each case. Sanction for disobeying the Committee's award is expulsion from the TUC, but this has only occurred in the case of two small unions.

'Procedures for the Avoidance of Disputes', known as the Bridlington Rules and laid down at the 1939 TUC, were developed from the Hull Rules of 1924. The Bridlington Rules require that no one who is, or who has recently been, a member of any trade union should be accepted into membership by another union without inquiry; that no union should accept a member of another union where inquiry shows that the member is under discipline, engaged in an ☼ Industrial Dispute, or in arrears with contributions; and that no union should start organizing activities at any establishment in respect of any grade of worker in which another union 'has the majority of workers employed and negotiates wages and conditions', unless by arrangement with that other union.

The Bridlington Rules comprise an injunction to cease poaching another union's (potential) members and do not provide a positive inducement to the rationalization of union jurisdiction. Further, the rules involve some restriction on the freedom of members to belong to particular unions.

In the USA jurisdictional conflict is bitter and ruthless; in Germany the problem is solved by industrial unionism (☼ Trade Union Types – Industrial Union). British unions prefer to tackle the problem by willingness to compromise on claims. A few unions steer a course between Scylla and Charybdis: the National Union of Public Employees has built itself up partly by a skilful exploitation of the gaps between other unions' spheres of influence. N.H.C.

S. W. Lerner, *Breakaway Unions and the Small Trade Union* (Allen & Unwin, 1961); John Hughes, Royal Commission on Trade Unions and Employers' Associations, Research Papers 5 (Part 1): *Trade Union Structure and Government* (HMSO, 1967).

Trade Union – at Law Before 1971 the term trade union covered, as far as the law was concerned, both trade unions of workers as well as employers' associations. The *Industrial Relations Act*, 1971, reserves the term 'trade union' for a *registered* organization of workers being an organization whose principal objects include the regulation of the relations between workers of that description and employers or organizations of employers or is a federation of workers' organizations. The term 'worker' includes a person working under a contract of employment or a

Trade Union – Membership

contract whereby he undertakes personally to perform any work or services for another party to the contract where that party is not a professional client.

The *Trade Union and Labour Relations Act*, 1974, defines a trade union as an organization of workers whose principal purposes include the regulation of relations with employers, or a federation of such organizations. The organization may be permanent or temporary. 'Worker' is defined to include employees, independent contractors and Crown servants. A trade union is an 'independent' trade union if it is not employer dominated, nor employer controlled, nor subject to interference by an employer tending towards such control. It is important to know whether a trade union is 'independent' since, while it would be an unfair dismissal if an employee was dismissed for refusing to join or to remain in a non-independent union, it would not be unfair if the union in question was an independent one.

The legal status of trade unions since 1974 is that what it was before 1971, i.e. the union is treated as an unincorporated association, but still enjoys some of the privileges of an incorporated body, e.g. it may sue or be sued in its registered name and it may enter into contracts in that name.

The registration of trade unions is voluntary. The Registrar of Friendly Societies maintains a register of listed trade unions. Registered trade unions enjoy certain advantages compared with unregistered ones, i.e. tax relief on provident income and easier transfer of property standing in their name. ⟺ Collective Bargaining; Industrial Disputes; Shop Steward; Strike – and the Law; Trade Union – Membership; Trade Union – Officers. w.f.f.

R. W. Rideout, *Principles of Labour Law* (Sweet & Maxwell, 1975)

Trade Union – Membership Trade union membership can be measured by total count or by 'density'. The density of membership is an index given by: actual union membership/potential union membership (number of civil employees) × 100. In the UK there are approximately 10 million trade union members spread unevenly among 23 million employees, an overall density of 45%. This is lower than that achieved in Sweden and Austria, where 66% of workers are trade union members, but higher than that in the USA, West Germany, France, Italy and almost every other non-Communist country in the world.

Viewed over the long run the growth of British trade union membership is impressive, despite its oscillations due to changes in the social and economic environment. Between 1892 and 1972 membership increased from 1·5 millions to 10 millions, while the number of employees increased from 14·1 millions to more than 23 millions, an increase in membership of 539% against an increase in potential membership of 67%. The overall density thus increased from 11% to 43%. Since the 1930s, however, growth has been much less impressive and the postwar picture is one of relative stability encompassing a decline in the growth rate of total membership and a decline in overall density from a peak of 45–7% in 1946–7. This has come about chiefly because of the changing pattern of employment, with a shrinkage in basic industries with a high union density – railways, coalmining, cotton, and manual employment generally – and an expansion of low union density industries which have proved difficult for unions to organize – professional services; insurance, banking and finance; distribution; chemicals; food, drink and tobacco; and white-collar occupations in all industries (⟨› Trade Union Types, White-collar Union). Traditionally women have been less ready to join unions than men, and less than a quarter of working women are union members compared with just over one half of employed men. However, over the last 20 years recruitment of women has proceeded at a faster rate than recruitment among men.

British union members have long been concentrated in a few large unions. Since the 1920s the trend has been for the number of unions to decline and the concentration to increase. From 1948–63 the number of unions decreased from 708 to 596 but the average size of unions increased. In 1963 the 18 largest unions each with over 100,000 members had 68% of total membership, whereas the 261 smallest unions with less than 500 members had 0·4% of total membership (⟨› Trade Union – Structure). By 1972 there were only 132 unions affiliated to the ⟨› TUC with a total affiliated membership of 9,894,881. Membership of the ten largest unions affiliated to the TUC in 1972 was:

Rank	Union	Membership (000s)
1	Transport and General Workers	1,643
2	Amalgamated Union of Engineering Workers	1,384
3	General and Municipal Workers	841
4	Local Government Officers	463
5	Electricians and Plumbers	419
6	Public Employees	397
7	Shop and Distributive Workers	319
8	National Union of Teachers	277
9	National Union of Mineworkers	276
10	Construction and Allied Trades	260

The older unions, like those of the Mineworkers and Railwaymen, are tending to move down the membership table while the younger ones, for example the Electricians and Public Employees, are moving up, in line with the changes in employment structure.

Trade union membership was not affected significantly by the ⟨› *Industrial Relations Act*, 1971, which laid down that every employee had the right to belong to a registered trade union (⟨› Trade Union – registration) of his choice, to take part in its activities at any appropriate time, and to stand as an official. He also had the right not to belong to any kind of trade union. This applied to all employees, whether manual, white collar, or managerial.

It was an ⟨› unfair industrial practice for an employer to refuse to engage an applicant, or to penalize him, for exercising his union membership rights and for a person to exert pressure on an employee to do so, except where an ⟨› agency shop agreement or ⟨› approved closed shop agreement was in force. An employer might, however, encourage employees to join a registered union which was recognized for bargaining purposes.

An employee claiming that his union membership rights had been infringed could apply to an ◊ Industrial Tribunal which was empowered to declare his rights and award compensation.

The 1971 Act was replaced by the ◊ *Trade Union and Labour Relations Act*, 1974. N.H.C.

Trade Union – Officers Trade unions depend heavily on their active members and from these are chosen both lay and full-time officials. The great majority are lay officials. Approximately 2600 are full-time. The lay representatives include ◊ Shop Stewards, workplace committee members, branch officers, district committee delegates, executive committee workers, national conference delegates and a number of national presidents and treasurers. Most full-time officials are employed chiefly as negotiators although they may carry the title of area, district, regional, divisional or national organizer. Another group of full-time officials are employed as branch, area, district, regional or divisional secretaries, and usually have both negotiating and administrative duties. The chief full-time official is the General Secretary. The post of General Secretary is an organizational post but it is also a symbol of a union's status, both in the trade union world and in the world at large. It is the key union office.

With the growth in size, complexity and geographical coverage of unions, they have found it increasingly necessary to delegate to full-time officials many of the functions originally exercised by rank-and-file members. Many decision-making functions have moved upwards from the branch into the hands of the General Secretary. It is he who controls the union's administration and normally the journal. He is often the only one having considerable knowledge of the separate specialist sections of the union. He thus carries considerable weight with his executive committee and so may effectively determine the strategy of national collective bargaining and joint operations with other unions. His post is often held for life; most of those General Secretaries who do have to face periodic elections are returned to office.

It is apparent that the central problem of union management is how to obtain administrative efficiency with the realities of democratic control. Unions attempt to achieve this in many different ways, setting up constitutional checks on the powers of leaders who, in the last analysis, must heed the pressure from the rank and file or face the consequences. While unions have not grown undemocratic they have developed centralized democratic bureaucracies. Vocal shop stewards, unofficial strikes (◊ Strike; Breakaway Union), are all indicative of counter-vailing forces to the centralizing trend. The internal structure of the union of the future will need to permit both strong central leadership and a greater degree of local autonomy than at present. Paradoxically, this is likely to call for an increase in the size of union staff, both of full-time officials and specialist support; for an improvement in the quality of union officers; and for better research and administrative departments. N H C.

H. A. Clegg, A. J. Killick and R. Adams, *Trade Union Officers* (Blackwell, 1961).

Trade Union – Politics Political action as practised by British trade unions is concentrated largely on Parliament, although union branches also take action on local government questions. The national political work of unions is carried on partly by the General Council of the ◇ TUC and partly by individual unions, which vary widely in their interest in parliamentary affairs. Some unions brief MPs concerning embryo or actual legislation; some support candidates at elections by contributing towards election expenses. If a union's nominee is elected, the union may also contribute towards the candidate's expenses as an MP. The miners, with over 30 sponsored MPs, form the largest group in Parliament, and a number of other unions are responsible for the candidatures of several members. The National Union of Teachers promotes candidates in all three parties. Most unions, however, have no members of their own in Parliament, and rely for assistance on trade union MPs or other members of the Labour Party.

Many unions also make contributions to the funds of the Labour Party and support it in publications, meetings and conferences. These political activities are subject to conditions prescribed by legislation, in particular the *Trade Union Act*, 1913, following the Osborne Judgment. This allows a union to spend funds for specified political purposes provided the majority of the members have balloted in favour of such political action and that the expenditure is made out of a separate fund. Members may contract out of payments into the political fund by formally indicating objection. This allows for Conservative and Liberal trade unionists, together with other objectors for whatever reason. It was noted in a PEP study in 1963 that 57% of the members of the Draughtsmen and Allied Technicians' Association contracted out of the union's political levy on behalf of the Labour Party, although this union was known as a militant and somewhat left-wing organization. At the end of 1970 there were 106 unions with political as well as other objects. These unions had political funds which stood at the end of the year at a total of £1.7 m.

It was largely as a result of action by the trade unions that the Labour Party was formed in the early years of the twentieth century, although socialist organizations also played a prominent part. In 1967 the number of unions affiliated to the Labour Party was 75, with an affiliated membership of 5·5 million. The membership of other organizations affiliated to the Labour Party was 21,000 and individual members numbered 734,000. This indicates the importance of the trade unions in the party from the point of view both of membership and of party funds.

There is some evidence that the Labour Party has become less necessary to the trade unions, and it is clear that the working relationship had its disadvantages. The trade union movement tolerates more constraints from a Labour than from a Conservative government, and it may be that unions encounter some difficulties in organizing white-collar workers because of the movement's connection with the Labour Party. ◇ Business Unionism. N.H.C.

Trade Union – Structure British trade unions, like those of Scandinavia, conform to a unitary system of industrial relations, so that there are no internal divisions on religious or political grounds as in many industrial relations systems on the mainland of continental Europe; nor is there the 'economic pluralism' typical of the American scene where unions raid each other for members, although some 'poaching' can occur (◇ Trade Unions – Jurisdiction).

The familiar classification of British unions by structural type (◊◊ Trade Union Types – Craft, General, Industrial, White-collar Unions) is inadequate to explain the nature of many of them. So also are the terms 'vertical unions', e.g. industrial and 'horizontal' unions, e.g. craft, with general unions appearing in both roles in different sectors of the economy. Since distinctions between such union types are increasingly blurred it is now more useful, in the terminology of Professor Turner of Cambridge, to think in terms of new categories according to the strategy and tactics of unions. Here the distinction is between 'closed' (military analogy, 'strong-point') unions, and 'open' (military analogy, 'broad front') unions. At the limits, a 'closed' union will delineate sharply its area of recruitment to a specific grade of worker, and sometimes to a specific industry and therefore region; an 'open' union will recruit all types of worker. In practice many unions are now intermediate types, 'open' in certain directions of recruitment interest but closed in others, e.g. the Amalgamated Union of Engineering Workers, descended from a craft union and with a 'closed' skilled nucleus, but now 'open' to the recruitment of supervisory grades and semi-skilled engineering workers. The degree of 'openness' of a union is a function of the attitudes of its membership and officers to recruitment.

Initiative in recruitment and amalgamation of unions has increasingly, from 1945, altered the balance of the trade union movement as a whole. Continuing change in the structure of the movement by natural growth reveals little sign of evolution towards industrial unionism, but the continued growth of large, 'open' unions. Industrial-type union organization appears more often as an aspect of internal union arrangements, or in the form of a very broad interest in one section of the economy. A number of unions organized basically on more strictly defined industrial lines are in numerical decline as regards membership.

Union development also shows a shift in the size structure of the movement:

% Total Membership by Size Group	End 1959	End 1965
Unions with under 25,000	14·9	12·0
25,000 and under 50,000	4·7	7·0
50,000 and under 100,000	13·4	12·9
100,000 and under 250,000	17·7 ⎫	11·7 ⎫
250,000 and above	49·3 ⎭ 67·0	56·4 ⎭ 68·1

This continuing shift towards large-scale relatively 'open' unions allows more economies of scale but appears unlikely to resolve the central structural problem of British unionism, namely the multiplicity of unions and overlapping in particular sectors or occupations.

Between the Bridlington Rules (◊◊ Trade Union – Jurisdiction) set up to limit inter-union competition in overlap areas and the activities of federations of unions operating in the same industry, there is a large and important hinterland of multilateral and bilateral union agreements; for example, on 'spheres of influence' and joint operation, for example in Joint Industrial Councils with multiple representation on the employees' side. Rationalization could better be accomplished by a more permanent and positive ⇔ TUC initiative through a Co-ordination and Development Committee set up on the lines of the present Disputes Committee. N.H.C.

John Hughes, Royal Commission on Trade Unions and Employers' Associations, Research Papers 5 (Part 1): *Trade Union Structure and Government* (HMSO, 1967).

Trade Union and Labour Relations Act The main purpose of the *Trade Union and Labour Relations Act*, 1974, was to repeal the *Industrial Relations Act*, 1971. It does this but re-enacts, with some changes, the part of that Act dealing with unfair dismissal. It also fills in some gaps left by the repeal. In particular, it provides legal immunities for those carrying out certain actions in contemplation or furtherance of a trade dispute. The Industrial Relations Code of Practice originally introduced under the *Industrial Relations Act* is retained. As before, the Code is not legally enforceable but continues as a set of guidelines, for example it may be used as a yardstick in Industrial Tribunal cases.

Repeal of the *Industrial Relations Act* thus abolishes *inter alia* the concept of the 'registered trade union', 'unfair industrial practices', the legal right not to belong to a trade union, the legally enforceable agency shop, compulsory cooling-off periods and strike ballots, the National Industrial Relations Court, and the Commission on Industrial Relations.

The *Trade Union and Labour Relations Act*, 1974, defines a trade union as an organization (whether permanent or temporary) consisting wholly or mainly of workers, whose principal purposes include the regulation of relations between those workers and employers. Central to the provisions affecting trade union membership is the concept of the 'independent trade union', which means a union which:

(a) is not under the domination or control of an employer or a group of employers or of one or more employers' associations; and

(b) is not liable to interference by an employer or any such group or association (arising out of the provision of financial or other material support or by any other means whatsoever) tending towards such control.

What is an 'independent trade union' has significance for the purposes of the Act in four areas:

Re dismissal:

(a) Only independent trade unions can conclude disciplinary procedure agreements which qualify for exclusion from the statutory unfair dismissal machinery.

(b) Only members of independent trade unions (or prospective members) are protected as such from dismissal on the grounds of union membership.

Re closed shops and the right to strike:

(c) Only independent trade unions can conclude union membership (i.e. closed shop) agreements.

(d) Only independent trade unions can conclude agreements which have the effect of restricting the individual employee's right to strike as part of his contract of employment.

A 'union membership agreement' is an agreement or arrangement which:
- (a) is made by or on behalf of, or otherwise exists between, one or more independent trade unions and one or more employers or employers' associations; and
- (b) relates to employees of an identifiable class; and
- (c) has the effect of requiring the terms and conditions of employment of every employee of that class to include a condition that he must be or become a member of the union or one of the unions which is or are parties to the agreement or arrangement or of another appropriate independent trade union.

The *Trade Union and Labour Relations Act* also reverses the presumption of the *Industrial Relations Act* that collective agreements are legally enforceable contracts and redefines 'trade dispute' to mean a dispute between employers and workers, or between workers and workers, connected with one or more of the following:
- (a) terms and conditions of employment, or physical working conditions;
- (b) engagement or non-engagement, or termination or suspension of employment, or the duties of employment, of one or more workers;
- (c) allocation of work or the duties of employment as between workers or groups of workers;
- (d) discipline;
- (e) membership or non-membership of a trade union;
- (f) facilities for officials of trade unions;
- (g) procedures on the above, including those for negotiation and consultation, and recognition matters.

The Trade Union and Labour Relations (Amendment) Bill at date (May 1975) proposes changes to the *Trade Union and Labour Relations Act*, 1974 as follows:
1. That protection against being dismissed in a closed shop situation be narrowed to cover only genuine religious objectors to union membership. It would no longer be valid to object to membership of a particular union on 'any reasonable grounds'.
2. That the definition of 'union membership agreement' (closed shop agreement) be amended so that only the parties to the agreement could specify other unions than themselves to which employees covered might belong. There would be no right to join 'any other appropriate union'.
3. That the rights of workers against being arbitrarily or unreasonably excluded or expelled from a trade union be repealed.
4. That the immunity from legal action in industrial disputes be extended to inducement or theatened inducement to breach of commercial contracts as well as contracts of employment, and to overseas disputes as well as disputes in Great Britain.

Adjustments made to this Bill in the House of Commons appear to have the effect of giving employers and unions much greater flexibility in operating union membership agreements than under the *Trade Union and Labour Relations Act*, 1974, or the (Amendment) Bill as originally published. N.H.C.

Trade Union Types – Craft Union A union where the basis for organization is the possession of certain trade skills.

Craft unions are typically associated with apprentice training which the union may control. Demarcation (⟡ Trade Union – Demarcation) of specific jobs, that is, the claiming of such jobs only for workers with particular trade skills, is characteristic of craft unions and is a device used by them for holding and strengthening the labour market position of workers with such skills. They control entry to these jobs completely in the ⟡ Closed Shop. New materials and methods may result in demarcation disputes between different types of skilled workmen and hence different craft unions, each concerned to minimize actual or imagined employment insecurity.

In their pure form craft unions are thus horizontal in character, seeking to unite all workers of a particular craft or trade irrespective of the industry in which they happen to be engaged. They were the earliest unions on the British scene, appearing as small, local, ephemeral societies in the eighteenth century; a number have continuous histories from the mid-nineteenth century, for example the engineers' union. They have a higher membership density and a higher membership participation in union affairs than is the case in other unions and, by virtue of their higher earnings originally, they tend to provide more and higher benefits from higher subscriptions.

A small number of unions of the pure craft type still exist, for example the United Patternmakers' Association, but for many years the share of craft unionism among British workers has declined. This has resulted from the decline of craftmanship, so that a number of unions containing men on skilled work would be better called skilled unions. It has resulted also because, in order to arrest their actual or relative decline in membership or influence, some former craft unions have enlarged their recruitment to embrace semi-skilled and unskilled workers, including women, although the original craft core has continued as an aristocracy and still provides the leadership, for example, in the Amalgamated Union of Engineering Workers. ⟡ Trade Union – Structure. N.H.C.

Trade Union Types – General Union A union with no limitation of recruitment interest, either occupationally or industrially.

General unions originated in the last two decades of the nineteenth century for labourers who had previously not been organized. Eventually they came to recruit workers in virtually unorganized, established industries like road passenger services; semi-skilled and unskilled workers in industries where craft unions were established, like engineering; workers of all grades of skill in new industries; and small groups of workers for whom craft or industrial unions were unable or unwilling to cater. Thus for workers who are industrially and occupationally mobile, general unionism offers continuity of membership. Because of their size, general unions have the advantages of economies of scale and provide efficient services to members, for instance legal, research and educational facilities.

Each of the general unions has its industrial strongholds. The Transport and General Workers' Union has its main strength in transport; the General and Municipal Workers' Union in public services, especially the gas industry and the manual work of local authorities; while most of the members of the Union of Shop, Distributive and Allied Workers are cooperative society employees. Even so, general unions have widespread membership, with the advantages of spread of interests and risks, and the concomitant managerial problems that go with considerable diversification. This means that they find it difficult to maintain effective democracy, the more so since they experience a high membership turnover. For this reason the Transport and General Workers' Union has provided for some autonomy to a number of trade groups within the organization, e.g. Docks, Road Passenger Transport, Road Commercial Transport, Building and Construction, Engineering, Chemicals, Municipal, Agricultural, etc. Even so, problems remain by virtue of the communication problems between the membership and the upper echelons of the union. ⟡ Trade Union – Structure; Trade Union – Officers; Trade Union – Government and Administration. N.H.C.

Trade Union Types – Industrial Union A union which seeks to organize all workers, of whatever craft, trade, occupation, or grade in a specific industry.

Industrial unionism tends to appeal to workers where there are production skills peculiar to an industry and not transferable to other industries; where there are conditions of work specific to one industry; and where there are promotion possibilities open through various grades of work. It has the advantage for members that it strengthens the unity of workers in the industry concerned and, since industrial unions tend to be large, they can provide efficient services. Further, such a vertically organized union can act decisively and with considerable strength in an industry because of the nature of its coverage. At the same time employers, usually organized on industrial lines, prefer to negotiate with a single union rather than a number who may not be in complete accord with each other.

Industrial unionism has been relatively unsuccessful in establishing itself in Britain, however, due to the persistence of craft interests; to too wide a coverage across many industries of general unions; and to the difficulties of organizing both manual and non-manual workers. Even such few industrial unions which are established, for example the National Union of Railwaymen and the National Union of Mineworkers, do not cover the whole of their industry. A better term for these, perhaps, would be single-industry unions, the nearest approach to an industrial union proper in Britain being the National Union of Boot and Shoe Operatives.

Historically, industrial unionism in Britain was in the main an offshoot of syndicalism in the early years of the twentieth century and did not have much importance until many years after the craft and general workers' unions were established. It was then advocated as both an efficient structure for trade union organization and as a method whereby workers could take control of an industry and, ultimately, of society. Since 1945 it has been resuscitated as a device for improving trade union efficiency and for reform of the union structure. Comparisons have been made with the (limited) industrial unionism of Sweden, the more complete example of the postwar German trade union movement, and the American examples typified by the United Automobile Workers. The ⟡ TUC reports of 1927 and 1946 accepted industrial unionism as a plausible ideal, and as an objective towards which organizational evolution might be influenced. Even the TUC, however, has now recognized that the complex of interests within the British trade union movement renders the achievement of this ideal impossible in Britain. ⟡ Trade Union – Structure. N.H.C.

Trade Union Types – White-collar Union A union in the 'white collar' or non-manual area of employment, including government administrators and executive officials; foremen and supervisors; professionals; scientists, technologists and technicians; artists, musicians and entertainers; clerical and administrative workers; salesmen, representatives and shop assistants.

Between 1911 and 1961 the number of white-collar workers in Britain increased by 147%, while the number of manual workers increased by only 2%, having decreased in total since 1931. In the same period the white-collar section of the labour force increased from 18·7% to 35·9%. Within the white-collar labour force as a whole, constituent groups have expanded differentially, the clerks, with an expansion of 260%, claiming most of the ground yielded by the manual workers. Scientific and technical occupations, though small in total numbers, have also experienced very high growth rates. Again from 1911 to 1961, the proportion of women in white-collar jobs increased from 29·8 to 44·5%. If present occupational trends continue, white-collar employees will outnumber manual employees during the 1980s as they do already in the USA.

The degree of unionization among white-collar employees is considerably less than that found among manual workers. In Britain 29% of white-collar workers belong to a union, against 51% of manual workers. Further, although white-collar unionism has increased considerably in absolute numbers since the end of the Second World War, it has merely kept abreast of the growth in the white-collar labour force and it has been insufficient to offset a decline in the density of manual unionism. Most white-collar unionism is concentrated in the public sector of the economy, the largest union of this type being the National and Local Government Officers' Association. With the possible exception of the distributive trades, manufacturing industry has the lowest density of white-collar unionism. The nature of the bureaucratic structure would appear to assist the growth of white-collar unionism in the public sector, but a major force in both public and private sectors has undoubtedly been government policies. Both world wars resulted in government policies which made it easier for unions in the private sector to exert pressure for recognition and harder for employers to resist it. Expansion of union membership among white-collar workers in private industry is limited chiefly by the recognition problem still facing the unions catering for these workers. ⟡ Trade Union – Structure. N.H.C.

G. S. Bain, *The Growth of White-Collar Unionism* (Clarendon, 1970).

Trades Council A locally based body representing trade union branches in the locality, usually a town or district.

Trades councils are in no sense TUC 'branches', yet are the counterparts of the ⟡ TUC at the local level. Over 500 are registered with the TUC but coverage is far from complete.

Trades councils function as local coordinators of trade union activity. They undertake recruiting campaigns; they raise funds, undertake propaganda and organize sympathetic action if requested to do so as a result of a dispute; they promote educational, social and cultural ventures among local trade union members; and they represent trade union interests in relations with local government agencies. In recent years the functions of trades councils have been expanded by the reception shown to them by government departments as the proper bodies to nominate trade union representatives to local tribunals, advisory bodies, planning bodies, hospital boards, etc.

With the centralization of much collective bargaining and the rise of local Labour parties in the twentieth century, their prestige and influence has diminished. The less interest shown in them, the more they fall prey to Communists and other minorities ($\Diamond$ Trade Union – Communism). As a consequence the TUC has attempted to develop the trades councils as its local agents since 1924 and from 1934 has instructed them to exclude Communists from office. The TUC has also prescribed model rules for them and 'reorganizes' those which misbehave. In particular, trades councils must regard themselves as policy-executing and not policy-making bodies and must not indulge in political activities. In consequence, most of the mixed 'Trades and Labour Councils', formerly so numerous, have been divided. The TUC has considerable powers over trades councils because the national unions wish them kept in their place.

In England and Wales trades councils have no representation at the TUC other than a simple fraternal delegate but in Scotland they may, and do, affiliate direct to the Scottish TUC. N.H.C.

A. Flanders, *Trade Unions* (Hutchinson, 1968).

Trades Union Congress A permanent association of British trade unions founded in 1868 to consider questions of importance to trade unionists and to give publicity to these considerations. Today the functions of the TUC can be said to be those of exercising influence; of defending the name of the unions by developing a public image of a responsible movement; and of providing research, publicity and representative services for the trade union movement as a whole. The TUC does not spend money on political action, nor does it have a political fund, although many of its affiliated unions are also affiliated to the Labour Party.

The TUC is composed solely of affiliated unions of which there were 132 in 1972. Affiliated unions range in size from the Transport and General Workers' Union with over 1·6 million members to the Wool Shear Workers' Trade Union with 20 members. Affiliated membership in 1972 was 9·894 million members.

The TUC operates through its Annual Congress, its General Council and its full-time staff of officials led by the General Secretary.

Affiliated unions are entitled to send to the annual Congress one delegate for every 5,000 members or part thereof. Congress has three main functions: to consider the report of work done by the General Council during the previous year, to transact business placed on the agenda by affiliated unions, and to elect the General Council for the coming year. Sitting members are normally re-elected. Decisions may be taken by voice, by show of hands or, more rarely, by formal vote. On such occasions voting is by card issued to union delegations according to membership on the basis of one vote for every 1000 affiliated members or part thereof. Such 'block voting' is sometimes said to favour the big battalions, and in some way to be undemocratic, but it is difficult to envisage alternatives which would be practicable. The business of Congress is conducted in public, in that meetings are televised and reported by the Press.

The executive body of the TUC is the General Council which has, in addition to the General Secretary and Assistant General Secretary, 37 members (1972). These are elected by the annual Congress to give centralized leadership on questions of broad policy for the whole trade union movement. Through the General Council continuous relations are kept up by the trade union movement with the Confederation of British Industry, the government, and numerous advisory and consultative bodies concerned with economic and social problems.

For purposes of representation on the General Council, unions affiliated to the TUC have been divided into 18 trade groups and seats allocated according to the size of the group. A nineteenth group ensures the contribution of the women trade unionists' viewpoint. Members of the General Council do not sit as representatives of individual unions or groups of unions, but are answerable to Congress as a whole. The General Council has, however, been criticized for being dominated by the large unions, even though in 1967, for example, the 37 members of the General Council came from 29 different unions and only 4 unions had more than one member on the Council. It could, however, be argued that the present structure of the General Council under-represents both the newer technologies and white-collar employments and overemphasizes the older and contracting sectors of the economy.

The General Council meets at least once a month and is mainly concerned with examining the detailed work carried out by the committees it appoints to deal with a particular range of subjects.

Neither the General Council nor Congress can override the autonomy of affiliated unions, but there is a strong moral obligation to carry out their decisions. Standing orders do give them certain disciplinary sanctions. The Electrical Trades Union was expelled from affiliation to the TUC until such time as it had rectified damage to the union by ballot-rigging Communist officials (◇ Trade Union – Communism).

The General Council does not normally intervene during a strike unless so requested by the union(s) involved, but it has the power to call union representatives together when there is a likelihood of negotiations breaking down so that other affiliated trade unionists not directly involved might suffer by unemployment or otherwise. If requested to intervene, the Council attempts to seek a fair settlement.

At the request of an affiliated union, the General Council may investigate a dispute between unions. The Disputes Committee of the TUC, a sub-committee of the Council, exercises a triple function: it is a fact-finding commission, a conciliating body and a judicial tribunal. The principles which guide the Disputes Committee in its decisions on inter-union disputes are those adopted at the 1939 Congress and known as the Bridlington Agreement (◇ Trade Union – Jurisdiction).

407

Training

The detailed work of the TUC is carried out by the permanent staff employed in various departments, for example, research and economic (trade union), organization, production (aimed at increasing efficiency), social insurance, international and education. This work is coordinated by the General Secretary whose potential influence as chief spokesman for the TUC is considerable.

It is sometimes said that the TUC should take more power over its affiliated members, but it could only do this with their consent. It had been noticed that many of the General Council members are clearly overworked, and that this might be overcome by electing for a term of years a full-time President and a small number of full-time officers. These would then have a better opportunity to develop the strategy and tactics of the trade union movement as a whole.

A larger TUC income through higher affiliation fees (itself a product of higher contributions paid by individual members to their unions) could be well spent on better publicity by the TUC to improve the image of the trade union movement; on better services, including education (the Swedish equivalent spends approximately 8 times the TUC expenditure on education); and on strengthening the TUC Regional Councils so that they could provide regional services in the fields of research, education and training, recruitment, legal advice, etc. Regional TUC services of this type could relieve trade union officers of hours of work and enable them to carry out their chief tasks much more effectively.

The TUC adopted a policy of non-registration (◇ Trade Union – registration) under the now defunct ◇ Industrial Relations Act. This caused 32 unions with approximately half a million members to have their affiliation to the TUC suspended.

The organization and methods of the Scottish Trade Union Congress resemble those of the TUC with which it closely works. It is, however, a distinct and separate institution which performs for trade unionists in Scotland many services which the TUC, by reason of its geographical remoteness, could not render as effectively. N.H.C.

Trade Unionism, evidence of the TUC to the Royal Commission on Trade Unions and Employers' Associations (TUC, 1967).

Training ◇ Industrial Training.

Training Officer The member of the staff of a company who has special responsibility for the training and education of employees (◇ Industrial Training). In a large firm he may be head of a department with several assistants and instructors. In small firms he may have other responsibilities as well as training. The duties of a training officer include advising his company on training policy and ensuring its implementation; organization of internal training courses and arranging for attendance at outside courses; and teaching, which may include, for example, some instruction in skilled work and the conduct of ◇ Induction courses for new recruits. The essential function of a training officer is to give a specialist service to production, sales, office and other 'line' managers – to advise and assist with the training of their staff – but this is qualified by his overall responsibility to the company for giving all employees equal opportunities for training and development so as to improve their individual contributions to the enterprise. As training is closely related to other aspects of ⇗ Personnel Management such as ⇗ Recruitment, transfer and promotion, the training officer is on the staff of the personnel manager, or works in close liaison with him. L.S.

A. Tegla Davies, *Industrial Training* (Institute of Personnel Management, 1962).

Training within Industry (TWI) A method of training supervisors within industry, first developed in the USA and introduced into Britain during the Second World War. TWI is a way of teaching the techniques of supervision under four headings: job relations, job instruction, job methods and job safety. Simple instruction manuals are available for each of the subjects. The Department of Employment has a group of specialist instructors in TWI who give the training to supervisors on the premises of an employer or to groups of supervisors from different firms on Ministry premises. L.S.

Department of Employment and Productivity: TWI, Pamphlets (HMSO).

Transfer Pricing One definition of an economic organization or entity is that it is an area of productive activity (or collection of working people) in which the control exercised by economic markets in the allocation of resources is replaced by a control process through administrative authority. A transfer pricing system is an attempt by a firm to decentralize decision-making amongst managers by the use of an internal pricing system which at the same time will encourage, motivate or 'coerce' the individual manager to make decisions which will achieve the firm's objectives. Thus it is an attempt to secure the advantages of the market price mechanism in achieving an efficient allocation of resources within the firm without relinquishing the advantages of being one economic unit.

As a firm uses a cost accounting system to allocate costs to divisions and productive centres of the firm which in turn are attached as unit costs (or 'price tags') to the goods and services, and as they are transferred from one division or centre to another, then, implicitly if not explicitly, it uses a transfer pricing system. However, in order to be effective a transfer pricing system should motivate managers to make decisions about buying-in and producing and selling goods and services which take account of the marginal and opportunity costs of resources. For such purposes it is clear that the use of fully allocated average accounting costs, probably the most frequently used transfer pricing basis, is likely to lead to uneconomic decisions. Consequently, suggestions have been made for the use of alternatives such as marginal or variable costs, market prices, market-based negotiated prices, market prices less a sales commission, etc. E.A.L.

J. Hirshleifer, 'On the Economics of Transfer Pricing', *Journal of Business*, Chicago, Vol. XXIX, No. 3, July 1965, pp. 172–84; L. R. Amey, *The Efficiency of Business Enterprise*, Ch. 7 and Appendix V (Allen & Unwin, 1969).

Transportation Method ⇗ Mathematical Programming.

Truck Acts The essence of the truck system is that an employee, as a condition of his contract of employment, is compelled to accept part of his remuneration in kind, i.e. in goods or services. There is evidence that the system had been in existence in England as far back as the fifteenth century and legislation was passed to deal with some of the abuses to which it gave rise. The building of canals and railways during the first half of the nineteenth century increased the complaints about the system and a series of Acts of Parliament, the first of which was passed in 1831, regulate the position today. These Acts apply only to 'workmen', defined as employees engaged in manual labour and exclude those employed in domestic service, managerial, clerical or other non-manual occupations. Any provision in a contract of employment of a 'workman' stating that wages are to be paid in any form other than legal tender is absolutely void as is also any actual payment made in this form. No deductions may be made from the wages of a workman on account of fines or for bad workmanship, unless the workman has either in writing consented to the deduction or a written notice giving details of proposed deductions is prominently displayed in the workman's place of employment. Payment of a workman's wages by cheque, postal or money order was also forbidden by the Truck Acts, but is now permitted by the *Payment of Wages Act*, 1960 subject to the workman's written consent. This Act also permits an employer to pay by postal or money order the wages of a workman who is off work due to sickness or is working away from the employer's premises, provided that a written notice is supplied to him indicating how the wages have been calculated. w.f.f.

G. W. Hilton, *The Truck System* (Cambridge, 1960).

Turnover ⟡ Labour Turnover.

U

Unfair Dismissal ⇨ Dismissal of Employees (Law).

Unfair Industrial Practices This is another concept introduced into English law by the *Industrial Relations Act*, 1971 and abolished subsequently by the *Trade Union and Labour Relations Act*, 1974. According to Professor Rideout unfair industrial practices were divided into two classes, namely those which specify some undesirable end and make it actionable to seek to achieve it either by any means or by strike or similar action. The second type of unfair industrial practice was that which laid down certain forms of industrial pressure applied in furtherance of an ⇨ industrial dispute which the law says may not be applied for any purpose whatsoever. The examples of both types of unfair industrial practice are too numerous to be given here in full and should be studied in one of the specialized books on labour law. Where a person alleges that an unfair industrial practice has been operated against him, he may complain to the ⇨ National Industrial Relations Court. The court could make a declaration stating the exact legal rights of the complainant, it could award him compensation for any loss that he had suffered or it could instruct the offending party to refrain from continuing the objectionable practice. Alternatively, a complaint could have been addressed to an ⇨ industrial tribunal which might make the above mentioned declaration, award compensation to the complainant or *recommend* his reinstatement if he has been dismissed as a result of an unfair industrial practice, w.f.f.

A. Campbell, *The Industrial Relations Act* (Longmans, 1971).

Union Shop ⇨ Closed Shop.

Unity of Command The principle that each subordinate shall report to, and receive instructions from, only one superior. The principle is dear to the hearts of the classical theorists and has been repeatedly reaffirmed, often with biblical support (Matthew 6:24, Luke 16:13). The problems which could arise if the principle is violated are obvious enough, conflicting instructions and divided responsibilities and loyalties, and, undoubtedly, many organizations suffer from a lack of clarity in their organizational structures. Nevertheless, research indicates that the successful violation of the principle is extremely common. Good coordination between the dual heads can considerably reduce the risk of their issuing conflicting instructions to their common subordinate and in the absence of conflicting orders the question of divided responsibilities and loyalties does not arise.

In recent years, however, although many managements have failed to recognize the fact, the principle of unity of command has been steadily eroded by the increasing use of functional authority (⇨ Functional 1). The near sacred regard in which unity of command has been held has unfortunately hampered the re-

Unofficial Strike

examination of the questions of personal authority and responsibility which the spread of functional authority has necessitated. ⟡ Authority; Functional 1 and 2; Responsibility. I.C.MCG.

Unofficial Strike ⟡ Strike – Causes, Forms, Remedies, Statistics.

V

Valuation of Assets The normal basis of valuing assets for accounting purposes has been in terms of historical cost (⟡ Accounting Conventions). Falls in value through business use have been recorded by writing off ⟡ Depreciation of fixed assets and in writing down stock-in-trade (which is normally valued at the lower of cost or market value); increases in value, on the other hand, have not normally been recorded, although some companies periodically revalue certain types of assets (e.g. land and buildings) which appreciate in value. There is a growing view that both depreciation and appreciation of assets should be recognized either in the published accounts or in the notes appended to them, although there are formidable difficulties in the way of annual valuations of all assets. Under proposals put forward by the Institute of Chartered Accountants in England and Wales changes in the value of non-monetary assets will in future have to be recorded. Such changes will, however, be determined from the general index of consumer prices and will not represent changes in actual market valuations of individual assets. E.A.L.

> J. C. Bonbright, *The Valuation of Property* (McGraw-Hill, 1937, reprinted by The Michie Company, Charlottesville, Virginia, 1965).

Value Analysis Value analysis is simply the application of the techniques of method study to the product design function. ⟡ Method Study.

The basis of the approach is identical to that used on the study and development of work methods, i.e.

(a) Select the product to be studied.
(b) Evaluate the purpose, design and cost of the product and its components.
(c) Develop designs for components and products to perform the function at less cost, i.e. develop designs of greater 'value'.
(d) Examine the various designs.
(e) Adopt the design with highest 'value'.
(f) Implement and review the results.

'Value' in this context is defined as the least cost for reliably providing the correct function, at the correct time and place and at a correct standard of quality. Value analysis therefore is a procedure which specifies the function of products or components, establishes the appropriate cost, creates alternatives and evaluates them.

Value analysis finds its greatest application where very large quantities of an item are being produced, so that fractional amounts saved on the manufacturing cost can result in substantial savings.

It has been criticized as a redundant discipline since analysis of value and comparison of alternative designs is a function carried out by all designers, and hence there is no need for an additional person, team or profession to perform the function. Whilst this may be true it is nevertheless equally true that re-evaluation of designs after a period of time often presents the opportunity for cost reductions, e.g. resulting from the use of newly developed materials, processes, etc.

The main achievement of value analysis has been to attract attention to the cost factor in the design function.

In practice a team approach is normally used with, for example, a value analysis 'engineer' acting as chairman to a team drawn from cost accounting; production, design and purchasing. ⟡ Design. R.W.

> American Society of Tool and Manufacturing Engineers, *Value Analysis in Manufacturing* (Prentice-Hall, 1967).

Values Fundamental beliefs, either generally or personally held, which serve as the criteria by which all social alternatives are appraised. Values always involve an emotional commitment in that people feel strongly that behaviour in accordance with the value is 'good', whilst behaviour in violation of the value is 'bad'. The value may not be something wholly attainable (e.g. absolute honesty) but may be, nevertheless, something towards which one should constantly strive.

Differences in values underline many of the differences in behaviour which occur in industrial organizations. Thus commonly among managerial values are beliefs in the sanctity of authority as an organizational principle and in the importance of personal advancement: whilst among shop floor values are beliefs in the importance of shared power leading to negotiated rules of behaviour governing the relationship between management and men, and in the importance of collective loyalty through which there can be general advancement. These conflicting values may lead managers to become over-concerned with the maintenance of managerial prerogatives whilst trade unionists assume the right to participate in organizational decision-making, to question orders and, where appropriate, to disobey. Similarly, managers may elaborate systems of individual incentive bonuses and merit rating whilst trade unionists press for equality of treatment.

Values are acquired by the individual, often during childhood as a result of family influences, but also during adulthood as a result of experience and widening social contacts. Values differ from one society or group to another and will change over time. For the individual, values do not change easily, although a process of modification usually takes place continuously during his lifetime. ⟡ Norm; Role. I.C.MCG.

> P. M. Blau and W. R. Scott, *Formal Organisations* (Routledge & Kegan Paul, 1963).

Variance ⟡ Measures of Dispersion.

Vendor Appraisal ⟡ Purchasing.

Vertical Integration ⟡ Patterns of Growth.

Vibration The most common sources of vibration are transport vehicles, such as ships, aircraft, cars and agricultural vehicles. The effects upon the human body may include discomfort, headaches, nausea, pain and permanent internal damage, in addition to severe decrements in working performance.

The type and severity of these effects depend upon the amplitude, frequency and duration of the vibration as well as the physiological and psychological condition of the individual.

Motion sickness results most commonly from very low frequency vibration. At higher frequencies severe discomfort and fatigue may occur. The natural frequencies of different parts of the body lie in the range 3–9 cps. Within this range resonance resulting in anatomical damage may arise from exposure. Experiments upon animals indicate that injury may result from displacement of the abdomen or from mechanical collisions between the lungs and the heart.

Numerous damping devices are available to protect the human from deleterious effects. Correct posture is of the utmost importance, and appropriate training procedures may assist people to cope. E.E.

L. J. Fogel, *Biotechnology: Concepts and Applications* (Prentice-Hall, 1963).

Vision The human eye comprises a roughly spherical case, fitted with a variable-diameter aperture (the pupil) controlled by the iris; a zoom, or variable focal length, lens; and a photo-sensitive layer, the retina, connected to the optic nerve.

A variety of mechanisms is involved in the visual perception of space. This includes the relative size and interposition of objects, perspective, and accommodation effects. Binocular cues are derived from convergence and stereoscopy.

Visual acuity is determined by the size of the retinal image, together with such factors as levels of illumination and contrast (⟡ Brightness; Illumination). Retinal image size is a function of object distance, R, and object size, S, and is usually measured in terms of visual angle. For general purposes this angle, A, is given by

$$A = \frac{S}{R} \text{radians}$$

Common defects in vision result from the inability of the lens to provide a sufficient range of accommodation. Short sightedness, or myopia, results from excessive convexity of the lens, such that the image falls short of the retina. Distant objects cannot then be focused sharply. The condition may be corrected by the use of a concave lens. Conversely, long sightedness or hypermetropia may be corrected by the use of a convex lens. There is a tendency towards long sightedness with increasing age. ⟡ Colour; Colour Blindness. E.E.

S. S. Stevens, *Handbook of Experimental Psychology* (J. Wiley, 1951).

Visualizing ⟡ Advertising.

W

Wage The payment made to workers for placing their ability and energy at the disposal of an employer.

'Money wages' must be distinguished from 'real wages', which are the goods and services money wages will buy. Real wages thus depend on the movement of prices. Rising prices during ✧ Inflation mean falling real wages if money wages remain unchanged. In some industries national agreements provide for the adjustment of wage rates according to changes in the Official Index of Retail Prices. Such wage systems are known as 'sliding scales' and they affect approximately 2 million workers. Sliding scales rarely, if ever, compensate fully for rises in the retail price index, and do not appear to be inflationary. The more recent 'threshold agreements', however, aim to compensate employees for price rises.

Ideally national agreements should set the frame, and the limits, within which ✧ Workplace Bargaining and plant and company bargaining about payment by results and other pay systems should operate. ✧ Wage Systems. In practice most national agreements merely set minimal standards for pay, with differentials for skill, for sex, and possibly for other dimensions, e.g. district.

Rates of pay are fixed in relation to a standard working week which at the present time is 40 hours for many industries. Time worked above this is 'overtime', which is paid at premium rates which may vary according to the time of the week in which overtime occurs and which may be calculated on piece rates, time rates, or flat payments for each hour of overtime. Postwar reductions in the standard working week have had a minimal effect on actual hours worked in Britain and many employees depend on overtime earnings. A high incidence of overtime in a company may indicate considerable underemployment in normal working hours. ✧ Productivity Bargaining. Shift pay is also paid at premium rates.

Holidays with pay are now typical of most British industries, calculations being made in a wide variety of ways, but often on time rates or average earnings.

It is possible to view a given wage as a function of supply and demand in a number of interrelated markets and indeed theories of wage determination have been developed mostly by economists. There are, however, important social and political determinants, e.g. traditional, legal, ideological and institutional factors combined historically to keep women's wages in general at a lower level than those of men. Thus the *Equal Pay Act*, 1970, embodied the principle of 'equal pay for equal work'.

A worker's earnings may be enhanced by various forms of ✧ profit-sharing and co-partnership but, strictly, these additions to income are not wages but appropriations from profits. Such schemes are regarded by some as a form of ✧ Industrial Democracy. ✧ Collective Bargaining; Fair Wages Clause; Wages Council. N.H.C.

Industrial Relations Handbook (HMSO, 1961); K. W. Rothschild, *The Theory of Wages* (Blackwell, 1954).

416

Wage Drift The tendency for wages paid to rise faster than would result from the increases agreed under industry-wide collective bargaining. Alternative names for this phenomenon are 'wages gap', 'earnings gap', 'earnings drift', and 'workplace margin'.

Wage drift in Britain is calculated for the economy as a whole by deducting the annual percentage increase in the Index of Hourly Wage Rates from the increase in average hourly earnings reported to the ⟨⟩ Department of Employment, excluding the estimated effect of overtime earnings.

Contributing factors to wage drift as defined are:

(1) The movement of labour to higher paid occupations, districts and industries.

(2) Productivity bargains at the workplace, plant and company level.

(3) Greater effort by workers on production bonuses, shift premiums, merit rates and other plus rates.

(4) Replacement of time work by piecework.

(5) Improved production methods with no change in piece rates.

But most significantly of all:

(6) Increases in actual (as distinct from nationally agreed) wage rates paid, or increased or 'incentive' earnings *not necessarily accompanied by greater effort* which occur 'autonomously' at the workplace. Sometimes this occurs because a firm wishes to maintain wage differentials when the pay of one group has risen.

This last factor contributing to wage drift is strongly associated with conventional payment by results systems. Even where management has good control, drift is likely to be 1 to 2% per annum; in an extreme case it might be 8% or more.

Wage drift under conventional payment by results systems is produced in four ways:

(1) The effect of many piece rate and incentive systems linking earnings with output is to increase hourly wages as productivity rises with technological change.

(2) The output per hour of workgroups tends to rise without any apparent change in job design or increase in effort the more of any given product is produced. Here observation challenges the widespread assumption that after an initial learning period a worker's output becomes constant.

(3) The collective bargaining process involved in fixing rates or times for new jobs. 'Loose rates' and high earnings are difficult to revise downwards, whereas ⟨⟩ Shop Stewards insist on review of 'tight rates'. This has been termed 'pieceworkers' creep'.

(4) The common assumption, indeed requirement under some collective agreements, that new rates or times must be fixed to give earnings at least as high as the previous task. Thus errors in the worker's favour and the 'learning curve' phenomenon combine to produce a 'ratchet' effect on earnings.

Conventional payment by results systems contribute to wage drift directly in that rising earnings from these systems are a significant element in total wage drift; and indirectly in that these greater earnings give rise to pressures elsewhere to restore wage differentials between work groups. This may occur not only in the firm, but in other firms in the same industry or district. Conventional payment by results systems can thus contribute significantly to cost inflation, more than off-setting the benefits of higher productivity obtained.

Wage drift has appeared in 'tight' labour market conditions but it seems that the actual mechanism of wage drift makes a contribution to the degree of drift. Firms in similar product and labour markets experience different degrees of drift, an indication that drift is amenable to managerial or management–union joint control ⟡ Collective Bargaining; Industrial Relations – Reform in Great Britain; Productivity Bargaining; Wage; Wage Systems; Workplace Bargaining. N.H.C.

National Board for Prices and Incomes, *Payment by Results Systems*, Report No. 65, Cmnd. 3627 (HMSO, 1968).

Wage Incentive Schemes ⟡ entries on Wage.

Wage Systems The two main forms of wage payment are by time (time rates) and by piece (piece rates). Even the simplest, i.e. 'straight', piece-rate systems often embody an element of time rates. 'Waiting time' pay (i.e. while waiting for work to arrive) is also based on time rates. Many workplace wage systems now embody 'payment by results', which attempt to establish a formal relationship between pay and output or effort. The least sophisticated version employs piece rates only, but most such systems in Britain are more complex and tend to be 'regressive', i.e. the effective pay per unit declines as output rises. Payment by results schemes are alternatively known as incentive (payment) schemes, as they are intended to provide a financial incentive to greater effort.

In most company wage structures, the pay packet is made up of a number of elements, including a fixed 'basic' amount, a variable 'output' element, and a 'fall-back' provision to give a minimum wage irrespective of production. A bonus on output or results may be calculated by the day, week, month, or other period.

In 1961 42% of workers in manufacturing industry were paid by results; 73% of all manufacturing industry workers were in plants where some were paid by results and where all therefore could be affected through the operation of the 'lieu bonus' and through maintaining differentials between one workgroup and another. Probably 8–9 million workers are affected by payment by results systems, the highest proportion of whom are in the metal trades and textiles. There is a limited movement away from payment by results in engineering, especially electrical and aircraft engineering, but an increased incidence in shipbuilding, chemicals, and iron and steel. The greatest geographical incidence is in the Northern Region and the least in London and the South East.

It is difficult to isolate the effect on labour productivity of payment by results schemes from other factors which are often associated with it, e.g. ⟡ Work Study, improved managerial organization; but it seems useful in many work environments. Quality may suffer however, and since workers, sometimes with the foreman's assistance, often hold back a 'bank' of finished work to reduce oscillations in earnings, so may production planning and control. Any beneficial effect on effort may be outweighed by the detrimental impact on labour costs. This can occur for many reasons, e.g. poor work study or ratefixing, a bargaining strategy by ⟨⟩ Shop Stewards, but it is most likely to happen because of management pressures, e.g. deliberately allowing pay standards to slip in order to retain or recruit scarce labour ⟨⟩ Wage Drift.

The term 'piecework' is applied also to incentive or premium bonus systems where effort is measured in time rather than output. A standard time is set for the job and a bonus paid in relation to time saved in performance. Such systems lend themselves to work study techniques, including the measurement of effort in 'standard minutes'. There are many types, e.g. Taylor Differential Piece Rate, Rowan System, Accelerating System, Bedaux System. 'Synthetic times' may be prepared for standard job elements and from these the time allowed for a job can be quickly determined (⟨⟩ Predetermined Motion Time Study, Synthetic Timing).

Under ⟨⟩ Rate-fixing (or ⟨⟩ Estimating) a time or price is set by a specialist rate-fixer or foreman. This is a subjective process and subject to ⟨⟩ Workplace Bargaining. In some industries (e.g. cotton) it is possible for trade unions and employers to agree piecework price lists (or standard times, e.g. the shoe industry) on an industry-wide or district basis, but it is much more usual for these matters to be bargained on the shop floor.

Where work study is involved in fixing wages, the ideal system is to start with ⟨⟩ Method Study and then proceed to ⟨⟩ Work Measurement. A common fault is to omit method study or perform it superficially. Timing (⟨⟩ Time Study) followed by ⟨⟩ performance rating, with the addition of ⟨⟩ Allowances for rest, contingencies, etc., then give the time for the job. This can be used as a basis for a rate, possibly with the addition of a bonus for performance. There is an element of arbitrariness in the process and bargaining may take place at any stage, but the system does produce work standards.

More recent and less conventional systems of payment by results are 'measured day work', 'high time rates', 'premium pay plan', and the Rucker and ⟨⟩ Scanlon systems. Payment by results systems normally apply to the individual worker but may be operated on a collective basis, e.g. for the gang, group, department, works.

Most union leaderships support or accept payment by results but there is less agreement at the workplace and much dissatisfaction with the constant bargaining; with the inversion of customary skill differentials (semi-skilled operatives on bonus systems often receiving more than skilled workers on time rates); and with the lack of pay packet stability.

'Direct workers' in production may well be paid by results while 'indirect workers' ancilliary to production, e.g. maintenance staff, are paid on time rates. The most common method of dealing with the resultant problem is to pay indirect workers a 'lieu bonus' calculated on the average bonus of direct workers. This may be illogical, and more indirect workers are now being paid on work study based incentive schemes, e.g. by using analytical estimating in the case of maintenance workers. ⟨⟩ Estimating.

Company wage arrangements should embody a formal structure of occupational rates and 'standard earnings', but in practice they are often irrational, even chaotic. A logical structure can be introduced by employing such devices as ⟨⟩ Job Evaluation ($\Diamond$ Job Analysis) with or without $\Diamond$ Merit Rating. $\Diamond$ Collective Bargaining; Industrial Relations – Reform in Great Britain. N.H.C.

> *Industrial Relations Handbook* (HMSO, 1961); National Board for Prices and Incomes, *Payment by Results Systems*, Report No. 65, Cmnd. 3627 (HMSO, 1968).

Wages Councils Wages Councils were set up in Britain by the *Wages Councils Act*, 1945 replacing the earlier Trade Boards. They provide machinery for an indirect form of statutory wage regulation. Wages Councils are set up by order of the Secretary of State for Employment for trades or industries in which, in the opinion of an independent commission, there exist either no or only inadequate facilities for collective bargaining. Each Council has a tripartite membership, consisting of an equal number of persons representing employers' and employees' interests together with three independent members, all of whom are appointed by the Secretary of State. The function of each Council is that of submitting proposals to the Secretary concerning either the remuneration to be paid in the trade or industry or the holiday entitlement of persons employed in it. The Secretary may either accept the proposals and embody them in a Wages Regulation Order which has the force of law or he may return the proposals to the Council for reconsideration. He may not make an order which deviates from the proposals submitted by the Council and may thus not substitute his own judgement for that of the Council. Before the proposals of the Council are submitted to the Secretary of State they are published in draft form in the London and Edinburgh Gazettes and a copy is also sent to every known employer in the industry. Employers and employees in the industry are given a fortnight in which to lodge objections with the Council.

Once the Secretary has made a wages regulation order, an employer would be guilty of an offence if he failed to pay an employee at a rate equal at least to that given in the order and the employee would also be able to recover by civil action from the employer any difference between the statutory wage and that actually paid to him. Special inspectors are appointed by the Secretary of State to ensure observance of the provisions of the Act. The Protection of Employment Bill which is likely to be enacted in 1975 provides that Wages Regulation Orders should be made by the appropriate Wages Council instead of by the Secretary of State. It also proposes that these Orders should deal with terms and conditions of employment and not just with wage rates. $\Diamond$ Collective Bargaining; Department of Employment and Productivity; Prices and Incomes Policy. W.F.F.

> F. J. Bayliss, *British Wages Councils* (Oxford, 1962).

Weber, Max (1864–1920) $\Diamond$ Bureaucracy.

Welfare That part of $\Diamond$ Personnel Management which is concerned with the physical and mental well-being of employees. Personnel management as a separate activity started as welfare and the first personnel managers were welfare officers or welfare superintendents, whose main duties were to look after the well-being of women and young people. This meant a concern with the conditions of work as well as with the personal, sometimes domestic, problems of employees. It soon led on to questions of ⟡ Recruitment and training and it was only a matter of time before the original concept of welfare was enlarged to include all aspects of the human side of enterprise and to include all employees. Today the expression 'industrial welfare' is usually restricted (1) to the provision of facilities such as cloakrooms, lavatories, rest rooms, canteens, social and sports clubs: (2) to ⟡ Fringe Benefits, many of which are designed to reduce hardship in sickness or old age, and (3) to personal counselling for those with domestic and other problems. One part of the ⟡ Factory Law lays down minimum standards of welfare provision and, in addition to the facilities mentioned under (1), it covers such things as drinking water, seats and first aid. Similar arrangements have been made for office workers and others under the *Offices, Shops and Railway Premises Act*, 1963. The law lays down minimum standards; many employers go further both from a sense of responsibility for the well-being of those who work for them and because good welfare facilities may help with recruitment and provide the right environment for good work. L.S.

R R. Hopkins, *A Handbook of Industrial Welfare* (Pitman, 1955).

White-collar Union ⟡ Trade Union Types – White-collar Union.

Whitley Committee ⟡ Joint Industrial Council.

Whitley Council ⟡ Joint Industrial Council.

Wholesaling That part of the distribution process of goods which offers the products of many manufacturers, in bulk, to a wide range of users or customers. It involves buying and selling, assembly, sorting and storage of merchandise. (⟡ Distribution Mix). Whilst in certain trades it has become traditional to exclude the use of separate institutions for the wholesaling function this is only generally achieved by reallocating it. The sorting function, in particular, carried out through wholesaling activity is widely thought to improve the efficiency of transactions. Special cases of wholesaling are to be found where sole agents are used, e.g. textile trade, and brokers. Recent trends in ⟡ Retailing, and increased size of manufacturing units, have led to pressures on wholesaling from both sides in the distributive process, and substantial changes have taken place in its structure (⟡ Branding). In groceries and other trades, multiple retail chains have taken the wholesaling function to themselves, and in this way imitated the Cooperative retail societies (⟡ Cooperative Movement). Wholesalers receive their revenue as a percentage mark-up on the value of the goods they handle. The percentage varies according to the speed at which the merchandise can be turned over and its value. Most trades have standard margins, which are generally lower than the margins obtained by retailers. One of the major costs incurred is in relation to warehousing, and mathematical techniques to minimize the costs both of storage and of delivery to various customers are well developed. ⟡ Routing Problems. G.S.C.W.

R. M. Hill, *Wholesaling* (Irwin, 1963).

Woodward, Joan ⟡ Technology and Organization.

Work

Work ⟡ Muscular Work.

Work Design (in Production) Work in this context is defined as those activities essential for production, and work design is concerned with work content, methods and procedures. Work is only one part of the 'job', consequently job design also concerns social relations, payment, supervision, etc.

Unfortunately there are no proven procedures or general rules for optimum work design, but merely a set of apparently conflicting requirements, resulting from experience, theory and hypothesis.

Certainly work design can be considered in two parts, i.e. work content and work method. (See diagram opposite.)

Work content is influenced by product design, equipment, layout and output. Work method is influenced by work content, technological constraints (e.g. production methods), organization, ergonomics, etc.

The two traditional bases for work design are work simplification to obtain the advantages of division of labour, and Gilbreth's Principles of Motion Economy (⟡ Motion Study). There is no question that both of these concepts have been and remain important, but also there is no question that they are insufficient in themselves.

Whilst ergonomic theory considers the total man/machine relationship, ergonomic practice is often confined to the physical relationship ⟡ Ergonomics.

The psychological needs of the worker are of paramount importance and should influence both work content and work method. It is frequently argued that continued work simplification will frustrate the needs of the individual and result in reduced productivity, and that job enlargement is necessary to increase productivity. Yet many ⟡ Job Enlargement experiments have not resulted in the expected improvement in productivity Clearly, it is unreasonable to expect different individuals to react in the same manner to the same work, or individuals in different geographical, or economic situations, to exhibit identical needs. The design of work for maximum productivity (i.e. minimum total cost, considering output, quality, labour turnover, etc.) is therefore a function of individual worker differences, situation, as well as physiological, technological and organizational constraints. (See Figure.) R.W.

G. Nadler, *Work Design* (R. D. Irwin, 1963).

Work Measurement A term covering the collection of methods used to establish the time required by a qualified worker to carry out a specified job at a defined level of performance.

Along with method study, it is a principal component of ⟡ Work Study.

Work Measurement methods are of two types:

(1) Direct ⟡ Time Study using a stop-watch or other suitable means of measuring the time required.

(2) Indirect methods of obtaining time required, i.e. (a) The synthesis of job times from previously collected data. (b) Predetermined Motion Time Systems (PMTS.) (c) Estimating from experience and by comparison with other jobs.

The object of a Work Measurement investigation is: (a) To obtain a time for a job which may be used during method study to compare alternative job methods,

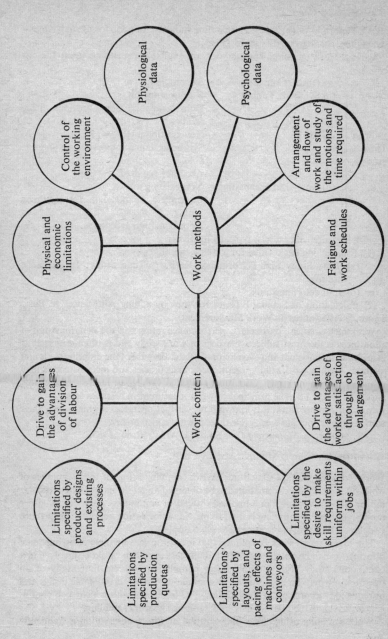

Relationship of factors determining work content and work methods. (From G. Nadler, Work Design)

(Basic Time) and/or (b) To establish a time standard for a job for use in payment, scheduling, costing, etc. (Standard Time).

Various work measurement methods are available depending upon the circumstances.

	(a) Direct Time Study	– Existing job.
	(b) Synthetic Timing	– Non-existing job. Data available from previous Time Studies.
Indirect Time Study	(c) PMTS	– Non-existing job. Synthetic timing impossible or undesirable. Accuracy required.
	(d) Analytical Estimating	– Non-existing job. Incomplete or no data for synthetic timing. Approximation acceptable.

A work measurement exercise typically involves:

(1) Establishing Basic Times for job elements either by:

(a) Time Study and Performance Rating ⟡ Time Study; Performance Rating.

or (b) Indirect Time Study.

(2) Calculation of Standard Times for jobs by adding Allowances to Basic Times. ⟡ Allowances (in Work Measurement).

Work measurement, particularly performance rating and the determination of allowances is the most subjective aspect of work study and is often criticized as inaccurate, inconsistent and even inappropriate. Because of the differing skills and methods used by work study practitioners, inaccuracies and inconsistencies may result in direct time study. Consistency is an advantage of indirect time study, particularly PMTS. The principal of work measurement assumes a single 'best' way of performing work, it is known however that operators normally vary their work methods and that work cycle times are not constant. R.W.

R. M. Barnes, *Motion and Time Study* (J. Wiley, 5th ed., 1963).

Work Planning Chart ⟡ Multiple Activity Chart.

Work Sampling (Ratio Delay Study) Work sampling is one of the techniques of work study by which information can be obtained about the nature of a particular job or activity. As the name implies, instead of continuous observation, either random or regular sampling is used to provide information about the occurrence of delays, utilization of resources, etc. (⟡ Sample.)

The advantage of work sampling is that in appropriate circumstances, adequate information can be obtained at substantially less cost than would be involved in a continuous study. For example, after completing a direct time study of an operation, it may be necessary to give an allowance for unavoidable delays and infrequently occurring ancillary duties. The frequency with which such contingencies arise and their nature may be determined by work sampling.

Work sampling using either photography or direct observation is frequently used: (1) to determine the utilization of machines, labour, etc.; (2) as a method of work measurement in clerical or other fairly irregular work activities; (3) to determine or verify work measurement contingency allowances.

Often the main objective is an analysis of activity as, for example, in ⟫ Memo-motion Photography. Such studies are frequently undertaken to determine the nature of activity or movement in an area, e.g. an analysis of the nature and quantity of traffic prior to plant layout or re-layout. R.W.

B. L. Hansen, *Work Sampling for Modern Management* (Prentice-Hall, 1960).

Work Study 'A generic term for those techniques, particularly method study and work measurement, which are used in the examination of human work in all its contexts, and which lead systematically to the investigation of all the factors which affect the efficiency and economy of the situation being reviewed in order to effect improvement.' (British Standard 3138.) (Also called Time and Motion Study – USA.) ⟫ Method Study; Work Measurement.

The primary object of work study is, by analysis of all the factors which affect the performance of a task, (1) to develop and install work methods which make optimum use of the human and material resources available; (2) to establish suitable standards by which the performance of this work can be measured.

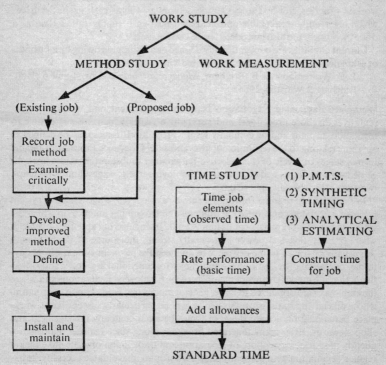

425

Working Capital

Work study is concerned with human work. It is not restricted to particular situations or industries but nevertheless finds its major application in relation to repetitive physical human work situations.

The complementary techniques of method study and work measurement are used:

(1) For an existing job: (a) Record existing work methods; (b) Critically examine those methods; (c) Develop and define improved methods; (d) Establish time standards for job; (e) Install and maintain work methods.

(2) For a proposed job: (a) Develop and define work methods; (b) Establish time standards for job; (c) Install and maintain work methods. R.W.

> R. M. Barnes, *Motion and Time Study* (J. Wiley, 5th ed., 1963); R. M. Currie, *Work Study* (Pitman, 2nd ed., 1963).

Working Capital Working capital is generally defined as the excess (or deficiency) of current assets over current liabilities. The relationship is often expressed as a ratio between these two categories.

Current assets may be defined as cash plus those assets which are held with the intention of converting into cash through a firm's ordinary selling process. Typical items included in the category of current assets are stocks of raw materials, work-in-progress, finished stocks, trade debtors as well as cash itself. Securities which are readily marketable and held as a near-cash supply rather than as a trade investment are also considered to be current assets.

Current liabilities are conventionally defined as all amounts owing by a business or estimated to be owing, which are payable within one year. E.A.L.

> J. F. Weston and E. F. Brigham, *Managerial Finance*, Chs. 4 and 6 (Holt Rinehart & Winston, 1966).

Workplace Bargaining Negotiation between management and workers' representatives on those procedural and substantive issues which are susceptible to regulation at plant and/or company level. 'Procedural' issues may be defined as anything relating to the resolution of grievances (◊ Grievance Procedure) and the formal stages or levels of ◊ Collective Bargaining. 'Substantive' issues are concerned with the terms and conditions of employment, e.g. wages, hours, holidays, overtime, fringe benefits and so on.

In factories where some form of incentive payment (◊ Wage Systems) system is in use, rate fixing constitutes the fundamental bargaining practice on which the whole edifice of workplace negotiation is built. In engineering and motor vehicles where ◊ Shop Steward power is generally strong, the source of their strength can usually be traced to the existence of an incentive payment system whose day-to-day operation provides ample opportunity for individual argument and collective action. Firms which are not members of ◊ Employers' Federations and where the employees are organized in large, general unions (◊ Trade Union – Structure) whose official apparatus is overstretched, will be particularly susceptible to workplace bargaining on a wide range of issues between company management and shop stewards. Even many federated firms have long since realized that the frequently unsatisfactory calibre of federation and trade union officials alike makes regular negotiation with company shop stewards an unavoidable necessity. It has been the experience of those companies which have engaged in ⟨⟩ Productivity Bargaining that detailed negotiation over aspects of job regulation peculiar to one plant or company inevitably concentrates negotiating activity within the confines of the company concerned.

The Donovan Report (⟨⟩ Industrial Relations – Reform in Great Britain) only confirmed what has in fact been manifestly obvious for some time – namely that national agreements between the officials of employers' associations and trade unions can only be enforced in those industries which have homogeneous technologies, where the firms tend to be more or less equal in size and profitability, and where there are no local or regional differentials in the labour market. Since no British Industry can claim to be in such a position, the whole formal system of ⟨⟩ Collective Bargaining at industry level has long been an inflationary charade. Basic terms and conditions of employment are still settled at national level but these are invariably geared to the needs and liabilities of the smallest, weakest, federated employers and are greatly supplemented by the bigger and more profitable companies, especially those operating in 'tight' regional and local labour markets. It is this margin of discretion above and beyond the minima agreed at national level which provides the scope for bargaining between individual employers and shop stewards. The bigger the employer, the more profitable his business and the stronger the trade-union representation in his establishment, the more scope there is for workplace bargaining. L.S. & N.H.C.

A. Flanders, *Industrial Relations: What is wrong with the System?* (Faber, 1965); A. I. Marsh, *Industrial Relations in Engineering* (Pergamon, 1965).

Works Committee ⟨⟩ Joint Consultation.

Works Council ⟨⟩ Joint Consultation.

Z

Zipf's Law The Principle of Least Effort, as expounded by G. K. Zipf, states that human behaviour is governed by an attempt to minimize the probable average rate of work required to achieve certain goals. Sometimes conscious efforts are made to minimize effort; the allocation of dots and dashes to serve as Morse symbols on the basis of letter frequencies serves as an example. Other instances of the conservation of effort seem without such systematic planning. Zipf produces a considerable volume of evidence in the form of statistical analyses of natural languages to show how his principle operates. He has shown that samples from a wide variety of sources conform to the rule that there is a simple linear relationship between the frequency of occurrence of any particular word, and its place in the rank order of occurrence frequencies. This relationship may be expressed in the form

$$\log p_n = A - B \log_n$$

where n signifies rank order of occurrence, p_n the frequency of occurrence, and A and B are constants. This same law has been derived from purely theoretical assumptions based upon the mathematical theory of communication by D. Mandelbrot. E.E.

G K Zipf, *Human Behaviour and the Principle of Least Effort* (Addison Wesley, 1949).

More about Penguins
and Pelicans

Some Penguin Education

Library of Management

Business Strategy

Editor: H. Igor Ansoff

Business Strategy introduces the reader to the explicit formulation
of the strategy of a firm. Part One looks at the ways in which
changes of policy come about. Part Two takes a look at the effect
the future will have on the firm and the individuals in it; while Part
Three compares two different approaches to the formulation of
strategy. The determination of the goals of the firm is discussed in
Part Four in a fascinating mixture of description (Galbraith),
prescription (Hayek) and cool analysis (Simon). Parts Five and Six
are devoted to case histories from Britain, France and the United
States of firms that needed to find a strategy to ensure their success.

'Catholic, exhaustive and commendably eclectic'
The Times Literary Supplement

H. Igor Ansoff is Dean of the Graduate School of Management and
Professor of Industrial Administration, Vanderbilt University,
Nashville, Tennessee.

Management is an international science whose boundaries are as
wide as the work men do and the organizations they work in.
Penguin Modern Management Readings bring together leading
articles and extracts, edited by distinguished authorities from every
field of management work and education.

Also published
Management and Motivation
Writers on Organizations

Some Other Penguin Reference Books

A Dictionary of Economics

Graham Bannock, R. E. Baxter and Ray Rees

A Penguin Dictionary of Economics is addressed to both the student and the general reader who wants to be able to follow economic discussions in the press and elsewhere, or whose daily work demands some familiarity with economic terms. It aims to provide a comprehensive companion to support other reading in a discipline which employs remarkably similar terminology in Britain and the United States.

This new dictionary, prepared by three practising economists, contains over 1,500 entries on economic terms and theory, the history of economics, and individual economists where they have made a definable contribution to contemporary economic thought. An elaborate system of cross-referencing makes the dictionary easy to use and extremely informative.

Also published
A Dictionary of Computers
A Dictionary of Commerce